# Time for EXPANSION BASEBALL

Edited by Maxwell Kates and Bill Nowlin
Associate editors: Len Levin and Carl Riechers

Foreword by Tal Smith

Society for American Baseball Research, Inc.
Phoenix, AZ

Time for Expansion Baseball
Edited by Maxwell Kates and Bill Nowlin
Associate editors: Len Levin and Carl Riechers

Book design: Rachael E. Sullivan
Society for American Baseball Research
Cronkite School at ASU
555 N. Central Ave. #416
Phoenix, AZ 85004
Phone: (602) 496-1460
Web: www.sabr.org
Facebook: Society for American Baseball Research
Twitter: @SABR

## FRONT COVER PHOTO CAPTIONS

1. (From left) Harry Craft, Bobby Shantz, Dick Farrell, Bob Aspromonte, and the rest of the 1962 Houston Colt .45s board a charter flight to Los Angeles in their travel cowboy uniforms. According to catcher Hal Smith, when two women asked the players who they were, one of the Colt .45s answered "[we] were the Tex Beneke Band." (Courtesy of the Houston Astros)
2. Montreal Expos pitcher Bill Stoneman with mayor Jean Drapeau. On April 17, 1969, the tenth game played in Expos'9; history, Stoneman no-hit the Philadelphia Phillies (Courtesy of the McCord Museum, Montreal).
3. Muriel and Ewing Kauffman take in a game at Royals Stadium with fellow Missouri baseball legend Stan Musial. Mr. and Mrs. K were largely responsible for bringing major league baseball back to Kansas City in 1969. (Courtesy of the Kansas City Royals)

## BACK COVER PHOTO CAPTIONS

1. Coco Laboy, Montreal Expos infielder, 1969 to 1973 (Courtesy of McCord Museum, Montreal)
2. The Kingdome, Seattle (Courtesy of David S. Eskenazi)
3. Houston Colt .45s 1963 program versus the St. Louis Cardinals (Courtesy of Frederick C. Bush)

# CONTENTS

## Florida Marlins

# 1998

## Arizona Diamondbacks

## Tampa Bay Devil Rays

# ACKNOWLEDGMENTS:
# THE MAKING OF THE BOOK

The genesis of this project took place in October 2016 as the Chicago Cubs were vying for their first World Series title in 108 years. Meanwhile, in my hometown of Ottawa, Ontario, the "saddest of possible words" became Osterer to Benmergui to Kates. Allow me to explain.

Irving Osterer is an avid sports fan and editor of the monthly bulletin of Congregation Machzekei Hadas, an Orthodox synagogue in Ottawa. That month, Irv decided to publish a baseball research paper that I had written. The article was spotted by congregants Joe Benmergui and Mindy Bullion who promptly sent it to my parents, David and Barbara Kates. When I saw the publication with my own eyes, I was bewildered, as it was a paper I did not even remember writing. The article answered the question "What is the only baseball team to wear an Israeli flag on their uniform?" It was the 2003 Houston Astros, as part of a memorial patch to the fallen astronauts on the Space Shuttle Columbia. Since one of the seven was Ilan Ramon, the first Israeli astronaut in space, the Israeli flag was affixed on the memorial patch.

Two years prior, in 2014, I had attended the SABR convention in Houston, where I had made a number of friends in the local baseball community. I decided to circulate the article amongst all of them. One of the people who replied was Jim Kreuz, a member of the steering committee of the Larry Dierker Chapter. Jim had attended my presentation of "The Bikers Beat the Boy Scouts: Facial Hair and the 1972 World Series" in Houston. Jim

soon invited me to return to the Bayou City to speak at a local meeting, which took place in February 2017.

Not long after, the steering committee of the Larry Dierker Chapter, which also included Bob Dorrill and Marsha Franty, was gracious enough to invite me for a return engagement. The date was set for November 12, 2018. But what to speak about? "How about something," I thought, "that encompasses both Toronto and Houston. How about...a statistical analysis on which of the 14 expansion drafts was the most successful?" Closer to home, I'd like to acknowledge Andrew and Elena North of the Centre for Canadian Baseball Research and Mike Henry and Alana Clarke, of Alumni Relations at University College (University of Toronto) for their contributions.

The next person I would like to acknowledge is the most important person in this entire project and that's Bill Nowlin. Bill and I first met at the SABR convention in Boston back in 2002. When I described the idea for my nascent research presentation to Bill, he surmised "that sounds like a good idea for a SABR book." Bill has been an excellent mentor and co-editor in this, my introduction to the production side of a SABR book. It was Bill who devised the format of this book: one article on the formation of each expansion team, followed by three biographies per team. Bill has presented an opportunity that has that have been both challenging and encouraging. He knew this was my first foray at editing a SABR project, allowed me to make mistakes, but made sure that I learned from them.

# Time For Expansion Baseball

The selection process of what players to include is also worth describing. We wanted to select players who were chosen in the various expansion draft who would be of interest to readers. Since we were drawing upon players representing 14 major league cities, we had the potential to tap into a large market segmentation of the baseball research community. All-Star players like Gil Hodges, Ted Kluszewski, Lou Piniella, and Maury Wills were chosen, as were fan favourites like Bobby Shantz and Brad Ausmus. Most of the biographies you are about to read have never been published before. Two Hall of Famers, Trevor Hoffman and Hoyt Wilhelm, were selections in expansion drafts, and you'll read about both. Wilhelm is particularly noteworthy because the Kansas City Royals selected him with the intention to trade him for younger players. Other players worth introducing include Dale Long, who hit home runs in eight consecutive games. Nate Colbert hit five home runs in a doubleheader after predicting as an 8-year-old that it was a feat he would never accomplish. Carl Morton won Rookie of the Year for the Expos while Mack Jones hit the first big-league home run on Canadian soil. Pete Vuckovich went on to win the Cy Young Award and play a supporting role in *Major League*. Charlie Hayes made the final out to win the 1996 World Series for the New York Yankees. You'll read about all these players and more.

Of course, thanks to all the writers who volunteered their time to chronicle the formation of expansion teams and to draft biographies of the players. Thanks to Carl Reichers and to Len Levin for providing the editorial and fact checking functions for the project, to Andy McCue for his role with the Business of Baseball Committee in bringing the project into reality, and to Marty Appel, whose rolodex of baseball contacts have been particularly helpful for interview purposes. Special acknowledgments are also extended to Deb Jayne and to Rebecca Mannis.

No SABR literary endeavour takes place without some element of serendipity. Through Mets fan Olga Nikiciuk, I was able to meet to Stan Manel. Brooklyn's own "Stan the Man"— at Citi Field during SABR 47 in New York. Stan had been an usher for the Mets "since the Polo Grounds." Stan provided a fantastic interview for our essay about the formation of the Mets. Several months later, I ran into Elliott Wahle at a synagogue function in Toronto. Elliott was one of the original employees of the Blue Jays and along with his wife Helene, provided us with some invaluable interview footage and photos. Another serendipitous moment took place when we were searching everywhere for Washington Senators photos. I suggested

to Bill Nowlin, "Have you tried John Blake at the Texas Rangers?" What I did not know, Bill was in the press box at Fenway Park as the Red Sox hosted the Rangers. Bill replied, "John Blake is standing 50 feet away from me."

Conversely, no SABR literary endeavour is without its share of sticky wickets. To name two, we had three different writers of the Montreal Expos essay withdraw from the project, all for valid reasons. But that's when the luck of the Irish worked in our favour. On St. Patrick's Day, I came across a paper about the formation of the Expos written by Danny Gallagher of the Renfrew, Ontario Gallaghers. Much like that other Daniel Joseph (Staub of the Expos), this one hit it out of the park when called upon to pinch-hit. Similarly, we lost communication with the author of the Bobby Abreu biography on account of the ongoing energy crisis in Venezuela. We are thankful to have Rob Neyer fill in relief, swapping Abreu for a biography of knuckleball pitcher Dennis Springer. And Andrew Sharp, who wrote up Duke Maas on even shorter notice.

Thanks to the National Baseball Hall of Fame and to Dwayne Labakas for allowing us to draw from their photography collections for the book. Finding photos of the expansion drafts themselves presented yet another challenge. Thanks to Mike Acosta, Jean Hastings Ardell, Mark Armour, Anne-Fred Beaulieu-Plamondon, Joy D. Benjamin, Matt Birch, Dan Boyle, Chris Brown, Bill Carle, Joshua "Cato" Cataldo, Bob Chandler, Wayne Chandler, Lisa Chisholm, John Cornell (aka "Mr. Shea Stadium"), Katie Davidson, Chris Dial, Jacques Doucet, Coi Drummond-Gehrig, Dave Eskenazi, Natalie Fiocre, Andre Gagnon, Maryrose Grossman, Lorraine Hamilton, Ana Hernandez, William Hickman, John Horne, Roger Kinney, Tom Larwin, Lori Leatherwood, Wayne McBrayer, Heather McNabb, Tim Mead, Curt Nelson, Ross Newhan, Paul Parker, Darrell Pittman, Jacob Pomrenke, John Schleppi, Robert Schultz, Marty Sewell, Alain Usereau, Rick Vaughn, Monica Vogan, Jeff Wheeler, Joel Zolondek, and Sam Zygner for providing leads on photos, if not the photos themselves. Special thanks to Hadley Barrett of the Topps Company for some extra-inning pinch-hitting to complete our photo complement.

Throughout the gestation of the project, one of our greatest sources of encouragement continued to emerge from the city of Houston. This included the Larry Dierker Chapter of SABR, the Pecan Park Eagle and its readership, and the Houston Astros. Thanks to Bob Aspromonte, Bill Brown, Frederick C. Bush, Larry Dierker,

Marsha Franty, Mickey Herskowitz, Greg Lucas, Bill Mc-Curdy, Wayne Roberts, Tal Smith, Joe Thompson, Mike Vance, Mark Wernick, and Jim "The Toy Cannon" Wynn. Another city who left its presence on the book is Washington DC. Thanks to Pete Cottrell, Barbara Mantegani, Dave Paulson, and Dave Raglin of the Bob Davids Chapter of SABR, and the members of The Expansion Washington Senators fan club for their own contributions.

Penultimately, THANK YOU for purchasing a copy of the book and reading as far as the introduction. Without your support, there would be no SABR and therefore, no book.

Lastly, I would like to acknowledge someone who unfortunately, will not be able to read the book. During the time this book was being prepared, my grandmother, Beulah Wagman, passed away. She was an avid fan of the Toronto Blue Jays and no doubt would have been proud that her grandson documented the story of how her favourite team became a reality.

It's time. It's time for expansion baseball.


Maxwell Kates

Houston, Texas, November 2018

# FOREWORD

## By Tal Smith

While I was somewhat oblivious to it at the time, my base-ball career began to change in the summer of 1960. I was in my third year working as an administrative assistant for the Cincinnati Reds, in what was then a three-person farm department.

My contact with Gabe Paul was somewhat limited. The Reds' general manager and the person who had listened to my pleas had eventually given me an opportunity to realize my dream of working in baseball. Even though the Reds' front office, like many teams in those days, con-sisted of only a dozen or so employees, most of my deal-ings with Mr. Paul consisted of running down the hall to provide him with the latest scouting reports on players in whom he was interested.

The Houston Colt .45s front office at the 1961 Nation-al League Expansion Draft, Netherland-Hilton Hotel Cincinnati. Back row l to r: Bobby Mattick, Paul Florence, Bobby Bragan, Grady Hatton; front row l to r: Tal Smith, Paul Richards, George Kirksey. (courtesy of Tal Smith)

This particular day though when I answered a summons from Miss [Frances] Levy to see Mr. Paul, I wasn't asked to bring any scouting reports. There were two gentle-men in his office whom Gabe introduced as Craig Culli-nan and George Kirksey. Gabe explained that they were from Houston and had a franchise in the newly created Continental League which was seeking major-league sta-tus. I was asked to acquaint them with the operation of our eight-team farm system and to answer any questions they might have about scouting and player development. I did as asked but then turned my attention back to the daily tasks, giving little thought to my meeting with the Houston delegation.

Soon thereafter though, there was another surprising de-velopment that piqued my curiosity. It was July and the Reds were on the road. I was enjoying an evening at home with my wife, Jonnie, and our 2-year-old daughter, Valerie, when the phone rang. It was Mr. Paul. He was in Chicago for a National League meeting. This was the first time he had ever called me at home. There was really little sub-stance to the call. When finished, I told Jonnie, "That was strange. I don't know why he called." As we subsequent-ly learned, that was the day the National League owners voted to expand. I suspect it is also the day that Gabe emotionally considered going to Houston if it got an ex-pansion franchise. Subconsciously perhaps, he was lining up those he might be able to take with him to help launch the expansion franchise. But, expansion was an exclusive issue for owners, or their representatives. I was more concerned with how Tony Perez and Pete Rose were doing in their rookie seasons at Geneva in the NYP and Johnny Vander Meer's need for another pitcher at Topeka.

Gabe Paul (l) with Pacific Coast League President Dewey Soriano at Sicks Stadium, Seattle, 1964. When Paul had left his position as general manager of the Cincinnati Reds in 1960 to head up the new franchise in Houston, his assistant Tal Smith joined him in the Bayou City. (courtesy of David S. Eskenazi)

The baseball season is long and the days are full. Time away from the daily grind is something most welcome. The baseball calendar was far different in my early years in the game prior to free agency. The one long break in the schedule was between the filing of reserve lists on October 16 and the winter meetings which usually began right after Thanksgiving. With this in mind, Jonnie and I began to plan a vacation trip to Durham, North Carolina where her mother and my parents both lived. Phil Seghi was the farm director for the Reds and my boss. I told Phil of our plans a couple weeks in advance. All was fine with Phil until one day he returned from his customary lunch with Gabe. Phil went on to say he had mentioned our vacation plans to Gabe, who seemed to take objection to my going at that time. I was somewhat chagrined by Mr. Paul's reaction and indicated such to Phil. We were anxious for the grandparents to see Valerie and proceeded with our plans with what I assume was the reluctant approval of Phil and Gabe.

We drove from Cincinnati to Durham in my 1955 Chevy which did not have a radio. Upon arrival my mother rushed out to greet us and quickly related that Gabe, Phil, and others in the Reds office had called. Now I understand why Gabe was reluctant for us to go on vacation. The day we arrived in Durham, October 25, 1960, was

the day Gabe stunned many by announcing he was leaving the Reds after some 25 years of service, the last nine as general manager. He was appointed general manager of the new Houston franchise in the first expansion of the major leagues since the formation of the American League in 1901.

The phone kept ringing as callers checked to see if we had arrived. Phil was the first one I spoke to, and he said Gabe wanted me to go to Houston with him and would be calling back shortly. I realized what an opportunity this might be and quickly accepted Gabe's offer to serve as his assistant and help develop the new organization. Jonnie, Valerie, and I had a very brief visit in Durham and turned the Chevy around the next day to head back to Cincinnati, pack up there and embark on our new journey in Texas.

And what a ride it turned out to be!

Tal Smith and Larry Dierker at the Astrodome, May 2018. Together they represent over 80 years of major-league baseball history in Houston. (courtesy of Mike Acosta)

We arrived in Houston and went to work for the new major-league team on November 1, 1960. We found Houston to be a very friendly and lively environment. It had the aura of the southwest – oil, cattle, cowboy boots, and 10-gallon hats. We have continued to make our home ever since with the exception of an interesting 21-month tour of duty in 1974-75 with George Steinbrenner's New York Yankees where we were reunited with Gabe Paul. Today Houston has become more cosmopolitan and developed into the fourth-largest city in the country while maintaining energy and spirit that is undaunted.

I am so thankful that I had the opportunity to be part of a new major-league franchise. It was an exciting and unique experience to help form the Colt .45s and to see the team develop. Upon moving into the Astrodome and being renamed the Astros in 1965, we continued to serve the club in many capacities over the years – a total of 35 years over three different time periods. There were many bumps in the road, but the memories of the wins, on and off the field, far outweigh the losses. Many of those great moments in the club's history are recounted in this book by Bill Nowlin and Maxwell Kates.

July 2, 2018

# INTRODUCTION

## BY MAXWELL KATES

The title, *Time for Expansion Baseball,* was adapted from Vin Scully's signature expression that began each of his broadcasts, "It's time for Dodgers baseball." Writers and analysts alike have argued that expansion was the natural conclusion to Scully's Dodgers moving west from Brooklyn to Los Angeles.

The major-league geographical atlas of 1951 was a virtual carbon copy of a map printed one half-century earlier. Apart from the St. Louis Browns, who relocated from Milwaukee, and the New York Yankees, who moved from Baltimore, none of the franchises had shifted locations as far back as 1903. The same way America underwent significant changes in the 1950s, so too did baseball. Inside a span of three years beginning in 1953, the Braves left Boston for Milwaukee, the Browns departed St. Louis for Baltimore, and the Athletics moved west from Philadelphia to Kansas City. Even so, Gordon Cobbledick of the *Cleveland Plain Dealer* had validity to describe baseball as a "sectional game" rather than a national one.[1] As seven of the 16 franchises were located within a 225-mile radius along the Eastern Seaboard, baseball left little appeal for fans outside the northeast and midwest.

In 1952, the Pacific Coast League (PCL) was given an "Open" classification above the AAA level. The move restricted American and National League teams from drafting PCL players and was considered a step towards becoming a third major league.[2] Any such plans ended in 1957 when the Brooklyn Dodgers and the New York Gi-

ants relocated to the Golden State. In 1959, Branch Rickey developed a plan to introduce the Continental League as a third major league but this idea, too, had short circuited before coming to fruition. How would major-league baseball respond to the American population moving south and west in increasing numbers? The solution was expansion. Hence the title, *Time for Expansion Baseball.*

The American League was the first to expand, adding the Los Angeles Angels and a new Washington Senators franchise in 1960. A year later, the National League welcomed the Houston Colt .45s and the New York Mets. Ten additional franchises were awarded before the expansion process concluded in 1998 with the Arizona Diamondbacks and the Tampa Bay Devil Rays. The full list is illustrated as follows:

| | | |
|---|---|---|
| Los Angeles Angels | 1961 | American League |
| Washington Senators | 1961 | American League |
| Houston Colt .45s | 1962 | National League |
| New York Mets | 1962 | National League |
| Kansas City Royals | 1969 | American League |
| Montreal Expos | 1969 | National League |
| San Diego Padres | 1969 | National League |

| | | |
|---|---|---|
| Seattle Pilots | 1969 | American League |
| Seattle Mariners | 1977 | American League |
| Toronto Blue Jays | 1977 | American League |
| Colorado Rockies | 1993 | National League |
| Florida Marlins | 1993 | National League |
| Arizona Diamondbacks | 1998 | National League |
| Tampa Bay Devil Rays | 1998 | American League |

**Notes**

1  Gaylon H. White, *The Bilko Athletic Club: The Story of the 1956 Los Angeles Angels* (Lanham, Maryland: Rowman & Littlefield, 2014), 44.

2  "Pacific Coast Year-by-Year Standings" in *2017 Pacific Coast League Sketch and Record Book* (Round Rock, Texas: The Pacific Coast League, 2017), 141.

# WHICH OF THE 14 EXPANSION FRANCHISES YIELDED THE MOST SUCCESSFUL DRAFT?

## BY MAXWELL KATES

Pat Gillick once observed that it should take 10 years for an expansion team to emerge into a contender.[1] The Hall of Fame executive would know; he oversaw the burgeoning of two of the 14 expansion teams. On one hand, his Astros were still a few years away from contending when he left Houston for the New York Yankees in 1973. On the other, after joining the Toronto Blue Jays on the ground floor in 1976, he watched their first pennant race in Year 7, winning the American League East two years later.

Each of the 14 expansion teams channeled their inner Pygmalion at different waves and speeds. In hockey, yes, it is possible to clinch a Stanley Cup berth in a team's first season, as evidenced by the St. Louis Blues and the Vegas Golden Knights. In baseball, however, the odds are stacked against the expansion teams. All 14 emerged from humble beginnings and rose to contend in their respective league or division, before retreating yet again to mediocrity. This essay will address the question of which expansion draft yielded the most successful team in its first decade of play. To illustrate the premise, the following three statistical metrics shall be used:

1. How well did the teams perform on the field in their first 10 years? This question will be answered by analyzing the different won-lost records and winning percentages.

2. For how long did the players selected in the expansion drafts contribute effectively to their teams? This question will be answered by examining the length of time expansion players remained on their teams as active players.

Within the realm of expansion players, it is important to note "drafted players" and "regeneration players." Drafted players were, quite simply, the players selected in each expansion draft. Regeneration players were the players received in trades for the drafted players. Both drafted and regeneration players are taken into account for the longevity analysis.

For example, the Montreal Expos selected Jesus Alou, Jack Billingham, and Skip Guinn in the 1968 expansion draft. Before the 1969 season, all three were traded to the Houston Astros for Rusty Staub. Three years later, in 1972, Staub was traded to the New York Mets for Tim Foli, Mike Jorgensen, and Ken Singleton. Alou, Billingham, and Guinn were "drafted" players. Staub was a "regeneration" player and so were the three Mets.

3. Of course, this part of the analysis assumes that a player on the roster after 10 years continues to display significant positive value. There is the argument that remaining on his team for 10 years may prove that he was not of significant enough value to be traded. The value of the drafted and regeneration players will be addressed by analyzing the statistical output of the players using wins above replacement (WAR).

It is the author's hypothesis that, given their relatively quick rise to contend and the length of time that they remained competitive, the Kansas City Royals shall score most points for their expansion draft, with the Toronto Blue Jays finishing second.

## PART I: WON-LOST ANALYSIS

One of the objectives used to analyze the success of each expansion draft was the won-lost records for the first 10 years of each franchise. Both the American and National Leagues adopted 162-game seasons prior to their first expansion drafts and the length of their seasons has not changed. Therefore, it should have been easy to assign point values for won-lost records. But what about strike seasons? Due to labor stoppages, complete seasons were not played in 1972, 1981, 1985, 1994, or 1995. What is the most accurate method to account for won-lost records in the incomplete seasons? The solution was to assign points based on winning percentages rather than wins whether the season was played to completion or not:

| | |
|---|---|
| .500 record | 1 point per season |
| .550 record | 2 points per season |
| .600 record | 3 points per season |

The big winner here was the Arizona Diamondbacks with 12. Posting a record of 100-62 in 1999, only their second season, the Snakes capitalized on their success by defeating the Yankees in the World Series two years later. However, most of the key players on the 2001 Diamondbacks, including Randy Johnson, Mark Grace, and Steve Finley, were free agents, posing zero correlation with the expansion draft held four years earlier. The Kansas City Royals finished a close second with 11 points. The Royals, in an era that predated free agency, first broke the .500 barrier in 1971 in only their third season. From 1972 to 1978, the Royals posted only two losing seasons.

At the other end of the spectrum, three teams scored no points. The Seattle Mariners did not post a winning season until 1991, their 15th year of existence, nor did the Montreal Expos until 1979, their 11th. As for the Tampa Bay Devil Rays, they perpetuated their role as the doormat of the American League East for their entire first decade, failing to register even a .440 winning percentage.

## PART II: EXPANSION PLAYERS

As defined earlier in this essay, expansion players consist of the following two components:

> Drafted Players - *Players selected in the expansion draft*
> Regeneration Players - *Players received in trades for players selected in the expansion draft*

Points were awarded to expansion players on the basis of five-year increments. If a drafted or regeneration player remains on his team's roster five years into the franchise history, he is awarded two points. Any player drafted or generated by the expansion draft who remained on the roster after 10 years is awarded five points.

Leading the way here were the Kansas City Royals with 53 points. The expansion draft generated trades for Hal McRae, Amos Otis, Fred Patek, Marty Pattin, and Kansas City native Steve Mingori. All remained active and productive on the Royals' roster in 1978 as they won their third consecutive American League West title. The Toronto Blue Jays were not far behind with 50 points. Expansion draft picks Jim Clancy, Ernie Whitt, and Garth Iorg all contributed to the Blue Jays' in their "Drive of '85," as did regeneration players Damaso Garcia and Rance Mulliniks.

On the other end of the scale, the Tampa Bay Devil Rays and Arizona Diamondbacks registered only 10 and 15 points, respectively. Only one expansion player, Brandon Lyon, remained in an Arizona uniform 10 years after the Diamondbacks joined the major leagues. No Devil Rays player can make the same claim.

## PART III: INDIVIDUAL STATISTICS

The third and perhaps most crucial metric to understand the effectiveness of the 14 expansion drafts is to analyze the statistical output of the players. Several problems arose with this particular analysis. Which statistics should be analyzed and how best to weight these statistics? Are runs batted in more important than home runs? Since most expansion teams posted poor aggregate records, would won-lost be of any significance at all? And how do you compare players across eras? In the 1960s, the mound was higher, fences were wider, and the ball did not travel as far. Every team played on natural grass surfaces during the first round of expansion. By 1977, when the Mariners and the Blue Jays were admitted into the American League, 10 of the 26 teams played on artificial turf.

To solve the problem, the home run, runs batted in, won-lost, and earned-run average were all shelved in favor of one all-encompassing statistic: wins above replacement (WAR). Unveiled by Bill James at the SABR convention in Milwaukee on July 13, 2001, WAR is defined as "the number of wins [a player is] responsible for beyond the replacement level at the player's position."[2] In other words, WAR is a statistical measure used to analyze the number of additional wins a player's presence is expected to contribute over that of a player of average capabilities. WAR encompasses pitching, fielding, and baserunning statistics as well as batting.

For the purpose of writing this essay, WAR is the simplest and most direct way to assess the collective output of the expansion players. This essay will adopt the Baseball Reference calculation of WAR. If a player's WAR is valued at 1, that is equal to one point in the expansion players' analysis. Suppose players selected in an expansion draft and others generated in trades for those players yielded 17 wins above replacement after subtracting negative from positive scores. That would be equal to 17 points in this analysis.

Among first year teams, the 1969 Kansas City Royals scored the highest WAR with 26.6. At the other end of the scale, the 1993 Colorado Rockies as a team score a WAR of only 6.1. The Royals continued to lead their expansion brethren with an aggregate WAR of 184.8 in their first decade of American League baseball. Hal McRae (15.7), Amos Otis (37.2), Fred Patek (21.5) and Al Fitzmorris (15.5) all contributed to the Royals and their strong finish between 1969 and 1978.

The Seattle Pilots-Milwaukee Brewers franchise also generated a high WAR of 151.1. Most of the output was the work of regeneration players. As general manager of the Brewers from 1970 to 1972, Frank Lane traded most of the roster he inherited. In return, Lane received players like Don Money (23.9 WAR with the Brewers through 1978) and Johnny Briggs (14.4) from the Phillies, George "Boomer" Scott (22.6) from the Red Sox, and Jim Colborn (12.5) from the Cubs. The Tampa Bay Devil Rays, meanwhile, posted an aggregate WAR of only 36.9 among their expansion players. The New York Mets were not much better with 41.8.

## THE ENVELOPE, PLEASE ...

Now for the results of the expansion draft analysis:

### 14. Tampa Bay Devil Rays   1998 to 2007   47 pts

Not surprisingly, the Tampa Bay Devil Rays generated the lowest overall score. During their first decade in the major leagues, the Rays finished in last place every year, winning as many as 70 games only once, in 2004. Five expansion players remained on their roster in 2003, combining for a WAR of -0.1. One positive spin about the draft is that at least it yielded one good season from each of Miguel Cairo (3.2 WAR), Quinton McCracken (2.1), and Tony Saunders (3.1) in 1998.

Aggregate WAR:  36.9

### 13. New York Mets  1962 to 1971   66 pts

A great miracle happened at Flushing Meadows when, in 1969, the New York Mets won the World Series in only their eighth season. However, most of the team's success in 1969 was attributed to the farm system and scouting department rather than the expansion draft. Only four players (Tommie Agee, Don Cardwell, J.C. Martin, Al Weis) were generated by trades from the expansion draft. Of the four, only Agee's WAR (5.2) was of any significance. In the seven intermediate seasons, the Mets averaged only 56 wins while producing a total WAR of 27.5 from its expansion players

Aggregate WAR: 41.8

### 12. Seattle Mariners   1977 to 1986   115 pts

Opening Day program for the 1977 Seattle Mariners. Although the Mariners avoided the cellar during their first season, they finished in last place five times between 1978 and 1986. (Courtesy of David S. Eskenazi)

Like the Devil Rays, the Mariners did not post one winning season among their first 10 in the American League. Their record was slightly better than Tampa Bay's; they finished in last place five times as opposed to 10. The Mariners did generate quality players, both through the expansion draft and through trades. The problem that the Mariners encountered under the ownership of Lester Smith and Danny Kaye, and, later, George Argyros, is that they could scarcely afford to keep players like Ruppert Jones, Rick Honeycutt, Floyd Bannister, and Richie Zisk. Only in 1987 did the luck of the Mariners' trident begin to point upward when they selected Ken Griffey Jr. as the first overall pick in the June amateur draft.

Aggregate WAR: 87.6

## 11. Arizona Diamondbacks   1998 to 2007  116 pts

The Diamondbacks rose meteorically to win 100 games in 1999, 92 games and the World Series in 2001, and 98 games in 2002. As was discussed earlier, the rapid ascent of the Diamondbacks is attributed more to their free-agent signings than the players they selected in the expansion draft. It should be emphasized that two key players in their playoff run, Luis Gonzalez (30.2 WAR) and Curt Schilling (25.9 WAR), were acquired in trades generated by the expansion draft. The Diamondbacks' reign atop the National League West was short, as the team plummeted to a record of 51-111 in 2004.

Aggregate WAR: 89.4

## 10. Houston Colt .45s-Astros  1962 to 1971  120 pts

In their first decade in the National League, the Houston franchise reached the break-even level only once, and that was exactly .500 (81-81) in 1969. The Colt .45s reaped immediate benefits from drafting pitchers Dick Farrell (16.7) and Bob Bruce (11.1). In addition, the draft generated a 1965 trade to the St. Louis Cardinals for Mike Cuellar (13.4). After yielding an aggregate WAR of 23.0 in 1962, expansion players yielded 16.2 wins above replacement to the Colt .45s in 1963 and 16.3 in 1964. Their contributions to the Astros after moving to the Astrodome were modest.

Aggregate WAR: 71.5

## 9. Colorado Rockies   1993 to 2002  126 points

The Rockies and their expansion players struggled in their first two seasons, posting a WAR of 6.1 in 1993 and 6.9 in 1994. Then in 1995, after moving from Mile High Stadium to Coors Field, the Rockies won a wild-card title with a record of 77-67. Two of the most prominent "Blake Street Bombers," Larry Walker and Ellis Burks, were free-agent signings. However, unlike the Arizona Diamondbacks, the Rockies' expansion players did contribute to their quick ascent. Dante Bichette, Vinny Castilla, Darren Holmes, Curtis Leskanic, Steve Reed, Kevin Ritz, and Eric Young Jr. were responsible for 21.2 wins above replacement for the 1995 Rockies. However, the early success of the Rockies was short-lived: Colorado contended again in 1996 and 1997 before retreating to mediocrity.

Aggregate WAR: 87.5

## 8. Montreal Expos   1969 to 1984   127 pts

The Expos were the third team who failed to reach the .500 barrier in its first decade in the major leagues, contending only in 1979 with a record of 95-65. Entering the National League with a record of 52-110 in 1969, the Expos fielded an above-average representation of quality players acquired through the expansion draft and trades. Players like Rusty Staub, Bill Stoneman, Ron Hunt, and Ron Fairly led the Expos to win an improbable "70 in '70" before appearing on the verge of contending as early as 1973. A global energy crisis, compounded by political uncertainty in Quebec, prompted the Expos to implement "Phase Two" in 1974. The most harmful trade in this austerity program sent Ken Singleton and Mike Torrez to the Baltimore Orioles for Rich Coggins and Dave McNally. Singleton and Torrez contributed a combined WAR

Rusty Staub of the New York Mets leads off 1st base in action against Mike Jorgensen and the Montreal Expos. On April 5, 1972, the two were traded for one another as Tim Foli and Ken Singleton were also sent north to Montreal. (Courtesy of the McCord Museum, Montreal)

of 48.3 before both players retired in 1984. Coggins and McNally, meanwhile, combined for a WAR of -1.0. Of the four teams celebrating their 10th anniversary in 1978, the Expos were the only one to post a losing record.

Aggregate WAR: 96.7

### 7. San Diego Padres   1969 to 1978   128 pts

Like their expansion brethren in Montreal, the Padres posted a record of 52-110 in 1969. The Padres, however, could not escape the basement of the National League West for another six years. Most of the players drafted by the Padres were prospects and therefore, remained on the roster longer than usual for an expansion team. The prize of the expansion draft was Nate Colbert, who was responsible for 17.2 wins above replacement in six years with San Diego. Although the Padres breached the .500 barrier in 1978 with a record of 84-78, their success was short-lived; they returned to last place in 1980.

Aggregate WAR: 89.1

### 6. Florida Marlins   1993 to 2002   137 pts

The Florida Marlins posted only one winning season in their first 10 years, a 92-70 record in 1997 on their way to winning the World Series. Many of the expansion players had already been replaced on the roster by free agents. However, the 1997 Marlins still included Jeff Conine (11.1 WAR), who was selected in the expansion draft, along with Gary Sheffield (13.0 WAR,

A Marlins fan celebrates the first Opening Day at Joe Robbie Stadium, April 5, 1993. Despite posting a record of only 64-98, the 1993 Florida Marlins set a franchise record for attendance which still stands today. (Courtesy of the Miami Marlins)

who was acquired in a 1993 trade for Trevor Hoffman. Sheffield was traded to the Los Angeles Dodgers in 1998 for Mike Piazza, a Wayne Huizenga "blockbuster" that generated deals for Preston Wilson and Mike Lowell. Sheffield notwithstanding, expansion players were generally unaffected by the scorched-earth policy that dismantled the Marlins after the 1997 World Series. The 1998 Marlins plummeted in the standings to finish 54-108 and would not contend again until 2003, when they won another World Series.

Aggregate WAR: 87.8

### 5. LA-California Angels   1961 to 1970   152 pts

As one of the two initial expansion teams, the Los Angeles Angels were not even expected to win 50 games in 1961. Instead they won 70, setting a record among first-year expansion teams that still stands. A year later, they breached the .500 barrier with a record of 86-76. The Angels were inconsistent in their first decade, posting four winning records but never two consecutively. What helped the Angels in this analysis were the wins above replacement contributed by two players. Jim Fregosi, selected in the expansion draft from Boston, provided a WAR of 45.2 between 1961 and 1970. Meanwhile, an expansion-day trade landed Dean Chance from the Washington Senators. In six seasons with the Halos, Chance posted a WAR of 20.5. The selection of Fregosi continued to pay dividends for the Angels in the 1970s. A 1971 trade sending him to the New York Mets brought Nolan Ryan to Orange County for eight seasons, from 1972 to 1979.

Aggregate WAR: 129.3

### 4. Toronto Blue Jays   1977 to 1986   167 pts

The Blue Jays started slowly in the American League East, averaging 58 wins a season between 1977 and 1980. By 1983, they entered their first pennant race and soon became the most consistent team in baseball, averaging 91 wins through 1993. As stated earlier, expansion draft picks Jim Clancy, Garth Iorg, and Ernie Whitt all remained Blue Jays in 1986, combining for 31.8 wins above replacement for the decade. The Blue Jays under Pat Gillick became adept in the trading department, generating Roy Howell, Damaso Garcia, and Alfredo Griffin in deals for expansion draft selections. The Blue Jays probably would have ranked higher were it not for the contributions of the farm system and the Rule 5 draft that augmented the team's success in the 1980s.

Aggregate WAR: 116.4

### 3. Seattle Pilots-Milwaukee Brewers 1969 to 1978 188 pts

Full ticket to Opening Day with the Seattle Pilots, April 11, 1969. While the Pilots defeated the Chicago White Sox, their next Opening day in 1970 would be played in Milwaukee as the Brewers. (Courtesy of David S. Eskenazi)

Ironically, two of the more successful drafts belonged to teams that posted only one winning season in their first 10 years. The expansion Senators perpetuated Washington's legacy as "first in war, first in peace, and last in the American League" until a sudden 86-win season in 1969 under new manager Ted Williams. The Milwaukee Brewers, having moved from Seattle in 1970, remained in their divisional doldrums until 1978. That is the year general manager Harry Dalton and manager George Bamberger imported "the Oriole Way" from Baltimore to reinvigorate "Bambi's Bombers" into a contender.

As stated earlier, when Frank Lane was appointed general manager of the Milwaukee Brewers in 1970, he inherited a franchise in disarray. True to his reputation, Lane concocted a series of mammoth trades to overhaul the roster by 1972. The deals brought a number of talented players to "Suds City," even if the Brewers' success as a team was not felt immediately. After five years of hitting "taters" over the fence at County Stadium, the Brewers traded George Scott back to Boston in 1976 for Cecil Cooper. "Coop" starred at first base for Milwaukee well into the 1980s, rapping 44 doubles in 1979 and batting .352 in 1980. The Brewers remained contenders in the American League East through 1983, winning the pennant in 1982.

Aggregate WAR: 151.1

### 2. Washington Senators 1961 to 1970 190 points

Both Milwaukee and Washington scored high points largely because of the acumen of their general managers in assessing the expansion players in trades. Late in the 1961 season, the Senators traded Dave Sisler to the Cincinnati Reds for Claude Osteen. The left-handed Osteen contributed nine wins above replacement before he was packaged to the Los Angeles Dodgers in 1964. Washington was able to negotiate for Frank Howard, Ken McMullen, Dick Nen, Phil Ortega, and Pete Richert in exchange for Osteen. The quintet of ex-Angelenos combined for 54.2 wins above replacement between 1965 and 1970. The Claude Osteen trade continued to generate quality players for the franchise long after it moved to Texas in 1971.

Aggregate WAR: 149.4

### 1. Kansas City Royals 1969 to 1978 249 points

True to hypothesis, the most successful expansion draft belonged to the Kansas City Royals. It was not even close, as they finished 59 points ahead of their nearest competitor. The explanation for the Royals' successful draft has already been analyzed. They contended as early as 1971, remained competitive for the remainder of the 1970s and all of the 1980s, while generating talented players from their draft choices who made positive contributions to the team.

No account on the early success of the Kansas City Royals would be complete without acknowledging Ewing M. Kauffman. Mr. K was not even a baseball fan, just a billionaire pharmaceutical magnate with fierce pride in his adopted hometown of Kansas City.

Young Kansas City Royals celebrate Cap Day at Municipal Stadium in 1969. They would have no idea that the Royals would emerge as the most successful of the fourteen expansion teams. (Courtesy of the Kansas City Royals)

He knew the psychological malaise associated with the Athletics moving to Oakland in 1967. The threat of an antitrust lawsuit followed and when the Royals came to town in 1969, Mr. K was happy to finance whatever was required to build a winner for Kansas City and keep them competitive.

Aggregate WAR: 184.8

# CONCLUSION

Using the criteria of won-lost analysis, the longevity of the careers of the expansion players, and the wins above replacement contributed by these players, it was determined that the Kansas City Royals conducted the most successful expansion draft of any team. While the Toronto Blue Jays and Milwaukee Brewers also became perennial contenders, the Senators slipped back to last place in 1970 before abandoning Washington a year later. Economic misfortunes were a main hindrance for many of the other teams. Some were underfunded while others were tight on money. Others still had the funds but spent profligately. Even the Brewers, despite their later successes, were born out of the bankruptcy of the Seattle Pilots in 1970.

Expansion has demonstrated to be a successful experiment for the National and American Leagues. As the nexus of gravity of American commerce and industry has shifted from the American Northeast to the Sun Belt, the Pacific Coast, and across the 49th Parallel, the population has migrated, bringing with its interest in baseball. No doubt Gordon Cobbledick would have marveled at how baseball has evolved as a truly national pastime with 30 franchises from coast to coast. It was time for expansion baseball.

*Disclaimer:* All figures for wins above replacement (WAR) are based on the statistics per Baseball-Reference. These figures have been rounded for presentation purposes. The reader should be aware that if one were to look up these wins-above-replacement figures on Baseball-Reference, the actual results may vary slightly.

**Acknowledgements:** Scott Crawford, Pat Gillick, Jim Kreuz, Len Levin, Barbara Mantegani, Bill Nowlin, Jacob Pomrenke, David Raglin, and Carl Riechers.

In addition to the undernoted source, the author relied on Retrosheet.org and Baseball-Reference.com to access information for this paper.

**Notes**

1 Interview with Pat Gillick, January 20, 2018

2 Paul Dickson and Skip McAfee, *The Dickson Baseball Dictionary, 3rd edition* (New York: W.W. Norton, 2011), 938.

# RICKEY'S FOLLY: HOW THE CONTINENTAL LEAGUE FORCED BASEBALL EXPANSION

## By Warren Corbett

President John F. Kennedy delivered the ceremonial first pitch in Washington's Griffith Stadium on April 10, 1961, to inaugurate baseball's new era. The debut of the new Washington Senators against the Chicago White Sox was the first game in the 10-team American League, marking the majors' first expansion since 1901.

The creation of the two AL expansion franchises, and the two new National League clubs that followed in 1962, came after more than a decade of hesitation, one step forward and two steps back, as American and National League owners struggled to cope with demands to bring big-league ball to growing metropolises outside the Northeast and Midwest. At last they capitulated under pressure from politicians and a baseball genius with wealthy backers.

"Probably no single program in baseball history," Commissioner Ford Frick wrote, "created more controversy, aroused stronger fan feeling, or brought more vituperative discussion, pro and con, than the movement of clubs and the expansion of the major leagues."[1] He should know; he turned backflips for years to delay expansion on the instructions of his masters, the owners.

Major-league baseball had been putting off expansion at least since the end of World War II, when the Pacific Coast League petitioned for big-league status. The PCL's ambition drew the predictable response: The majors stiff-armed the Westerners. But two PCL markets were too

big to ignore. By the 1950 census, Los Angeles was the fourth-largest US city in population, with San Francisco 11th. The National Football League had put a franchise in Los Angeles in 1946 and absorbed the San Francisco 49ers as part of its merger with the All-America Football Conference in 1950. Some baseball executives thought a westward move was overdue.

In 1954 former owner Bill Veeck produced a bullish report on the booming LA market that could have been written by the chamber of commerce.[2] The next year an American League realignment committee headed by White Sox general manager Frank Lane released a financial analysis of a 10-team league, complete with sample schedules. Lane concluded that the existing clubs could make a profit by putting new teams in Los Angeles and San Francisco, despite increased travel costs.[3]

But nothing happened. Many owners believed there were not enough big-league-quality players to stock new teams. No owner wanted to give up home dates with the Yankees or Dodgers in return for games against no-name expansion clubs with no-name players.

Then, in the fall of 1957, Walter O'Malley seized Los Angeles. O'Malley's bold move of his Brooklyn Dodgers, hauling Horace Stoneham's Giants in his ample wake, was the catalyst for expansion.

New York Mayor Robert Wagner, having lost the Dodgers and Giants and facing re-election, did what any fearful politician would do: He appointed a committee. Its chairman was William Shea, a politically connected lawyer who became the prime mover in an urgent drive to bring another big-league team to New York. "I thought it was a very easy job to be accomplished," Shea recalled with Big Apple arrogance, "that all I had to do was get some people with money together and go out on a white charger and pick up a franchise somewhere in the hinterlands.

"Well, I soon found out that it wasn't going to be done."[4]

Commissioner Frick declared the city "open territory," meaning the Yankees could not block another team from moving in.[5] Shea targeted small-market franchises in Pittsburgh and Cincinnati, but their owners had no interest in becoming the New York Pirates or the Brooklyn Reds. Throwing more cold water, NL President Warren Giles told Shea the league had no plans to expand. Giles was reported to have said, "Who needs New York?"[6]

Another politician was stung by the loss of the Dodgers. Brooklyn's congressman, Emanuel Celler, was chairman of the House Judiciary Committee and a longtime critic of baseball's exemption from antitrust laws. In 1958 he proposed legislation to end the exemption. Furious lobbying by the majors defeated his bill. The House voted instead to exempt all professional sports leagues from antitrust restrictions, but the Senate buried the bill, at least temporarily.

Facing pressure from Washington and agitation from New York, the majors held their ground. The frustrated Bill Shea saw no clear path to his goal, but someone else did. Branch Rickey, the farsighted executive who had invented the farm system and brought racial integration to baseball, declared that a third major league was inevitable. In a May 1958 interview with *The Sporting News*, Rickey said forming a new league was preferable to expanding the existing majors and creating "too many also-rans."[7]

Rickey was soon talking to Shea, and he found an eager audience. Within six months Shea announced that he was lining up backers for a third league. Speaking to reporters at Toots Shor's saloon, he revealed that "a substantial baseball man" was advising him. "I'm hopeful [the majors] will give the new league cooperation," Shea said. "But if they don't take you in, you have to go on your own."[8]

While he traveled the country rounding up partners, Shea found his most important supporter in Washington. Tennessee Senator Estes Kefauver, chairman of the antitrust and monopoly subcommittee, believed in enforcing antitrust laws and didn't believe in monopoly. It was Kefauver who had blocked the House bill granting antitrust immunity to sports leagues. In February 1959 he introduced his own legislation to put all professional leagues, including baseball, under antitrust law. In addition, the bill limited teams to controlling just 80 players. (Some teams had more than 400 in their farm systems.)[9] Kefauver was attacking the economic foundation of the baseball business.

Feeling the heat, the majors adopted their first policy on expansion in May 1959. After a special owners meeting, the majors announced they would "favorably consider" recognizing a third league — with a big if: if the new circuit's cities were larger than the smallest current big-league market (Kansas City, population around 450,000); if it had stadiums seating at least 25,000; and if the new teams reached a financial settlement with the minor leagues whose territory they invaded. If those and other criteria were met, the American and National Leagues might embrace a competitor.[10]

On July 27 Shea formally launched his new circuit. It now had a name, the Continental League, and commitments from backers in five markets: New York, Houston, Minneapolis-St. Paul, Denver, and Toronto. Shea listed 11 other cities that were interested. Taking the majors at their word, he said, "We are therefore proceeding on the basis of the complete and unqualified cooperation of the two existing major leagues."[11]

The next day Senator Kefauver opened hearings on his antitrust bill. Commissioner Frick testified that the majors were "on the level" in pledging cooperation with the upstarts: "I feel deep in my heart that the new Continental Baseball League will become a reality."[12] Not all baseball men toed the company line. American League President Joe Cronin sniped, "Calling a league a major league doesn't make it a major league."[13] Kefauver didn't push his legislation, but he warned that he would be watching: "You might say baseball is under surveillance, even under a shotgun."[14]

With Kefauver's threat of a shotgun marriage, the baseball establishment agreed to talk with the Continentals. At the first meeting of the three leagues, on August 18 in New York, Shea played his ace. Branch Rickey walked into the room as the first president of the Continental League. Although he was 77 years old, Rickey was still a formidable force in the eyes of his former rivals. His league might be a mirage, but Rickey was flesh and blood and baseball genius. "It was at that moment that the owners knew we were for real and that we meant business," said one of the Houston financiers, Craig Cullinan Jr.[15]

Rickey argued that it would be easier to find 200 players for eight new teams that would compete among themselves than to find 100 to stock four expansion teams capable of competing in the existing majors. He envisioned a round-robin World Series among the champions of all three leagues by 1963. "The fans will devour it," he exclaimed.[16]

But the majors pointed to their criteria for recognition of a new league. The Continental had only five teams, and not all had big-league-sized stadiums. They had reached no agreements to pay off the minor-league clubs that would be displaced.

Then Washington Senators owner Calvin Griffith tossed a stink bomb into the party. Griffith, with his team losing games and money, wanted out of Washington. He was laying plans to move to Minneapolis-St. Paul. His fellow AL owners put him off, fearing a congressional backlash if they abandoned the nation's capital. But wheels were beginning to turn. At the October league meeting, President Cronin appointed a committee to study expansion.[17]

Rickey now saw that his trust had been misplaced. He told the Continental owners that the majors were undermining the new league. For the first time, he said the Continental might have to "go outlaw."[18] That meant raiding the majors and minors for talent and mounting a court challenge to the reserve clause, which bound players to their teams for life. But several Continental owners were leery of going to war. While publicly committed to the new venture, they wanted to stay on the majors' good side in case the existing leagues decided to expand.

Acquiring players was the Continental's biggest challenge. Baseball had no pipeline of college talent as in football. The majors controlled virtually all professional players through their farm systems. Without their cooperation, Rickey confidently maintained that the player pool could be expanded by tapping Latin America and Japan, and making full use of African-American talent.

Rickey's plan represented a radical departure from baseball history and tradition. The Continental League would operate a central scouting bureau and a farm system controlled by the league, not individual teams, with all clubs drafting players from the pool. The teams would share local television revenue.[19] The goal was to level the financial playing field so there would be no Yankee dynasty and no charity case like the St. Louis Browns. Branch Rickey, conservative Republican and fervent anti-communist, wrote a constitution for socialism in baseball.

At the winter meeting in December 1959, the majors continued to insist that they had no plans to expand. Rickey put up a bold front, saying, "The Continental League is as inevitable as tomorrow morning, if not as imminent."[20] Commissioner Frick declared, "The Continental League can have our endorsement, too, as soon as they settle certain things."[21]

Frick's public expressions of support served to keep Congress at bay while pushing expansion down the road to some unspecified date in the misty future. Some saw it as a cynical ploy. New York Daily News columnist Dick Young wrote, "Did you ever have the feeling that someone is being too nice to you, and it has you worried?"[22]

"Expansion is coming," Frick said, "but it will not come by fiat, by pressure or the threat of legislation." He picked the wrong place to strike a defiant tone: at the Touchdown Club in Washington, with Senator Kefauver in the audience. Kefauver thought the commissioner had "disparaged Congress."[23]

The senator struck back in February 1960 with new legislation that might have been titled the Continental League Relief Act. His bill provided that each major-league team could control no more than 40 players; the rest would be eligible to be drafted by other clubs. Shea and Rickey enthusiastically endorsed the legislation, but Commissioner Frick denounced it as "vicious" and "discriminatory." He predicted that it would kill the minor leagues, since the majors would no longer subsidize farm clubs if they stood to lose most of the players in the draft.[24]

The Continental League had filled out its circuit of eight teams with the addition of Dallas-Fort Worth, Atlanta, and Buffalo, and announced that it would begin play in 1961. If the Kefauver bill failed, Shea said, the Continentals' choice was "war or quit."[25]

The Senate opened debate on June 28. For procedural

reasons, the first vote came on an amendment that would extend baseball's antitrust exemption to other sports leagues. When that was adopted by 45 to 41, it was obvious that Kefauver's proposal to eliminate the exemption would fail, so sponsors pulled the bill from consideration. The majors had won, but the margin, with 41 votes against the antitrust exemption, was far too close for comfort.[26] Frick later admitted, "Baseball was scared."[27]

"Panicked" is more like it. After dawdling for 14 years since the Pacific Coast League pushed for expansion, the owners moved faster than a speeding Ty Cobb to quash the threat to their monopoly. Within days after the Senate vote, they invited the Continental principals to meet for a discussion of how "to implement expansion via Continental League or increased membership."[28]

The summit meeting, in Chicago on August 2, opened with fireworks. The Dodgers' Walter O'Malley lectured the Continentals, "Your having rocked the boat makes it hard for the major leagues to meet you halfway." Shea angrily replied that he had no choice but to appeal to Congress, since the majors had stonewalled him.[29] At one point O'Malley roared, "Goddammit," then turned to the pious Continental president and said, "Excuse me, Mr. Rickey."[30]

After both sides vented, Milwaukee owner Lou Perini offered a compromise: The majors would expand, taking in four Continental franchises immediately and the other four within a few years. The "four now, four later" proposal was the first concrete step toward a settlement.

The Continental delegation retired to caucus in another room and erupted in loud cheers. Chicago writer Jerome Holtzman commented, "The Continental League went phffft – and disappeared into the hot air from whence it came."[31]

At that moment Rickey's last shot at glory died. The jubilant Continentals ignored his warning to read the fine print. O'Malley had not said which four cities would come first or when the other four would be added.

But the old man had served his purpose. Just by being Branch Rickey, he had forced the majors to take the league seriously. Houston's Craig Cullinan said, "It was ridiculed as a sham, but on the contrary it was an enormous success because it ran what became the biggest bluff in the history of professional sports."[32] All Continental cities except Buffalo were eventually accepted into the majors, though Denver had to wait 33 years.

Rather than savoring victory, the majors dissolved into backbiting and chaos. The pressure for expansion revealed a rift between the American and National Leagues, which were separate and highly competitive organizations. Major-league baseball had no management structure suitable for a large business, which the game had become. With the docile Frick in the commissioner's office, the cartel lacked strong leadership. Owners O'Malley and Del Webb of the Yankees stepped into that void as the de facto leaders, two businessmen protecting their private interests rather than pursuing the greater good of the game.

O'Malley fired the opening shot in an intramural baseball war. As chairman of the NL expansion committee, he engineered a unanimous vote on October 17 to award franchises to New York and Houston. The owners were Continental League backers: heiress Joan Whitney Payson in New York and Craig Cullinan Jr., R.E. Smith, and Judge Roy Hofheinz in Houston. The new clubs would begin play in 1962, giving them a year and a half to prepare.

New York's addition was a foregone conclusion. Houston was "considered by many the ripest plum available for plucking by big league baseball," as *Sports Illustrated*'s Roy Terrell put it.[33] Both leagues had coveted the nation's seventh-largest city. Del Webb, chairman of the AL expansion committee, fumed that the Nationals "pulled a fast one on us" by taking unilateral action. He added, "This was O'Malley's doing."[34]

O'Malley had stepped on a hornet's nest. He had his own agenda: to keep the American League out of Los Angeles, or at least delay as long as possible. But LA was now the third-largest city, and Commissioner Frick had declared it, like New York, open territory for expansion.[35] The AL couldn't pass it up. And Webb wouldn't pass up a chance to sting O'Malley.

Meeting in New York on October 26, the AL pulled its own fast one. The owners voted to allow Calvin Griffith to take his Senators to Minneapolis-St. Paul. To mollify Congress, they awarded Washington an expansion franchise. The second expansion team would go to Los Angeles.[36]

The AL's decision blew up the agreement with the Continental League. Continental owners in Minnesota were shut out, and Los Angeles had never been part of the third league. (The Continentals had avoided challenging O'Malley, even rejecting an investor group that included Frank Sinatra.)[37] Bill Shea, now kibitzing from the sidelines, described the AL action as "one of the lowest blows below the belt in the history of sports."[38]

But O'Malley wasn't giving up without a fight. He leaned on the commissioner, and Frick about-faced, saying that O'Malley was entitled to compensation for the invasion of "his" territory. Hank Greenberg, the slugger turned executive who had secretly been promised the LA franchise, refused to kowtow to O'Malley and dropped his bid.[39] That left the American League scrambling.

The AL, in its haste to upstage the Nationals, had voted to put expansion teams on the field in 1961. Opening Day was less than six months away. There was no turning back; the old Washington Senators were loading the truck for Minnesota and the new Washington franchise had been awarded to a syndicate led by retired Lieutenant General Pete Quesada. The league couldn't play with nine teams. "Never has the baseball picture been more muddled, millstoned or mired in uncertainty as it is today," the Associated Press's Joe Reichler wrote.[40]

Singing cowboy Gene Autry threw his white Stetson into the ring to save the day. The AL jumped at his bid for the Los Angeles franchise. But O'Malley had the whip hand, and he used it. After three days of negotiations at an emergency meeting in St. Louis in December, Autry agreed to O'Malley's terms. He paid the Dodgers $350,000; agreed to play one year in the city's tiny minor-league park, Wrigley Field; and then become O'Malley's tenant when the new Dodger Stadium was ready.[41] The AL got a team in LA, and O'Malley got everything else.

At last expansion was a fact. It was a windfall for the 16 legacy teams. Each new club paid $2.1 million for the ragtag players they drafted – "crumbs from the table," Rickey called them.[42] As Rickey had predicted, the expansion teams took up residence at the bottom of the standings. Only the Angels posted a winning record in their first seven years. The "Miracle Mets" won the 1969 World Series and reached the Series again four years later, but no other expansion club made it to the championship round until 1980.

Would baseball have been better off if the Continental League had succeeded? Professional football followed that model; the American Football League was born as an outlaw in 1960 and persevered through years of heavy financial losses until it merged with the NFL to create the colossus of American sports. Baseball expanded its two leagues four more times, with stumbles at every turn,

while its claim to be the national pastime became a relic of history.

**Notes**

1  Ford C. Frick, *Games, Asterisks and People* (New York: Crown, 1973), 119.

2  Special Research Committee for Major League Baseball in Los Angeles, "Progress Report on the Los Angeles Major League Baseball Project" (1954), commonly known as the Veeck report, in the author's files.

3  American League Realignment Committee, "Is a Ten-Club League Practicable?" (the Frank Lane report), January 30, 1955, in American League Papers, BA MSS 125, Series III Box 20 Folder 4, at the National Baseball Hall of Fame library, Cooperstown, New York.

4  Murray Polner, *Branch Rickey* (New York: New American Library, 1982), 252.

5  "Frick Favors New York as Open," *Washington Post and Times Herald*, December 7, 1957: A12.

6  Arthur Daley, "Sports of the Times," *New York Times*, November 18, 1958: 48.

7  J.G. Taylor Spink, "'Third Major Must Come Soon' – Rickey," *The Sporting News*, May 21, 1958: 1.

8  Dick Young, "Third Major League Gets New York Go-Ahead," *Chicago Tribune*, November 14, 1958: C1.

9  United Press International, "Kefauver Offers Sport Control Bill," *Chicago Tribune*, February 4, 1959: B1.

10  United Press International, "Majors to Accept Bids From 3d League," *Chicago Tribune*, May 22, 1959: E1.

11  Dan Daniel, "35,000 Minimum Capacity for Continental Loop Park," *The Sporting News*, August 5, 1959: 8.

12  United Press International, "Frick Talks Baseball Harmony," *New York Times*, July 30, 1959: 32.

13  Dave Brady, "Majors Told to Play Ball With Third Big League," *Washington Post and Times Herald*, August 1, 1959: A11.

14  Lee Lowenfish, *Branch Rickey, Baseball's Ferocious Gentleman* (Lincoln: University of Nebraska Press, 2007), 556.

15  Clark Nealon, Robert Nottebart, Stanley Siegal, and James Tinsley, "The Campaign for Major League Baseball in Houston," *Houston Review* (undated reprint), 22. houstonhistorymagazine.org/wp-content/uploads/2014/02/7.1-The-Campaign-for-Major-League-Baseball-in-Houston-Clark-Nealon-Robert-Nottebart-Stanley-Siegal-James-Tinsley.pdf, accessed November 1, 2017.

16  Lowenfish, *Branch Rickey*, 564-565.

17  Daniel, "A.L. Lays Expansion Groundwork, Will Study Twin

Cities' Request," *The Sporting News*, October 28, 1959: 5.

18  Michael Shapiro, *Bottom of the Ninth* (New York: Henry Holt, 2009), 141.

19  Dick Gordon, "Player Pool Plan Aired By B.R. in Twin-City Visit," *The Sporting News*, January 13, 1960: 9.

20  Oscar Kahan, "Mahatma Dares Majors to Attempt Expansion," *The Sporting News*, December 16, 1959: 12.

21  "Third Major Standards Set; Don't Need Mediator – Frick," *The Sporting News*, January 13, 1960: 9.

22  "Dick Young Finds Love Feast 'Too Mushy'; He's Suspicious," *The Sporting News*, September 2, 1959: 16.

23  Brady, "Blast by Frick Scorches Ears on Capitol Hill," *The Sporting News*, January 27, 1960: 6.

24  Brady, "Frick Clears Sacks Testifying Against Kefauver Sport Bill," *The Sporting News*, May 25, 1960: 9.

25  Shapiro, *Bottom of the Ninth*, 188.

26  Lowenfish, *Branch Rickey*, 568-569, 571-572; Robert Reed, *Colt .45s: A Six-Gun Salute* (Houston: Lone Star Books, 1997), 31.

27  Frick, *Games, Asterisks and People*, 128.

28  Shapiro, *Bottom of the Ninth*, 208-209.

29  Reed, *Colt .45s*, 34.

30  Lowenfish, *Branch Rickey*, 573.

31  Jerry Holtzman, "Big Timers Clearing Decks for Expansion," *The Sporting News*, August 10, 1960: 3.

32  Reed, *Colt .45s*, 34.

33  Roy Terrell, "'The Damnedest Mess Baseball Has Ever Seen,'" *Sports Illustrated*, December 19, 1960, si.com/vault/1960/12/19/585926/the-damndest-mess-baseball-has-ever-seen, accessed October 20, 2017.

34  Shirley Povich, "Griffith's Decision Made Purely on Impulse," *Washington Post and Times Herald*, October 27, 1960: D1.

35  Associated Press, "Ford Frick Believes L.A. Should Be Open Territory," *Los Angeles Times*, August 15, 1960: IV-3.

36  Joe King, "A.L. Speeds Expansion – 10 Teams in '61," *The Sporting News*, November 2, 1960: 3.

37  Shapiro, *Bottom of the Ninth*, 124.

38  "League's Action Scored by Shea," *New York Times*, October 27, 1960: 46.

39  Al Wolf, "Several Groups to Bid for New L.A. Franchise," *Los Angeles Times*, November 19, 1960: II-3.

40  Joe Reichler, "Muddled Baseball Picture May Be Cleared Up at Meetings This Week," Associated Press-*Washington Post and Times Herald*, November 27, 1960: C2.

41  Frank Finch, "It's Official! Angels to Play in 1961," *Los Angeles Times*, December 8, 1960: IV-1; Andy McCue, *Mover and Shaker: Walter O'Malley, the Dodgers, & Baseball's Westward Expansion* (Lincoln: University of Nebraska Press, 2014), 292-293.

42  Shapiro, *Bottom of the Ninth*, 216.

# MIS-MANAGEMENT 101 –
# THE AMERICAN LEAGUE EXPANSION OF 1961

BY ANDY MCCUE AND ERIC THOMPSON

Responding to six decades of demographic change, the National and American leagues moved to expand as the 1960s dawned. While the National League took a measured approach to analyzing markets, identifying ownership groups and giving them time to organize, the American League followed a stumbling, reactive path. One new franchise was given merely eight days to find personnel and plan for an expansion draft. And then, to conform to a Byzantine set of rules, the league president had to secretly revise the draft with a series of mandated trades before announcing the results.

The path to expansion for both leagues was a combination of new markets and old politics.

By 1953, the 50-year-old lineup of American and National League cities had been left in the demographic dust. Population had moved from the northeast quadrant to the vibrant cities of the West and South. The less financially successful clubs in two-team cities were finding it increasingly difficult to compete.

This situation was ameliorated with the moves of the Boston Braves to Milwaukee (1953), the St. Louis Browns to Baltimore (1954), and the Philadelphia Athletics to Kansas City (1955). But these shifts barely strayed from the Northeast. There was talk of further franchise shifts, or maybe expansion, but nothing actually happened. That pattern was shattered in late 1957 with the announcement that the National League's New York Giants and Brook-

lyn Dodgers would move to San Francisco and Los Angeles.

The reaction in New York was swift. Within a few weeks, the Mayor's Baseball Committee, headed by well-connected lawyer William Shea, was created to bring National League baseball back to the city.

The reaction in major-league baseball was slower. It wasn't until December of 1958 that the owners formed the Major League Baseball Expansion Committee and it was here that the American League's stumbles began.

For its representatives, the National League owners chose two powerful owners, Walter O'Malley of the Dodgers and Philip Wrigley of the Cubs. Wrigley was a well-connected, wealthy owner, who'd played a quiet role in the westward expansion of the National League. O'Malley was particularly important because the implicit assumption behind any expansion was that if the National League wanted back into New York, the American League would have to be allowed into Los Angeles

The American League owners chose Arnold Johnson, the man who had just moved his Athletics to the smallest market in major-league baseball, and George Medinger, a minority shareholder and a vice president of the Cleveland Indians. No Del Webb, whose Yankees were now the sole major-league team in New York. No Tom Yawkey.

Six months later, the expansion stew was complicated by

the unveiling of Branch Rickey's plan for a third major league to be called the Continental League. Rickey promised to respect major-league baseball's player contracts, but he was clearly eyeing their best existing and potential markets. The Continental League loomed as a bigger threat as Rickey began to put together impressive ownership groups in major cities.

In New York, Shea was quickly won over to the Continental camp, and he brought with him Joan Payson, who'd been a minority owner of the Giants and bitterly regretted their move to San Francisco. Her brother was publisher of the *New York Herald-Tribune* and US Ambassador to Great Britain. Other old money quickly joined. There was Dwight Davis, Jr., whose father had funded tennis' Davis Cup, and George Herbert Walker, a merchant banker with strong ties to the Harriman empire and the grandfather of eventual president George Herbert Walker Bush.

In Houston, it was all new money, but there was a lot of it. Craig Cullinan was Texaco. R.E. "Bob" Smith and "Bud" Adams had extensive oil and real estate interests in the Houston area. Roy Hofheinz was Smith's partner in many ventures and a former mayor of Houston. The Denver group was headed by Bob Howsam, owner of the minor-league Denver Bears but with powerful political connections through his father-in-law, former Colorado governor and U.S. Senator Edwin C. Johnson. In Toronto, it was media mogul Jack Kent Cooke. In Minneapolis, Rickey rounded up members of the Dayton-Hudson department stores and Hamms Brewing families, as well as George Pillsbury.

Rickey's Continental League would leave several legacies. It had coalesced viable ownership groups and educated them about dealing with major league baseball. And it had scared major league baseball.

In Washington, DC, Edwin C. Johnson's connections had brought about legislation to limit the number of players major-league teams could keep under contract, and he had aided New York Representative Emanuel Celler's antitrust hearings on baseball. In Houston, Bud Adams had struck fear into the hearts of the owners. In addition to his baseball interests, Adams was a major player in the creation of the American Football League. In 1960, his Houston Oilers drafted the Heisman Trophy winner from LSU – Billy Cannon. The Los Angeles Rams of the National Football League had offered Cannon $10,000. Adams offered $110,000 and the idea of competing for amateur talent with that kind of money reverberated through

major-league baseball.[1]

In August 1960, the two leagues met and announced each would absorb two teams from the Continental League. While the National League immediately began to examine the potential markets and to interview the possible ownership groups, the American League owners argued over internal issues, such as existing teams' desires to move and the possibility of ownership changes. Arnold Johnson had died that spring and other teams were thought to be on the market. The American League began its reactive spasms.

As the Washington Senators' 1961 media guide proclaimed, 'A Team is Born,' with general manager Ed Doherty, manager Mickey Vernon, and president Elwood 'Pete' Quesada (Courtesy of John Schleppi)

On October 10, Webb pushed the American League's somnolent Expansion Committee into going after Houston.[2] The next day, O'Malley announced the Houston Continental League group had applied for membership in the National League. Six days later, President Warren Giles announced Houston and New York, with its Continental League ownership group, would join the National League for the 1962 season.[3]

The 1960 census would soon show that the markets underserved by major-league baseball were New York, Los Angeles, and Houston. The National League was now in all three, the American in one. But, American League sources were sounding confident about the Dallas-Ft. Worth market, another growth area.[4]

A few days later, the American League revealed Calvin Griffith would be allowed to move his Washington Senators to Minneapolis-St. Paul and two expansion teams would be created in cities to be named.[5] To one-up the National League, Webb said it might add another two teams by 1964 and that its expansion teams would start play in 1961, a year before the National League. These teams had no general managers, no managers, no players, no ticket sales department and a spring training that would begin in four months. Webb glossed over the fact that these moves broke the August agreement to choose ownership groups from the Continental League, a decision Rickey characterized as "the dictionary definition of perfidy."[6] *The Sporting News* and other commentators suggested the Americans' pace was too headlong.

On November 17, 1960, American League president Joe Cronin announced that one of its expansion teams would replace the Senators in Washington and that it would petition major-league baseball to be allowed into the Los Angeles area.[7] The promising market of Dallas-Ft. Worth fell out of the saddle. Cronin set the expansion draft for November 25. In those eight days, including a weekend and the Thanksgiving holiday, the league would have to resolve the Los Angeles situation. The Washington team would have eight days to prepare for the draft. The Los Angeles team, whose ownership group was not known, would have less.

November 25 passed with no resolution of the Los Angeles situation and no expansion draft. On November 28, the Senators lurched into life by taking Ray Semproch and John Gabler in the minor-league draft. The Los Angeles team didn't participate because it didn't exist yet.

By December 6, the AL had negotiated hastily with Walter O'Malley to get into Los Angeles and slapped together an ownership group headed by former country music star and radio/tv entrepreneur Gene Autry. Autry's organization would have eight days to prepare for the December 14 draft and less than three months before spring training.

For the draft, the Los Angeles team would be aided by several factors. Autry quickly hired former Braves manager Fred Haney as general manager and recently dismissed Giants manager Bill Rigney as field manager. Both were familiar with many major-league players, although more heavily in the National League. Walter O'Malley ordered

Roland Hemond joined the Los Angeles Angels' on the ground floor in 1961, remaining with the Halos until 1970. Here is Hemond in 1961 with prospects Dan Ardell (l) and Tom Satriano (Courtesy of Angels Baseball)

his staff to turn over the Dodgers' scouting reports on American League minor leaguers. But the big prize was Los Angeles-area resident Casey Stengel, recently fired as New York Yankees manager and very miffed about it. Stengel gave Haney and Rigney a full rundown on Yankees minor leaguers.

So, on the chilly morning of December 14, Haney and Rigney from the Angels as well as manager Mickey Vernon, general manager Ed Doherty, and farm director Hal Keller of the Senators climbed to the sixth floor of the IBM Building in Boston, where President Joe Cronin kept the American League's offices. Keeping the number of people in the room to six was designed to protect the secrecy of the players the existing eight teams had, or hadn't, protected.

Those teams had been required to expose 15 players from their 40-man rosters. Seven of those players had to come from the roster as of August 31, 1960, just before the September callups of minor leaguers. As would a different set of rules by the National League a year later, the process maximized protection for the existing franchises and minimized quality for the expansion teams. Each player selected would cost $75,000.

The league had created a complicated set of draft rules. Each team first had to select 10 pitchers, then two catchers, six infielders, four outfielders, and finally six players from those remaining. To make it even more complex, no existing team could lose more than seven players and no expansion team could take more than four players from any one existing team. Crucially, Bill Rigney recalled, the American League didn't inform drafting teams of this rule.[8]

The pitching and catching selections went smoothly enough, starting with the Angels choosing Eli Grba and the Senators taking Bobby Shantz, both from the Yankees. But, with the 27th pick, the Angels took infielder Coot Veal from the Tigers. They already had selected pitchers Bobby Sprout and Aubrey Gatewood, catcher Bob Rodgers, and third baseman Eddie Yost from Detroit. Four picks was the limit in the rules and Veal took them over it.

Nobody at 540 Boylston Street raised a red flag. With the outfielder picks, things got really messy. With the 40th pick, the Angels took outfielder Ken Hunt from the Yankees, their fifth choice from New York. Four picks later, they took yet another Tiger – outfielder Neil Chrisley. Washington quickly joined the mess, taking Marty Keough and

Jim King from Cleveland with the 41st and 43rd picks, giving them six picks from the Indians, in addition to the two taken by the Angels. The Indians and Tigers had now lost eight players and still nobody said, "Stop."

With the miscellaneous players, the situation got worse. The Angels took their fifth players from both the Red Sox and White Sox while the Senators took their fifth from Baltimore and Kansas City. Finally, Cronin stepped in after the Angels took Julio Becquer from the Twins with the 55th and penultimate pick. He ordered Washington to drop catcher Red Wilson, one of their Indians' picks, and, because of the inflexibility of the rules, replace him with another catcher – Pete Daley of Kansas City. While reducing the Senators' Indians picks to five, this raised their Athletics selections to six. Cronin then had the Angels drop Neil Chrisley and take Faye Throneberry of the Twins. Then, Washington took its last regular pick, pitcher Rudy Hernandez from the Twins.

The scorecard now read: Boston, Detroit, Chicago, and New York had lost seven players, but five each were to the Angels; Boston and Cleveland had lost seven, but five to the Senators; Kansas City had lost seven but six were to Washington. Only the Twins losses were according to the rules.

Cronin now ordered trades to rectify the mistakes. To balance the Red Sox, the Senators sent pitcher Bob Davis of Kansas City to the Angels for Boston infielder Jim Mahoney. Cleveland and Detroit were evened out when the Angels shipped Coot Veal to the Senators for Cleveland infielder Ken Aspromonte. Kansas City and New York's losses were brought into line with the rules when Washington traded infielders – Ken Hamlin to the Angels for Bud Zipfel.

One last trade was needed. The Senators had too many Orioles. The Angels had too many White Sox. Finally, with Cronin leaning in, the deal was struck. The Senators sent outfielder Joe Hicks to the Angels for a 19-year-old pitcher named Dean Chance who had spent the 1960 season at Fox Cities of the Three-I League. Hicks would have 389 more major-league plate appearances, batting .221. Dean Chance would win 20 games twice and a Cy Young Award.

Joe Cronin emerged from the draft and walked down Boylston Street to the Venetian Room of the Sheraton Plaza Hotel, where reporters awaited the results. He supplied each team's list of 28 choices and acknowledged

Both the Angels and the Senators remained in their original venues only for the 1961 season. Just as the Angels left Wrigley Field for Chavez Ravine in 1962, so did the Senators leave Griffith Stadium for District of Columbia Memorial Stadium. Here is a brick from Griffith Stadium after it was demolished in 1965 (Courtesy of John Schleppi)

one small glitch when they found the Indians had lost eight players. This was an oblique reference to replacing Red Wilson with Pete Daley. Cronin did not mention the Throneberry for Chrisley switch nor the four trades that made the picks conform to the draft rules. Neither of the expansion franchises would win a postseason game until 1979, nor a postseason series until 2002.

The material on the management of the expansion draft is available in the American League records at the National Baseball Hall of Fame and Museum and was confirmed by Hal Keller in a phone interview on October 30, 2010.

**Notes**

1 Michael Shapiro, *Bottom of the Ninth* (New York: Times Books, 2009), 193-4.

2 Ibid., 240-1.

3 *Los Angeles Times*, October 18, 1960: IV, 1.

4 Joe King, "N.L. Opening Door for Houston – Dallas Likely A.L. Addition." *The Sporting News*, October 19, 1960: 6.

5 *Los Angeles Times*, October 27, 1960: IV, 1.

6 Roy Terrell, "The Damndest Mess Baseball Has Ever Seen," *Sports Illustrated*, December 19, 1960: 18.

7 *Los Angeles Times*, November 18, 1960: IV, 1.

8 Tyler Kepner, "Expansion the Hard Way by 1961 Angels," *Press-Enterprise* (Riverside, California), November 12, 1997.

## TABLE 1: Largest U. S. Cities and Their MLB Franchises

| | 1900 | | 1930 | | 1950 | | 1960 |
|---|---|---|---|---|---|---|---|
| 1. | New York (3) | | New York (3) | | New York (3) | | New York (1) |
| 2. | Chicago (2) | | Chicago (2) | | Chicago (2) | | Chicago (2) |
| 3. | Philadelphia (2) | | Philadelphia (2) | | Philadelphia (2) | | Los Angeles |
| 4. | St. Louis (2) | | Detroit | | Los Angeles | | Philadelphia |
| 5. | Boston (2) | | Los Angeles | | Detroit | | Detroit |
| 6. | Baltimore | | Cleveland | | Baltimore | | Baltimore |
| 7. | Cleveland | | St. Louis (2) | | Cleveland | | Houston |
| 8. | Buffalo | | Baltimore | | St. Louis (2) | | Cleveland |
| 9. | San Francisco | | Boston (2) | | Washington | | Washington |
| 10. | Cincinnati | | Pittsburgh | | Boston (2) | | St. Louis |
| | | | | | | | |
| 11. | Pittsburgh | 14. | Washington | 12. | Pittsburgh | 11. | Milwaukee |
| 13. | Detroit | 17. | Cincinnati | 18. | Cincinnati | 12. | San Francisco |
| 15. | Washington | | | | | 13. | Boston |
| | | | | | | 21. | Pittsburgh |
| | | | | | | 22. | Cincinnati |
| | | | | | | 27. | Kansas City |
| | | | | | | | |
| | 13 | | 14 | | 14 | | 10 |

The number in parentheses after the city name indicates the number of franchises in that city. The number at the bottom of the columns is the number of the 16 franchises which are in the top 10 cities. The American League lineup of 1903 is used to locate franchises.

## TABLE 2: After Outfielders

|              | Los Angeles | Washington | Total |
|--------------|:-----------:|:----------:|:-----:|
| Baltimore    | 1           | 2          | 3     |
| Boston       | 4           | 2          | 6     |
| Chicago      | 2           | 1          | 3     |
| Cleveland    | 2           | **6**      | **8** |
| Detroit      | **6**       | 2          | **8** |
| Kansas City  | 1           | 4          | 5     |
| Minnesota    | 1           | 3          | 4     |
| New York     | **5**       | 2          | 7     |

The draft began to stray from the rules with the Angels choice of OF Ken Hunt from the Yankees — their fifth choice from New York. By the end of the OF choices, several violations had occurred. The large, bold numbers indicate where the choices had exceeded the limits of no more than seven players lost by any one team, and no more than four to any one of the expansion teams.

## The Hidden Trades

Washington traded Bob Davis (KCA) to Los Angeles (LAA) for Jim Mahoney (BOS).

Washington traded Ken Aspromonte (CLE) to Los Angeles (LAA) for Coot Veal (DET).

Washington traded Ken Hamlin (KCA) to Los Angeles (LAA) for Bud Zipfel (NYY).

Washington traded Dean Chance (BAL) to Los Angeles (LAA) for Joe Hicks (CWS).

## TABLE 3: After Adjustments

|              | Los Angeles | Washington | Total |
|--------------|:-----------:|:----------:|:-----:|
| Baltimore    | 2           | **5**      | 7     |
| Boston       | **5**       | 2          | 7     |
| Chicago      | **5**       | 2          | 7     |
| Cleveland    | 2           | **5**      | 7     |
| Detroit      | **5**       | 2          | 7     |
| Kansas City  | 1           | **6**      | 7     |
| Minnesota    | 3           | 4          | 7     |
| New York     | **5**       | 2          | 7     |

Even with changes ordered by American League President Joe Cronin, the draft still finished with many rules violations. No existing team had lost more than the mandated seven players, but the limit of no more than four from one existing team to an expansion team still was broken for seven of the eight franchises, as indicated by the large, bold numbers.

# A SEASON IN HOMER HEAVEN:
# THE BIRTH OF THE LOS ANGELES ANGELS

### By Warren Corbett

"I don't give a damn about O'Malley."

Hank Greenberg was furious. The 6-foot-4 Hall of Famer towered over Commissioner Ford Frick, who had just told him what he did not want to hear: Before Greenberg could put an American League expansion team in Los Angeles, he would have to pay tribute to Dodgers owner Walter O'Malley. Tribute in the form of cash.

"I don't give a damn about O'Malley," Greenberg roared.

"I don't give a damn about O'Malley, either," the commissioner replied. "And I don't give a damn about Hank Greenberg or anybody else. But I do give a damn about what is proper. This thing that you propose to do is not fair, not right, not decent!"[1]

Greenberg had won the American League owners' private blessing to acquire the Los Angeles franchise as part of an expansion

In the spirit of Western films, a popular genre of the time, Albie Pearson, Billy Moran, Leon Wagner, and Lee Thomas of the Angels channel their inner John Wayne, brandishing bats to be rifles in the dugout at Chavez Ravine, 1962. (Courtesy of Angels Baseball)

plan that would send the Washington Senators to Minnesota and create a replacement team in the nation's capital in 1961. The former slugger, who had been a part-owner of the Indians and White Sox, had lined up investors and traveled to California to negotiate a stadium lease and radio-TV contracts.

Frick had previously declared Los Angeles and New York "open territory." This gave expansion teams a green light to move into those cities without interference from the Dodgers or Yankees.[2] But after O'Malley threw his considerable weight around, Frick was persuaded to see the error of his ways. Now the commissioner said O'Malley deserved compensation for the expenses he had incurred to bring the first major-league club to Los Angeles.

"This was a complete about-face," Greenberg said.[3] He wouldn't stand for it. He walked away, leaving the AL's expansion plan in "frightful chaos," as one writer put it.[4] The league had already awarded a franchise to Washington. It needed a 10th team to balance the schedule. The National League rejected interleague play with nine-team circuits.

With Opening Day only four months away, AL owners were facing ridicule over their bungled expansion when they met in St. Louis on December 5. Just as in the movies, the hero in the white hat came riding to the rescue. Gene Autry, the Hollywood singing cowboy who had built a fortune through investments in oil wells, real es-

34

tate, and radio stations, put in a bid for the Los Angeles franchise. The league welcomed a famous, popular – and rich – man who wanted to own a ballclub.

The oft-told story is that Autry went to the AL meeting hoping to secure radio rights for the new franchise, and instead came away owning it. In fact, published reports identified him as a bidder for the team before the meeting, and he said he decided to pursue it as soon as Greenberg dropped out: "I thought it was all Greenberg. When it appeared it wasn't, the thought occurred to me that I'd like that franchise."[5] Autry had already chosen his general manager, who was at his side at the meetings in St. Louis: Fred Haney, a Los Angeles resident who had managed the Milwaukee Braves to NL pennants in 1957 and 1958. The cowboy and his partner in the radio business, former Stanford football All-American Bob Reynolds, were majority owners of the new team.[6]

But O'Malley would not accept competition in the market unless it was on his terms. At the least, he wanted another year of exclusivity in Los Angeles. Then he would move into his new ballpark at Chavez Ravine and the AL expansion team could be his rent-paying tenant. O'Malley also wanted an effective veto over the American League owners. One of Greenberg's partners was C. Arnholt Smith, who with his brother John owned the San Diego club in the Pacific Coast League and had bankrolled the opposition to the Dodgers' ballpark plans. Another prospective bidder was Kenyon Brown, whose Los Angeles television station had editorialized against the Dodgers' deal to acquire land from the city.

At a meeting that lasted until 3:00 AM on December 7, O'Malley exacted a stiff price to allow the American League club to begin play in 1961. Autry had to pay the Dodgers $350,000 for a ticket of admission to enter Los Angeles, partial reimbursement for O'Malley's payment to the Pacific Coast League for invading its territory. Instead of sharing the 90,000-seat Los Angeles Memorial Coliseum with the Dodgers, the AL team would play its first season at Wrigley Field, the city's minor-league ballpark, with a capacity of about 23,000, counting standing room, and few parking spaces. Beginning in 1962, the upstart franchise would move into the new Dodger Stadium, paying a minimum $200,000 in rent, or 7.5 percent of gate receipts. O'Malley would keep all parking revenue and some of the take from concessions.[7]

The deal was worth around $750,000 a year to the Dodgers, but that didn't faze Autry. "For me, it's the realization of a lifetime dream," he said.[8] He had played semipro ball in his youth and claimed to have been invited to a Cardinals tryout camp. While filming his movies, he had organized pickup games during breaks, and had once owned a share of the Pacific Coast League's Hollywood Stars.

Los Angeles's new team adopted an old name, the Angels, after the Coast League club. When the franchise was awarded on Tuesday, December 6, Haney had only six days to prepare for the player draft that would stock the roster.

It was a frantic week. Back in Los Angeles on Thursday, Haney was introduced to the media as general manager. The first question from reporters: Would the Angels hire Casey Stengel, recently fired by the Yankees? Autry acknowledged that the 70-year-old Stengel was his first choice as manager.[9] But on Monday, the club named Bill Rigney, who had managed the Giants for 4½ years. Autry said Stengel had turned down the job because he had sold his life story to a magazine on the condition that he would not manage in 1961.

Instead, Stengel served as the Angels' first scout. Haney had been managing in the National League, so Stengel spent hours giving a rundown on the players who were available in the draft. The Dodgers and Giants also shared their scouting reports.

AL President Joe Cronin hosted the draft at his office in Boston on Wednesday, December 14, after a snowstorm forced a delay. That didn't make the eligible players look any better. Each of the existing teams made available seven players from its 25-man roster and eight minor leaguers from the 40-man. They were derided as castoffs, rejects, and retreads, but they would cost the expansion clubs $75,000 apiece.

The Angels and the new Washington Senators picked players by position: pitchers, then catchers, infielders, and outfielders. Haney won the first coin toss and tapped Eli Grba, a right-hander who had achieved little success with the Yankees but was recommended by Stengel. Leaving the mighty Yankees for a certain loser, Grba remembered, "I was kind of disappointed and pissed. But then you get calls from writers and congratulations from people. ... [Y]ou felt that you were really wanted."[10]

The Angels chose several former All-Stars: pitcher Ned Garver; the "Walking Man," Eddie Yost; and sluggers Ted Kluszewski and Bob Cerv – all past their 34th birth-

Eli Grba with Angels' owner Arte Moreno on Opening Night 2011. As part of the Angels' 50th anniversary commemoration, Grba threw out the first pitch as 'the First Angel.' (Courtesy of Angels Baseball)

days. The well-known names gave a sheen of respectability to the roster. "We felt we needed names to combat the Dodgers," Autry said.[11] He tried to sign Gil McDougald, the Yankees' sterling jack of all infield trades, but not even a $50,000 contract offer, plus a free home in Los Angeles, could shake McDougald's decision to retire.[12]

A pair of teenage unknowns proved to be the Angels' prizes. Jim Fregosi, an 18-year-old shortstop in the Red Sox farm system, had played only one season in Class D. Rigney had spotted him in winter ball in the San Francisco area. Fregosi developed into a six-time All-Star, but is best known as the man who was traded for Nolan Ryan.

Because of a mixup in the draft, Cronin ordered the two teams to swap several players.[13] That's how the Angels got 19-year-old right-hander Dean Chance, who was originally chosen by Washington out of the Orioles organization. Chance won the Cy Young Award in 1964.

In the minor-league portion of the draft, Haney picked up Albie Pearson, the 1958 AL Rookie of the Year, who had been demoted, and first baseman Steve Bilko. They were quite the odd couple: Pearson, 5-feet-5 and 140 pounds, and Bilko, who squashed the scales at more than 250.

Bilko was a local favorite, one of the most popular players in the history of the Pacific Coast League Angels. He had won three consecutive Most Valuable Player Awards from 1955 through 1957 while twice hitting more than 50 homers, but his strikeouts kept him from holding a major-league job. "This could be my last chance," Bilko wrote to Haney when he sent in his signed contract. "I couldn't think of a better place to make a last stand than Wrigley Field."[14]

Haney knew the exquisite little ballpark well – he had played there decades earlier – and he shaped his roster for its contours by acquiring big boppers Bilko, Kluszewski, and Cerv. Most recently the site of the television show *Home Run Derby*, Wrigley was homer heaven with power alleys in right- and left-center just 345 feet from the plate. A two-story house across 41st Street beyond the left-field wall was peppered with so many flying baseballs that *Los Angeles Times* columnist Ned Cronin wrote, "No one would think of sitting down to dinner without wearing a fielder's glove."[15]

The Angels and Senators each paid $2.1 million for 28 players, and the Angels laid out another $100,000 for Bilko and Pearson. Rigney said, "I think the players we picked will give us the nucleus of a decent ball club."[16] Optimism was part of his job description as he tried to stoke fan interest.

But the pitching staff shaped up as a potential disaster area. Grba's six victories for the Yankees in 1960, primarily in relief, were the most by any of the new Angels. None of the pitchers had been a regular starter. Their combined record was 26-41.

As Haney scrambled to create an organization, everything was makeshift. The team's first office was upstairs over a bar. Farm and scouting director Roland Hemond, whom Haney had recruited from the Milwaukee Braves, recalled an electric massage chair downstairs that shook the floor, and cowboy pickers and singers rehearsing next door. Haney used his California contacts to hire some experienced scouts, and Hemond brought in several he had known with the Braves. Hemond began scrounging for unaffiliated minor-league teams to patch together a farm system.[17]

The Angels established their spring-training headquarters at Autry's Melody Ranch Hotel in Palm Springs, California, and the owner saddled up on a bicycle to lead a parade of players to the ballpark. Former President Dwight D. Eisenhower attended the first intrasquad game. Stengel later visited from his home in Glendale, California, to look the team over.

Most prognosticators thought the expansion clubs would struggle to win 50 games. One prominent writer, Dick Young, said 40 was more realistic.[18] *Sports Illustrated* predicted that the Angels would show some power in their miniature ballpark, but "almost everything else looks weak."[19]

The history of the Los Angeles Angels began in Baltimore on April 11 with a bang. Two bangs, actually. Kluszewski and Cerv hit back-to-back home runs in the first inning. Grba limited the Orioles to six hits as the Angels won, 7-2. "I've seen a lot of things to remember in my day," Autry said, "but I'll never forget that afternoon as long as I live."[20] The castoffs, rejects, and retreads were undefeated with 161 games to go.

They lost their next eight. The schedule makers had done the Angels no favors. They were set to open with 13 road games, but eight of them were rained out. The season was more than two weeks old on April 27 when the club finally came home to Wrigley Field for the first time.

Ticket holders walked a red carpet into the park, but only 11,931 turned out on a Thursday afternoon. "This is the life," one fan exulted. "A beer in my hand, a roof over my head and a seat near the diamond." Dodgers games at the Coliseum offered none of those amenities.[21] Rigney put both of his mammoths in the lineup, Kluszewski at first base and Bilko making the first appearance of his life in right field. Bilko delivered a fine lumbering catch, but neither managed an extra-base hit. The Angels dropped their eighth straight, losing to Minnesota, 4-2.

Oh, it was bad. The club sank to last place and stayed there for most of the first half. Haney turned over every rock in search of players; 46 men wore the cap with the halo on top in 1961.

Two early trades added power. On April 13, Haney acquired Leon Wagner, one of the Giants' surplus outfielders, who had slipped down to the minors. Getting his first opportunity to play regularly, Wagner led the Angels with 28 homers. On May 8, Bob Cerv was swapped back to the Yankees with pitcher Tex Clevenger for pitchers Ryne Duren and Johnny James and rookie outfielder Lee Thomas. Thomas shuttled between first base and right field, hitting 24 homers with an .844 OPS.

In Duren and Art Fowler, the Angels had a pair of hard-drinking veteran right-handers, so Rigney made them roommates. "We got along fine," Duren said later, "except the night he got drunk and was going to stick me with a knife over some gal or something." Fowler filed for divorce: "I went to Rigney and told him Duren was too much. He didn't drink too much, but it took only three drinks and he was drunk."[22]

Haney's deals turned the club around in the second half.

From June 27 until the end of the season, the Angels played one game over .500. The strategy of building the lineup for Wrigley Field worked; the club went 46-36 at home. But Wrigley punished pitchers. The home team and its visitors combined for a major-league record 248 home runs in the fiendish confines.

The Angels were good at hitting homers, but not much else. Only two teams allowed more runs and none made more errors. The infield was a revolving door. And the club could not win on the road, losing 55 of 79 decisions.

They lost their final game to finish eighth with a 70-91 record, ahead of the Senators and Kansas City Athletics. No first-year team has ever done better. Steve Bilko gave Wrigley a fitting farewell. With two out in the ninth, he pinch-hit and hammered a 400-foot home run over the left-field wall. Bilko's .940 OPS in part-time play led the team.

Angels owner Gene Autry leads his players in a bicycle ride through the streets of Palm Springs, California, March 1962. As Autry owned the Melody Ranch Hotel in Palm Springs, the desert community became a natural fit for the Angels' as their spring training camp. (Courtesy of Angels Baseball)

A winning home record didn't fill the seats. Even the Yankees' first visit failed to draw as many as 20,000 for any of the three games. The season attendance, 603,510, was ninth in the league, better than only the expansion Senators.

No fan enjoyed it more than Gene Autry. With his movie and television career behind him, he seized on the ballclub as his new passion. After nearly every road game, he called the clubhouse to congratulate the winning pitcher or commiserate with Rigney when the Angels lost. "[H]e rarely missed a game," Rigney said. "I've been in baseball almost 25 years and I can't remember any other owner who showed such interest in his players."[23]

Rigney acknowledged the club's poor pitching and leaky defense, but he was encouraged by the late-season performances of rookie shortstop Jim Fregosi, switch-hitting

Buck Rodgers at Tiger Stadium in 1961. The former Detroit farmhand was drafted by the Angels in 1960 and spent nine years with the Halos as a player and four as a manager. (Courtesy of Dwayne Labakas)

catcher Bob "Buck" Rodgers, and third baseman Tom Satriano, a bonus baby who came straight from the University of Southern California's NCAA champions.

With high hopes for the youngsters and confidence in the players he had already acquired, Haney made few significant moves in the offseason. The Opening Day roster in 1962 included only eight holdovers from the team that had begun the previous season. Rodgers took over as the regular catcher and finished second in the Rookie of the Year voting. Dean Chance was right behind him in the balloting and became the club's ace pitcher. By August Fregosi had claimed the shortstop job. A Rule 5 draft pickup, Bo Belinsky, spun a no-hitter on May 5 while exasperating Rigney with his after-hours pursuit of Hollywood starlets. And the mix-and-match roster climbed into the pennant race.

On July 4 the Angels took over sole possession of first place. That lasted only one day, but they hung in close behind the Yankees until the final two weeks of the season. An 86-76 record was good for third place. *The Sporting News* named Haney the Major League Executive of the Year and Rigney Manager of the Year.

Although attendance nearly doubled in the Angels' first year in Dodger Stadium, Autry was never happy as O'Malley's tenant. He said the Dodgers owner was "a difficult landlord" who treated the Angels like a stepchild.[24] In 1966 the renamed California Angels moved into their own home, a gift from the city of Anaheim, but their attendance still lagged far behind the Dodgers'.

The early success on the field didn't last. The club fell back to the bottom half of the standings for most of the 1960s and 1970s. The Angels didn't reach postseason play until 1979, after free agency arrived and Autry became one of the biggest spenders.

## Additional Sources

Parts of this story are adapted from the author's SABR BioProject biography of Gene Autry.

Rick Reichardt, who played for the Angels from 1964 to 1970. Despite Gene Autry's deep pockets, which allowed the Angels to sign bonus babies like Reichardt, the team remained inconsistent for its first decade and beyond. (Courtesy of Angels Baseball)

## Notes

1 Dick Young, "Frick Threatens to Veto A.L. Move Here," *Los Angeles Times*, November 16, 1960: IV-1. This is Frick's account of the meeting in his office on November 9.

2 Associated Press, "Ford Frick Believes L.A. Should Be Open Territory," *Los Angeles Times*, August 15, 1960: IV-3.

3 United Press International, "New L.A. Club 'Impossible,'" *Pasadena* (California) *Independent*, December 2, 1960: 22.

4 Frank Finch, "Rumors Have AL Expanding," *Los Angeles Times*, December 4, 1960: H5.

5 Jeanne Hoffman, "Autry Set to Build Angels in 120 Days," *Los Angeles Times*, December 13, 1960: IV-5.

6 Minority owners of the Golden West Baseball Club were Kenyon Brown, former owner of Los Angeles TV station KCOP; Paul O'Bryan, a Washington, DC, lawyer; and Joseph A. Thomas, a banker in New York and Florida. All three had previously owned shares of the Detroit Tigers. Brown soon dropped out, possibly because of O'Malley's antipathy, and was replaced on the board of directors by Leonard Firestone of the tire family.

7 Finch, "It's Official! Angels to Play in 1961," *Los Angeles Times*, December 8, 1960: IV-1; Andy McCue, *Mover and Shaker: Walter O'Malley, the Dodgers, & Baseball's Westward Expansion* (Lincoln: University of Nebraska Press, 2014), 292-293.

8 Hoffman, "Autry Set to Build."

9 "Bob Kelley Says," *Long Beach* (California) *Independent*, December 9, 1960: 53.

10 Fran Zimniuch, *Baseball's New Frontier* (Lincoln: University of Nebraska Press, 2013), 47.

11 J.G. Taylor Spink, "Looping the Loops," *The Sporting News*, May 3, 1961: 6.

12 Associated Press, "Declined Job," *Tampa Times*, March 10, 1961: 14. The Yankees allowed the Angels to talk to McDougald, who had retired when he learned he was exposed to the expansion draft. He didn't want to leave his janitorial business in New York.

13 Under the rules, each expansion team was limited to choosing four players from any one existing club. When league officials tallied the results of the draft, they found several violations of that limit and had to shuffle some players. Andy McCue and Eric Thompson, "Mis-Management 101: The American League Expansion for 1961," *The National Pastime* (SABR, 2011), sabr.org/research/mis-management-101-american-league-expansion-1961, accessed February 6, 2018.

14 Gaylon H. White, *The Bilko Athletic Club* (Lanham, Maryland: Rowman & Littlefield, 2014), 36.

15 Ned Cronin, "Cronin's Corner," *Los Angeles Times*, September 15, 1956: 15.

16 Al Larson, "Angels Shortchanged on Mound," *Long Beach* (California) *Independent*, December 15, 1960: 30.

17 Roland Hemond, with Jean Hastings Ardell, "A Whole New Franchise: Creating the 1961 Los Angeles Angels in 120 Days," *The National Pastime* (SABR, 2011), sabr.org/research/whole-new-franchise-creating-1961-los-angeles-angels-120-days, accessed February 6, 2018.

18 Bob Burnes, "Writers Size Up Expansion Outlook," *The Sporting News*, December 28, 1960: 2.

19 "Los Angeles Angels," *Sports Illustrated*, April 10, 1961, si.com/vault/1961/04/10/624833/los-angeles-angels, accessed December 29, 2017.

20 Braven Dyer, "Autry – Players' Pal and Rootin', Tootin' Fan," *The Sporting News*, April 4, 1962: 27.

21 Al Wolf, "Wrigley Like Good Old Days," *Los Angeles Times*, April 28, 1961: IV-2.

22 Danny Peary, ed., *We Played the Game* (New York: Black Dog & Leventhal, 1994), 515.

23 Dyer, "Autry."

24 Al Carr, "When and Will Angels Move?" *Los Angeles Times*, February 9, 1964: 14.

## LOS ANGELES ANGELS EXPANSION DRAFT

| PICK | PLAYER | POSITION | FORMER TEAM |
|---|---|---|---|
| | | | |

### REGULAR PHASE

| PICK | PLAYER | POSITION | FORMER TEAM |
|---|---|---|---|
| 1 | Eli Grba | p | New York Yankees |
| 2 | Duke Maas | p | New York Yankees |
| 3 | Jerry Casale | p | Boston Red Sox |
| 4 | Tex Clevenger | p | Minnesota Twins |
| 5 | Bob Sprout | p | Detroit Tigers |
| 6 | Aubrey Gatewood | p | Detroit Tigers |
| 7 | Ken McBride | p | Chicago White Sox |
| 8 | Ned Garver | p | Kansas City A's |
| 9 | Ted Bowsfield | p | Boston Red Sox |
| 10 | Ron Moeller | p | Baltimore Orioles |
| 11 | Ed Sadowski | c | Boston Red Sox |
| 12 | Buck Rodgers | c | Detroit Tigers |
| 13 | Eddie Yost | 3b | Detroit Tigers |
| 14 | Coot Veal | ss | Detroit Tigers |
| 15 | Bud Zipfel | 1b | New York Yankees |
| 16 | Jim Mahoney | ss | Boston Red Sox |
| 17 | Gene Leek | 2b | Cleveland Indians |
| 18 | Jim Fregosi | ss | Boston Red Sox |
| 19 | Bob Cerv | of | New York Yankees |
| 20 | Ken Hunt | of | New York Yankees |
| 21 | Joe Hicks | of | Chicago White Sox |
| 22 | Neil Chrisley | of | Detroit Tigers |
| 23 | Earl Averill | of | Chicago White Sox |

### ADDITIONAL PHASE

| PICK | PLAYER | POSITION | FORMER TEAM |
|---|---|---|---|
| 24 | Fred Newman | p | Boston Red Sox |
| 25 | Jim McEnany | of | Chicago White Sox |
| 26 | Ted Kluszewski | 1b | Chicago White Sox |
| 27 | Don Ross | ss | Baltimore Orioles |
| 28 | Julio Becquer | 1b | Minnesota Twins |

### MINOR LEAGUE PHASE

| PICK | PLAYER | POSITION | FORMER TEAM |
|---|---|---|---|
| 29 | Steve Bilko | 1b | Detroit Tigers |
| 30 | Albie Pearson | of | Baltimore Orioles |

# DUKE MAAS

## By Andrew Sharp

Duke Maas pitched in the American League during seven seasons from 1955 to 1961, most notably with the New York Yankees. He appeared in relief in the 1958 and 1960 World Series.

Maas won the game that clinched the 1958 pennant for New York. In 1959 he started 21 games, fashioning a 14-8 won-loss record for a Yankees team that finished a disappointing four games over .500. He played his entire career, cut short by arthritis in his arm, having shaved two years off his age.

Maas told *The Sporting News* in 1957 that he didn't like his given name, Duane, so he adopted the nickname Duke as a child.[1] The 1957 *Baseball Register* said his father gave him the nickname. His father was a second-generation dairy farmer in Utica, Michigan, where Duane Frederick Maas was born on January 31, 1929, the younger of two sons of Frederick and Mabel (Weier) Maas.[2] Duane's brother, Lawrence, was born in 1926. Their paternal grandfather had emigrated from Germany.[3] His mother also was of German descent.[4]

"They say milking cows strengthens your wrists, and I did a lot of that as a kid," Duke told Watson Spoelstra of the *Detroit News* while he pitched for the Tigers. With chores to do on the family's 60-acre farm, Maas didn't play organized baseball until he made the Utica High School varsity as a senior. Utica, in Macomb County, is about 25 miles from Detroit.[5]

"Pitchers on the baseball team got to leave an hour early," Maas told an Associated Press reporter in 1955 about his motivation. "So I tried out for the team and made it. That was in 1948, and I've been pitching ever since."[6]

After graduation, Mass pitched for a Utica team in the semipro Macomb County Federation League, winning 12 and losing twice, His high-school coach, Barney Swinehart, wrote to the Detroit Tigers to see if they would take a look at Maas, a slim 5-foot-10 right-hander.[7] In the fall of 1948, he and Swinehart went to Briggs Stadium for a tryout, but the Tigers' longtime chief scout, A.J. "Wish" Egan, wasn't available to see Maas when he arrived.

"Mr. Egan had been ill and wasn't there the first day," Maas told *The Sporting News* in March 1955.[8] "So I went back the following day. He signed me that afternoon." Tigers general manager John McHale gave Maas $500 and a $150-a-month contract.[9]

The 20-year-old Maas was assigned to Roanoke Rapids in the Class-D Coastal Plain League at the beginning of the

1949 season. He went 3-5 with a 4.01 earned-run average before moving on to Dunn-Erwin in the Class-D Tobacco State League. Although he was 3-2, his ERA was 5.25. He yielded nearly a hit per inning. With both teams, his control was shaky – 10 walks every nine innings overall.

The results, at least in the won-lost column, were better in 1950 for Jamestown, New York, in the Class-D Pennsylvania-Ontario-New York (PONY) League. Maas was 12-7, starting 19 of 30 games. He cut down on his walks and hits per inning, but his ERA was still 4.47.

With the Korean War raging, Maas was drafted into the Army. He was stationed first at Fort Campbell, Kentucky, before being sent to Germany to serve with the occupation force there for 14 months. He had no opportunity to pitch. He even had to play the outfield on an Army team at Fort Campbell. "I couldn't make the club as a pitcher," he said in 1955.[10]

Released from the military, Maas was sent in 1953 to Durham, North Carolina, the Tigers' affiliate in the Class-B Carolina League. His won-lost record for a losing team was 6-16, but his overall performance improved significantly. His ERA dropped to 3.03 and he cut his walks per nine innings to less than four. The next season was a breakout for Maas: 18-7 combined at Double A and Triple A with a 2.37 ERA. He was the Eastern League's top pitcher at Wilkes-Barre with three shutouts and a 1.10 ERA when he was promoted to Buffalo in the International League.

Maas's 1954 season earned him a trip to spring training with Detroit in '55. His impressive performance there won him a spot in the Tigers' rotation to start the season. Veteran Tigers manager Bucky Harris called Maas "the surprise package" among the young pitching prospects.[11] At first, Maas seemed as if he would be.

With the Tigers being blown out by the White Sox, Maas made his major-league debut on April 21, 1955, at Briggs Stadium. His team was down, 9-1, when he took the mound in the eighth inning to face Chico Carrasquel, who grounded out to short. Nellie Fox then grounded to second and Minnie Minoso grounded to third. The ninth wasn't quite as smooth: Maas hit a batter and walked another, but escaped without a run scoring.

His first big-league start came at home on April 30 against Washington. It didn't go well. Maas lasted just 2⅓ innings. He gave up just two hits, but walked five. Merci-

fully, Maas yielded only two runs. The Tigers won, 11-7.

Five days later, Maas started and won his first major-league game as the Tigers scored the winning run with two outs in bottom of the ninth on Al Kaline's triple. Maas went the distance, allowing six hits and walking two.

"Everybody tells me the first victory is the toughest," Maas told reporters. "I don't see how they possibly could come any tougher."[12]

After being knocked out early at Washington in his next start, Maas pitched another complete game at home to beat the Red Sox, 9-3. The Tigers were up 9-0 in the eighth when Maas yielded a meaningless three-run homer. He followed that with a complete-game, 3-2 victory over Cleveland on May 21. At that point, Maas was 3-1 with three complete games and a 3.27 ERA.

Although he shut out the Orioles twice – on June 5 and June 18 – he was knocked out in four innings or less in four of his next five starts. His ERA was 4.81 when he was optioned to Buffalo on July 18. A rookie named Jim Bunning replaced him in the rotation.

That fall, Maas married the former Nancy Gail Seeman, a 19-year-old local beauty pageant queen in Michigan, in a ceremony noted in *The Sporting News*. His "bride carried a satin catcher's mitt and her "bridesmaid's bouquets were arranged in shapes of baseball bats and balls."[13] The couple's first child, Kevin, was born on Father's Day in 1957. Another son and daughter – twins Randy and Robin – were born on September 8, 1960.[14]

After his demotion to the minors, Maas admitted to experiencing arm trouble, but in the spring of 1956, he told *The Sporting News*, "My arm felt good again at the end of last season."[15] And he again was making an impression on his manager.

"He is a fighter … who is always in top condition to pitch," Harris said.[16] The 1956 season was one to forget for Maas, however. His record was 0-7 with a 6.54 ERA when he was shipped in mid-July to Charleston in the American Association, the Tigers' top farm club. There, he straightened himself out, winning six of nine decisions, including two shutouts, with a 2.39 ERA. He sharpened his control, walking just nine in 64 innings.

Maas began working more on a slider in the offseason, and it helped him make the Opening Day roster in 1957. That pitch "moves six to 12 inches just before it reaches the plate," catcher Frank House said praise of Maas early in the season.[17]

When Frank Lary was hit by a line drive on April 26, 1957, Maas relieved him and pitched six scoreless innings. Put back in the rotation, he won his first five starts, completing four of them. After beating Washington on May 19, he was 6-1 with a 1.74 ERA.[18]

"I've finally mastered control of my pitches," he told an Associated Press reporter. "It's just a matter of using my head instead of my arm. I've always felt I could be a consistent winner in the big leagues. ... It's about time I made something out of myself."[19]

On June 14, 1957, Maas hit his lone major-league homer in beating the Red Sox. He was never much at the plate with just 6 hits in 80 plate appearances that season; he had a .117 lifetime batting average.

His victory over Boston was his seventh, but wins were hard to come by after that. Maas didn't win again until August 1. He lost seven of his last nine decisions to finish 10-14 with a 3.28 ERA in 26 starts and 19 relief appearances over 219 1/3 innings. He saved six games. The game starts and innings pitched in '57 would be Maas's career highs. Despite his heavy workload, Maas went to the Caribbean during the offseason to pitch in Puerto Rican Winter League.[20]

On November 20, 1957, Maas was involved in a 13-player transaction, which remains the third largest in history, between Detroit and Kansas City. Billy Martin, sent to Detroit, was the key player for the Tigers in deal. The Athletics also sent an aging Gus Zernial and five others to Detroit. Maas and Bill Tuttle were the keys among the seven players acquired by the Athletics.

The next season, Maas found himself on the New York-Kansas City shuttle. The Athletics, a team that seemed as if it were still a Yankees farm club, shipped Maas and 41-year-old Virgil Trucks to New York on June 15 in exchange for Bob Grim and Harry Simpson. "The Yankees dropped by their favorite store in Kansas City and picked up an item that may turn out to be the year's biggest bargain," columnist Red Smith wrote of the Maas deal.[21] Indeed, Maas helped the Yankees secure the 1958 flag, going 7-3 in 13 starts and 9 relief appearances. He started and won the pennant-clincher, on September 14.

Before the World Series began, Maas was presumed to

be in line to start the third game against the Milwaukee Braves,[22] but when Bob Turley was knocked out in the first inning of Game Two, Maas was brought in. Rather than douse the fire, he added fuel. Maas got a fly-ball out before a walk and a single allowed both runners Turley had left on base to score. Still, all Duke needed was to retire the opposing pitcher. Lew Burdette would have none of it. His three-run homer turned the game into an early rout and sent Maas to the showers with an ERA of 81.00.

Down three games to one, the Yankees came back to beat Milwaukee, but New York's run of 14 pennants in 16 seasons hit a bump in 1959. Although New York fell to third place, Maas was second on the team in victories with 14. He beat the Indians five times and the Red Sox four. Nine of his 21 starts came as regular member of the rotation from May 27 to July 11, but otherwise he was the classic spot starter/long man, pitching out of the bullpen 17 times. In all four of his saves, he pitched two innings or more.

His 1959 performance had earned Maas a solid chance to be a consistent starter, but he experienced arm trouble during spring training and into April 1960.[23] He lasted five innings in his only start of the season, on June 1. Between June 4 and July 21, he never pitched more than two innings in a game. He appeared just four times in June, an indication his arm might have been bothering him.

Nevertheless, Maas received a vote of confidence – in public, at least – from manager Casey Stengel. "Nobody likes the Duke but me," Stengel said about stories that Maas was on the trading block. "He's coming along."[24] Yet New York newspapers had reported earlier that the Yankees tried and failed to pass Maas through waivers so he could be sent to Triple-A Richmond.[25]

Maas pitched 3 1/3 innings to earn a save on August 6. He had three more before the season ended, the last a four-inning save on September 21. The 70 1/3 innings he threw in 35 games were his fewest since 1956, when he spent half the season in the minors. Still, he finished 1960 with a 5-1 record.

In Game One of the 1960 World Series, Maas pitched two innings, yielding an RBI double to Bill Virdon in the sixth in the 6-4 Yankees loss to the Pirates. This turned out to be the last moment in the spotlight for him. The arthritic condition of his pitching arm grew worse before the start of the 1961 season. Neither the Yankees nor the expansion Los Angeles Angels must have been aware of this, however.

Maas was among the seven players on the August 31, 1960, Yankees' roster exposed to the expansion draft in December to stock the Angels and the new Washington team. (The Yankees and the other seven teams had to make an additional eight players available from the 40-man rosters.) The Angels made Maas the third pick – all three from New York – in the draft, but then traded him back to the Yankees on April 4, 1961, for infielder Fritz Brickell.

"Maas was one of two or three I hated to make available to the other clubs," Ralph Houk, the new Yankees' manager, said of the deal to reacquire the pitcher.[26] "If he doesn't make it, we will have lost nothing but an infielder on whom we had not counted," said general manager Roy Hamey.[27]

That spring, Maas moved his family to California, where his wife and three children remained, even after he was traded back to New York, for about a year before returning to their home in Utica.[28]

Although the Yankees apparently never raised the issue, it's hard to believe the Angels did not recognize that Maas had a sore arm during spring training. He didn't pitch in a game for New York until April 23. Maas retired just one of the three batters he faced – on a sacrifice bunt. He was charged with two runs. After yielding a run-scoring triple to Brooks Robinson, he walked off a big-league mound for what turned out to be the final time.

Maas remained on the active roster until May 20, when he was optioned to Richmond in the International League. He reported there after several more days of treatment on his sore arm.[29]

Soon, it was obvious that Maas no longer could pitch effectively. He gave up 36 hits – six of them homers – in 27 innings over nine games at Richmond. His ERA was 7.67. His arm trouble did not improve. At 32, he called it quits. That fall, his Yankee teammates awarded him a $750 share of their 1961 World Series money.

In late October of 1961, the Yankees released Maas to Amarillo of the Double-A Texas League, although he never played there.[30] Returning to Utica, his Michigan hometown, he was hired by the traffic department at the Ford Motor Co. plant there,[31] where he worked until shortly before his death.

According to his son Randy, Duke Maas attended the Yankees' Old Timers Game in New York in August 1967. Maas and his wife divorced in 1968.[32]

As his rheumatoid arthritic condition deteriorated, he was admitted to St. Joseph's Hospital in Clinton Township, Michigan, in late November 1976, where he remained for two weeks until he died of congestive heart failure on December 7.[33] Maas was 47. He is buried in Utica Cemetery.

## Sources

I gratefully acknowledge the help of Randy Maas, Duke's younger son, with this essay.

The statistical details on the player's career and games are from baseball-reference.com and retrosheet.org.

## Notes

1 Watson Spoelstra, "Hudlin Coaching Straightens Out Tigers' Curving," *The Sporting News*, May 15, 1957: 10.

2 1940 U.S. Census, accessed through familysearch.org. Throughout his pro career, team rosters listed Maas as having been born on January 31, 1931, as did *Baseball Register*. His 1976 obituary by the Associated Press correctly listed his age as 47. United Press International had him at 45. Today, all sources note his correct birthday, but I found no mention of when the discrepancy first was noted.

3 Ibid.

4 Telephone conversation with Randy Maas, Duke's younger son, July 23, 2018.

5 Watson Spoelstra, "Hats Off," *Sporting News*, May 29, 1957: 23.

6 Syd Kronish, Associated Press, "Chance to Beat School Bell Started Maas on Hill Career," *Mason City* (Iowa) *Globe Gazette*, June 4, 1955: 9.

7 Spoelstra, "Hats Off."

8 "Rookie Lives Near Park, But Has Seen Few Tiger Games," *The Sporting News*, March 30, 1955: 17.

9 Spolestra, "Hats Off."

10 Spoelstra, "Pair of Rookie Righties Brace Bengals on Mound," *The Sporting News*, June 1, 1955: 14.

11 Spoelstra, "Bucky Plans to Join Casey and Richards as Pitching Juggler," *The Sporting News*, March 30, 1955: 17.

12 United Press, "Duke Maas Wins First Tiger Game; Kaline Stars," *Holland* (Michigan) *Evening Sentinel*, May 6, 1955: 11.

13 "Maas' Bride Carries Satin Catcher's Mitt at Wedding," *The Sporting News*, November 23, 1955: 15.

14  "Stafford After Third," *World Telegram and Sun* (New York City), September 9, 1960: page unknown, from clip file for Maas at Hall of Fame and Museum.

15  Spoelstra, "Maas Could Fill Tigers Need of 'Another Hurler'," February 15, 1956: 22.

16  Ibid.

17  Spoelstra, "Hats Off."

18  Ibid.

19  Dave Diles, Associated Press, "Duke Maas Is Using Head, Winning," *Gettysburg Times*, June 24, 1957: 5.

20  Telephone conversation with Randy Maas, July 23, 2018.

21  Red Smith, "Dealing From Fright," *New York Herald Tribune*, June 17, 1958: B1.

22  Harold Rosenthal, "Ford Seen Yankees' Series Key Again," *New York Herald Tribune*, September 25, 1958: B1.

23  Tommy Holmes, "Yanks Deal Brickell to Angels to Regain Maas," *New York Herald Tribune*, April 4, 1961: 29.

24  Dan Daniel, "Ol' Prof Scribbles Question Marks on Yanks' Curvers," *The Sporting News*, June 1, 1960: 8.

25  Daniel, "Stengel Tells Why James Had to Go," (New York) *World Telegram and Sun*, July 28, 1960: page unknown, from the Maas clip file at the Hall of Fame.

26  Holmes, "Yanks Deal."

27  Daniel, "Yankees Need a Hitter," *World Telegram and Sun*, April 4, 1961; page unknown, from Maas clip file at the Hall of Fame.

28  Telephone conversation with Randy Mass, July 23, 2018.

29  John Drebinger, "Tie Broken in 8th," *New York Times*, May 21, 1961: S1.

30  Daniel, "Gibbs Tops List of 9 Newcomers on Yank Roster," *The Sporting News*, October 25, 1961: 7.

31  William Hickey, "Where Are They Now?" *Baseball Digest*, July 1966: 82.

32  Telephone conversation with Randy Maas, July 23, 1968.

33  Associated Press, "Ex-Tiger Maas Dies, *Escanaba* (Michigan) *Daily Press*, December 8, 1976: 20, and telephone conversation with Randy Maas, July 23, 2018.

# TED KLUSZEWSKI

## BY PAUL LADEWSKI

The area known as Argo is located eight miles west of Chicago's old Comiskey Park in Summit, Illinois, a lowdown five-figure village in Cook County known for a corn milling and processing plant that is among the largest of its kind – and has the odor to prove it. It was also home to Ted "Klu" Kluszewski, the 6-foot-2, 225-pound mountain of a man with the famous 15-inch biceps, whose legend in baseball history will live even longer and go farther than the home runs he hit decades ago.

Kluszewski has often been referred to as one of the most underappreciated players of the post-World War II era; one whose accomplishments as a player and a coach have remained under the radar far too long. In the mid-1950s "Klu" was the original "Big Red Machine," a long-ball hitter and run-producer without peer. In the four seasons from 1953 to 1956, he averaged 179 hits, 43 homers, and 116 RBIs, numbers every bit as impressive as those of Eddie Mathews (152-41-109) of the Milwaukee Braves and Duke Snider (180-42-123) of the Brooklyn Dodgers

in the same period. It's not a stretch to believe that if Kluszewski had stayed healthy and productive for four or five more seasons, he would have joined Mathews and Snider in the Hall of Fame. Despite an abbreviated career, his 251 homers while he was with rank fifth on the Reds' all-time list.

Born on September 10, 1924, Theodore Bernard Kluszewski attended Argo High School in Summit, where he excelled in football. His father worked in a local factory. As a youth, Klu's baseball experience consisted mostly of sandlot games. Indiana University recruited him primarily as a football player, but he also played baseball there, and his 1945 season ranks as one of the best for a two-sport athlete in the school's history. As a center fielder, Kluszewski hit .443, a school record that stood for 50 years; then the star end and kicker helped lead the Hoosiers to their only outright Big Ten football championship. The squad, which also included future NFL players Pete Pihos and George Taliaferro, finished with a 9-0-1 mark, the only unbeaten Hoosiers football team.

If not for World War II, Kluszewski most likely would have embarked on a professional football career. During that time the Reds held spring training at the Indiana campus in Bloomington because major-league teams were forbidden to train in the South. One day they invited the kid to take some hacks at batting practice. As legend has it, "Big Klu" promptly launched a few rockets over an embankment nearly 400 feet away. After they picked up their jaws off the ground, team officials offered him a $15,000 contract, which he accepted.

With the bonus in hand, Kluszewski married Eleanor Guckel in February 1946. Eleanor was a fine athlete herself, excelling at softball, and Klu later credited her with helping his major-league career by taking films of him at bat and in the field from seats close to the field.

Making his professional debut for the Reds' Columbia (South Carolina) farm team in the Class-A South Atlantic League in 1946, Kluszewski was an immediate sensation, leading the league with a .352 batting average and driving in 87 runs in 90 games. He made his Cincinnati debut in April 1947, but logged only 10 at-bats with the Reds, spending most of the season with Memphis of the Double-A Southern Association. Again he tore up the league, winning the batting crown with a .377 average.

In 1948 Kluszewski returned to Cincinnati to stay for 10 full seasons. It wasn't long before his large biceps prompted Klu to cut off the sleeves of his jersey, one of the boldest fashion statements in baseball history. At first, he did it because the sleeves were restricting his swing, but after a while it became part of his persona. "I remember the first time that I saw Ted in those cut-off sleeves," former White Sox teammate Billy Pierce said of his trademark style nearly a half-century later. "They were good-sized. He was a big man. A big man."[1]

Despite those massive arms, Kluszewski did not immediately become a home-run hitter at the major-league level. He hit only 12 as a rookie in 1948, and just eight in 1949, though he showed overall improvement as a hitter by lifting his batting average 35 points from .274 to .309. He showed his power potential for the first time in 1950, hitting 25 home runs and driving in 111 runs to go along with a .307 batting average. After a dip in 1951 (.259-13-77), Klu had 16 home runs in 1952 while raising his average to .320. His big breakthrough came a year later.

In 1953 Kluszewski finally blossomed as big-time slugger, as his .316 batting average, 40 home runs, and 108 RBIs translated into a seventh-place finish in the Most Valuable Player vote. A career year followed in 1954, when he led the NL with 49 home runs. He hit .326 (fifth overall), slugged .642 (third), drove home 141 runs (first), and finished a close second to New York Giants outfielder Willie Mays in the MVP vote. In the All-Star Game at Cleveland, he delivered an RBI single and a two-run homer in consecutive innings, the latter of which broke a 5-5 tie in

an eventual 11-9 loss. Klu was at his best when the stars came out, as he hit .500 in four midsummer classics.

Kluszewski did the brunt of his damage at the cozy confines of Crosley Field, which produced one of the highest home-run rates of the decade, but he wasn't known for front-row jobs. What separated Kluszewski from the rest of the musclemen was his off-the-charts discipline at the plate. He totaled 31 fewer strikeouts (140) than home runs (171) in his four peak seasons. Of the ten times in major-league history that a player hit at least 40 homers with fewer strikeouts, three were by Kluszewski. The others on the list: Lou Gehrig (twice), Johnny Mize (twice), Mel Ott, Joe DiMaggio, and Barry Bonds.

"Everybody moves at his own pace," Billy Pierce said many years later. "I mean, we had a Nellie Fox who jumped around all the time. Sherm Lollar couldn't move very fast no matter what happened. But both gave you everything they had on the field and Ted was the same way. He worked at his own pace, and he had a pretty good career that way."[2]

Kluszewski didn't make many mistakes in the field, either, although his detractors argued that the low error totals were the result of an inability or reluctance to move more than one step either way. If you believe in range factors, though, Big Klu was well above average in this regard before his achy back came into play. He led the league in fielding percentage in a record five consecutive seasons, largely the result of excellent hands and nimble footwork.

"Everybody knows Ted could hit a baseball," said the late Bill "Moose" Skowron, the former New York Yankees first baseman who crossed paths with Big Klu many times in their careers. "What some people don't know is that he was a hell of a first baseman and a hell of a nice guy, too. And he always played in those short-sleeve shirts. He was built like a rock, you know."[3]

Kluszewski might have had a long run as one of baseball's top sluggers if not for a back injury that resulted from a clubhouse scuffle during the 1956 season. The disc problem proved to be Delilah to Klu's Samson, as he would never be the same power hitter again. After the 1957 season, one in which Klu was limited to a half-dozen homers and 21 RBIs in 69 games, he was dealt by the Reds to Pittsburgh in return for Dee Fondy, another veteran first baseman.

In 1958, his only full season with the Pirates, Kluszewski produced a mere four home runs and 37 RBIs in 100 games, but he had a positive influence on a young, talented team that was on the move. Before he left, Klu made history at Forbes Field on May 9, when he went deep against Philadelphia Phillies pitcher Robin Roberts leading off the 12th inning, the 19th walk-off homer to decide a 1-0 game since the turn of the century.

Big Klu began the 1959 season with the Pirates, but was reduced to part-time status behind Dick Stuart and Rocky Nelson. He had started only 20 games and logged just 122 at-bats by late August when the White Sox, looking to add power for the stretch and (hopefully) the World Series, traded outfielder Harry "Suitcase" Simpson and minor-league pitcher Bob Sagers for Kluszewski on August 25.

While the 34-year-old Kluszewski was deep into the back nine of his career at the time, news of his return to Chicago was well received by South Siders. "Certainly, the attitude of the fans was positive about the trade," said John Kuenster, who covered the 1959 pennant-winners as a *Chicago Daily News* beat writer. "Ted was a nice guy, a popular guy. He was well known in the area and his return was very well received there."[4] At the very least, the consensus went, Klu could do no worse at the position than 35-year-old warhorse Earl Torgeson, a .226 hitter at the time, or 24-year-young prospect Norm Cash, a .231 hitter who was new to the pressure of a pennant race.

Besides, the righty-dominated lineup had been rather "Kluless" for months. The veteran lefty provided a much-needed option for a "Go-Go" Sox team that was overly dependent on speed and defense at the time. "We didn't have a regular first baseman," Pierce recalled. "When we got Ted, we all thought it was a very, very good thing for us, because he gave us a strong left-handed hitter with a good reputation. We never thought he was past his prime but that he would help us. We were very glad to have him on our ballclub."[5]

What Kluszewski lacked in glitzy numbers, he made up for in stature. His mere physical presence gave the Second City a sliver of security, a reason to flex its own muscles for a change. "Ted was a quiet fellow, but he had been with a winner in Cincinnati and had many accomplishments in his career," Pierce said. "A fellow like that is a kind of automatic leader on the team. He gave us stability, which was very good for us."[6]

As it turned out, Kluszewski didn't quite turn back the

clock in the final weeks of the regular season, but he had his moments. The most significant took place in Chicago on September 7, when the White Sox defeated the Kansas City Athletics in a Labor Day doubleheader. In the opener Kluszewski contributed a key run-scoring hit in a 2-1 victory; in the nightcap he slugged a pair of homers and drove home five runs in a 13-7 rout. As a result of the sweep, the White Sox maintained a 4½-game lead over the second-place Cleveland Indians, who scored an emotional sweep of the Detroit Tigers by 15-14 and 6-5 scores the same day.

While Kluszewski had rather modest statistics in the final 32 games of the regular season – .297 batting average, 2 homers, 10 RBIs – the hidden numbers suggest the White Sox were deeper and better because of him. "Ted was a great asset for us," Pierce said. "He was an important cog in the middle of the lineup."[7] With Klu as protection in the cleanup spot, outfielder Jim Landis immediately picked up the pace in the third hole. The offense produced more runs (4.5 vs. 4.3 per game) and team won at a higher rate (.625-.607) with Big Klu than without him.

But it was his performance in the 1959 World Series against the Dodgers that made South Side fans forever remember the Kluszewski trade as one of the greatest Brinks jobs in White Sox history; a local boy who made very, very good one unforgettable season. In the six World Series games, Kluszewski hit .391, slugged three home runs and drove in 10 runs. His 1.266 OPS (on base plus slugging) was just plain silly.

Kluszewski smashed two home runs in an 11-0 rout of the Los Angeles Dodgers in the Series opener. "Oh, man, the two home runs that Ted hit...," Pierce smiled at the thought of them. "That was exciting. I mean, there we were in the World Series. ... The fans were excited, we were excited, everybody was excited."[8] Witnesses said Comiskey Park never rocked the way it did in the moments after Kluszewski took reliever Chuck Churn for a ride to the upper deck in the fourth inning. The two-run blow not only sealed the victory, but it did much to "chuck" Churn, as it turned out. The pitch was his last in the big leagues.

Until outfielder Scott Podsednik went deep to decide Game One of the 2005 World Series, the monster blast stood as the most memorable home run in team history. "There was a similar feeling with the two home runs," said John Kuenster. "They gave White Sox fans a reason to think, 'Maybe we will win this thing after all,' although in the case of the 1959 team, it didn't turn out that way."[9] Alas, the Dodgers won four of the next five games to become world champions.

Kluszewski left the team for the Los Angeles Angels in the expansion draft after the 1960 season – he had hit .293 with 5 homers in 81 games – but not before he was involved in the most controversial play of the 1960 campaign. In a game at Baltimore on August 28, Kluszewski hit a dramatic pinch-hit, three-run homer against Orioles starter Milt Pappas in the eighth inning to give his team a 4-3 lead. Or so it seemed. The umpire crew agreed that time had been called before the pitch was thrown and the home run was wiped out. After teammate Nellie Fox was ejected from the game, Kluszewski flied out to end the threat. The White Sox went on to drop a 3-1 decision and fell three games out of first place.

Before Kluszewski retired one year later, he exacted a sliver of payback at the same site. In the first game in Los Angeles Angels history, Big Klu took Pappas deep with a man on base in the first inning, the first home run in franchise history. One inning later he greeted rookie John Papa with a three-run homer to set the wheels in motion for a 7-2 victory. Kluszewski finished his final big-league season with a .243 batting average, 15 home runs, and 39 RBIs in 107 games.

Kluszewski returned to the Reds after retiring as a player, and his impact on the team was no small one. He was the Reds' hitting coach for nine seasons in the 1970s, a decade that the Big Red Machine dominated as few other offenses in NL history had done. In 1986, after he had become a hitting instructor in the Reds' minor-league system, Kluszewski suffered a heart attack and underwent emergency bypass surgery. On March 29, 1988, a massive heart attack took his life. He was 63 years old.

That the funeral service in suburban Cincinnati was a virtual Who's Who said as much about Kluszewski the person as Big Klu the athlete. Rose, Johnny Bench, and Tony Perez were among those who paid their respects. Stan Musial and Joe Nuxhall did, too. During the 1988 season the Reds wore black armbands in memory of their late teammate. There wasn't an arm large enough to do justice to Big Klu, a big man in more ways than one.

**Notes**

1 Billy Pierce, interview with author, August 2008.

2 Ibid.

3 Bill Skowron, interview with author, August 2008.

4 John Kuenster, interview with author, September 2008.

5 Pierce.

6 Ibid.

7 Ibid.

8 Ibid.

9 Kuenster.

# ELI GRBA

## By Chuck Johnson

On December 6, 1960, the American League awarded Los Angeles and Washington, D.C., expansion franchises that would play in the league beginning in April 1961. With only four months to put a franchise together, Los Angeles owner Gene Autry first hired Bob Reynolds as team president and Fred Haney as general manager. When it came time to pick a field manager, their first choice was Casey Stengel, who had been fired by the New York Yankees after the 1960 season. Stengel turned down the offer but provided insight on players he thought would be of immediate help to the Angels. With just eight days to prepare for the expansion draft, the three executives took Stengel's advice to heart, and on December 14 they chose right-handed pitcher Eli Grba of the Yankees, making him the first player ever chosen in an expansion draft and the first player in Angels history.[1]

A native of Chicago, Eli Grba was born on August 9, 1934. His father, Joseph Grba, left the family early on, leaving his mother, Eva, to raise her only child as a single parent. Working as a waitress during the day and a factory worker at night, she afforded Eli the opportunity to participate in sports as a child. He became a three-sport star at Bowen High School on Chicago's South Side. "Basketball was my favorite," Eli said, "even after I made the major leagues I played semipro in the offseason, sometimes as many as 40 games."[2]

Baseball was the sport that came calling, however, as Grba's exploits at Bowen and in summer leagues attracted the attention of Boston Red Sox scout Chuck Koney. After graduating in the spring of 1952, Grba signed with the Red Sox and was sent to play at Salisbury, North Carolina, of the Class-D North Carolina State League.

"Sheriff Robinson was my first manager," Grba recalled. "As a matter of fact, Robinson was my manager my first three seasons in the minors." A catcher during his 13-year minor-league playing career, Robinson was making his managerial debut with Salisbury in 1952 and, Grba said, "We just hit it off."

Grba learned his lessons well, as he was an all-star that first season in Salisbury and again in 1953 with Corning of the Class-D Pony League, where he led the league in games started, innings pitched, and strikeouts.

After one more solid season under Robinson's tutelage, with San Jose in 1955, the Red Sox placed Grba placed on the fast track, bypassing three levels of competition and moving him up to Triple-A San Francisco (Pacific Coast League) for 1956.

San Francisco was managed that season by Eddie Joost and then, after Joost was fired in June, future Hall of Famer Joe Gordon. Not wanting to tip the cart and upset the veteran pitchers on the staff, Joost at the start of the season dispatched Grba, the youngest full-time pitcher on the staff, to the bullpen. "I went from over 220 innings the previous two years to less than 100 (93⅓)," Grba said. "I was a starter, and I wanted to pitch."

Grba reported to spring training in 1957 with the Red Sox but finished it with the New York Yankees. On March 14 he and outfielder Gordon Windhorn were traded to the Yankees for outfielder Bill Renna. "I hated the trade," Grba said, "I grew up a White Sox fan and (the Yankees would) come in and beat us all the time."

Before he could establish himself with his new team, however, another team soon came calling: the U.S. Army. With the start of the season just two weeks away, Grba tried, unsuccessfully, for a deferment. After being inducted, he was sent to Fort Jackson, in Columbia, South Carolina. He later was stationed at Fort McPherson, in Atlanta, Georgia. Over the course of the next two years, he played baseball and basketball for his base teams, and upon his discharge he reported to St. Petersburg, Florida, for spring training with the Yankees in 1959.

The Yankees sent Grba to Triple-A Richmond to start the season. Grba had gotten stronger during his Army hitch and was throwing harder, but the Yankees thought he needed a third pitch to complement his fastball and curve. In spring training coach Ralph Houk "asked what I thought I needed to get to the major leagues," Grba said. "I never could learn a changeup, so I just said a slider." After a brief session with minor-league pitching coach Eddie Lopat, Grba was throwing a modified slider, or cutter as it came to be called. Again Grba pitched out of the bullpen.

His work paid off, as Grba was recalled by the Yankees in July. He reported to the team at Boston's Fenway Park, where he made his major-league debut in relief on July 10, pitching a hitless inning. The next day manager Casey Stengel sent him to the mound again, and this time he was reached for three runs (two of which scored on a wild throw) in 2⅔ innings. His first major-league start and win came eight days later in Yankee Stadium against his favorite team as a child, the White Sox. It was a 6-4 victory, and all four runs off Grba were unearned.

Grba spent the rest of the season with the Yankees, winning two games and losing five with a high 6.44 ERA. He reported to spring training in 1960 confident in his role with the team, but things didn't go exactly as planned. "I made the team," Grba said, "I even rode the team train back to New York." But once in New York manager Stengel had a change of heart, and Grba was sent down to Richmond.

Grba pitched well in Richmond, going 7-1 in nine starts before being recalled in early July. He remained with the Yankees for the rest of the season, winning six games and losing four (3.68 ERA) in a mix of starting and relief roles. He was on the Yankees' World Series roster against the Pittsburgh Pirates, although his only appearance came as a pinch-runner for Elston Howard in Game Six.

Shortly after the World Series, which the Yankees lost on Bill Mazeroski's Game Seven walk-off home run, the Yankees advised Grba that he would be among the players they would leave unprotected in the coming expansion draft. The Angels selected Grba first overall, and in 1961 he reported to spring training in Palm Springs, California.

As the season opener approached, Angels manager Bill Rigney selected Grba to start the first game in the franchise's history, so on the cool, windy afternoon of April 11, 1961, Grba took the mound in Baltimore in front of 37,352 fans. The Angels scored seven runs in the first two innings and went on to win, 7-2. Grba pitched a complete-game six-hitter. The weather on the East Coast at the time played havoc with the schedule; two rainouts in Baltimore were followed by another in Boston and then two more in New York before Grba's next start, which came against his former teammates in Yankee Stadium on April 20. In his return to New York, Grba gave up a pair of homers and five RBI to Mickey Mantle as the Angels lost, 7-5.

On April 27 Grba was tabbed by Rigney to start the Angels' home opener, against the Minnesota Twins at Wrigley Field.[3] He went 6⅓ innings, allowing six hits and four runs, three on a home run by Twins catcher Earl Battey, as the Angels lost, 4-2.

Grba won 11 games and lost 13 in 1961, finishing second on the pitching staff in wins, innings, and starts. He spent the entire 1962 season with the Angels as well (8-9, 4-54 ERA), but, in his own words, "drinking was starting to affect my pitching."

Manager Bill Rigney had had enough. The Angels tried to trade Grba twice[4] and finally sold him to the Hawaii

Islanders of the Pacific Coast League. Grba bounced around the minor leagues for the next few years, even making the International League all-star team with Toronto in 1964, before his drinking finally forced him out of the game as a player in 1967.

"I was drinking heavy and I didn't care about anything," Grba said, "My priorities were all gone. Bob Lemon saw me one day and said, "I've never seen a pitcher lose his stuff as fast as you did.""

Grba bounced around from job to job and rehab center to rehab center until, in his words, he "hit the limit" on August 1, 1981. Living and working at a detox center in El Monte, California, he was sneaking back into his room at 2:30 A.M. when he lost his balance and fell to the floor. Realizing then how he had disappointed those closest to him – family, friends, and teammates –he decided right then that things had to change.

As of 2018, he is still sober, 33 years and counting.

Grba's sobriety also afforded him a chance to get back into the game. In 1982 he was hired as the pitching coach for the Milwaukee Brewers' Triple-A team in Vancouver. After a year in Waterbury with the Angels' Double-A team, Grba tried his hand at managing with Reno in the California League in 1989.

With the help of Philadelphia Phillies general manager Lee Thomas, a good friend, Grba joined the Phillies organization and spent two years with Rookie-level Princeton as[1] a scout under farm director Del Unser. He scouted for five seasons, retiring after the 1997 season.

Grba and his fourth wife, Regina, were residing in Florence, Alabama, in 2015. He has two children from previous marriages, a son, Nick, and a daughter, Stacy, and two grandchildren. Nick spent 26 years with the Air Force, served in Iraq and Afghanistan, and retired with the rank of staff sergeant. Stacy also served overseas in the Air Force.

In 2011, the Angels celebrated their 50th anniversary as a franchise. Among the events were ceremonies honoring people who were part of Angels' history since the beginning. The first person the Angels honored was the first player in franchise history, Eli Grba.

"What I think about sometimes is about how I messed it up," Grba said of how he let drinking destroy his career and three marriages. "Baseball has been a secondary

thought to me ever since I got sober, I didn't leave the Angels the way I wanted."[5]

For most of the 43,853 fans in attendance on April 8, 2011, Grba's appearance was a symbolic one, but for Eli it was sentimental. "It's nice to be recognized as the first, nice to be remembered, and it's an honor."

He went out to the mound and threw a strike, just as he had done 50 years earlier.

## Sources

In addition to the items cited in the Notes, the author also consulted Baseball Reference.com, Retrosheet.org, and The Sporting News via Paper of Record.

## Notes

1 Roland Hemond, "A Whole New Franchise," *The National Pastime,* 2011.

2 All quotes in this article are from the author's phone interview with Eli Grba on December 6, 2014, emails between the author and subject on December 7, 8, 14, and 23, 2014 and an email between co-author Chuck Boyer and Eli's niece Karen Milovich on December 17, 2014.

3 The Angels played home games in 1961 at Wrigley Field in Los Angeles. They played home games in Dodger Stadium beginning in 1962 and remained there until Anaheim Stadium opened in 1966.

4 Chris Foster, "Managing Day by Day," *Los Angeles Times,* August 2, 1989.

5 Marcia C. Smith, "Original Angel Grba Takes Mound," *Orange County Register,* April 8, 2011.

# THE WASHINGTON SENATORS
# BEGIN A NEW TERM

## By Chris Jones

Every two years, the nation's capital sees senators leave town and new senators arrive to take their place. After a while, the suits all begin to look the same; only the bodies filling them out are different. The dance of those coming and going is typically confined to Capitol Hill. But between October 1960 and April 1961, it made its way approximately two miles north and into the national pastime.

On October 2, 1960, the Washington Senators played the final game of the season at Griffith Stadium. A little more than six months later, on April 10, 1961, the Washington Senators took the field at Griffith Stadium once again, this time for Opening Day. The uniforms looked the same (exactly the same, actually, as 60 unused uniforms were purchased from outgoing owner Calvin Griffith, who had ordered them before receiving approval to move the prior Senators club to Minnesota.)[1] But the players filling those uniforms out were most assuredly different.

And "different" may be the most glowing term by which the new roster could be described. One writer went so far as to tell Senators fans to "have heart," reasoning that because the American League had only 10 teams, "no matter how bad the new Washington club may turn out to be, it can't finish eleventh like its 1899 predecessor."[2] The writer was correct: The 1961 Washington Senators did not finish in 11th place. But they did finish tied for last.

Even fielding a team for the 1961 season was a monumental undertaking for the Senators and their expansion

brethren, the Los Angeles Angels. It began on October 26, 1960, when the major-league owners met in New York and determined that the American League would expand from eight to 10 teams for the 1961 season. It had been an open secret for some time that Griffith wanted out of Washington, despite his public assurances to the contrary. In fact, *The Sporting News* dated on the same day as the owners' meeting quoted Griffith as saying, "That's a lot of baloney and sounds like somebody's pipe dream. It is news to me that the American League will discuss transferring the Washington club elsewhere."[3]

Behind closed doors, however, Griffith sensed his opportunity and pounced. Most of the other owners wanted

Washington Senators' owner Elwood 'Pete' Quesada and President John Fitzgerald Kennedy attend Opening Day 1961 at Griffith Stadium. (Courtesy of the John F. Kennedy Presidential Library)

to keep a team in Washington. A balance was therefore struck: The existing Senators were permitted to relocate to Minneapolis-St. Paul and the two expansion franchises were awarded to Los Angeles and Washington.[4] Optimism did not exactly abound for the new additions. Former Dodgers boss Branch Rickey even predicted that "the new clubs in Washington and Los Angeles will throw in their franchises before the playing season is a month old."[5]

Bidding for ownership of the new franchise was underway immediately. The two primary contenders had military backgrounds: Elwood R. "Pete" Quesada, a former US Air Force lieutenant general who was in 1960 the chief of the Federal Aviation Agency,[6] and John J. Bergen, a former Navy admiral who was then the chairman of the Graham-Paige Corp.[7] In *The Sporting News,* Shirley Povich wrote that "the inter-service rivalry that used to stir the wrath of Capitol Hill is still aflame, but it no longer is regarded as a menace to national security. It has been transferred to the bidding for the new Washington franchise in the American League that is now up for grabs."[8]

Quesada had the upper hand from the word go – or perhaps even before that. There were reports that Calvin Griffith had conferred with Quesada as early as the previous summer about possibly bidding for a new Washington franchise. In Griffith's words, "[C]ertainly Quesada got his bid in almost before the ink was dry on the newspapers announcing the American League expansion."[9] Griffith also publicly supported Quesada's bid.[10] And so it was no surprise when ownership of the new Washington franchise was awarded to Quesada, who led a group of 10 local investors.[11] Two of Quesada's primary backers in the group were Washington automobile dealer Fred Akers and banker George Garrett, who was a former US ambassador to Ireland.[12]

Senators' manager Mickey Vernon and Tigers' manager Bob Scheffing meet President Kennedy on Opening Day 1962, the first at District of Columbia Memorial Stadium. (Courtesy of the John F. Kennedy Presidential Library)

With Quesada at the helm, it seemed certain that the new club would not fail for lack of strong leadership. A former lieutenant described his service under Quesada during World War II:

> When the Battle of the Bulge came, I was ordered to supervise the last convoy leaving Verviers for Liege, Belgium, a retreat of some 18 miles. But it had to be made along the only road into Liege along the Meuse River. It was a bright, moonlit night and we were strafed constantly by German planes. It took us something like 12 hours to negotiate 18 miles.
>
> When I finally got the convoy into Liege, with a loss of one truck, I was told that General Quesada wanted to see me. I figured here was my medal for valor, finally. Instead, Pete chewed me out for losing the truck. And then he smiled and said: "I guess, Bob, you thought you were going to get a medal for pulling that convoy through. But even the loss of one radar-equipped truck hurts."[13]

True to form, Quesada acted quickly and decisively in naming the first manager of the new club within 24 hours. He received rave reviews from the local populace by selecting former Senators first basemen and fan favorite Mickey Vernon.[14] Quesada also announced the hiring of retiring American Association President Ed Doherty as general manager.[15]

The quick hiring of Doherty was especially important because Quesada intended to remain with the FAA until the change of administration on January 20, "out of my sense of duty."[16] There was therefore the "need for a general manager with a quick grasp of the needs of a figuratively rudderless club."[17] For his part, Doherty stated his intention to be aggressive in the front office:

> There will be instant dealing after we learn who we draw in the player pool. ... We know we can't stand still on the 28 players we select. I know, too, that other clubs, including those in the National League, will be ready to deal for some of them.[18]

At the minor-league meetings in Louisville in late November, Commissioner Ford Frick announced that the new Washington franchise was officially certified and open for business,[19] and was "entitled to all rights and privileges, including the right to select two players in a special draft [and] to file waiver claims..."[20]

And so it was that on November 28, 1960, the new Senators acquired their first two players in the Flag Room of the Kentucky Hotel in Louisville, selecting pitchers John Gabler and Ray Semproch in the special draft, held after the regular minor-league draft.[21] The right-handed hurlers formed the beginnings of what Doherty hoped to be a respectable pitching staff. Semproch had won 13 games for the Phillies in 1958 before succumbing to arm trouble in 1959, but had rebounded to go 11-2 at Spokane in 1960. Gabler, who had been property of the Yankees, had a 2.71 earned-run average for Richmond in 1960, and the Yankees were reportedly "miffed when he was claimed by Doherty off the Richmond roster."[22] The next day Washington signed 30-year-old free-agent infielder Danny O'Connell.[23]

Mickey Vernon filled out his coaching staff, hiring Sid Hudson as the pitching coach and George Case, Rollie Hemsley, and George Susce as coaches.[24] So it was that "the new Washington Senators closed the week with more coaches than ball players – four to three. ..."[25] The disparity would be short-lived, though, as the coming expansion draft, to be held at AL President Joe Cronin's offices in Boston, permitted the Senators and the Los Angeles Angels to select players for $75,000 apiece.[26]

The Senators' brain-trust endured an arduous trek to even make it to the draft. With a severe snowstorm looming, Quesada suggested taking the train to Boston instead of flying. "It didn't look like there was a chance of making it to Boston by plane," Doherty said.[27] *The Sporting News* described the ordeal:

> With two newspapermen (Francis Stann and Moe Siegel) along, Farm Director Hal Keller, Doherty and [Burton] Hawkins[28] headed for the Hub. Their train was frozen up outside of New Haven, Conn., Monday morning, December 12. They occupied a cold, foodless car for about six hours before they were transferred to a coach for Boston. This, too, was cold and without food.
>
> Instead of arriving here at 8 a.m., the Washington delegation arrived here at 5 p.m., nine hours later. "And to complete the voyage," Doherty related, "I slipped off the train and landed in a snow pile."[29]

Safe in Boston at last, the Senators and Angels brass convened on December 14 to commence the expansion draft. It was decided that the draft would be conducted by category, with the clubs selecting players by position: pitchers, catchers, infielders, and finally outfielders. Angels general manager Fred Haney won a coin toss for the right to select first in three of the four categories, draft-

A couple of New Englanders reunited in the White House: Massachusetts' Dave Powers and Connecticut's Jimmy Piersall. After many years with the Red Sox, Piersall played outfield for the Senators in 1962 and 1963. (Courtesy of the John F. Kennedy Presidential Library)

ing Yankees pitcher Eli Grba first overall.[30] The Senators made pitcher Bobby Shantz (also from the Yankees) their first selection.[31] In addition to Shantz, the Senators came away with catcher Pete Daley (A's), infielder Coot Veal (Tigers), and outfielder Willie Tasby (Red Sox) with their first selections in each player category.[32] And despite selecting first only in the outfielder portion of the draft, the Senators insisted that they came away with the two players they were most after – Shantz and Tasby.[33]

A problem arose when the league went to tally the results of the draft. The draft rules provided that "no existing team could lose more than seven players and no expansion team could take more than four players from any one existing team."[34] But nobody bothered to keep track of such things while the draft was underway. As a result, after the last pick was made, it was discovered that numerous violations had occurred. To rectify the situation, Cronin ordered the clubs to swap players to bring the draft in line with the rules.[35]

The worst fortune the Senators had in the post-draft swaps was the trade of pitcher Dean Chance to the Angels for outfielder Joe Hicks, which occurred because the "Senators had too many Orioles" and the "Angels had too many White Sox."[36] Hicks went on to hit .221 in only 389 more major-league plate appearances, while Chance won 128 big-league games, including 20 in 1964, made two All-Star Game appearances and received the Cy Young Award.

Overall, the Senators had selected 28 players ranging in age from 22 (Bud Zipfel) to 38 (Gene Woodling) in the major-league portion of the draft, and selected another

(Counter clockwise from left) Manager Ted Williams, along with Senators' players Frank Howard, Darold Knowles, Dick Bosman and team owner Robert Short flank President Richard M. Nixon on the cover of the 1970 team program. After contending in 1969, the Senators reclaimed their familiar position of 'first in war, first in peace, and last in the American League'. (Courtesy of Robert Schultz)

three players off the minor-league rosters of the existing teams.[37] For some players, being drafted gave new life to their careers. Woodling, for example, had no interest in moving to the West Coast to join the Angels at age 38, later stating that "that would have made a farmer out of me. ... I would have retired to my Ohio farm before I would sign with Los Angeles."[38] He was willing to play in Washington, however, and went on to lead the 1961 team in hitting with a .313 average.[39]

For other players, even being made available for the expansion draft by their former clubs was a cold dose of reality. Chuck Hinton said that "people gave you who they didn't want. I'm not going to say that I was in that category, but as far as the Orioles were concerned, I guess I was. They never thought that I would be drafted, so that's one reason they put me on the list."[40]

And while the baseball talent assembled may have been less than awe-inspiring, one writer noted that "the Senators should rank among the brainiest in the majors, at least scholastically. ... Pitcher Dave Sisler is working for his master's degree in industrial engineering...Catcher Dutch Dotterer is working for his master's in Latin-American studies."[41] But even Commissioner Ford Frick could provide only backhanded optimism after the draft, predicting that the Angels and Senators "will win at least 50 games," which as one writer noted would be a 50-112 record and a .309 winning percentage.[42]

Ed Doherty kept his word and immediately went to work on the trade market after the draft. Only two days after drafting Bobby Shantz as the Senators' number-one selection, Doherty flipped the left-hander to the Pittsburgh Pirates for pitcher Bennie Daniels, infielder Harry Bright,

and first baseman R.C. Stevens.[43] Shantz could barely conceal his relief at not having to pitch for the expansion Senators, admitting that his wife wanted him to quit baseball anyway and that he had been "hoping" that he would not get drafted by Washington in the first place.[44] Manager Mickey Vernon was familiar with all three of the newly acquired players from having been a coach for Pittsburgh in 1960, and was said to have "recommended the deal heartily."[45]

Vernon's support notwithstanding, the Senators' agreement to the deal with Pittsburgh is perhaps most notable because of the corresponding trade proposal from the Cardinals that the team turned down. St. Louis was said to have offered a package of players, including future Hall of Fame pitcher Bob Gibson, to the Senators for Shantz.[46] Gibson, who had yet to start more than 12 games in a season, went on to win 251 games and strike out over 3,000 batters in his 17-year career. By contrast, of the three players acquired from the Pirates, Daniels had the biggest impact on the Senators, winning 12 games in 1961 and a total of 37 in his five years with the team.[47] Bright and Stevens combined for only 159 hits (151 from Bright) with Washington.[48]

After the Pittsburgh trade, Senators farm director Hal Keller described his plans to infuse more talent, and bodies, into the pipeline: "After the first of the year, Sheehan and I will start signing as many as 30 full-time scouts. ... You begin to acquire ball players when you get the right kind of scouts."[49] Scout Jack Sheehan, who had already been brought in, had spent more than 20 years as the chief scout for the Cubs and White Sox.[50]

Now that the Senators had some semblance of a roster, Doherty and the rest of the front office went to secure a site for spring training. Pompano Beach, Florida, put on a full-court press to bring the new club to town, even agreeing to borrow $30,000 to improve the city's Municipal Stadium.[51] The effort succeeded; the Senators signed a lease to hold spring training there for at least five years.[52] The playing field in Pompano Beach "is one of the finest any big league team will have," Doherty said.[53] Calvin Griffith also made good on his promise that "whoever gets the Washington franchise will get most reasonable rental terms for Griffith Stadium during the year before the new Washington stadium is completed in September 1961."[54] Doherty's agreement to a one-year lease of Griffith Stadium for the 1961 season was said to be "at a favorable rental."[55]

Low expectations notwithstanding, the Senators got off to a hot start in spring training, winning their first three contests.[56] They finished the spring with an American-League best 15-10 record, and "an enthusiastic crowd of over 500 waited for four hours in the rain at National Airport to give their new 'first place' Senators a heroes' welcome when they arrived in Washington for the first time."[57]

On April 10, 1961, the new Washington Senators officially began play, opening the season against the Chicago White Sox before a crowd of 26,725 at Griffith Stadium. The Senators put up a valiant fight before falling, 4-3. The game was said to mark the beginning of something much more significant:

> The election of John F. Kennedy as President of the United States became official at 1:27 p.m. on April 10. This was certified when he stood up in his box seat at Griffith Stadium and threw out the opening ball to start a new major league season, even as every President before him since William Howard Taft in 1910.[58]

Among the highlights of an overall unremarkable season was a 5-3 victory on April 21 over the "old" Senators (now Twins) in Minnesota. Another was a five-game winning streak in early May that included the sweep of a two-game series at Yankee Stadium. Dick Donovan, who led the team before 1961's second All-Star Game with a 2.39 earned-run average, was the team's lone All-Star representative and pitched two scoreless innings.

Perhaps the game circled on most Washington calendars was May 26, when the Minnesota Twins made their first appearance back in town. The Twins were "good-naturedly booed by the partisan Washington fans when they were introduced," and in the end the new Senators bested the old Senators yet again by the score of 4-3.[59] The Twins also participated in the final game at Griffith Stadium, on September 21, in front of a minuscule crowd of 1,498.

In the end, though, the Senators could not avoid a 100-loss season, finishing at 61-100. Things did not improve significantly for the Senators in the ensuing years, though not for lack of effort. Before the 1962 season, the club traded Opening Day starting pitcher and All-Star representative Dick Donovan, along with Gene Green and Jim Mahoney, to the Indians for Jim Piersall. Donovan proceeded to win 20 games for the Indians in 1962 and finished fifth in the MVP voting. Piersall regressed from a

.322 average in Cleveland in 1961 to .244 for Washington in 1962.

Over the next 10 years, the futility spawned slogans such as "Off the Floor in 64" and a reprise of "First in War, First in Peace, and Last in the American League."[60] And then the end came yet again. On September 21, 1971, owner Bob Short received approval to move the club out of Washington and to the Dallas-Fort Worth Metroplex after the 1971 season.[61]

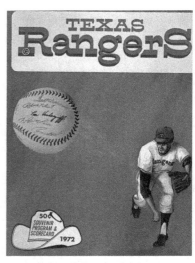

The Senators ended 71 years of American League baseball in Washington in 1971, moving to the Dallas-Ft. Worth Metroplex after the season where they become the Texas Rangers in 1972. (Courtesy of Bill Nowlin)

## Sources

In addition to the sources noted in the Notes, the author also accessed Retrosheet.org and Baseball-Reference.com.

### Notes

1 Shirley Povich, "Doherty Beams Over Nat Depth of Mound Staff," *The Sporting News*, January 18, 1961: 20.

2 Leo Fischer, "Grab-Bag Picks Could Bring Big Surprise," *The Sporting News*, January 4, 1961: 20.

3 James R. Hartley, *Washington's Expansion Senators (1961-1971)* (Germantown, Maryland: Corduroy Press, 1997, 1998), v.

4 Ibid.

5 Dan Daniel, "A.L.'s Expansion Drive Too Hasty, Mahatma Claims," *The Sporting News*, November 30, 1960: 16.

6 Hartley. In 1967 the FAA was renamed the Federal Aviation Administration.

7 Shirley Povich, "Showdown Is Near on Bidding for New Club in Washington," *The Sporting News*, November 16, 1960: 4.

8 Ibid.

9 Bob Addie, "Cal Tipped Quesada on Club Shift Last Summer," *The Sporting News*, November 23, 1960: 15.

10 "Showdown Is Near."

11 Hartley.

12 Shirley Povich, "Vernon Saluted as Capital Pick for Pilot's Post," *The Sporting News,* November 30, 1960: 20.

13 Bob Addie, "Ex-Lieutenant Recalls His Old Boss, Gen. Quesada," *The Sporting News,* November 30, 1960: 20.

14 "Vernon Saluted as Capital Pick."

15 Ibid.

16 "Showdown Is Near."

17 "Vernon Saluted as Capital Pick."

18 Ibid.

19 Shirley Povich, "Now It's Official – Capital's New Nats Open for Business," *The Sporting News,* December 7, 1960: 6.

20 Oscar Kahan, "Bill Veeck Busiest Selector – Chooses Four for Pale House," *The Sporting News,* December 7, 1960: 13.

21 Ibid.

22 "Now It's Official."

23 Hartley.

24 Shirley Povich, "Nats to Sprinkle Vets With Youth in Player Picks," *The Sporting News,* December 14, 1960: 24.

25 Ibid.

26 Dan Daniel, "Hidden Factors in 75-Gee Price Tag," *The Sporting News,* December 14, 1960: 10.

27 Hy Hurwitz, "Senators' Brass Snowbound, Arrived in Hub 9 Hours Late," *The Sporting News,* December 21, 1960: 4.

28 Burt Hawkins was the club's traveling secretary.

29 "Senators' Brass Snowbound."

30 Bob Hunter, "Haney Landed Power Sockers for L.A. Crew," *The Sporting News,* December 21, 1960: 3.

31 Hy Hurwitz, "Grba, Shantz First Hurlers to Be Nabbed," *The Sporting News,* December 21, 1960: 3.

32 Ibid.

33 Shirley Povich, "Beaming Nats Land 'Most Wanted' Pair – Shantz and Tasby," *The Sporting News,* December 21, 1960: 5.

34 Andy McCue and Eric Thompson, "Mis-Management 101: The American League Expansion for 1961," The National Pastime (Phoenix: SABR, 2011), sabr.org/research/mis-management-101-american-league-expansion-1961, accessed April 22, 2018.

35 Ibid.

36 Ibid.

37 Hartley, v-vi.

38 "Beaming Nats Land 'Most Wanted' Pair."

39 Hartley, 196.

40 Hartley, vi.

41 Bob Addie, "Three of Four A.L. Starters Needed Relief," *The Sporting News*, March 8, 1961: 8.

42 Bob Hunter, "Angels, Senators Hoping to Top 50-Win Forecast," *The Sporting News,* December 21, 1960: 22.

43 Les Biederman, "Buccos Beef Up Bull Pen in Deal for Lefty Shantz," *The Sporting News,* December 28, 1960: 11.

44 Dan Daniel, "Yanks Revive Advance Camp as Cushion for Draft Losses," *The Sporting News,* December 28, 1960: 12.

45 "Buccos Beef Up Bull Pen."

46 Oscar Kahan, "Bing Clicks Heels Over Prize Pair, Landrum, Cicotte," *The Sporting News,* December 28, 1960: 13.

47 Hartley, 245.

48 Hartley, 208, 219.

49 Shirley Povich, "Nats Clear Decks for Quick Start in Free-Agent Grabs," *The Sporting News,* December 28, 1960: 22.

50 Ibid.

51 Joe Shabo, "Pompano Beach Clears Way for Okay as Nat Spring Base," *The Sporting News,* January 4, 1961: 25.

52 Shirley Povich, "Nats' Doherty Clears Decks for Club Debut," *The Sporting News,* January 11, 1961: 11.

53 Ibid.

54 "Showdown is Near on Bidding for New Club in Washington."

55 "Nats' Doherty Clears Decks for Club Debut."

56 Shirley Povich, "Nats Flashing New Hill Gem – Joe McClain," *The Sporting News,* March 22, 1961: 25.

57 Hartley, 1.

58 Shirley Povich, "Kennedy Sets Presidential Mark With Fireball Pitch," *The Sporting News,* April 19, 1961: 3.

59 Hartley, 4.

60 Hartley, 37, 91.

61 Hartley, 136.

## WASHINGTON SENATORS EXPANSION DRAFT

PICK PLAYER  POSITION  FORMER TEAM

### REGULAR PHASE

| 1  | Bobby Shantz | p | New York Yankees |
| 2  | Dave Sisler | p | Detroit Tigers |
| 3  | Johnny Klippstein | p | Cleveland Indians |
| 4  | Pete Burnside | p | Detroit Tigers |
| 5  | Carl Mathias | p | Cleveland Indians |
| 6  | Ed Hobaugh | p | Chicago White Sox |
| 7  | Hal Woodeshick | p | Minnesota Twins |
| 8  | Tom Sturdivant | p | Boston Red Sox |
| 9  | Bob Davis | p | Kansas City A's |
| 10 | Hector Maestri | p | Minnesota Twins |
| 11 | Dutch Dotterer | c | Kansas City A's |
| 12 | Red Wilson | c | Cleveland Indians |
| 13 | Ken Aspromonte | 2b | Cleveland Indians |
| 14 | Dale Long | 1b | New York Yankees |
| 15 | Ken Hamlin | ss | Kansas City A's |
| 16 | Bob Johnson | ss | Kansas City A's |
| 17 | Billy Klaus | 2b | Baltimore Orioles |
| 18 | John Schaive | 2b | Minnesota Twins |
| 19 | Willie Tasby | of | Boston Red Sox |
| 20 | Gene Woodling | of | Baltimore Orioles |
| 21 | Marty Keough | of | Cleveland Indians |
| 22 | Jim King | of | Cleveland Indians |
| 23 | Chuck Hinton | of | Baltimore Orioles |

### ADDITIONAL PHASE

| 24 | Dean Chance | p | Baltimore Orioles |
| 25 | Chet Boak | 2b | Kansas City A's |
| 26 | Gene Green | c | Baltimore Orioles |
| 27 | Dick Donovan | p | Chicago White Sox |
| 28 | Rudy Hernandez | p | Minnesota Twins |

### MINOR LEAGUE PHASE

| 29 | Leo Burke | 3b | Baltimore Orioles |
| 30 | Haywood Sullivan | c | Boston Red Sox |
| 31 | Joe McClain | p | Minnesota Twins |

# DALE LONG

## By Gregory H. Wolf

Baseball fans love streaks. And though the number 8 is not as recognizable as 56 or 2,632, it is nonetheless a cherished part of the national pastime's lore. After bouncing around the minor leagues for 11 seasons, 30-year-old Dale Long was the unlikely center of national media attention in 1956, his second full season with the Pittsburgh Pirates. A powerful pull hitter, the left-handed slugger walloped a home run in eight consecutive games, bettering the previous big-league record by two. That accomplishment, later tied by the New York Yankees' Don Mattingly in 1987 and the Seattle Mariners' Ken Griffey Jr. in 1993, defined Long's career and propelled him to fleeting stardom and baseball immortality.

Richard Dale Long was born on February 6, 1926, in Springfield, Missouri, to Elmer Euphrates and Mary (Lomax) Long. He was the fourth of five children (Lilian, Milton, Louise, and youngest sibling Janet) born between 1915 and 1931. Just months after Dale's birth, the family relocated to Oshkosh, Wisconsin, and then to Fond du Lac and later to Green Bay, where Dale attended kindergarten, while the elder Long looked for employment in the unforgiving times of the Great Depression. When his parents separated, Dale moved with his father to Berkshire County, in Western Massachusetts, about 40 miles east of Albany, New York. Dale attended Cheshire elementary school and Williston Academy, a boarding school in East Hampton, and finally Adams High School, near the historical district of Farnams in the town of Cheshire, where the elder Long worked as manager of the US Gypsum plant. Always big for his age, Dale naturally gravitated to sports. Local newspapers, the *Berkshire Eagle* and the *North Adams Transcript*, regularly reported about his accomplishments on the gridiron, hardwood, and diamond as the seasons changed.

Dale left Massachusetts before his senior year and moved in with his mother in Green Bay.[1] When he discovered that he was not eligible to play sports in Wisconsin, he made another abrupt decision: He quit school and enlisted in the US Navy, in August 1943, during the height of World War II. Rising to the rank of seaman 2nd class, Long served on the USS PCS 1451, a patrol craft sweeper, which sought enemy submarines. A noncombat injury prematurely ended his stint in the military, and in May 1944, he was honorably discharged.[2] He subsequently moved in with his brother, Milton, in Green Bay. In an interview conducted by SABR's Gerry Tomlinson in the 1980s, Long stated bluntly about his teenage years, "I didn't really like baseball."[3] His preference was football, which dominated the sporting landscape in Green Bay. According to Long, the legendary Packers coach Curly Lambeau offered the 18-year-old, a robust 6-foot-4, 200-pound fullback, a contract after a tryout, but his mother would not sign it on behalf of her still minor son to embark on a career in football.[4]

Dale had a stroke of luck. Packers assistant coach Red Smith also coached baseball for the Milwaukee Brewers of the American Association and saw the teenager play in a local semipro league in Green Bay.[5] Upon his recommendation, Brewers skipper Casey Stengel offered Long a contract that his mother gladly accepted.[6] Long played in just one game, going 0-for-4, before leaving the team and returning to Farnams to re-enroll in high school. Once again starring in football and basketball, Long left school in late March of 1945 to participate in the Brewers' spring training.

Long's decade-long odyssey to the big leagues is a study in dedication and persistence. He had stints with 13 minor-league teams before he finally secured a permanent job, with the Pittsburgh Pirates in 1955. Along the way, he was the property of six big-league clubs; was thrice selected in the minor-league or Rule 5 draft; had a brief, but disastrous cup of coffee in the majors in 1951, but persevered, his mighty left-handed home-run stroke always attracting interest.

Long initially made his mark as a sturdy contact hitter, batting .306 and .330, with little pop (seven combined home runs), in Class D and C, respectively, in his first two full seasons in Organized Baseball, primarily in the Cincinnati Reds farm system. The first baseman-outfielder's glaring weakness was his fielding, which was an albatross Long carried with him until he hung up his spikes as a 38-year-old in 1964. Given his outright release by the Reds in 1947 and signed by the Boston Red Sox, Long emerged as a slugging threat the following season with the Class-B Lynn (Massachusetts) Red Sox. An imposing presence at the plate, he paced the New England League in runs batted in (119) and tied for second in home runs (18). Chosen by the Detroit Tigers in the 1948 minor-league draft and then by the New York Yankees in the 1949 draft, Long took a big leap forward in 1950, in his second season in the Class-A Eastern League, pacing the circuit in round-trippers (27) and setting a new league record with 130 RBIs (in 133 games) with the Binghamton (New York) Triplets. Given the Yankees surfeit of sluggers, Long's outstanding season barely registered on the franchise's radar, and he was selected by the Pirates on November 16 in the 1950 Rule 5 draft.

At the Pirates spring training in 1951, GM Branch Rickey made national headlines by deciding to convert the 25-year-old Long into a catcher. There had not been a regular left-handed-throwing starting catcher in the majors since Jack Clements in the late nineteenth century; and Jiggs Donahue who caught 45 games in 1900-1902, had been the last southpaw backstop. Even the lack of a left-handed catcher's mitt did not derail the Mahatma's plan. On March 20, Long debuted wearing the tools of ignorance in an exhibition game against the San Diego Padres of the Pacific Coast League. "I knelt down to give the sign to some new kid who could really blaze that ball," recalled Long years later. "In my head, I called for a curve. But I put down one finger for the fastball instead. I'm squatting there, looking for the curve and, whoosh, here comes the fastball. The only thing I could do was reach out and catch it with my bare hand."[7] Long played in the field only once for the Pirates in 1951, at first base against the New York Giants, and walloped a home run into the upper left-field deck in the Polo Grounds on May 5. Rickey gave up on the project and released Long, whom the lowly St. Louis Browns signed on June 1. Installed at first, Long saw action in 34 games (2 home runs, 11 RBIs, .238 batting average) before he was optioned to the San Francisco Seals in mid-July. He waited 3½ years to play in another big-league game.

In the offseasons, Long lived in Farnams and Berkshire County, where he married local resident Dorothy Robak in 1946 and with whom he had two children, Dale Jr. and Johnny. Long also played semipro football and basketball in the late 1940s and refereed high-school and college football games.

One can only imagine what Long thought when the Pirates purchased him after the 1951 season. Sportswriters commented that Rickey's experiment with the player as a catcher set back his development by a year or more. Assigned to the New Orleans Pelicans of the Double-A Southern Association, Long teamed with future Pirates slugger Frank Thomas to finish 1-2 in round-trippers (33 and 35, respectively). Promoted to the Hollywood Stars in 1953, Long enjoyed his best season in professional baseball, leading the PCL in home runs (35) and RBIs (116), and was named the league's MVP. On September 11, he had the novelty of playing all nine positions.

Long must have felt as though his chance to make it back

to the big stage was slipping away. He played winter ball in 1953-1954 with Caguas, in Puerto Rico, and reported to the Pirates spring training in 1954, but was jettisoned well before camp ended. After another injury-riddled but productive (23-68-.280 in 410 at-bats) season with Hollywood, the 29-year-old Long was reluctantly back at the Bucs' spring training in San Bernardino, California, but wanted assurances from Pirates brass that he'd get a fair shake in what seemed like his last shot with the Bucs. Were it not for endless support of Stars skipper Bobby Bragan, whom Long considered the "finest thing [that] happened to me in baseball," the ballplayer might have called it quits.[8]

The Pirates, coming off their third consecutive last-place finish, expected little from Long in 1955. Initially slated as Preston Ward's backup at first, Long collected four hits in the first game of a twin bill against the Philadelphia Phillies at Connie Mack Stadium on April 24 and wrestled the job away from the veteran. Long, described as "the newest of [manager] Fred Haney's rascals," whacked three doubles and drove in a career-best six runs on May 5 against the Milwaukee Braves at Forbes Field, and quietly emerged as the Pirates' most feared slugger.[9] Three hits against the Reds in the first game of a doubleheader at home on June 5 gave the slugger 17 safeties in his last 28 at-bats to push his average to .351. Three days later, he hit his first walk-off home run to give the Bucs a 2-1 victory over the Chicago Cubs. "Maybe my break will be an object lesson to others," Long said when asked about his success. "A lesson for players never to give up; a lesson to owners to give a man a fair test."[10] Haney detected a difference in Long's swing. "Pitchers used to take him out on a high, hard one inside," said the skipper after Long belted two homers for the first of four times in his career, and collected four hits in the first contest of a twin bill against the Reds at Crosley Field on June 19. "They don't anymore. He's powering this pitch for distance."[11] Al Abrams, sports editor of the *Pittsburgh Post-Gazette*, noted that Long helped give the Bucs "respectability" and took umbrage at the player's snub from the All-Star Game.[12] The Bucs finished in the cellar again, though they avoided the 100-loss collar for the first time since 1951. Long was consistent at the plate (16-79-.291) while slugging a team-high .513 and tying Willie Mays for the league lead with 13 triples. He also paced the circuit in errors at first base (13) for the first of three times (also in 1956, 1961).

Enthusiastically greeting the hiring of mentor Bragan as the new Bucs skipper in 1956, the 30-year-old Long got off to a torrid start. He was batting .384 when he arrived at Forbes Field on May 19 to play the Cubs in a game that set him on path to unimaginable, indeed career-defining, fame. Armed with his standard 35-inch, 35-ounce bat, Long belted a home run and drove in four runs, and secured the Pirates' win with a game-ending unassisted twin killing with the tying run at the plate. The next day, the largest crowd (32,346) in five years at Forbes Field saw Long bash two more home runs and drive in seven runs as the Pirates swept the Braves in a doubleheader. Three days later, he walloped a monstrous blast, widely described as one of the longest ever at Forbes Field, over the 436-foot sign in right-center field to extend his home-run streak to five consecutive games.[13] "I didn't care what they threw up there or who was throwing it, I could hit it," said Long, in the midst of an epic groove.[14] Suddenly cast into the national spotlight, Long victimized the Phillies at Connie Mack Stadium to tie the major-league record of homering in his sixth consecutive game, held by High Pockets Kelly (1924), Walker Cooper (1947), and Mays (1955). Long took sole possession of the record in his next game when he spanked a knuckleball from the Phillies' Ben Flowers over the right-field wall. National and local media outlets wanted a piece of Long. When the Pirates' next game was rained out, Long took a train from Philadelphia to New York to appear on the nationally televised *Ed Sullivan Show*. On the verge of exhaustion, mentally and physically, because of the media circus, he returned to Philadelphia, traveled with the club back to Pittsburgh to kick off a series against the Brooklyn Dodgers. The largest crowd for a night game at Forbes Field in six years (32,221) watched Long blast a low inside curveball from Carl Erskine over the right-field wall to extend his home-run streak to eight games.[15] Long's accomplishment even reached the US government where Pennsylvania Senator James H. Duff (R) lauded him on the Senate floor.[16] The Bucs' seventh victory in their last eight games pushed their record to 19-14, the first time the club had been five games over .500 since 1948, and just 1½ games off the NL lead. Long's streak ended on May 29 when the Dodgers' Don Newcombe held him hitless in four at-bats. "I was just plain tired," said Long. "I couldn't get my bat around."[17]

Long went 15-for-30 and drove in 19 runs during his epic streak and was sitting atop the leaderboards in home runs (14), RBIs (37, tied with Ken Boyer of the St. Louis Cardinals), and batting average (.411) when his glass slippers broke. On June 6 he severely pulled a muscle in his left leg; he was further hampered by a bruised right shin from foul tips. "I tried to play hurt, and by doing that, everything went down the drain," recalled Long. "I didn't help myself of the club. I couldn't turn my foot."[18] He hit a dismal .151 with just one homer in his next 27 games leading into the All-Star break. Chosen as starting first sacker in his only midsummer classic, Long fanned twice. Little changed in the second half for Long, whose slump continued while the Pirates crashed and burned, too, at one point losing 25 of 33 games, and finishing in seventh place (66-88). Long paced the club with 27 home runs and 91 RBIs while batting .263.

Feted throughout the offseason, Long was presented awards by the Dapper Dan Club of Pittsburgh and the city's chapter of the Baseball Writers Association of America, and was a regular on the speakers' circuit, giving at least 50 talks.[19] At the Pirates spring training in Fort Myers, Long reflected on the stress following his home-run feat. "[A]ll of a sudden I'm famous. Maybe some people are built to handle all that. I'm not," he said. "The outside pressure kept mounting until I was ready to explode."[20] While Long vowed to be a more consistent contact hitter, Pirates beat writer Les Biederman reported that the club was generally unhappy with his play.[21] When Long fanned four straight times in the third game of the 1957 season, he landed in Bragan's doghouse and was benched, much to the delight of the boo birds at Forbes Field. Pittsburgh sportswriter Al Abrams unapologetically called for his trade.[22] On May 1, Long was the guest of honor at a testimonial dinner as the Pirates team MVP for the 1956 season when Bragan informed him that he had been traded along with outfielder Lee Walls to the Chicago Cubs for first sacker Dee Fondy and utilityman Gene Baker.[23]

Coming off a last-place finish and trying to avoid their 11th straight losing season, the Cubs welcomed the slugger to join superstar Ernie Banks. Long blasted a home run in his first game as a North Sider in a loss to the Phillies in the City of Brotherly Love, and also whacked round-trippers in in first two games as a Cub at Wrigley Field, both losses, the latter against his former teammates. After 13 games in blue, Long had five home runs and was slugging .625; however, his productive start was followed by 11 inconsistent weeks, during which he was benched often against left-handed pitchers and battled wrist injuries. After hitting .300 against southpaws in 1956, he managed a paltry .186 average in 1957. While the Cubs tied the Pirates for the NL's worst record, Long unexpectedly emerged over the last two months of the season as one of the hottest hitters in baseball, batting .340 and slugging .541.

Long (21-62-.305, as a Cub) teamed with Banks (43-102, .285) and Walt Moryn (19-88-.289) to form one of the most potent trios in the NL in 1957, yet the Cubs were so talent-poor that they had a major-league-low 33 players in spring training, in 1958.[24] Touted as a potential 100-RBI man, the 32-year-old Long avoided the streaks, both hot and cold, that had characterized his big-league career thus far; however, he also battled chronic pain in his back, which he had injured sliding into the dugout attempting to make a catch in late May.[25] In what proved to be his final full season as a starter, Long batted .271-20-75 in 142 games. The Cubs led the majors with 182 round-trippers, yet even that lofty number did not translate into a winning season or a first-division finish. A level-headed, pragmatic player, Long scoffed at the notion that he was disinterested or lacked a burning fire to succeed, a critique that had dogged him in Pittsburgh. "A ballplayer is forced to pace himself at times so that he's able to summon that extra reserve when the pressure's on," he said. "Some people interpret that as a lack of desire."[26] In the first game of a doubleheader against his former team on August 20 in the Windy City, Long might have had a fleeting nightmare about Branch Rickey and the Mahatma's plan to make him a catcher. A series of events conspired to force Long to don the tools of ignorance, thus becoming the first southpaw backstop in the majors since 1902.[27] The Cubs' fifth option at catcher, Long moved from first base, kept the same mitt, and secured the final two outs on five pitches to preserve the Cubs' 4-2 win.[28] A similar situation occurred again on September 21 in Los Angeles. Long caught the ninth, though the results weren't as good: he was charged with a passed ball and dropped a third strike, though he threw out the runner in a 2-1 defeat.

Long was the odd man out with the Cubs fighting to play .500 ball in mid-July of 1959. Removed as the primary first baseman in favor of Jim Marshall, he made only 11 starts from July 14 through the end of the season, collecting just 9 hits in 60 at-bats, punctuated by a horrendous September (1-for-25). Described by *Tribune* sportswriter Richard Dozier as one of skipper Scheffing's "dog house boys," the disgruntled veteran was the subject of fruitless offseason efforts by the Cubs to unload him.[29] At the end of spring training, GM John Holland found a taker, and sold the 34-year-old to the San Francisco Giants on April 5, 1960.

Long's final four seasons in the big leagues probably evoked memories of his way up the ladder. He was traded, released, sold, or drafted five times, and wore the colors of four different teams. Managing just 9 hits in 54 at-bats for the Giants, Long was sold to the New York Yankees on August 21. The Bronx Bombers, in a fierce three-way pennant race with the Baltimore Orioles and Chicago White Sox, wanted a power-hitting left-handed pinch-hitter to take advantage of Yankee Stadium. Long delivered. Playing for his first winning team as a big leaguer, he went 15-for-41 with 3 home runs, batted .366 and slugged .707. His final hit of the season was a walk-off two-run home run off Arnold Earley to give the pennant-winning Yankees a come-from-behind 8-7 victory over the Red Sox in the Bronx. In the David versus Goliath World Series, the heavily favored Yankees faced the Pirates. Long made three pinch-hit appearances and connected for a single in the ninth inning of Game Seven. He was eventually lifted for pinch-runner Gil McDougald, who scored the tying run. The game and the Series were decided in the bottom of the frame when Bill Mazeroski clouted his immortal home run to the amazement of the Forbes Field faithful.

Made available in the 1960 expansion draft, Long was chosen by the Washington Senators with the 28th overall pick. Counted on to be the club's main source of power, Long got off to a slow start, hitting just .156 by the end of April. Defying expectations, the 35-year-old slugger found the fountain of youth. He tied his career best with three runs and four hits, including a double and home run, on May 27, kicking off a 13-game stretch in which he batted .360 and slugged .660. The Senators surprised baseball by playing .500 ball as late as June 15 before a 10-game skid revealed their true identity. Long, however, kept rolling, and emerged as one of the team's most productive players along with Willie Tasby and Gene Green. After starting 77 of the club's first 94 games and slugging a robust .500, Long was pulled from the order and made only 15 starts the rest of the season. While the press reported on rumors of Long's imminent trade back to the Yankees, a look behind the scenes revealed Long's dissatisfaction with losing and a troublesome relationship with skipper Mickey Vernon. By the end of August, team owner and President Elwood Quesada made national headlines by publicly chastising and fining Long, Tasby, and Green as malcontent loafers and disruptive to the team.[30]

Unable to unload Long in the offseason and with no other viable options at first, Washington brought the discontented veteran back in 1962. Like his team, Long struggled and then was finally traded to the Yankees for Don Lock on July 11. "Long is the kind of player any contending club can use," said first-year Yankees manager Ralph Houk. "Dale is a powerful left-handed hitter and that's good in our park."[31] On July 27, Long blasted a solo shot off Turk Lown in the 12th inning to give the Yankees a dramatic 4-3 victory over the White Sox. Given its forgiving right-field wall (314 feet down the first-base line), Yankee Stadium was tailor-made for the pull-hitting Long. One can only wonder what he could have accomplished had he played his career there. As a 36-year-old, he provided a punch, hitting .298 in 94 at-bats. The Bombers repelled challenges from the Minnesota Twins and Los Angeles Angels to capture their third straight pennant and faced the Giants in the World Series. In Game One Long replaced Moose Skowron at first base to start the seventh, then in the bottom of that frame sent Billy O'Dell's first pitch into right field to drive in Roger Maris and give the Yankees a 4-2 lead in their eventual victory. He started Game Two and went 0-for-3 while Jack Sanford shut out the Yankees on three hits. Long did not see action again in the Series, which the Yankees took in seven games.

Long appeared in his third World Series in 1963, but not as a player. Released by the Yankees on August 2, he signed on as a bullpen coach. New York's sluggers ran into the buzzsaw of the Los Angeles Dodgers pitchers and were swept in four games. "Playing for a winner in the twilight of a mediocre career," said Long 20 years after retiring, "it feels real good."[32]

Not yet ready to call it quits, Long attempted a comeback with the Cubs as a nonroster invitee in spring training in 1964. He subsequently had a brief stint with the Jacksonville Suns in the International League. Homerless in 24 Triple-A games, Long was released, ending a professional baseball career that spanned parts of 21 seasons. He finished with 132 homers and 467 runs batted in, and batted .267 in 10 big-league seasons; he also walloped 166 round-trippers in the minors.

"It wasn't easy," said Long bluntly about his transition to life after baseball.[33] Unable to find a coaching or managing job, he sold sporting equipment and pharmaceuticals, operated a tavern in North Adams, Massachusetts, and became a minor-league umpire for several years, beginning in 1965.[34] He also served as a TV sports commentator in northeastern New York and operated the Dale Long baseball camp in Rexford, New York. "I love baseball," said Long, "but it really keeps you down. Everything in my house is related to the game. But you have to forget."[35] By the mid-1970s Dale found steady work with General Dynamics in Saratoga Springs, New York, building nuclear submarines in the company's Electric Boat Division, and rose to the rank of supervisor.[36] In the mid-1980s, he surprisingly returned to baseball and served as a field representative for the National Association, then the governing body of the minor leagues.

On January 27, 1991, Dale Long died at the age of 64 at Ormond Memorial Hospital, near his home in Palm Coast, Florida. He had been suffering from cancer. He was survived by his wife, Dorothy, and his two sons. A service was held at Light's funeral home in Schenectady, and Long was buried at Cheshire cemetery, in Cheshire, Massachusetts.

## Sources

In addition to the sources cited in the Notes, the author also accessed Retrosheet.org, Baseball-Reference.com, the SABR Minor Leagues Database, accessed online at Baseball-Reference.com, SABR.org, and *The Sporting News* archive via Paper of Record.

## Notes

1 A child of the Depression Era, Dale moved around a lot. The following sources were valuable in piecing together his year prior to professional baseball: Cleon Walfoort, "Road From Green Bay to Homer Record Was Torturous for Long of Pirates," *Milwaukee Journal* [undated article found in Long's player file at the National Baseball Hall of Fame]; Charles Einstein, "'Big Guy' at Pittsburgh," *New York Times Magazine*, June 10, 1958; Jack Rice, "Dale Long Liked Pro Football But Mom Said 'No'; Pirates Star High on Bragan," June 10, 1956 [unsourced article from Long's player file.]

2 "Dale Long to Join Milwaukee League Club Next Monday," *North Adams* (Massachusetts) *Transcript,*" March 22, 1945: 8.

3 Gerald Tomlinson interview with Dale Long, SABR.org. [Undated, 1980s].

4 Les Biederman, "Long-Range Plan by Rickey Behind Experiment on Long," *The Sporting News*, March 21, 1951: 8.

5 Gerald Tomlinson interview with Dale Long.

6 "He's Pulling for Yanks," *The Sporting News*, August 26, 1953: 23.

7 "Former Slugger Dale Long Dies at 64," *Los Angeles Times*, January 29, 1991.

8 Al Abrams, "Sidelights on Sports," *Pittsburgh Post-Gazette*, May 24, 1956: 22.

9 Jack Hernon, "Dale Long Stars in Fourth Straight," *Pittsburgh*

*Post-Gazette*, May 6, 1955: 25.

10 Les Biederman, "Hats Off!," *The Sporting News*, June 22, 1955: 19.

11 Al Abrams, "Monday Morning's Sports Wash," *Pittsburgh Post-Gazette*, June 20, 1955: 20.

12 Al Abrams, "Trouble in the Balkans," *Pittsburgh Post-Gazette*, July 6, 1955: 18. Long was easily the Pirates' best player at the All-Star break. He led the team in home runs (9), RBIs (44), and batting average (.300); much better than the slashline for Frank Thomas (11/28/.214) who earned his second consecutive All-Star berth. Abrams admitted that the NL had two more deserving players at first base (the Reds' Ted Kluszewski and the St. Louis Cardinals' Stan Musial), while Thomas could join the senior circuit's fly-chaser corps.

13 Jack Hernon, "Long Swats 436-Foot HR as Bucs Win, 6-0," *Pittsburgh Post-Gazette*, May 24, 1956: 22.

14 Bill Madden and Jack Lang, "Dale Casts Long Eye on Mattingly," *New York Daily News*. Undated article, 1987. [Player's Hall of Fame file.]

15 Lester J. Biederman, "32,000 Cheer Long's Record No. 8," *Pittsburgh Press*, May 29, 1956: 15.

16 "Duff Lauds Long on Senate Floor*,"* *Pittsburgh Press*, May 29, 1956: 15.

17 Walfoort.

18 Bill Madden and Jack Lang.

19 "Long Says '56 Home Run Feat Boosted Income About $8,000," *The Sporting News*, February 6, 1957: 29.

20 Les Biederman, "Long's Homer Spree Also Had Drawback," *The Sporting News*, March 13, 1957: 10.

21 Les Biederman, "Bucs Uneasy at First Base," *The Sporting News*, March 27, 1957: 19.

22 Al Abrams, "Sidelights on Sports," *Pittsburgh Post-Gazette*, April 22, 1957: 18.

23 Jack Rosenberg, "Long Story, Happy End," *Chicago Sunday Tribune Magazine*, July 13, 1958: 29.

24 Edward J. Prell, "Cubs Have Few Clippings: Just Five Made Headlines," *The Sporting News*, April 2, 1958: 16.

25 *The Sporting News*, June 4, 1958: 23.

26 Rosenberg.

27 The events leading to Long's appearance were almost comical. Emergency fourth-string catcher Jim Bolger (who had never caught in the majors) pinch-hit for starter Sammy Taylor. With third-string catcher Moe Thacker out with a torn ligament in his knee, Cal Neeman replaced Taylor. With one out in the ninth, Neeman was tossed arguing balls and strikes. See "Dale Long First Lefty Catcher in Majors Since '02," *The Sporting News*, August 27, 1958: 15.

28 "Who's on 1st? No Long, He's Catching," *Chicago Tribune*, August 21, 1958: F5.

29 Richard Dozier, "Cubs Hurlers in Shape to Open Camp," *Chicago Tribune*, February 29, 1960: F3.

30 United Press Internarional, "Slump Ridden Nats to Bench 3 Players," *Morning Call* (Allentown, Pennsylvania), August 31, 1961: 52.

31 Til Ferdenzi, "Houk Presses Soft Pedal on Yanks Runaway Chorus," *The Sporting News*, July 28, 1962: 20.

32 Gerald Tomlinson interview with Dale Long.

33 "Dale Long," *Inside Sports*, April 1981: 57.

34 Associated Press, "Dale Long Begins Road Back in Majors – As Ump," *The Record* (Troy, New York), February 1, 1965: 26.

35 "Dale Long."

36 "Where Are They Now?" *1979 Yankee Scorebook*, 2nd edition. [Long's Hall of Fame player file.]

# BOBBY SHANTZ

## BY MEL MARMER

Almost every scout considered him too short (5-feet-6½) to be a major-league pitching prospect. One scout was not deterred, however, and dared to sign the left-hander, setting off Bobby Shantz on a 16-year odyssey in the major leagues. Shantz reached the heights of success early in his career by winning the American League's Most Valuable Player Award in 1952. He also bore the depths, nearly quitting baseball in midcareer because of serious arm injuries.

During four seasons (1953-1956) nursing those injuries, Shantz won just 13 games against 26 losses. Traded by the Kansas City Athletics to the New York Yankees before the 1957 season, Shantz enjoyed success again working mostly as a relief pitcher. He pitched in two World Series and except for a freakish bad break he might have been a surprise hero of the 1960 Series. In 1964 his career came full circle when he returned to Philadelphia, where he had begun. Shantz figured in that season's dramatic conclusion, though hardly for the expected reasons.

Robert Clayton Shantz was born on September 26, 1925, to Wilmer and Ruth Eleanor (Ebert) Shantz in Pottstown, Pennsylvania a city of 20,000 people 40 miles northwest of Philadelphia. His father worked at a Bethlehem Steel mill. In 1927 brother Wilmer Jr. (Billy) was born, and in 1929 the family moved to larger quarters in the suburbs with a big back yard where they could play sports.

Wilmer Sr. loved baseball and was considered a good semipro third baseman. Offered a minor-league contract by the Chicago White Sox, he was advised by his father, Clayton, to "turn it down, and play for the love of the game instead." Clayton had played baseball, too, and had had a bad experience as part-owner of a local baseball team.[1]

Wilmer taught his sons to play baseball and football when they were toddlers. One of Bobby's favorite games was devised by Wilmer to reward throwing strikes.[2] Perhaps this early training was responsible for the excellent control Bobby demonstrated in the major leagues; in nine of his 16 seasons he struck out more than twice as many batters as he walked.

At the age of 6 Bobby suddenly became sick one day. He was sent to the hospital with a high fever and was not expected to live through the night. He survived, and his mother remained by his bedside for a week.[3] Bobby recovered completely and enjoyed a happy childhood. In addition to baseball and football, his favorite pursuits were fishing at nearby Sanatoga Lake, taking part in family snowball fights, and trapping small animals.[4]

Despite tough economic times, the Shantzes were able to obtain sports equipment by redeeming hundreds of cereal box tops given to them by that a friend of the family, a cook at a local school.[5]

Young Bobby helped to organize a baseball team called the Sanatoga Pee Wees. As a 4-foot-4-inch teenager he pitched for a neighborhood team, Lower Pottsgrove. The family took trips to Philadelphia to watch the Athletics play, and Bobby's only dream was to play baseball. Could he play baseball professionally one day, being so much smaller than the other boys?

Shantz made the Pottstown High School baseball team as an outfielder. His manager told him to forget about being a pitcher because he was too small. He never showed off the snappy curveball he'd been practicing for years with his brother in their backyard. He played well for the high-school team though it did not have a good record. He was also a fine diver on the varsity swim team.

Perhaps Bobby's serious childhood illness had impaired his growth, for when he graduated from high school in 1943, he was still less than five feet tall. He got a job as a busboy in the cafeteria of the nearby Jacobs Aircraft plant, and he made the plant baseball team, though he sat on the bench.

The family moved to Philadelphia when Bobby's father took a job at a shipyard there. The family's relocation was a good break for Bobby and Billy. Their new neighborhood was a hotbed of sports activities and gave the brothers more opportunities to play ball. Bobby played sandlot baseball and Pop Warner football, and continued to grow. In 1944 he got a $75-a-week job at the Disston Saw Company as a glazer, shining saws. His draft board called him in, but he was rejected for military service because he was one inch below the minimum 5-foot height requirement. Though Bobby was short, his hands were comparatively large and strong which helped him to excel at athletics.

In the spring of 1944 Bobby played for the Holmesburg Ramblers, a youth baseball team that played in the competitive Quaker City League. He played center field, and his brother Billy, who had dropped out of high school in the tenth grade, was a catcher.

One day Bobby threw batting practice, and the team's manager saw his fine overhand curveball with its sharp downward break and immediately added him to the pitching staff.[6] Bobby compiled a 9-1 record and played the outfield in games he didn't pitch, batting .485 from the cleanup spot.

Shantz continued to excel in other sports besides baseball. "Shantz was a 'big star' in the neighborhood who could throw, kick, and run,' according to Brud Williamson, the son of the Holmesburg Ramblers' coach. "Without question, he was the most modest guy I ever met. Boulevard Pools used to put on diving exhibitions with professional divers. We talked them into letting Bobby dive one summer, and he stole the show. He was a great gymnast too, and he could beat anyone in ping-pong or bowling, any sport he tried."[7]

Meanwhile, Shantz had grown an inch, enough to pass his Army physical, and was sworn in on December 28, 1944.[8] After three months of basic training, he headed to Fort Knox, Kentucky, to be trained to drive tanks. But his feet barely reached the pedals and he was transferred to a mortar outfit. In June of 1945, two months before the end of World War II, he arrived in the Philippines.[9] At camp in Batangas he played inter-divisional ball, sharing pitching duties with the White Sox' Gordon Maltzberger. Later, he played against a team of touring major leaguers at Rizal Stadium in Manila. Shantz pitched and lost the game, 4-2, but his performance against established major leaguers helped to build his confidence.[10] Shantz also pitched well in games against the highly regarded service team the Manila Dodgers. (The Dodgers gave Shantz a tryout but rejected him, which only inspired him to work harder.[11]) Discharged from the Army in 1946, Corporal Shantz had grown to 5-feet-6½ and weighed 139 pounds. He returned home to work at the saw company in the fall of 1946. He played quarterback and punted for a Pop Warner League football team, but hurt his back and quit football for good so he would not jeopardize his baseball career.

In 1947 Shantz signed to play sandlot baseball for the Souderton, Pennsylvania His Nibs team in the East Penn League, rated equivalent to a Class-B minor league. He went 8-0, and 1-1 in the postseason. In the championship game, Shantz pitched a four-hitter, hit a double, and scored a run. Fans held a Bobby Shantz Day and showered him with cash and gifts. Shantz's reputation spread. Admirers arranged a game against a team featuring Curt

Simmons, another highly-touted left-handed pitcher who had just signed for a large bonus with the Philadelphia Phillies.[12]

Fans from the East Penn League and their counterparts from the Lehigh Valley League set up the match game for charity. Bobby and his team from the East Penn League faced Simmons and his former team from the Lehigh Valley League.

A left-hander from upstate Egypt, Pennsylvania, Simmons had recently signed with the Philadelphia Phillies for $65,000, and had spent the last few months in Class-B ball. The Phillies had called him up the week before and he had pitched a complete-game 3-1 win, a five-hitter, over the New York Giants.

On the big day, October 6, 1947, fans filed into the stadium. The exhibition game benefited a memorial park, and all 2,500 seats were sold out. Shantz had injured his wrist playing touch football the day before. It was swollen and he had difficulty throwing. Manager Glick worked on the wrist and bandaged it. Bobby asked Glick to warm him up out of sight of the fans, and said that if he felt okay, he'd try to pitch.[13] The thought of disappointing the fans who had come to watch him pitch made him uneasy. After warming up for a while, Shantz was ready to call it quits. Glick, however, got an idea. He produced a book and told Bobby to rest his hand on a flat surface. To Bobby's surprise, Glick lifted the book and thwacked Bobby's swollen wrist with it. "Perhaps he figured I had something like carpal tunnel syndrome, and that the sudden smack would fix it. I don't know. But, it worked! I was able to go out on the mound and pitch." [14] Shantz won the game, 4-1. He allowed five hits, struck out 14, and walked one. Simmons allowed eight hits, struck out nine, and walked three. Bobby and Curt later became good friends and golf buddies.

Scouts from all of the major-league teams admired Bobby's competitiveness but passed him up because of his height. Phillies' scout Jocko Collins liked Shantz very much but felt he was too small for the rigors of major-league baseball. "He thought I had one heck of a curve ball but was just too small," Shantz told a biographer. "When he met me years later, he apologized. 'I sure made a mistake with you, Shantzy,' he said. "I told him I didn't blame him, that I had doubts myself."[15] The Tigers and Browns offered contracts to play in the Class-D minor leagues, but Shantz was not interested in them. Tony Parisse, a former Athletics catcher and Bobby's batterymate on the Souderton His

Nibs, warned him not to sign a "D-Ball contract," fearing that teams that offered that wouldn't take him seriously.[16] Tony recommended Shantz to A's scout Harry O'Donnell, as did Souderton's third baseman, Bill Hockenbury.

O'Donnell signed Shantz to an "A-Ball" contract in November 1947. Bobby convinced the A's that his brother Billy was a good catcher and that they should sign him, too, as a part of the deal. At least he wouldn't be lonely in Lincoln, Nebraska, in the Class-A Western League. Bobby was 22 years old and Billy was 20. The A's accepted. Billy was soon sent down to Class-C ball, but Bobby wasn't lonely very long. He went out on a date with Shirley Vogel of Lincoln, a student at the University of Nebraska, and they hit it off very well. They married a year and a half later. The couple had four children: Bobby, born in 1954, followed by Kathy, Teddy, and Danny, born in 1965.

In his first year of professional baseball, with the Lincoln A's, Shantz was the talk of the league. He pitched 28 games and went 18-7 with a WHIP (walks and hits per innings pitched) of 1.093, struck out 212 batters in 214 innings, and had an ERA of 2.82. In a game against Des Moines, he faced 32 batters and threw only 17 pitches for balls.[17]

After just the one minor-league season, Shantz went north from spring training with Philadelphia in 1949. He was sent down for more experience, but was quickly recalled when another pitcher was injured. After a brief relief appearance on May 1, Shantz relieved Carl Scheib on May 6 against the Detroit Tigers with the bases loaded and none out in the fourth inning and held the Tigers hitless for the next nine innings, though he walked seven. In the top of the 13th inning the A's went ahead, 5-3. Shantz allowed two hits and a run in the bottom half of the inning, but won his first major-league game, 5-4.

Shantz finished his rookie season with a 6-8 record and a 3.40 ERA. In 1950, he was 8-14 (the A's were 52-102). For the first half of 1951, he was a so-so 8-8, then won 10 of his next 12 games, and was the American League's most effective pitcher for the second half of the season. He was chosen for the American League team in the All-Star Game, but didn't get in the game.

In his first three major-league seasons Shantz improved from year to year. He was doing very well with a fastball, curve, and change up, but felt he needed another pitch. That pitch was the knuckleball. Shantz had experimented with it since he was a boy throwing to his father and his brother in their backyard.[18] Athletics manager Connie Mack had forbidden him to throw the knuckler in a game, but when Jimmie Dykes succeeded Mack in 1952 he told Shantz, "Throw the knuckleball. I am not Mr. Mack."[19] Shantz credited A's catcher Joe Astroth with helping him perfect the pitch. Some contemporary writers assumed that Chief Bender, the Athletics' great pitcher, who was working with Shantz at the time, helped him with the knuckleball, but Shantz said in an interview in 2011 that it wasn't true. "Mr. Bender helped me to become a more confident pitcher, Joe Astroth helped me with the knuckleball," he said.[20]

Shantz also threw a few varieties of the curveball. He was best known for his classic over-the-top curve that broke sharply down, and as much as a foot across. But he also threw a tighter-breaking curveball, and on occasion, what was then called a "nickel curve," thrown more from the side than a regular curve, and which came to be called a slider. Shantz once said he felt the slider was dangerous to throw because if it did not move as expected, it would come over the plate and be easy to hit.[21]

Shantz had a breakout year in 1952. After 18 starts, he was 15-3. By his 16th complete game, he had racked up three shutouts. A person's size was fair game back then, and sportswriters referred to him in terms like "the midget southpaw" and "toy pitcher." The press speculated that he could become the first 30-game winner in 18 years.

Named to the American League All-Star team for the second time, Shantz pitched in the All-Star Game, played that year in Philadelphia. He entered the game in the bottom of the fifth inning and struck out Whitey Lockman looking, Jackie Robinson swinging, and Stan Musial looking. Shantz wanted to see if he could duplicate Carl Hubbell's 1934 feat of striking out the side twice in an All-Star Game, but rain came and washed out the game with the National League ahead, 3-2.

Shantz finished the season 24-7, and was named the American League MVP with 83 percent of the vote. Five days before the end of the season, on September 23, he broke his left wrist when he was hit by a fastball from the Senators' Walt Masterson. Connie Mack had warned Shantz that batting right-handed and leaving his pitching hand "exposed" could result in just such an injury.[22] Shantz had tried batting left-handed but gave up the idea because he could not control the bat as well. The injury healed over the offseason.

Shantz started 33 games, completed 27, and pitched five shutouts. In 279 innings he struck out 152 and allowed 77 earned runs, for a 2.48 earned-run average.

On May 21, 1953, pitching against the Red Sox, Shantz injured his left shoulder. A tendon had separated from the bone, and it was the beginning of three difficult years. His shoulder eventually healed, but it would require treatment for the remainder of his career.

Among treatment possibilities, a novel experimental surgery was proposed: A tendon would be taken from another part of the body to replace the one that had separated. Shantz rejected this and opted to let nature take its course.[23] Until his body healed completely, it was rough going. Shantz made only 16 starts in 1953 and was 5-9 with a 4.09 ERA.

On Opening Day 1954, Shantz had a 5-2 lead over the Red Sox when he reinjured his shoulder. He pitched in only one other game that season. In 1955, the Athletics' first year in Kansas City, he was 5-10 and in 1956, in which he pitched almost entirely in relief, he was 2-7, There were occasional flashes of brilliance. On April 29, 1955, Shantz pitched a shutout, his first since 1952, before 33,471 in Kansas City to defeat the Yankees, 6-0. On April 19, 1956, in one of only two starts he made that season, Shantz five-hit the Tigers and the A's won, 4-1. After that, he experienced pain in his right side, and manager Lou Boudreau made him a reliever. Trainer Jim Ewell wrapped hot water bottles around Shantz's arm between innings to prevent it from stiffening which helped for a long time.

Before the 1957 season, Shantz was part of a 13-player trade between the Athletics and the Yankees. Yankees manager Casey Stengel intended to use him exclusively as a relief pitcher but an injury to left-hander Whitey Ford forced him to use Bobby as a starter.

While Ford was out and other Yankees pitchers struggled, Shantz, healthy for the first time in years, kept the Bronx Bombers in contention. He had a record of 9-1 at the All-Star break with an ERA of 2.25. He completed seven games and earned his third selection as an All-Star, though he did not pitch in the game. Bobby finished the season with a record of 11-5 and led the American League in ERA at 2.45. He started 21 games, completed nine, and saved five games. He was awarded the first Major League Gold Glove Award given to a pitcher.

Yankees pitching coach Jim Turner advised Shantz to throw the sidearm curve less often because it consumed too much energy, and to follow through more on his fastball. Most of all, Turner harped on Shantz to keep his pitches down. He also taught him to throw the sinker.[24]

In the 1957 World Series against the Milwaukee Braves, Shantz started the second game in Yankee Stadium. He struck out the side in the first inning, but gave up a run in the second and three runs in the fourth, and was the losing pitcher in the Braves' 4-2 win. In the bottom of the second inning with the score tied 1-1 and two men on base, Shantz drove a Lew Burdette pitch toward the left-field corner that left-fielder Wes Covington made a miraculous catch on. Covington snared the ball backhanded to end the inning and change the complexion of the game. Shantz pitched in relief in two other games as the Yankees fell to the Braves in seven games.

Shantz was considered one of the game's finest fielding pitchers, "The kind that managers dream of and so seldom find. He goes with the Brecheens, Burdettes, and Haddixes," broadcaster Mel Allen said of him during the 1960 World Series.[25] He won the American League Gold Glove for a pitcher in 1958, 1959, and 1960. Traded to the National League, he won National League Gold Glove Awards in 1961, 1962, 1963, and 1964. After the award began, Shantz won it every year he played. Only pitchers Bob Gibson, Jim Kaat, and Greg Maddux won more.

Shantz pitched solely in relief in 1960, appearing in 42 games and posting 11 saves. The Yankees won the pennant and Shantz figured in one of the most dramatic World Series games played. He pitched an inning in relief against Pittsburgh in Games Two and Four. Bob Turley started for the Yankees in Game Seven, at Forbes Field. Shantz began warming up in the first inning in case he'd be needed. Turley was roughed up early and the Yankees trailed 4-0 when Shantz entered to begin the third inning. He held the Pirates to one hit for five innings as the Yankees took a 7-4 lead. (During the 1960 season Shantz hadn't gone more than four innings in a game.) Leading off the bottom of the eighth, pinch-hitter Gino Cimoli got the second hit off Shantz, a bloop single to short right-center field. Bill Virdon followed with a sure double-play ball toward shortstop Tony Kubek. But the ball took a bad hop and struck Kubek in the Adam's apple. Kubek went down, unable to make the play. Dick Groat drove in Cimoli with a single to left field. Jim Coates relieved Shantz and the Pirates eventually went ahead, 9-7. The Yankees tied

it in the top of the ninth but in the bottom of the inning, Bill Mazeroski hit his famous home run off Ralph Terry to win the World Series for the Pirates. Instead of becoming a hero, Shantz had wound up responsible for three Pittsburgh runs. Ironically, after Stengel lifted Shantz, Coates failed to cover first base on a ground ball hit to the first baseman by Clemente. It was the type of play that Shantz routinely made, and which helped to earn him eight Gold Gloves. Coates then gave up a three-run home run to Hal Smith.

Still, Shantz said that while his fondest memories occurred early in his career with the Athletics, his time with the Yankees was the most satisfying because the team went to the World Series three of the four years he was there, 1957, 1958, and 1960.[26] He did not participate in the 1958 World Series because of an injured finger.

The 1961 season found Shantz pitching for his erstwhile World Series foes. The major leagues held an expansion draft in the offseason and Shantz was left unprotected by the Yankees. He was selected by the new American League expansion Washington Senators, and two days later the Senators traded him to the Pirates. Shantz began the season in the bullpen but between May 23 and July 22, he started six games. In the first start he was out-dueled by Lew Burdette of the Braves, 1-0. Shantz was 6-3 as the Pirates finished in sixth place.

Another expansion draft was held after the season and Shantz moved again, selected by the National League Houston Colt .45s. On April 10, 1962, he started Houston's first-ever game, defeating the Chicago Cubs with a complete game five-hitter. After each inning, trainer Jim Ewell placed a steam-heated pad on Shantz's pitching arm to keep it from stiffening. A week later, on April 17 he had a no-decision against the Mets, and on the 27th he lost a 2-1 decision to the Braves in what turned out to be the last start of his career.

On May 7 Shantz was traded to the St. Louis Cardinals for pitcher John Anderson and outfielder Carl Warwick. Reunited with his buddy Curt Simmons, Shantz pitched out of the bullpen in 28 games, with a 5-3 record, 4 saves, and a 2.18 ERA with the Cardinals. He pitched a season-high six innings on August 26, 1962 to earn a win over Pittsburgh. In 1963, Shantz made a career-high 55 appearances with a 2.61 ERA and 11 saves. He was adept at shutting down the opposition and was brought into crucial situations at any time in a game. Left-hander Shantz and 25-year-old right-hander Ron Taylor were the mainstays of the Cardinals' dependable bullpen. The Cardinals won 93 games yet finished six games behind the Los Angeles Dodgers.

In January 1964 Bobby's father died suddenly on a bitterly cold night. Bobby was playing in an alumni/faculty basketball game at Pottstown High School. The PA announcer had just told the crowd a car in the parking lot had its headlights on. Wilmer Shantz realized it was his car and ran out to the lot to turn off the headlights. He ran back to the gym, settled into a seat and collapsed with a fatal heart attack, in Bobby's arms.

Taylor and Shantz were not as effective in 1964 as they had been in 1963. Taylor regained his 1963 form for a while, but Shantz, now 38 years old, did not, and starting pitchers were pressed into duty for relief chores. On June 15 Shantz was dealt to the Cubs in the six-player trade that netted the Cardinals speedy 25-year-old outfielder Lou Brock.

Bobby did not pitch well for the Cubs. The team fell out of contention quickly, and sold Shantz to the Phillies on August 15. The city where he began in the major leagues was gripped in pennant fever, and then disbelief as the Phillies blew a 6 1/2 game lead down the stretch and finished in a tie for second place, one game behind the Cardinals.

Shantz's finest performance of 1964 came on September 17 when he defeated the Dodgers' Don Drysdale, 4-3. He relieved Rick Wise in the first inning and allowed just three hits and one run in 7 ⅔ innings. However, by exhausting Shantz in long relief, Phillies manager Mauch left his bullpen short-staffed and had to use a left-hander just up from Triple-A two days later with dire results; a game-ending steal of home plate. During the Phillies' epic 10-game collapse, Shantz lost to the Braves on September 26, giving up a bases-loaded triple to Rico Carty in the ninth inning. Three days later he made what turned out to be his final appearance in Organized Baseball, pitching two-thirds of an inning in relief against the Cardinals.

Shantz was asked to return to the Phillies for 1965 but instead retired from baseball.

His odyssey ended with a career record of 119-99 and a 3.38 ERA.

After his baseball career, Bobby managed a dairy bar and restaurant in Chalfont Pennsylvania next to the bowling alley he co-owned with his former A's catcher, Joe As-

troth. The bowling alley was sold in 1966 but Shantz worked at the restaurant until he retired in 1986. After retiring, Shantz golfed regularly at a course owned by his friends Curt Simmons, and Robin Roberts.

In 1994 Bobby received the first of a number of honors in his retirement. He became the 41st member to be inducted into the Philadelphia Baseball Wall of Fame. His plaque hung in Veterans Stadium, Philadelphia, but is now located in the Philadelphia Athletics Historical Society in Hatboro, Pennsylvania. In 2009 Shantz was invited to attend the showing of a previously unknown film of the seventh game of the 1960 World Series, but declined to attend, saying, "I'd rather face a tough hitter with the bases loaded than speak in public. It's not my forté."[27]

In 2010, Bobby received two additional honors. He was inducted into the Philadelphia Sports Hall of Fame, and Pottstown High School renovated its baseball field and dedicated it in his honor: Bobby Shantz Field. A metal plaque with a photograph of Shantz can be seen by the entrance to the field.[28]

**Sources:**

In addition to the sources cited in the Notes, the author also relied on *Baseball Digest*, Baseball-Reference.com, *The Sporting News*, and

Berksmontnews. *Shantz Field*, December 22, 2010.

Gordon, Bob. *Game of My Life, Memorable Stories of Phillies Baseball* (Champaign, Illinois: Sports Publishing LLC, 2008).

Reiser, Jim. *The Best Game Ever, Pirates vs. Yankees October 13, 1960* (New York: Carroll & Graf Publishers, 2007).

SABR Oral History, Bobby Shantz, 1991, by Bob Ulster.

*Christian Science Monitor,* July 18, 1952.

Delaney, Ed. *Bobby Shantz, Most Valuable Player Series* (New York: A.S. Barnes, 1953).

*Pittsburgh Pirates Baseball's Greatest Games: 1960 World Series Game 7*. Major League Baseball Productions. A&E Home Video, 2010. DVD.

**Notes**

1 Bobby Shantz. *The Story of Bobby Shantz as told to Ralph Bernstein.* (Philadelphia: J.B. Lippincott, 1953), 21.

2 Ibid., 26.

3 Ibid.

4 Ibid., 27.

5 Ibid., 28.

6 Ibid., 34.

7 Robert Gordon and Tom Burgoyne. *Movin' On Up, Baseball and Philadelphia, Then, Now, and Always* (Moorestown, New Jersey: Middle Atlantic Press, 2004), 93.

8 Shantz, *The Story of Bobby Shantz,* 36.

9 Ibid.

10 Ibid., 37.

11 Ibid., 38.

12 Ibid., 44.

13 Personal interview with Bobby Shantz, January 13, 2011.

14 Telephone interview with Bobby Shantz, January 20, 2011. All information from interviews with Shantz came from the personal interview, with this one exception.

15 Bobby Shantz, 51.

16 Ibid.

17 He may have thrown 219 innings, instead of 214. See *The Sporting News*, September 5, 1948: 33.

18 Interview with Bobby Shantz.

19 Ibid.

20 Ibid.

21 *Baseball Digest*, September 1957: 50.

22 Interview with Bobby Shantz.

23 Ibid.

24 *Baseball Digest*, September 1957: 44

25 Mel Allen, *Pittsburgh Pirates Baseball's Greatest Games: 1960 World Series Game 7.* Major League Baseball Productions. A&E Home Video, 2010. DVD.

26 Interview with Bobby Shantz.

27 Ibid.

28 www.philadelphiaathletics.org/event/shantzfieldupdate.htm

# TOM STURDIVANT

## By Bill Nowlin

Right-hander Tom Sturdivant pitched 10 years in the major leagues, for seven different teams over both leagues (wearing seven different uniform numbers).

His first team was the New York Yankees, the team that first signed him, and he won Game Four of the 1956 World Series for them, evening the series against the Dodgers at two games apiece. It was his only world championship, though he helped lead the Yankees to another pennant in 1957. Sturdivant finished his career with a 59-51 record, with an earned-run average of 3.74.

Thomas Virgil Sturdivant was born in Gordon, Kansas, on April 28, 1930. Gordon is in Butler County, about 20 miles east-southeast of Wichita. It served as a station on the Atchison, Topeka and Santa Fe Railway.

At the time of the 1940 US census, Tom's family had moved to Oklahoma City. Elbert E. "Pete" Sturdivant (1907-91) worked as a telegraph operator for an oil pipeline company. His wife, Ethel (Moudy) Sturdivant (1905-95), worked as an assistant in a fur repair shop. Tom had

an older brother, Bobby Joe (1926-96). The family's ancestry was, Tom reported, "Dutch-English-French-Indian."[1]

Sturdivant was signed out of Oklahoma City's Capitol Hill High School by legendary New York Yankees scout Tom Greenwade on May 24, 1948.[2] Greenwade wasn't as legendary as he would become; later that year he first approached another Oklahoman, Mickey Mantle, and signed him early in 1949. Sturdivant, like Mantle, was seen as an infielder at the time, though he had pitched in American Legion ball; an article in Little Rock's *Arkansas Gazette* shows him pitching for Bill Mosier's Tires of Oklahoma City against the visiting Little Rock Doughboys, losing 4-2.[3] He's seen the following year throwing a 6-0 shutout against the Legion team in Hastings, Nebraska, and hitting an inside-the-park home run with a man on board.[4]

He was placed with the Quincy (Illinois) Gems in the Class-B Three-I League, where he played third base.[5] In 21 games, Sturdivant hit .338. The Yankees moved him to Norfolk, where they had a need. The Norfolk Tars were also a Class-B team (in the Piedmont League); there he hit .241 in 36 games. Early in 1949, Greenwade enthused about his potential to a writer for the *Kansas City Star*: "What a boy if we can find a position for him. ... Great speed and a rifle arm. Used to be a high-school pitcher in Oklahoma City, you know. And one of the greatest. He set some kind of record. More than 100 innings without being scored on. When he wasn't pitching he was playing short. He likes to play the infield. He might, with that arm and speed, make a real outfielder."[6]

Though he threw right-handed, Sturdivant batted from the left side. He stood an even 6-feet tall and played at 170 pounds. In 1949, he returned to Quincy and played in 109 games, batting .255. He played again at Quincy in 1950, hitting .246 in 68 games. There he also pitched in at least a couple of games.[7]

In 1951, Sturdivant was one of a couple of dozen Yankees prospects brought – as an infielder – to Arizona for early schooling under Casey Stengel, prior to spring training. As it happens, Sturdivant was called to military service and saw no professional baseball in 1951.

He spent 1951 and much of 1952 in the US Army. While there, he decided that "if he was going to fashion a baseball career, for himself, he would have to turn to pitching."[8] He pitched a fair amount in the Army. A "leg injury that slowed him down on the bases" which he had suffered at Quincy was said to have contributed to his decision.[9]

Tom married Paula Reba Whitten on May 9, 1952; she went by the name Reba. Tom and Reba had two sons, Tommy and Paul.

He was discharged from the Army in time to get into 17 games for the Texas League's Beaumont Roughnecks in 1952; he was 3-3 with a 3.56 ERA. Beaumont was Double-A baseball, and so were the Birmingham Barons (Southern Association), where he pitched a full season in 1953, working in 47 games – all but three as a reliever – and finishing with an earned-run average of 2.98 and a record of 10-7. He struck out 104 batters in 139 innings.

Sturdivant was advanced to Triple A in 1954, pitching for the Kansas City Blues. He started 20 games and relieved in a dozen others, and went 8-9 (3.57). He struck out 133 and walked 59 in 169 innings of work.

Over the winter, Sturdivant "received quite a few tips from his fellow townsman, Allie Reynolds, … and … the Chief said he thought Tom had a chance of making the Yankees as a reliefer."[10] Sturdivant said he had first met Reynolds in the fall of 1950, and that Reynolds had given him a few tips.[11] Yankees manager Casey Stengel came to appreciate his talent during spring training: "I'm very impressed with his work. He has improved considerably since training started. … [W]e learned that he can be a

fighter … and that's what we want with this club."[12]

In 1955, Sturdivant did indeed make the Yankees out of spring training. He made his major-league debut against the Boston Red Sox, in Boston's home opener, on April 14. It didn't go well. The Red Sox were ahead, 5-2, when Stengel called him in to pitch the bottom of the seventh. The first batter he faced was Boston's starting pitcher, Willard Nixon. Nixon tripled to center field. Sturdivant walked the next batter but then struck out Eddie Joost. Faye Throneberry doubled in Nixon. In the bottom of the eighth, a walk, hit batsman, sacrifice, and a two-run single by Red Sox relief pitcher Ellis Kinder boosted the score to Boston 8, New York 4. Sturdivant had got his feet wet, but most of the damage was done by the opposing pitchers.

Six more relief appearances followed and Sturdivant brought his ERA down to 2.87. Then he got his first decision, a win, in the second game of the May 22 doubleheader against the visiting Baltimore Orioles. It was 3-2 Orioles when Sturdivant took over for Whitey Ford in the top of the seventh. Yogi Berra's two-run homer gave the Yankees the lead. Sturdivant singled (in his second big-league at-bat), and scored. Though he gave up a two-run homer in the top of the ninth, and was replaced, he still earned the win.

They weren't all wins, though. In fact, Sturdivant lost the next time out – and had to wait until 1956 before he booked his second win. He appeared in 33 games in 1955 and finished 1-3 (3.16). His one start resulted in the third loss, giving up just two runs in a 3-1 loss in Kansas City on July 22.

The Yankees lost to the Brooklyn Dodgers in the seven-game 1955 World Series. Sturdivant pitched the final two innings in Game Three and the final inning in Game Four, but both games had seen the Dodgers sufficiently ahead by the time he came in.

Sturdivant joined the Yankees on a post-Series tour of Japan; he and Johnny Kucks combined on a three-hit shutout of the Chunichi Dragons during the seventh game of the visit.

After arriving for spring training in 1956, Sturdivant expressed extra appreciation for the help he had been given by Yankees pitching coach Jim Turner.[13]

In 1956, Sturdivant both started and relieved, with considerable success. But he didn't appear in a game until May 13. In fact, the Yankees had determined to send him to Denver on waivers when it was time to cut rosters in May, but Detroit's Bucky Harris declined to waive – prompting the Yankees to give their pitcher a closer look.[14] Stengel assigned Sturdivant a start against Baltimore on May 13 and he threw seven innings of one-run, two-hit ball before tiring in the eighth and giving up two more runs, losing a game in which his teammates scored only one run. Eleven days later, he had won three games in relief. He got a second start on June 16 in Cleveland and won a complete game, giving up just two hits and one run while striking out 11. When the Indians visited Yankee Stadium on July 13, he shut them out on two hits.

Seventeen of the 32 games in which Sturdivant appeared were starts. He finished the season 16-8 with a 3.30 ERA. Only Whitey Ford (19-6) and Johnny Kucks (18-9) had more wins.

The team earned a return to the 1956 World Series, again facing the Dodgers. In Game Two, a high-scoring 13-8 Brooklyn win, Sturdivant was one of seven Yankees pitchers. He worked two-thirds of an inning in the third, and was charged with one run. He started and won Game Four, evening the Series up at 2-2. Though he walked the first batter in each of the first three innings, gave up a leadoff double in the fourth, saw the first batter reach due to an error in the fifth, and faced a bases-loaded situation with one out in the bottom of the ninth, Sturdivant held steady. He allowed two runs on six hits, a complete-game effort. "Yogi called 'em and I threw 'em," he said after the game, crediting Berra for his pitch-calling and Casey Stengel for his confidence.[15]

Some had said that Sturdivant didn't have one overpowering pitch, but Ed Rumill quoted Ted Williams: "Maybe he hasn't got a thing. But I notice one thing. He keeps winning." Rumill added his own thoughts: "He has everything. … Tom lacks overpowering pitches, particularly the fast ball that he could throw right by the good hitter in the clutch. But he spots his fast one smartly. He throws a good curve. He has a pitch that breaks like a screwball, in on a right-hander and away from a lefty. The young Yankee throws all the conventional pitches, then he throws them as change-ups. Then when he gets ahead on a hitter, a tricky knuckler comes out of the bag."[16]

After the game, Sturdivant said, "Five months ago I thought I was gone. Today I'm a winning World Series pitcher. How can you figure it? I'm just numb – absolutely numb."[17]

His signing scout, Tom Greenwade, who'd signed him as an infielder, was pleased: "Look at him now. If any pitcher ever was a self-made man, he is that."[18]

As Jack Hand of the Associated Press wrote, "Tom Sturdivant, almost released by the club in May, squared the World Series for the New York Yankees at two games each. … [He] blew his fast ball and low-breaking curve past the Dodgers in the best pitching job in the series."[19]

That status was short-lived, overshadowed when Don Larsen threw a perfect game the very next day. When the Yankees also won Game Seven, Tom Sturdivant was a world champion.

One remarkable note regarding that World Series: Whitey Ford, Sturdivant, Larsen, Bob Turley, and Johnny Kucks threw five consecutive complete games, Games Three through Seven.

Casey Stengel had had a little fun with the writers after Game Four, as recounted by Arthur Daley of the *New York Times*: " 'Try to get rid of him on waivers,' said Ol' Case with a sly leer, 'but Bucky Harris keeps claimin' him. Since I'm stuck with the feller I put him to work pitchin' and he wins – big. That makes me a genius.' Ol' Case stuck out his chest, put a hand to brow in the manner of Rodin's Thinker and hammed it up dreadfully."[20]

Sturdivant had batted .313 (20-for-64) in 1956, leading all major-league pitchers in hitting. He had five RBIs. After his 10-year career was done, his lifetime batting average was .183, with a total of 10 RBIs.

In 1957, he had an even better regular season, leading the league in winning percentage (16-6, .727 – tied with Dick Donovan of the White Sox), with three more wins than anyone else on the Yankees' pitching staff. He was second in the league in ERA; his 2.54 was just behind that of teammate Bob Shantz (2.45). It was a well-balanced staff that led the Yankees into the World Series yet again. Sturdivant had seven complete games, two of them shutouts. At one point, into the May 24 game, he rode a string of 31 consecutive innings without giving up an earned run.

Sturdivant wasn't a pitcher who hesitated to work inside. There were some harsh words thrown his way in 1956, and on June 9, 1957, in Detroit, after the first two batters in the third inning homered back-to-back, and his next pitch sailed over Ray Boone's head. Boone charged the mound, and Sturdivant gave no quarter, heading toward Boone. Benches cleared, and both were ejected. The pitcher claimed, "It was a high fast one that got away from me."[21] Both were assessed $100 fines.

The Milwaukee Braves won the National League pennant in 1957 and faced the Yankees in the World Series. The Yankees started Ford, Shantz, and Larsen, holding back Sturdivant until Game Four. They won Games One and Three. Sturdivant, however, pitching against Warren Spahn, got hammered for four runs in the bottom of the fourth, thanks to home runs by Hank Aaron (to left field on a knuckleball) and Frank Torre (to right). Stengel pinch-hit for him in the top of the fifth. Only Elston Howard's three-run homer in the top of the ninth prevented Sturdivant from bearing the loss. The Braves won it in 10.

The Series went to seven games. Don Larsen started Game Seven, and was knocked out of the box after giving up three runs in 2 ⅓ innings. Lew Burdette (3-0 in the Series) shut out New York. Sturdivant pitched an uneventful sixth and seventh. They were his last innings in postseason play.

Sturdivant was a holdout in spring training 1958, but seems to have finally signed on the last day of February, for a reported increase of $4,000 and a total salary of $18,000.[22] The 1958 season was far from satisfying; he lost one and then won one (both to the Red Sox) in April, but the win was a 12-7 game, with all seven runs earned. He threw 158 pitches in the game, and walked seven. He didn't pitch from April 22 to May 28. After June 12, he was 1-4 with an ERA of 6.00 and banished to the bullpen. The problem was unspecified "arm trouble" and resulted in Stengel leaving Sturdivant (and Don Larsen, for that matter) off the list of Series eligible.[23] Alternatively, the AP said Sturdivant was on the disabled list with an injured heel.[24] In fact, both bothered him, and his record for the year was 3-6 (4.20) in just 15 appearances. (The *Boston Globe* later reported that he'd been fooling around in the outfield before a game, and one of his Yankees teammates had stepped on his heel and spiked him badly enough to cost him six weeks — and also cost him a $250 fine for horseplay.)[25]

At the last minute, both Larsen and Sturdivant were certified as eligible for the 1958 World Series, and they both earned wins in the season-ending doubleheader on September 28. Larsen won Game Three in the Series; Sturdivant did not appear.

He was included in many trade rumors after the season. During the offseason, Sturdivant worked for an oil company in Oklahoma City. He was a holdout again in the spring of 1959, but came around at the last minute. There was talk of him being packaged in a deal with the Washington Senators, but then he threw five innings of two-hit ball in a late-spring game. He started three games and relieved in four others, going 0-2 with a 4.97 ERA. Then on May 26, he was traded to the Kansas City Athletics, with Johnny Kucks and Jerry Lumpe, for Héctor López and Ralph Terry. Just a year and a half earlier, Kucks and Sturdivant had been seen as two of the better prospects in baseball, both just coming into their own.

Stengel was on the mark when he said, "The two pitchers, Kucks and Sturdivant, just couldn't get going for me, and I felt we had to do something. Maybe a change of scenery will do them good."[26] It did not. Sturdivant never truly got back what he had had. He was 2-6 (4.65) for Kansas City in the remainder of 1959.

On December 3, the Boston Red Sox traded catcher Pete Daley to the Athletics for Sturdivant. Red Sox skipper Billy Jurges saw Sturdivant as a likely starter: "His trouble is that his arm is weak. He has to start all over again and strengthen it. I've talked to a lot of the men in the league who liked what they saw of him late last season."[27]

When the Red Sox gathered at Scottsdale for spring training, it was said that Sturdivant looked to be the best-conditioned player in camp.[28] He pitched very well during the exhibition season, so well that he was named the starting pitcher for Opening Day in Washington. President Dwight Eisenhower threw out the first pitch; Camilo Pascual pitched a three-hitter for the Senators, and Sturdivant was hit for six runs (five earned) before parting in the fourth inning. By season's end, he had started two more games, and relieved in 37, eating up innings. His record was 3-3 (4.97).

After the season, the Senators franchise moved to Minneapolis/St. Paul and became the Minnesota Twins. A new Senators franchise was founded and in the December 14, 1960, expansion draft, Sturdivant was taken by Washington, the 16th overall pick.

He had a difficult start with the new Senators, going 2-6 with a 4.61 ERA (the team finished 61-100) — but then on June 29 he was dealt to the Pittsburgh Pirates organization, his contract sold to their affiliate, the Columbus Jets. At the same time, the Senators purchased the contract of another right-handed pitcher, Tom Cheney.[29]

This time, the change of scenery really did seem to help. Arriving in the National League in midseason, Sturdivant was 5-2 for the Pirates with a 2.84 ERA. The two losses were in a 4-3 game and a 2-1 game that lasted 11 innings, the third in a stretch of six consecutive complete games. Sturdivant credited Columbus manager Larry Shepard with helping turn his season around. "One thing he noticed was that I seemed to be flinging or flipping the ball, instead of firing it. Maybe because I'd been hit so hard in the American League I was timid about throwing strikes. But Shepard put me right to work. He threw me in there every fourth game, my arm got stronger, and my confidence returned. I started throwing more knuckleballs for strikes and I started winning."[30] In six starts for Columbus, he was 5-1 with a 1.80 earned-run average.

In 1962, Sturdivant had a solid year with the Pirates, appearing in 49 games (12 starts, 37 as a reliever) and recorded a 3.73 ERA, with a 9-5 record. He holds a minor distinction as the first pitcher who ever lost to the New York Mets (9-1, on April 23).

The knuckleball did become Sturdivant's "money pitch."[31] He was quoted as saying he often started slowly: "I don't know what it is. I've always had trouble starting the season. It's just one of those things. Maybe it's the weather – but my knuckleball just won't act right till late in the season."[32]

The Detroit Tigers had themselves gotten off to a very slow start as a team in 1963; hoping to improve their pitching staff, they acquired Sturdivant from the Pirates on May 4. He'd only pitched 8 1/3 innings for the Pirates but had given up six earned runs. He was not at all displeased with the trade. "I asked the Pirates to trade me because I get nervous when I don't pitch."[33]

After reporting to the Tigers, Sturdivant pitched in 28 games, all in relief, and had a 3.76 ERA (he was 1-2) before having his contract sold (via waivers) to the Kansas City Athletics on July 23. In his second stint with Kansas City, he appeared in 17 games, with a very consistent ERA of 3.74. His record was 1-2.

Sturdivant began the 1964 season with the Athletics, but pitched only 3 2/3 innings before he was released on May 2.[34] One week later, on May 10, he signed as a free agent with the New York Mets.[35] This reunited him with manager Casey Stengel. It was Sturdivant's last year in the major leagues. He wasn't used much; he relieved in 16 games,

throwing 28 2/3 innings, He had neither a win nor a loss and had an ERA of 5.97. His last game was on June 21. Two days later, the Mets put Sturdivant on waivers for the purpose of giving him his unconditional release.

Even before the season began, Sturdivant had decided he would like to try his hand at politics, to run as a Republican candidate for the Oklahoma State Senate. He had filed on February 28. Allie Reynolds had filed just the day before.[36] Sturdivant said that, if elected, he would retire from baseball.[37]

On July 5, perhaps reflecting an attempt to build up local support, he signed on with the Oklahoma 89ers, the Triple-A affiliate of the Houston Colt .45s. With Oklahoma City, he started 5-0 but finished 6-3 with a 3.89 ERA.

There were three prominent sports figures all running for political office in Oklahoma – Sturdivant, Reynolds, and football coach Bud Wilkinson, but come election on November 3, not one of them was elected.

After retiring as a player, Sturdivant went into the freight and truck leasing business, but he kept up some associations with the game. In 1976, he organized an "Allie Reynolds Appreciation Day" in Oklahoma, hoping in part to boost Reynolds' chances for the Baseball Hall of Fame. In later years he also took part in some baseball fantasy camps.

Tom and his second wife, Elaine, married in 1980. As one might expect, Tom favored the Yankees, and the Sturdivants made sure to subscribe to the television package that enabled them to watch all the games.

Sturdivant worked for RR Trucking, and later became an executive with Rollins Trucking Company in Oklahoma City. "He worked for two or three companies and then we started our own company, King Truck Leasing," Elaine said. "It was really hard work. I worked there a while, but for someone as high-strung as Tom, it maybe wasn't best for husband and wife to work together."[38]

He was also active civically, on the boards of both Metro Technology Centers and the Integris Hospice of Oklahoma City.

Just before the year, while traveling in Texas, Sturdivant suffered serious misfortune. "Tom had a really bad car accident, and he just wasn't the same afterward. He rolled a pickup five times."[39] After being hospitalized in Texas for a few weeks, he was brought back to Oklahoma and underwent a couple of surgeries. He lived another nine-plus years. "It wasn't much of a life for him," Elaine added, but that was the hand fate had dealt.

As it happens, the Sturdivants' pastor in Oklahoma City was former ballplayer Don Demeter. He remained Elaine's pastor in the year 2017.

On Valentine's Day 2009, Elaine woke and found Tom on the floor. He had suffered some form of seizure. He was rushed to the hospital where, having never woken up, he died two weeks later at Oklahoma City's Integris Southwest Medical Center on February 28, 2009. He was survived by Elaine. His two sons had predeceased him, Paul in 2002 and Tommy in 2006.[40]

## Sources

In addition to the sources noted in this biography, the author also accessed Sturdivant's player questionnaire from the National Baseball Hall of Fame, the *Encyclopedia of Minor League Baseball*, Retrosheet.org, Baseball-Reference.com, Rod Nelson of SABR's Scouts Committee, and the SABR Minor Leagues Database, accessed online at Baseball-Reference.com.

## Notes

1 Tom Sturdivant player questionnaire, National Baseball Hall of Fame.

2 "31 Scouts Sent Five or More to Big Time," *The Sporting News*, May 24, 1961: 13.

3 "Doughboys Win Two at Oklahoma City," *Arkansas Gazette*, July 8, 1946: 7.

4 "Oklahomans Win Again," *Omaha World-Herald*, July 24, 1947: 10.

5 Dan Daniel, "Casey Glad Bucky Blocked Sturdivant's Minor Ticket," *The Sporting News*, June 27, 1956: 5.

6 Ernest Mehl, "A Scout Keeps His Eye on 'His Boys' in Practice," *Kansas City Star*, March 28, 1949: 14.

7 SABR's Minor-League Database shows him in one game, 1-0 in nine innings, an apparent six-hit shutout, but the September 8 issue of the *Daily Nonpareil* of Council Bluffs, Iowa, shows him starting another game, one that Quincy lost.

8 Dan Daniel.

9 Dry, "The Dope Bucket," *Daily Illinois State Journal* (Springfield, Illinois), April 13, 1955: 14. The injury was a spiking that "ripped my leg," he told Joe Reichler of the Associated Press. See Joe Reichler,

"Tom Sturdivant Awoke as Casey's 'Sleeper'; Now Stengel Rests Easy," *Richmond* (Virginia) *Times Dispatch,* June 26, 1955: 81.

10 George C. Burton, "Sturdivant Looms as Bullpen Sleeper," *Jersey Journal* (Jersey City), April 1, 1955: 13.

11 Red Smith, "Yankee Rookie Sees Stadium First Time; Ole' Case Tells a Story," *Boston Globe*, April 10, 1955: C46.

12 Ibid. Stengel raved more to Joe Reichler midway into the season. See the Joe Reichler article referenced above.

13 George C. Burton, "Sturdivant Likes Life in Big Time," *Jersey Journal* (Jersey City), March 5, 1956: 11.

14 Dan Daniel.

15 Will Grimsley, "Casey's Confidence, Berra's Calls Won It," *Atlanta Constitution*, October 8, 1956: 6.

16 Ed Rumill, "Young Tom Sturdivant Masters Brooklyn to Even Up World Series at 2 All," *Christian Science Monitor*, October 8, 1956: 11.

17 Joe Reichler, Associated Press, "Big Hurling Surprise of Yankees is 'Numb,'" *Advocate* (Baton Rouge), October 8, 1956: 10.

18 Daniel, "Dodgers Call Knuckler Vital," *New York World Telegram Sun*, October 8, 1956.

19 Jack Hand, "Sturdivant Evens Series by Foiling Dodgers, 6-2; Mantle, Bauer Homer," *Atlanta Constitution*, October 8, 1956: 1.

20 Arthur Daley, "How to Become a Full-Fledged Genius," *New York Times*, October 8, 1956: 32.

21 Louis Effrat, "Yankees Check Tigers on Run Set Up by Attempted Steal with Bases Filled," *New York Times*, June 10, 1957: 44.

22 John Drebinger, "Yanks Hope to Use McDougald and Kubek as Keystone Pair," *New York Times*, March 1, 1958: 20.

23 United Press International, "Stengel Leaves Larsen, 2 Others Off Series List," *Boston Globe*, September 10, 1958: 35.

24 Associated Press, "Larsen Off Series List," *New York Times*, September 10, 1958: 44.

25 Bob Holbrook, "Daley Becomes A's Regular," *Boston Globe*, December 4, 1959: 39.

26 John Drebinger, "Yanks Get Lopez, Terry from A's," *New York Times*, May 27, 1959: 40.

27 Bob Holbrook.

28 Ed Rumill, "Sox New Hurler Has Right Idea," *Christian Science Monitor*, February 29, 1960: 11.

29 Bob Addie, "Senators Buy Cheney, Sell Tom Sturdivant," *Washington Post*, June 30, 1961: B1.

30 Ed Rumill, "AL Discard Wins with NL Pirates," *Christian Science Monitor*, August 31, 1961: 6.

31 Publicity biography, issued prior to the 1963 season, preserved in Sturdivant's player file at the National Baseball Hall of Fame.

32 Ibid.

33 Watson Spoelstra, "Sturdivant Knuckler Perking Up Bengals," *The Sporting News*, May 18, 1962: 10.

34 United Press International, "A's Sturdivant Given Unconditional Release," *Chicago Tribune*, May 3, 1964: B2.

35 United Press International, "Mets Sign Sturdivant Released by A's," *Chicago Tribune*, May 10, 1964: C2.

36 "Sturdivant, Reynolds Pitch Bonnets Into Political Ring," *The Sporting News*, March 14, 1964.

37 "The Clubhouse," *Boston Traveler*, August 7, 1964: 36.

38 Author interview with Elaine Sturdivant, June 15, 2017.

39 Ibid.

40 Tom Sturdivant, 78, dies; CAPITOL HILL GRAD PITCHER WON 16 GAMES FOR YANKEES IN '56, '57," *The Oklahoman* (Oklahoma City), March 1, 2009.

# THE COLT .45s AND THE 1961 EXPANSION DRAFT

STEPHEN D. BOREN AND ERIC THOMPSON

On October 10, 1961, the National League held the expansion draft to provide players for the Houston Colt .45s and the New York Mets. While the American League had held a seemingly similar expansion draft on December 14, 1960, the National League draft had the following distinctions:

It was held earlier in the year.

There were three distinct price levels for draftable players.

It was less cumbersome to implement.

There were different draft selection requirements.

It was held before the Rule 5 Draft.

As in the 1960 American League draft, the eight established National League teams were required to name 15 available players on their 40-man roster—including seven players from their 25-man roster.[1] The due date for the National League lists was September 20 for the draft that would occur on the day after the 1961 World Series ended, more than two months earlier than the American League draft had taken place in 1960.

In the previous AL draft, all the players in the expansion pool were available for $75,000 each to the new teams. However, the National League draft had three prices for players: $50,000, $75,000, and $125,000. Each expansion team was required to select 16 players: two from each established team's available player list at $75,000 (regular phase), then at most eight players, one from each established team at $50,000 (optional phase) from the players remaining. At that point, in a major departure from the AL system, each established team was to submit two additional names from their August 31 active roster: "premium players." From this list of 16, each expansion team was required to choose four players at $125,000 each (premium phase), and no established team could lose more than one premium player.

If an expansion team purchased the maximum number of players—16 at $75,000 each, eight at $50,000 each, and four at $125,000 each—the total cost would be $2.1 million. That cost represented the team's entry fee into the National League and was equal to the amount paid by the AL expansion teams for 28 players at $75,000 each. While these prices for

A 1962 Houston Colt .45s yearbook, published by Jay Publishing Co. (Courtesy of Frederick C Bush)

players do not seem high in 2014, they were quite pricey in 1961 even after discounting the entry fee involved. The consumer price index was 29.9 in 1961, compared to 233.5 in 2013.[2] Adjusting 1961-dollars to 2013-dollars at a rate of $7.81, would yield prices of $585,750, $390,500, and $976,250.[3] The sale of players was a financial bonanza to each of the eight established teams.

The American League had required that each new team draft 10 pitchers, followed by two catchers, six infielders, four outfielders, and then six players unrestricted by position. The NL draft did not have any position requirements. In the AL draft no established team was supposed to lose more than seven players and an expansion team could take no more than four players from any established team. Unfortunately Joe Cronin forgot about these requirements while he conducted the AL draft and the selections needed to be rearranged after the draft was seemingly over because the Tigers and Indians had lost <u>eight</u> players each![4] The NL draft did not make this mistake.

While these differences were significant, the most significant distinction was the date of the draft. The AL draft was held more than two months after the season ended. Thus before the 1960 American League expansion draft, the lists of available players had not been distorted by any of the following roster changes:

Retirements (e.g. Ted Williams)

Unconditional releases

Sale and optioning of players to minor-league teams

Promotion of prospects

Addition of players taken in the Rule 5 Draft held on November 28

After the 1960 season ended but before the 1960 draft, the Cleveland Indians had released Jack Harshman and sold **Billy Moran** to the International League, the Orioles had released Jim Busby, Del Rice, and Dave Philley, the Yankees had released Jim Hegan, and the White Sox had released Bob Rush and Mike Garcia and dropped Don Ferrarese, Jake Striker, Frank Barnes, and Al Worthington.[5],[6] With only eight days between the end of the season and the NL draft, no roster modifications by any of the eight established National League teams had yet taken place.

The greatest inequity of the NL expansion draft was that few blue chip minor-league prospects were included on the 40-man rosters. Most promoted their top minor leaguers on October 17, 1961, seven days after the draft and the last day to modify the 40-man roster before the Rule 5 and Rule 3 Drafts. These players had been exempt from the expansion draft in October and now were protected in late November as well. A partial list of these prospects follows.[7]

Meanwhile, many "deadwood" players promoted in September to be showcased for the expansion draft, but not taken, were then shuffled off the 40-man roster to make room for superior minor-league talent.

The list of players made available for the NL expansion draft follows.[8]

The general managers in Houston and New York, Paul Richards and George Weiss, were not happy with the players made available. Richards commented, "I figured the lists of players would be bad, but they're worse than I thought they would be."[9]

Thirty of the available players were 31 years old or older. Nineteen had eight years or more of major-league experience including many with correspondingly high salaries. Of the 120 available players, 23 were rookies who ended their baseball careers without ever appearing in a single major-league game—19 additional players never played at the major-league level after 1961. Twenty-one were journeyman players who had spent seven or more seasons in the minor leagues.

At the AL expansion draft there were five coin tosses, one for each position category. At the NL expansion draft there was one coin toss with the winner selecting to go first in the regular-optional phase or the premium phase. The Colts won the coin toss and elected to go first in the regular-optional phase.

The Colts decided that shortstop Ed Bressoud of the Giants was the best player available and selected him. He had been the backup to Jose Pagan and played in only 59 games the past season while hitting a mere .211. On November 26 he was traded to the Red Sox for the erratic Don Buddin, another shortstop. After 40 games in 1962, Buddin was hitting .163 and was sold to the Tigers. They did well with their second pick, Bob Aspromonte, who had a successful career with Houston. Incidentally, his brother Ken had been selected by the Senators and traded to the Angels at the draft table in the AL expansion draft.[10] Their third pick was light-hitting shortstop Bob Lillis, who did have a long career Houston as a player, coach, and manager.

Fourth and fifth picks, Dick Drott and Al Heist, were both from the Cubs and were both busts. Drott was called to eight months of active military duty on November 2 and appeared in only six games.[11] Heist was on the disabled list for a month, played in only 27 games, and batted only .222.[12] In 1963, Drott went 2–12 in his final year in the majors. Heist was in the minors all season.

Sixth pick Roman Mejias was a power hitting success in 1962 for the Colts and became one of their most popular players. In 1962, Mejias led the team in batting, home runs, runs batted in, runs scored, hits, and stolen bases. After the season he was traded to the Red Sox for the reigning AL batting champion, Pete Runnels. Unfortunately, Runnels lost his batting eye when he joined the Houston team and was released in early 1964.

Seventh pick George Williams, like Drott, was called to active military duty soon after the draft.[13] Williams played in only five September games for the Colts in 1962, played in the minors in 1963, and was sent to the Cardinals after the season. Eighth pick Jesse Hickman never played in a major league game with the Colts. It is very likely that Paul Richards mistook him for Jim Hickman, who was also available in the expansion draft. It wasn't the first time a G.M. made such a mistake: The St. Louis Browns took Garvin Hamner in the 1947 minor-league draft, thinking that they were selecting his brother Granny.[14] Ninth pick Merritt Ranew was a backup catcher for one season, then was traded away and spent most of his career in the minors. Their 10th pick Don Taussig hit only .200 in 16 games, but the Colts received part of their investment back when the Braves drafted him in the minor league phase of the 1962 Rule 5 Draft.

Their 11th pick, Bobby Shantz, started three games on the mound for the Colts before being traded to the Cardinals for Carl Warwick and John Anderson on May 7, 1962. Warwick became the Colts' regular center fielder for 1962. Since the Washington Senators had selected Shantz in the 1960 AL expansion draft, Shantz bore the distinction of being the only player selected in both drafts.[15]

Their 12th pick was Norm Larker, who had lost the 1960 batting title by making an out in his final plate appearance. However, he hit only .263 for the Colts and was traded

after the 1962 season. Their 13th pick, Sam "Toothpick" Jones, never pitched for the Colts. Jones was quickly traded on December 1 to the Tigers for Bob Bruce and Manny Montejo. Bruce pitched in the Colts starting rotation for five years. Jones won only four games during the remainder of his career. Their 14th pick was Paul Roof, who never played major league baseball, although his brothers Phil and Gene did. Again, perhaps he was mistaken for Phil who was also in the draft.

Their 15th pick was Ken Johnson who was a decent pitcher for Houston for several seasons during his 13-year major league career. His main claim to fame was pitching a nine-inning no-hitter for the Colts on April 23, 1964, but losing the game 1-0 when he and Nellie Fox made errors in the ninth inning. Their 16th pick, Dick Gernert, hit .208 in 10 games and was quickly released on May 17, 1962.

Their 17th pick and first $50,000, optional pick was Ed Olivares. Olivares was on the disabled list during the entire 1962 season and never played again in the majors.[16] Eighteenth pick Jim Umbricht pitched effectively out of the bullpen for two years before he, unfortunately, died of cancer in 1964. Nineteenth pick Jim Golden was back in the minors in 1963 and traded for Nellie Fox after that season.

Golden was the last optional pick taken in the draft because Weiss and Richards refused to spend any more money. By leaving 11 optional choices unused, the Mets saved $300,000 and the Colts $250,000 on the anticipated $2.1 million expected expenditure by each team. Both general managers intended to use that money to develop their teams: Weiss to purchase retreads at his own price, Richards to acquire and develop young talent.

At that point a representative from each established team made known the identity of their team's two premium players. The list follows of the 16 premium players, two from each established team, made available for the NL expansion draft.[17]

The premium player choices were marked by the presence of three "bonus babies" from the mid-1950s. Those three, Bob L. Miller (Cardinals), Joey Amalfitano (Giants), and Jay Hook (Reds), were the first three players taken in the premium phase. Since the Mets chose first in the premium phase, Miller and Hook became Mets. The Colts took Amalfitano with their first premium pick. Their original teams actually turned a tidy profit when they received

$125,000 each! On the humorous side, when Amalfitano discovered that he had been purchased for that princely sum, he said, "I'll have to go out and get another life insurance policy. I'm worth more than I thought."[18] Amalfitano lasted only one season with Houston but enjoy a long career as a major-league coach and manager.

Their second premium pick, Dick "Turk" Farrell, was an all-star pitcher for the Colts, and was their jewel of the draft. Their third premium pick, Hal W. Smith, was their regular catcher in 1962 and their third string catcher the next season, before he was released. Their final premium pick, Al Spangler, was a regular outfielder for three seasons before being traded away. Spangler had the distinction of being the final player taken in the NL expansion draft as well as the last player to bat in an eight-team National League. The regular, optional, and premium choices made by the Colts and Mets follow.[19]

After the draft, Paul Richards had changed his tune. Richards was quoted, "I was frightened a week ago when I did some talking, but had I known that we would get the team we did, I never would have opened my mouth."[20]

George Weiss saw much work ahead saying, "We did as well as we expected to do, maybe a little better, but please don't think this will be our starting club on opening day. We plan to purchase many more players and have some deals in mind." [21]

When the Colts and Mets left 11 optional choices at $50,000 each untaken, the following players were still available who went on to play at least five years at the major league level after 1961.[22]

Passing over Vic Davalillo is understandable since he had been a pitcher in the Reds' organization through the 1961 season rather than an outfielder, the position he played throughout his 16-year major-league career. However, infielder Dick Allen became NL rookie of the year in 1964 and AL Most Valuable Player in 1972. In 1961, Allen was in his second year in Organized Baseball and had batted .317 with 21 home runs and 94 runs batted in as a second baseman at Magic Valley in the Class-C Pioneer League. Allen finished his major-league career with a .292 average and 351 home runs.

Also untaken was Eddie Fisher, a highly regarded 25-year-old pitcher in the Giants' farm system who had posted a record of 47–28 with a 3.23 ERA in his four minor-league seasons. Fisher became the main piece in the Giants' No-

vember 30, 1961, trade with the White Sox for Billy Pierce and Don Larsen. Fisher followed with 12 successful years in the AL posting an 80-61 record with a 3.25 ERA. He was AL Fireman of the Year in 1965.

Other noteworthy names included Robin Roberts, Jerry Zimmerman, Jim Brewer, and Ray Culp. The Colts and Mets left some experienced talent and potential talent untaken.

The National League kicked off their first season as a ten-team league in 1962. The Houston Colts managed to duplicate the Los Angeles Angels' feat of 1961 by finishing in eighth place but with only a 64–96 record compared to the Angels' record of 70–91 in 1961. The Cubs, who lost 103 games, had the dubious distinction of finishing ninth, six games behind the Colts.

The Colts featured an everyday lineup of veterans. Norm Larker, Joey Amalfitano, Bob Lillis, and Bob Aspromonte covered the infield. Al Spangler, Carl Warwick, and Roman Mejias held down the outfield posts. Hal Smith was the regular catcher. All, except Warwick, were taken in the expansion draft. Dick Farrell, acquired in the expansion draft, and Bob Bruce, acquired from the Tigers in the December trade for Sam Jones, each won 10 games. Don McMahon, purchased from the Braves on May 9, 1962, and Jim Umbricht, acquired in the expansion draft, anchored the bullpen.

The Colts had heavily invested in young talent. Waiting in the wings for the opportunity at the major league level were catcher Jerry Grote, outfielders Ron Davis and Rusty Staub, and pitchers Dave Giusti and Chris Zachary. The future looked bright for Houston.

*Acknowledgement*

Portions of the information used here were obtained free of charge from and is copyrighted by Retrosheet. Interested parties may contact Retrosheet at www.retrosheet.org.

## References

Rules governing the American League expansion draft of 1960:

J. G. Taylor Spink. Ed. *Baseball Guide and Record Book 1961* (St. Louis: Charles C. Spink and Sons, 1961), 110-112.

Rules governing the National League expansion draft of 1961:

J. G. Taylor Spink. Ed. *Baseball Guide and Record Book 1961* (St. Louis: Charles C. Spink and Sons, 1961), 119-120.

Daniel, Dan. "N.L. Execs Okay Grab-Bag Plan in Marathon Huddle," *The Sporting News*, July 5, 1961: 5-6.

Statistical data for players included in all lists and for players drafted by Houston: retrosheet.org and SABR minor-league database included in baseball-reference.com.

Description of 1962 Houston season compiled from retrosheet.org.

## Notes

1  The 25-man roster as of August 31.

2  http://www.bls.gov/cpi/tables.htm

3  http://inflationdata.com/inflation/Inflation_Calculators/Inflation_Calculator.asp

4  Letter of May 13, 1973, from Hal Keller, farm director of the Texas Rangers, to Cliff Kachline, historian of the National Baseball Hall of Fame, on file in the 1961 American League Expansion Draft folder in the A. Bartlett Giamatti Research Center at the National Baseball Hall of Fame, Cooperstown, New York.

5  http://www.retrosheet.org/boxesetc/1960/YM_1960.htm

6  EdwardPrell, "In the Wake of the News," *Chicago Tribune*. September 23, 1961: 4, 1..

7  List compiled from BASEBALL, Office of the Commissioner, Official Bulletin No. 23, November 14, 1961, pages 2-3.

8  List compiled from information in 1962 National League Expansion Draft folder in the A. Bartlett Giamatti Research Center.

9  Clark Nealon, "Colts Get Frick Okay to Set Up 40-Man Roster," *The Sporting News*, October 11, 1961: 15.

10  Letter of May 13, 1973, from Hal Keller, farm director of the Texas Rangers, to Cliff Kachline, the historian of the National Baseball Hall of Fame, on file in the 1961 American League Expansion Draft folder.

11  BASEBALL, Office of the Commissioner, Official Bulletin No. 26, December 20, 1961: 2.

12  BASEBALL, Office of the Commissioner, Official Bulletin No. 14, August 15, 1962: 3.

13  BASEBALL, Office of the Commissioner, Official Bulletin No. 23, November 14, 1961: 3.

14  Frank Yeutter, "Gran-D Young Man of the Phillies," *Baseball Digest*, July 1950: 11.

15  Shantz could not compare with former NBA player George Wilson. Wilson was selected in three NBA expansion drafts (May 1, 1967 by the Seattle Super Sonics from the Chicago Bulls, May 6, 1968 by the Phoenix Suns from the Seattle, and May 11, 1970 by the Buffalo Braves from the Philadelphia 76ers) http://www.basketball-reference.com/players/w/wilsoge01.html

16  BASEBALL, Office of the Commissioner, Official Bulletin No. 8, April 25, 1962, page 3.

17  List compiled from information in 1962 National League Expansion Draft folder.

18  *Milwaukee Sentinel*, October 11, 1961: 11.

19  List compiled from http://www.retrosheet.org/boxesetc/1961/10101961.htm.

20  Clark Nealon. "Colts Corralled Slick Infielders, Richards Chirps," *The Sporting News*, October 18, 1961: 7.

21  Bob Burnes. "Draft Gives Colts, Mets Solid Send Off," *The Sporting News*, October 18, 1961: 7.

22  List compiled from retrosheet.org.

## HOUSTON COLT .45S EXPANSION DRAFT

PICK   PLAYER                POSITION   FORMER TEAM

### REGULAR PHASE, $75,000 PER PLAYER

| | | | |
|---|---|---|---|
| 1 | Eddie Bressoud | 2b | San Francisco Giants |
| 2 | Bob Aspromonte | 3b | Los Angeles Dodgers |
| 3 | Bob Lillis | ss | Los Angeles Dodgers |
| 4 | Dick Drott | p | Chicago Cubs |
| 5 | Al Heist | of | Chicago Cubs |
| 6 | Roman Mejias | of | Pittsburgh Pirates |
| 7 | George Williams | ss | Philadelphia Phillies |
| 8 | Jesse Hickman | p | Philadelphia Phillies |
| 9 | Merritt Ranew | c | Milwaukee Braves |
| 10 | Don Taussig | of | St. Louis Cardinals |
| 11 | Bobby Shantz | p | Pittsburgh Pirates |
| 12 | Norm Larker | 1b | Los Angeles Dodgers |
| 13 | Sam Jones | p | San Francisco Giants |
| 14 | Paul Roof | p | Milwaukee Braves |
| 15 | Ken Johnson | p | Cincinnati Reds |
| 16 | Dick Gernert | 1b | Cincinnati Reds |

### REGULAR PHASE, $50,000 PER PLAYER

| | | | |
|---|---|---|---|
| 17 | Ed Olivares | 2b | St. Louis Cardinals |
| 18 | Jim Umbricht | p | Pittsburgh Pirates |
| 19 | Jim Golden | p | Los Angeles Dodgers |

### PREMIUM PHASE, $125,000 PER PLAYER

| | | | |
|---|---|---|---|
| 20 | Joe Amalfitano | ss | San Francisco Giants |
| 21 | Turk Farrell | p | Los Angeles Dodgers |
| 22 | Hal Smith | c | Pittsburgh Pirates |
| 23 | Al Spangler | of | Milwaukee Braves |

Houston Colt .45s team executive George Kirksey (l) observes (from left) outfielder Aaron Pointer, manager Harry Craft, and outfielder Rusty Staub model the team's new uniforms at spring training in Apache Junction, Arizona. Pointer's sisters were, in fact, the Pointer Sisters. (Courtesy of the Houston Astros)

General manager Paul Richards conducts a Cactus League hitting clinic for the Colt .45s. Wearing #41 with his back to the camera was pitcher Paul Roof; years later, his brother Phil became the first player ever acquired by the Toronto Blue Jays. (Courtesy of the Houston Astros)

The position players in the clubhouse (from left) oufielder Al Heist, infielders Bob Lillis, Bob Aspromonte, and Joe Amalfitano, and outfielder Al Spangler. (Courtesy of th Houston Astros)

The pitchers with manager Harry Craft (from left) Dick Farrell, Jim Golden, and Bobby Shantz, (Courtesy of the Houston Astros)

The Houston Colt .45s were Cactus League Champions in 1962 and again in 1963. They would not win the World Series until 2017, but it was well worth the wait (Courtesy of the Houston Astros)

A 'Here Come the Colts' booklet featuring Bob Aspromonte. One of the most talented players selected by the Colt .45s in the expansion draft, the Brooklyn native set a   franchise record for grand slam home runs that was broken only in 2011, (Courtesy of Mark Wernick)

A 1964 Colt .45s program versus the Milwaukee Braves. In three major league seasons, the Colt .45s never finished higher than eighth place or won more than 66 games. The team moved indoors in 1965, relocating from Colt Stadium to the Astrodome and rebranding itself as the Houston Astros.. (Courtesy of Frederick C Bush)

# HERE COME THE COLTS

## By David E. Skelton

Manager Harry Craft. The former Cincinnati Reds' outfielder piloted the Houston Colt .45s from their inaugural 1962 season until midway through 1964.

In 1958, three years before a major-league expansion team took the field for the first time, Milwaukee Braves owner Lou Perini, one of the lone voices in baseball's hierarchy pushing for extending into other regions of the country, complained, "Baseball men have always been averse to changes. ... They simply can't continue to sit back and do nothing."[1] In fact, Perini, who had owned the Braves since 1945, when they were the Boston Braves, misjudged the glacial pace of decision-making among his fellow owners. In 1939, six years before Perini purchased his club, Warren Giles, the Cincinnati Reds' general manager, first raised the possibility of realigning and potentially expanding major-league baseball.[2]

Presumably shelved with the onset of the Second World War, the subject gained traction during the 1946 winter meetings after Organized Baseball mushroomed from 12 leagues to 43 within a 12-month span. Despite this enormous growth, major-league owners remained steadfast in their opposition to expansion. "They are content to rake in their profits and defy any other cities to crash into their select group," said Perini ally and former baseball executive Larry MacPhail.[3]

Beginning in the late 1940s, Houston and several other cities and regions around the country were often used as a pawn in the owners' decades-long strategy of placating the US Congress when the House Monopoly Subcommittee, while reviewing baseball's antitrust exemptions, began to push for expansion. In the mid-1950s, with the advent of the Douglas DC-7 airliner, which revolutionized domestic air travel, the owners turned an earnest eye toward expanding into the lucrative West Coast. But the subject of expansion reverted to mere lip service after the Brooklyn Dodgers and New York Giants moved to Los Angeles and San Francisco, respectively, after the 1957 season. It wasn't until two years later, when the owners were threatened by the formation of a third major league – and it won backing from key members of Congress – that the owners moved positively toward expansion.

Immediately after World War II, baseball experienced a renaissance unlike anything before or since. Besides the frenzied growth of the minor leagues in 1945-46, amateur leagues nationwide also grew at an alarming rate. This unexpected surge caught many by surprise. In March 1947, after a 10-day strike by its employees, the Hillerich & Bradsby Company, maker of the Louisville Slugger bat, asked Organized Baseball to "specify ... orders [of] *reasonable quantities*" [emphasis added] to allow the firm to meet the demands of its other customers.[4] That year the pockets of the major-league owners were lined handsomely when attendance more than doubled from prewar years. In July, in a seemingly halfhearted response to this surge, the National League established a committee to explore the likelihood of expansion along the West Coast. Five months later, as Perini was floating the possibility of two 12-club circuits that, in various iterations, included Milwaukee, Montreal, Toronto, and four California sites (Texas received only lukewarm consideration), the senior circuit took a nonbinding vote during the winter meetings in favor of a 10-club league.

The proposal proved short-lived when the American League, citing increased travel costs and other factors, voted 5 to 2 against the proposal. (Cleveland Indians owner Bill Veeck, an expansion proponent, inexplicably abstained from voting.) In August 1948, while attempting to ease the disappointment of prospective major-league owners during an official visit to Houston, Baseball Commissioner A.B. "Happy" Chandler said, "We definitely are not opposed to other cities moving into major league baseball. ... But when and if the occasion arrives ... it should be done gradually."[5] This sentiment was still being echoed 10 years later when retiring AL President Will Harridge remarked that "[e]xpansion is going to come, but we should let it develop naturally."[6]

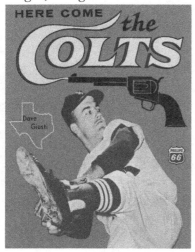

Who pitched for the Houston Buffs, the Houston Colt .45s, and the Houston Astros? Dave Giusti, that's who! Later in his career as a St. Louis Cardinal, Giusti was selected by the San Diego Padres in their expansion draft.

One of the many prospective owners not placated by Chandler's soothing words was Texas millionaire oilman Richard Wesley Burnett. A moderately successful businessman from the small East Texas town of Gladewater, Burnett became fabulously wealthy in 1944 after discovering an oil and gas field in southwest Arkansas. An ardent baseball fan, Burnett had acquired several low-level minor-league clubs before setting his sights toward greater goals.[7] In 1948, after purchasing the Dallas Rebels of the Double-A Texas League for $550,000, Burnett, in concert with league President J. Alvin Gardner, began negotiations with club owners in the Pacific Coast League to form a third (and possibly fourth) major league. Though nothing came of this, neither Burnett's nor Gardner's goal of attaining big-league status ever diminished. "Maybe ... I will not live to see it, but the time is not too far distant when this country will see four major leagues in existence," declared the visionary Gardner in 1949. "Houston promise[s] to become one of the largest metropolitan centers in the United States and [I envision] the time when Houston, along with Dallas, would be in the majors."[8]

The idea of three or four major leagues was certainly not unique to Burnett and Gardner, and it continued to gain traction over the next dozen years. In 1952, Philip K. Wrigley, the Chicago Cubs owner, not only came out in favor of four circuits, but took the additional step of divesting himself from ownership of the PCL's Los Angeles Angels to clear the city's path from conflict in its quest for a major-league club. After initially coming out in favor of expanding the existing leagues, Lou Perini, who for years was the subject's most consistent advocate, eventually endorsed a three-league arrangement. "[T]he so-called 'world championship' [is] confined to practically one-quarter of the country's area," he sniffed. "[I]t's not very national in scope."[9] Continuing to turn a blind eye to Texas, Perini looked even farther south by suggesting the placement of teams in Mexico City and Havana. When Ford Frick replaced Chandler as commissioner in 1951, he maintained the gradualist position of his predecessor before eventually championing a three-league arrangement. When doing so, he became one of the fiercest advocates for placing a club in Houston.

But this growing chorus of expansion advocates continued to face stiff opposition. In 1953, when the National League announced that it would begin independent pursuits toward expansion apart from the American League, AL President Will Harridge complained that this would be in violation of the circuits' National Agreement. The divide between the pro- and anti-expansion camps was not limited to an NL-AL conflict alone. Though Bill Veeck, now owner of the St. Louis Browns, found support for expansion among a few of his fellow AL owners, Harridge's position often aligned with that of Bob Carpenter and Horace Stoneham, owners of the NL

Philadelphia Phillies and New York Giants, respectively. The anti-expansion camp cited a multitude of reasons for their opposition: there weren't enough quality players to go around; there would be increased costs in salaries, operating expenses, travel and training expenses; and there would be a need to address the territorial rights (investment and property rights) of the minor-league owners whose cities were targeted. Moreover, at a time when major-league owners could not or would not conceive of a schedule increase from 154 games to 162 games, the greatest concern was lost revenue. With reference to two 10-club leagues, Branch Rickey, an expansion advocate, explained, "[T]his would mean a different sharing of the gate receipts. Instead of one-eighth, it would mean a one-tenth split. And there are some clubs having trouble with the financial problems playing 77 games."[10]

A break in the opposition camp came before the 1953 winter meetings when, after the Browns announced their move to Baltimore, the AL appointed a three-man committee to conduct a study on expansion and realignment. (A fourth person would be added to the committee a year later.) In 1954, outspoken Chicago White Sox general manager Frank Lane, who was selected to chair the committee, was not shy about expressing his disdain toward members of the anti-expansion camp, "brand[ing] them as reactionaries still hobbled by horse-and-buggy thinking."[11] Moreover, Lane was a strong proponent of placing a major-league club in Texas. His support, like that of Gardner's before him, was well warranted. While the United States had witnessed a brisk 61 percent increase in population increase from 1910 to 1950, during the same period Texas's population had nearly doubled, from 3.9 million to 7.7 million. If Gardner and Lane had had the ability to gaze into the future, they would have known that, over the next 40 years, the state would realize a more than twofold increase to 16.9 million people. In 1948, the National Association had issued a statement saying, "[V]arious sections of the country have developed greatly and increasing population ... should eventually result in expansion of major league baseball to such territories."[12] By the 1950s the Lone Star State, with its burgeoning population, was certainly making its case for consideration.

From 1953 through June 1958, discussions surrounding expansion, if they happened at all, took a variety of forms. Interleague play, an idea strongly advocated by Indians GM Hank Greenberg, was introduced alongside expansion. During the 1954 winter meetings, factions within the NL presented a proposal for immediate expansion that included reducing rosters from 25 players to 23, but it was defeated. Three years later, the AL also considered immediate expansion to 10 clubs during a five-year interim phase with the option of reverting to eight clubs if necessary. The proposal never went beyond talk. The only concrete action taken during this period came in May 1955 when the commissioner's office

Relief pitcher Don McMahon. Acquired by the Colt .45s from the Milwaukee Braves midway through the 1962 season, he pitched for Houston through 1963.

hired a public-relations firm to study expansion among other items. The task generated even more studies, a process that prompted sportswriter Dan Daniel to sarcastically opine that "[t]he reports advise expansion, but do not counsel haste."[13] In May 1958, Bill Furlong, a Chicago-based sports scribe, piled on by writing that "all the talk about expanding the majors seems as far from reality as a trip to the moon."[14] [This was four years before President John F. Kennedy announced a goal of reaching the moon.] Conspicuously absent from these four-plus years of discussions and proposals was the matter of multiple circuits. On October 22, 1953, Warren Giles, now the NL president, who in 1939 had first raised the potential of major league expansion, in a speech in Milwaukee, roundly dismissed the three- or four-circuit concept. It proved to be the first nail in the multiple circuits' coffin. Except for the short-lived Continental League, the idea never gained much attention again.

The inaction of the major-league owners created a vacuum that was eventually filled by a variety of competing factions. In October 1957, New York City Mayor Robert F. Wagner announced plans for the appointment of a citizens committee to seek an NL team to replace the departed Giants and Dodgers. Within a year, the origins of the Continental League were established when the committee threatened to set up a third major league. Meanwhile, 1,600 miles to the southwest, Houston, which had grown to become the largest city in the nation without a big-league club, was making its own presence felt. On June 19, 1958, George Kirksey, a former United Press

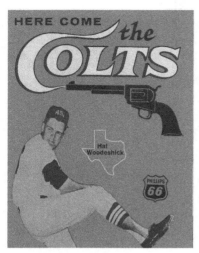

Relief pitcher Hal Woodeshick, an All-Star for the Colt .45s in 1963.

sportswriter who now was the executive secretary of the newly established Houston Sports Association, made formal application with the NL for placement of an expansion team in the Texas city. Thirteen days later he made the same filing with the AL. "[W]e believe we're ready for the big leagues," Kirksey said. "We'd like serious consideration for membership."[15]

Former Houston Mayor Roy Hofheinz and oilmen K.S. "Bud" Adams Jr., future owner of the Houston Oilers of the NFL, and Craig F. Cullinan Jr. were among Kirksey's many powerful allies. Over the preceding years the Houston Sports Association had approached the owners of the Indians and three other clubs in failed attempts to purchase those teams and relocate them to Houston.[16] Two weeks after the AL filing, the citizens of Harris County, Texas, by voted overwhelmingly in favor of a $20 million bond to build a new multipurpose stadium in Houston. The Houston Sports Association was the driving force that had brought the bond issue to the fore, a task made all the easier by the influence of a member of the county's Board of Park Commissioners, former major-league player and manager Eddie Dyer. In November, in a move similar to what Philip Wrigley did for Los Angeles six years earlier, the Cardinals ended their nearly 40-year affiliation with the Houston Buffaloes by selling the minor-league club to Milton Fischmann and a business associate, former Cardinals All-Star shortstop Marty Marion. New York and Houston were hardly alone in their pursuit of a major-league club. Within two years of Houston's $20 million bond approval, Seattle floated a similar bond for the same purpose, while Denver, New Orleans, and Buffalo, among other cities, also competed for recognition. On December 3, 1958, in response to these developments, the NL approved a resolution appointing an independent research organization to conduct a survey on expansion. A day later, in a similarly bold move, the AL approved an identical motion.

Years of surveys, studies, and overall foot-dragging were rapidly ending. Congress, which in 1951 had made a pitch for expansion before being placated with pledges of imminent action, by the late 1950s was no longer swallowing empty promises. "The owners' failure to expand has had Congress looking down their throats for several years now, and understandably," MacPhail said. "There are congressmen and senators eager to make political capital out of baseball and the game could lose the favored status it gained from the Supreme Court decisions. If Congress puts baseball under some of the antitrust laws, well, the owners asked for it. So far the owners have gotten away with their vague promises of expansion, but there has been no sign they have been acting in good faith."[17] But in May 1959, the NL, seemingly disregarding the number of times Commissioner Frick was hauled before Congress to testify about antitrust exemptions, expansion, and other matters, vetoed a proposal for expansion to 10 clubs. (The AL didn't even bother to bring the issue up.)

"Expansion is coming," Frick said. "[B]ut it will not come by fiat, by pressure or by the threat of legislation." New York's mayor had already appointed attorney William A. Shea to chair the city's baseball committee. Within days of his appointment, Shea announced the formation of the Continental League on July 27, 1959. New York, Toronto, Denver, Minneapolis-St. Paul, and Houston formed the nucleus of the proposed league, with the Houston Sports Association and the Marion-Fischmann group each having bid separately for Houston's entry. "The question is no longer whether Houston will be in the major leagues but when and in what league," Shea declared.[18] Further pressure was put on the major-league owners after he projected a 1961 opening for the new circuit.

But the Continental League's path to major-league status was hardly a smooth one. In August 1959, with Houston among half of the Triple-A American Association's 10 cities targeted for either major-league expansion or inclusion in the new circuit, the Association's executives claimed an expected $5 million loss in territorial rights. Without declaring a specific amount, the Triple-A International League also weighed in with anticipated losses in the millions of dollars. "[N]ot want[ing and likely lacking the ability] to pay for territorial damages," Shea started engaging in merger talks with the major-league owners.[19] These negotiations came to fruition in Chicago on August 1, 1960, when the Continental League agreed to fold after securing a firm commitment from the major-league owners to expand to two 10-club circuits by 1962. The parties reached a general agreement that the AL would expand into Toronto and Minneapolis-St. Paul (plans that were torn to shreds by the Washington Senators' move to Minnesota, plus the owners' desire for a California presence); the National League would expand into New York and Houston. Two months later, the Houston Sports Association made its second application for entry into the National League.

Notably absent from this process were the Buffaloes, owners of Houston's territorial rights. In August 1959, shortly after the Marion-Fischmann contingent applied for entry into the Continental League, a Houston group unaffiliated with the Houston Sports Association purchased the majority interest in the club. Shortly thereafter, the owners expressed their goal of entry into the major leagues via expansion. But by February 1960, this new entity was instead engaged in merger talks with the Houston Sports Association. Talks quickly turned bitter as both sides took a hard-line negotiating stance and discussions collapsed in July. Negotiations eventually resumed, with the parties about $240,000 apart, before another impasse was reached. Finally, in October, with considerable political weight behind it, the Houston Sports Association presented a take-or-leave-it offer to the Buffaloes in the amount of $362,000. (A final settlement was reached at slightly under $400,000.) The offer appears to have been taken in part because the Buffaloes owners' focus had since shifted to Missouri, where they were busy placing a bid for ownership of the Kansas City Athletics. Within days of the settlement the NL rewarded the Houston Sports Association by selecting Houston among its two expansion entries. "[Houston] has made the most progress of all the cities seeking major league franchises," Giles said. "It has definite plans to build a ball park ... and has started its organization."[20]

One of the first steps taken by the quartet of Robert E. "Bob" Smith (considered the world's largest independent oil operator), Hofheinz, Cullinan, and Bud Adams, who collectively owned 51 percent of the new franchise's stock, was to hire a general manager. Wasting no time, on October 25 the team lured Reds GM Gabe Paul from Cincinnati with a three-year contract. Paul brought Reds executive Tal Smith with him to oversee the farm system and the scouting system, and immediately hired former major-league infielder and manager Bobby Bragan as the personnel director. "First and foremost in our format ... will be a master scouting system second to none," Paul declared.[21] Next the organization announced a February 1961 construction start date for a domed stadium to be ready by Opening Day 1962. Though this projected schedule was found to be overly optimistic, it proved to be one of the few missteps in Houston's relentless pursuit of a major-league franchise.

Ken Johnson. On April 23, 1964, Johnson held the dubious distinction as the first to pitch a nine inning no-hitter and lose. He took a 1-0 defeat to the Cincinnati Reds.

**Sources**

In addition to the sources cited in the Notes, the author consulted Baseball-Reference.com. The author wishes to thank Mickey Herskowitz and Tal Smith for their invaluable assistance.

**Notes**

1  Bob Wolf, "Perini Predicts Two Ten-Team Majors by '63," *The Sporting News*, March 26, 1958: 30.

2  Jack Walsh, "So What? Fans Ask After Celler Hearing," *The Sporting News*, October 31, 1951: 8.

3  Shirley Povich, " 'Expand or Regret,' MacPhail Warns," *The Sporting News*, July 29, 1959: 2.

4  John Hillerich, "To ALL Clubs in Organized Baseball," *The Sporting News*, March 19, 1947: 24.

5  "Chandler Favors Gradual Expansion," *The Sporting News*, September 1, 1948: 2.

6  Edgar Munzel, "Harridge Retirement Marks End of Era," *The Sporting News*, December 10, 1958: 4.

7  "Burnett, Richard Wesley," "Handbook of Texas Online," Texas State Historical Association, June 12, 2010. Accessed July 30, 2017 (,bit.ly/2hdiOgZ ).

8  "Gardner Predicts Four Major Loops for U.S.A.," *The Sporting News*, January 19, 1949: 15.

9  "Big Leagues Too Limited in Area, Contends Perini," *The Sporting News*, August 18, 1948: 6.

10  "No Immediate Expansion to West Coast Seen by B.R.," *The Sporting News*, December 8, 1954: 2.

11  J.G. Taylor Spink, "Lane Calls Ten-Club Foes Reactionary," *The Sporting News*, December 22, 1954: 1.

12  Edgar G. Brands, "Coast's Major Aspirations Dealt New Setback," *The Sporting News*, December 22, 1948: 2.

13  Dan Daniel, "Daredevil Dan Foresees Yank-Brave Repeat," *The Sporting News*, December 31, 1958: 16.

14  "Quotes," *The Sporting News*, May 28, 1958: 18.

15  Jack Gallagher, "Houston Ready to Join N.Y. in Bid to N.L.," *The Sporting News*, November 26, 1958: 3.

16  One of the parties the H.S.A. approached appears to have been Calvin Griffith. In July 1958, the Washington Senators owner petitioned the AL for approval to relocate his club to either Houston, Dallas, Toronto, or Minneapolis. The request was denied.

17  Shirley Povich, " 'Expand or Regret,' MacPhail Warns," *The Sporting News*, July 29, 1959: 1, 2.

18  Clark Nealon, "Two Houston Groups to Bid for Third Major Franchise," *The Sporting News*, June 3, 1959: 17.

19  Jerry (Jerome) Holtzman, "Big Timers Clearing Decks for Expansion," *The Sporting News*, August 10, 1960: 4.

20  "Giles Explains Why Houston Should Land N.L. Franchise," *The Sporting News*, October 19, 1960: 4.

21  Ray Gillespie, "500 Scouts to Hunt Houston Talent," *The Sporting News*, November 9, 1960: 1.

# BOB ASPROMONTE

## By Mark Wernick

April 10, 1962, is an important date in the history of baseball in Houston, Texas. It marked the culmination of years of effort by George Kirksey, Craig Cullinan Jr., Roy Hofheinz, and R.E. "Bob" Smith to bring major-league baseball to Houston. The newly minted Houston Colt .45s played their first official National League game, defeating the Chicago Cubs 11-2. Nine professional baseball aspirants staked their claim to be consistent starters for the Colt .45s. Of these nine, only Al Spangler and Bob Aspromonte carried over to the 1963 Opening Day lineup card. And only Aspromonte carried over to the 1964 Opening Day lineup card. Aspromonte's name appeared in every Opening Day starting lineup for Houston through 1968, the year he was traded to the Atlanta Braves. Aspromonte, fondly nicknamed "Aspro" in Houston, never started on Opening Day during his two seasons in Atlanta. After his trade to the New York Mets in 1971, Mets manager Gil Hodges penciled in Aspromonte as his Opening Day third baseman. Aspro batted .296 in eight Opening Day starts, going 8-for-27 with six runs and four RBIs.

Along with the distinction as the only original Colt .45 to appear in Houston's first seven Opening Day lineups, Aspromonte achieved a number of franchise firsts. He was the first expansion-draft selection to take the field for the team. He was their first batter, hitting leadoff in the first inning on Opening Day. Aspromonte connected for the first hit, singling to left field on the first pitch from Cubs starter Don Cardwell. Moments later, Aspromonte scored the first run when Al Spangler tripled down the right-field line. He drew the first base on balls and subsequently scored the second run; while he was on base, Roman Mejias hit the first home run. Aspro stole the first base, taking second base in the eighth inning ahead of Mejias' second home run of the day. He was the first player to reach base four times in a game, going 3-for-4 with a walk. On April 24, 1965, Aspromonte became the first Houston player to homer in the newly opened Astrodome against Vern Law as part of a 5-0 Astros victory over Pittsburgh.

Apart from these significant firsts, Bob Aspromonte also has two historic "lasts." In addition to being the final original Colt .45 to start on Opening Day for Houston in 1968, he was the last active player in baseball (he retired in 1971) to wear the uniform of the Brooklyn Dodgers. He had one at-bat for Brooklyn in September of 1956 as an 18-year-old fresh out of Lafayette High School.

Robert Thomas Aspromonte was born on June 19, 1938, to Angelo and Laura Aspromonte. He was the youngest of their three sons, all of whom played professional baseball. The Aspromonte boys were raised in the Bensonhurst section of Brooklyn, an area that was noted for its large constituency of Italian and Jewish residents. Aspromonte felt fortunate to be raised in a family and neighborhood where he was surrounded by athletic activities. Most of the Aspromonte household were fans of the Dodgers. Young Bob became the outlier when he developed a fondness for the New York Yankees, to the consternation of the rest of his clan.

As a child and teenager, Aspromonte participated in the Brooklyn Grasshopper, Little League, Kiwanis, Shore Parkway, and Coney Island baseball leagues, helping several of his teams to win titles. He was an all-star in the Coney Island and Kiwanis Leagues and won a Kiwanis Most Valuable Player Award. He captained his high-school baseball team during his senior year. In addition to baseball, Aspro played basketball at Lafayette. He came off the bench on his high-school varsity team, most of whose players were Jewish. Pertinent to that topic, Aspromonte noted that Hall of Famer Sandy Koufax was two years ahead of him at Lafayette, and won notoriety not in baseball but basketball. He said that Koufax, who pitched very little in high school, was the team's first baseman.

Aspro's brother Ken, older by seven years, played for six teams in a seven-year major-league career, followed by three seasons in Japan and another three managing the Cleveland Indians. Their father, Angelo, was a respected infielder in Brooklyn sandlot baseball in his youth. He augmented his youngest son's interest in baseball by taking him to an Interstate League game in 1950. Bob was 12 at the time. Their main objective was to see a talented 19-year-old outfielder play for Trenton. The prospect would hit .353 in 306 at-bats. His name was Willie Mays, and the following year, he was called up to the New York Giants.[1]

Aspromonte's fond memory of this experience with his father was complemented by the influence of his brother Charles. Eleven years his senior, Charles mentored Bob's early development. After playing baseball in Bensonhurst, Charles played at New York University on his way to the Kingston Colonials and Sunbury A's, Class-B affiliates in the Philadelphia Athletics farm system. Charles played with and tutored young Bob, even acting as his guide and agent to steer him professionally. Since Bob was only 17

when he tried out with the Dodgers, Charles had to act as his legal guardian through the signing process. This was not just because Angelo was busy supporting his family – he worked for 50 years as a brick mason – but because Charles, from his years in college and professional baseball, had acquired the know-how and confidence to guide his younger brother. As Aspro remembered, Angelo's support for his sons' athletic pursuits was a given: "I work. I want you guys to play baseball, because you have the talent."[2]

After graduating from high school, Aspromonte was invited to try out with five different teams, including the St. Louis Cardinals and the Brooklyn Dodgers. As an early admirer of Marty Marion, Aspromonte was tempted to sign with the Cardinals. Ultimately, however, he was influenced to sign with the Dodgers due to their strong local connection. It helped that his friend Michael A. Napoli Jr. also played in the Brooklyn system. Brooklyn scouts Al Campanis and Steve Lembo recommended Aspromonte to general manager Buzzie Bavasi, who invited him to his office to discuss terms. Aspro's first contract with the Dodgers was for $7,000 for two years.[3] Here is how Campanis assessed Aspromonte in his scouting report:

"What first attracted my attention was his batting form. He does things naturally up there. He's smart and always seems to know what he's doing. He's got an old head on a pair of young shoulders. And he not only can hit the long ball occasionally, but he seldom strikes out – usually gets a piece of the ball … that's an important asset."[4]

Initially, Aspromonte aspired to attend Long Island University to obtain a bachelor's degree in physical education. However, the urge to turn professional led him to the Dodgers, who signed him on July 20, 1956.[5] The Dodgers sent Aspromonte to Macon in the Class-A Sally League. After playing 13 games, he was recalled to Brooklyn in September. His big-league debut took place on September 19. As part of a 17-2 rout of the Cardinals, Walter Alston sent Aspro to pinch-hit for Sandy Amoros in the eighth inning. He laced a couple of line drives foul off pitcher Don Liddle before swinging for a third strike.

Although Aspromonte played only the one game for Brooklyn, he was invited to accompany the Dodgers on a goodwill trip to Japan after the World Series. Aspromonte spoke fondly of his memories of Japan.

Aspromonte was in awe of the famed Dodgers surrounding him. He remembered that Jackie Robinson was one of the first to take an interest in him. Robinson noticed that Aspromonte played infield with a large outfielder's glove. With unmistakable reverence, Aspromonte recalled that Robinson gave him one of his own smaller gloves and invited Aspro to work out with him. Sandy Koufax had preceded Aspromonte to the Dodgers by one year, and the Dodgers put the two Lafayette alumni together as roommates that September.

Military service remained compulsory for young American males in 1957. However, it marked the first year of a new program that allowed recruits to join the Army for six months before participating in the Reserve for the next seven years. Walter O'Malley's son Peter was one year older than Aspromonte. As Aspromonte remembered, he "really took care of me."[6] The elder O'Malley arranged for Peter and Aspro to enter the freshly launched Army Reserves program together.

Upon his discharge from the Army, Aspromonte was returned to Macon, where he hit .311 in 48 plate appearances. From there he was sent to Class-D Thomasville of the Georgia-Florida League. Aspro hit .263 in 228 plate appearances with a .344 on-base percentage, including five doubles, three triples, and his first professional home run. Impressively, he struck out only 14 times, demonstrating an early flair to make contact. In 1958, the Dodgers' first year in Los Angeles, they assigned Aspromonte to Class-A Des Moines of the Western League. Playing alongside Ron Fairly, he hit .263 in 531 plate appearances with only 48 strikeouts.

In 1959 the Dodgers promoted Aspromonte to their Triple-A International League affiliate in Montreal, where he was reunited with former Brooklyn teammate Sandy Amoros. As the Royals' starting shortstop, he hit .259 in 451 plate appearances. Also on that Montreal team was a 31-year-old pitcher named Tom Lasorda, who went 12-8 with a 3.83 ERA.

After batting .412 with the Dodgers in spring training, Aspromonte finally made the Dodgers' Opening Day roster in 1960. With Maury Wills at shortstop, Jim Gilliam at second base, and Charlie Neal and Daryl Spencer as fellow utility players, Aspro's playing time was limited to 21 games. Aspromonte demonstrated a flash of his potential at Los Angeles Coliseum on May 5. He went 4-for-5, including his first big-league home run. In the bottom of the 10th, Aspromonte hit a bases-loaded, two-out, two-strike single to drive home Wally Moon with the winning run.

Then Aspromonte went 5-for-37, prompting the Dodgers to option him to Triple-A St. Paul, where he could see more playing time. There he blossomed. He hit .329 with a .390 on-base percentage and 27 extra-base hits in 411 plate appearances, striking out only 38 times. After Aspromonte hit .330 in the Venezuelan Occidental League, missing the batting title on the season's last day, the Dodgers kept him in Los Angeles for the entire 1961 season. Still, he took the field for only 15 games and only five as a starter. He was not getting the playing time he needed in order to develop.

Then the National League expanded to include new teams in New York and Houston. On October 10, Houston general manager Paul Richards won the coin flip to determine who would pick first in the expansion draft. Aspro was selected as the third overall pick.[7] Though initially disappointed not to have been chosen by New York, as it would have brought him home, he soon warmed to the idea of playing in Houston.

In his first season in Houston as the Colt .45s' third baseman, he played in 149 games in 1962, including 142 at third base. His slash line was .266/.332 with 18 doubles, 4 triples, and 11 homers. Although they trailed the pennant-winning San Francisco Giants by 36½ games, these numbers do not tell the whole story of "the little expansion team that could."

The Giants' record at Candlestick Park was 61-21, and the Colt .45s were the only team to win a season series there in 1962 with a record of 5-4. Only a pair of solo home runs by Willie Mays and Ed Bailey in the season finale gave the Giants a 2-1 victory and prevented the Los Angeles Dodgers from advancing straight to a World Series vs. the Yankees. Aspromonte went 2-for-4 in a losing effort for Dick Farrell. Despite a 64-96 eighth-place finish, Houston's expansion team was in position to affect the outcome of the pennant race on the last day of the season.

While finishing 1963 with a record of, 66-96, the season proved to be more difficult for both the Colt .45s and Bob Aspromonte. He played in only 136 games, with a .214/.276 slash line. Star reliever Jim Umbricht was diagnosed with cancer and began treatments at Houston's M.D. Anderson Hospital; he died on April 8, 1964.[8] Despite these lows, the season had its highlights for Aspromonte. On May 12, the Colt .45s behind Don Nottebart trailed the Cubs 1-0 entering the bottom of the ninth inning. With two outs, 19-year-old rookie Rusty Staub tripled to drive home Johnny Temple and send the game into extra innings. Meanwhile, Umbricht, pitching while fighting cancer, preserved the tie with two scoreless innings. Then in the bottom of the 10th, Aspromonte hit a walk-off homer off Bob Buhl.

Also in 1963, an unusual and extraordinary human-interest story involving Aspromonte and a 9-year-old boy named Billy Bradley reached its zenith. The story actually began on April 30, 1962. While drinking water at a fountain in El Dorado, Arkansas, Billy was struck by lightning. Although he survived, the bolt robbed him of his vision. Billy's family took him to Houston for ophthalmology treatments with Dr. Louis Girard. While undergoing a series of surgeries to restore his eyesight, Billy listened to the Colt .45s on the radio. He soon adopted Bob Aspromonte as his favorite player.

Eventually the Colt .45s were notified of Billy's request for Aspromonte to visit him at Houston's Methodist Hospital. Accompanied by teammate Joe Amalfitano, Aspro visited Billy on May 7, 1962, bringing a glove, a ball, a transistor radio, and Colt .45s pajamas as gifts. Before the players left, Billy asked Aspromonte to hit a home run that night against the Dodgers. Aspro countered that while he was not a home-run hitter, he would try to honor the boy's request.[9]

Houston built a 5-0 lead by the second inning, only to trail the Dodgers 6-5 in the seventh. With two runners on base in the bottom half of the inning, Aspromonte came to bat. He was 2-for-3 to that point with two singles. On a 3-and-1 pitch from lefty Pete Richert, Aspromonte lined a three-run homer to provide the margin of victory in Houston's 9-6 win. At the same time, he consummated the improbable scenario of delivering on an offer to hit a home run for a child.

The Bradley family returned to Houston in 1963 for additional eye treatments. Aspromonte took them to lunch on June 11, and again Billy asked Aspromonte to hit a home run for him. Battling chronic back pain, Aspromonte was struggling through perhaps his worst season in uniform. Although batting a feeble .198, he nevertheless told Billy that he would try to deliver another home run for him against the Cubs.[10]

The Cubs and the Colt .45s went into extra innings deadlocked at 2-2. Pitcher Hal Woodeshick led off the 10th inning with a single against Lindy McDaniel and was lifted for pinch-runner Bob Lillis. Ernie Fazio bunted and

a throwing error by Ernie Banks advanced the runners to scoring position. Brock Davis was walked to load the bases for the struggling Aspromonte. One-for-four on the night with a single, Aspro faced his final chance to deliver on Billy's request. Accordingly, he hit a 2-and-2 pitch on the screws, delivering a walk-off grand slam to left field. A humbled Aspromonte averred that he could not have done this on his own, that he had help coming from somewhere.[11]

On July 26 Billy Bradley was in Houston again to see Dr. Girard. Once again he met with Aspromonte and once again he requested a home run. Aspro was homerless since the grand slam, and his hitting had deteriorated even further to .176 over his last 20 games. This time Aspro told Billy he was pushing his luck and suggested instead that Billy settle for a couple of base hits.

By this time Billy's eyesight had been partially restored and he was able to watch the game at Colt Stadium. Tracy Stallard of the Mets had loaded the bases with Al Spangler, Rusty Staub, and Jimmy Wynn when Aspromonte came to bat in the bottom of the first. Astonishing even himself, Aspro once again hit a grand slam.[12]

Houston broadcaster Gene Elston was aware of the human-interest story involving Billy Bradley and referred to it on the air. The game was interrupted to retrieve the ball and Aspromonte and Bradley hugged. A New York sportswriter asked Aspromonte, "Are you doing it for the boy, or is the boy doing it for you?" Aspro replied, "It's almost spooky, isn't it? But if Bill will stick around, I'll be tempted to buy him a season ticket. It's a great thrill to see how happy it makes the boy."[13]

After the 1963 season, Aspromonte undertook a series of eight rigorous daily 90-minute isometric exercises in his Brooklyn home to strengthen the "worn out" lumbar disc in his lower back. At times the pain was severe enough to prevent him from bending down. After the offseason of rest and exercises, the acute pain from which he suffered in 1963 had largely been eliminated.[14]

Indeed, Aspromonte recovered to have one of his best seasons in 1964. His slash line over 608 plate appearances in 157 games was .280/.329/.392. He set career highs with 69 RBIs and 12 home runs, including two more grand slams. He led the Colt .45s with a .280 batting average, and he had a .973 fielding percentage, still (as of 2018) a record for Houston third basemen, and a National League record at that time.[15] In 1964 the Colt .45s duplicated their 1963 record of 66-96 and their ninth-place finish, but the resurgent Bob Aspromonte with a 66-point gain in batting average trailed only the 70-point gain by teammate Bob Lillis as the National League's most improved hitters.[16]

The Houston Chapter of the Baseball Writers Association of America voted Aspromonte as the team's Most Valuable Player for 1964. Although both the Reds and Dodgers sought him in a trade, Vivian Smith, wife of co-owner Bob Smith, put the kibosh on any trade talk for Aspromonte.[17]

In 1965, the club abandoned Colt Stadium, moving into a space-age sports facility. Officially known as the Harris County Domed Stadium, the venue quickly became known as the Astrodome as the team was rechristened the Astros. Lum Harris was now the manager and by season's end, Bob Smith would sell his share of the club to Roy Hofheinz.

On April 9, 1965, a crowd of 47,879 watched Mickey Mantle hit the first home run in the inaugural exhibition game in the Astrodome as the American League champion New York Yankees suffered a 2-1, 12-inning exhibition loss to the nascent Astros. Three days later, the Astros hosted the Philadelphia Phillies in the first official game at the Dome. Aspromonte caught the ceremonial first pitch from astronaut Alan Shepard.[18] Aspro managed one infield single in four at-bats in a 2-0 loss to Philadelphia. After an eight-day road trip that ended with a win, the Astros set a team record by embarking on a 10-game winning streak including nine at home. Aspromonte expressed great satisfaction from contributing 11 game-winning hits to the Astros cause in 1965.[19]

After winning 12 of their first 18, the Astros soon plummeted to familiar territory, ninth place, with a record of 65-97. Though Aspromonte's slash line was a respectable .263/.310 in 152 games, he managed only five home runs and 52 RBIs in the pitcher-friendly confines of "the Eighth Wonder of the World." Early in the year, he received an encouraging letter from Billy Bradley. Following his surgeries, Billy's eyesight recovered. With the help of corrective lenses, Billy resumed playing baseball. The letter contained a newspaper article with a note that read, "This one's for you, Bob. I didn't hit you a home run, but I pitched you a no-hitter."[20]

Roy Hofheinz fired both manager Lum Harris and general manager Paul Richards after the 1965 season. Under new manager Grady Hatton, the Astros improved to eighth place in 1966, with a record of 72-90. Aspromonte's solid fielding continued, with a National League-leading .962 for third basemen. His batting tapered to .252/.297 with 52 RBIs and 8 home runs, but he added two more grand slams to his final career total of six, a Houston record that stood until July 25, 2011, when Carlos Lee hit his seventh grand slam in an Astros uniform.[21]

In 1967 Aspromonte enjoyed his finest year in a Houston uniform. He set career highs with 24 doubles and a .294/.354/.401 slash line in 137 games. Along with 6 home runs and 58 RBIs, he matched his 1963 high of five triples. The Astros announced that H.B. "Spec" Richardson was the new general manager on July 27 in midst of a ninth-place, 69-93 campaign.

Aspro's playing time began to diminish in 1968 as young third baseman Doug Rader was being groomed for the position. Even so, Aspromonte participated in yet another historic event on April 15, 1968. Astros ace Don Wilson and Tom Seaver of the Mets locked horns in a tremendous duel that contributed to a record that has lasted half a century. Seaver was pitching a two-hit shutout when he was pulled from the game after 10 innings. Wilson, meanwhile, pitched a shutout of his own through nine. Then the bullpens took over, holding the stalemate for what amounted to almost another two full games. When the Astros came to bat in the bottom of the 24th inning, the score was still deadlocked at 0-0. Norm Miller singled off pitcher Les Rohr, Jim Wynn was walked intentionally, Rusty Staub grounded out, and John Bateman was intentionally walked, when Aspromonte came to the plate.

Aspro was 0-for-8 with one walk. Still adept at making contact, he laced a grounder to short that Al Weis failed to handle cleanly, allowing Miller to score the winning run. Bob Aspromonte had a walk-off E-6, and the Astros defeated the Mets 1-0 in what remains as of 2018 the longest reciprocal shutout by two major-league teams.[22]

By 1968, America had entered one of the most turbulent periods in its history. Civil unrest began to offset the promise of Camelot and the Great Society. On June 6, only two months after Dr. Martin Luther King was assassinated, presidential candidate Robert F. Kennedy was shot and killed in Los Angeles.

President Lyndon B. Johnson declared June 9, the day after Kennedy's funeral, as a national day of mourning. Baseball Commissioner William Eckert ordered that no games on June 8 should start until after the burial, and that while games would continue on June 9, Eckert proclaimed that any player could "pay respects" if desired by sitting out to observe the day of mourning.[23]

Despite the option given the players by the commissioner, players who opted out were threatened with consequences. The Astros were scheduled to host the Pirates as Aspromonte, Staub, player representative Dave Giusti, and Pittsburgh's Maury Wills all opted not to play. Giusti noted that the entire team voted to abstain, but rescinded amid a threat of "very definite economic pressures" from GM Richardson.[24] A question of team retaliation for Aspro's stance on the Robert Kennedy matter arose. His playing time continued to decrease, and with it came a decline in production. His 1968 slash line fell to .225/.285/.284.

Perhaps hard feelings lingered over these June events. Giusti was traded to St. Louis. Staub was soon traded to Montreal. By 1968, Bob Aspromonte was the only remaining member of the original 1962 Colt .45s still with the franchise. One of the team's most popular players in its short history, Aspro was their second drafted player, their first-ever batter and position player, and the last player from the team's first Opening Day lineup. On December 4 that player was gone, traded to the Atlanta Braves for Marty Martinez.

With Paul Richards as the Braves' general manager and Lum Harris their manager, Aspromonte was not the first Houston alumnus to find his way to Atlanta. He was reunited with former teammates Sonny Jackson, Ken Johnson, and Claude Raymond in the Braves' fourth season in Georgia. The 1969 season also marked the first in the divisional era. Both the American and National Leagues had realigned to each form two divisions, East and West, of six teams apiece. Atlanta and Houston found themselves in the National League West.

Since Clete Boyer was the Braves' regular third baseman, Bob Aspromonte became a part-time player, filling in in left field, third base, second base, and shortstop. His slash line was .253/.304/.348 in 215 plate appearances with 3 home runs and 24 RBIs. Every National League West team except San Diego factored into the pennant race and as late as September 10, Aspro's former team was two games out of first with a record of 75-65. But the Astros declined after that to finish at exactly .500, while Aspro's new team won the first-ever National League West Division title with a record of 93-69.

The 1969 National League Championship Series marked Aspromonte's first and only postseason experience. The Braves' opponents were the unlikely New York Mets. Having lost at least 89 games and finished no higher than ninth place in their first seven seasons, little was expected from the Mets in 1969. As late as May 27, the Mets won-lost record stood at 18-23. However, they soon caught fire and by August, they passed the Chicago Cubs to finish at 100-62.

Aspromonte's postseason experience was limited to three pinch-hit appearances and no action in the field. In Game One, in Atlanta, he grounded out for Phil Niekro in the eighth inning as Tom Seaver picked up a 9-5 decision. Aspro was again sent in as a pinch-hitter in Game Two, in Atlanta. Batting for Cecil Upshaw, he popped up in the eighth inning. With Ron Taylor taking the 11-6 victory, the Braves faced elimination as the series headed to New York. Aspromonte once again pinch-hit for Upshaw, this time facing Nolan Ryan to lead off the ninth inning. The young flamethrower retired Aspro on a pop fly. Two outs later, the Mets had swept the Braves and went on to face the Baltimore Orioles in the World Series.

In 62 games as a reserve player in 1970, most of Aspromonte's time in the field was spent at third base, with a few games at shortstop, left field, and first base. In 142 plate appearances, his slash line was .213/.282/.236 with no home runs and 7 RBIs. Atlanta fell to a 76-86 record and a fifth-place finish in the National League West.

Aspro had maintained a friendly connection with Gil Hodges during the decade since they were teammates with the Dodgers. After Joe Foy's disappointing campaign in 1970, the Mets were in the market to upgrade at third base. Hodges turned toward his former teammate, and Aspromonte was happy to play for his old friend and mentor. Having left Foy unprotected, the Mets lost him to the Washington Senators in the Rule 5 Draft. Meanwhile, the Mets traded pitcher Ron Herbel to Atlanta for Aspromonte. Aspro had worn number 14 for his entire career to honor Hodges, and this became the basis of some good-humored teasing when Aspromonte told Hodges he wanted to wear the number for the Mets. Hodges was not surrendering 14, and he assigned Aspro number 2.[25]

Aspromonte was given a renewed opportunity as a starter in 1971 as Hodges penciled him into the Opening Day lineup at third base, his eighth and final Opening Day start. After a slow beginning, Aspro peaked on May 18 with a 3-for-4 outing against former Atlanta teammate

Mike McQueen that included two solo home runs, bringing his batting average to .283. He was still hitting a respectable .270 in June when a calf muscle injury interrupted his momentum. Aspro was limited to 38 games in the second half of the season and was unable to sustain his prior level of performance.

On September 25, Aspromonte pinch-hit for left fielder Dave Marshall in the bottom of the 15th inning to score Tim Foli from second base with the game-winning run. The walk-off proved to be Aspro's final hit, in his next to last major-league game. His last appearance took place on September 28 when he started at third base. Hitless in three official at-bats, Aspro drove in his final run when Cleon Jones scored on his sacrifice fly in a 5-2 loss to the Cardinals and Steve Carlton. Aspromonte's 1971 slash line was .225/.285/.301 in 104 games, with 5 home runs and 33 RBIs.

The Mets finished a disappointing 1971 season with a record of 83-79, tied for third place with the Cubs. Needing to upgrade at third base again for 1972, the Mets traded Nolan Ryan to the California Angels for Jim Fregosi, releasing Aspromonte. Sparky Anderson still thought Aspro could play and invited him to spring training with the Reds in 1972. Although Aspromonte was featured on a 1972 Topps card with Cincinnati, he failed to make the team and hung up his spikes.[26]

Aspro's final career slash line was .252/.308/.336. He finished with 1,103 hits and 60 home runs. The disciplined hitter's strikeout totals in his eight seasons as a regular ranged from 44 to 63, topping 60 only once. By contrast, 20 major-league players had 60 or more strikeouts in the first two months of the 2018 season.

After retiring as a player, Aspro decided to make Houston his year-round home, ultimately persuading both of his brothers to join him. They formed a partnership to obtain a Coors distributorship in 1975, which they named Aspromonte-Coors Distributing Company.[27]

Bob Aspromonte managed the distributorship, which by 1981 was valued in the range of eight figures. He implemented several innovative business strategies that improved both company profitability and personnel loyalty and morale. He ran Aspromonte-Coors until 2000, when he sold his majority interest. Aspromonte remained active in the Houston community, lending his name to the YMCA, the Lions Eye Bank Foundation, and Houston Eye Associates.

There is an epilogue to the Bill Bradley story. In 2003 Aspromonte was blinded in one eye after a car battery exploded in his face. When Bradley, now 51, learned of the injury, he contacted Aspro to offer support. The same ophthalmologist who restored Bradley's sight, Dr. Louis Girard, operated on Aspromonte and eventually helped him to overcome substantial damage to his eye.[28]

Aspromonte remained a revered figure throughout the Houston community. He said he was particularly proud of receiving the Ellis Island Medal of Honor, a humanitarian award honoring American diversity and fostering tolerance, respect, and understanding among religious and ethnic groups.[29]

In 2005 Aspro was inducted into the Texas Baseball Hall of Fame. In 2011, Bob and Ken were both elected to the National Italian American Sports Hall of Fame in Chicago. For the silver anniversary of the franchise in 2012, the Astros created a Walk of Fame outside Minute Maid Park. Their first honoree was Bob Aspromonte: "Aspro the Astro." And on April 10, 2012, the 50th anniversary of the franchise's first game, Aspromonte threw out the ceremonial first pitch. Away from the game, he retained a powerful reverence for the bond of family, which includes his brothers along with three generations of nieces and nephews.[30]

"In all my years in baseball," remarked fellow Houston baseball legend Larry Dierker, "I have never known a player with more class than Bob Aspromonte."[31]

## Sources

In addition to the sources cited in the Notes, the author relied on Baseball-Reference.com and Retrosheet.org.

Thanks for assistance to Bob Aspromonte, Mark Kanter, Maxwell Kates, and Liubov Wernick.

## Notes

1 Author interview with Bob Aspromonte, February 24, 2018. Unless otherwise indicated, all direct quotations or unattributed memories come from this interview.

2 Interview with Bob Aspromonte, February 24, 2018.

3 Joe Reichler and Budd Theobald, "Bob Aspromonte" in Here Come the Colts (New York: Prentice-Hall Inc., 1962), 10.

4 Ibid. Cockroach, "From Brooklyn to the Bayou City: Bob Aspromonte" on Astros County: Your Neighborhood Astros Blog and Grill, January 27, 2017, astroscounty.com; accessed June 3, 2018.

5 Cockroach.

6 Interview with Bob Aspromonte, February 24, 2018.

7 Robert Reed, *A Six-Gun Salute: An Illustrated History of the Houston Colt .45s, 1962-1964* (Houston: Lone Star Books, 1999), 59.

8 Bill Brown and Mike Acosta, *Deep in the Heart: Blazing a Trail from Expansion to World Series* (Houston: Bright Sky Press, 2013), 29.

9 Brown, 31.

10 Ibid.

11 Reed, 124.

12 Ibid.

13 Ibid.

14 Mickey Herskowitz, "Aspromonte Leaves Drydock – Worn-Out Back Disc Repaired," *The Sporting News*, February 1, 1964: 23.

15 Cockroach.

16 Chuck Pickard, "Colts' Lillis Boosted Bat Mark 70 Points – Majors' Best Gain," The Sporting News, November 7, 1964: 25.

17 Clark Nealon, "Houston Picks MVP – Aspro the Astro," The Sporting News, January 23, 1965: 7.

18 Cockroach.

19 Interview with Bob Aspromonte, February 24, 2018.

20 Reed, 124.

21 Brown, 30.

22  Norm Miller, To All My Friends ... from Norm Who? (Houston: Double Play Productions, 2009), i.

23 Cockroach.

24 Associated Press, "Houston's Staub, Aspro Don't Play," Dallas Morning News, June 10, 1968: 2.

25 "National League Rosters, Uniform Numbers, " The Sporting News, April 17, 1971: 38.

26 1972 Topps #659, Brooklyn: Topps Chewing Gum Inc., 1972.

27 Rich Marazzi and Len Fiorito, "Bob Aspromonte" in Aaron to Zuverink, (New York: Avon Books, 1984), 16.

28 Brown, 31.

29 neco.org/medal-of-honor.

30 Interview with Bob Aspromonte, February 24, 2018.

31 Mickey Herskowitz, "Players Don't Come Classier Than Aspromonte," Houston Chronicle, February 14, 2001.

# EDDIE BRESSOUD

## By Bill Nowlin

Eddie Bressoud played over 1,000 big-league games as a shortstop in a 12-year career, primarily for the New York and San Francisco Giants, and the Boston Red Sox. He played 10 or more games at each of the other three infield positions, and one inning in left field. He was a .252 career batter who had his best season in 1962, after he was the first selection of the Houston Colt .45s in the 1961 expansion draft, but was then traded to the Red Sox for Don Buddin.

Bressoud was born in Los Angeles on May 2, 1932. His father, Charles Bressoud, had been born in South America – in Lima, Peru, of French parents; he came to the United States in 1917 arriving via Colon, Panama.[1] At some point he met and married New Jersey native Josephine Mibielle. The two had seven children. Edward Francis Bressoud was the fourth-born. Charles work as a clerk in the sales department of a lumber firm and then as its purchasing agent.

Eddie attended schools in the Los Angeles area, going to Mount Carmel High at first but graduating from the city's George Washington High School in 1950. He was named All-City in baseball. Bressoud also played American Legion ball and some semipro baseball.

He later attended El Camino Junior College and Los Angeles City College, and received a bachelor of science degree in physical education from UCLA. While playing ball, he went to San Jose State in the offseasons and earned a master's degree in education. All along, he had his mind on being prepared to earn a living. In 1962, midway through his playing career, he said, "I'll play baseball as long as it's profitable, and when it isn't, I'll switch to teaching and coaching."[2] He had said, "I've seen too many players wind up their careers unprepared for the future."[3]

Right after high school, however, Bressoud had been signed to a New York Giants contract. Accounts differ as to the signing scout, but it appears he was signed by Walter "Dutch" Ruether, on the advice of Evo Pusich.[4] "That's exactly right," Bressoud said. "But Evo Pusich did all the work for it. He signed Mike McCormick, Chuck Essegian, myself, and probably two or three others who reached the big leagues. He was a spectacular man."[5] He was reportedly given $4,000.[6]

Bressoud's first professional assignment was to the 1950 Springfield (Ohio) Giants in the Class-D Ohio-Indiana League. He got into 70 games, batting .240. In both

1951 and 1952 he played Class-A baseball in the Western League for the Sioux City Soos. He hit .230 in 1951 with 53 RBIs in 149 games, but led the league in fielding by shortstops with a .949 fielding percentage. In 1952, he appeared in 155 games and boosted his average to .255, with 68 RBIs, while leading the league in putouts (302), assists (487), and double plays (105). He was named to the All-Star second team.

The Korean War was underway and the United States armed forces needed men; Bressoud served in the Marine Corps from January 1953 to January 1955. Five months into his service, he married high-school sweetheart Eleanor Griesser on June 6 in Los Angeles. He played baseball in the Marines into August 1953, even playing for the Marine Corps Recruit Depot team in the all-Marine championships in Quantico, but then spent 11 months stationed on the side of Mount Fuji in Japan.

When Bressoud returned Stateside, it was to spring training with the Giants in 1955 and then to Triple A, playing in the American Association for the Minneapolis Millers, and it seemed he hadn't skipped a beat, either at bat on the field. He hit .251, with 19 homers, and drove in 74 runs. The Millers won the American Association pennant by eight games over second-place Omaha, and then the Little World Series against the International League champions. Despite finishing 18½ games out of first place, the Rochester Red Wings won the I.L. playoffs. Minneapolis beat Rochester, four games to three.

It looked as if 1956 was shaping up to be a good year. Bressoud was seen by some as a possible successor to Alvin Dark at shortstop for the New York Giants.[7] He himself had his sights set on taking the shortstop position away from Alvin Dark on the Giants, and didn't hesitate to say so. Louis Effrat of the *New York Times* wrote, "Some kids aim high. Ed Bressoud, for example, believes that at the age of 23 and after only one season of Triple-A ball, he is ready to become a regular with the Giants." Effrat averred that "there is nothing brash about Bressoud. He is not a pop-off guy."[8] He was confident in his own abilities, and by the end of March it was a possibility that manager Bill Rigney would have Dark moved to third base and Bressoud installed at short.[9] It wasn't to be – at least not right away. On April 8, Bressoud was assigned to Minneapolis once more. Nonetheless, sports pundits had seen him as "the most captivating rookie the Giants had presented in their camp for years."[10]

On June 14, Alvin Dark was one of eight players in a 4-for-4 trade with the St. Louis Cardinals; Red Schoendienst was the Giants' principal target. Because they knew they had Bressoud, they felt freer to make the trade. Bressoud was called up from Minneapolis – and had his major-league debut that very same day.

The Giants were in Milwaukee. Bressoud was the starting shortstop, batting second in the order. Warren Spahn of the Braves struck him out his first time up. He reached on an error in the third inning, but picked up his first big-league RBI on the play. He was 1-for-4 in the game, with a single in the eighth inning.

Bressoud collected one or more base hits in each of his first six games. He played fairly steadily through August 14, though Daryl Spencer took over more of the work at shortstop. Bressoud was hitting .227 with 9 RBIs when the Giants elected to send him on option back to Minneapolis on the 16th. He had appeared in 49 games. For the Millers, he hit .269 over a total of 86 games.

In 1957, Bressoud began the season again with Minneapolis, brought up to appear in his first Giants game on July 5, replacing Andre Rodgers.[11] He hit safely in his first five games back, homering to kick off a rally on July 5 and then with four consecutive multi-hit games. All in all, Bressoud fared much better at the plate in his 49 major-league games in 1957, batting .268, but drove in only one more run (10). He hit five homers, oddly hitting all of them in 21 days in July and then not another before the end of the season. He mostly played shortstop but appeared in an even dozen games at third base, albeit less effectively. He hit .286 in 81 games for Minneapolis; it was the last year he was in the minors.

The Giants moved the franchise to San Francisco beginning in 1958 and Bressoud played there through 1961, almost exclusively at short.

Early in the 1958 season, personal tragedy struck. His wife, Eleanor, was hospitalized on April 24, the day before her 26th birthday, and died following surgery for a brain tumor on April 29. When initially hospitalized, Eddie was told the prognosis was as dire as could be. Rigney told him to go home and spend those last few days with his family. Even when he returned to the Giants, Rigney said, "he still was like a man having a bad dream."[12] Bressoud moved into his sister's home, where she could take care of his and Eleanor's two children, Edward and Steven.

Bressoud had a living to earn and returned to work in the

second game of the May 4 doubleheader against the Pirates, winning the game for the Giants with an RBI single off Roy Face in the bottom of the 10th. He appeared in only 66 games that year, and hit .263.

In 1959 and 1960 Bressoud played in over 100 games. He hit .251 in 1959, but then .225 in 1960. It was 1959 that Bressoud considered one of his most exciting seasons in baseball. The Giants really made a run for the pennant, and were in first place from July 4 to as late as September 19, with only six games to play. The team had dipped to second place for just one day, July 29. They finished third, but it had been quite a run. Before the 1967 season began, he called it his biggest thrill in baseball, "being in the thick of the pennant fight."[13] Bressoud had 26 RBIs and he scored 36 runs, but his contribution to the team's success was noted in early September. An Associated Press story said that the day he'd become a regular, July 3, "brought a major turning point for the pennant contenders. He solidified a shaky infield and has contributed some timely hits."[14] In Bressoud's first 19 games as a regular, reported Bob Stevens, he hit .406 and was involved in 11 double plays.[15] After the Giants season was over, Stevens still credited him as key, writing of "Bressoud, without whose excellent play the Giants would never have been in a contending position."[16]

Still, Bressoud acknowledged his shortcomings at the plate, during spring training in 1960. "I'm not a good hitter, and I know it. I'm trying to improve, but I concentrate on my glove. A team like this, with a lot of hitting, can carry a guy like me."[17] There were some big hits, like the three-run inside-the-park home run on May 7 to beat the Pirates, 6-5. The 43 RBIs he had in 1960 were his high point with the Giants.

After the season, the Giants toured Japan, playing against the Tokyo All-Stars. Bressoud kicked off the October 30 game at Tokyo's legendary Korakuen Stadium with a "towering home run into the left-field bleachers in the first inning."[18]

In 1961, now playing for a Giants team that had Alvin Dark as manager, Bressoud saw much less work. He struggled with a nagging leg injury at the beginning of the season and appeared in just 59 games that year, batting .211. After the season, Bressoud said, "The manager evidently felt he had a better shortstop in Jose Pagan."[19]

On October 10, 1961, the expansion draft was held to help populate two new teams for the National League –

the Houston Colt .45s and the New York Mets. Houston won the coin toss and its first choice in the draft was Eddie Bressoud.[20]

Bressoud never played for Houston. In fact, he was earmarked for the Boston Red Sox even before the Colt .45s drafted him. In discussions during the World Series, Mike Higgins of the Red Sox talked with GM Paul Richards of Houston. The Sox had tried to obtain Bressoud from the Giants, but failed, and so a deal was struck whereby Houston would draft Bressoud and then swap him to the Red Sox for Boston shortstop Don Buddin. Buddin was no fan favorite in Boston, and Higgins was looking for someone steadier in the field. Columnist Dan Daniel quoted an unnamed Boston writer: "Mike Higgins would not have dared to open the 1962 season with Buddin still on his club. The fans hooted Don all last summer."[21]

The trade was done at the winter meetings, on November 26. Houston manager Harry Craft said Buddin was a good ballplayer "and he'll be a lot better ballplayer once he gets out of Boston."[22]

Bressoud was told the job was his unless he lost it. He was pleased at the opportunity. On first hearing he's been traded, he admitted, "I know so little about the American League that I'm not even sure Tom Yawkey is still alive and owns the Red Sox. ... I have never even seen Fenway Park, but I have certainly heard a lot about it. I'm strictly a right-handed pull hitter so maybe I can do some damage with that short left field wall."[23] He said playing for the Red Sox "is going to be like starting a new career."[24] Bressoud's former manager, Bill Rigney, with the Los Angeles Angels at the time, said, "I wish we could have landed him. He knows how to play shortstop and he'll be a threat in Fenway Park with his bat."[25] Richards later suggested that the trade he regretted most might be Bressoud-for-Buddin.[26]

Bressoud had remarried, in Alameda on February 7, 1959. He had met Carol Mathews, an airline stewardess, while on a flight with the Giants. They soon had a daughter, Michelle. In 1966, he talked about the need for a baseball spouse to be flexible and for children to be "socially mobile." He said, "A girl who married a ball player, under any circumstances, has to be an extraordinary woman. There are problems unique to our business. There is always a new environment, new companions, new shopping areas, new living conditions and most of all the constant uprooting of children from place to place. The children have to learn to be socially mobile. Mine, fortunately, have enough gray matter to understand the situation. Our kids are socially gregarious."[27] Maury Allen added that Bressoud took the family to Florida each spring, then to the city in which he was playing, and moved them back to California for the winter. He wanted to be involved in raising his children, and not leave that responsibility to his wife for the whole of the baseball season.[28]

In many respects, Bressoud's Red Sox years were his best years. He was nervous, of course, playing in his first AL game, and in as unique a field as Fenway Park. "When I went out to my position, I was a bit shaky. But once I made the first play, I felt at home."[29] In 1962, Bressoud played in 153 of the team's 160 games. He collected one or more base hits in each of his first 14 games. His .277 batting average was his best to date, as were his 14 homers, 40 doubles, 9 triples, and 79 runs scored. The 68 runs batted in proved to be the best season of his career. The downside was that the 28 errors he committed were the most among shortstops in the American League.

For the first time in nearly a decade, the Red Sox had a reliable shortstop. "All I wanted was a chance to play," he said. "The Red Sox made me feel like I was wanted. They told me that the shortstop job was mine."[30] Higgins said he wasn't surprised that he hit better in the American League, particularly playing half his games at Fenway Park. Bressoud said he liked both the better background for batters at Fenway, and the fact that the fans were closer to the players.[31] A year-end wrap-up concluded, "Bressoud was as valuable as any player on the team, as much as anyone the reason why the 1962 Sox finished eighth instead of tenth."[32]

Over the winters, Bressoud coached basketball and baseball at Los Altos High School.[33]

In 1963, he hit a career-high 20 homers, the most by any shortstop in the league; his batting average, though, dipped to under .250 for a good part of the season, though a strong finish brought it up to .260 at the end. Even at midseason, when Bressoud was hitting around .240, Boston columnist Arthur Sampson wrote, "Acquiring him was one of the most profitable transactions the Red Sox have made in some time."[34] Bressoud himself had written a column for the *Boston Globe* in April, an instructional one on playing his position.[35]

In 1964, with his master's degree now in hand, Bressoud was named to the American League All-Star team by manager Al Lopez, because Luis Aparicio was out with an injury. He did not see action in the game. He topped his own start-of-the-season hitting streak with one or more hits in each of his first 20 games. He didn't go without a hit until May 10. (He set a Red Sox record in the process, besting outfielder Elmer Smith, who had hit in his first 18 games back in 1922.)[36] His batting average at year's end was .293, the best of his career and the highest on the Red Sox that year. His 86 runs scored also led the team and stand as a personal career-best.

Bressoud had one last year with the Red Sox in 1965, under new manager Billy Herman. There was talk before the season of trading him when his value was high, and the Red Sox taking their chances with rookie Rico Petrocelli at shortstop. Bressoud's average fell off to .226 in 328 plate appearances in 1965, down from 644 the year before. He played in 107 games, just a few more than rising Red Sox star Petrocelli.

After the season, Bressoud was traded to the New York Mets on November 30 for outfielder Joe Christopher. It was not a major move for either team. Indeed, suggested United Press International, it was "a deal which produced nothing but a lot of yawns."[37]

The 1966 Mets finished in ninth place (so, for that matter, did the Red Sox.) Though originally seen as a utilityman, Bressoud became a solid member of the team, third in homers, fifth in both runs scored and runs batted in, but he finished seventh in batting average (.225) and struck out 107 times, 26 more than anyone else on the team.

Bressoud started wearing eyeglasses toward the middle of the season. On June 10, he had a game in which he hit two homers, one of them a three-run homer. He'd fought wearing them initially, since they would steam up on him or otherwise be uncomfortable, but the order came down from the front office and he complied. "I see better with the glasses," he said. "I can pick up the ball real well now. For a long time, I had been unable to see the spin on the ball, but I can see that now, too." Once he got the order, though, "There no longer was any choice. I had to wear them. You'd be surprised how that changed things. From then on, they didn't seem to bother me."[38] On June 15 and June 17, he hit another two three-run homers.

For the Mets, he played seven or more games at each of the four infield positions. "I like the idea of moving around," he said. "It improves my value."[39]

In the offseason, he worked substitute teaching in the

Fremont and Mountain View/Los Altos high-school districts, often overseeing lunch periods and school senate meetings. He even promoted a Big Mama Thornton concert.[40]

Just before the 1967 season, on April 1, Bressoud was traded to the St. Louis Cardinals as part of a five-player transaction that was as much as anything a trade of Bressoud for infielder Jerry Buchek.[41] The Cardinals wanted him as a backup for shortstop Dal Maxvill. Bressoud didn't see much playing time, mostly being used as a late-inning replacement. In contrast to the 1962 and 1964 seasons, when he started off with hitting streaks, in his first 29 plate appearances in 1967, extending over 20 games and all the way through June 7, he failed to get a base hit, though he did draw six walks. Finally, on June 8, he singled to left field in the bottom of the fifth and came around to score.

Bressoud was happy with the Cardinals, though, saying, "This is the greatest spirit I've ever seen around a ballclub, and I've been around 16 years. I've never been happier with any other club, and that's saying a lot when you know you're not going to play much."[42]

It was a tough year at the plate, all in all, though. Bressoud hit .134 for the season (in 76 plate appearances over 52 games) and he had only one RBI – a home run in the bottom of the third inning on August 9 against the Dodgers. He came up to the plate in the bottom of the 10th with the bases loaded and nobody out. He popped up to first baseman Wes Parker, who dropped the ball. The run scored, but it was unearned and not an RBI.

The Cardinals won the 1967 National League pennant and played the Red Sox in the World Series. Bressoud made the roster and appeared for last-inning defense in two games, Game Two and Game Five, for one inning each time. He had no fielding chances, but on October 12 celebrated becoming a world champion as St. Louis beat Boston in the Game Seven finale, 7-2. That very day, Bressoud announced his retirement. He began work as head baseball coach for De Anza Junior College of Cupertino, California.[43]

It was the end of Bresoud's career as a professional ballplayer, but a wonderful way to end a career. He said, "Winning this World Series meant far, far more to me than I could ever say."[44]

In late November, Roland Hemond of the California

Angels signed Bressoud as scout, to work under Rosey Gilhousen.[45] "The person who got me the job," Bressoud explained, "was Bill Rigney, who I had played for."[46] He scouted for two years, during which time he also, twice, managed a minor-league team, both times taking over in midseason. In 1968, he replaced Tom Sommers managing Idaho Falls (Pioneer League) In June 1969, he was named manager of the San Jose Bees (California League), taking over for Tom Morgan.[47]

Bressoud's post-baseball career was devoted to teaching. "I went to school in the offseason for 14 years. I got my master's degree and I started coaching for DeAnza Community College after we played in the 1967 World Series. I taught there for 24 years. I retired in 1990."[48]

As of the time of the July 2017 interview, Ed and Carol Bressoud were married for 58 years. "I'm looking at her right now," he said, "and she's spectacular."

One of his sons is currently "a cowboy and the other one is the CFO of a newspaper chain." A cowboy? "He was working with PG&E in their geothermal plant up in the mountains, and he had a ranch up there."[49]

## Sources

In addition to the sources noted in this biography, the author also accessed Bressoud's player file and player questionnaire from the National Baseball Hall of Fame, the *Encyclopedia of Minor League Baseball*, Retrosheet.org, Baseball-Reference.com, Rod Nelson of SABR's Scouts Committee, and the SABR Minor Leagues Database, accessed online at Baseball-Reference.com.

### Notes

1 Speaking of his father, Ed Bressoud said, "His father [Ed's paternal grandfather] was a pharmacist, and the company sent him to Peru. He was there at the time of the war in 1917 and the French government wanted to bring him into the army. He decided to go to the United States instead." Interview with Ed Bressoud on July 27, 2017.

2 Hy Hurwitz, "Astute Eddie Works Toward Master's Degree in Education," *The Sporting News*, June 9, 1962: 3.

3 Hy Hurwitz, "Bressoud Likens Trade to Starting New Career," *Boston Globe*, December 10, 1961: 91.

4 Joe King, "That Bright Flash on Giants' Roster Is Eddie Bressoud," *The Sporting News*, April 4, 1956: 15, 16. See also Margery Miller Welles, "Bressoud, the Giants' New Infielder," *Christian Science*

*Monitor,* July 6, 1956: 19.

5  Interview with Ed Bressoud on July 27, 2017.

6  Jack McDonald, "Giants' Gems Bargain Counter Pickups," *The Sporting News,* August 19, 1959: 1, 6. Bressoud explained that "$2,000 was the signing bonus and then I got $125 a month for six months." Bressoud interview.

7  "Who Is Ed Bressoud? Giants Next Shortstop," *New York World Telegram & Sun,* February 3, 1956.

8  Louis Effrat, "Rookie on Giants Seeks Dark's Job," *New York Times,* February 29, 1956: 41.

9  Louis Effrat, "Rookie Looms as Giants' Shortstop," *New York Times,* March 31, 1956: 9.

10 Joe King, "That Bright Flash on Giants' Roster is Eddie Bressoud."

11 Joe King, "Phenom Rodgers Fades, Bressoud Back with Giants," *The Sporting News,* July 17, 1957: 11.

12 Lester J. Biederman, "Bressoud Starts New Life for Himself, Giants," *Pittsburgh Press,* July 20, 1958.

13 Biographical summary, 1967, in Bressoud's player file at the National Baseball Hall of Fame.

14 Associated Press, "Ed Bressoud Big Factor in Giants' Race to Top," *Greensboro* (North Carolina) *Daily News,* September 9, 1959: 15.

15 Bob Stevens, "Bressoud Bounces From Wings, Grabs Spotlight on Giants," *The Sporting News,* July 22, 1959: 9.

16 Bob Stevens, "Giants Fall Made Fans Feel Like Morning After," *The Sporting News,* October 7, 1959: 14, 18.

17 Jack Mann, "Bressoud Won't Give Up, in Baseball or Anything," *Newsday,* March 15, 1960.

18 Associated Press, "Homer Wins for Giants,' *Boston Record,* October 31, 1960: 15. The game-winning homer that earned the headline was Willie McCovey's in the top of the ninth.

19 Larry Claflin, "Bressoud Cheers Trade to Sox; Minoso Swapped to Cardinals," *Boston Record American,* November 28, 1961: 22.

20 Milton Richman, United Press International, "45 Players Picked by Mets and Colts," *Atlanta Daily World,* October 12, 1961: 7.

21 Dan Daniel, "Over the Fence," *The Sporting News,* December 13, 1961: 10. Buddin was characterized as "Bootin' Buddin" and it was said his license plate read "E-6." He made 23 errors in 1961 (for a .956 fielding percentage), while Bressoud – with a much better reputation as a fielder – committed 28 errors in 1962, though his fielding percentage was .965. Over the course of their careers, Buddin's fielding percentage was .954 and Bressoud's was .963.

22 Bob Holbrook, "Sox Trade Buddin for SS Bressoud," *Boston Globe,* November 27, 1961: 25. Holbrook's story details the talks leading up to the trade.

23 Larry Claflin.

24 Hy Hurwitz, "Bressoud Likens Trade to Starting New Career."

25 Ibid.

26 Mickey Herskowitz, "Colts Like Kasko – He's a Glove Whiz, Off-Field Comedian," *The Sporting News,* September 12, 1974: 18.

27 Maury Allen, "Teacher With Class," *New York Post,* July 22, 1966.

28 Ibid.

29 "'Shaky' Bressoud Feels at Home After 1st Play," *Boston Globe,* April 11, 1962: 47.

30 Dick O'Connor, "Small-Fry Cagers Coached, Polished by Tutor Bressoud," *The Sporting News,* January 12, 1963: 33.

31 James Enright, "'11 or 12' Pitchers Throw Spitters in A.L., Bressoud Says," *The Sporting News,* April 11, 1964: 20.

32 Ray Gillespie, "Diamond Facts and Facets," *The Sporting News,* December 22, 1962: 18.

33 Dick O'Connor, "Small-Fry Cagers Coached, Polished by Tutor Bressoud," *The Sporting News,* January 12, 1963: 33.

34 Arthur Sampson, "Pats' Acquisition Looks Good," *Boston Herald,* July 18, 1963: 37.

35 Eddie Bressoud, "Powerful, Accurate Arm SS Most Important Asset," *Boston Globe,* April 7, 1963: 79.

36 "Bressoud Tops Foxx Mark; Hits in 14 Straight Tilts," *The Sporting News,* May 9, 1962: 23.

37 UPI, "Twins Eye 2d Sacker, Hit a Snag," *Augusta* (Georgia) *Chronicle,* December 1, 1965: A13.

38 Barney Kremenko, "Specs Giving Vet Bressoud New Bat Vim," *The Sporting News,* June 25, 1966: 19.

39 Barney Kremenko, "Bressoud's Bat Breathing Fire Into Hit-Hungry Mets," *The Sporting News,* July 16, 1966: 40.

40 Dick O'Connor, "Action! Bressoud Is Always on Go in High School Post," *The Sporting News,* December 31, 1966: 41.

41 Dick Young, "Bing, Stan Swing That Deal; Bressoud Goes for Buchek," *New York Sunday News,* April 2, 1967: 132.

42 Neal Russo, "Did Card Flag Team Go Down with Gibson?" *The Sporting News,* July 29, 1967: 28.

43 "Bressoud to Coach JC Team," *San Francisco Examiner,* October 13, 1967.

44 Ibid.

45 UPI, "Bressoud Is Now Cal Angel Baseball Scout," *San Francisco Examiner,* November 27, 1967.

46 Interview with Ed Bressoud on July 27, 2017.

47 "Bressoud Takes Helm," *The Sporting News,* June 28, 1969: 48.

48 Interview with Ed Bressoud.

49 Ibid.

# BOB LILLIS

## BY PAUL GEISLER

A strong, quiet leader. Steady and determined. One of the best minds in baseball. All apt descriptions of the often-overlooked player, coach, and manager Bob Lillis.

In 1928, Perry Reed Lillis, born in Michigan, married Lillian Pearl Porterfield, from Oklahoma. The couple had two sons: Jack Howard Lillis, born in 1928, and Robert Perry "Bob" Lillis, born June 2, 1930, at Altadena, California. Perry worked several different jobs, supporting his family through the 1930s, including as a wholesale-grocery stockman and a building construction clerk.

Bob recalled that he always seemed to have a baseball in his hands. "My father played a lot of semipro baseball and once had a tryout with the Angels as a pitcher. He taught me a lot."[1]

On March 17, 1940, both 10-year-old Bob and 11-year-old Jack were baptized at Messiah Lutheran Church, in Pasadena, California.

Bob received recognition as All-Southern California shortstop while at Pasadena High School, which both his parents also attended. As a 140-pound member of the football squad, he starred as a quarterback and running back and earned All-Foothill League, League Player of the Year, and All-CIF and All-Southern California honors.[2] He also lettered in basketball and track.

After high school, Bob moved on to Pasadena City College, which won the 1949 Western States Junior College baseball championship, 1-0, over Los Angeles City College. Lillis picked up the only hit for Pasadena when he singled, advanced on a fielder's choice and a walk, then scored when a batter was hit by a pitch with the bases loaded.[3] Lillis joined the inaugural class of the Pasadena City College Sports Hall of Fame, in 1961.

After spending one year at PCC, Lillis transferred to the University of Southern California. With the Trojans baseball team, he found early success at the plate, and at one point in April 1950, he led the California Intercollegiate Baseball Association with a .643 batting average. Rated as a top major-league prospect, the slick-fielding shortstop gained valuable experience and skills under USC coach Rod Dedeaux, a former shortstop himself who once played for the Brooklyn Dodgers. Dedeaux "helped me tremendously with pointers on fielding, how to play hitters, give signs, etc.," Lillis said.[4] He "taught me more than I can ever say."[5]

In 1951, at 160 pounds and 5-feet-11, the right-handed Lillis led the Pacific Coast Conference with a .313 batting average. The Brooklyn Dodgers grabbed him away from his All-American (second team in 1950 and 1951) collegiate career in June 1951, when scout Lefty Phillips[6] signed him to a professional contract, reportedly worth $15,000, to play at Pueblo in the Class-A Western League. After 37 games there, Lillis moved to Newport News of the Class-B Piedmont League for 39 games. A few years earlier, his older brother, Jack, had signed with the Dodgers and played for a little over four years in their minor-league system.

On December 31, 1951, the 21-year-old Lillis married 20-year-old Gloria Jeanne Keithley in Los Angeles, California.

After the baseball season, Lillis returned to classes at USC, then in 1952 he joined Elmira of the Class-A Eastern League, where his brother had played second base just the year before. With a remarkably close physical resemblance to his brother, some thought Jack had returned to play shortstop. "They look more like twins than most twins," said a local sportswriter.[7] Jack left baseball and moved to Las Vegas, later to become chief sales manager for an auto-sales agency there.[8]

With Newport News in 1951, Lillis lined an attempted bunt to the pitcher, who completed a triple play. In an almost identical play the next year at Elmira, he popped a bunt attempt to the pitcher, who again completed a triple play. Lillis may well be the only batter ever to bunt into two triple plays two years in a row.

Back with Newport News in 1953, Lillis made the Piedmont League All-Star team with a .291 batting average. He teamed with second baseman Charley Neal to set a league record with 199 double plays.

In 1954 military training interrupted Lillis's minor-league service when he was drafted into the US Army. The timing seemed awkward for the shortstop the Dodgers had hoped to groom to replace Pee Wee Reese. Lillis continued to play baseball while in the Army with the Fort Ord, California, team. He posted a .350 batting average for the all-Army and all-Service champion.

Bob and Jeanne celebrated the birth of their first child, daughter Joy Lynn, born in California in May 1955.

After two years of Army duty, Lillis returned to the Dodg-

ers farm system in 1956 with St. Paul of the Triple-A American Association, where he restarted his pursuit of the Dodger shortstop position. He "covers shortstop like a tarpaulin," commented Max Macon, his manager at St. Paul.[9] Joe Hennessy of the *St. Paul Pioneer Press* wrote that Lillis "came out of two years of military service to give one of the most convincing demonstrations at his position in some years."[10] Lillis also impressed with his speed and power. The annual poll of American Association managers named him the league's best baserunner.[11] He hit 18 home runs for St. Paul that year, especially significant since he never hit more than three in any other professional baseball season.

In the offseason Lillis joined several other Dodgers farmhands for an exhibition trip to Japan. His fine showing on the trip moved him ahead of Don Zimmer and Chico Fernandez in competition for a starting position on the Dodgers. General manager Buzzie Bavasi recognized Lillis's defensive skill, commenting, "His style resembles [Pee Wee] Reese's. He doesn't have a lot of power. Those 18 home runs were hit in a short ballpark. He's a right-handed hitter, and left field in St. Paul is 265 feet away."[12]

The Lillis family received a sad setback in March, when Jeanne suffered a miscarriage.

The Dodgers, now with three shortstop prospects, fielded several trade requests. The Philadelphia Phillies especially sought Lillis, while Brooklyn hoped to land a pitcher or outfielder. Finally, just at the start of the 1957 season, the Phillies acquired Chico Fernandez from the Dodgers, who kept Zimmer on the Brooklyn roster and sent Lillis back to St. Paul.

Lillis made the American Association All-Star team in 1957, and earned the title "iron man," not missing a game throughout the season. Despite the earlier trade, the Phillies reportedly offered Brooklyn $200,000 for Lillis during the season.[13] The Saints fans voted him the team's most valuable player, and he made the *Look* American Association team at shortstop. He was slated to join the Dodgers in the September call-up but stayed with St. Paul, which was in the playoffs. He seemed almost certain the join the Dodgers in 1958, and rejoin his former infield partner Charlie Neal, who would shift to second base after playing shortstop for Brooklyn in 1957. Although Lillis had yet to play in a major-league game, Brooklyn manager Walt Alston called him "as good a fielder as there is in the National League."[14]

Lillis signed a contract with the Dodgers for the 1958 season and joined the team for spring training, with his ability to hit big-league pitching remaining the only major question. "I honestly can say I don't feel nervous," he said as he headed to Vero Beach. "I'll just do my best."[15] He came out of the spring with the highest batting average (.324) of any Dodger with 30 or more at-bats. Manager Alston noted that Lillis "has more 'bulldog' and spirit than most people think. He's aggressive, fast, and covers a lot of ground."[16] That year, the Dodgers began their first year in Los Angeles, but Lillis found himself back with the Saints to start the season.

Although again named to the American Association All-Star team, Lillis did not play in the game because he severely tore ligaments on both sides of his left ankle on June 17 in a collision with teammate Lacy Curry. In early August, with his ankle still swollen, he received the call from the Dodgers to join the team.

In July 1958, Bob and Jeanne welcomed their second daughter, Jan Robin, born in Minnesota.

Lillis played in his first major-league game on August 17, in the second game of a doubleheader, in which the Dodgers beat the St. Louis Cardinals 9-3. Lillis batted once, in the eighth inning, and grounded out to shortstop. He went hitless for his first 10 plate appearances, then got his first hit on September 1, a line-drive single to left field off Johnny Antonelli of the San Francisco Giants in the fifth inning.

Lillis hit his first home run on September 24. He would hit only two more in his career. Lillis hit the ball over what was the shortest fence in modern major-league history. A baseball field had been squeezed into the oblong-shaped Coliseum while Dodger Stadium was being built. The 40-foot-high screen in left field was only 250 feet from home plate. "It almost scraped the screen coming down. But, nevertheless, it was a home run."[17]

Lillis ended 1958 with a .391 batting average in 20 games played and finished with a 12-game hit streak. After the season he took a job selling cars in Alhambra, a Los Angeles suburb. He made his first sale to fellow Dodger and USC Trojan Ron Fairly.

Entering the 1959 season, Lillis found himself squared off for the starting shortstop position with Don Zimmer, who had played 110 games at short the prior season and did not relish the competition. "The only thing Lillis can

do better than me is run from home to first, commented Zimmer. "After that, I've got him shaded."[18] Lillis seemed to have an inside track, but both players flopped at the plate in the spring games. Manager Alston picked Zimmer to start the season "because he has more power, and I wanted as much sock as possible on opening day."[19]

Lillis served mostly as a second-string shortstop and pinch-runner through May, then found himself playing in the Pacific Coast League for the Spokane Indians by his 29th birthday, when rookie Maury Wills joined the Dodgers as the regular shortstop. Lillis won most valuable player honors for Spokane, despite playing in only 103 games there. He also received a one-fourth share of the Dodgers' World Series earnings.

Several offseason trade offers focused on Lillis and Zimmer, with Zimmer finally going to the Chicago Cubs during 1960 spring training. Lillis spent the full 1960 season with the Dodgers, mostly as backup shortstop and occasional pinch-runner and utility infielder. Limited to just 60 at-bats, he managed a .267 batting average. On October 1, on the last weekend of the season, he and Maury Wills each had five hits in a 14-inning loss to the Cubs at the Coliseum.

In 1961 Lillis had a firm hold on the Dodger utility-infielder job. The team continued to get trade offers for him from several other clubs, including the Phillies, the Cardinals, the Detroit Tigers, and the Minnesota Twins, plus four new teams formed in 1961-1962.

Lillis played sparingly at the start of 1961, entering only 19 games in April and May and producing just one hit in nine at-bats. Then, just before his 31st birthday, the Dodgers traded him and Carl Warwick to the Cardinals for Daryl Spencer. Although he batted only .217 from June through September, Lillis accumulated 230 at-bats in 86 games, compared with 186 at-bats in 117 games total with the Dodgers since 1958.

After the season the National League held an expansion draft to stock its two new franchises, the Houston Colt .45s and the New York Mets. Houston took Lillis with its fifth pick. Lillis saw the draft as a major opportunity for both himself as well as for several other players. "Most of us didn't have a chance to play every day. Now we could show everybody what we could do. Being drafted was not a bad thing," he said.[20]

First slotted as a utility player, after the first 10 games of the season, he finally at age 31 had a starting position on a big-league team. "I don't mind having to fight for my job," he commented. "I've waited quite a while to be in the position I'm in now, but I know I've got to fight to keep it."[21]

Lillis started the 1962 season very slowly at the plate. Through May 23, he had a .146 batting average in 103 at-bats and only four runs batted in. Ironically, pitching coach Cot Deal suggested that he try whipping his bat through the zone to achieve a higher velocity on his swing, more like his free-swinging minor-league days.[22] Despite a slump in July, he batted .280 in 354 at-bats the rest of the season, to finish with a .249 batting average for the year. He finished strong, hitting .314 in the last 48 games. He also ranked among the hardest batters in the league to strike out, with only 23 whiffs in his 492 plate appearances.

Lillis commanded shortstop most of the season and shifted to second base when the Colts brought up J. C. Hartman to play short. The team also tried Don Buddin (batted .163) and Ernie Fazio (batted .083) at short, with little success.

Probably to his surprise, as much as to anyone else's, Lillis received the nod of the baseball writers as the most valuable player for the first season of the Colt .45s. Several also began to see him as a strong candidate for a manager's job in the future. "He just has the looks," Colts coach Lum Harris said. "When a preacher and a bootlegger walk into a room, you can tell them apart. That's how it is in baseball."[23] Also, in April 1962-64, National League sportswriters listed Lillis as the "best managerial material" on the Houston team.[24] Former high-school teammate Dick Williams got a similar rating with the Red Sox in 1964.

In 1963 Lillis played in 147 games, with 124 at short, the most of his career for both numbers. He hit the last of his three career home runs on May 21. He did not homer again, in 1,345 more at-bats. At age 33, he stood among the oldest on a Colts team that averaged 27 years old.

Lillis served for several years as the Houston player representative, and in March 1966, the team representatives made the major decision to hire Marvin J. Miller of Pittsburgh, a former labor union leader, as the executive director of their association.

Lillis, who turned 37 years old in 1967, started the season

with the indefinite assignment as coach and possible utility player, then joined the active player roster before the end of April. He played in only 37 games, 13 of them as a pinch-hitter, and posted a .244 batting average for his final season, giving him a .236 career batting average. When no team claimed him from waivers, Bob Aspromonte became the last original Colt .45 left on the team.

Lillis had a close relationship with longtime teammate Aspromonte, and they often roomed together. Lillis once suggested that "Aspro" take up a hobby, like coin collecting. He even gave him some rare quarters out of his own collection. When asked how he was liking the new endeavor, Aspromonte said, "Those quarters worked fine in the laundry machine."[25]

The Astros named Lillis chief scout for southeast Texas, then a year later instructional director of their minor leaguers. "I'm not retiring," he said. "I'm just going into another phase of the game."[26] Astros manager Leo Durocher (1972-73) named him to the Astros coaching staff for the 1973 season, where he remained the next nine seasons under managers Preston Gomez (1974-75) and Bill Virdon (1975-82). Lillis received strong consideration for the top position in 1975 when Houston finally picked Virdon.

Lillis compiled a book of notes on each National League pitcher to assist Astros baserunners in getting their jump from first base. "We talk to Bob before a game, and when we get on base we know what we have to do against any pitcher," said speedster Enos Cabell. Cabell stole 35 bases in 1976, part of a club record 150 steals for the season.[27]

The Astros used an experimental walkie-talkie communication system in 1981, linking general manager Al Rosen's box with the dugout during game to position players correctly defensively. Rosen's assistant Tony Siegle viewed the field from upstairs and talked with Lillis in the dugout. "We have a chart on how we want every infielder and outfielder to play each opposing hitter," explained manager Virdon.[28]

On August 10, 1982, Houston announced the firing of Virdon as manager and named Lillis interim manager, through the end of the season. On his way out, Virdon praised Lillis as "one of the best people I know and without a doubt the best coach anyone could have."[29]

In the one major change that Lillis made, he declared, "I am not a platoon manager."[30] Virdon had used 59 different batting orders in 111 games in 1982 before his exit, and in 1980 he wrote out a record 97 different lineups.

The Astros sat in fifth place in the Western Division, at 49 wins and 62 losses, when Lillis took over. Although he managed a winning record of 28 wins and 23 losses for the rest of the season, Houston stayed in fifth place throughout. He reportedly made good game decisions and demonstrated a positive firmness and rapport with the players as well as with the media.[31]

Major discussion ensued during the offseason as to whom the Astros would chose as their next full-time leader. Upper management seemed to prefer a younger pick or a "big-name" player, and they courted Joe Morgan, still playing for the San Francisco Giants in 1982. Popular opinion favored Lillis, a member of the Houston organization since its beginning. Lillis received a two-year extension on his coaching contract, guaranteeing his presence with the team either way.

Morgan opted to sign a player's contract with the Phillies, and the Astros finally offered Lillis a one-year contract as manager on November 2. Not bothered by the short tenure of the contract, he responded, "If I do well, I won't have to worry about it. If I don't, no one will have to tell me." He explained his first major task as putting together "a team that will jell and have the right chemistry."[32] Television announcer and former Astro Larry Dierker predicted success, saying, "Lillis will relate better to the average ballplayer than a big-name player who turned manager. ... The best teachers in this game are the guys who weren't the best players."[33]

At the start of the 1983 season, Lillis joined seven other big-league managers who did not start 1982 with the same club: Steve Boros with the Oakland Athletics, Russ Nixon with the Cincinnati Reds, Doug Rader with the Texas Rangers, Mike Ferraro with the Cleveland Indians, Joe Altobelli with the Baltimore Orioles, Bill Virdon with the Montreal Expos, John McNamara with the California Angels, and Billy Martin with the New York Yankees.

The Astros endured a rough spring exhibition season, with only three wins and 16 losses. With his typical understated, low-key confidence, Lillis noted, "We didn't peak too soon."[34] He also spoke calm words of reassurance. "We waded through the misfortune. We proved we can handle adversity."[35]

The beginning of the new season brought its own set of

woes, as Houston lost its first nine games. State legislators in Albany, New York, conducted their third annual "Billy Martin 'Yer Out' Poll," and Lillis received the most votes as the manager most likely to lose his job before the All-Star break.[36]

Their early disappointments did not hold sway, and the Astros soon put together some winning streaks, reaching 12 wins in 17 games at one point. Their win against the San Diego Padres on June 17 put them over .500 winning percentage, with 33 wins and 32 losses. On July 16 the Houston record stood at 47-41. The ever-positive Lillis opined, "There isn't a person in our clubhouse who doesn't believe we can be a contender the second half of the season."[37] By September, the Astros had compiled the best record in the National League, not counting their opening losing streak. They finished the season with 85 wins – a winning record – and claimed third place in their division.

With the surprising turnaround, Lillis came in second in voting for the National Manager of the Year, just one vote behind Tommy Lasorda of the Dodgers. He also won the Texas Sports Writers Association Pro Coach of the Year award for 1983. He signed a two-year contract to manage the Astros through the 1985 season.

Houston lost the first game of the next season but won the second, leaving the memories of the 0-9 start of 1983 in the past until the team lost the next five games. The Astros played very inconsistently, dropping to 10 games below the .500 mark by June 10, then rebounded to an even 62-62 record on August 18, perhaps inspired by a team meeting called by Cabell, one of the team leaders. In the end, they captured second place in the division, but with a losing record of 80 wins and 82 losses.

Again during 1984, Lillis used his innovative expertise with statistics and radio communication. He compiled comprehensive charts on each batter's tendencies, which he updated every day with input in a computer. This time they employed a three-way system, with Billy Joe Bowman from the press box and Gene Colman with a radar gun in the home-plate tunnel relaying messages to the dugout with a direct-line FM radio setup.[38] The system proved effective; on June 14 the team knocked out 10 hits against Fernando Valenzuela in a 3-1 win, after Lillis spent six hours entering information in the computer before setting his lineup.[39]

A drop in home attendance – down 122,000 from the year

before – accompanied the disappointing finish, and some speculated that Lillis might not fulfill the second year of his contract. But owner John McMullen and general manager Rosen showed no intentions to make a change. Even with that lackluster season, Lillis ranked fourth in the National League Manager of the Year voting, with one vote.

During the offseason, Lillis kept contact with his players and sought their thoughts about the needs and opportunities of the year ahead. "I'm trying to get input from everywhere and everyone. Just exactly what our plan of attack in the spring will be remains to be seen."[40]

The Astros had good contact hitters, without much power, hitting only 79 home runs in 1984, with Jose Cruz producing a paltry team-best of 12. Although they shortened the fences in the Dome, Houston did not add home-run punch over the winter.

In the 1985 version of the "Billy Martin 'Yer Out' Pool," Lillis ranked first in National League managers likely to lose their job by midseason.[41] Owner McMullen hosted Yogi Berra at Shea Stadium at an Astros game against the Mets, sparking speculation that he might fire Lillis and hire Berra sometime soon, but McMullen had made a point to tell Lillis about the Berra visit the day before, to allay any possible consternation.[42]

The Astros actually performed moderately well, winning 10 of 20 games in April, and hung on to a record of 43 wins and 45 losses at the All-Star break. Lillis made his first big-league All-Star appearance in 1985 as a member of Dick Williams's National League coaching staff. The team hit a midseason slump and had fallen to 11 games under the .500 mark by August 26. The Astros then made a remarkable recovery and won nine of their next 10, part of a 27-12 (.692) finish to the season. Their overall record stood at 83-79, tied with San Diego for third place in the division, 12 games behind the division champion Dodgers.

In mid-September McMullen, promising to "shake up his struggling Houston Astros,"[43] fired Rosen and replaced him with Dick Wagner, formerly with the Cincinnati Reds. Lillis fell next. At the end of the season the Astros fired him also but offered him a job in the organization. Saying he preferred more aggressiveness to Lillis's "nice guy" style, Wagner said, "To be a manager, you've got to have a little Billy Martin in you to get the respect of the umpires."[44] Whitey Herzog shared his thoughts with a group of reporters about the Lillis dismissal: "I think Lil-

lis did a real good job. He just can't sit here and BS with you guys like I can."[45]

Lillis completed his managerial career a winner, with 276 wins and 261 losses, a winning percentage of .514.

He did not accept the Astros job offer, preferring to work on the field instead. "I'm going to put my name out and let people know I'm available and, preferably, would like to have a job at the major-league level," he said.[46] He received consideration from Toronto for the managerial opening with the Blue Jays. In the end he took a coaching position with the Giants, joining Rosen, who became the San Francisco general manager after leaving Houston, and his longtime friend and now Giants manager, Roger Craig. As Craig assembled his coaching staff, he chose Lillis to sit next to him in the dugout. "I think he was the best manager in the NL last year. He's the most solid baseball man I've never known," said Craig.[47] Lillis stepped in and managed the Giants during a three-game absence of skipper Craig in September 1991.

Craig often relied on Lillis for key strategy decisions, and used him as a special infield instructor, most notably with Robby Thompson, Jose Uribe, and Royce Clayton. While with the Giants, Lillis coached in the 1987 National League playoffs and the 1989 World Series. He joined Craig's coaching staff for the 1990 All-Star Game.

Al Rosen resigned in November 1992, after a dismal 72-90 season by the Giants, and Bob Quinn Sr., replaced him. The shift also meant a change in managers, from Craig to Dusty Baker, who stuck with Lillis as his bench coach. Baker wanted to draw upon Bob's wealth of knowledge, and likened him to "a library."[48]

At age 65, Lillis announced his retirement after the 1996 season, completing a career of 46 years of professional and military baseball. He moved to Orlando, Florida, where he spent time with his family and enjoyed watching his two grandsons play Little League baseball.[49]

Besides his stellar fielding with a light bat, Lillis became widely recognized for his unflappable demeanor and calm confidence in tense times as well as joyous ones. "He loses his temper as infrequently as he loses a groundball hit directly to him," wrote a longtime sports scribe.[50] He even got along with the ruling authorities on the field, receiving only three ejections in his career: once as a player, once as a manager, and once as a coach. Two days after his major-league debut, first-base umpire Ed Sudol tossed him for disputing a call at first base. Then 27 years later, with 10 games left as manager of the Astros, Lillis got the thumb from umpire John Kibler over an interference noncall. And finally in 1989, as a coach with the Giants, Lillis argued a call with umpire Ed Montague at first base during the last game of the season. "I thought he was out. I didn't say anything; I just threw my hands up," Lillis said.[51]

The soft-spoken fielding virtuoso with bright blue eyes and "crewcut brown hair [that] stands straight up, like porcupine quills"[52] entered every season in a tenuous posture, unsure of his eventual role with the team. His steady nature and deep love for the game led him to "just do my best."

## Sources

In addition to the sources cited in the Notes, the author also consulted Ancestry.com, baseballalmanac.com, baseball-reference.com, and retrosheet.org.

## Notes

1  Paul Zimmerman, "Lillis Battles with Zimmer at Shortstop," *Los Angeles Times*, March 6, 1968: 71.

2  pasadenasportshalloffame.org/bob-lillis.html.

3  "Pasadena Is Jaycee Baseball Champion," *Bakersfield (California) Californian*, May 25, 1949: 29.

4  Halsey Hall, "Lillis Studies Hurlers," *Minneapolis Star*, July 3, 1957: 18.

5  Paul Zimmerman, "Experts Agree Dedeaux Best," *Los Angeles Times*, April 5, 1961: 78.

6  Phillips also signed Don Drysdale, Ron Fairly, and Larry Sherry from the Southern California area for Brooklyn.

7  Jim Morse, "Morse Code," *Star-Gazette* (Elmira, New York), June 22, 1951: 9.

8  Hank Ives, "Sad Week for Sports," *Pasadena Independent*, January 25, 1967: 14.

9  Byron Hollingsworth, "The Morning After," *Tampa Tribune*, July 1, 1956: 25.

10 Charles Karmosky, "The Sportscope," *Daily Press* (Newport News, Virginia), July 13, 1956: 14.

11 Halsey Hall, "Kirkland Rated Best AA Outfield Arm," *Minneapolis Star*, September 5, 1956: 56..

12 Jimmy Cannon, "Campy Is Key to Dodger Building Program in '57," *Dayton* (Ohio) *Daily News*, November 17, 1956: 6.

13 "American Association," *The Sporting News*. July 31, 1957: 38.

14 "Lillis Signs," *Miami News*, December 30, 1957: 28.

15 Mannie Pineda, "Bobby Lillis Departs for Big Dodger Trial," *Pasadena Independent*, February 27, 1958: 17.

16 George Lederer, "Dodger Pitching Stale," *Long Beach Independent*, March 31, 1951: 21.

17 John Wilson, "Astros Welcome Gladding to Fill No. 1 Fireman Role," *The Sporting News*, January 27, 1968, p. 36

18 "Bunts and Boots," *The Sporting News*, March 11, 1959: 27.

19 George Lederer, "Don Comes on Fast After Bad Spring," *Long Beach Independent*, April 26, 1959: 38.

20 David Casstevens, "Unprotected Might Find Valley Haven," *Arizona (Phoenix) Republic*, November 18, 1997: 12.

21 Mickey Herskowitz, "Lillis Credits Swat Spurt to 'Good Deal,'" *The Sporting News*, February 9, 1963: 3.

22 "Bob Lillis One of .45s Best Glovemen," *La Marque* (Texas) *Times*, August 31, 1962: 7.

23 Charley Eskew, "Point of View," *Austin American-Statesman*, April 24, 1962: 15.

24 *The Sporting News*, April 18, 1962: 10; April 20, 1963: 14; and April 25, 1964: 12.

25 "Putt Powell's Putting Around," *Amarillo Globe-Times*, March 11, 1977: 26.

26 John Wilson, "Astros Give Lillis Snappy A-OK Grade as Front-Office Rookie," *The Sporting News*, January 20, 1968: 34.

27 "Cabell, Cedeno Reach Accord," *Longview* (Texas) *News*, March 24, 1977: 23.

28 "Astros Walkie-Talkie for Defense Positions," *Galveston Daily News*, May 28, 1981: 16.

29 "Lillis Becomes Astros Manager at 52," *Galveston Daily News*, August 12, 1982: 17.

30 Harry Shattuck, "Lillis Declares Halt to Platoon System," *The Sporting News*, August 30, 1982: 47.

31 "1983 Astros Pilot? Lillis Has an Edge," *The Sporting News*, October 18, 1982: 34.

32 "Lillis Promises '83 Astros Will 'Jell,'" *New Braunfels* (Texas) *Herald-Zeitung*, November 3, 1982: 10.

33 "Bob Lillis Manager of Houston Astros," *Ukiah* (California) *Daily Journal*, November 3, 1982: 8.

34 Mark Heisler, "The New Fernando Goes Tonight," *Los Angeles Times*, April 5, 1983: 73.

35 "Ailing Astros Open with Dodgers Today," *Del Rio* (Texas) *News Herald,* April 5, 1983: 14.

36 Bob McCoy, "Idol Thoughts," T*he Sporting News,* May 30, 1983: 8.

37 "Astros Make Good on Lillis' Forecast," *The Sporting News,* July 25, 1983: 25.

38 "When Bowman Speaks, Astros Lillis Listens," *Paris* (Texas) *News,* May 8, 1984.

39 Gordon Edes, "Dodgers Fail to Support Valenzuela," *Los Angeles Times,* June 15, 1984: 35.

40 "Lillis Seeks Consistency in 1985," *The Sporting News,"* October 29, 1984: 44.

41 Bob McCoy, "'Yer Out' Again," *The Sporting News,* May 27, 1985: 8.

42 Milton Richman, "Despite the Speculation, Yogi's Not Headed for Houston," *Petaluma* (California) *Argus-Courier,* May 6, 1985: 6.

43 "Astros Choose Ex-Reds Chief to Fill Top Job," *Austin American-Statesman,* September 14, 1985: 3.

44 "Astros' Housecleaning catches Lillis' Job," *Longview News-Journal,* October 8, 1985: 13.

45 Tom Friend and Gordon Edes, "Cards Run Better Than They Fly," *Los Angeles Times,* October 9, 1985: 48.

46 "Lillis Turns Down a Front Office Job," *Petaluma Argus-Courier,* October 16, 1985: 10.

47 Mike Barnes, "New Giants' Manager Promises Major Changes," *Auburn* (California) *Journal,* December 10, 1985: 10.

48 Mark Newman, "Managing Just Fine," *The Sporting News,* September 13, 1993.

49 Paul Geisler, Conversation with Bob Lillis' daughter Joy, July 31, 2018.

50 Herskowitz.

51 Nick Peters, "Giants Lose, So Does Clark," *Santa Cruz* (California) *Sentinel,* October 2, 1989: 27.

52 Herskowitz.

# "THE NAME IS METS – JUST PLAIN METS"

## By Leslie Heaphy

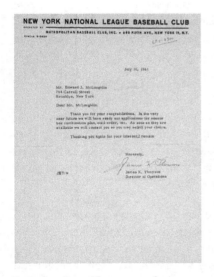

Letter from James Thomson to a fan in response to an enquiry about season tickets to the 'New York Metropolitan Baseball Club, July 10, 1961. (Courtesy of James Cornell)

As part of the National League expansion in 1962, a franchise was awarded to New York City. From 1962 to the current day the Metropolitans' ownership has been fairly stable. Joan Payson and her family maintained control of the club until they sold the team in 1980 to the publishing firm Doubleday and Co. Nelson Doubleday bought out the company in 1986 with his partner Fred Wilpon. In 2002 Wilpon and Sterling Equities bought out Doubleday and as of 2018 have remained the primary owners. This relative stability in ownership for the Mets has not prevented them from experiencing incredible highs and lows during the franchise's history. Two World Series, in 1969 and 1986, brought the Mets to the highest honor in baseball while they began their existence with the worst record in major-league history in 1962.

### Birth of the Metropolitans

In 1957, when the Brooklyn Dodgers and New York Giants left New York for the West Coast, Gotham City fans were left reeling and looking for a replacement. The 1958 season would be the first since 1882 for New York not to host a National League team. A number of groups stepped forward and talks developed about who might emerge to take over this market.

Late in 1957, New York Mayor Robert Wagner Jr. appointed a committee to bring National League baseball back to the city. While luminaries such as former Attorney General James Farley, department-store mogul Bernard Gimbel and real-estate impresario Clinton Blume sat on the panel, the real power was attorney William Shea. Shea hoped to lure one of the league's weaker members to New York. However, as talks with the Cincinnati Reds, Pittsburgh Pirates, and Philadelphia Phillies all failed, he decided to propose the creation of a third league, to be called the Continental League. Shea even coaxed Branch Rickey out of retirement to spearhead efforts to establish the league.

With Rickey at the helm, the league would initially field eight teams, including a New York entry, with plans to expand to 10. After nearly half a century as a major-league player, manager, and executive, Rickey knew that any challenger league would require strong ownership to provide the money to develop a front office, sign players,

Program from the groundbreaking ceremony at Flushing Meadow Park on October 28, 1961. Shea Stadium opened in 1964, just in time for the New York World's Fair. (Courtesy of James Cornell)

and, perhaps, build a stadium. In New York, the Continental League found its potential owners in the city's old money.

The group was led by Joan Whitney Payson and her husband, Charles Shipman Payson. Her minority partners included George Herbert Walker Jr., an executive with merchant banker Brown Brothers Harriman (and uncle of President George Herbert Walker Bush), and Dwight F. Davis Jr., son of the founder of tennis's Davis Cup. Another was Payson's stockbroker, M. Donald Grant.[1] As a member of Horace Stoneham's board, Grant had been the only director to vote against the Giants moving out west. He voted "no" on behalf of Payson, who would rather have had the Giants than the extra money.[2]

After two years of resisting the Continental League, the National and American Leagues finally rallied around to the idea of expansion in late 1960. They also faced pressure from the US Congress, who threatened baseball's exemption from antitrust laws if they did not agree to expansion. According to the announcement from National League President Warren Giles, two teams would be added to the National League through ownership groups from the Continental League groups. National League play was to begin in New York and Houston in 1962.[3]

The decision gave Payson the distinction of being the first female major-league-baseball franchise owner in four decades and the first who did not own the franchise without inheriting it. She first became involved in baseball by buying one share of stock in the New York Giants in 1950 and gradually increased her involvement to a 10 percent share by the mid-1950s. Before the Giants moved to San Francisco, she gave some thought to investing more heavily to keep the franchise in New York. However, she sold her shares when the Giants followed the Dodgers to the West Coast. Payson's interest in baseball came from

her mother but it was not her only sporting interest. She also invested heavily in horse racing, owning a stable with her brother, Jock Whitney.[4]

Joan Whitney was born in New York in February 1903 to a family with an impressive lineage dating back to their arrival in Massachusetts from England in 1635. Her father, William Payne Whitney, came from a family line that included Henry B. Payne, a Democratic senator from Ohio in the 1850s. Payne Whitney had not only inherited money but added to his fortune with investments in banking, tobacco, railroads, mining, oil, and Greentree Stables.

His own father, William C. Whitney, served as secretary of the Navy during the first Grover Cleveland administration and owned a streetcar line in Boston. Payne Whitney's uncle, Col. Oliver Payne, left his fortune to his nephew when he died in 1917. Joan's mother, Helen Hay Whitney, of Cleveland, was the daughter of John Hay, who began his career as assistant private secretary to President Abraham Lincoln. Hay went on to serve as secretary of state under Presidents William McKinley and Theodore Roosevelt. Joan and her brother inherited her father's fortune upon their father's death in 1927.

Joan Whitney married Charles Shipman Payson when she was 21. Their marriage at Christ Church in Manhattan was a huge social event uniting two old-time wealthy families in 1924. During the course of their marriage they had five children, three girls and two boys. Joan continued to oversee and invest her own money in horses, art, and, ultimately, the New York Mets.[5]

After paying $1 million for her primary investment, Mrs. Payson moved quickly to organize and name her new ballclub. In March 1961, the first major management decision was made: to hire George Weiss as president and general

'Meet the Mets' brochure from 1962. Most of the players were past their prime while former New York Giants pitcher John Antonelli retired before the season even began. (Courtesy of James Cornell)

manager. Weiss's tenure with the New York Yankees from 1932 to1960 had been incredibly successful, as attested by his ultimate election to the National Baseball Hall of Fame in 1971. Weiss insisted on bringing on board Casey Stengel as the new manager.[6] Then in May 1961, Payson hosted a gathering at her Manhattan home to name the new team. According to some of those present, Payson's personal favorite was the Meadowlarks but the New York Metropolitans was chosen. The Metropolitans had been the name of the American Association club in New York from 1882 to 1887. Payson herself announced the name at the Savoy on May 8, 1961, indicating that the team would be known by the nickname Mets. A new logo was commissioned from sports cartoonist Ray Gotto and unveiled in November 1961. The colors incorporated Dodgers blue and Giants orange to encourage support from fans of these former franchises.

M. Donald Grant first met Joan Payson at a club in Florida in 1950. Over a game of cards the conversation had shifted to what each of them would buy with their money. Payson and Grant both wanted to buy the New York Giants. From there a lifelong friendship and working relationship began. Grant was born in Montreal in 1904, the son of Michael Grant, a professional hockey player. He eventually found his way to New York to make his fortune. He started as a night clerk and worked his way up to being a managing partner in Fahnestock and Company while also serving on the board of the Mets.[7] Grant went to work for Payson after selling his one percent share of the Giants to her. Eventually she came to own 10 percent of the club and Grant represented her on the board of directors. While Grant was a minority owner of the Mets, Mrs. Payson claimed that her investment was about 85 percent of the team.[8] Grant served as the chairman of the board until he resigned in 1978.

One of the biggest concerns for Payson and the other major-league owners was where the Mets would play. Plans were immediately underway to construct what was to be known as Flushing Meadows Stadium, a 55,000-seat ballpark with a price tag of $15 million. However, it would never be ready for the first season. One proposal was to share Yankee Stadium for a year or two, but Yankees ownership was not interested in anything less than a long-term rental agreement. The Mets then turned to the Polo Grounds, the former home of the Giants, which was scheduled to be razed. Mayor Wagner worked to delay the destruction, allowing the Mets to play their inaugural home opener on April 11, 1962, a game they lost

The interior of the 'Meet the Mets' brochure which featured manager Casey Stengel and visiting stars from around the National League. Later added to the coaching staff were Hall of Famers Rogers Hornsby and Red Ruffing. (Courtesy of James Cornell)

11-4 to the St. Louis Cardinals. The Mets went on to have the worst record (40-120) of any major-league team since 1935 and an attendance of only 922,530 for the season. They ended the season in 10th place, 60½ games out of first place.[9]

When Shea Stadium finally opened for the Mets to play their home opener on April 17, 1964, it was supposed to be the state of the art in ballparks. Usher Stan Manel, an employee of the Mets since 1962, commented that moving from the Polo Grounds to Shea "was like moving from the basement to the penthouse."[10] Sadly, the reality was different, though the outcome of that first game was as expected. The Mets lost to the Pittsburgh Pirates, 4-3. When Shea Stadium was first proposed, the venue was planned to be part of urban planner Robert Moses' vision for all of Flushing Meadows. Moses originally used the idea to try to entice Walter O'Malley to move the Dodgers from Brooklyn to Queens.

Shea and Moses had to find a way around an existing New York state law that prohibited the city from borrowing money to build a stadium. The only way around the law was to prove that the stadium could pay for itself from rent and event revenue. If the new team paid a substantial annual rent, then 30-year bonds could be paid off and no borrowings were required. All Shea and Moses had to do was convince others that the idea could become a reality. With the endorsement of the *New York Times* and local dignitaries Stengel and Weiss and civic leader Bernard Gimbel, the deal was reached and construction began. The Mets were never able to live up to that monetary commitment, which would cause difficulties when Fred Wilpon wanted a new ballpark three decades later. The Mets were also granted exclusive rights to Shea during the course of the baseball season by Parks Commission-

A ticket stub to the first Opening Day for the Mets at the Polo Grounds on April 13, 1962 - a Friday. Perhaps ominous for the day of the month, the Mets were defeated by the Pittsburgh Pirates, 4-3. There would be 119 more losses before the 1962 season was over. (Courtesy of James Cornell)

er Newbold Morris. One of the other features of Shea Stadium was the fact that the park was built for multiple tenants, a trend for municipal stadium development in the 1960s. Due to his efforts in bringing National League baseball back to New York, William Shea became the logical person to name the new ballpark after.[11]

The ballpark was dedicated the day before the home opener in 1964 with Shea, Wagner, Moses, Stengel, Payson, and many dignitaries in attendance. Shea christened the new field with water from the Harlem River and the Gowanus Canal. The Polo Grounds had stood on the banks of the Harlem, and its water represented the lost Giants, while the canal ran through Brooklyn near an early field of the Dodgers.

Manel, the usher, described the home opener in the following way:

> Over 50,000 fans showed up on opening day. There was a great traffic jam outside the ball park. some fans did not get to their seat until the sixth inning. The paint was still wet in some places. The score board was not yet completed. The color of your ticket matched the color of the level on which the seat was located. The crowds were great. Over 1.7 million fans came out that season. The 1964 Worlds Fair was located across the road.[12]

Shea Stadium was plagued by financial issues and water concerns throughout its life. Since Shea was built on marshland, it had constant drainage issues. Those issues were compounded when the outfield fences were moved in and the drainage pipes were then outside the fences. The planned 80,000-seat expansion and dome did not

happen because of financial shortfalls. The financial woes would continue to plague the Mets for their entire tenancy, and later affected how the city dealt with the desire by both the Mets and Yankees for new ballparks.[13]

Part of the blame for the terrible start can be placed squarely on the shoulders of the aging and increasingly disengaged Casey Stengel. But the 1961 expansion draft was the primary trouble. Each National League team had to make 15 players available for the Houston and New York teams to draft. The draft was scheduled for the period before major-league teams had to add blue-chip prospects to their 40-man rosters and thus be eligible for selection. The Mets selections came primarily from players at the end of their careers or players without any big-league experience yet. Coupled with the declining skills of Casey Stengel, who was the oldest manager in the major leagues at the time, the Mets got off to a dismal start.

The draft was scheduled for October 10, 1961, and would be conducted in three phases. Each team could select four premium players ($125,000 each), 16 players at $75,000 each, and three at $50,000 each. Houston won the coin toss and received the first pick. The selections alternated through the allowed 45 picks. Together the teams spent $3,650,000 for the drafted players. The Mets used their first pick to select Hobie Landrith from the Giants. Landrith was included in a trade with Baltimore on June 7, 1962, that brought Marvelous Marv Throneberry to New York. When the draft was complete, the Mets had selected 22 players for under $1.8 million, which left room for acquiring players such as Frank Thomas from the Braves. The best player they selected was clearly Gil Hodges, an eight-time All-Star and three-time Gold Glove winner nearing the end of his playing days. After retiring, Hodges managed the Mets to their first World Series win, in 1969.[14]

Payson and her fellow board members did not lose heart, bolstered by the unexpected attendance success in spite of the team's on-field performance. The team drew over a million fans in its second year, despite another dismal performance, and then shot to 1.7 million, second in the league, the year Shea Stadium opened. Stan Manel said, "If you came to our ball park, we gave you nine full innings of baseball. Not the eight and a half you get with a winning team. We did however draw over 900,000 fans, with 55,000, at a double header on Memorial Day with the Dodgers. We drew over a million the second year."[15] The success continued for much of the next two decades.

Owner Payson did not get involved in many of the day-to-day decisions of the ballclub. She preferred to remain in the background and be the team's number-one fan. She attended games regularly, took care of the players and even decorated part of her house in Mets colors. One of the few personnel decisions she weighed in on was bringing Willie Mays to the Mets in 1972, as he had been her favorite player with the Giants. Much of the operational work was done by the general managers, front-office staff, and M. Donald Grant; though Grant indicated in an interview that he was credited with more input in decisions than he ever gave. He claimed he never interfered in the choices made by the general managers but just offered advice and counsel.[16]

With the expansion of the National League, New York once again had its entry in the league and the fans had the new "lovable losers" to root for. Joan Payson took her love of the game to the next level when she purchased the franchise and was lucky enough to be the owner while the Mets rose from the doldrums to the highest honor, winning the World Series in 1969.

**Notes**

1  Dick Young, "The Mets Are Born: NL Votes to Return to NY in 1962," *New York Daily News*, October 18, 1960; Peter Bendix, "The History of the American and National League, Part I," beyondthe-boxscore.com/2008, November 18, 2008; Mike Barry, "Payson's Legacy," antonnews.com, May 18, 2012.

2  George Vecsey, *Joy in Mudville* (New York: McCall Publishing Company, 1970), 13.

3  Vecsey, 15-16.

4  Joseph Durso, "Joan Whitney Payson, 72, Mets Owner, Dies," *New York Times*, October 5, 1975.

5  "Payne Whitney Dies Suddenly at Home," *New York Times*, May 26, 1927.

6  Burton A. Boxerman and Benita W. Boxerman, *George Weiss: Architect of the Golden Age Yankees*, (Jefferson, North Carolina: McFarland & Company, Inc., 2016), 164.

7  Murray Chass, "Mets Chairman M. Donald Grant, 94, Dies," *New York Times*, November 29, 1998. In Donald Grant file, National Baseball Hall of Fame and Library, Cooperstown, New York.

8  Durso.

9  Mike Dodd, "MLB Expansion Effects Still Felt 50 Years Later Around the Leagues," *USA Today*, April 11, 2011.

10  Email Correspondence with Stan Manel, May 2018.

11  Chris Strohmaier, "Shea Stadium, Robert Moses, and an Era of Ballparks," amazinavenue.com/2014/10/13/689131/mets-shea-stadium October 3, 2014; Jack Lang, "Yanks in Shea Stadium? Idea En-

rages Mets," *Long Island Press*, September 18, 1971, in Donald Grant file; "History of Shea Stadium," New York Mets, accessed June 5, 2018, newyork.mets.mlb.com/nym/ballpark/history.jsp.

12  Email correspondence with Stan Manel.

13  Eric Barrow, "Shea Stadium: Mets First Miracle," *New York Daily News*, October 23, 2008.

14  "1961 MLB Expansion Draft," Baseball-reference.com; Vecsey, 31-33.

15  Email correspondence between author and Stan Manel, May 2018.

16  Dick Young, "Don Grant: I Took Blame for Things I didn't Do," *New York Daily News*, November 25, 1978, in Donald Grant file.

## NEW YORK METS EXPANSION DRAFT

| PICK | PLAYER | POSITION | FORMER TEAM |
|---|---|---|---|
| **REGULAR PHASE, $75,000 PER PLAYER** | | | |
| 1 | Hobie Landrith | c | San Francisco Giants |
| 2 | Elio Chacon | ss | Cincinnati Reds |
| 3 | Roger Craig | p | Los Angeles Dodgers |
| 4 | Gus Bell | of | Cincinnati Reds |
| 5 | Joe Christopher | of | Pittsburgh Pirates |
| 6 | Felix Mantilla | 2b | Milwaukee Braves |
| 7 | Gil Hodges | 1b | Los Angeles Dodgers |
| 8 | Craig Anderson | p | St. Louis Cardinals |
| 9 | Ray Daviault | p | San Francisco Giants |
| 10 | John DeMerit | of | Milwaukee Braves |
| 11 | Al Jackson | p | Pittsburgh Pirates |
| 12 | Sammy Drake | ss | Chicago Cubs |
| 13 | Chris Cannizzaro | c | St. Louis Cardinals |
| 14 | Choo Choo Coleman | c | Philadelphia Phillies |
| 15 | Ed Bouchee | 1b | Chicago Cubs |
| 16 | Bobby Gene Smith | of | Philadelphia Phillies |
| **REGULAR PHASE, $50,000 PER PLAYER** | | | |
| 17 | Ed Olivares | 2b | St. Louis Cardinals |
| 18 | Jim Umbricht | p | Pittsburgh Pirates |
| **PREMIUM PHASE, $125,000 PER PLAYER** | | | |
| 19 | Jay Hook | p | Cincinnati Reds |
| 20 | Bob Miller | p | St. Louis Cardinals |
| 21 | Don Zimmer | 3b | Cincinnati Reds |
| 22 | Lee Walls | of | Philadelphia Phillies |

# CHOO-CHOO COLEMAN

## By David E. Skelton

No team in history compares to the 1962 Mets, a completely inept club that bumbled its way to becoming New York City's "Loveable Losers." And no two players represent this label better than Marvelous Marv Throneberry and Clarence "Choo-Choo" Coleman, the team's first baseman and catcher, respectively, whose on-field antics contributed to an inaugural record 120-loss season. Coleman, who retired after a four-year major-league career, subsequently disappeared from public view over the next five decades, an absence that, combined with his memorable nickname, contributed to his near-cult-figure status. Absent but never forgotten, his career was perhaps best captured in a 1972 letter to *The Sporting News* from a fan who claimed that Coleman "play[ed] the game for the fans, for spirited fun."[1]

Clarence Coleman was born on August 25, 1935, the seventh of eight children of John Henry and Elnora (Pittman) Coleman, in Orlando, Florida. He was the grandson of William and Lottie Coleman, who were born a decade after Abraham Lincoln issued the Emancipation Proclamation. In the late 1800s, William and Lottie married and eventually raised eight children on a farm south of Macon, Georgia. Around 1919, their second eldest child, Clarence's father John, married Elnora. The union produced two children born in Georgia before the family moved to Florida around 1923. They settled into a small house west of downtown Orlando, 10 miles or so northeast of present-day Disney World.

The house bordered a community park that included a baseball field and tennis courts, access to which helped Coleman hone his athletic skills both before and during his enrollment at Orlando's Jones High School in the 1950s. It was also around this time that Coleman earned the nickname "Choo-Choo" for a fleet-footedness likened to that of a speeding train. The name would stick with him the rest of his life. Another trait that followed him into adulthood was Coleman's shy, quiet nature, a characteristic borne from embarrassment over a childhood stutter. Though the stutter improved with age, it never disappeared. A superb athlete, Coleman turned to sports as his primary means of communicating. "In high school, Choo-Choo was a baseball catcher, played basketball and tennis, and was probably a better tennis player," recalled Coleman's niece, Linda Milhouse Hibbler, years later. "But he loved baseball."[2]

In 1955, shortly after graduating from high school, Coleman signed with the Florida State League's Orlando C.B.s, a Class-D affiliate of the Washington Senators. The signing was facilitated by one of Coleman's childhood friends who was playing for the team. The excitement Coleman experienced after joining the team quickly turned to disappointment when he saw very little usage: 20 at-bats in 17 games. When the same pattern surfaced midway through the following season, Coleman bolted the team and signed with the Indianapolis Clowns. One year removed from the Negro American League, the club, owned by Syd Pollock, barnstormed with Coleman throughout the nation.[3]

By 1958, Coleman had returned to Orlando and once again signed with the local club. Though he played 38 games in the outfield, Coleman received the bulk of the catching duties for the unaffiliated Orlando Flyers and continued doing so the next season when the club became the Class-D affiliate of the Los Angeles Dodgers. In June 1959, at the season's midpoint, the left-handed hitter led the league with 55 RBIs. Though he slowed in the second half, he still finished among the circuit leaders. He also placed among the leaders with 15 stolen bases. Defensively, Coleman presented a mixed bag. His strong arm contributed a league leading 74 assists by a catcher while his 18 errors trailed only one other backstop. Despite these miscues, Coleman was selected to the league's All-Star squad in a poll of managers and sportswriters. It was around this time that Coleman, now 23, started representing himself as two years younger to attract major-league interest.

The ploy worked when Coleman opened the 1960 season in Class A, with the Macon Dodgers of the South Atlantic League. His ascension within the organization continued when, despite a pedestrian .195/.271/.312 line in 26 games, he was advanced to the Triple-A Montreal Royals in the International League just weeks later. Except for a near-league-leading 12 errors, a yield that trailed only his future Mets teammates Chris Cannizzaro and Jesse Gonder, he drew rave reviews for his defense. "[Coleman is] the best lowball catcher I've ever seen," Royals manager Clay Bryant claimed.[4] Moreover, Coleman responded well to the promotion with a .258 average in 291 at-bats while placing among the league leaders with 10 stolen bases. When the season ended, he joined a group of African-American stars that included Hank Aaron and Curt Flood on a 33-game barnstorming tour throughout the South. On November 28, the Philadelphia Phillies selected Coleman with the first pick in the annual Rule 5 Draft. Cleveland Indians GM Frank Lane, who had made no secret of his desire to select the backstop, grudgingly acknowledged that Coleman was "a fine draft choice. [He will] make them a pretty good catcher in a year or so."[5]

Lane's prediction appeared prescient when Coleman got four hits including a ninth-inning game-winning RBI single in a March 14, 1961, Grapefruit League game against the St. Louis Cardinals. A month later, in a sportswriters' nationwide poll, he was tabbed as the Phillies' "Hottest Young Prospect."[6] Though he was unable to unseat sophomore catcher Clay Dalrymple from the starting catcher job, Coleman prevailed in competition with four others for one of the two backup roles.

On April 16, 1961, Coleman made his major-league debut at San Francisco's Candlestick Park pinch-hitting for pitcher Chris Short. Representing the tying run in a 5-2 deficit, he was struck by the pitch from veteran right-hander Sam Jones.[7] The rally was quickly extinguished when pinch-hitter Bobby Del Greco grounded into a double play. Coleman's first official at-bat came four days later when he was again called upon to pinch-hit, this time for shortstop Ruben Amaro with two strikes on the batter. He grounded out to Milwaukee Braves first baseman Joe Adcock after fouling off four pitches. "I always remembered that," Coleman recalled more than 60 years later. "That's tough, man!"[8]

On April 28, following two additional pinch-hit appearances, Coleman collected several major-league firsts: his first base hit, an eighth-inning single to right field against Cardinals reliever Lindy McDaniel, his first RBI and run scored, and his first appearance at catcher. Coleman got his first start 10 days later, while his first extra-base hit – an RBI double against future Hall of Famer Don Drysdale – came on May 9. On May 27, he was robbed of his first career home run on a brilliant catch by Cincinnati Reds center fielder Vada Pinson.

But opportunities for additional play proved fleeting when, through mid-June, only five of Coleman's 26 appearances came as a starter, while 19 came either solely or initially as a pinch-hitter or pinch-runner. After the Phillies signed free-agent outfielder Elmer Valo on June 17, Coleman was no longer the sole left-handed hitter on the bench. Following a June 20 appearance as a defensive replacement he was assigned to the Spokane Indians, a Dodgers Triple-A affiliate in the Pacific Coast League. Coleman did not take the demotion well and it initially affected his play. Breaking out of his slump with grand slams on successive nights against the Salt Lake City Bees on July 26-27, he finished among the team leaders in several categories including his 13 home runs and a .518 slugging percentage. Though recalled by the Phillies in September, Coleman was left unprotected in the first National League expansion draft. On October 10, he was selected by the Mets with the 28th pick.

Before their inaugural 1962 season, the Mets drafted or acquired primarily older players in the belief that a veteran presence would result in immediate success. Despite hitting the first home run in Mets history during a March 11, 1962, exhibition against the Cardinals, Coleman did not make the final cut prior to the start of the regular season – a demotion he again did not take well. Assigned to the Triple-A Syracuse Chiefs, Coleman suffered through a series of injuries that contributed to a dismal .195/.275/.279 line in just 226 at-bats as he split his time between catcher and the outfield.

But as bad as things were in Syracuse, events were much worse in New York. In July, while en route to a modern-record 120-loss season, the Mets lost veteran catcher Sammy Taylor due to a fractured finger. On July 16, Coleman was recalled. Eleven days later, in his first start, he got a bunt single and came around to score the only run of the game in a 1-0 win over Cardinals flamethrower Bob Gibson. A week later Coleman connected for his first major-league home run, a two-run pinch-hit homer against Reds reliever Jim Brosnan. Citing Coleman's "high potential," Mets manager Casey Stengel turned increasingly toward the 26-year-old for the club's catching needs.[9] He finished the season with a .250 average in 152 at-bats with career highs in runs (24), doubles (7), homers (6), and RBIs (17). Moreover, of the seven catchers the Mets used in 1962, Coleman had the highest fielding percentage of anyone with 92 or more innings behind the plate. His only error came when he attempted to pick off a runner at first and sent the ball sailing past a seemingly oblivious Marv Throneberry. "The official scorer must have reasoned that anybody who tried a pickoff with Marvelous Marv deserved an error, just for bad judgment," sportswriter George Vecsey cracked years later.[10] During the winter Coleman was assigned to the Florida Instructional League, where coach Solly Hemus worked with him at catcher and at second base and outfield as well.

But the gains made by Coleman in 1962 inexplicably evaporated. He opened the 1963 season as the Mets starting catcher, but after a 1-for-20 start was quickly moved into a platoon role. He especially struggled on the road with a miserable season-long .107 average in 121 at-bats.

Moreover, except for his strong-armed capabilities that placed him among the league leaders in erasing baserunners, Coleman's defensive strides of the preceding season collapsed to near league-leading yields in passed balls (11) and errors by a catcher (15). As if to add salt to the wound, his horrid 5-for-49 slump beginning on August 28 contributed to a final .178/.264/.215 line. Seeking to reclaim his abilities, Coleman traveled to Central America to play winter ball in the Nicaraguan League – the first of four consecutive winters in which he did so.

The confidence Stengel had previously shown in Coleman appeared to have completely dissipated when the catcher reported to 1964 spring training and found himself competing with five other backstops for the starting job. Moreover, Hall of Fame catcher Bill Dickey was brought in to work almost exclusively with catcher Jesse Gonder, a powerful slugger acquired the season before, on his defense. Coleman's chances of recapturing the starting job were further reduced when he suffered a fractured thumb on March 8 that sidelined him for a month. Days before the start of the regular season, he was optioned to the Buffalo Bisons in the Triple-A International League. Injuries followed Coleman to Buffalo and he was unable to get regular play until midway through the season. He finished with a .285/.357/.488 line with 10 home runs in 172 at-bats – good enough to warrant a recall in September but not enough to garner additional play.

In 1965, the Mets used no fewer than seven catchers, not one of whom was named Coleman. Seemingly an afterthought in the minds of management, the 29-year-old was one of the first players assigned to Buffalo during spring training. Once again, injuries marred his season as Coleman got a mere 150 at-bats. The following year, having been removed from the 40-man roster, he attended Mets spring training as a nonroster invitee.

As inexplicable as Coleman's descent had been three years earlier, his ascent in 1966 was just as hard to explain. One of many observers who noticed the marked improvement was Stengel, by now the former manager, who visited the Mets camp during spring training. "[Coleman]'s looked real good," Casey remarked. "[M]aybe he's ready to make it this time."[11] These words appeared prophetic when Coleman earned the third-string catcher role behind youngsters Jerry Grote and John Stephenson. After sitting on the bench on Opening Day, Coleman started in five of the club's first six games. The last start came on April 23 against the Braves in Atlanta Stadium in what proved to be Coleman's last appearance in the major leagues. Three weeks later he was shipped to the Triple-A Jacksonville (Florida) Suns for veteran backstop Hawk Taylor. Coleman finished the season there as backup to once-prized catching prospect Greg Goossen before proceeding to Nicaragua for another winter season. In a preview of his much longer hibernation, he then seemingly dropped off the face of the earth for the next two years.

In July 1967, the Mets extended an invitation to Coleman to attend the fifth anniversary of their inaugural team but he did not show. Though he would later shrug off this two-year absence as a fishing hiatus, a darker side eventually emerged. Former teammate Larry Bearnarth later claimed that Coleman had confided in him that "he'd been in Philadelphia ... and was starving."[12] Coleman's next sighting came in the spring of 1969 when he was spied in uniform at the Mets minor-league training camp at St. Petersburg, Florida. In a short letter of apology to Mets farm director Joe McDonald, specifics of which were never fully divulged, Coleman asked for and received a tryout. He was eventually assigned to the Triple-A Tidewater Tides in the International League.[13]

The Tides' inaugural season coincided with the circuit's experiment with the designated hitter, making Coleman one of the first DH's in the league's history. His presence also brought a thrill to Jeff Terpko, Buffalo's 18-year-old right-hander, who described Coleman as his "boyhood idol" after the two faced off against each other in a June 5 contest. "I watched him every night that first year (1962) when the Mets started," Terpko said.[14] In a five-player platoon Coleman received the bulk of play behind the plate and carried a .300 average through the first half of the season. His veteran presence helped stabilize a young staff that included 19-year-old Jon Matlack as the club proceeded to the International League crown.

By 1970, Coleman had parted ways with the Tides and launched a two-year (possibly three-year) stint with the Mexico City Reds in the Triple-A Mexican League. In his first year, Coleman was among the league leaders in hitting throughout the season's first half, and his team-leading 15 homers helped the Reds to a runaway first-place finish in the Northern Division. But at no point during this or subsequent years was he able to attract major-league attention. He hung up his spikes after the 1972 season.

Throughout his career Coleman had spent most of his offseasons following in his father's footsteps as a carpenter, though he also worked as a butcher and house painter

at various times. In 1961, he met Suzie Mae Starks on the public tennis courts across from his parents' house. They married in October. The union produced a son, Clarence Jr., and a daughter, Elnora Vanessa, before dissolving in divorce years later. A subsequent marriage in Chesapeake, Virginia, to Odessa Dejetta, whose son-in-law owned a Chinese restaurant, resulted in Coleman launching a lengthy second career as the restaurant's primary chef before he opened his own establishment. In 1994, after Odessa's death, Coleman moved to Bamberg, South Carolina, 80 miles northwest of Charleston, where he married Lucille Middleton, a South Carolina native who was the sister of his brother-in-law.

Around 2010 Lucille fell victim to Alzheimer's disease. Coleman, who was struggling with his own health concerns after contracting diabetes, was compelled to place her in a nursing home and moved into the home of his niece Linda Milhouse Hibbler in Bamberg. Sometime before this last move, Coleman, through the tenacity of Lou Cafiero, a diligent New York sports collector, was rediscovered. In 2012, in his first flight in 35 years, he traveled to New York, where he was an instant hit among the attendees at a large autograph show.

Coleman returned home from his trip to New York and resumed his twin passions of gardening and watching sports on television. But in early 2016 doctors discovered that he had colon cancer. The disease was so far along that there was little to be done. On August 15, 2016, 10 days shy of his 81st birthday, Coleman died in nearby Orangeburg, South Carolina. He was buried at Holy Temple COGIC Church Cemetery in Bamberg. The year proved to be heartbreaking for fans of the original 1962 Mets as outfielder Jim Hickman had died in June and catcher Chris Cannizzaro died in December.

One would be excused for thinking that someone with a career .197/.266/.281 line in 462 at-bats would have been long forgotten in the dustbin of history of marginal players who reached the major leagues. This is hardly the case with Coleman. Though the recollections may not be among the most flattering, they possess an inviting allure that rarely fails to bring a smile to those who cherish the memory of the hapless 1962 Mets. Author Roger Angell is among the many writers who have carried Coleman's memory forward. In his 1972 release of *The Summer Game,* Angell wrote:

> "Coleman, who is eager and combative, handles outside curve balls like a man fighting bees. He is quick

on the basepaths, but this is an attribute that is about as essential for catchers as neat handwriting."[15]

A decade later, 1962 Met Richie Ashburn, in a recollection for *The Sporting News*, cited a time when Coleman launched a game-winning pinch-hit homer after Stengel had called time, walked onto the field and whispered something in his ear. "After the game, the writers asked Coleman what Casey whispered ... and Coleman said, 'He told me to hit a home run.'"[16]

There are stories about Coleman's inability to remember the names of his teammates – everyone was "Bub" – or the fact that, because of his shyness, he was never the easiest person to interview. Yet another, as related by pitcher Bob Miller, describes an incident in which the right-hander called Coleman to the mound to change the signs with a runner on second base. Returning to his position behind the plate, Coleman promptly forgot what they'd just agreed to and repeatedly put down one finger for a fastball. Miller "laughed so hard he fell off the mound" and was called for a balk.[17] But the most amusing tale of all was the one uncovered by sportswriter Jay Dunn in 2016:

> Coleman's signature play happened one day when he missed the tag on a runner trying to score. Since the runner also missed the plate the umpire made no call. Under 1962 rules, the run would count unless the Mets tagged the runner before the next pitch was thrown. By the time a teammate pointed this out to Coleman, the runner had retreated to the visitors' dugout. Dutifully, the catcher took the ball trundled to the dugout intent on making the necessary tag.
>
> It was a long way to the dugout in the Polo Grounds [the Mets' home field]. By the time Coleman got there he could no longer remember who he was supposed to tag. No problem. He started down the bench tagging everyone wearing a uniform. The base runner figured out what was happening and, with nothing to lose, burst out of the dugout and made a mad dash for the plate. Coleman had to throw the ball to a teammate to complete the out.
>
> That was probably the only time in baseball history that a rundown play occurred between home and the dugout.[18]

These many rich, possibly apocryphal tales of Coleman will remain forever in the memories of baseball historians. Among these, perhaps no one captured him more than his former batterymate Larry Bearnarth, who claimed

that Coleman "love[d] baseball more than anything in the world."[19] That same love has been reciprocated by fans many times over.

## Sources

In addition to the sources cited in the Notes, the author consulted Ancestry.com and Baseball-Reference.com. The author wishes to thank Linda Milhouse Hibbler, Coleman's niece, and SABR members Joseph Wancho, chair of the Minor Leagues Research Committee, and Bill Mortell for their invaluable assistance.

## Notes

1 "Voice of the Fan," *The Sporting News*, October 28, 1972: 6.

2 Phone interview with Linda Milhouse Hibbler, August 14, 2017.

3 "Choo Choo Coleman: Farewell to a Good 'Bub,'" Baseball Happenings, August 15, 2016. Accessed August 29, 2017 (bit. ly/2wQn50R).

4 Allen Lewis, "Phils Placing Top Price on Twirling Trio," *The Sporting News*, December 14, 1960: 33.

5 Ibid.

6 "Names to Watch? Scriveners Spill Lowdown," *The Sporting News*, April 19, 1961: 2.

7 Through 2017, Coleman is one of only 29 known players to be hit by a pitch in his first major-league plate appearance.

8 "Choo Choo Coleman: Farewell to a Good 'Bub,'" Baseball Happenings.

9 Dan Daniel, "Rivals Pepper Mets With Trade Offers – Jackson No. 1 Target," *The Sporting News*, November 17, 1962: 19.

10 George Vecsey, "Deconstructing the Legend of Choo Choo," *New York Times*, January 23, 2012. Accessed September 1, 2017 (nyti. ms/2iNizu6).

11 Barney Kremenko, "Ol' Case's Verdict: 'Mets Much Better Than Ever Before," *The Sporting News*, April 16, 1966: 36.

12 Kevin Duffy, "The Passing of a Legend: Original Met Clarence 'Choo-Choo' Coleman Has Died," SBNation, August 16, 2016. Accessed August 29, 2017 (bit.ly/2gofAas).

13 Ibid.

14 "International League," *The Sporting News*, June 21, 1969: 46.

15 Joe Pollack, "A Top Writer Captures Heart, Pace of Baseball," *The Sporting News*, July 8, 1972: 38.

16 Richie Ashburn, "Richie Remembers Mets," *The Sporting News*, September 29, 1986: 16.

17 Michael Carlson, "Remembering Choo Choo Coleman," Irresistible Targets, August 18, 2016. Accessed October 16, 2017 (bit. ly/2gmhlpg).

18 Jay Dunn, "A Comedy of Errors from Baseball's Vault," *The Trentonian*, August 31, 2016. Accessed September 4, 2017 (bit.ly/2eUM-dJd).

19 Kevin Duffy, "The Passing of a Legend: Original Met Clarence 'Choo-Choo' Coleman Has Died."

# GIL HODGES

## BY JOHN SACCOMAN

*"Not getting booed at Ebbets Field was an amazing thing. Those fans knew their baseball, and Gil was the only player I can remember whom the fans never, I mean never, booed."*—Clem Labine[1]

*"... epitomizes the courage, sportsmanship and integrity of America's favorite pastime."*—back of a 1966 Topps baseball card.

*"Gil Hodges is a Hall of Fame man."*—Roy Campanella[2]

*"If you had a son, it would be a great thing to have him grow up to be just like Gil Hodges."*—Pee Wee Reese[3]

*"Gil Hodges is a Hall of Famer; he deserves it and it's a shame his family and friends have had to wait so long."*—Duke Snider[4]

*"He [Hodges] was such a noble character in so many respects that I believe Gil to have been one of the finest men I met in sports or out if it."*—Arthur Daley, *New York Times*.[5]

Gil Hodges was born Gilbert Ray Hodge on April 4, 1924, at Princeton, Indiana, in the state's southwestern corner. The origin of the discrepancy between his birth name of Hodge and the name by which he became well-known is unclear; however, the family name was Hodges at least by the time of the 1930 US census. Gil's parents were Irene K. (née Horstmeyer) and Charles P. Hodges. When Gil was 7 years old, the family, including older brother, Robert, and younger sister, Marjorie, moved 30 miles north to Petersburg. Big Charlie, as Gil's father was known, did not want his two sons to work in the coal mines as he did. (Big Charlie lost an eye and some toes in various mining

accidents and died of a heart embolism in 1957.)

Charles Hodges taught his sons how to play sports, and Gil was a four-sport athlete at Petersburg High School. He ran track and played baseball, basketball, and football, earning a combined seven varsity letters. In 1941, like his brother before him, Hodges was offered a Class-D contract by the Detroit Tigers, but he declined it and instead enrolled at St. Joseph's College on an athletic scholarship. St. Joseph's, 100 miles north of Indianapolis, had a well-regarded physical education program, and Hodges had designs on a college coaching career. He played baseball and basketball for the Pumas and was a member of the Marines ROTC.

After his sophomore year, Hodges was offered a contract by a local sporting-goods store owner and part-time Dodgers scout, Stanley Feezle. The lure of playing in the major leagues was too much this time, and Hodges left St. Joseph's and signed with Brooklyn, which then sent him to Olean, New York. He worked out with the Class-D Oilers but did not appear in a game.

Brooklyn called up the 19-year-old Hodges late in the 1943 season. He made his debut at Crosley Field on October 3, the Dodgers' last game of the year. Facing Cincinnati's Johnny Vander Meer, Hodges went 0-for-2 at the plate and made two costly errors at third base. Eleven days later, he entered the Marine Corps and was sent to Hawaii, first to Pearl Harbor and later Kauai. Hodges served as a gunner in the 16th Anti-Aircraft Battalion. From Hawaii he went to Tinian, in the South Pacific. In April 1945, Sergeant Hodges, now assigned to his battalion's operations and intelligence section, landed on Okinawa with the assault troops and was subsequently awarded the Bronze Star. Don Hoak, a future Dodgers teammate, said, "We kept hearing stories about this big guy from Indiana who killed Japs [Japanese soldiers] with his bare hands."[6] Discharged in February 1946, Hodges went to spring training with Brooklyn.

The solidly built Hodges stood 6-feet-1½-inches tall and weighed 200 pounds. He batted and threw right-handed, and was considered big for a baseball player of that era. However, Hodges was a gentle giant, often playing the role of peacemaker during on-field brawls. His hands were so large that teammate Pee Wee Reese once remarked that he could have played first base barehanded but wore a mitt because it was fashionable.

Dodgers President Branch Rickey sent the now 22-year-old Hodges to the Newport News (Virginia) Dodgers, the club's entry in the Class-B Piedmont League, where he was converted from infielder to catcher. Hodges played in 129 games, hitting .278 with 8 home runs for Newport News. For his efforts, Hodges was named to the all-league team. He went to the historic and tumultuous Dodgers 1947 spring training and made the team. He was the second-string catcher but played just 24 games behind the plate as the backup to Bruce Edwards.

On May 17 at Forbes Field, Hodges, batting for pitcher Harry Taylor, singled off Pittsburgh's Fritz Ostermueller for his first major-league hit. Hodges hit his first major-league home run on June 18, at Chicago's Wrigley Field. His blast came in the seventh inning against Cubs starter Hank Borowy and broke a 3–3 tie.

Hodges appeared in 28 games overall in 1947, hitting an anemic .156. He clearly needed more playing time, but he was not going to get it behind the plate. With Roy Campanella on the way to take over for Edwards, another position change for Hodges was in order. The next spring, Dodgers manager Leo Durocher subsequently wrote, he "put a first baseman's glove on our other rookie catcher, Gil Hodges. ... Three days later, I'm looking at the best first baseman I'd seen since Dolph Camilli."[7]

In 1948 Hodges played 96 games at first base, but he was the catcher in 38 games, as well. With 13 errors at first, his fielding percentage was .986, the only year he played regularly that he fielded under .990. In addition, he contributed 11 home runs and 70 runs batted in for the third-place Dodgers. He would not drive in fewer than 100 runs over the next seven seasons, nor would the Dodgers finish lower than second place over the next eight campaigns.

On December 26, 1948, Hodges married the former Joan Lombardi, from the Bay Ridge section of Brooklyn. The couple made a permanent home in Brooklyn, one of the few Dodgers to do so, and raised four children, Gil Jr. (who would spend some time as a player in the New York Mets minor-league system), Irene, Cynthia, and Barbara. (As of 2018, Joan Hodges still lived in that house in Brooklyn.) This no doubt made Gil "one of them" in the eyes of the fans. Walter O'Malley, the Dodgers' owner, stated, "If I had sold or traded Hodges, the Brooklyn fans would hang me, burn me, and tear me to pieces."[8] The very busy Hodges used the GI Bill to earn his degree at Oakland City College in Indiana during the 1947 and 1948 offseasons.

By 1949 the Brooklyn Dodgers were poised for the most productive period in the franchise's history. The fabled lineup was in place: Roy Campanella behind the plate, Hodges at first, Jackie Robinson at second, Pee Wee Reese at short, Billy Cox at third, Duke Snider in center, and Carl Furillo in right with a rotating cast in left. The team did not disappoint; Brooklyn won the National League pennant, edging the St. Louis Cardinals by one game. Hodges was now a key contributor. His first career grand slam came on May 14 off the Boston Braves' Bill Voiselle. Hodges hit for the cycle on June 25 in a 17-10 victory at Forbes Field. He hit a single, a double, a homer, and then a triple before hitting his second homer of the game in the ninth. He was 5-for-6 with four RBIs for the day.

Hodges appeared in his first All-Star Game and went 1-for-3 with a run scored. For the season, he tied with Snider for the team lead in home runs with 23, and his 115 RBIs were second on the team to Robinson' 124. Brooklyn's pennant euphoria was short-lived, however, as the Dodgers lost the World Series to the New York Yankees in five games. Hodges drove in four of the team's 14 runs in the Series.

The next two years, 1950 and 1951, brought consecutive second-place finishes. Hodges' power numbers continued to improve: He averaged 36 home runs and 108 RBIs for the two seasons. He established his career high in runs scored in 1951 with 118, one of three seasons in which he topped 100. He also established a career high in strikeouts, 99, which led the league. (He finished in the NL top 10 in strikeouts 11 times in his career.)

In the 1951 All-Star Game, Hodges went 2-for-5, including a two-run homer. However, his biggest day came on August 31, 1950, when he became the fourth major leaguer to hit four home runs in a nine-inning game. He went 5-for-6 and had 9 RBIs that night at Ebbets Field, hitting the home runs off four different Braves pitchers. His 17 total bases tied a major-league record.

The Dodgers won pennants in 1952 and 1953, only to fall again each time to the Yankees in the Series. In 1952, Hodges hit 32 home runs and drove in 102, while in 1953 he had 31 home runs and 122 RBIs, despite hitting just .181 through May 23.

The slump with which Hodges began the 1953 season actually had carried over from the 1952 World Series and cemented the legendary bond between Hodges and the Brooklyn fans. In the seven-game Series, he went 0-for-21 with five walks. Instead of booing their first baseman, the Ebbets Field faithful embraced him, cheering him warmly, sometimes with standing ovations, before each at-bat.

In his classic *The Boys of Summer*, Roger Kahn wrote, "The fans of Brooklyn warmed to the first baseman as he suffered his slump. A movement to save him rose from cement sidewalks and the roots of trampled Flatbush grass. More than thirty people a day wrote to Hodges. Packages arrived with rosary beads, rabbits' feet, mezuzahs, scapulars."[9]

In his book, *The Game of Baseball*, Hodges recalled that slump in his typical humble fashion: "The thing that most people hear about that one is that a priest [Father Herbert Redmond of St. Francis Roman Catholic Church] stood in a Brooklyn pulpit that Sunday and said, 'It's too hot for a sermon. Just go home and say a prayer for Gil Hodges.' Well, I know that I'll never forget that, but also I won't forget the hundreds of people who sent me letters,

telegrams, and postcards during that World Series. There wasn't a single nasty message. Everybody tried to say something nice. It had a tremendous effect on my morale, if not my batting average. Remember that in 1952, the Dodgers had never won a World Series. A couple of base hits by me in the right spot might have changed all that."[10] Undoubtedly, his experience of the slump helped him later in his managerial career, when he took over struggling expansion teams.

The 1954 season saw the Dodgers finish in second place and Hodges post career highs in batting average (.304), home runs (42), RBIs (130), and slugging (.579). It was his second consecutive year over the .300 mark. Hodges had 19 sacrifice flies, yet another career high, which also led the major leagues by a wide margin. On the last day of the regular season, September 26, Hodges had a solo shot and provided the only run rookie Karl Spooner needed for a 1-0 Dodgers victory. The homer was the 25th Hodges hit at Ebbets Field in 1954, establishing a new club record. His 42 homers and 130 RBIs were both second in the National League in their categories. It was the closest he would come to winning a home-run or RBI title.

In 1955 the Brooklyn Dodgers won their first and only World Series. Hodges, now 31 years old, contributed 27 homers, 102 RBIs, and a .500 slugging percentage to the Dodgers' first-place finish. Brooklyn clinched the '55 pennant on September 8 with a 10-2 drubbing of Milwaukee, the earliest a team had clinched the pennant in the 80-year history of the National League. For the fifth time in nine years, they met the Yankees in the World Series. Hodges hit .292 (7-for-24) with a homer, three walks and five RBIs. Hodges drove in the only two runs scored in the seventh and deciding game of the Series, and recorded the final putout on a throw from Reese.

Hodges would appear in two more World Series, 1956 and 1959. He continued to play as a regular over the span of those years, averaging 26 home runs and 82 runs batted in. Hodges homered once in each Series; in the 1956 seven-game loss to the Yankees, he had a hand in 12 of the Dodgers' 25 runs, and he batted .391 in the 1959 Los Angeles Dodgers Series win over the Chicago White Sox. In that Series, he won Game Four with a solo homer in the bottom of the eighth that snapped a 4-4 tie. In all, Hodges played in 39 World Series games, compiling a .267 average (35-for-131) with 5 homers, 21 RBIs, and 15 runs scored.

Hodges was active for parts of four more seasons, but

knee and other injuries limited his playing time. Despite the Dodgers' move to Los Angeles, the Hodges family maintained their home in Brooklyn, and after the 1961 season, the newly formed New York Mets selected Hodges in the first National League expansion draft. He hit the first home run in Mets history, on April 11, 1962. Overall, he appeared in 54 games for the woeful '62 Mets, hitting .252.

Hodges began 1963 as an active player, but retired when the two-year-old Washington Senators asked him to be their manager. After clearing waivers, he was traded to Washington for outfielder **Jimmy Piersall** on May 23, ending his playing career. Fittingly, Hodges's last major-league hit was an RBI single, on May 5, 1963, against the San Francisco Giants. He had hit his 370th and final home run on July 6, 1962. Until April 19 of the next season, when **Willie Mays** hit career home run 371, Hodges had the most home runs by a right-handed batter in National League history.

Each season after Hodges' arrival, the expansion Senators improved on their record from the previous season, peaking with a 76-85 record in 1967. On December 4, 1964, the Senators engineered a seven-player trade with the Dodgers. The Senators received Hodges' former teammate, slugging outfielder **Frank Howard**, pitchers **Phil Ortega** and **Pete Richert**, first baseman **Dick Nen**, and third baseman **Ken McMullen**.

These players were the core of the Senators franchise for the next several years and helped Hodges bring the team from 10th place to their surprising sixth-place finish in 1967. Although he had one year left on his contract, Hodges would not be around to guide the Senators in 1968. When **Wes Westrum** resigned as manager of the New York Mets in September 1967, the Mets sought out Hodges as his replacement.

Joan Hodges had never been more than an infrequent commuter to Washington, and Hodges still had financial interests in bowling alleys in Brooklyn. Given his popularity in the New York area, he was a natural fit for the Mets. While Senators general manager **George Selkirk** did not want to lose Hodges, he eventually relented, aided by a Mets payment of $100,000 and a player to be named. (Pitcher **Bill Denehy** was sent to the Senators on November 27.) Hodges then signed a three-year, $150,000 contract to manage the Mets.

The Mets had never finished above .500, but they were just

four games below that mark at the 1968 All-Star break. They could not maintain the pace, however, and lost 46 of the remaining 80 games. On September 24, 1968, the 44-year-old Hodges suffered a "mild" heart attack during a game in Atlanta. In addition to the stress, which he always kept bottled up, and his father's early death from an embolism, he also had developed a smoking habit on Okinawa, contributing factors for an attack so early in life. The '68 Mets did move up one position in the standings, to ninth place, a 12-game improvement over 1967. There was little in their second-half performance that would predict the much greater improvements still to come.

Hodges' first winning season as manager came with the 1969 Mets, a team that went 100-62, 27 wins more than the previous year. They were led by rising star pitchers **Tom Seaver**, **Jerry Koosman**, and promising youngster **Nolan Ryan**, as well as left fielder **Cleon Jones** and center fielder **Tommie Agee**.

On July 8, 1969, the Mets were in second place in the National League Eastern Division, 5½ games behind the Chicago Cubs. They were entering a nine-day stretch during which they would play 10 games, six of them against the Cubs, and four against the expansion Montreal Expos (now the Washington Nationals). The New York sports press referred to this as "9 crucial days," which would determine if the Mets were contenders or pretenders.

In the game against the Cubs on July 8, the Mets, down 3-1 heading into the bottom of the ninth, rallied for three runs to win the contest. Included in the rally were doubles by two pinch-hitters, **Ken Boswell** and midseason acquisition **Donn Clendenon**. The next night was Tom Seaver's self-titled "Imperfect Game," a one-hitter with the only blemish a one-out base hit by the 26th batter to face him, **Jimmy Qualls**.

The Cubs won the final game of the series, and in the press conference afterward, Hodges was characteristically guarded, with a message for his team as well. When asked, "Did the team let down today?" he replied, "We'll take seven more in a row and lose one anytime. ... We took two out of three. ... [W]e're in good shape."[11]

After taking two of three from Montreal (one game called because of rain), the Mets traveled to Chicago to face the Cubs. Still five games back at the beginning of the series, the Mets lost the first game 1-0 before taking the next two, ending up, on July 17, four games out of first.

Hodges' level-headedness and humor were certainly a factor in guiding the team through this season. When asked about the last three batters in the Expos lineup getting eight hits in the lone Expos' win, he said, "They can beat you as well as anyone else. They have a bat in their hands, don't they?" When asked if pitching was his greatest concern now, he replied, "No, hitting is." When a reporter leaves, saying that he can't stand the quiet of this press conference, Hodges quipped, "I can't stand the quiet either, but I can't leave."[12]

In another veiled message to his team, when a reporter asked Hodges if he would call the Mets a team of destiny, he said, "No, I wouldn't."[13] However, on September 1, the Mets were five games behind the Cubs. The Cubs proceeded to go 9-17 in September and October, while the Mets finished the season winning 38 of their final 49 games, including a 23-7 September.

What is truly remarkable about Hodges' managerial achievement, besides the 27-win improvement from the previous season, was the fact that the Mets had only two players (Jones and Agee) who had enough plate appearances to qualify for a batting title. In fact, Hodges platooned at catcher, right field, and all the infield positions. While the Mets did not finish above the league average in any major offensive statistic, they had only one more run allowed than the league-leading St. Louis Cardinals. Projecting wins based on runs scored and runs allowed (Bill James' Pythagorean Projection), the Mets were expected to have 92 wins. They wound up with an even 100.

The Mets beat the Atlanta Braves, with four future Hall of Famers on their roster, in three straight games in the NL playoffs. The New Yorkers outscored the Braves by an aggregate score of 27-15. In the first game, despite five earned runs surrendered by eventual Cy Young Award winner Tom Seaver, the Mets won 9-5, capped off by a five-run rally in the top of the eighth that included a two-run single by pinch-hitter **J.C. Martin**. The Mets accomplished this victory without an appearance by eventual World Series MVP Clendenon, as the Braves did not start any lefty hurlers.

In the World Series, Hodges and the Mets defeated the heavily favored Baltimore Orioles (also with four future Hall of Famers, including manager **Earl Weaver**) in five games, making the Mets the first expansion team to win a World Series. The Mets had lost the first game but swept the next four, outscoring the Orioles 14-5 in the process, a dominating effort by his young pitching staff.

The bottom of the sixth inning in the clinching Game Five has become a part of the Gil Hodges legend. The Mets, up three games to one in the Series but losing 3-0 and facing a return to Baltimore for a sixth game, had Cleon Jones leading off. Orioles lefty **Dave McNally**, with a 1-and-1 count, bounced a curveball at Jones's feet for ball two. Or did it hit Jones? He pointed to his foot, claiming the latter. The ball had bounced 50 feet into the Mets dugout. Hodges came out with the (a?) ball with a black smudge on it, convinced home-plate umpire **Lou DiMuro** that it had struck Jones, and Cleon was waved to first. Clendenon then hit a McNally offering to left for a home run that cut the Baltimore advantage to 3-2. The Mets went on to win, 5-3.

What happened with the shoe-polish incident? Did Hodges bring out the actual game ball with a shoe-polish smudge? **Ed Kranepool**, on the bench because a lefty was pitching, said that Hodges brought out a smudged ball from a bucket of discards.[14] Hodges asserted that it was the actual ball with the actual smudge.[15] Koosman recalled that he picked up the errant ball and Hodges told him to rub it on his own shoe, perhaps to enhance the mark that was already there.[16] Jones acknowledged that "Gil Hodges would never do anything dishonest."[17] In any case, Hodges' reputation for fair play and never being thrown out of a game for arguing might have been a factor in the reversal of the call. The play was so unusual that it was a plot point in the movie *Frequency*, in which a time-traveling Mets fan predicts the incident during the game itself to prove that he is from the future.

Hodges was voted Manager of the Year for turning the lovable losers into world champions. The Mets finished with identical 83-79 records in each of the next two seasons. For Hodges, there would be no more championships.

The spring of 1972 saw the first modern players strike. On April 2, Easter Sunday, Hodges played golf at the Palm Beach Lakes golf course in Florida with coaches **Joe Pignatano**, **Rube Walker**, and **Eddie Yost**. The first two were old Brooklyn Dodger pals, while Yost had been with Hodges since the Senators days. As they walked off the final hole of their 27-hole day toward their rooms at the Ramada Inn, Pignatano asked Hodges what time they were to meet for dinner. Hodges answered him, "7:30," and then he fell to the pavement.[18] He was pronounced dead of a coronary at 5:45 P.M. in West Palm Beach. He was just 47 years old.

The Mets were scheduled to open the season in Pittsburgh on April 7, the day of the funeral, but the players agreed to forfeit the game to attend. The Pirates graciously canceled the game, which was not played anyway because of the lingering strike. Coach **Yogi Berra** took over the stunned Mets as Hodges' replacement and led the Mets back to the World Series in 1973.

Hodges' funeral Mass easily could have been held at St. Patrick's Cathedral in Manhattan, but that would have not been in keeping with his unassuming ways. During his funeral Mass, held at his Flatbush parish church, Our Lady Help of Christians, Father Charles Curley said, "Gil was an ornament to his parish, and we are justly proud that in death he lies here in our little church." Repeating the story of Father Herbert Redmond's concern for Hodges' slump, Father Curley said, "This morning, in a far different setting, I repeat that suggestion of long ago: Let's all say a prayer for Gil Hodges."[19] Hodges is buried in Brooklyn's Holy Cross Cemetery.

In the years since Hodges' death, much attention has been given to his absence from the Hall of Fame. He has received well over 3,000 Hall of Fame votes, including the Baseball Writers Association of America (BBWAA) vote for the first 15 years of eligibility (1969 to 1983), and the various incarnations of the Veterans Committee subsequent to that. In 11 of his years on the BBWAA ballot, he finished with more votes than at least one and as many as 10 men who were ultimately elected to the Hall. In all, 25 Hall of Famers received fewer votes than Hodges at one time or another on the BBWAA ballot. Some were elected by the writers, some by the Veterans, but 13 never received more votes than Hodges during the years that they were both on the BBWAA ballot at the same time.

Hodges led all major-league first basemen of the 1950s in home runs (310), games (1,477), at-bats (5,313), runs (890), hits (1,491), runs batted in (1,001), total bases (2,733), strikeouts (882), and extra-base hits (585). He made the All-Star team eight times, every year from 1949-55 and again in 1957, the most of any first baseman of the time. In addition, Hodges was considered the finest defensive first baseman of the era, winning Gold Gloves the first three years they were given out (1957-59, and there were no separate AL and NL awards). Also, he was second among all players in the 1950s in home runs and RBIs, third in total bases and eighth in runs. Not to mention the managerial feat of 1969. Did his premature death cause people to forget about his greatness?

The bridge that spans the East Fork of the White River in northern Pike County, Indiana, is now named the Gil Hodges Memorial Bridge. A space was left at the bottom of the stone monument to someday include the wording of Hodges' Cooperstown plaque.

### Notes

1 gilhodges.com.

2 Marino Amoruso, *Gil Hodges: The Quiet Man* (Middlebury, Vermont: Eriksson, 1991), 141.

3 Amoruso, 165.

4 Amoruso, 168.

5 Arthur Daley, "A Fond Farewell to Gil Hodges," *New York Times*, April 4, 1972: 49.

6 Joseph Durso, "Hodges, Manager of Mets, Dies of Heart Attack at 47," *New York Times*, April 2, 1972: 1.

7 Durocher, *Nice Guys Finish Last* (New York: Pocket Books, 1975), 245.

8 Mort Zachter, *Gil Hodges: A Hall of Fame Life,* (Lincoln: University of Nebraska Press, 2015), 124.

9 Roger Kahn, *The Boys of Summer* (New York: Signet, 1973), 318.

10 Gil Hodges (with Frank Slocum), *The Game of Baseball* (New York: Crown, 1970), 16-17.

11 Paul Zimmerman and Dick Schaap, *The Year the Mets Lost Last Place* (New York: Signet, 1969), 94.

12 Zimmerman and Schaap, 117.

13 Zimmerman and Schaap, 146.

14 Tom Clavin and Danny Peary, *Gil Hodges: The Brooklyn Bums, the Miracle Mets, and the Extraordinary Life of a Baseball Legend* (New York: New American Library, 2012), 344.

15 Clavin and Peary, 343.

16 Clavin and Peary, 344.

17 Ibid.

18 Amoruso, 118.

19 Red Smith, "Gil and His Guys Last Time Around," *New York Times*, April 7, 1972: 17.

*Appendix*

Listed here are the 25 players whom Gil Hodges finished ahead of in the BBWAA voting at least once. An asterisk (*) indicates a player who never received more votes than Hodges in any season that they were on the ballot together.

Phil Rizzuto

*Red Schoendienst

*Bobby Doerr

*George Kell

Bob Lemon

*Richie Ashburn

*Hal Newhouser

Early Wynn

Enos Slaughter

Johnny Mize

Pee Wee Reese

*George Kell

Duke Snider

*Nellie Fox

Robin Roberts

Eddie Mathews

Don Drysdale

*Jim Bunning

*Bill Mazeroski

Hoyt Wilhelm

*Luis Aparicio

*Ron Santo

Juan Marichal

*Billy Williams

*Joe Torre

Source: James, Bill, John Dewan, Neil Munro, and Don Zminda, *STATS All-Time Baseball Sourcebook* (Skokie, Illinois: STATS, Inc., 1998), 2384-2387.

# HOBIE LANDRITH

## By Alan Cohen

*"The first thing you have to have is a catcher. Because if you don't have a catcher, you're going to have a lot of passed balls and you're going to be chasing the ball back to the screen all day."*

-- Casey Stengel, 1962[1]

*"I've never played any other position, except the first year when (at age 10) I was playing for a team in the Detroit Amateur Baseball Federation. I wasn't big enough to get into the equipment, but that's what I wanted to be. I used to go out to the stadium and look at Birdie Tebbetts. He's the guy who gave me the idea of keeping up a steady flow of chatter. The Tigers seemed to go better when he was yelling at them. I've been doing it for so long now, I guess it's second nature."*

– Hobie Landrith, March 1949[2]

The young faces looked at the camera as they posed for pictures to be included in the program for the 1946 Esquire All-American Boys Baseball Game in Chicago. One face was that of a sandlot player from Detroit who had turned 16 on March 16 of that year. He was already well known in Detroit, having begun playing at the age of 10 and having played for the Battalion Seven team that won the championship in the Detroit Baseball Federation in 1944.[3] He was selected to go to the Esquire Game after being one of 14 players invited to a tryout at Briggs Stadium on July 6. 1946. The five-man selection committee included Tigers manager Steve O'Neill, Tigers coach Frank Shellenback, Tigers scout Aloysius "Wish" Egan, Tigers broadcaster and former player Harry Heilmann, and writ-

er Lyall Smith of the *Detroit Free Press*. As Landrith said in 1953, "Wish Egan, the Tigers' chief scout, began buying me free dinners when I was 13 years old."[4]

Hobart Neal Landrith was born on March 16, 1930, in Decatur, Illinois. His parents, Charles X. and Edna Irene Spalding Landrith, had nine children – eight boys and a girl. Hobie's father had been born Xelpho Landrith on March 24, 1903, but was also known during his life as Charles X. Landrith. The family moved from Illinois, where Hobie's father had been a truck driver, to Michigan after Hobie was 7. The Landrith brothers all played baseball, and several were catchers. For more than a decade, the family virtually monopolized the catching position at Northwestern High School in Detroit. In Michigan, Hobie's father owned a meat-refrigeration business. His older brother Charles, who was born in 1923, started the tradition behind the plate. Hobie's older brothers also included Ellis, born in 1925, Carl, born in 1927, and Don, born in 1929. After Hobie came Johnny, born in 1934, Bob (1938), and Dale, who born in 1946 and was a 6-month-old infant when Hobie played in the Esquire game in 1946. The one sister, Phyllis, was one year older than Johnnie.[5]

After playing on the varsity at Michigan State in his freshman year, Hobie went east to represent the *Detroit Times* in the Hearst Sandlot Classic in August 1948. It was a busy month for the young player. No sooner had he got to New York than he was summoned back to Detroit to play for his Joe Gentile's Crew team in the Michigan Class-D Detroit Amateur Baseball Federation championship game. Sponsor and coach Joe Gentile said, "The kid is good. He has everything. Good arm. Good fielder. Good hitter. At Michigan State, he's considered the greatest prospect ever to hit Lansing. And every major-league club has made offers."[6] His teammates passed on the offer of a steak dinner by team sponsor Joe Gentile and pooled the money that Gentile would have spent on dinner to fly Landrith back and forth from New York to Detroit.[7] He flew back to New York after the game in Detroit and was the first player on the field when practice resumed on August 23.[8]

Before the 1949 season, Landrith signed with Cincinnati Reds farm director Fred Fleig for a reported bonus of $16,000. He had elected to sign with Cincinnati, rather than the Tigers, after Detroit signed Frank House to a large bonus, and Hobie felt he had a better chance to advance with Cincinnati.[9] He spent the season with Charleston in the Class-A Central League. He batted .250 with 23 extra-base hits in 304 at-bats. On April 23, Hobie took a weekend off before the season began and married Peggy Higdon, his childhood sweetheart. The wedding took place in Ashland, Kentucky, about 65 miles west of Charleston. Hobie and Peggy had six children.

Landrith's first professional game came on April 28 in the brand-new Watt Powell Park in Charleston in front of 8,000 fans. He doubled and homered in four at-bats and wasted little time in injecting his "peppery" personality behind the plate.[10]

After displaying "hustle and scrap"[11] in spring training in 1950, Landrith was slated to play with Tulsa in the Texas League but broke his ankle in the team's opener against Dallas and was placed on the disabled list. In the final stages of his recuperation, he served as the bullpen catcher with Cincinnati. He started working out with the Reds on June 12, and in July, when he came off the disabled list, he stayed with the team.[12] He made his debut on July 30, 1950, starting behind the plate when the Reds played the Braves at Braves Field in Boston. In his very first major-league at-bat, he singled off Vern Bickford, but was left stranded. His second time up, there were runners at the corners with one out. He grounded to second, forcing the runner at second base, but beat the throw to first. A run scored, and Landrith had his first career RBI.

Landrith spent most of 1951 with Buffalo in the Triple-A International League but was overmatched at the plate, batting only .191. Nevertheless, he was called up to the Reds late in the season and started four games with Cincinnati. He went 5-for-13. The following season, the "squeaky-voiced holler guy from Michigan State"[13] was with Tulsa in the Double-A Texas League and batted .300. He again joined Cincinnati in September, and this time got into 15 games, batting .260. His best game that season was on September 10, when he hit safely in each of his first four at-bats against the Braves. For the night, he went 4-for-5 with a double as the Reds won, 6-5 in 10 innings.

Landrith spent each of the next three seasons with Cincinnati, but played in only 143 games over all. In 1953, he backed up Andy Seminick and started 41 games. He batted .240 with three home runs and 16 RBIs. His first big league homer came off Chicago's Bubba Church leading off the top of the sixth inning at Wrigley Field in an 8-4 Cincinnati loss.

In 1954, with Seminick starting 75 games behind the plate and rookie Ed Bailey 53, Landrith started only 26. However, he made the most of his opportunities. On July 19, the Redlegs were playing the Giants at Crosley Field and Harry Perkowski was pitching a masterpiece for the home team. When Landrith replaced Seminick in the 11th inning, his batting average stood at .190 (8-for-42), and it had taken him parts of five major-league seasons to reach the 100-career-game mark.

The game was scoreless entering the bottom of the 12th inning. With one out, Landrith stepped in against the Giants' Al Corwin. After taking the first pitch for a ball, he slammed the second into the 28th row of the right-field bleachers. The Reds had a 1-0 win and Landrith had his fifth homer of the season. Although his batting average stood at only .209, more than half of his hits were home runs and his slugging percentage stood at .558. The homer was no cheapie, but it was his last of the season. He ended the year with a .198 batting average (16-for-81) with five homers and 14 RBIs in 48 games.

On April 30, 1955, Seminick and three other players were traded to the Phillies for catcher Smoky Burgess and two other players. Burgess was installed as the first-string catcher and Landrith started only 20 games during the season. Appearing in 43 games, he made 98 plate appearances, batting .253. Although a backup, he was doing well at the plate until he suffered a broken collarbone in an exhibition against Cleveland on June 26 and missed two months. After his return, he slumped and finished the season with only four homers and seven RBIs.

*"I knew it was a homer when I heard the crack of the bat. Boy what sweet music that was."* Cincinnati first-base coach Jimmy Dykes, May 8, 1955.[14]

The 1955 season was one with few highlights for Landrith, but he had timely home runs. On May 8, he started the second game of a doubleheader against the Cubs at Crosley Field. It was only his fourth start in the Reds' first 23 games. It would prove the most memorable. Entering the bottom of the sixth inning, Landrith knotted the score, 3-3, with a homer off Bob Rush. The score continued at 3-3 into the ninth inning. Those in the crowd of 15,086 who stayed for the last out would not be disappointed. Harry Perkowski came on in relief for Rush and the first batter he faced was his former batterymate, Landrith, who pulled the fourth pitch of the at-bat over the right-field fence and the Reds had a come-from-behind win. It would be more than three months until his next meaningful blast, an eighth-inning pinch-hit homer on August 29 off Robin Roberts that tied a game between the Reds and Phillies. The Reds went on to win the game, 4-3.

After the 1955 season, Cincinnati traded Landrith to the Chicago Cubs for Hal Jeffcoat. Cincinnati manager Birdie Tebbetts, for whom Landrith had grown to have great respect, said, "He's a good receiver with sufficient experience, he's a pepperpot behind the plate, and he's a better than average hitter with good power. If I didn't have a good left-handed hitter like Smoky Burgess catching for me, I'd never have let Hobie go."[15]

The left-handed-hitting Landrith was given opportunities in the early part of the 1956 season and made the most of them. He started five of his team's first six games and was batting .400 (6-for-15) after going 5-for-9 against the Reds in a three-game series at Wrigley Field, "because I had a pretty good idea of what sort of pitch would be coming."[16] However, Landrith's bat cooled off and although he appeared in a career-high 111 games, he batted only .221 and was once again on the trading block.

The Cubs traded Landrith to the Cardinals after the 1956

season. He was part of an eight-player deal. Once again, he was a backup at St. Louis, getting into 75 games in 1957, batting .243 with 3 homers and 26 RBIs. For the first time, Landrith was with a contender; the Cardinals finished in second place with an 87-67 record. He became the personal catcher for Sad Sam Jones down the stretch. On September 5, Jones pitched a four hitter and Landrith went 2-for-4 with three RBIs, as the Cardinals defeated the first-place Braves 10-1 to pull within 6½ games of the league lead.

Ten days later, In the second game of a doubleheader against Pittsburgh on September 15, Landrith again caught Jones and the Cardinals won 11-3 to pull within 2½ games of the league-leading Braves. Landrith went 3-for-5 with three RBIs. But the Cardinals were not able to gain any further ground and finished the season eight games out of first place.

Landrith's second year with St. Louis was disappointing. His average dropped to .215 in 70 games. The Cardinals finished tied for fifth place with a 72-82 record. At the end of the season, Landrith was traded to the San Francisco Giants with Billy Muffett and Benny Valenzuela for Ernie Broglio and Marv Grissom.

*"Hobie seems to be the spirit of the team, with a line of chatter that can be heard from the bleachers."*[17]

Landrith was with the Giants for three seasons. He was the regular catcher in the first season and the team made a run at the pennant. He had been at first expected to back up Bob Schmidt behind the plate, but his ability to handle pitchers made him a regular. He was also known for his talkative nature behind the plate. In 1959, Landrith batted .251 and had career highs in runs (30), hits (71), and doubles (14). *Sports Illustrated* said his main value was in handling the pitching staff, particularly Sad Sam Jones. Jones and Landrith had been teammates at Chicago and St. Louis and in 1959 with the Giants, Jones had his best season, going 21-15 with a league-leading 2.83 ERA. On September 17, Jones (making a rare relief appearance) and Landrith entered the game in the eighth inning with the Giants ahead 11-5. The Giants won the game 13-6 and extended their league lead over the Dodgers to two games with eight games remaining in the season. But the Giants lost their next five games and finished in third place.

Landrith was expected to be the starter in 1960. However, a spring-training injury sidelined him, and he didn't start a game until May 2. Even though he was not expected to contribute much offensively, Landrith slumped to the point where he lost playing time. After his first 30 games, he was batting only .181, and Schmidt got most of the starts behind the plate. Landrith's bat warmed up over the last three months of the season and he batted .280 after the disastrous start to raise his average for the season to .242. One of his starts in 1960 proved to be his most memorable day of the season behind the plate. On July 19, against the Phillies at Candlestick Park, rookie Juan Marichal made his debut for the Giants. Over the first six innings, 18 Phillies came up and 18 Phillies were retired. Marichal lost his opportunity for a perfect game in the top of the seventh inning. Then, with two out in the eighth inning and the Giants leading 2-0, Clayton Dalrymple broke up the no-hitter with a single. It was the Phillies' only hit. Marichal went on to complete the 2-0 shutout.

The 1961 season was Landrith's last with the Giants. In the offseason, they had acquired Ed Bailey from Cincinnati. Bailey, like Landrith, batted from the left side, very much a plus at San Francisco's Candlestick Park. They had also added rookie Tom Haller, with whom Landrith formed a lasting friendship. Landrith started only 18 games in 1961, batting .239 in 71 at-bats. At season's end he was not protected in the expansion draft.

On October 10, 1961, the New York Mets selected Landrith with their first pick in the expansion draft. Although he would gain a certain amount of fame as the Mets' first draft pick, he was with them a relatively short time before being sent to the Baltimore Orioles for Marv Throneberry. With the Mets Landrith batted .289 with one homer and seven RBIs.

His days with the Mets provided few highlights, and his defense was not quite as advertised. He made the first of his errors on Opening Day, overthrowing second base on an attempted steal, and had three passed balls in 21 games behind the plate with New York. His passed-ball ratio with the Mets was far worse than his prior career mark of one passed ball per 19 games caught.

But there was one memorable day – May 12. In the opening game of a doubleheader against the Braves at the Polo Grounds, Landrith entered the contest as a defensive replacement in the eighth inning and came to bat for the first time with two outs and a runner on first in the bottom of the ninth. Warren Spahn of the Braves had a 2-1 lead. Landrith hit the ball neither long nor far, but his fly ball down the short right-field line had just the distance to clear the fence near the foul pole and the two-run homer

gave the Mets their sixth win of the season. It was the third walk-off homer of his career.

The Mets won the second game as well for their first-ever doubleheader sweep. Landrith was behind the plate, and the score was 7-7 going into the ninth inning. Gil Hodges hit the Mets' second walk-off homer of the day. Landrith went 1-for-3 to bring his average to .409. Relief pitcher Craig Anderson was credited with wins in each game, bringing his record to 3-1. Anderson would never win another game. He lost his last 16 decisions in 1962 and went winless in three decisions over the following two seasons, establishing a record (since broken) for consecutive losses by a National League pitcher.

Baltimore needed Landrith's services because regular catcher Gus Triandos was injured. Landrith got into 60 games with the Orioles and batted .222 with 4 homers and 17 RBIs. His last start of the 1962 season, on September 12, was his longest game – 16 innings. The Orioles faced the Washington Senators that evening, and Tom Cheney set a major-league strikeout record with 21 strikeouts (albeit in extra innings). In the bottom of the eighth inning, Landrith became one of Cheney's victims.

In May 8, 1963, Landrith was sold to the Washington Senators. Washington was his last stop as a player. In 42 games with the Senators, he batted .175 with one homer and seven RBIs. After leaving the Senators as a player, he stayed on as a coach for former Mets teammate Gil Hodges. He left baseball after the 1964 season.

For his career, which included parts of 14 seasons, Landrith batted .233 with 34 homers and 203 RBIs in 772 games.

Hobie played for several managers during his major-league career, and his favorite was Birdie Tebbetts, for whom he played in Cincinnati. The two had first met when Landrith was a schoolboy in Detroit, working out with the Tigers and Tebbetts was catching with the Tigers. Landrith would mimic the infectious spirit displayed by Tebbetts, a chatterbox behind the plate. It was Tebbetts who instilled in Landrith the need to communicate effectively with pitchers. Hobie explained: "Birdie told me once that when a pitcher gets in trouble, call time out and talk to the guy. Even if you don't know what his trouble is, he said tell him something, anything, to get his mind off his troubles."[18]

Landrith remembered that first day of spring training with the New York Mets in 1962 when Casey Stengel came onto the field looking like a character out of a Norman Rockwell painting – "on pant leg up, one down. His socks were a mess. His hat was cocked,"[19] – and shared his wisdom with his new team. Speaking with Everett Feay of the *Fresno Bee* in 1966, Landrith said, "I can't copy his style, but he started out with, 'Fellas, there is one or two reasons why you are here. Either you are a younger fella that is not good enough to take the place of an older fella, or you're an older fella replaced by a younger fella and you want to go on in the game. We're gonna win. Whatever your problems, we're gonna correct them and win. I'm used to winning, and we're gonna win here and we're gonna correct your problems and win' He went on from there."[20]

Stengel's lessons were not lost on Landrith. On June 10, 1963, when he was with Washington, Claude Osteen was shutting out the Yankees, 1-0, in the top of the ninth, and the Yankees had runners on second and third with one out. Two right-handed batters were coming up and manager Hodges was tempted to remove the left-handed Osteen. But Landrith reminded Hodges of a lesson he learned from Stengel: In that situation, go with your best guy and have him pitch inside and induce the batter to pop up. Harry Bright, the next batter, did pop up for the second out, and Osteen retired Hector Lopez on a liner to right field for his victory. Speaking with Harvey Zucker of the *Jersey Journal* in 2003, Landrith remembered, "Casey would say throw the first pitch to the first batter at the belt buckle. The batter will be so surprised he won't be able to resist and will pop it up. Then throw the next batter a sinker low and away." Things worked out the right way and "Osteen thought I was someone special after that."[21]

During the offseasons toward the end of his playing career, Landrith worked as the business manager at a hotel near his home in California. After his playing years, he worked in public relations with the Reynolds C. Johnson Company, a distributor for Volkswagen of North America. He managed public relations for an organization serving more than 50 dealerships in California, Utah, and Nevada.

Landrith's son David, another catcher, was selected out of high school in the sixth round of the 1979 draft by the Cleveland Indians. He decided to go to college at the University of Arizona and was drafted by the Kansas City Royals in the 12th round of the 1983 draft. He batted .242 in two minor-league seasons. A generation later, David's daughter Robin was the catcher for the Baylor University women's softball team.

Landrith and his wife relocated to Sunnyvale, California, when he was with the Giants and they raised their six children there. He retired from Volkswagen after 30 years and remained part of the Giants family, appearing at many events and reunions over the years.

## Sources

In addition to the sources included in the notes, the author used Ancestry.com, Baseball-Reference.com, Hobie Landrith's player file at the National Baseball Hall of Fame and Museum, and the following:

Baker, Bob. "Detroit Star Wanted Man," *Dayton Herald*, September 8, 1948: 26.

Swope, Tom. "No Giant Sees Third Against Perkowski," *Cincinnati Post*, July 20, 1954.

Author interview with Hobie Landrith, November 19, 2013.

## Notes

1 Jack Bluth "Speaking of Sports," *San Mateo* (California) *Times*, October 30, 1963: 13.

2 Ritter Collett, "Journal of Sports," *Dayton* (Ohio) *Journal Herald*. March 12, 1949: 6

3 "After Prep Job," *Detroit News*, March 31, 1945: 11

4 Earl Lawson, "Seven Landrith Brothers All Catchers," *Cincinnati Times-Star*, March 7, 1953

5 Bob Latshaw, "6 Months Old and Fated to Catch," *Detroit Free Press*, July 31, 1946: 14.

6 Bob Baker, "Detroit Star Wanted Man," *Dayton Herald*, September 8, 1948: 26.

7 "Hobey Costs Mates a Feed," *Detroit Free Press*, August 23, 1948: 17.

8 Edgar Hayes, "Lindley to Play First for Hearst Stars," *Detroit Times*, August 24, 1948: 18-C.

9 Cy Kritzer, "Landrith Eyed Tigers Until House Received Big Bonus," *The Sporting News*, April 25, 1951: 25.

10 George Maskin, "Rookie's Big Night," *Detroit Times*, April 29,

1949: 26-C.

11 John L. Ferguson, "Landrith's Sock Surge Sparks Tulsa's Climb," *The Sporting News*, August 13, 1952: 31.

12 "Landrith, Rookie Catcher, Makes Debut with Reds," *The Sporting News*, August 9, 1950: 4.

13 Ferguson, "Landrith's Sock Surge."

14 Earl Lawson, "Hobe's Homers Give Redlegs Split with Cubs," *Cincinnati Times Star*, May 9, 1955.

15 Edgar Munzel, "Chiti-Landrith Catching Rivalry to Be Renewed by Cubs Mates," *The Sporting News*, January 11, 1956: 14.

16 Tom Swope, "Ex-Red Hottest Cub," *Cincinnati Post*, April 24, 1956

17 *Sports Illustrated*, April 11, 1960.

18 Jack Bluth, "Speaking of Sports," *San Mateo Times*, April 27, 1966: 41.

19 Keven Manahan, "A Real Original," *Newark Star Ledger*, November 11, 2006.

20 Everett Feay, "Landrith, Retired Giants Catcher, Finds It Hard to Sit on Sidelines," *Fresno Bee*, April 17, 1966: 12-S.

21 Harvey Zucker, "Hobie Knows: Losing's Not Easy," *Jersey Journal*, May 16, 2003.

# EXPANSION, ROUND TWO:
# HOW CHARLIE FINLEY BLEW UP BASEBALL

## By Warren Corbett

The cartel that ruled the national pastime was called Organized Baseball, but its second round of expansion in 1969 turned into a model of disorganization. The American and National Leagues could not agree on whether, when, or how to expand. The result was a radical restructuring of both leagues that abolished the traditional pennant races.

The turmoil was Charlie Finley's fault. Who else?

Almost from the moment the multimillionaire insurance salesman bought the Kansas City Athletics in 1960, he began agitating to leave town. He courted Dallas-Fort Worth, Louisville, Seattle, Oakland, and possibly Venus and Mars. Other American League owners repeatedly told him to stay put, once threatening to take the franchise away from him.[1]

In 1967 Finley forced the issue. He refused to sign a new lease on the Kansas City ballpark and announced plans to move to Oakland. He had worn down his fellow owners. They approved the move at a meeting in Chicago on October 18.

To salve the wound, the league promised Kansas City a new franchise as part of an expansion to 12 teams no later than 1971. When AL President Joe Cronin broke the news to Kansas City officials, they erupted. Voters had just authorized construction of a new baseball stadium, but it couldn't be built without a team to pay rent. Mayor

Ilus Davis threatened a lawsuit. Even more ominous, US Senator Stuart Symington of Missouri vowed to sponsor legislation to end baseball's cherished exemption from antitrust laws.

Faced with a threat to the foundation of his employers' monopoly, Cronin moved faster than he ever had in his days as a Hall of Fame shortstop. With the clock ticking toward midnight, he rounded up as many owners as possible and called them back into session. He could reportedly find only five of the 10; the others had gone out on the town or gone home. Before the sun rose, Cronin

Missouri State Senator Stuart Symington throws out the first pitch on Opening Day for the Kansas City Royals, April 8, 1969, as Ewing and Muriel Kauffman look onwards. The threat prompted to remove Major League Baseball's antitrust exemption after the Kansas City A's moved to Oakland. The legal action prompted the American League to add two new teams, Kansas City and Seattle, in 1969. (Kansas City Royals)

The coin toss to see who would pick first at the American League expansion draft, October 15, 1968. (From left) Cedric Tallis, Ewing Kauffman, Joe Cronin, Dewey Soriano, Marvin Milkes. (Kansas City Royals)

announced that the league would expand in 1969, with teams in Kansas City and Seattle.

It was 1960 all over again, one league charging helter-skelter into expansion without consulting the other. For the AL, it was payback; in 1960 the Nationals had struck first to grab the booming Houston market. This time both leagues had eyes on Seattle and the untapped Pacific Northwest. NL President Warren Giles thought the leagues had agreed to work together, and Commissioner William Eckert had appointed a committee to plan an orderly expansion at some future date. Instead, the American League sowed disorder.

Putting the Athletics in Oakland was a mortal danger to the NL's San Francisco franchise. "It's a question of whether we can both survive," Giants owner Horace Stoneham said.[2] (His team did, but he didn't. Stoneham went broke and was forced to sell in 1975.)

What would the National League do? "We don't want to go off half-cocked," Giles cautioned.[3] The chairman of the NL expansion committee and the most powerful voice in league councils, Walter O'Malley of the Dodgers, said, "I feel if we must expand we have to do it now."[4] But the owners were divided, and expansion required a unanimous vote.

A 12-team American League and a 10-team National League was an unworkable combination. The AL would get two more slices of network television money and two more picks in the amateur draft. The AL planned to split into two divisions, cutting the regular season to 156 games with a playoff series to determine its representative in the World Series. The playoff would steal the spotlight

from the final week of the NL pennant race.

The last obstacle to AL expansion fell in February 1968 when Seattle voters approved construction of a new stadium. The National League bowed to the inevitable at a five-hour meeting on April 19. The league would go along with the Americans and add two teams in 1969. Five hopeful cities were preparing bids: Milwaukee, Dallas-Fort Worth, San Diego, Buffalo, and Montreal.

Montreal was by far the largest contender, with a metropolitan population exceeding 2.5 million, but local sportswriter Lloyd McGowan didn't think much of the city's chances. It had had no baseball since the Triple-A Royals folded in 1960. "Nowadays Montreal is primarily a hockey, horse racing and football city," McGowan wrote.[5]

City officials asked 10 leading businessmen to pledge $1 million each for shares of the team. Charles Bronfman, a 36-year-old heir to the Seagram whiskey empire, anted up. When his wife, Barbara, objected, Bronfman assured her, "Well, it's never going to happen anyway."[6]

Montreal's mayor thought otherwise. Jean Drapeau, who held the office for 29 years, pursued big dreams and let lesser men sweat the details. He sent a letter to the National League promising to build a domed stadium by 1971. Never mind that the city council had not voted to fund such a project. The mayor had a favorite saying: "There are no problems, only solutions."[7]

National League owners met in Chicago on May 27 to decide which cities would win the precious title "major league." San Diego appeared to be a lock; it had Walter O'Malley's support, and his longtime general manager, Buzzie Bavasi, was part-owner. The other bidders came with baggage. Montreal is outside the United States and most of its residents speak French. Milwaukee was

Action at Sicks Stadium as the Seattle Pilots take on the Boston Red Sox, July 27, 1969. (David S. Eskenazi)

the biggest US market in the running, but some owners hadn't forgiven the city for suing baseball when the Braves moved to Atlanta. Dallas-Fort Worth faced a roadblock in Houston's Judge Roy Hofheinz, who wanted his Astros to be the lone star in Texas. Buffalo's ballpark was in such a rough neighborhood that the Triple-A club had moved night games to Niagara Falls.[8]

The meeting slogged on through 16, 17, 18 ballots. A dinner with the commissioner was canceled. At 10:00 P.M. President Giles emerged, his white hair like smoke rising from the Vatican. The anointed: San Diego and Montreal. Bronfman said most of the Montreal owners were "flabbergasted."[9] Mayor Drapeau's dream dome had made the sale. The national pastime went international.

Now the issue was how to operate 12-team leagues. Division play and postseason playoffs were too radical for the tradition-bound National League owners. They argued that the playoffs were a gimmick that would rob the World Series of some of its luster. A five-game playoff was a crapshoot that might produce a World Series between the third- or fourth-best teams in each league. To those objections, the American League had a simple response: Without divisions, who would buy tickets to see a 12th-place team?[10]

The logical solution would be to split the two leagues into three eight-team circuits. Logic be damned. "How in the world would we ever decide what teams to put in which leagues?" Giles said. "I don't think we could ever get agreement on that."[11]

The two leagues finally did agree to operate under the same rules. The Nationals caved, although the resolution was called a compromise. The NL accepted division play and playoffs. In return, the AL dropped its plan for a 156-game schedule, magnanimously consenting to keep the revenue from six additional games. The 162-game slate would be unbalanced, with 18 games against each division opponent and 12 against each of those in the other division.

One sure thing about the split into divisions: Some teams wouldn't be happy. The Chicago White Sox, a founding member of the American League, landed unwillingly in the Western Division along with five come-lately cities: Anaheim, Kansas City, Seattle, Oakland, and Minneapolis-St. Paul. No traditional rivals there, and the White Sox' West Coast night games would last until around midnight Central Time, a TV ratings-killer.

The National League map caused even more teeth-gnashing. The Mets didn't want to give up games against the Dodgers and Giants, with their nostalgic fans in New York, and had to be persuaded that a coast-to-coast division wouldn't fly. Houston, Los Angeles, San Francisco, and San Diego were the only natural Western teams. St. Louis and Chicago were closest, but they didn't want to be stuck with so many late California games. Cincinnati and Atlanta from the Eastern time zone agreed to join the Mostly Western Division, enticed by the additional dates with the Dodgers and Giants.

The insolvency of the Seattle Pilots by early 1970 was so dire that the club could not afford to repay its debts to fellow American League owners, as evidenced by this letter from Charlie O. Finley. (David S. Eskenazi)

Like the first expansion in 1960, the chaotic second round showed that the organization of Organized Baseball was obsolete. Baseball still lacked the strong management structure needed to run a large business. The industry faced game-changing challenges: a newly militant players union and declining popularity. The owners and the Players Association signed their first collective-bargaining agreement in 1968, limiting the owners' absolute power over players. The next spring a Louis Harris poll found that football had surpassed baseball as America's most popular sport for the first time.[12] And the latest expansion franchises would bring more complications.

Kansas City Royals' prospects of the future, 1968-1969 (from left) Lance Clemons, Paul Splitorff, Jim York, Don O'Riley. (Kansas City Royals)

**Notes**

1  Mark Armour, "Charlie Finley," SABR Baseball Biography Project, sabr.org/bioproj/person/6ac2ee2f, accessed February 22, 2018.

2  Bob Stevens, "Giants More Than Slightly Worried at Invasion by Finley," *The Sporting News*, November 4, 1967: 32.

3  Jerome Holtzman, "N.L. Owners Unload Weapons, Vote Against a Fight for Seattle," *The Sporting News*, November 25, 1967: 30.

4  Shirley Povich, "This Morning," *Washington Post*, March 22, 1968: D1.

5  Lloyd McGowan, "Little Chance for N.L. Team in Montreal," *The Sporting News*, May 4, 1968: 30.

6  Charles Bronfman with Howard Green, *Distilled* (New York: HarperCollins, 2017), location 1371.

7  Ibid., location 1363.

8  C.C. Johnson Spink, "We Believe," *The Sporting News*, April 6, 1968: 14.

9  Ted Blackman, "Baseball Holds Draft Here in October," *Montreal Gazette*, May 29, 1968: 41.

10  Edward Prell, "N.L. Rejects Two-Division Proposal," *Chicago Tribune*, May 29, 1968: C1.

11  Dick Kaegel, "Cool It! That's What Club Brass Will Do in Wake of Big Fuss," *The Sporting News*, June 15, 1968: 4.

12  Louis Harris, "Harris Poll: Football Now No. 1 Sport," *Fort Lauderdale* (Florida) *News*, April 23, 1969: 6B.

# MR. K BRINGS BASEBALL BACK TO KANSAS CITY

## By Joseph Thompson

Charles O. Finley never seemed to connect with the people of Kansas City after acquiring ownership of the Athletics in 1961.[1] In the six years that he owned the club in Kansas City, Finley failed to field a winning club, he often looked to relocate the club to a different city, constantly sparred with other baseball owners and officials over radio and television rights, and failed repeatedly to try and build a new ballpark. American League owners became fed up with Finley's antics in Kansas City and his constant requests to move the franchise. They finally granted him his wish and approved the Athletics' move to Oakland in 1967. As part of the arrangement that granted Finley's departure, the people of Kansas City received a new franchise called the Royals. The owner of the expansion club, Ewing M. Kauffman, committed himself to the people of Kansas City. His commitment to produce a successful franchise quickly set him apart from other expansion clubs as a model of franchise excellence on and off the field.

On October 18, 1967, American League owners gave Finley the go-ahead to move his Athletics to Oakland. At the same meeting, major-league owners voted to expand each league by two teams no later than 1971.[2] A delegation from Kansas City, including Mayor Ilus Davis and Missouri Senator Stuart Symington, protested the American League's decision to wait until 1971 to expand. Symington threatened to hold congressional hearings that promised to strip away baseball's antitrust status if the league failed to replace a team in Kansas City before 1971.

Mayor Davis threatened legal action to stall the Athletics from moving.[3]

American League President Joe Cronin called another meeting with the owners to discuss an adjusted plan for expansion in the wake of threats by the Kansas City delegation. The owners agreed to move expansion up two years, to 1969. As added appeasement, the owners agreed that Kansas City would receive a new franchise, not one moved from another city. Frank Cashen of the Orioles recalled, "One thing I'll never understand is the events of that day. Voting in the morning to allow Finley to leave Kansas City. Then voting in the afternoon to expand into Kansas City because we considered it one of the hotbeds of baseball. As an American Leaguer, I have to say I think that was a disgraceful proposition to have occurred in one day. Expansion was forced, and I'm not sure at all that it

Royals players (l to r) Chuck Harrison, Roger Nelson, and Bob Oliver unveil the original team uniforms and jacket, 1968. (Courtesy of the Kansas City Royals)

was good for baseball – as far as comparing the caliber of the game before that expansion before that expansion and now."[4]

Expansion in 1969 included two new teams for the American and National Leagues. In the National League, the San Diego Padres would be joined by the major leagues' first team in Canada, the Montreal Expos. In the American League, the Seattle Pilots would join the new club in Kansas City. These four clubs were part of baseball's "second wave of expansion," as described by historian Fran Zimniuch in *Baseball's New Frontier: A History of Expansion, 1961-1998*. This wave of expansion changed the game forever.[5]

Manager Joe Gordon addresses the Kansas City Royals in spring training, 1969. It was Gordon's second term at the helm of a Kansas City team, having managed the A's in 1961. (Courtesy of the Kansas City Royals)

Baseball's second wave of expansion called for a complete restructuring of the divisional format in baseball. The one-division leagues became circuits with two divisions, East and West. The division leaders would hold best-of-five playoffs, or Championship Series, to determine the pennant winners. They would then face each other in the World Series.[6] The expansion San Diego Padres joined the National League West Division along with the Atlanta Braves, Cincinnati Reds, Houston Astros, Los Angeles Dodgers, and San Francisco Giants. The new Montreal Expos were in the National League East along with the Chicago Cubs, New York Mets, Philadelphia Phillies, Pittsburgh Pirates, and St. Louis Cardinals. The American League East featured the Baltimore Orioles, Boston Red Sox, Cleveland Indians, Detroit Tigers, New York Yankees, and Washington Senators. The expansion Seattle Pilots and Kansas City Royals joined the American League West along with the California Angels, Chicago White Sox, Minnesota Twins, and Oakland Athletics.[7]

At a Chamber of Commerce luncheon in Kansas City

in 1967, Gabe Paul, president and general manager of the Cleveland Indians, spoke of the need for someone or some group to put forth the financial effort to make sure Kansas City received the expansion club promised to it by the American League. In attendance was a local business leader who loved sports and felt a sense of civic pride in helping bring a new baseball franchise to his beloved Kansas City.

Ewing Kauffman, 51, was a native Missourian who made his fortune in pharmaceuticals. Kauffman had started Marion Laboratories in 1950 using $5,000 of his own money as a stake. He was a salesman during the day and order filler at night in the basement of his Kansas City home.[8] Marion Laboratories became the largest drug-marketing organization in Missouri and ranked 41st among the nation's 900 pharmaceutical companies by 1968.

Kauffman's passion for sports focused not on baseball but on breeding race horses. His hobby, which included horses purchased from the actor Desi Arnaz, had earned him a profit of over $375,000.[9] In fact, Kauffman did not really like baseball but was willing to help bring major-league ball back to Kansas City. "I raised my hand and said I would be willing to put in a million dollars," Kauffman said, "not really doing it from anything but a civic standpoint."[10]

The cost set by the American League for owning a new major-league franchise in Kansas City reduced the number of potential owners. The franchise fee totaled $5,300,000 plus an additional $600,000 for the major-league pension fund. Only four other groups made serious bids to become the new owners: Alex Barket, president of the Civic Plaza National Bank; Richard Stern, president of Stern Brothers; Crosby Kemper Sr., retired chairman of the City National Bank; and John Latshaw, vice president of Hutton & Co. who represented a group of civic leaders. The four groups plus Kauffman met with the American League screening committee as potential owners.[11]

Baseball supporters, businessmen, and civic leaders convinced Ewing Kauffman that he alone should be the new owner of the club. Sportswriter Ernie Mehl told Kauffman in late 1967 that "we need to show the American League there is somebody in Kansas City that is somewhat interested in baseball and financially can afford it."[12]

Kauffman agreed and persuaded Commerce Trust to grant him a $4 million letter of credit to help him purchase the team. He received another letter of credit for $6 million for operating reserves for the club if he became the sole owner of the team.[13]

Kauffman's meeting with American League officials placed him as the favorite to land the franchise. A number of national newspapers called his selection as the new owner "a foregone conclusion" because the American League owners preferred sole owners over syndicates.[14] He assured the major-league owners in November 1967 of his commitment to the people of Kansas City and his plans to run the team. "If I get the ball team," he said, "I'll do what I did with the stable (referring to his horse-breeding experience) – hire professionals and turn the operation over to them. I'll lay down the financial policy. The baseball end, I'll leave to the baseball men." All of the owners – including Charles O. Finley himself, voted to approve Kauffman as the owner of the Kansas City franchise.[15] Announcing the selection of Kauffman, American League President Joe Cronin said on January 11, 1968, "Mr. Kauffman was chosen because of his fine business background, his connections in the public relations field, and his unending desire to own a major league franchise."[16]

Kansas City Royals' 1969 pitching staff (from left) Bill Butler, Mike Hedlund, Dick Drago, Wally Bunker, Roger Nelson, Tom Burgmeier. (Courtesy of the Kansas City Royals)

Kauffman promised his fellow townsmen that he would build a franchise that the people of Kansas City could be proud of. "Kansas City has been good to me and I want to show I can return the favor," he said.[17] He vowed that the club would remain in Kansas City during his lifetime, and that after his death his estate would be "legally bound to sell the club to Kansas City interests."[18]

Kauffman was praised for his commitment to the city. His message to the mayor and to the potential fans of the new club removed the "onus of absentee ownership which plagued the A's and their fans for 13 years," said *The*

*Sporting News.*[19] Dick Young of the *New York Daily News* wrote after Kauffman received the franchise that readers should be prepared "for all sorts of jokes like changing the name from the Kaycee A's to the Kaycee LSD's."[20]

To run the ballclub, Kauffman in January 1968 chose Cedric Tallis from the California Angels as his new general manager and executive vice president, then, as he had promised, stepped back and allowed Tallis to set up the baseball operation. Tallis hired front-office staff, established a minor-league system for the club with its first teams in Dubuque, Iowa, and Corning, New York. The Royals hired baseball veterans including Charlie Metro from the Chicago Cubs as director of personnel, Lou Gorman from the Baltimore Orioles as director of player development, and former Kansas City Athletics manager Joe Gordon to run the club on the field.[21] Kauffman and Tallis assembled a baseball management staff loaded with experience to help him field a solid expansion club. Kauffman's next moves to solidify Kansas City's new major-league franchise utilized his marketing skills. He started the process of getting the Kansas City community and its baseball fans excited about their new club.

Kauffman turned to the people for suggestions on a team name and colors. The team received over 17,000 name suggestions, including Plowboys, Pythons, Canaries, Bovines, Bengals, Badgers, Salukis, and Batmen. Some names paid homage to Kansas Native American nations, among them the Pawnees, Osages, and the Kansa. A few names like the Kauffs, Kauffies, and Kawsmonats referred to Kauffman himself, but as historian Roger Launius wrote in his history of baseball in Missouri, "[E]veryone agreed that those names were just plain silly."[22]

The board of directors agreed on the name Royals, a name submitted by Sanford Porte, a bridge engineer from Overland Park, Kansas. Porte suggested the Royals name because of "Missouri's billion-dollar livestock income, Kansas City's position as the nation's leading stocker and feeder market and the nationally known American Royal parade and pageant." Porte later added that "royalty stands for the best."[23] Porte also played a role in the colors of the team and suggested a logo and a mascot. He said the team mascot should be a "champion American Royal stallion like the west's golden Palomino," and the colors royal blue and white with an emblem of a royal blue crown on a white diamond. For his winning entry, Porte received an expense-paid trip to the All-Star Game in Houston that summer.

Bat Day at Municipal Stadium, 1969. (Courtesy of the Kansas City Royals)

Kauffman, his wife, Muriel, and Tallis turned to the Kansas City-based greeting card giant Hallmark for help creating a logo. Hallmark held a contest among its designers. The logo had to contain blue, gold, and a crown. Designer Shannon Manning, submitted a logo representing a modern version of home plate, topped by a gold crown. As for the "KC" and the "R" in the logo lettering he explained, "And at the time, in the later '60s and early '70s, one of the more popular type styles was what they called 'swash,' these are modifications of the swash letters. They add a little flair to the image." Muriel Kauffman had wanted a horse's head in the loop of the "R" in the logo, but the final logo did not go with that. "I guess Mrs. Kauffman was a horse lover because she wanted a horse head inside the loop of the R, they didn't do that," Manning said.[24]

Kauffman's marketing experience helped him build a loyal fan base in the relatively small major-league baseball market of Kansas City. One of his first deals involved the radio and TV broadcast rights. Just a month after the franchise was awarded to him, Kauffman signed a three-year sponsorship contract with the Schlitz brewery. When the Athletics moved to Kansas City in 1955, the brewery was the original sponsor for the club. The broadcasting contract with the Royals, worth over a million dollars a season, provided radio coverage for the team in Missouri, Kansas, Oklahoma, Colorado, Nebraska, South Dakota, Iowa, and Arkansas.[25] The company also agreed to sponsor television broadcasts for 30 road games but no home games. Broadcasting no home games and only a few road games was the norm at the time. The cross-state St. Louis Cardinals aired the same number of road games, while other teams aired nine or fewer games. On the other hand, the expansion Seattle Pilots never even secured a broadcast deal, which probably helped fuel their demise after only one season in the Pacific Northwest.[26] *The Sporting News* called the broadcasting contract between the Royals and Schlitz the best ever for a Kansas City team because

Charles Finley never received more than $156,000 per year in radio and television rights while in Kansas City.[27]

Kauffman created a team of boosters known as the Royal Lancers to help promote the team and push ticket sales. Membership in the exclusive sales force was limited to those who sold at least 75 season tickets for the inaugural 1969 season. It included some of Kauffman's sales force from Marion Laboratories. Members of the club received team privileges including a Royals Lancers blazer, a Lancers club at Municipal Stadium, and a three-day trip for two to the team's new spring-training facility at Fort Myers, Florida. *The Sporting News* reported that season-ticket sales by October 1968 had reached 6,334 for 1969, more than the top season-ticket sales for the Kansas City Athletics. A month later, the Royals set an American League record for season-ticket sales when their number reached 7,022. Kauffman did not plan on stopping there. "We'll reach 10,000," he said.[28]

Kauffman trusted Cedric Tallis to help make the team a success. Tallis and his staff agreed that the best way to build a sustaining winner was to focus on obtaining young players and teaching them the fundamentals of the game instead of trading for more experienced veteran players. "We won't take players just because they have names," Tallis said. "We have to build with young players; we're going for prospects."[29] The Royals aggressively pursued and signed young players at a rate far outpacing the new expansion clubs and most other clubs. They had signed 29 of their 56 picks by July 1968, including their first pick of the expansion draft, Kenneth O'Donnell, a shortstop from Neptune, New Jersey. Jack McKeon, a scout for the Royals, liked what he saw of O'Donnell, saying, "He's the best-looking infielder I've seen in three years."[30]

The Royals and the Seattle Pilots participated in the expansion draft held in Boston on October 15, 1968. The 30 players obtained in the draft cost the Royals $175,000 each. Roger Nelson, a 24-year-old hard-throwing right-handed pitcher from the Baltimore Orioles, was the club's first pick. The Royals then selected Joe Foy, a third baseman from the Boston Red Sox, and left-handed pitcher Jim Rooker from the New York Yankees. They expected Nelson and Rooker to lead their rotation for the inaugural 1969 season and for Foy to start at third.[31] The Royals' 49th pick was 46-year-old knuckleballer Hoyt Wilhelm. "I consider it an honor that Kansas City would draft me," Wilhelm said. "I also was a little bit surprised that anybody would take a chance on me."[32] On July 24,

1968, while pitching for the White Sox, Wilhelm had broken Cy Young's record for most games pitched. His time with the Royals, however, did not last long. Less than two months after drafting him, the Royals, in their first major-league-level trade, sent him to the California Angels for utility infielder Ed Kirkpatrick and rookie catcher Dennis Paepke. Tallis said the move emphasized the Royals' "youthful approach."[33] Ike Brookens, a right-handed pitcher from the Washington Senators, became the Royals' final selection on draft day. "By the start of spring training in Fort Myers," Cedric Tallis said, "we should have at least 120 players."[34] The team and its signed players then headed out on a bus tour around Kansas and other states to help promote the new team. The caravan greeted fans and the media in Leavenworth, Atchison, Lawrence, Topeka, Manhattan, Junction City, Salina, Emporia, and Wichita in Kansas, as well as cities in Nebraska, Iowa, Missouri, Arkansas, and Oklahoma.[35]

Municipal Stadium had been the former home of the Athletics and on June 4, 1968, the Royals signed a four-year lease with the city to play their games there. Originally named Muehlebach Field, after local brewer George E. Muehlebach, the ballpark, near the heart of the city, was built in 1923 for $400,000. The Muehlebach Brewing Company was founded by Swiss immigrant George Muehlebach Sr. When he died in 1905, his son took over the brewery and went on to leave his mark on Kansas City's baseball history. George E. Muehlebach, a former player on his father's local team, the Pilsners, purchased the minor-league Kansas City Blues of the American Association in 1917. Eventually, the Kansas City Monarchs of the Negro Leagues became a tenant of Muehlebach Field.[36] The New York Yankees purchased the field for their minor-league team in 1937 and renamed it Ruppert Stadium in honor of the Yankees owner, Col. Jacob Ruppert. When the Athletics left Philadelphia for Kansas City in 1955, the facility was renamed Municipal Stadium and an upper deck was added. The ballpark also became the home of the Kansas City Chiefs of the American Football League and the Kansas City Spurs of the North American Soccer League in 1968-1969.[37]

Kauffman had plans for a much bigger stadium project. Ground was broken for the Jackson County Sports Complex on July 11, 1968. The new sports complex consisted of a 45,000-seat ballpark for the Royals and a 75,000-seat football stadium for the Chiefs. The project cost the taxpayers of Jackson County $43 million and was scheduled to open in 1970.[38] Delays in construction caused by two

major strikes and inflation increased the total cost of the project to $70 million by the time Royals Stadium opened in April 1973.[39]

A crowd of 17,688 made their way into Municipal Stadium on April 8, 1969, to watch the Royals play the Minnesota Twins in the major leagues' quick return to Kansas City. Senator Symington threw out the first pitch. The Royals team that took the field had little to no major-league experience but that did not stop them from giving the fans of Kansas City something good to cheer for. Lou Piniella, a 26-year-old rookie acquired from the Seattle Pilots, provided four hits for his new team that day. But pinch-hitter Joe Keough proved to be the Opening Day hero. His single in the bottom of the 12th inning off Twins reliever Dick Woodson gave the Royals a 4-3 walk-off win.

Opening Day provided the fans of Kansas City with a win but the team experienced expansion club growing pains. That first season the team surprised no one by finishing with a record of 69-93. In 1970, they finished 65-97.[40] They made a run at contention in 1971, but finished a distant second, 16 games behind the Oakland Athletics, who were beginning their run as the most powerful team in the 1970s. Kansas City's former Athletics won three straight World Series (1972-74) and locked up the division for five years beginning in 1971.

Kauffman understood that the other owners in baseball were not going to help him build a winner in Kansas City. "The only thing I could do," he said, "was to go outside the normal baseball avenues open to us and try to find better players. So I came up with the idea that you didn't have to play baseball all your life to be a good baseball player. That's what the old-timers in baseball thought. I thought that if you had the physical attributes necessary to be a baseball star, you could be taught baseball."[41]

Happy Birthday, Mr. K! Royals pitcher Moe Drabowsky presents a birthday cake to Ewing Kauffman as his wife Muriel and 'Royal Lancer' Lester Milgram look onwards, September 1969. (Courtesy of the Kansas City Royals)

Kauffman challenged his baseball people to devise innovative ways to build a contender for a division title and possible World Series victory within 10 years. The club brainstormed and although no one can receive full credit, those involved with the Royals at the time said later that the answer came from Syd Thrift in the scouting department.[42] Syd's idea challenged the traditional norms of baseball establishment by searching for athletic players who were often passed up on their baseball abilities. Kauffman funded his innovative new training program, the first of its kind in the major leagues, called the Royals Baseball Academy.

Situated in Sarasota, Florida, the academy opened in 1970. Kauffman hired scientists, including a young researcher from NASA and the Naval Research Laboratory named Dr. Raymond Reilly, and physicians who focused on four physical abilities necessary to succeed in baseball: speed of foot, excellent eyesight, quick reflexes and overall agility, and outstanding body balance. Athletes who showed that they had these skills, in the eyes of the instructors at the academy, could learn how to become successful in baseball. Several players who attended the academy made it to the major leagues, including future manager Ron Washington, and the Royals' double-play combination from 1977 to 1984 of shortstop U.L. Washington and second baseman Frank White. The academy, although an innovative baseball experiment, proved too costly for the club to maintain. In 1974 the experiment ended when the academy closed its doors.[43] The Royals Baseball Academy demonstrated Kauffman's willingness to challenge traditional methods in building a successful major-league club, and his dedication to building a winning tradition for the Royals.

Jack McKeon, Royals manager in 1973, believed his team could win the American League pennant after the team thumped the Texas Rangers on April 10. "This team believes it can win a pennant," McKeon said. "I believe we can win it. There's no question about it. The atmosphere in this stadium and on this club is contagious … exciting."[44] In an era of cookie-cutter sporting venues, Ewing Kauffman built a unique ballpark. Designed by Kivett & Myers, a sports stadium architectural firm in Kansas City, Royals Stadium featured new-age technologies like a $2 million, 10-story-high electronic scoreboard shaped like the Royals crest. The ballpark's 322-foot water fountain was the world's largest privately funded water fountain. The fountain spectacular lit up the Kansas City sky with a combination of lights and dancing water jets that illuminated when a Royals player hit a home run. The water spectacular was a dream come true for the proud owner.[45] "The scoreboard and water display will be so spectacular," Kauffman said, "they will border on making the stadium a dream world."[46] Kauffman used his own money to fund the extras; for Opening Night he arranged to have the game televised in color at his own cost.[47]

Kauffman Stadium was the first American League park to be fully carpeted with an artificial surface. The team used that surface to build a winner based on speed and pitching.[48] On August 2, 1973, a 20-year-old third baseman drafted by the club in 1971 from El Segundo High School in California made his debut against the Chicago White Sox. George Brett became the most popular Royals player and the foundation for what became one of the most successful teams of the expansion era. In his 20-year career, he was the centerpiece for a Royals franchise that won six AL West crowns, American League pennants in 1980 and 1985, and the 1985 World Series championship.

### Notes

1 John Helyar, *Lords of the Realm: The Real History of Baseball* (New York: Villard Books, 1994), 77.

2 Fran Zimniuch and Branch Rickey, *Baseball's New Frontier: A History of Expansion, 1961-1998* (Lincoln: University of Nebraska Press, 2013), 76.

3 Roger D. Launius, *Seasons in the Sun: The Story of Big League Baseball in Missouri* (Columbia: University of Missouri Press, 2002), 89; Zimniuch and Rickey, 77-80; Mark Rieper, "Fifty Years Ago Today, Ewing Kauffman Became the First Owner in Royals History," royalsreview.com/2018/1/11/16878996/fifty-years-ago-today-ewing-kauffman-became-the-first-owner-in-royals-history, January 11, 2018. Accessed April 7, 2018.

4 Launius, 89.

5 Zimniuch and Rickey, 77-80.

6 Charles C. Alexander, *Our Game: An American Baseball History* (New York: Henry Holt, 1992), 271.

7 Ibid.; Zimniuch and Rickey, 79.

8 "Celebrate the Legacy," Ewing Marion Kauffman Foundation Website, kauffman.org/emk/marion#epitomeofentrepreneurship. Accessed March 2, 2018.

9 "Sunrise in Kansas City," *The Sporting News*, January 27, 1968; "Celebrate the Legacy."

10 Launius, 93.

11 "Kansas City Owner to be Named by A.L. Today," *Chicago Tribune*, January 11, 1968; Alexander, 270; Zimniuch and Rickey, 79.

12 Launius, 93.

13 Ibid.

14 "American League Gives Franchise," *Baltimore Sun*, January 12, 1968; Launius, 95.

15 Launius, 93.

16 United Press International, "Kauffman Heads Kansas City Club," *New York Times*, January 12, 1968: 77.

17 "Ewing Kauffman and the Story of the Royals," Ewing Marion Kauffman Foundation Website, kauffman.org/who-we-are/our-founder-ewing-kauffman/ewing-kauffman-and-the-story-of-the-kansas-city-royals. Accessed March 1, 2018.

18 "American League Gives Franchise."

19 "Sunrise in Kansas City."

20 Dick Young, "Young Ideas," *The Sporting News*, February 3, 1968: 14.

21 Joe McGuff, "Old Home Week for Pilot Joe Gordon in Kaycee," *The Sporting News*, September 21, 1968; "Royals Sign Gordon to One-Year Pact," *Baltimore Sun*, September 10, 1968; Launius, 95.

22 Launius, 95.

23 "Kansas City Royals Need Some Players," *Sarasota Herald-Tribune*, March 22, 1968; "Kansas City Directors Name New Baseball Club the Royals," *Hartford Courant*, March 22, 1968; Launius, 95.

24 Cynthia Billhartz Gregorian, "The Man Who Designed Iconic Kansas City Royals Logo in '60s Recalls How He Did It," *Kansas City Star*, March 28, 2018. https://www.kansascity.com/sports/mlb/kansas-city-royals/article207123729.html Accessed April 6, 2018.

25 "Royals Sign Three-Year Contract," *Independence* (Missouri) *Examiner*, May 8, 1968.

26 Ibid.; Launius, 95; Max Rieper, "A History of Royals Broadcasters," *SB Nation: Royals Review*, royalsreview.com/2016/11/28/13651720/a-history-of-royals-broadcasters. Accessed March 30, 2018.

27 Joe McGuff, "$3 Million Air Pact to Bolster Royals in Their '69 A.L. Debut," *The Sporting News*, June 1, 1968: 17.

28 "Royals Top K.C. Mark," *The Sporting News*, October 12, 1968: 16; Sid Bordman, "Royals Set A.L. Season-Ducat Mark," *The Sporting News*, November 2, 1968: 45; Launius, 95.

29 Launius, 96.

30 Joe McGuff, "Royals Post High Mark in Scouting Players," *The Sporting News*, July 6, 1968: 16.

31 Zimniuch and Rickey, 77-80; Bordman, 41.

32 Paul Cox, "45-Year Old Wilhelm 'Honored' to Join the Royals as a Draftee," *The Sporting News*, November 9, 1968: 44.

33 "Angels Deal 2 Players to Kansas City for Wilhelm," *Chicago Tribune*, December 13, 1968.

34 Zimniuch and Rickey, 77-80.

35 Matthew Pozel, "5 Ways Ewing Kauffman Changed Baseball," Ewing Marion Kauffman Foundation Website, March 28, 2018. Accessed April 1, 2018.

36 Jason Roe, "A Beer Baron Is Born," Missouri Valley Special Collections, Kansas City Public Library. kchistory.org/week-kansas-city-history/beer-baron-born. Accessed March 1, 2018; David B. Stinson, "Kansas City Municipal Stadium – Muehlebach, Ruppert, and Blues," Deadball Baseball. deadballbaseball.com/?tag=muehlebach-field. Accessed June 18, 2018.

37 Ibid.

38 Joe McGuff, "Kaycee Starts on Stadiums," *The Sporting News*, July 27, 1968: 9.

39 Bill Richardson, "Royals' Brand New Stadium – Fit for a King," *The Sporting News*, April 14, 1973: 9.

40 Neil Amdur, "Royal Welcome for Kansas City," *New York Times*, April 8, 1969; "Royals Edge Twins, 4-3 in 12 Innings," *Boston Globe*, April 9, 1969.

41 Launius, 96.

42 Sam Mellinger, "Forty Years Later, Royals Academy Lives On in Memories," *Kansas City Star*, August 2, 2014. kansascity.com/sports/spt-columns-blogs/sam-mellinger/article940797.html. Accessed April 6, 2018.

43 Matthew Pozel, "5 Ways Ewing Kauffman Changed Baseball"; Launius, 96.

44 "Kansas City All Agog Over Streaking Royals," *Los Angeles Times*, April 19, 1973.

45 'Huge Scoreboard Big Hit in New K.C. Park," *Baltimore Sun*, March 16, 1973.

46 Bill Richardson, "Royals' Brand New Stadium – Fit for a King," *The Sporting News*, April 14, 1973: 9.

47 "Royals Stage Spectacular," *Washington Post*, April 10, 1973.

48 William Leggett, "Now Comes the Big Blue Machine," *Sports Illustrated*, April 23, 1973.

## KANSAS CITY ROYALS EXPANSION DRAFT

| PICK | PLAYER | POSITION | FORMER TEAM |
|------|--------|----------|-------------|
| 1 | Roger Nelson | p | Baltimore Orioles |
| 2 | Joe Foy | 3b | Boston Red Sox |
| 3 | Jim Rooker | p | New York Yankees |
| 4 | Joe Keough | of | Oakland A's |
| 5 | Steve Jones | p | Washington Senators |
| 6 | Jon Warden | p | Detroit Tigers |
| 7 | Ellie Rodriguez | c | New York Yankees |
| 8 | Dave Morehead | p | Boston Red Sox |
| 9 | Mike Fiore | 1b | Baltimore Orioles |
| 10 | Bob Oliver | 1b | Minnesota Twins |
| 11 | Bill Butler | p | Detroit Tigers |
| 12 | Steve Whitaker | of | New York Yankees |
| 13 | Wally Bunker | p | Baltimore Orioles |
| 14 | Paul Schaal | 3b | California Angels |
| 15 | Bill Haynes | p | Chicago White Sox |
| 16 | Dick Drago | p | Detroit Tigers |
| 17 | Pat Kelly | of | Minnesota Twins |
| 18 | Billy Harris | 2b | Cleveland Indians |
| 19 | Don O'Riley | p | Oakland A's |
| 20 | Al Fitzmorris | p | Chicago White Sox |
| 21 | Moe Drabowsky | p | Baltimore Orioles |
| 22 | Jackie Hernandez | ss | Minnesota Twins |
| 23 | Mke Hedlund | p | Cleveland Indians |
| 24 | Tom Burgmeier | p | California Angels |
| 25 | Hoyt Wilhelm | p | Chicago White Sox |
| 26 | Jerry Adair | 2b | Boston Red Sox |
| 27 | Jerry Cram | p | Minnesota Twins |
| 28 | Fran Healy | c | Cleveland Indians |
| 29 | Scott Northey | of | Chicago White Sox |
| 30 | Ike Brookens | p | Washington Senators |

# BOB OLIVER

### By John Struth

Robert Lee "Bob" Oliver played baseball with the Kansas City Royals in 1969, their inaugural season, getting his first real opportunity to show off his baseball skills at the age of 26. He toiled in the minor-league systems of the Pittsburgh Pirates and Minnesota from 1963 to 1968, receiving a cup of coffee with the Pirates as a September call-up in a 1965. For a few years he was a successful power hitter with the Royals and California Angels. However, by 1974 his skills had diminished and he was out of major-league baseball by July 1975. His story is one of perseverance, as he overcame the obstacle of race that still lingered in the Deep South and in the institution of baseball, as he began his professional career.

Bob Oliver was born in Shreveport, Louisiana on February 8, 1943. His father was a mill worker and by the late 1940s the family had located to Plumas County, in California's Sierra Nevada.[1] The Oliver's subsequently moved to Highland, California, just outside Sacramento, where young Bob completed high school. His father died when he Oliver was 12 years old. At that young age he began to work in construction, mowed lawns, and delivered groceries to supplement his mother's earnings as a "domestic."[2]

Still, Oliver found time to letter in baseball, basketball, and football at Highland High School. In his senior year he was named to the All-Sacramento team in all three sports.[3]

Following high-school graduation in 1961, Oliver attended American River Junior College, where he lettered in baseball and basketball. He was named to the All-Valley Conference team in both sports in 1962. Subsequently, Oliver was elected into the school's athletic hall of fame. He also played for the Haggin-Grant Post American Legion team of Sacramento, helping it to a conference championship, hitting two home runs in the deciding game.[4] He was signed to his first contract by Bob Fontaine of the Pittsburgh Pirates.

In 1963 Oliver began his professional career, playing for the Pirates' Class-A affiliate in Gastonia, North Carolina. He had immediate success on the diamond, with the Pirates winning the Western Carolinas League pennant that season. Oliver batted .281 with 13 home runs, scored 82 runs, and drove in 84 runs, leading his team in that category.[5] He was chosen to the league all-star team.[6] However, off the field he struggled. In a radio podcast interview with Carly Lundblade, Oliver remembered how unprepared he was for the prejudice he encountered. He called home and was prepared to quit. Oliver recalled that his mother told him, "Let this be a good lesson to you." From that conversation he learned discipline. He also said that it hardened him. He didn't look at people the same way any longer.[7]

Oliver moved to Kinston of the Class-A Carolina League for the 1964 season. Though his power numbers were down from the previous year, he continued to impress the Pirates' brass. And his team won the Eastern Division title with a record of 79-59. After the season, he was assigned to the Florida Instructional League.

In 1965 Oliver earned a promotion to Double-A Asheville of the Southern League. Asheville finished second with an 80-60 record, losing out by a percentage point to the Yankees' Columbus [Georgia] affiliate, which finished with a record of 79-59 with 1 tie. Oliver continued his development, as his power numbers improved over the previous season.

In May Oliver was named the Topps Chewing Gum Southern League Player of the Month, an honor bestowed by the league's sportswriters and broadcasters.[8] Most promising for Oliver, his on-field performance earned him a call-up to the Pirates at season's end, along with Jim "Luke" Walker. Oliver played in his first major-league game on September 10, 1965. The *Pittsburgh Press* reported, "Rookie Bob Oliver made his debut, lifting a fly at bat and grabbing one fly ball in the field."[9] Oliver saw limited action, playing only three games.

To start 1966, Oliver was promoted to Triple-A Columbus [Ohio]. He played in 32 games, batting a paltry .177 with two doubles in 79 at-bats. After the slow start he was sent back down to Asheville, where he heated up. In 85 games he drove in 78 runs and batted .314.

During the 1965 and 1966 seasons, Oliver continued to experience the reality of segregation in the Deep South. In a 2012 radio interview he marveled at the leadership of Joe Solimine, a white teammate from New York City. After not being allowed to dine in a restaurant, Oliver remembered that Solimine rallied his teammates, arguing, "If these guys are good enough to be on the field with us, they should be good enough to eat at a restaurant with us. So, if they can't go in here and eat I'm not going to eat either."[10] This left a lasting impression on Oliver and it was a gesture that helped sustain him in the face of Jim Crow.

In 1967 Oliver was again assigned to the Pirates' Dou-

ble-A affiliate, now based in Macon, Georgia. Now 24 and entering his fifth full season of minor-league play, Oliver led the team in home runs and slugging, base hits, runs scored, and runs batted in. He was among the team leaders in batting average. In the field, Oliver played first base, shortstop, third base, and the outfield.[11]

The Pirates traded Oliver to the Minnesota Twins for Ron Kline during the offseason. In 1968 he was assigned to the Twins' Triple-A affiliate in Denver of the Pacific Coast League. He led the team with 93 runs batted in and finish second on the team in home runs with 20. That season he also established himself in the outfield, playing only a handful of games in the infield.

Baseball expansion was Oliver's ticket to the major leagues. Now 26, he had toiled in the minor leagues since 1963. In 1969 the major leagues expanded by introducing four new teams. The Kansas City Royals and Seattle Pilots joined the American League and the San Diego Padres and Montreal Expos entered the National League. Oliver was the 19th pick by by Kansas City in the October 1968 expansion draft.[12]

On March 20, while battling for a roster spot, Oliver had a scare. In the ninth inning, he was caught in a rundown between second and third after he had "looped a double over first." He wrenched his ankle on the play and "was helped from the field. X-Rays were negative, and the swelling was minor."[13]

Oliver fought for a position in spring training. While batting only .240 through March 25, he was aided by the fact that Steve Whitaker (.148) and Ed Kirkpatrick (.172) were struggling to hit.[14]

Oliver made the Royals' Opening Day roster. He got off to a slow start, with one hit in his first 23 at-bats, playing sporadically throughout April. In early May, Oliver got hot. On May 4 he went 6-for-6. He began by singling in the second inning, though he was later picked off second base to end a Royals rally. He led off the fourth inning with a double off Eddie Fisher. In the fifth, Oliver rapped a two-run homer. He led off the seventh inning with a single off Phil Ortega. This began a six-run eruption for the Royals. In his second at-bat that inning, Oliver singled off George Brunet. This plated the sixth run of the inning. Not yet finished, Oliver came to bat one more time, in the ninth inning. Facing Tom Murphy, he singled to left, making him a perfect 6-for-6.[15]

On July 4 the Royals played the Seattle Pilots. Entering the seventh inning, Fred Talbot and Roger Nelson were battling in a taut game, 2-2. The Royals then erupted for six runs. Their bats continued ringing in the eighth. With Jim Bouton pitching, Oliver hit a home run with the bases loaded. Oliver said of the grand slam, "I hit the ball good, but I thought it would be up against the wall (in right center). I didn't know it was in until I saw Tommy Harper stop at the fence. I'm thankful for the wind."[16] It was the Royals' first grand slam.

In August the *Kansas City Times* reported, "Joe Gordon also plans to stick with an infield that places Bob Oliver at third base. Oliver, who has taken a refresher course in the Joe Gordon short stride batting method, seemed to have learned his lesson well in his last game. He went 4-5 in Washington. 'He can be some hitter,' Gordon sums it up."[17]

In his rookie campaign, Oliver played in 118 games, batting .254 in 394 at-bats with 13 homers.

Charlie Metro replaced Joe Gordon as manager of the Royals in 1970. The Royals made a concerted effort to play Oliver every day by assigning him a permanent third-base role. The Royals got off to slow start, losing frequently. Oliver also struggled at third base. During a question-and-answer session held by the Tigers and Royals a fan asked "if some of Oliver's misplays might be because of a dissatisfied attitude tracing back to a desire to play first base." Noting that Oliver couldn't break into the outfield, his most natural position, Royals GM Cedric Tallis said, "Oliver asked me, 'Do you think Kirkpatrick plays third base better?' I said, 'No' and he volunteered to play third."[18]

Appearing to refute Tallis's statement, Oliver was interviewed about his third-base play in mid-May. By that point he was acclimating to the position and had reluctantly come around after, he said, he had a conversation with his mother while the Royals were in Oakland: "When we played Oakland, my family was there to see me play. They asked me how I liked playing third base and I told them I didn't dig it. My mom, who's a baseball nut, told me to forget it and go out there and do my thing. She has very positive ideas. She's a great woman."[19]

In early May, with the Royals scuffling, they played a series against the Orioles. In eight at-bats, Oliver had six hits, including two doubles and a home run. On May 7 he knocked in four runs and hit a 430-foot two-run home

run to left that broke a 4-4 tie. The Royals lost the game on a two-out walk-off homer by Frank Robinson. After the game, Oliver lamented, "Something has to turn. Our luck has to change." He said little about his drive that crashed the seats in left, a shot of about 430 feet. "Home run. He hung a slider on me."[20]

There was growing dissention on the team, with some teammates accusing others of lying down or not trying. Fingers were pointed at manager Metro. With a 19-33 record, he was fired on June 9. Oliver said, "First, I had to see a man lose his job. You can only get out there and do your job. The manager can't do it for you. ... I just went out there and went along with the program. If he gave us exercises, I did them. If he had us get to the park at 3 o'clock, I got there. Baseball is a good job, it beats getting up early every morning and carrying a lunch pail. ... We should all wake up and play the way we should."[21]

While the team never recovered from its slow start, it played slightly better under Bob Lemon than it had under Metro's tutelage. Still, by year's end the Royals finished with a worse record than in the previous season. By September, when Oliver had returned to first base, his hitting continued to be a highlight. Sportswriter Joe McDuff wrote that Oliver was modest about his hitting accomplishments, saying, "I'm not in a class of Harmon Killebrew, Willie Stargell, or Willie Mays. They all have the that type of swing you need to be a consistent home run hitter." Manager Lemon, for his part, said, "[T]here's really no telling yet how far he can go."[22]

By season's end Oliver led the team with 27 home runs, 83 runs scored, and 99 RBIs. In July he was batting near .300, but he finished the season batting .260. Importantly, Oliver became a spokesman of sorts, someone who spoke to issues like manager firings and team play. He expressed discomfort at situations and accepted responsibility for his play.

Oliver got out quickly to begin the 1971 season, hitting three home runs in the first two weeks. But he went into a prolonged power outage that lasted the entire season. While he slumped, the Royals were playing decent ball. They challenged Oakland early and finished second in the division with an 85-76 record, 20 games better than their 1970 record.

Oliver's loss of power cost him playing time. He played in just 128 games, down from a career-high 160 games the year before. Many of his appearances were as a pinch-hitter. He batted .244, and his other offensive numbers were down significantly from the previous season.

Oliver hit well through 1972 spring training but this did not continue in the early stages of the regular season. In an article on a luncheon sponsored by the Royals in April, beat writer Gib Twyman wrote, "Oliver was introduced by Buddy Blattner, the Royals announcer, as the club's leading home run hitter. He has one."[23]

Oliver never found his power stroke. The Royals were dissatisfied with his production. He too may have been dissatisfied with the team. Max Reiper wrote, "There were rumblings that Oliver was upset at the lack of African Americans on the team, particularly since the trading of Pat Kelly. However, in public, Oliver had nothing but pleasant things to say about the Royals."[24]

Oliver was traded to the Angels for Tom Murphy on May 5, 1972. Asked his opinion of the trade, he said, "Unhappy and happy, I guess. It's tough to leave a club that you've been with this long. It's been a long association, and I've made some good friends. ... I'm not really surprised because they've been trying to trade me for me for two years."[25]

The trade to California was the elixir Oliver needed. He got regular playing time, primarily at first base, and rediscovered the pop in his bat. On July 30, he exacted some revenge on the Royals. "I really wanted to do something to beat that team. ... I was trying with all my might to hit one out."[26] And he did, an 11th-inning walk-off home run that beat the Royals, 4-3.

Oliver could be prickly. In a July interview discussing the Angels pitching staff, he said, "The pitching here hasn't done its job. ... This is the major leagues? It's hard to accept those statistics. You can't pitch like that up here and expect to win."[27]

Oliver firmly established himself as the Angels' everyday first baseman. He hit 19 home runs with the Angels, who hit only 78 as a team.

During the offseason Oliver along with Sal Bando and umpire Chris Pelekoudas went to West Germany and ran baseball clinics at US Army bases. In their spare time they enjoyed the local cuisine. Oliver apparently enjoyed the cuisine too much and gained about 20 pounds. "I drank some beer," he said. "They had quite a bit of it. It was something drinking the beer, eating the cheese and trying

all the foods they had."[28]

This caused some consternation in spring training. One result was that new manager Bobby Winkles put Oliver through a rigorous training regimen. Winkles had Oliver running in a rubber body suit. At 6-feet-3, Oliver's ideal playing weight was 220 pounds. Initially after the regimen began he gained four pounds, getting up to 240. Oliver said, "It's not as hard now as when I started. But the first couple of days, if I'd had $600,000 in the bank, give or take a few dollars, I'd have said forget it. It's the hardest spring training I've had in ten years. ... You live it up during the winter and you have to pay the price."[29] Winkles was not above using other motivational means to get compel Oliver's compliance to dieting. He publicly stated that Jim Spencer had jumped ahead of Oliver for the first-base job.

Oliver got off to a slow start in 1973, not hitting his first home run until late April. He finally got his hitting stride and took off in May, tying an Angels record with 26 RBIs that month.

Oliver could be very descriptive. In an article on Wilbur Wood, he used this metaphor to describe Wood's knuckleball: "It's like riding in a DC-9, the knuckleball flight. Everything is up and down."[30]

Oliver finished 1973 with similar stats to 1972. He batted .265, drove in 89 runs and hit 18 home runs.

During the offseason, Oliver, like many players at the time, took on part-time work. He was interested in serving his community in some capacity. In a conversation with his barber, he learned that the Santa Ana Police Department had many job vacancies.[31] After inquiring at the department, he was hired as a school resource officer. His work extended beyond the school. He and his partner, Tom Taylor, patrolled the neighborhood and responded to calls, wrote traffic summonses, and as the *Los Angeles Times* reported, "He has 'umpired' family fights and made arrests."[32] Oliver found the work with students rewarding, by and large. He was comfortable engaging them. But the work could be difficult and traumatizing as well. On one occasion Oliver and his partner responded to a stabbing. At the scene he came on a 17-year-old youth who died at his side. Officer Taylor noted, "It was the only time I saw Bobby get tight, When the kid was lying there dying. There was nothing we could do. The heck of it was that we drove by those kids five minutes before it happened and they waved at us."[33]

Oliver was not sure he would return to the department when he completed his stint. Though he appreciated the experience, he said, "It was a lot different than I thought it would be. ... You can't solve problems in a matter of hours. It takes time. You have to be devoted and it takes a lot of patience. ... I don't know yet. I really enjoyed Tom. Your training officer makes it or breaks it. ... My wife, Hazel, would prefer that I not return. She jumps every time the phone rings after I should have gotten home. ..."[34]

The high-school principal said, "We definitely hope he returns. He really fits right in, he and Taylor. They're damn good. They're to be commended. They're not just here during school hours. They're here for extracurricular activities that I know aren't part of their normal working hours. They're dedicated and concerned."[35] Taylor joked, "If he doesn't come back next year, we'll issue a warrant on him and bring him back. ... I hope Bob decides to come back next year."[36] Oliver left the position in February to report for spring training.

Oliver did not have a good 1974 season with the Angels. They were a poor team. Over the course of the season the players endured three managers. Whitey Herzog, in an interim role, replaced Winkles for four games. The Angels then brought in Dick Williams, who managed them through the second half of the season. Because the team was doing so poorly, Angels brass decided to play and evaluate their prospects. As a result, playing time dropped off and Oliver was frequently benched. He had no problem voicing his disappointment and bewilderment. "My name is nobody. ... Everybody loves a winner. They talk to you, take an interest, you know? But when you're losing, or not playing, they avoid you."[37] He went on, "I can take not playing. But what I don't like is not knowing why I'm not playing. ... I don't begrudge the rookies being brought up ... but I do object to them being given my position. I say let them earn it, don't just give it to 'em."[38]

But as much as he was upset, Oliver was also searching to understand his poor performance. "It happens every time I have a big year. It happened in 1971 after I had a big year in Kansas City. And now, it's happening to me again here. I'm a man, I can understand it if they'd only explain it to me. ... I think my versatility has hurt me in some ways. It's good to be a jack of all trades, but you'd better be a master of one."[39]

Finally, he expressed anger, and voiced his perception of the implicit racism that held sway. "It's always their way.

They don't consider what's fair for the player. ... I can't speak up, though. Being black, it won't do me any good. ... It's just some players can get away with things. It's like when Winkles left. He blamed Robby [Frank Robinson]. But why couldn't it have been (Nolan Ryan's) fault? I'm not saying it was, but it's just that type of thing that goes on in baseball."[40]

Playing time didn't improve.

On September 11, the Orioles claimed Oliver off waivers to help them down the stretch drive. At that point in the season the Orioles trailed the Yankees by two games, with a record of 74-67. When Oliver left the Angels, they had a record of 57-87. Frank Cashen, the Orioles general manager, was tempered in his assessment of Oliver, saying, "Oliver has not had a really good year, but he is only 31. He plays first base well, a little bit of third base, can play the outfield and is a good physical specimen with a real good arm."[41]

A bit more positive was Earl Weaver, who said, "Bob might give us a little power. We were fortunate to get him. Paul Blair added, "Not too bad. We need some power. Bob can give us a lot of positions."[42]

While Oliver played only nine games with Baltimore, he did contribute to their eventual division championship. On September 27 the Orioles and Brewers went into the 17th inning scoreless. Oliver came to the plate with the bases loaded. "I was just trying to hit a fly ball," he said. "Murphy threw me a fastball and I topped it." The ball rolled 45 feet. Don Money tried to barehand it for a play at the plate and missed it, and Bobby Grich scored the winning run. The play was ruled a fielder's choice, but as the paper noted, "Bob Oliver will probably remember this one more than he does his hits."[43]

By season's end the Orioles overtook the Yankees and won the Eastern Division. They lost to Oakland in the playoffs, three games to one. Oliver did not appear in the postseason.

At the winter meetings in December 1974, Oliver's contract was purchased by the Yankees. As reported in the *New York Daily News*, "The Yankees also got into the act. They sent Bill Sudakis to the Angels, in return for right hander Skip Lockwood to complete a complicated deal which represents payment for Bob Oliver. Presumably the Orioles owed the Angels a player for Oliver but by sending him to New York that obligation was transferred to the Yankees…."[44]

On July 7, 1975, Oliver was placed on the deactivated list to make room for a returning Lou Piniella. That deactivation effectively ended his major-league career. To that point in the season he had batted only 38 times. He had five hits and a .138 batting average.

Murray Chass of the *New York Times* commented, "When a player's most frequent position is a seat on the bench, he has two choices: He can, as Rick Dempsey did earlier in the season, complain vociferously and bitterly to the manager; or he can, as Bob Oliver did, remain silent and wait his chance to play.

"Oliver said, 'I'm disappointed, but I'm a better man than to go around ripping people. You feel like it, but what are you going to gain by doing it? … I knew the handwriting was on the wall. What bothers me is I went to (manager Bill Virdon) before the trading deadline and I'm sure he knew it was coming. Why didn't he trade me to another club or sell me or release me? He waited until now, when it's tough to catch on with anybody and it's pretty crummy. If this is the end of my career, I hate it to end like this – by the Yankees not giving me a chance. I don't think it was right or fair."[45]

Oliver hung around a few more seasons. In 1976 he played at Triple-A Oklahoma City, the Phillies' affiliate. Now 33, he was the oldest player on the roster. The next year he returned to the Columbus Clippers, once again the Pirates' affiliate. He hit 17 home runs. Finally, at 35, in 1978 he played in 15 games for with Iowa, the Triple-A affiliate of the White Sox. After one season with Veracruz of the Mexican League in 1979, Oliver decided to hang up his spikes.

Oliver remained close to the game. He struggled to find work coaching and did not get a chance until he managed the Sacramento Steelheads, an independent minor-league team, in 1999.[46] He was an instructor in Dusty Baker's and Orlando Cepeda's baseball academies numerous times. Oliver ran his own baseball academy for many years, alongside his son Tony. His other son, Darren had a 20-year major-league career.

Oliver has also worked for an oil company and when he and his wife, Hazel, returned to the Sacramento area, took work at McKesson Health.[47]

He told an interviewer that two things stood out in his experience. One was the undercurrent of racism. When playing in the minor leagues the racism was overt. It came from the fabric of the community and he felt it deeply.[48] Had his mother not been supportive, and for the kindness of teammate Joe Solimine, Oliver might have given up his dream. He found a resilience to carry on. But it left scars. He implicitly pointed fingers at the baseball bureaucracy for its unstated racism. Inferences to reduced opportunities, and different treatment filtered through his thinking and statements.[49]

A second theme was that baseball teams didn't know how to use him. He was essentially a 6-foot-3, 220-pound utilityman. He insisted throughout his career that first base was his best position. However, he was constantly moved around to third base and in the outfield. Oliver never felt as comfortable in those positions. A look at his worst seasons shows they coincided with his being shuffled from one position to another.

Off the field Oliver cared about his community. His work on the Santa Ana police force focused on children, making connections. After he was traded to the Yankees, he made several, appearances to speak to inner-city youth. As he put it, he kept it real![50] His work at baseball academies focused on teaching. His own academy specialized in at-risk children and children with diabetes.

All statistics come from Baseball-Reference.com.

**Notes**

1 Dave Moller, "Big League Veteran Joins Baseball Camp," *Feather River* (California) *Bulletin*, August 18, 1993: 18.

2 Steve Jacobson, "Oliver Serves as an Inspiration to Youth," *Democrat and Chronicle* (Rochester, New York), March 26, 1975: 47.

3 1972." Baseball Hall of Fame Library, Bob Oliver player file.

4 Ibid.

5 1963 Gastonia Pirates, Baseball Reference, baseball-reference.com/register/team.cgi?id=b5ce4bd9.

6 "Greenville Will Meet WCL Stars," *High Point* (North Carolina) *Enterprise*, July 7, 1963: 21.

7 Carly Lundblade interview with Bob Oliver, March 6, 2012. blogtalkradio.com/psyched-up-radio/2012/03/06/bob-olivers-mlb-highlights.

8 "Bob Oliver Is May's Top Player," *Asheville Citizen-Times*, June 14, 1965: 12.

9 Lester Biederman, "Veale Keeps Pirates Hot in Pennant Race," *Pittsburgh Press*, September 11, 1965: 6.

10 Carly Lundblade interview with Bob Oliver.

11 1967 Macon Peaches, Baseball Reference, baseball-reference.com/register/team.cgi?id=7e40f88f.

12 Max Reiper "The 100 Greatest Royals of All-Time – #67 Bob Oliver," royalsreview.com/2018/5/25/17394868 /here-are-your-1972-kansas-city-royals, February 20, 2008.

13 Sid Bordman, "Bill Butler Shows Style," *Kansas City Times*, March 21, 1969: 28.

14 Sid Bordman, "Royals Get Ax Ready," *Kansas City Times*, March 25, 1969: 23.

15 Bradford Lee, "Bob Oliver," April 16, 2018, royalsreview. com/2018/4/16/17245136/.

16 "Pilots Crash Twice," *Daily Chronicle* (Centralia Washington), July 5, 1969: 6.

17 Dick Wade, "Rain Gives Royals Rest," *Kansas City Times*, August 16, 1969: 5.

18 Bill Sharp, "Oliver, McLain Targets of Questions," *Kansas City Times*, April 30, 1970: 54.

19 Joe McGuff, "Oliver Does Royally at Kansas City Hot Spot," *Kansas City Star*, May 9, 1970, article in Bob Oliver's player file at the National Baseball Hall of Fame Library.

20 *Kansas City Times*, May 8, 1970: 19.

21 Sid Bordman, "Tension Follows Metro Out Door," *Kansas City Times*," June 10, 1970: 53.

22 Joe McDuff, "Oliver Having a Ball at Royal Gateway," *Kansas City Star*, September 12, 1970.

23 Gib Twyman, "Royals Play Luncheon for Laughs," *Kansas City Times*, April 26, 1972: 26.

24 "The 100 Greatest Royals of All Time."

25 Sid Bordman, "Oliver to Angels for Tom Murphy," *Kansas City Times*, May 6, 1972: 53, 59.

26 "Oliver Successful in Striking Back Against the Royals," *Emporia* (Kansas) *Gazette*, July 31, 1972: 6.

27 Phil Furer, "Oliver Blames Pitching for Poor Angels Record," *San Bernardino County Sun*, July 6, 1972: 61.

28 Ron Rapoport, "It Was a Wonderful Winter; Now Oliver's Paying for It," *Los Angeles Times*, March 19, 1973: 33, 36.

29 Ibid.

30 Staff, "Wilbur Wood's knuckleball: A Big Winner," *Los Angeles Times*, June 1, 1973: 47, 56.

31 "The Law and Mr. Oliver," *California Angels 1974 Scorebook*: 26-27.

32 Dave Distel, "Bob Oliver Swaps Uniforms: Angel Player Is Also a Cop," *Los Angeles Times*, February 12, 1974: 37, 43.

33 "The Law and Mr. Oliver."

34 Ibid.

35 Distel.

36 "The Law and Mr. Oliver."

37 Ryan Rees, "My name is nobody…," *San Bernardino County Sun*, July 28, 1974: 34, 36.

38 Ibid.

39 Ibid.

40 Ibid.

41 Lou Hatter, "Orioles Acquire Angels' Bob Oliver," *Baltimore Sun*, September 12, 1974: 43, 45.

42 Ibid.

43 Ken Nigro, "Orioles Win 1-0 in 17th," *Baltimore Sun*, September 28, 1974: 27, 29.

44 Phil Pepe, "Tug Dealt to Phils; Sudakis an Angel," *New York Daily News*, December 4, 1974: 103.

45 Murray Chass, "Irate Oliver Says Farewell to Yanks," *New York Times*, July 8, 1974.

46 "The 100 greatest Royals of All Time."

47 Ibid.

48 Carly Lundblade interview with Bob Oliver.

49 Ibid.

50 Jacobson.

# ELLIE RODRIGUEZ

## By Steven Schmitt

Ellie Rodriguez loved to catch. The catching position put him in the center of the action of a baseball game, from his sandlot days in the Bronx Federation League and a Spanish league in New York City to a nine-year major-league career with five teams. In 1969, Rodriguez was the Kansas City Royals' only selection to the All-Star Game.[1]

Eliseo Rodriguez Delgado was born in Fajardo, Puerto Rico, on May 24, 1946, to Francisco Rodriguez and Juana Delgado. Francisco farmed and Juana cared for Eliseo, his older brother, Jimmy (who owned Jimmy's Bronx Café in the 1980s), and two sisters, Daly and Iris. As of 2018, only Eliseo and Daly survive. In 1953, Francisco moved his family from the depressed economy of Puerto Rico to New York City. He worked primarily on tomato farms in New Jersey to support the family, who lived at 174th Street and Boston Road, 10 streets from Yankee Stadium. While at PS 61 in the Bronx, Rodriguez played stickball with a pitcher, batter, and outfielder. They drew

the strike zone with chalk on the wall of the building and used brooms and a red rubber ball. "We'd get up in the morning and be in the schoolyard," he said.[2]

From about age 12, Eliseo walked to Yankee Stadium with Jimmy to watch Mickey Mantle, Whitey Ford, Elston Howard, and Yogi Berra, who became Rodriguez's boyhood idol. "The way he hit and the way he caught, he got my attention."[3] Today, Rodriguez advises young players in his Roosevelt Baseball School, founded in 1994 at San Juan, to watch and learn from the best. "When you're young, you watch and learn," Rodriguez said. "I used to watch all those good catchers," naming Berra, Howard, Cleveland's Jim Hegan, and Brooklyn's Roy Campanella among those he learned from.

Rodriguez played sandlot baseball but boxing became his first real competitive sport after an incident near Herman Ritter Junior High. "One time I got out of school and these guys started pushing me around," he recalled. "My brother said, 'We've got to get you in the gym so you know how to defend yourself.' We got in the gym and learned how to fight." Rodriguez honed his skills at the St. Mary's park and recreation center on 38th Street. At age 16, he entered the *New York Daily News* Golden Gloves competition as a novice 175-pound middleweight and won two bouts – one by technical knockout and the other on a decision. When he broke the middle finger on his right hand during a sparring session, he turned exclusively to baseball.

Rodriguez graduated from James Monroe High School in 1964. His Spanish League team, El Gardel – which had won 16 games in a row – defeated an amateur team from Puerto Rico for the championship at New York's Central Park. Catcher Rodriguez threw out "four or five" basestealers and former Kansas City Athletics scout Felix Delgado told him, "When you get back to New York, I'm going to send a scout there to sign you." Two days later, scout Tommy Giordano signed Rodriguez to a contract that carried a $4,000 bonus and a progressive bonus of $7,500.

"When you signed and went to Double-A, you got $1,000," Rodriguez explained. "When you got to Triple-A, you got $1,500. When you reached the big leagues, you got $5,000." Eventually Rodriguez received the entire bonus from his beloved Yankees. In 1964, he played 17 Rookie League games for Daytona Beach and then batted .354 for Wytheville (Virginia), another Rookie League team in the Kansas City organization. "I hit particularly well against the Yankees," Rodriguez recalled. "They got a real good report on me." Rodriguez also played well defensively, thanks in part to instruction from Wytheville's manager, former major-league catcher Gus Niarhos, and due in part to footwork Rodriguez learned as a boxer. "It's all about your quick feet and release," he said. "If you're quick on your feet, that gets your body in position to throw the ball quickly."

After the season the Yankees selected Rodriguez in the first-year player draft and sent him to Class-A Greensboro (North Carolina), where in 1965 he drove in 45 runs in 108 games and hit .272. He played most of the next two seasons with two minor-league teams, making the 1966 Southern League All-Star team with the Double-A Columbus (Georgia) Confederate Yankees. He moved up to the Triple-A Syracuse Chiefs in 1967, batting .248. The Yankees kept Rodriguez on the major-league roster as a condition of his draft selection. "They brought me to spring training every year," he said.

Rodriguez spent the offseason of 1967-68 playing for the Puerto Rican League champion Caguas Criollos. He had an 11-game hitting streak and hit the first grand slam of the season on November 5. Caguas won the league title over the defending champion Santurce Crabbers, 17-2, on January 28 at San Juan before a record crowd of 21,812.[4]

One of five catchers on the Yankees' 1968 spring-training roster, Rodriguez had a shot to make the team. National Guard duty for players in those days, when the military

draft was still in effect, opened the door for hopefuls like the 21-year-old Rodriguez. Yankees manager Ralph Houk chose his 25-man roster with an emergency catcher in mind.

"This is his fourth visit to the Yankee training camp," Jim Ogle wrote of Rodriguez in *The Sporting News,* "but the first time he has been more than a face and a number." Rodriguez told Ogle, "This is the first time I ever came here with the feeling that I was part of the team. In the past there was always an Elston Howard or Jake Gibbs and a couple of others. I knew it was only a question of how long I would be around. Believe me, when I come up, I'll be ready."[5] Syracuse manager Gary Blaylock said, "Rodriguez could step in and catch in the majors right now. He still needs a little work on his hitting, but there isn't a better young catcher in baseball."[6]

His dream of playing for the Yankees came true on Sunday afternoon, May 26, 1968, at Yankee Stadium, in the first game of a doubleheader against the Chicago White Sox. With catcher Frank Fernandez on weekend military duty, Rodriguez caught ace pitcher Mel Stottlemyre for the entire game. The Yankees won, 5-1. Rodriguez went 0-for-3 but threw out White Sox center fielder Ken Berry trying to steal. For the highly regarded prospect, his chance came quickly and was a day to remember. He drove 4½ hours from Syracuse, arriving at Yankee Stadium at 11:30 in the morning. "I'm dressing and Ralph Houk said, 'You're playing, you're in there.'" Clubhouse manager Pete Sheehy had Rodriguez's uniform 23 in the training room. There was one empty locker – next to Mickey Mantle. "Welcome to the Yankees," said the Mick, who told Sheehy, "He going to dress right here."

Of the 23,966 in attendance, 30 or more were Rodriguez's family and friends – his parents, siblings, and "10 or 15 cousins." He got free tickets from Mantle, his roommate Bobby Murcer, and other teammates. "Other friends paid for tickets," Rodriguez recalled. Traveling back and forth between Syracuse and New York over the summer (rejoining the Yankees during Fernandez's month-long military hitch in June, a weekend in July, and a mid-September call-up), Rodriguez played nine games for the Yankees, starting and completing six with a 1.000 fielding average in 44 chances, throwing out three of six would-be basestealers, and batting .208.[7] He got his first hit on May 31, 1968, off Detroit Tigers southpaw Mickey Lolich, whom Rodriguez tagged for three of his 16 career home runs.

Rodriguez caught for Caguas manager Luis Arroyo during

the 1968-69 Puerto Rican League season. On October 15, 1968, he became property of the new Kansas City Royals, a second-round selection in the American League expansion draft.[8] Before the 1969 season, Houk told Kansas City manager Joe Gordon that Rodriguez would be his starting catcher. Elston Howard called Rodriguez "one of the very best defensive catchers in the league."[9] Two months into the season, Rodriguez had raised his batting average from .186 to .275 with 17 hits in 43 at-bats over a three-week stretch. "He's going to be my catcher," said Gordon. "Everyone has had a chance at the job and he's won it."[10] With his family and friends in attendance for a weekend series at Yankee Stadium June 9-11, Rodriguez collected 5 hits in 13 at-bats, belted a three-run homer, and gunned down two basestealers. His hitting improved after he decided to use a 36-ounce bat and just meet the ball.[11]

His first-half play earned Rodriguez selection to the 1969 American League All-Star team, the Royals' only representative. Though a batting slump resulted in Rodriguez and John "Buck" Martinez sharing catching duties in the second half of the season, Rodriguez caught 90 games, 83 as a starter, and threw out 24 of 53 basestealers. Despite a modest .236 average with 2 home runs and 20 RBIs, Rodriguez seemed to have secured a regular job in the major leagues. New manager Charlie Metro declared that he wanted Rodriguez to catch every day in 1970. "He may even catch some doubleheaders," Metro said. "I definitely believe in one guy doing the catching."[12]

On June 9, 1970, the Royals replaced Metro with coach Bob Lemon, who platooned Rodriguez with left-handed-hitting Ed Kirkpatrick. "I don't see why he can't become one of the best catchers in the league," Lemon said of Kirkpatrick.[13] In 1969, Kirkpatrick had hit 14 homers in 315 at-bats, mostly as a corner outfielder. The following year, he out-homered Rodriguez 18 to 1, and threw out 46 percent of potential basestealers, starting 80 games behind the plate. Meanwhile Rodriguez, who had started 36 of 52 games under Metro, became a part-time player on the trading block. "He didn't like me at all," Rodriguez said of Lemon, who started Rodriguez in 33 of 100 games. Rodriguez's lack of power became an obstacle to playing regularly.

In his return to the Puerto Rican League for the 1970-71 season, Rodriguez momentarily returned to boxing when he punched Mayaguez pitcher Bill "Spaceman" Lee outside the Caguas ballpark on November 20, 1970, causing

Lee's face to strike a handrail on a stairway leading into the ballpark and breaking four front teeth. Earlier in the season, Rodriguez had homered and doubled off Lee, who warned, "Next time, I'll stick it in your ear." On November 16, Lee surrendered a home run to Caguas first baseman Willie Montanez.[14] Lee said that Montanez showed him up doing "the cha-cha-cha" around the bases. The Mayaguez catcher warned Rodriguez to watch out. Lee hit Rodriguez with a pitch. Rodriguez charged the mound and took a swing at Lee, who blocked the punch and decked Rodriguez with a left hook. The umpire ejected Rodriguez from the game.[15] On the 20th, Rodriguez saw Lee get off the Mayaguez team bus. Rodriguez recalled, "He was the first guy I saw and I hit him with one shot." Lee went back to Boston to get his teeth fixed that weekend. The feud reached the major leagues on May 24, 1973, when Lee hit Rodriguez with a pitch at Fenway Park. Rodriguez charged the mound and the Boston fans booed. The Red Sox won, 10-1.[16]

In response to Mayaguez fans throwing rocks at the Caguas team bus after Caguas had won two straight games, Rodriguez said, "One of these days, I'm going to do something that has never been done in Puerto Rico." On November 22, 1977, Rodriguez homered for Bayamon off Tony Chévez at Isidoro Garcia Stadium in Mayaguez and ran around the bases backwards, a la the Mets' Jimmy Piersall, who performed a similar act after hitting his 100th career home run on June 23, 1963. After Rodriguez touched home plate, umpire John Shulock said, "The home run's good but you're out of the game." Rodriguez received $500 from an overjoyed owner.[17]

On February 2, 1971, Rodriguez was sent to the Milwaukee Brewers for veteran utilityman Carl Taylor. Rodriguez became the Brewers' regular catcher, leading the AL in runners caught stealing. In 1972 he stood closer to the plate, stopped batting from a crouch, held the bat straight up, and on the advice of batting coach Harvey Kuenn used a lighter bat and started hitting to all fields. Batting second in the order, Rodriguez led the Brewers with a .285 average and made the American League All-Star team. Over a 16-game stretch in May, he batted .360 and hit a two-run homer into the upper deck at Tiger Stadium May 25 to give Milwaukee a 2-0 victory.[18] By season's end, Rodriguez had nailed half of the runners who tried to steal on him. Brewers pitcher Jim Lonborg called Rodriguez a rock behind the plate. "(He) stays low and gives you a constant target," Lonborg said. "You know if you throw the ball where his glove is, it usually will be in the strike zone."[19]

Still, Rodriguez knew he had to compete for his starting job with Darrell Ray Porter, the Brewers' number-one selection in the June 1970 amateur draft. In 1973, the Brewers surprised the experts and their delirious fans, leading the American League Eastern Division in June. They took seriously new manager Del Crandall's order to have fun. Rodriguez had earned the starting job, but he fractured his left wrist on a foul tip at Cleveland on April 18. Porter started every game from April 19 to May 20. When Rodriguez returned, he emerged as the team leader. On June 2, he caught all 13 innings and drove in all three runs in a 3-2 victory over the Chicago White Sox at County Stadium. With Rodriguez catching every day, the Brewers on June 17 went one game up in the East Division. A crowd of 6,000 fans greeted the team bus on its arrival in Milwaukee. Rodriguez and rookie second baseman Pedro "Pete" Garcia were carried off the bus to start a two-hour celebration. "He was my roomie," Rodriguez said. "(Our team) had good chemistry that year."[20]

The Milwaukee miracle became a mirage in one month. From June 18 to July 15, the team posted an 11-19 record and Rodriguez's average dropped 25 points to .275. Porter, primarily a designated hitter in the first half of the season, became the regular catcher, with 16 home runs and 67 RBIs, compared with Rodriguez's zero homers and 30 RBIs. "I haven't done too much lately," Rodriguez admitted, "and Darrell is. The big thing is to win."[21] Porter said, "Ellie is one of the best catchers in the game and he helped me as much as anybody."[22]

The day Rodriguez got a hit to beat the Chicago White Sox, Crandall yelled from the dugout, "How in the world can anybody think of trading you?," referring to rumors that Milwaukee GM Jim Wilson denied before the June 15 trading deadline.[23] To his surprise, Rodriguez was traded October 22, 1973, three weeks after the season ended. Once again, he had lost the battle of the big bats and missed six weeks because of injuries. "They wanted to play Darrell Porter," Rodriguez recalled, "so I got traded. Same thing with the Yankees – Thurman Munson coming up, I gotta go." The Brewers sent Rodriguez, pitchers Skip Lockwood and Gary Ryerson, and outfielders Joe Lahoud and Ollie Brown to the California Angels for veteran left-handed starter Clyde Wright and catcher Art Kusnyer.

Rodriguez was considered the key player coming from Milwaukee but the ex-boxer would again fight for a starting job. He played regularly for manager Bobby Winkles,

but in midseason, two-time World Series winner Dick Williams took over and called Rodriguez "the dumbest catcher in baseball," later claiming that he did not apply himself and did not hustle.[24] Future Hall of Fame pitcher Nolan Ryan said the opposite and praised Rodriguez's handling of pitchers. "He's a good thinking catcher," Ryan said. "Like most good catchers, he wants to win. He has that drive behind him. The thing I like about him is the way he picked up my pitching pattern. He takes command. You'll see him moving infielders around all the time."[25]

Rodriguez led the American League in putouts (782), assists (75), and runners caught stealing (56), setting a single-season club record. On June 14, he caught 13 innings of a 15-inning victory over Cleveland, setting an American League record of 21 putouts in an extra-inning game, 19 on Ryan strikeouts over the same 13 innings. On August 12, Ryan fanned 19 in nine innings in a 4-2 victory over the Boston Red Sox, tying a major-league mark with Rodriguez calling the shots and setting a record for putouts in a nine-inning game. Ellie caught a career-high 137 games – 125 as a starter - and set individual batting marks with seven home runs and 36 RBIs.

So what was the deal with his future Hall of Fame manager? "He didn't like me," Rodriguez said. "He never did like Latinos. He jumped all over me, he jumped all over Ed Figueroa. In Montreal, he jumped all over Tony Perez, a Hall of Famer."

On June 1, 1975, Rodriguez caught Ryan's fourth career no-hitter. Activated just hours before the game after missing a month with an injured ankle, Rodriguez called Ryan's gem "better than going 4-for-4 and hitting a home run. I just want to catch his fifth." Rodriguez predicted that Ryan would win 30 games someday. "His fastball is unbelievable," he said. "And his curve's second only to Bert Blyleven's."[26] In 2018, Rodriguez called Ryan "the greatest competitor that I can recall."

Rumored to be traded along with Figueroa to Cleveland, Rodriguez knew that catching Ryan's fifth no-hitter was not likely. On June 15, the Angels bought veteran catcher Andy Etchebarren from the Indians and named him the first-string catcher. By spring training 1976, Ed Herrmann had been acquired from the Yankees.[27] On March 31, 1976, the Angels shipped Rodriguez to the Los Angeles Dodgers for outfielder Orlando Alvarez and cash.

In 36 games, 21 as a starter, Rodriguez batted .212 with

9 RBIs. After suffering a fractured collarbone in Puerto Rico during the 1976-77 winter league, Rodriguez opened the 1977 major league season on the disabled list. The Dodgers released him on May 2. That summer, the Pittsburgh Pirates signed Rodriguez and sent him to Triple-A Columbus. On July 25, Rodriguez caught Rod Scurry's Triple-A debut, a no-hitter.[28] On July 30, Rodriguez homered and drove in four runs against Pawtucket but the comeback ended with a .224 average in 49 games.

For the next three seasons, Rodriguez played in the Mexican League. In 1978, he caught for the Cordoba Cafeteros under manager and former Angels teammate Winston Llenas, then co-managed the Coatzacoalcos Azules in 1979 and played for the Saltillo Saraperos in 1980. His last active year was 1982 with the Monclova Acereros. Rodriguez said that the players "made more money in Mexico and didn't want to leave their country."[29]

Eventually, Rodriguez's shoulders and knees told him it was time to retire as a player. Then former major-league general manager Joe Klein recruited Rodriguez to sign Latin American players as player-development director and chief Puerto Rican scout for the independent Atlantic League of Professional Baseball. Rodriguez signed former major leaguers Raul Mondesi, Rubén Sierra, and Andres Galarraga, among others. In 2018, he was signed to manage the Road Warriors, a traveling Atlantic League team that replaces the former Bridgeport (Connecticut) club and awaits construction of a new stadium in Texas.[30]

As of 2018, Rodriguez still coached at the Roosevelt Baseball School in San Juan, Puerto Rico, where youngsters from age 6 to 18 learn the basics of playing the game. Major leaguers Angel Pagan and René Rivera both came out of Roosevelt, Rodriguez said.

After Hurricane Maria tore through Puerto Rico in September 2017 leaving more than three million people without electric power and scrambling for food, water, and cash, Puerto Rican League owners suspended the 2017-18 season in November but resumed play on January 5 after negotiating a $500,000 pool to be shared equally among four teams.[31] Fans got free admission and parking to games. Evaristo "Varo" Roldàn Stadium in Gubaro, capacity 2,500 and a half-hour south of San Juan, was jammed for the opening pitch of the season on January 5. Hiram Bithorn Stadium in San Juan and Isidoro Garcia Stadium in Mayaguez hosted games without lights.[32]

Six months after the storm, volunteers continued to provide providing equipment, trucks, clothing, food and water for the recovery effort, though "we have to import produce from other places," including South America, Rodriguez said.[33]

In 2018, his 55th season in professional baseball, Rodriguez said he was grateful and amazed at the sport's role in his life journey. "It changed my whole life," he told the author. "If I hadn't signed that (bonus) contract, I don't know if I'm talking to you right now."[34]

## Sources

In addition to the sources cited in the Notes, the author consulted Baseball-Reference.com. He wishes to express his appreciation for the assistance of Jorge Colón-Delgado.

## Notes

1 Russell Schneider, "Indians Seeing Red Over Sims Shutout on All-Star Balloting," *The Sporting News,* July 26, 1969: 20.

2 Author interview with Eliseo Rodriguez on February 27, 2018.

3 Author interview with Eliseo Rodriguez on January 26, 2018. Unless otherwise indicated, all quotations from Rodriguez came from this January interview.

4 Miguel Frau. "Caguas Muscle Brings Playoff Crown," *The Sporting News,* February 10, 1968: 39.

5 Jim Ogle. "An Ex-Ring Warrior Catches Yankee Eye in Fight for Mitt Job," *The Sporting News,* March 23, 1968: 23; Tom Owens. "Jake Gibbs Remembers Teammate Thurman Munson," *Baseball by the Letters,* baseballbytheletters.com/2010/04/18/jake-gibbs-remembers-yankees-teammate-thurman-munson-2/. Accessed February 8, 2018; Rodriguez interview.

6 Ogle.

7 Rodriguez interview; Ogle, "Stott Steady Pillar Supporting Yanks' Riddled Slab Staff," *The Sporting News,* June 15, 1968: 18; Ogle, "Yanks Tab Rocky, Lindy to Buttress Bench and Bullpen, *The Sporting News,* August 3, 1968: 16. Baseball Reference, baseball-reference.com/players/r/rodriel01.shtml. Accessed February 8, 2018.

8 The Yankees decided to protect their 1968 number one amateur free agent draft choice Thurman Munson who made an immediate impression batting .301 for the Double-A Binghamton, New York Triplets of the Eastern League.

9 Larry Claflin. "Pilots Select Vets, Royals Corral Kids;" "Plucked From A.L. Bag, *The Sporting News,* October 26, 1968: 11,18; Ogle, "Solaita Delights Yanks – Swings Home-Run Bat," *The Sporting News,* October 12, 1968.10.

10 Joe McGuff. "Ellie's Heavy Bat Rewarding Royals," *The Sporting News*, June 28, 1969: 22.

11 McGuff; Rodriguez interview.

12 McGuff, "Metro Sees .500 Plateau Just Over K.C. Horizon," *The Sporting News*, April 11, 1970: 43.

13 McGuff, "Royals Take 'Difficult Step' – Metro Out, Lemon In*," The Sporting News*, June 20, 1970: 21; Sid Boardman. "Kirkpatrick Eager for Royal Finish," *The Sporting News*, August 1, 1970: 20.

14 Rodriguez, January 26, 2018; Interview, Bill Lee, March 11, 2018; Miguel Frau. "Native P.R. Players Get Strong Value in Power," *The Sporting News*," December 5, 1970: 55.

15 "Chapter III Unfolds in Rodriguez-Lee Feud," *The Sporting News*, December 12, 1970: 63.

16 "Old Feud Flares Again; It's Lee Versus Rodriguez," *The Sporting News*, June 9, 1973: 16.

17 Jorge Colón-Delgado, email communication, March 16, 2018; Chris Jaffe, "50th Anniversary: Jimmy Piersall's 100th homer," *The Hardball Times*, June 23, 2013, fangraphs.com/tht/tht-live/50th-anniversary-jimmy-piersalls-100th-homer/. Accessed March 15, 2018; Rodriguez interview, February 27, 2018.

18 Larry Whiteside. "Brewers Discover Dynamite in Rodriguez' Bat," *The Sporting News*, June 17, 1972.

19 Whiteside.

20 Lou Chapman. "Scent of Second Miracle Descends Over Milwaukee," *The Sporting News*, July 7, 1973: 8.

21 Lou Chapman. "Rookie Porter Takes Over No. 1 Brewer Backstop Post," *The Sporting News*, August 11, 1973: 16.

22 "Ellie Rodriguez Leads Cheers for Brewers," *Wausau* (Wisconsin) *Daily Herald*, July 3, 1973: 17: Lou Chapman. "Brewers' Booming Porter as A.L.'s Premier Catcher," *The Sporting News*, April 13, 1974: 12.

23 Chapman. "Hot Brewers Thankful They Kept Rodriguez," *The Sporting News*, June 30, 1973: 19. "Ellie Rodriguez Leads Cheers for Brewers," *Wausau Daily Herald*, July 3, 1973: 17.

24 Dick Miller, "Rodriguez Wins Wings as Angels' Greybeard," *The Sporting News*, May 10, 1975: 13; Dick Miller, "Angels Are Seeking Bids on Rodriguez," *The Sporting News*, October 8, 1975: 32.

25 D. Miller, "Angel Hurlers High on Ellie, Better Than Scouts Reported," *The Sporting News*, June 1, 1974: 16.

26 D. Miller, Ryan's Pace: Four No-Hitters in Two-Year Span," *The Sporting News*, June 14, 1975: 5. "Ryan Laughs at Law of Averages," *The Sporting News*, May 17, 1975: 3.

27 D. Miller, "Rodriguez to Get Reprieve, but Andy Remains as No. 1," *The Sporting News*, February 7, 1976: 41; D. Miller, "Herrmann Eager to Share Angel Catching Duties," *The Sporting News*, March 13, 1976: 36.

28 John McNeely, "Scurry Scuttles Foe in AAA Debut," *The Sporting*

*News*, August 13, 1977: 34.

29 Rodriguez interview, February 27, 2018.

30 "Atlantic League of Professional Baseball." atlanticleague.com/clubs/league-directory/. Accessed March 11, 2018; Rodriguez interview, February 27, 2018.

31 Jorge Castillo, "After Hurricane Maria, things remain far from normal for Puerto Ricans. But they do have baseball," *Washington Post*, January 19, 2018. www.washingtonpost.com/sports/after-hurricane-maria-things-remain-far-from-normal-for-puerto-ricans-but-they-do-have-baseball. Accessed March 15, 2018.

32 Pedro Gomez, "80th version of Puerto Rican winter league begins despite Hurricane Maria devastation," ESPN.com, www.espn.com/mlb/story/_/id/21972859/80th-version-of-puerto-rican-winter-league-begins-despite-hurricane-maria-devastation. Accessed March 15, 2018.

33 Jim Wyss, "Puerto Rico assessing Hurricane Irma damage amid widespread power outage," *Miami Herald*, September 8, 2017. http://www.miamiherald.com/news/weather/hurricane/article172023172.html. Accessed March 11, 2018; http://www.daily-chronicle.com/2018/03/07/acmtyt2. "Puerto Ricans Still Stranded in Hotels 6 Months after Hurricane Maria," *Daily Chronicle*, March 7, 2018. Accessed March 11, 2018; Rodriguez, February 27, 2018.

34 Rodriguez interview, February 27, 2018.

# HOYT WILHELM

## BY MARK ARMOUR

During the first half of Hoyt Wilhelm's major-league career, the attention he received usually focused on his freak pitch — a knuckleball — which he likely threw better than any man in history. In the latter half of his career, he was equally renowned for his advanced age — he had become an "old" knuckleballer.

Wilhelm was called "Old Folks" when his career had more than a decade to run. Nearly every story written about Wilhelm in the 1960s speculated on how much longer he could get batters out. Could he throw the knuckleball until he was 42? How about 46? Wilhelm patiently gave variations of the same answer: "I am pitching as well as I ever have. I have never felt better. I see no reason why I can't pitch a few more years."[1] Every July 26, his birthday, a cake would appear, and Hoyt would be asked again about how it felt to be 43, or 47. In his Carolina drawl, Wilhelm would bring the subject back to how he was pitching, how he was feeling. When Wilhelm died in 2002, his death certificate revealed

something unexpected. His birth date was discovered to have been July 26, 1922, one year earlier than had been presumed for his entire career. It is not uncommon for a baseball player to have lied about his birth date – in fact, it is somewhat of an honored tradition. It was nonetheless startling to discover that Hoyt Wilhelm, probably the most famous "old" player in history, was actually older than we had thought

James Hoyt Wilhelm was born in Huntersville, North Carolina, a farming town just north of Charlotte. His parents, John and the former Ethel Stanley, were tenant farmers, and raised 11 children. Wilhelm never liked talking about himself, but we know that his family was very poor.

Wilhelm was asked thousands of times how he learned to throw a knuckleball, and usually claimed that he taught himself in high school after seeing a picture of Dutch Leonard gripping a baseball. Emil "Dutch" Leonard was then pitching for the Washington Senators, who were the closest major league team to North Carolina. Leonard dug his index and middle fingers into the ball's seam – he did not use his knuckles. Wilhelm began experimenting with the pitch and soon could throw it pretty well. After horsing around with it amongst his friends, Wilhelm began to throw the knuckler for his high school team (Cornelius High School, about five miles from home).

Before Wilhelm, the knuckleball was an old pitcher's pitch, something a veteran might turn to at the end of his career to eke out another year or two. A pitcher who threw it would do so along with his usual assortment of pitches-its slower speed and unusual movement made it a fine "changeup."

Wilhelm broke both molds — he threw it as a teenager, and he threw it nearly every pitch. Most young kids give up on the knuckleball quickly because the pitch cannot be thrown to a location, which is how a pitcher is taught to throw. Wilhelm soon discovered that he could just aim the ball right down the middle of the plate, knowing full well that it would end up somewhere else, but maximizing his chances of keeping it in the strike zone.

After high school, Hoyt passed up the chance to attend Davidson University and signed a contract to play ball 12 miles from home in Mooresville, a team in the Class-D North Carolina State League. Wilhelm was not a prospect--he was a big guy who had some success in high school, which got him a chance to pitch for the local pro team.

In 1942, he managed a 10-3 record for Mooresville, before being drafted into the Army. He spent three years in the service, seeing a lot of combat in Europe and receiving the Purple Heart for wounds he received at the Battle of the Bulge. We do not know a lot about his war experience because, as with everything else, Wilhelm never made a big deal of it.

Returning stateside, he pitched two more seasons at Mooresville, compiling records of 21-8 and 20-7. Although these were fine years, he was still a 25-year-old, pitching in the lowest level of the minor leagues. Scouts were looking for big guys who threw hard, and as a Charlotte newspaper famously reported, "Wilhelm is never going any place. He throws like a washer-woman."[2] The New York Giants finally drafted him after the 1947 season and he spent the next two seasons at Jacksonville (Sally League) and Knoxville (Tri-State League).

During his stay in the Sally League, at a game in Columbus, Georgia, he spotted Peggy Reeves sitting in the stands. Wilhelm asked a vendor to get her phone number, and he asked her for a date. For the next three years, Hoyt and Peggy corresponded faithfully and saw each other whenever he got back to Columbus. In September 1951, they were married.

Meanwhile, after winning 17 games for Jacksonville in 1949, he was finally promoted to Minneapolis (American Association), the highest rung in the Giants minor-league chain. Over the next two years, Wilhelm finished 15-11 and 11-14, mainly as a starter. He spent the winters of 1950-51 and 1951-52 playing winter ball in Cuba. In July 1951, still a minor leaguer, he turned 29 (although everyone thought he was 28).

Wilhelm went to his first big-league training camp in 1952 and impressed his manager, Leo Durocher, enough to make the roster. The Giants were the defending league champions, and featured a strong starting rotation, so Durocher sent his new knuckleballer to the bullpen, reasoning, "The knuckler can fool 'em for four or five innings, even if Wilhelm doesn't have the hard stuff to go nine."[3] After waiting 10 years to get a shot, Hoyt was in no position to complain.

In his first season, Wilhelm pitched 71 games (a rookie record at the time) and 159 innings, all in relief. He finished 15-3 with 11 saves and won the league's ERA title (2.43), the first and only time a full-time relief pitcher has done so. In Wilhelm's first major-league at-bat, against the Braves' Dick Hoover at the Polo Grounds, he hit a home run--the only one he ever hit. For all this, he finished fourth in the league's MVP voting.

His fabulous knuckleball began to attract attention for how difficult it was to catch. After selecting Wilhelm to the 1953 All-Star team, National League manager Charlie Dressen expressed concern whether Roy Campanella would be able to catch him, and Hoyt did not pitch.

The next season saw Wilhelm involved in a couple of run-ins with the police in Westchester County, north of New York city. In June, he was cited for driving 60 miles per hour in a 25-mile-per-hour zone in Tarrytown, and was further charged with disorderly conduct for using "abusive language" to the desk sergeant who tried to book him at the station. The very next day, on the Sawmill River Parkway, a patrol car was turning into a gas station with sirens on and red light flashing, when Wilhelm drove into the cop car broadside. Hoyt suffered a bruised right arm and hurt his back, and his wife Peggy, another passenger, and the police officer, all suffered minor injuries as well.[4]

These incidents did not hurt Wilhelm's pitching, as he had a great 1954 season (12-4, 2.10 ERA in 111 innings) to play a key role in the Giants pennant. In the World Series, Hoyt pitched 2 1/3 innings over two games, allowing a single hit and no runs during the Giants' sweep of the Indians.

Over the next two years, 1955 and 1956, Wilhelm's ERA rose to 3.93 and 3.83 amid concern that he had been overused in his first few years. For his part, Wilhelm believed that his struggles were related to pitching less frequently.

In February 1957 the Giants traded Wilhelm to the Cardinals in order to reacquire first baseman Whitey Lockman. New York needed a first sacker because Jackie Robinson, acquired from the Dodgers after the 1956 season, chose to retire, and Bill White was drafted into the army. Hoyt wasn't particularly effective in 1957 (4.25 ERA in 40 games), but the reason he was let go in September, according to general manager Frank Lane, was that the team's catchers were having difficulties catching Wilhelm's knuckleball.

The Indians picked Wilhelm up and kept him most of the next season (2.49 ERA in 90 innings), before they waived him in August 1958. Wilhelm was still pitching effectively, but now in his mid-thirties, he seemed to be nearing the end of his career. A 35-year-old knuckleballer, even one with a 2.49 ERA, is not allowed many bad outings before being sent on his way.

Catching his knuckleball was a continual problem. In Wilhelm's first 16 seasons (1952-1967), his team led its league in passed balls in every year but one (1953). The Giants' Ray Katt was charged with four passed balls in a single inning catching Wilhelm in 1954. The catchers of the 1958 Indians (mainly Russ Nixon and Dick Brown) allowed a league-leading 35 passed balls. The next year, without Wilhelm, the same catching corps was charged with six.

The Orioles claimed him on waivers in August 1958. Orioles' manager Paul Richards thought Wilhelm might make a good starter, reasoning: "I'd always wondered why he'd been used in relief, coming in with men on base where one passed ball could hurt him. I thought that perhaps, if Hoyt started, the runners wouldn't get on base to begin with."[5] In September, Wilhelm started four times, and in the last start tossed a 1-0 no-hitter against the Yankees. The final batter, Hank Bauer, laid down two bunts that rolled foul before eventually popping to second base.

In 1959, Wilhelm started the season 9-0 with an ERA under 1.00, prompting former manager Leo Durocher to express some regrets: "If I ever had any idea he could go the distance like that I'd have used him as a starter when I had him on the Giants. Maybe I made a big mistake."[6] On May 22, he took a no-hitter into the eighth against New York, settling for a one-hitter. He shut out the Yankees again six days later. Hoyt came back to earth in the second half, but still finished 15-11 with a 2.19 ERA, good enough for his second ERA crown.

Richards still occasionally went to his star in the middle of a game: on August 6, Wilhelm came into a 1-1 game in the ninth inning against the White Sox, and proceeded to throw 8 2/3 innings of no-hit ball before finally allowing a safety. The game ended in a tie after 18 innings.

The Orioles of this era had a promising collection of young starting pitchers, dubbed "The Kiddie Corps": Milt Pappas, Chuck Estrada, Steve Barber, Jack Fisher, and Jerry Walker. The oldest (Estrada) was 22 in 1960, and all of them were above average or better major-league pitchers in their early 20s. When Wilhelm struggled a bit early in the 1960 season, Richards moved him back to the bullpen. The Orioles' reasoning--going with the young guns--appears sensible. After all, Wilhelm turned 38 years old that summer, and had proven flexible enough to excel in relief. How could Richards have known that Hoyt had more than a decade of great pitching ahead of him, and that he would outlast most of the Orioles' vaunted young guns?

Wilhelm successfully returned to full-time relieving and was named to the All-Star team in each of the next two seasons for the Orioles. In the 1961 All-Star Game, Wilhelm entered a tie game in the eighth inning in San Francisco. After retiring the first two hitters in the ninth, he walked Ken Boyer. Paul Richards, managing the American League team, came to the mound and, in an unusual move, relieved catcher Yogi Berra, who was uncomfortable catching Hoyt with a man on base. New catcher Elston Howard's passed ball in the 10th contributed to Wilhelm's loss.

During the 1962 offseason the Orioles traded the 40-year-old Wilhelm to the White Sox in a six-player swap in which the Orioles landed shortstop Luis Aparicio. The Orioles had acquired Hoyt for the waiver price back in 1958, and had wrung four great years out of him. Now approaching 40, few could have imagined that Wilhelm had more than a year or two left. In fact, he was just hitting his stride.

Many of the stories surrounding the trade concerned whether the White Sox catching corps, primarily Camilo Carreon, J. C. Martin, and Sherm Lollar, would be able to handle Wilhelm's knuckler. Gus Triandos, who had had some success with Wilhelm early on in Baltimore, was vocally celebratory when the Orioles dealt him away prior to the 1963 season. Hoyt was typically nonchalant: "I don't believe the catchers here will have any trouble if they just stay loose and relaxed."[7]

In 1963, major-league baseball deployed a new strike zone, which extended from the bottom of the knees to the top of the shoulders (formerly it reached from the top of the knees to the armpits). During the next six years, run scoring in both leagues dropped to levels not seen since 1919 (with the exception of the American League during World War II). A larger strike zone helps all pitchers, but especially those, like Wilhelm, that have little idea where the ball is going.

Over the next six years, while with the White Sox, Wilhelm put together one of the best sustained stretches of relief pitching ever. In 1963, his ERA "soared" to 2.64 in over 136 innings (he had three starts). Thereafter his ERA decreased for four consecutive years (1.99, 1.81, 1.66, and 1.33) before finally inching up to 1.73 in 1968-still not a bad year for a pitcher turning 46. More than a situational pitcher, Wilhelm averaged well over 100 innings a season, throwing 144 in 1965. Run production was historically low, but no one else consistently pitched as well. His ERA in the 1960s was 2.18.

Wilhelm did not have to do much to stay in shape, other than a little walking. He was an avid fisherman and hunter, but claimed that seven weeks in spring training was time enough for exercise. He was also apparently a fairly prodigious eater. Hoyt and Peggy spent a lot of time together, going to a movie, or dinner, and were often referred to as good, plain folks. Hoyt never talked much, even with his friends, and seemed uncomfortable with the increased attention as he continued to beat back Father Time.

During spring training in 1966, Wilhelm sustained the only significant injury of his career when a pitching machine broke the middle finger of his pitching hand while he was taking bunting practice. At the time, the White Sox had the best pitching staff in the league and an excellent bullpen. Accordingly, on his return Wilhelm began to share the late-inning situations that resulted in saves. The White Sox usually produced very high team save totals, but spread them around among an excellent relief corps that also included, at various times, Jim Brosnan, Bob Locker, and fellow knuckleballers Eddie Fisher and Wilbur Wood.

Throughout the 1960s, the fame of Wilhelm's phe-

nomenal knuckleball, and its effect on catchers, continued to spread. When Wilhelm came to the American League in 1958, the league record for passed balls in a game was four, set by John Henry of the Washington Senators in 1911. Over the next five years, Wilhelm's team tied this record seven times while he was pitching. The 1959 Orioles were charged with 49 passed balls, 30 more than any other team. The 49 were split between Gus Triandos with 28 and Joe Ginsberg with 21, the two highest totals for any catcher in the 1950s.

Catchers did not particularly enjoy being on the receiving end of Wilhelm's deliveries. Wes Westrum, his primary receiver with the Giants, later said that the night after catching Wilhelm he would wake up shaking. Catching him so baffled J. W. Porter that the catcher used a first baseman's mitt. In 1960, the Orioles began using a specially designed catcher's mitt (designed by manager Paul Richards) for Wilhelm that measured 42 inches in circumference. When the rules were changed in 1965 to prohibit gloves larger than 38 inches, the White Sox designed a new one with a hinged thumb, one of the first of its kind.

There were several other excellent knuckleball pitchers whose careers overlapped Wilhelm's, including Eddie Fisher, Phil Niekro, and Wilbur Wood. None of them had the consistent problems with catchers that Wilhelm had, an indication that Wilhelm's knuckleball moved much more than theirs did. Ted Williams, who knew a thing or two about pitchers, once stated categorically: "Don't let anybody tell you they saw a better knuckleball than Wilhelm's."[8] Sportswriter Jim Murray described the difficulty in hitting Wilhelm: "Part of the trouble is, the ball comes to the plate like a kid on the way to a bath."[9]

Wilhelm began to draw more and more attention for his age. When asked by Edgar Munzel of *The Sporting News* his secrets of longevity, Hoyt mentioned his knuckleball, which does not wear the arm, his being a relief pitcher, the oversized mitt, and his durable body.[10]

In 1968, as Wilhelm approached Cy Young's record of 906 games pitched, manager Eddie Stanky decided that he would start Wilhelm in game number 907. Unfortunately, Stanky was fired on July 12, and Hoyt broke the record against the Athletics in relief on July 24. Even then, Hoyt refused to consider his accomplishment special. "The next 900 won't be so tough," he allowed.[11]

The White Sox left Wilhelm unprotected in the 1968

expansion draft, most likely reasoning that no one would want a 46-year old knuckleballing reliever. However, the Kansas City Royals drafted Hoyt and traded him to the Angels for outfielder Ed Kirkpatrick and catcher Dennis Paepke. Despite the newly-reduced strike zone, Wilhelm had another excellent season in Anaheim, throwing 65 innings with a 2.47 ERA.

In September 1969, Wilhelm was traded (for farmhand Mickey Rivers) to the Atlanta Braves, who were trying to win the NL West and needed help in the bullpen. He provided it brilliantly, with two wins, four saves and a 0.73 ERA in eight games. When the Braves won the division by three games, Wilhelm received much of the credit. He arrived too late to be eligible for the NL playoffs, which the Braves lost in three straight to the Miracle Mets.

Wilhelm continued his excellent pitching for the Braves in 1970 (6-4, 3.10) and was selected to another All-Star Game (he did not play). On May 10, Wilhelm pitched in his 1,000th game against the Cardinals, which received a lot of attention. With the Braves out of the race this time around, they sold Hoyt to the Chicago Cubs with only 10 days left in the season. Wilhelm was ineffective this time (four runs in 3 2/3 innings), and was traded back to the Braves after the season. The "rental" was suspicious enough that Commissioner Bowie Kuhn investigated the matter, but he let the trade stand.[12]

In 1971, the Braves gave Wilhelm just 2 1/3 innings of work in April before releasing him. Hoyt hooked on with Tommy Lasorda's Spokane Indians of the Pacific Coast League, hoping for a recall to the Dodgers. After eight games, including six starts (his first since 1963), Hoyt went to Los Angeles in the midst of the 1971 pennant race. In 17 2/3 innings, he gave up just two runs and logged three saves, but the Dodgers fell a game short of the San Francisco Giants.

The next season he threw just 25 innings for the Dodgers (4.62 ERA) before drawing his release on July 21, just five days before his 50th birthday (which everyone thought was his 49th). One wonders whether the Dodgers, or another team, would have let him pitch a while longer had they known his true age. The story of a 50-year-old man pitching in the major leagues would have garnered quite a bit of publicity. Nevertheless, his pitching career was over.

Hoyt managed in the Atlanta Braves system for two years, spending 1973 with Greenwood of the Western Caroli-

nas League and 1974 with Kingsport of the Appalachian League. He then spent 22 years coaching in the minors, most of them as a roving instructor for the Yankees.

Hoyt and Peggy settled after his playing career in Sarasota, Florida, and they lived there the rest of his life. The Wilhelms raised three children: Patti, Pam, and Jim.

In 1985, Wilhelm became the first relief pitcher to be inducted into the Hall of Fame. It took him eight tries to be voted in, and his omission became an annual opportunity for many celebrated writers (Leonard Koppett, Tom Boswell, and Jim Murray, among others) to take up his cause.

One can speculate on what Wilhelm's career might have been like had he been a starter. He threw in a regular rotation only once in his career and led the league in ERA. Over all, he pitched 384 lifetime innings as a starter, with an ERA of 2.36. He finished his career with a record of 143-122, and 227 saves (the most ever until the 1980s).

Could he have had a Phil Niekro-type career? Might it have been better? Wilhelm may have been a better pitcher than Niekro, albeit in many fewer innings. It seems reasonable to conclude that had he stayed as healthy and effective as a starter for as long as he did as a reliever Wilhelm could have won well over 300 games. Either way, he had a unique and wonderful career.

## Sources

In addition to the sources cited in the Notes, the author also consulted:

Armour, Mark L. and Daniel R. Levitt, *Paths to Glory*. Brassey's, 2003.

Cairns, Bob. *Pen Men*. St. Martin's Press, 1992.

Greene, Lee. "Suddenly, Wilhelm's A Mystery," *Sport*, September, 1959.

National Baseball Hall of Fame. File on Hoyt Wilhelm.

Shaap, Dick. "Hoyt Wilhelm, Nothing But Knucklers," *Baseball Stars of 1960*. Pyramid, 1960.

Porter, David L., *Biographical Dictionary of American Sports*, Greenwood Press, 2000.

Shapiro, Milton. *Heroes of The Bullpen*. Messner, 1967.

The Sporting News. *One For the Book*. The Sporting News Publishing Company, 1970

Thorn, John. *Relief Pitcher*. Dutton, 1979.

Vincent, David, Lyle Spatz and David W. Smith. *The Midsummer Classic*. Bison Books, 2001.

Young, Dick. "Can A Relief Pitcher Last," *Sport*. July 1960.

**Notes**

1 Edgar Munzel, "Wilhelm Fires Duster at Father Time," *The Sporting News*, March 18, 1967: 3.

2 Lee Greene, "Suddenly, Wilhelm's a Mystery," *SPORT*. September 1959: 32.

3 Dick Schaap, "Hoyt Wilhelm: Nothing But Knucklers," (Ray Robinson, ed.) *Baseball Stars of 1960* (New York: Pyramid, 1960), 57.

4 "Wilhelm Loses One Traffic Case, Gains Delay on Other," *The Sporting News*, June 30, 1954: 20.

5 Schaap, 58.

6 Greene, 30.

7 Edgar Munzel, "White Sox Mittmen Pass Exam—Handle Hoyt Without a Hitch," *The Sporting News*, March 30, 1963.

8 John Steadman, "Wilhelm's Knuckler Best Ever," *Baltimore News-Post*, 1962. (from Wilhelm's Hall of Fame file, specific date unknown.)

9 Jim Murray, "Wilhelm is Wonder Man as Pitcher," *The Sporting News*, April 5, 1969: 62.

10 Munzel, 3.

11 Bill Furlong, "The Next 900 Won't Be So Tough," *SPORT*, November 1968: 98.

12 Jerome Holtzman, "Wilhelm Deals Were on Up-and-Up, Kuhn Says," *The Sporting News*, December 19, 1970: 37

# "LES EXPOS SONT LA" – THE EXPOS ARE HERE

## By Danny Gallagher

Gerry Snyder, Charles Bronfman, and John McHale. Three of the biggest names in Montreal Expos history.

Without Snyder's efforts, there very likely would have been no Expos in Montreal. Most of the media laughed at him when they found out he was pursuing a major-league baseball franchise for Montreal.

"Nobody believed me," Snyder said years later. "The people on radio and television thought it was a big joke. Oh, yeah. Whenever I'd see them at a golf tournament or whatever, they'd have these sarcastic looks on their faces. They'd say, 'Good luck, you'll need it.'"[1]

When Snyder was informed by National League owners at Chicago's Excelsior Hotel on May 27, 1968, that Montreal had been granted a franchise, only two reporters, Marcel Desjardins and Gerry Champagne, both from *La Presse*, were on hand to record the occasion. Jack Varnas, Snyder's brother-in-law, had also tagged along to keep him company in Chicago.

Six years earlier, in 1962, Snyder, a Montreal city councilor and vice chairman of the municipal government's executive committee, and Lucien Saulnier, the committee's chairman, sat in the New York office of Commissioner Ford Frick to promote Montreal as a potential expansion city.

"Do you have a stadium?" Ford asked, almost immediately.

"No" was the answer.

"Well, when you have a stadium, come back to me," Frick said.[2]

The meeting lasted only 10 minutes and Snyder and Saulnier left for Montreal rather dejected. Not until 1967 did Snyder get the feeling that perhaps Montreal had a chance at a franchise.

"All of a sudden out of a clear blue sky, the American League announced that it was expanding by two teams to Kansas City and Seattle for the 1969 season," Snyder remembered. "I said to myself, 'Hey, chances are good that the National League will also expand by two teams.

Montreal Expos' manager Gene Mauch and New York Mets' manager Gil Hodges post    prior to the first game in franchise history, Shea Stadium, April 8, 1969. The Expos won, 11-10. (Courtesy of the McCord Museum, Montreal)

Montreal Expos' owner Charles R. Bronfman wearing his familiar uniform number 83 at spring training, West Palm Beach, Florida, March 1969. (Courtesy of the McCord Museum, Montreal)

So I started going to a number of NL meetings and I'd meet up with the expansion committee, which included Walter O'Malley of the Dodgers. I got along good with O'Malley."[3]

"Whenever I'd speak to him on the phone, he'd always say, 'Bonjour, Gerry, comment allez-vous? Look Gerry, you don't have to come to LA to see me. I know what Montreal can do. I made a lot of money there with the Montreal Royals Triple-A team."[4]

From that point on, Snyder was optimistic because of O'Malley's support. But the media still wasn't convinced.

"I was getting criticized from all quarters," Snyder said. "The reporters were saying there was no hope in hell that the league would expand to a foreign country. Veteran newspaperman Jacques Beauchamp would always say afterward that the biggest mistake he made was not following me through the routine of getting a franchise. When we got the franchise, it was that much more pleasurable."[5]

The 1960s had been a wonderful decade for Montreal. In 1962, the same year Frick rejected Snyder and Saulnier, Montreal Mayor Jean Drapeau shocked his citizens when he arranged for Expo 67 to be staged in Montreal. Three years later, Montreal's impressive subway system opened for the first time. Snyder's coup of bringing major-league baseball to Montreal was icing on the cake for the decade.

Snyder had told major-league owners that the Autostade, a sports stadium built by the automakers for Expo 67, would play host to the Expos' games in 1969. In the end, the Autostade was ruled unsuitable for baseball after officials visited Montreal in June of 1968. National League President Warren Giles was not worried. Paraphrasing Mayor Drapeau, he told a press conference that "we have no problems, we only have solutions."[6]

Baseball was not unfamiliar ground for Gerry Snyder as he attempted to bring a team to Montreal. "No question," he said. "I'd been an athlete. I was a softball player in both Montreal and in the Air Force wherever I was stationed for five years. I brought major-league baseball to Canada. I didn't bring the Expos to Montreal. What the Expos did after was not my responsibility."[7]

Snyder's coup involving the new franchise didn't end there. He coaxed minority shareholders to come on board with $1 million each to pay the $10 million franchise fee. He persuaded Jean-Louis Levesque of Blue Bonnets Raceway to be the first investor. Eventually, majority owner Charles Bronfman was the second investor.[8] All this time, Snyder was also introducing eventual Expos President John McHale to Bronfman. At the time, McHale was baseball's deputy commissioner after serving a stint as general manager of the Milwaukee/Atlanta Braves.

"Bronfman didn't know McHale from a hole in the ground and neither did I," Snyder said. "I'd found out about McHale from this guy [William Daley] who was chairman of the board of the Pennsylvania Railroad. He was also half an investor in the Seattle Pilots and he was a former investor in the Cleveland Indians."[9]

"Before we'd gotten the franchise, O'Malley said this guy wanted to talk with me. So we talked and he said, 'I have someone in mind whom you should consider as the guy running your organization. I won't tell you now who he is because he's in baseball.' So we left it at that. So when we got the franchise, the first guy to call was him. He told me about McHale and the next morning, McHale and I talked. I told him we'd talk later in the week."[10]

Snyder soon arranged for McHale to come to Montreal to meet Bronfman. Snyder would pick McHale up the airport and then take him back for his return flight. This routine happened several times and at one point, McHale took Snyder aside and said he'd like to get him involved with the team because he appreciated Snyder's role in landing him a job with the Expos.

"Then one time when McHale was in town, I found out he'd already left for the airport. When I found that out, I said there's something wrong," Snyder said. "I heard from different sources that McHale was not to hire me, that he'd have to forget his commitment to me. I heard they had turned me down. I never trusted McHale after that. It was a typical American thing. Any typical American, he brought in half a dozen Americans to work full time for him. ... Over the years, McHale didn't want to see me. He wasn't my type of guy. When we'd meet, he'd say how glad he was to see me and then he was done."[11]

Snyder's treatment for many years by the Expos left him bewildered but not despondent. Wouldn't you be a little ticked off? Just think, Snyder persuaded major-league owners to award a franchise to Montreal, he brought investors on board and he arranged for McHale to be part of the ship's upper-management staff. Snyder received no position with the organization. He received no money for his efforts. No commission for bringing the franchise to Montreal, no commission for bringing investors on board and no bonus from Bronfman for recommending McHale.

"I got two season tickets every year the team was at Jarry Park,» Snyder said. «Once they moved to Olympic Stadium in 1977, that all stopped. I got nothing else. I was a politician and they didn›t want to get involved in paying me off. Heck, Bruce McNall, when he was the majority owner of the Los Angeles Kings, was paid $25 million by the NHL for bringing the Disney franchise into the league. No question, I should have received more recognition.

"The guy who got New York the Mets franchise for 1962 had a stadium (Shea) named after him. I took 25 years before I threw out the first pitch before an Expos game. It was under Claude Brochu and the new regime. Name 24 people who did more for the franchise than me. But I've never regretted getting involved. I'm very pleased to have brought a franchise to Montreal and helped out a little."[12]

For his part, McHale was driven around the city of Montreal in 1968 looking for a suitable venue for a team to be called the Expos.

National League President Warren Giles and Montreal Expos' President John McHale at the National League Expansion Draft, Montreal, October 14, 1968. (Courtesy of the McCord Museum, Montreal)

"We

looked at DeLorimier Downs. There was nothing there. No way," McHale said. "The Autostade, where the Alouettes played, was awful. It was already leased to the Alouettes." Then two journalists, broadcaster Russ Taylor and *La Presse's* Marcel Desjardins, suggested National League attorney Bowie Kuhn (a future commissioner), Warren Giles, and General William Eckert (the current commissioner) check out Jarry Park.[13] It was about 6 P.M. when Giles and several others from the Montreal contingent arrived at Jarry Park, just as an all-star junior game was about to take place.

"When we reached the site, the city's director of recreation said there were only about 3,500 seats at the time but said up to 30,000 seats could be ready in time for the first pitch of the first home game in 1969. We told the recreation guy to get going on it," McHale said.[14]

So Jarry Park became the home of the Expos with about 28,000 seats, a quaint, romantic park where fans could be up close to their heroes on the field. In less than five months, the park was transformed into a wonderland, complete with a press box.

"Snyder was a great lobbyist with major-league clubs," McHale said.[15]

But there was another pothole to overcome. A group of original investors including Blue Bonnets' Levesque backed out of the deal to be part of the Expos' consortium, leaving the chance that Montreal would not get the team.

"Cities like Buffalo and Milwaukee (Bud Selig was part of the Milwaukee group) that didn't get franchises were standing by to take over from Montreal and offering more money," McHale said. "Then Charles Bronfman came along. He felt it would be an embarrassment to Quebec and Canada if the franchise got away. Charles said he would put up the money if I would stay and run the franchise for him."[16]

McHale was born in Detroit and attended Catholic Central High School there and from 1939-45 he attended the University of Notre Dame in South Bend, Indiana, where he graduated cum laude in economics and was a football letterman for the Fighting Irish. Somewhere in there, McHale's university studies were interrupted by three years in the US Navy during World War II.

McHale went on to play in the Detroit Tigers' mi-

Montreal mayor Jean Drepeau with (from left) John Bateman, Jim 'Mudcat' Grant, and Maury Wills on Opening Day in New York, April 8, 1969. (Courtesy of the McCord Museum, Montreal)

nor-league system before getting to play in the big leagues for five seasons, beginning in 1943. And from there, his administrative career took hold when he began working for the Tigers in 1948. By 1957, McHale had advanced to become general manager, a title he held for two years.[17]

Then he moved to Milwaukee to become the president and GM of the Braves, who later moved to Atlanta. He stayed with the Braves until 1966 and then he made another move, this time becoming the deputy commissioner of baseball for a year. That's when the Montreal offer came forth. He stayed with the Expos until 1986 when he stepped down and was replaced by Claude Brochu. However, McHale did continue with the Expos as vice chairman of the board of directors until 1990, when he retired.

Shortly thereafter, he joined Japan Sports Systems as president of JSS-owned minor-league clubs in Vancouver, British Columbia, and Visalia, California. He also was president of the Association of Professional Baseball Players of America and a director of the National Baseball Hall of Fame in Cooperstown. At one time, he was a member of the Chairman's Council of Intracoastal Health Systems Inc. in West Palm Beach, Florida. For many years, he lived in Palm City, Florida, where he died in 2008.

When the Expos had a chance to get Rusty Staub from Houston, this is how the original trade went down: Staub to the Expos for Jesus Alou and Donn Clendenon. Then Clendenon pulled his shocker. The slugger said that he had retired so the Expos trade with the Astros was off on January 22, 1969.[18] The Astros and Expos were both unhappy with the turn of events after both teams publicly announced the trade.

"It was a shock to all of us," recalled longtime Expos handyman Jim Fanning. John McHale arranged to go and visit Clendenon, who had said he was out of baseball to pursue a career as an executive with the Scripto Pen company. McHale convinced Clendenon to unretire and got the slugger to sign a two-year contract at a salary suggested by the player himself. So Clendenon, who was the Expos' sixth pick overall in the expansion draft, became an Expo. Clendenon, a first baseman, belted 17 homers and drove in 87 runs for Pittsburgh in 1968 and Fanning recalled that "we were getting a front-line player."[19]

Houston would not accept the trade and asked that it be redone. On April 8, 1969, Alou returned to Houston along with Jack Billingham, Skip Guinn, and $100,000. The Expos also received pitchers Leo Marentette, Howie Reed, and Steve Shea from the Astros.[20]

Courtesy of Bronfman, here's a tale out of spring training in 1969 about an unlikely immortal by the name of Joe Moock. He had just hit the Expos' first-ever home run at spring training and Bronfman ambled over to manager Gene Mauch to say something.

"That Mook guy will never make the team," Bronfman said.

"Well, I don't think he'll make the team because he doesn't have the talent," Mauch said.

"No, he won't make the team because of the name he has. You don't want any competition."[21]

Bronfman had a chuckle over the Mook-Mauch story and he came back with another yarn about the time Mauch got a tad wary of his boss in the infant stages of the Expos before they hit the field.

"Gene had heard I wouldn't be an on-hands owner," Bronfman recalled. "Well, John McHale, Jim Fanning, Gene, and I were sitting and I told Gene I wanted a uniform with a number. I had the feeling he thought I would want 4, which was his number but I told him I wanted 83. He probably thought, 'Now, he's asking for a football number.' There was dismay on his face. I laughed and said: 'I just want to be able to put the uniform on once in a while and have some whiskey with you.' (83 was one of the Seagram brand names produced by Bronfman's company). Gene was vastly relieved when I told him that."[22]

Bronfman can be a funny guy when he wants to be. Mostly, though, his quiet, modest, humble, soft-spoken demeanor is what endears him most to those who meet him. He was the ideal out-of-the-spotlight owner, who didn't seek publicity. The fame that vaulted him from the obscurity of the Seagram boardrooms to the glare of professional sports wasn't something he flaunted.

To the relief of the team executives and managers who worked for him, Bronfman never did interfere with the baseball operations department while he maintained majority control. That majority control is something Bronfman never originally sought in the early days of the franchise. He wasn't even involved in the process that netted the city of Montreal a franchise. The spadework that resulted in that magnificent coup had been orchestrated by Snyder and Mayor Jean Drapeau.

Bronfman did agree to be one of 10 shareholders, who would throw in $1 million each to play the $10 million expansion fee. Bronfman also consented to be chairman of an administrative board responsible for attracting financial support for the team.[23]

"I never thought I'd be a majority owner," Bronfman said. "Our letter of agreement for $1 million was on the basis that we could get a domed stadium."[24]

Montreal did get a retractable roof in the 1980s but its operational capacity was a nightmare, the joke of the major leagues. In any event, when Levesque backed out as majority owner of the Expos in their infant stages, Bronfman decided to assume a larger percentage of the club's ownership.

When Opening Day of the franchise came on April 8, 1969, it was of tantamount importance. Some 44,541 Canadians and Americans were on their feet at Shea Stadium in New York as the US and Canadian national anthems were being sung.[25] This was the first time "O Canada" had ever been sung prior to a major-league game and some of the Americans had even joined in the chorus.

"Tears were rolling down my face," Bronfman recalled. "I was very, very happy. You have to understand that I was an inheritor. I inherited wealth and I inherited a position with Seagram so when I pioneered the first major-league team in Canada, it was very special to me. Maureen Forrester was singing 'O Canada' that day and I remember Drapeau very good. He was quite non-plussed. The winds were blowing and the airplanes were flying over. Drapeau said, 'How can they play with these airplanes making noise?' He couldn't quite understand that."[26]

As was the case with Expos employees and fans, Bronfman suffered through the team's growing pains, including a horrendous 20-game losing streak that first season. The streak was broken at Dodger Stadium but there was some heavy breathing going on before the game was over.

"Elroy Face was pitching for us," Bronfman said. "We led 4-1 but the Dodgers cut the lead to 4-3 and they had two men on base in the ninth. Willie Crawford hit a ball and it looked like it was going out but Rusty Staub leaped up and made a great catch."[27]

Mauch lasted seven seasons and when he was fired after the 1975 season, Bronfman and McHale thought they had Tommy Lasorda lined up to be manager. Lasorda had been a popular pitcher with the Montreal Royals' Triple-A team in the 1950s and showed potential in the Los Angeles Dodgers organization as a manager.

"Gene no longer had control of the club," Bronfman said. "He wanted to go with veterans but we had a young club. We were serious about Tommy. We thought he was coming. I remember I was in Israel and I got a phone call from John McHale in Denver. John said, 'We lost Tommy Lasorda.' I was heartbroken. If we had gotten him, he would've been with us for a long time."[28]

Instead, Lasorda stayed with the Dodgers for a long time after becoming their big-league manager, beginning late in the 1976 season when Walter Alston decided to retire. "I ran into Tommy some point later and I said, 'Tommy, you used us, you bugger.' But he said he had too much Dodger Blue in him," Bronfman said.[29]

In an experiment that failed miserably, the Expos gave Karl Kuehl the manager's post. K.K. had been a highly

Gary Carter poses with a fan at the Expos' spring training camp in Daytona Beach, Florida, in 1976. The Expos their rise in the National League East beginning in the late1970s to excellence in player development, signing future All-Stars and Hall of Famers like Carter. (Courtesy of the McCord Museum, Montreal)

admired man in the Expos' minor-league system but he was out of his element at the major-league level. The Expos finished with 55 wins and 107 losses.[30] Kuehl didn't last the season. The final day epitomized how the season went.

"It was a cold, rainy, miserable, rotten day. It was the way the season ought to end," Bronfman said. "Karl was in over his head. He didn't earn the respect of the players."[31]

Dick Williams was hired a few months later but the Expos still endured their ninth consecutive losing season in 1977 and that's when Bronfman thought very seriously about withdrawing his ownership. He had become very frustrated.

"I felt as a group that we hadn't done our jobs," Bronfman said. "I know that was one of my worst periods."[32]

Coming to Bronfman's rescue was minority shareholder Lorne Webster, who persuaded his buddy to stay on. Bronfman was glad he did. The Expos came ever so close in 1979 and 1980 and finally in 1981, they came within a whisker of going to the World Series.

Bronfman was happy with his role in ownership until late in the 1989 season when the Expos folded and gave away the NL East, which they had led for 37 consecutive days at one point. Bronfman had given general manager Dave Dombrowski the mandate to improve the team during the course of the season and D.D. did just that, trading pitchers Randy Johnson, Brian Holman, and Gene Harris to Seattle for veteran pitcher Mark Langston.[33]

Langston should have been the catalyst to push the Expos over the top but he too, like the Expos, faltered the last two months. Bronfman was devastated and he made the decision to get out.

"I was very bitter," Bronfman said. "I had a Plan A, Plan B, and Plan C. Plan A was to sell the club to someone who would keep the team in Montreal; Plan B was to sell to someone who would agree to keep the team in Montreal for five years; Plan C was to sell to the highest bidder anywhere."[34]

In the end, team President Claude Brochu and Jacques Menard of Burns Fry put a consortium together to keep the team in Montreal.

**Notes**

1 [1] Jacques Doucet and Marc Robitaille, *Il Etait Une Fois Les Expos, Tome 1: Les Annees 1969-1984* (Montreal: Editions Hurtubise Inc., 2009), 28.

2 Danny Gallagher, *You Don't Forget Homers Like That: Memories of Strawberry, Cosby, and the Expos* (Toronto: Scoop Press, 1997), 163.

3 Danny Gallagher and Bill Young, *Remembering the Montreal Expos* (Toronto: Scoop Press, 2005), 19.

4 Gallagher, *You Don't Forget Homers Like That*, 164.

5 Gallagher, *Remembering the Montreal Expos*, 20.

6 Brian Schecter, ed., *Les Expos, Nos Amours* (Montreal: TV Labatt, 1989).

7 Gallagher, *Remembering the Montreal Expos*, 20.

8 Gallagher, *Remembering the Montreal Expos*, 21.

9 Ibid.

10 Ibid.

11 Gallagher, *You Don't Forget*, 165.

12 Gallagher, *You Don't Forget*, 166.

13 Schecter, *Les Expos, Nos Amours*.

14 Gallagher, *You Don't Forget*, 164.

15 Gallagher, *Remembering the Montreal Expos*, 23.

16 Ibid.

17 Denis Brodeur and Daniel Caza, *Les Expos du Parc Jarry au Stade Olympique* (Montreal: Les Editions de l'Homme, 1996), 25.

18 Brodeur, 15.

19 Gallagher, *Remembering the Montreal Expos*, 60.

20 John Robertson, *Rusty Staub of the Expos* (Scarborough, Ontario: Prentice-Hall of Canada Inc., 1971), 91.

21 Gallagher, *You Don't Forget*, 84.

22 Ibid.

23 Charles Bronfman and Howard Green, *Distilled: A Memoir of Family, Seagram, Baseball, and Philanthropy* (Toronto: Harper Collins Publishers, 2016), 76.

24 Gallagher, *Remembering the Montreal Expos*, 26.

25 Doucet, 72.

26 Gallagher, *You Don't Forget*, 85.

27 Gallagher, *Remembering the Montreal Expos*, 26-27.

28 Gallagher, *Remembering the Montreal Expos*, 27.

29  Gallagher, *You Don't Forget,* 86.

30  Brodeur, 47.

31  Gallagher, *Remembering the Montreal Expos,* 27.

32  Ibid.

33  Brodeur, 273.

34  Gallagher, *You Don't Forget,* 87.

## MONTREAL EXPOS EXPANSION DRAFT

| PICK | PLAYER | POSITION | FORMER TEAM |
|---|---|---|---|
| 1 | Manny Mota | of | Pittsburgh Pirates |
| 2 | Mack Jones | of | Cincinnati Reds |
| 3 | John Bateman | c | Houston Astros |
| 4 | Gary Sutherland | ss | Philadelphia Phillies |
| 5 | Jack Billingham | p | Los Angeles Dodgers |
| 6 | Donn Clendenon | 1b | Pittsburgh Pirates |
| 7 | Jesus Alou | of | San Francisco Giants |
| 8 | Mike Wegener | p | Philadelphia Phillies |
| 9 | Skip Guinn | p | Atlanta Braves |
| 10 | Bill Stoneman | p | Chicago Cubs |
| 11 | Maury Wills | ss | Pittsburgh Pirates |
| 12 | Larry Jackson | p | Philadelphia Phillies |
| 13 | Bob Reynolds | p | San Francisco Giants |
| 14 | Dan McGinn | p | Cincinnati Reds |
| 15 | Jose Herrera | ss | Houston Astros |
| 16 | Jimy Williams | 3b | Cincinnati Reds |
| 17 | Angel Hermoso | of | Atlanta Braves |
| 18 | Mudcat Grant | p | Los Angeles Dodgers |
| 19 | Jerry Robertson | p | St. Louis Cardinals |
| 20 | Don Shaw | p | New York Mets |
| 21 | Ty Cline | of | San Francisco Giants |
| 22 | Garry Jestadt | p | Chicago Cubs |
| 23 | Carl Morton | p | Atlanta Braves |
| 24 | Larry Jaster | p | St. Louis Cardinals |
| 25 | Ernie McAnally | p | New York Mets |
| 26 | Jim Fairey | of | Los Angeles Dodgers |
| 27 | Coco Laboy | 3b | St. Louis Cardinals |
| 28 | John Boccabella | c | Chicago Cubs |
| 29 | Ron Brand | c | Houston Astros |
| 30 | John Glass | p | New York Mets |

# MACK JONES

## By David E. Skelton

Certainly there were easier scenarios than facing Bob Gibson for one's first major-league appearance, but the Milwaukee Braves' Mack Jones made his debut on July 13, 1961, in St. Louis look like child's play. His four consecutive hits, including a run-scoring double in his second at-bat, tied a National League record and reinforced the can't-miss label assigned to the 22-year-old fleet-footed youngster.[1]

When in 1966 Jones, dubbed Mack the Knife[2], galloped out to center field in Atlanta Stadium, fans of the brand-new Atlanta Braves hoped he would reinforce the aging bats of Eddie Mathews and Hank Aaron. His 31 home runs for Milwaukee the season before had given them reason for that hope.

Mack Fletcher Jones was born to Georgia natives Mack and Inell (Willis) Jones on November 6, 1938. (He was their only child together; Mack Sr. had two children from a previous marriage).[3] Mack Sr. and his wife, 13 years

his junior, scraped out a living together near the Chattahoochee River as a construction laborer and maid, respectively. Their children attended Henry McNeal Turner High School in Atlanta, where Mack developed a sterling reputation in sports, becoming, among other things, an all-state halfback. The racism he encountered then, and later in his life, is reflected in his remark that he "had scholarship offers from just about every [African-American] college in the country."[4] Apparently no other colleges would consider this multi-talented athlete. At any rate, it was baseball that had the greater allure.

In 1957 Mack was discovered by Julian Morgan while playing with the Atlanta Yankees, an all-black amateur team. A former minor-league pitcher, Morgan was associated with the Atlanta Crackers of the Double-A Southern Association, a Milwaukee farm club, and he persuaded Milwaukee to sign Jones the following year. Jones raced through Class-C and Class-B ball, eliciting this report from Braves assistant farm director Roland Hemond: "He's a carbon copy of [budding prospect] Lee Maye and in one respect is ahead of Maye. He has a better knowledge of the strike zone than Maye did at the same stage of his career."[5]

In 1960 Jones was promoted to the Louisville Colonels of the Triple-A American Association, where he was teamed with Maye until the latter was called up to Milwaukee. Mack's superb season was capped by a late-season 19-game hitting streak that propelled him and the team to a Junior World Series triumph over the International

League's Toronto Maple Leafs. That winter Milwaukee traded longtime center-field stalwart Bill Bruton to the Detroit Tigers with the expectation that a replacement would be found among a vast number of prospects. When Jones received the starting nod in the first exhibition game the following spring, it provided a clear indication of the esteem in which the 22-year-old lefty slugger was held. But a poor Grapefruit League campaign resulted in a return to Louisville, setting in motion a pattern that exhibited itself over the next three seasons.

From 1961 to 1963, Jones spent portions of each season between the Braves and Triple A, lighting up the latter while struggling with the former. An all-star campaign with Louisville in 1961 resulted in his promotion to the majors, with his four-hit major-league debut quickly followed by a .151 swoon. A blistering start to the 1962 season, in which he hit .333 with a slugging percentage of .520, secured Jones the right-field post as Aaron shifted to center, but Mack soon fell into another slump that, if not for another demotion to the minors, might have established a single-season strikeout record (He had 100 in 333 at-bats). Despite his four stolen bases against the Philadelphia Phillies on June 11, 1963 – one shy of the league record – Jones struggled at the plate and was once again returned to minors. Perhaps one of his managers at Milwaukee, Birdie Tebbetts, best described these ups and downs when he said, "I'm never going to be able to give up on this kid, but neither can I afford to get too excited. … He's the kind of player who is going to go from one extreme to the other."[6]

But it appeared that the Braves had indeed given up on Jones in the spring of 1964 when manager Bobby Bragan said, "I have no plans for him."[7] The acquisition of outfielder Felipe Alou, on top of still another poor spring for Jones, ensured yet another demotion. This time the Braves appeared poised to cut the strings altogether. In 1964 Mack was traded conditionally to the Detroit Tigers' International League affiliate in Syracuse. From there he blazed a rapid track back to the major leagues.[8]

Few minor-league teams have ever had the offensive heft of the 1964 Syracuse Chiefs. Led by the explosive bats of Willie Horton, Jim Northrup, and Jones, the Chiefs led the league in nearly every offensive category. Jones ran the board by leading the league in runs scored (109), triples (18), home runs (39), RBIs (102), and slugging percentage (an eye-popping .630). Until a late-season drought, he threatened the 17-year-old league record for home runs.

His efforts earned him the Topps-George M. Trautman International League Player-of-the-Year award. Chiefs manager Frank Carswell was given considerable credit for Mack's charged output: "Carswell has done a fine job on Jones," said Braves farm director John Mullen. "Mack is much more aggressive. … He's really attacking the ball."[9] It was not long before Jones was brought back into the Braves' fold. Doing a 180-degree turn, Bragan now exclaimed that Jones was "very much in the running" for the center-field berth.[10]

Center field would not simply be handed over to Jones. In 1964 the outfield trio of Aaron, Rico Carty, and Maye had batted .328, .330, and .304, respectively. Mack still had his challenges before him. But from the outset, an injury-plagued 1965 campaign saw Bragan use players in a variety of circumstances – for example, 11 players manned both first base and left field – that afforded playing time for Mack and all his teammates. Injuries notwithstanding, Milwaukee remained in contention until the final weeks of the season, and when an opportunity arose to bolster their pitching rotation, Maye was traded six weeks into the schedule to the Houston Astros. The vacancy assured Mack even more playing time, and in the first seven games after the trade he went on a .385 blitz. The home runs followed shortly thereafter; with only three homers prior to Maye's departure, Jones went on to produce an average of one home run every 4.6 games (including his first career grand slam, on June 5) and racked up a season total of a career-high 31. "I finally felt I belonged," Jones explained. "I started hitting away and I gradually got my confidence back."[11]

Jones's home-run total, combined with those of five other Braves, set a National League record for the most teammates (dubbed Milwaukee's version of Murderers' Row) with 20 or more. (The 2003 Atlanta Braves tied this record.) In addition, Mack was one of three Braves slugging 30 or more round-trippers, tying a major-league mark. (His 30-plus home runs were matched by nine other NL players in 1965, marking the first time 10 National Leaguers attained the 30-homer level in the same season. Among this select company, and with his first full season behind him, Jones appeared to have permanently arrived in the major leagues.

The 1965 season was played in the shadow of one overriding reality – it would be the last of the Braves' 13 seasons in Milwaukee. A pending move to Atlanta was met with player reaction ranging from ambivalence to deepest sorrow, but for one – Mack Jones – the thought of wearing the name of his hometown across his chest was met with sheer excitement. The community was similarly enthralled and Mack became a local celebrity. An Atlanta radio station catering to an African-American audience contracted with him for a series of sports broadcasts, and the Braves made him part of their winter caravan (where his humor was oft cited) to solicit season-ticket holders from the same audience. The buzz brought Mack to exclaim, "I think this [move to Atlanta] is going to be the greatest break in my life."[12] But elation was soon tempered by an injury that affected the remainder of his playing career.

Though Jones felt discomfort in his right shoulder from the outset of spring training in 1966, he and the team doctor felt it would subside. Instead, the pain got progressively worse and, on the day before the season began, he underwent an operation to remove a nickel-sized bone chip. The timing could not have been worse. The personal angst was palpable as Jones was forced to watch while his teammates took the field on April 12 for the first major-league game in his hometown. He returned to the lineup on May 14 in St. Louis only to be forced to leave the game early the next day after being hit in the head by a Gibson fastball, and miss the next two games entirely. On May 20 he celebrated his first game in Atlanta with two home runs, and slugged seven round-trippers in his first 22 games. Bragan credited his return for the team's surge in June, and called Jones, Aaron, Carty, and Alou "the best composite outfield in the game."[13] Mack's seven home runs and 17 RBIs in his final 28 games helped the team close on a strong note and set great expectations for the next season.

The misfortunes that befell Jones in 1967 are perhaps best exemplified by the events of April 16, when he was struck by a first-inning pitch from the Dodgers' Don Drysdale, then was hit again during a pickoff play at first and had to be removed for a pinch-runner. The Braves had spent the winter fending off trade inquiries for Jones– including an aggressive offer from the Chicago White Sox – and his promising start (.300 in his first 20 at-bats) seemingly confirmed the team's decision to hold on to their prized slugger. But another strong close to the season (.342 in his final 79 at-bats) only served to mask the difficulties he encountered in between. After 16 games Jones was batting .189, and he had a horrific five-game stretch in mid-June when he struck out in 13 of 20 at-bats. Even the heavens appeared to conspire against him. On June 29 in Atlanta,

after batting.296 with seven RBIs in nine games, he drove in four runs with a home run and a double against Houston, but a heavy rain washed out the game, along with that day's statistics, in the top of the fourth inning.

Suspicions that the 1966 operation was affecting Jones's play – he later admitted that the shoulder "never was fixed right"[14] – became evident when manager Billy Hitchcock (who'd replaced Bragan during the preceding year) explained his reasons for shifting Mack from center field to left in August of 1967: "[W]e kept hoping that Jones' throwing arm would come around. But it hasn't. Runners have been taking the extra base on Mack. … It could be that because Mack thinks he hasn't done the job on defense, it has affected his hitting. Perhaps this move will ease the pressure."[15] The shift may indeed have contributed to his strong finish, but Mack's season-long output was a mere shadow of the preceding year.

Jones had plenty of company during the disappointing campaign. The Braves' league-leading 782 runs scored and second-highest team batting average (.263) in 1966 dissolved to 631 and .240 in 1967, and that dropoff, combined with an oft-injured or ineffective pitching staff, contributed to the franchise's worst season in 15 years and a seventh-place finish. A season full of finger-pointing intensified as the campaign ground to a close, and in one instance general manager Paul Richards felt compelled to deny rumors that he'd ordered Hitchcock to play Jones. Richards made clear his desire to clean house, and before the World Series had ended, he had made two trades involving eight players. Jones was traded to the Cincinnati Reds along with first baseman Jim Beauchamp and pitcher Jay Ritchie for outfielder Deron Johnson. "I had a feeling I was going to be traded," Mack said. "Sometimes playing in your hometown can be bad psychologically. Some people expect too much of you."[16]

The Reds looked to Jones as their left-field replacement for the traded Tommy Harper, but they complicated matters by acquiring outfielder Alex Johnson from the St. Louis Cardinals. In spring training Johnson won the starting role, relegating Mack to the bench. Jones derived some satisfaction on the occasions when he played– including a three-run home run and a double on August 14 to lead the Reds to a victory over his former Atlanta teammates – but he had only 234 at-bats and a .252 average. Left unprotected in the October expansion draft, he was selected by the Montreal Expos. The Expos immediately began receiving trade offers for Mack, including one from the Reds. "We hated to lose [him]," Reds general manager Bob Howsam explained.[17]

Jones was projected as the Expos' center fielder, but the arm problems that followed him north forced a move to left field. Still, he smacked the first home run hit on Canadian soil, and became a fan favorite. (Jarry Park's grandstand and bleacher area abutting Mack's perch in left was christened Jonesville. He sported a .373-7-26 line 30 days into the season, and the baseball-hungry Montreal fans offered standing ovations the moment Mack emerged from the dugout. "Never have I seen a man applauded for a strikeout," said Expos manager Gene Mauch after just such an occasion.[18] He hit his 100th career home run on May 9 and followed with his second career grand slam the next day. (He hit another on July 26 in Atlanta.) He was bypassed in favor of Rusty Staub as Montreal's sole All-Star Game representative, and despite a severe slump (.187 with only one homer during a 26-game stretch), he still finished among the team leaders in every offensive category.

The only cloud that marred Jones's fine season was the challenge that every African-American encountered – the unsightly face of racism. On a road trip to Houston in mid-May, Mack's ire was raised when an unruly fan used a contemptuous racial epithet. "Any time I hear that filthy word, my reaction is violent," said Jones.[19] Tempers cooled and the game proceeded, but one wonders if the words from his high school's namesake before the Georgia House of Representative in 1868 – "[a]m I a man? If I am such, I claim the rights of a man" – may have echoed through Mack's strong reaction.

Though Jones spent two more seasons with the Expos, he did not regain the success of his debut campaign. He never fully recovered from a slow start in 1970 that relegated him to pinch-hitting duties, and before long the moniker Mayor of Jonesville became a distant memory to the fans in Montreal. Before the 1971 season the team rejected trade inquiries in hopes that the preceding season was merely an anomaly. Hitting coach Larry Doby worked closely with Mack in Florida. Jones was the Opening Day starter in left field but returned to the bench after going hitless in his first four games, and was used sparingly thereafter. An unsuccessful pinch-hit at-bat on July 1 against Atlanta dropped his batting average to .165 and represented his last appearance in the major leagues. He was released seven days later. Mauch's comments reflected the feelings of fans and teammates alike: "This is one of

the saddest days since the Expos were born. I hate to see Mac[k] leave us."[20] In 1,002 major-league games and 3,091 at-bats, Jones collected 133 home runs and 415 RBIs to accompany a .252 batting average. His hit-by-pitch total of 77 placed him among the career top 200 (as of 2014).

Jones returned to Atlanta and resumed his offseason career in insurance. He dedicated much time coaching youth baseball and football, and this avid fan could often be found in front of a television watching sports. In 1998 he was one of six players (including Hall of Famer Grover Cleveland Alexander) honored as inaugural inductees in the Syracuse Chiefs' Baseball Wall of Fame. Jones joined five others – including Hall of Famer Grover Cleveland "Pete" Alexander – in the first induction class. He was inducted into the International League Hall of Fame in 2013.

Mack Jones was diagnosed with stomach cancer in October 2003 and succumbed to the disease on June 8, 2004, at age 65. He was survived by his second wife of 30 years, Esther; two children; two stepchildren; and three grandchildren. His only son, Rontae, apparently inherited some of Mack's athleticism – at various times he had tryouts the Braves, Expos, and Florida Marlins.

"I know everybody has slumps, but not like mine," Jones said in 1963. "I get in one and my average goes down, down, down."[21] Conversely, when he was hitting his stride, this streak hitter was nearly impossible to get out. Perhaps no one captured Mack Jones's value more than his teammate Hall of Famer Hank Aaron: "I admired Mack for his talent. He was tremendously gifted … [and] a good guy in the clubhouse. I wish he had played longer."

### Author's Note:

The author wishes to thank Mack Jones's widow, Esther, and son, Rontae, for their time and assistance in ensuring the accuracy of this narrative. Further thanks are extended to Terry Sloope, Bill Nowlin, Len Levin, and Russ Lake for their editorial and fact-checking assistance.

### Sources

In addition to the sources cited in the Notes, the author also consulted Ancestry.com, Baseball-Reference.com, mlb.com, and thedeadballera.com/Obits/Obits_J/Jones.

Mack.Obit.html

Thanks as well to Rontae Jones and Esther Jones for telephone interviews on September 9, 2013, and to Rontae Jones for email correspondence on September 12, 2013.

**Notes**

1  "Vet Covington and Rookie Jones Run 1-2 in Tepee Picket Derby," *The Sporting News,* January 18, 1961: 12.

2  Jones's nickname "Mack the Knife" was a reflection of the popular 1959 hit song by recording artist Bobby Darin. Other athletes of the era with the same first name – Kuykendall (minor-league baseball), Herndon (college basketball), and Herron (football) – were all similarly tagged.

3  1940 Census records refer to Inell as "Snellen." Conversations between surviving members of the Jones family and the author suggest her first name was Inell.

4  "Mack Likes New Scenery in Cincy," *The Sporting News,* February 10, 1968: 35.

5  "Dressen, Taking Over, Charts Busier Summer for Papooses," *The Sporting News,* December 30, 1959: 15.

6  "Bell's Busy Bat Helps to Calm Storm in Tepee," *The Sporting News,* June 23, 1962: 19.

7  "Bragan to Continue Platooning Strategy," *The Sporting News,* February 15, 1964: 8.

8  The Braves sent Mack to the Detroit Tigers for outfielder Purnal Goldy, although each team retained the rights to their original player. See *The Sporting News,* November 28, 1964: 7.

9  "Chiefs' Jones, Northrup Hit Chuckers With HR Arrows," *The Sporting News,* August 15, 1964: 29.

10  "Braves Drill on Assembly Line; Squad Broken Up Into 3 Shifts," *The Sporting News,* March 6, 1965: 23.

11  "Braves' Eyes Flash and Crackle as Jones Turns on the Juice," *The Sporting News,* September 18, 1965: 16.

12  "Atlanta Togs Fit Perfectly, Jones Beams," *The Sporting News,* December 11, 1965: 23.

13  "Braves' Garden Best, Bragan Boasts," *The Sporting News,* July 23, 1966: 21.

14  "Stoneman Aiming to Soften Batter With New Pitches," *The Sporting News,* March 28, 1970: 29.

15  "Aaron Moves to Center In Tepee Picket Switch," *The Sporting News,* August 26, 1967: 29.

16  "Mack Likes New Scenery in Cincy," *The Sporting News,* February 10, 1968: 35.

17  "Draft Blows Fog Over Cardenas' Future," *The Sporting News,* November 2, 1968: 34.

18  "Raps at Playing Surface Annoy Expos," *The Sporting News,* May 3, 1969: 20.

19  "Robertson Turns Ignition as Starter for Expos," *The Sporting News,* June 7, 1969: 23.

20  "Mike Marshall No Longer Hero in Montreal," *The Sporting News,* July 24, 1971: 24.

21  "Maye, Jones Out Front in Picket Race," *The Sporting News,* March 16, 1963: 23.

# CARL MORTON

## By Tom Hawthorn

The rookie Carl Morton was tapped by manager Gene Mauch to start just the fourth game in the history of the Montreal Expos. The 25-year-old right-hander made his major-league debut on April 11, 1969, at Wrigley Field in Chicago. The expansion Expos, who had to fill a roster with rejects, castoffs, and hopefuls from older clubs, had gone 1-2 on their inaugural roadstand in New York. Meanwhile, the Chicago Cubs had scored 24 runs against the Philadelphia Phillies in a three-game sweep at Wrigley.

Morton, a college-educated redhead from Oklahoma, whose childhood baseball hero was Mickey Mantle, had been moved from the outfield to the mound only two seasons earlier. He arrived at spring training fighting for a spot in the bullpen. By the time the Expos headed north from West Palm Beach, Florida, Morton had been named a fourth starter on a rotation including Jim "Mudcat" Grant, Bill Stoneman, and Larry Jaster. The rookie's tough first assignment featured a Cubs lineup including Ernie Banks, Billy Williams, and Ron Santo.

The temperature was in the high 40s and the sky clear as Morton got to work with a repertoire including a solid fastball, a curve, and a combination slider-curve he liked to call a slurve. "When I went to the mound, I told myself it was just another game," he said. "Same ball and same kind of field we played on last year at Shreveport."[1]

Morton got through his first inning by inducing three groundouts. He avoided serious trouble through the following innings, giving up a walk in the second, a single in the third, a walk in the fourth, and a single in the fifth. The Cubs touched Morton for three singles in the sixth but failed to score, as Glenn Beckert was out at the plate on a fielder's choice. After giving up another single in the eighth and a walk in the ninth, Morton completed nine innings without giving up a run. Unfortunately for him and his Expos, Cubs pitcher Joe Niekro also completed nine shutout innings. The Cubs went on to win the game, 1-0, in the 12th.

Four days later, Morton started only the second major-league game to be played outside the United States. He lasted only four innings against the St. Louis Cardinals in another no-decision. He gave up three earned runs on three hits, including home runs by Mike Shannon and Vada Pinson, while issuing one base on balls. He struck out six.

In his third start, against the Cubs at Jarry Park on April 20, Morton again left after the fourth inning, this time after surrendering four runs. He gave up just one hit, a single, but walked five. He took the loss, while Ferguson Jenkins of the Cubs pitched a complete game to become the first Canadian to win a major-league game on Canadian soil.

Morton lost his next two starts, both against the Pirates, lasting 4⅔ innings at Forbes Field and falling, 8-2, to the Pirates on April 25 and unable to get out of the second inning in a 4-2 loss at Jarry Park on May 3. Two weeks later, the pitcher, who was 0-3 with a 5.40 earned-run average, was optioned to the Vancouver Mounties of the Pacific Coast League.

The Triple-A team served as a farm club for both the Expos and the expansion Seattle Pilots, so Morton wound up on a staff including Jim Bouton, who was keeping a diary that season that would be the basis for his controversial bestseller, *Ball Four.* Morton went 8-6 in 18 starts, completing seven games, including a shutout. He returned to the parent club in September, making three inconsequential relief appearances.

It was an inauspicious debut for the 6-foot, 195-pound pitcher, who would be back with the Expos to start the 1970 season. Big Red, as he was sometimes called, was expected to handle long relief assignments, but got a start in chilly San Francisco against the Giants in the second game of a doubleheader. Manager Mauch wanted to save staff ace Steve Renko for a coming warm-weather gig in San Diego. On April 26, Morton gave up just two singles through five scoreless innings as the Expos recorded three runs. In the Giants' sixth, Bobby Bonds' single was followed by a two-out home run by Ken Henderson, but Morton got out of the inning to gain his first major-league win as the Expos called on reliever Claude Raymond, a Quebec native, to hold the Giants off in the ninth.

The performance earned Morton another start and he beat the Dodgers on a three-hitter at Dodger Stadium. He picked up a third consecutive victory against no losses against the Giants in a 15-8 blowout at Jarry Park. The pitcher went 3-for-5 at the plate with a double and a pair of singles.

Morton attributed his success to a 95-cent paperback copy of *Psycho-Cybernetics*, a book on the science of motivation and self-confidence by Maxwell Maltz, a cosmetic surgeon. "Last year I had negative goals," Morton told Montreal baseball writer Ted Blackman in 1970. "I doubted that I could succeed in the majors and, naturally, I fulfilled my negative goal. Now, I believe I will make it."[2]

The pitcher said he reread the book before every start and considered it a form of self-hypnotizing.

By July, it seemed possible Morton might win 20 games, but he got stuck after his 14th victory and failed to record a win in four consecutive starts in August. By season's end, Morton had compiled an 18-11 record with 10 complete games and four shutouts, an outstanding performance for a rookie pitcher in an expansion team's sophomore campaign.

Morton won National League Rookie of the Year honors with 11 of 24 votes from the Baseball Writers Association of America. Cincinnati Reds outfielder Bernie Carbo was runner-up with eight votes, followed by Philadelphia Phillies shortstop Larry Bowa with three and Houston Astros outfielder César Cedeño and Reds pitcher Wayne Simpson with one apiece. The prize was the first major award to be won by an Expos player. Morton also got two votes for the Cy Young Award, which was won by Bob Gibson of the St. Louis Cardinals with 118.

Late in the season, Morton bemoaned his fate to be in a pitching stable lacking a bona-fide star. "I'd give my right arm to watch Gibson pitch every fourth day," he said in September after defeating the Pirates in Pittsburgh for his 17th victory. "Just think what you could learn from him."[3]

The award-winning rookie season was followed by two disappointing campaigns as Morton went 10-18 and 7-13 before the Expos traded him to the Braves for pitcher Pat Jarvis during spring training in 1973. The right-hander got a measure of revenge on his return to Montreal, limiting his old team to three singles over six innings to earn a win. "I wanted to come back and show these people I'm a big-league pitcher," Morton said after the game. "I think a lot of people didn't believe it last year."[4] He was a productive and successful starter for the Braves by winning 15, 16 and 17 games in successive seasons, pitching more than 250 innings in each of those campaigns.

Morton won only four games in 1976 and was traded with four other players to the Texas Rangers for slugging outfielder Jeff Burroughs.

Released by the Rangers, Morton traveled from camp to camp during spring training in 1977 before signing a minor-league contract with the Philadelphia Phillies. He spent the season with the Oklahoma City 89ers of the

American Association. After his final appearance, he went to the bullpen, dug a hole in the dirt and tossed his cap in before covering it with dirt. "They tried to bury me," he explained. "This is my way of burying the season."[5]

Morton had an 87-92 record in the majors over parts of eight seasons with a 3.73 ERA. He compiled 13 shutouts and registered 51 complete games. His playing days over at age 33, Morton returned to Oklahoma to help Gene Shell coach the Golden Hurricane baseball team at the University of Tulsa. Shell had been his high-school coach.

Although he grew up in the Sooner State, Carl Wendle Morton was born in Kansas City, Missouri, on January 18, 1944, to Merle V. and William Clyde Morton, a school-teacher. As a boy, Carl dreamed of playing in the New York Yankees outfield alongside his idol – Oklahoma's favorite son, Mickey Mantle.

"I saw him play twice," Morton said on the day of his major-league debut. "Our kid team took a train excursion to Kansas City when the Yankees were playing there." He never got a chance to meet the Hall of Famer, who retired before Morton's debut.

By his senior year at Daniel Webster High School in Tulsa, the outfielder's games attracted scouts from several teams. At 18, he turned down a large bonus (reports cite $80,000 and $150,000), choosing instead to play for the Sooners at the University of Oklahoma. After his sophomore college campaign, he signed with the Milwaukee Braves, who assigned him in his first season to farm teams at West Palm Beach, Florida, and Yakima, Washington. The 1966 season saw him in Kinston, North Carolina, where he hit 13 home runs in 317 at-bats, though an anemic .227 batting average made it unlikely he'd make the major-league roster anytime soon.

At spring training in 1967, Atlanta general manager Paul Richards told the prospect he was to move from the outfield to the mound. Considering he was struggling against the slider and figured it was better to throw one than try to hit one, Morton quietly but eagerly accepted his new position. He went 10-9 with Kinston before graduating to Shreveport, Louisiana, in 1968, where he was 13-5.

"The Braves thought I had a better chance to reach the majors as a pitcher," he said. "Why did they put me in the expansion draft? Well, I think they thought they were set in pitching."[6]

The Braves left the prospect unprotected in the expansion draft to stock the expansion Expos and San Diego Padres. Montreal general manager Jim Fanning, who had worked with Morton in the Braves system, selected the pitcher in the fifth round, number 45 overall.

On April 12, 1983, Morton went for a morning jog in Tulsa. He collapsed in the driveway of his parents' home and died of a heart attack an hour later at Tulsa Osteopathic Hospital. He was 39. He left his wife, Karen, and a son, Brent David Morton, from his marriage to his first wife, Sandi, as well as a stepdaughter, Lori Watts. He was buried at Memorial Park Cemetery in Tulsa, which would be the final resting place for his father, who died three years later, and his mother, who died in 1994.

In 2007 the *Tulsa World* listed the top 100 baseball players from Oklahoma to mark the centennial of statehood. Mantle was number 1, while Morton was number 52.[7]

## Sources

In addition to the sources cited in the Notes, the author also consulted Retrosheet.org and Baseball-Reference.com.

## Notes

1 Edward Prell, "Rookie Makes Dazzling Big League Start," *Chicago Tribune,* April 12, 1969: 69.

2 Ted Blackman, "Red Hair, Strong Arm – Morton Ticket to Montreal," *The Sporting News.* May 23, 1970: 26.

3 D. Byron Yake, "Morton Tosses 'Book' at Buccos," *Indiana* (Pennsylvania) *Gazette,* September 24, 1970: 54.

4 "Morton Homecoming Sets Back the Expos," *Nanaimo* (British Columbia) *Daily News,* June 8, 1973: 11.

5 "Former Pitcher Carl Morton, 39, NL Rookie of the Year in 1970," *Philadelphia Inquirer,* April 14, 1983: 56.

6 Prell.

7 Barry Lewis, "Oklahoma Centennial Top 100 Baseball Players." *Tulsa* (Oklahoma) *World,* July 8, 2007. tulsaworld.com/archives/oklahoma-centennial-top-greatest-oklahoman-baseball-players/article_228edfa6-55b9-58b5-a41b-e00a3c10455a.html (Retrieved January 5, 2018).

# MAURY WILLS

## By Glen Sparks

Harsh sunshine beat down on the Los Angeles Coliseum floor. Two men, drenched in sweat, practiced baseball drills while local temperatures soared past 100 degrees in the spring of 1960. Maury Wills, an eager Dodger infielder, and Pete Reiser, an enthusiastic LA coach, worked together for nearly two weeks.

"You can't quit," Reiser said over and over to his pupil. "You have to keep at it. These things don't come overnight."[1]

"Overnight?" What did Wills think about that? … Overnight? … Ever?

Wills had endured a long and often frustrating road to the major leagues. He toiled eight seasons in the minors and nearly quit a few times. The Dodgers finally called him up in June of 1959. The rookie batted .260 over 83 games and helped LA win the National League pennant. He hit .250 in the World Series; the Dodgers knocked off the Chicago White Sox in six games.

But Wills began the 1960 season in a funk. Dodgers manager Walt Alston started pinch-hitting for him as early as the third inning. Discouraged, Wills asked Reiser for help. The coach, a former Brooklyn Dodgers phenom, told Wills to meet him at the Coliseum the following morning.

Reiser stood on the pitcher's mound at the Dodgers' home field and threw one ball after another, yelling at Wills to hit each offering to the opposite field. At one point, Wills complained about the heat wave. Reiser brushed off his pupil and kept going. "Would you rather take a little heat here with the Dodgers or go back to the 'bus and wool-shirt circuit' in Spokane (one of the many minor-league stops for Wills)?" he asked.[2]

That comment probably made Wills cringe. No way did he want to go back to the minors, not at the age of 27. He had spent enough time riding the bus and playing ballgames in rickety parks for crummy pay and lousy meal money.

The slump continued. *These things don't come overnight.* Eventually, he broke out of it and earned back his starting job. Baseball writers voted him 17th for the National League MVP that season. The hard work had paid dividends.

Wills went on to play 14 big-league seasons and retired with 2,134 hits and a .281 batting average. Of course, he also stole bases. He did that better than almost everybody, retiring with 586 thefts. Wills led the National

League in steals six times, broke the single-season mark, and earned a Most Valuable Player award. Fans in LA, and often in other stadiums, yelled, "Go! Go! Go!" as soon as he reached first base. Usually, he took off, daring the opposing catcher. Former Dodgers executive Buzzie Bavasi wrote in his memoir that Wills "was electrifying in his prime, in the early '60s."[3]

Born on October 2, 1932, in Washington, D.C., Maurice Morning Wills grew up in the district's Anacostia neighborhood, along with four brothers and eight sisters. His father, Guy Wills, born in 1900 in Maryland, worked as a machinist at the Washington Navy Yard and part-time as a Baptist minister. His mother, Mable Wills, born in 1902, also in Maryland, worked as an elevator operator.

Maury began playing organized baseball at age 14, in a local semipro league. He starred in baseball, basketball, and football at Cardozo High School in Washington, earning all-city honors in each sport as a sophomore, junior, and senior. On the diamond, Wills pitched and played third base. He also got married during his senior year to his high-school sweetheart, Gertrude Elliott. The couple had six children and later divorced.

Several colleges liked Wills for his gridiron skills. He played quarterback on offense, safety on defense, and kicker on special teams. Wills, though, opted to pursue a professional baseball career. "Football was my first love, but baseball was my true love," he explained.[4]

Wills signed with the Dodgers in the summer of 1950. The young ballplayer had hoped for a $6,000 bonus. Brooklyn scouts Rex Bowen and John Curry offered him a new suit of clothes. The negotiations continued. Finally, the scouts got up to leave. Bowen offered $500. "Take or leave it," he said. Guy Wills thought about it for a second. "We'll take it," he said.[5]

Wills reported to the Hornell (New York) Dodgers of the Class-D Pennsylvania-Ontario-New York League, in 1951. He batted .280 and stole 54 bases. The Dodgers promoted him to the Class-C Santa Barbara Dodgers of the California League in 1952. Wills, though, felt comfortable in New York and asked to stay there for one more season. He did and stole another 54 bases.

In 1953, Wills split time between the Pueblo (Colorado) Dodgers of the Class-A Western League and the Miami Sun Sox of the Class-B Florida State League. Combined, he hit .286 in 111 games and returned to Pueblo the next

year. He put together another solid season and earned a promotion in 1955 to the Fort Worth Cats in the Double-A Texas League. It was a tough campaign. Halfway through, Wills' batting average had dropped to .220. The Dodgers demoted him back to Pueblo in 1956. "It was a bitter pill to swallow and nearly caused me to lose faith in myself and my career," Wills said.[6] Even so, he hit .302 and stole 34 bases during his Pueblo encore.

The Seattle Rainiers, a Pacific Coast League club, purchased Wills' contract on a conditional basis. The 24-year-old hit .267 in 1957 and stole 21 bases. The Dodgers exercised their claim on the journeyman prospect and in 1958 assigned him to the Spokane (Washington) Indians, also in the PCL. Manager Bobby Bragan, a former big-league catcher, mentored Wills. "He took a big interest in me and just being around him made my baseball life worth living," Wills said. "I had just about given up on myself."[7] Bragan improved Wills' attitude and encouraged him to switch-hit. The natural right-hander could reach first base even faster by batting left-handed. Why not try it? Bragan asked.

Wills replied, "Bobby, I'll try anything once."[8]

Within a few weeks, Wills had the hang of it. "You're a switch-hitter now, kid," Bragan said.[9] But Wills worried that he might be stuck forever as a minor leaguer. In the spring of 1959, the Dodgers once again sold him, again on an option basis, this time to the Detroit Tigers. Wills, playing mostly in B games, went 11-for-23, and stole eight bases. The Tigers, though, had traded for shortstop Rocky Bridges. Wills returned to the Dodgers, who sent him back to Spokane. "But I didn't feel despondent," Wills said. "Being in spring training with the Tigers and having a chance to make the big leagues was the greatest experience I had had in my career."[10]

The Dodgers needed another shortstop. Pee Wee Reese, a future Hall of Famer, had retired after the 1958 season. One option was Bob Lillis, who like Wills, had languished in the minors for several years. Lillis batted .391 in 20 games for LA in 1958. He began slowly in 1959, though, and lost his job. Don Zimmer, a six-year veteran, took over as the starter. Zim, however, broke a toe in early June, and Bragan recommended Wills for a promotion to Los Angeles.[11] Wills, batting .313 with 25 stolen bases at Spokane, not surprisingly, said, "I sure was hoping to get a chance to play in the majors."[12]

Wills played his first game for the Dodgers on June 6,

1959, and went hitless in four at-bats. His batting average stood at a meager .175 after one month in LA. Finally, he began to rap groundballs that eluded infielders. Thanks to a burst of speed, he beat out plenty of throws to first base from opposing shortstops and third basemen. His batting average began climbing. Zimmer, meanwhile, returned from his toe injury but battled a season-long funk. He hit only .165 in 97 games and went to bat just one time in the World Series. Wills played in all six games.

On April 8, 1960, the Dodgers traded Zimmer to the Chicago Cubs for pitcher Ron Perranoski, infielders Johnny Goryl and Lee Handley, and $25,000. Wills struggled until he began practicing with Reiser under that blazing sun. By the end of the season he had hiked his batting average to .295 and stolen a league-high 50 bases. No National League player had swiped 50 bases in one season since Max Carey notched 50 for the Pittsburgh Pirates in 1923. "It was like magic," Wills wrote about his sudden hot streak. "My entire attitude had changed from that of despair to one of eager anticipation. I couldn't wait to get up to the plate."[13] The Dodgers finished 82-72, good for fourth place.

Wills enjoyed another solid season in 1961. (The Dodgers dealt Lillis to the Cardinals early in the campaign.) His batting average slipped from the previous campaign, to .282, but he still led the league with 35 stolen bases. He made his first All-Star team, won his first Gold Glove and finished ninth in the MVP voting. Los Angeles ended up 89-65, in second place, four games behind the Cincinnati Reds. Hints of the glorious, but brief, reign of LA left-hander Sandy Koufax had emerged. The 25-year-old from Brooklyn battled control problems in his first six seasons. He won 18 games in 1961 and led the National League with 269 strikeouts.

The Dodgers moved out of the oddly shaped Los Angeles Coliseum (251 feet from home plate to the left-field wall) after the 1961 season and into Dodger Stadium. The new ballpark favored pitchers, especially on cool nights when the heavy marine layer moved in from the coast. Koufax and Don Drysdale, a hard-throwing right-hander and a hometown product from LA's San Fernando Valley, were primed to form a dynamic 1-2 pitching combination.

Wills supplied speed and bursts of energy. He set a goal of stealing at least 50 bases in 1962 and reached that mark by the 104th game, on July 27 against the San Francisco Giants. His self-confidence had soared. "Every time I

get on base, I feel like I'm going to make it when I go," Wills said. "I've eliminated in my mind the fear of failure."[14] How much did Wills mean to the LA offense? One late-summer game offers an example. On August 26 against the New York Mets, he walked, stole second, and scored on a Tommy Davis single in the first inning. Two innings later, he reached on an infield single, stole second, sprinted to third on a Willie Davis bunt, and raced home after Tommy Davis hit into a double play. In the sixth, Wills ripped an RBI double, stole third, and scored on a Jim Gilliam single. "Thus did Maury Wills, perhaps the greatest base stealer in modern baseball history, demonstrate once more his tremendous value to the Los Angeles Dodgers," according to one article.[15]

Off the field, Wills enjoyed playing his banjo in the team clubhouse, on the team plane, and in nightspots from LA to Las Vegas and New York City. He also liked to mingle with Hollywood movie stars. He claimed to have had an affair in 1962 with actress/singer Doris Day, who was a big Dodgers fan. "Doris Day is a lovely lady, and we did see each other," Wills wrote in his 1991 book, *On the Run*. "And, yes, we were lovers."[16] The two met at Dodger Stadium and began dating, according to Wills. Rumors began to circulate throughout the summer. The whispers grew louder. Day and Wills were both married. Plus, Day being white and Wills being black mattered to many people in early-1960s America.

Reporters asked Wills about the relationship. Bavasi ordered Wills into his office and "made it clear that the club wouldn't look kindly on the public relations nightmare likely to ensue if white fans learned that one of the team's star players was dating America's girl-next-door," Michael Leahy wrote in his book *The Last Innocents*, about the Dodger teams of the Koufax-Wills era. Bavasi ordered Wills to stop seeing Day.[17] (Day in her autobiography wrote that she and Wills were simply friends and that "we certainly saw each other alone anywhere."[18])

Wills agreed to Bavasi's temperamental demand and kept running. He stole 46 bases in 51 attempts by midseason. Could he break Ty Cobb's single-season mark of 96, set in 1915 for the Detroit Tigers? No major leaguer had even stolen 60 bases since George Case swiped 61 for the 1943 Washington Senators.

Stealing bases nearly every day didn't come easy. Wills' hamstrings burned from all the sudden starting and stopping on the basepaths. He kept running. Some opposing groundskeepers packed sand into the clay around first base to make the dirt soft and slippery and more difficult for Wills to get traction. He kept running. Wills stole four bases on September 7, giving him 82 for the season and breaking the National League mark of 81, set by Bob Bescher of the Cincinnati Reds in 1911. He was closing in on Cobb.

Late in the year, Commissioner Ford C. Frick tossed Wills a curveball. He said that Wills would have to break Cobb's stolen-base mark in 154 games, the same number of scheduled games in 1915. Due to expansion, the National League lengthened its season to 162 games in 1962. The American League did that the previous year, also following expansion. (Cobb actually played in 156 games for the Tigers in 1915. Two games ended in ties, and the Georgia Peach notched a stolen base in one of them.)

Wills ran past Cobb on September 23, stealing two bags in a 12-2 loss to the St. Louis Cardinals and getting to 97 thefts, in the Dodgers' 156th game. "As far as I'm concerned, I was right on schedule," Wills said. "He (Cobb) did it in 156 games and what's good enough for Cobb is good enough for me."[19] He also declared, "I'm going for 100 steals."[20]

Wills reached the century mark on September 26 in a 13-1 shellacking of the Houston Colt .45s in game number 158. He did not steal a base in the next four games, all Dodgers losses. LA, which had taken over first place on July 8, picked a bad time to go cold. The Giants, meanwhile, had gotten hot. They caught the Dodgers on the final day of the scheduled season. Both teams ended the regular campaign with impressive 101-61 won-lost records. A best-of-three playoff would determine the NL pennant winner.

San Francisco won the opening matchup, 8-0, and Wills did not steal a base. LA took the second game, 8-7; Wills notched steal number 101. The Giants, despite Wills going 4-for-5 at the plate and stealing three bases, took the pennant in the third game by knocking off the Dodgers, 6-4, on October 3 at Dodger Stadium "It's horrible, and it's true," Wills said afterward. "But you just can't understand it. It's like a nightmare."[21]

Mostly, though, Wills enjoyed a dream season for the Dodgers. He not only stole a record 104 bases, opposing catchers threw him out just 13 times.[22] He also set a major-league record in 1962 by playing in 165 games. He went to bat 695 times and hit safely 208 times for a .299 batting average. Wills topped the NL with 10 triples. And he smacked a career-high six home runs. Writers voted

him the league's Most Valuable Player. "This is the best award a player can get," Wills said.[23] All that running and sliding, though, left Wills battered. Late in the season, *Los Angeles Times* columnist Jim Murray wrote, "His body is so bruised he constantly looks as if he had just crawled out of a plane wreck."[24]

In his book *It Pays to Steal*, published in 1963, Wills asked himself rhetorically, "Do I think I'll ever steal 104 bases again?" He answered, "No, I can't believe I did it to this day. I don't see how I can ever come close again. The physical beating I took is more than I want to endure."[25]

Indeed, Wills swiped just 40 bags in 1963. He still led the National League in that category, although catchers threw him out 19 times. The shortstop batted .302, just a little bit higher than in 1962, but he played in 31 fewer games and scored 47 fewer runs. Even so, the Dodgers, thanks in large part to Koufax (25-5, 1.88 ERA, 306 strikeouts, and 11 shutouts), captured the league pennant. The team finished 99-63, six games ahead of the second-place St. Louis Cardinals, and swept the New York Yankees in the World Series. Wills batted just .133 (2-for-15) in the Series with one stolen base and one run scored.

The 1964 Dodgers slumped to 82-80 and finished tied for sixth place with the Pittsburgh Pirates. Koufax made only 28 starts but went 19-5 with a 1.74 ERA. Drysdale compiled an 18-16 won-lost mark despite posting a 2.18 ERA. Wills hit .275 with 53 steals and led the league for the fifth straight year. Poor offense did in the Dodgers, who averaged just 3.7 runs scored, third from last in the 10-team National League. Tim McCarver, a longtime catcher for the Cardinals and other teams once said, "We used to kid around that a Dodger rally consisted of a Maury Wills bunt for a single, Wills stealing second base, Wills moving to third on a sacrifice, and then Wills scoring on a wild pitch."[26]

The Dodgers rebounded in 1965. They went 97-65 and captured the NL pennant. Koufax set a major-league record with 382 strikeouts. He and Drysdale combined to win 49 games. Wills didn't steal 100 bases, but he did swipe 94. He hit .286 and scored 92 runs. Late in the campaign, Philadelphia Phillies manager Gene Mauch said, "Maury Wills is the greatest slider and the quickest starter in the history of the game. He gets the base stolen the first five feet. He's the most unafraid runner I've ever seen."[27] Wills enjoyed his best World Series that year. He batted .367 (11-for-30) against the Minnesota Twins and stole three bases but was caught twice. The Dodgers knocked off the

Twins in six games. Koufax pitched brilliantly, going 2-1 with a 0.38 ERA.

It figured that some pitchers and catchers might eventually catch up with Wills. He admitted as much during the 1966 season and mentioned strong-armed backstops Jerry Grote of the New York Mets and Randy Hundley of the Chicago Cubs. "The pitchers have come up with some new moves, which make it more difficult to get a good jump. When (the catchers) throw 10 inches over the bag, I'm dead."[28] Wills swiped 38 bases in 1966 but was caught 24 times. He batted .273. Rarely inclined to take a walk, he posted just a .314 on-base percentage and scored only 60 runs. Once again, Koufax led the Dodgers to a pennant. He went 27-9, struck out 317 batters and fashioned a 1.73 ERA. Writers voted him baseball's Cy Young Award winner for the third time. The Baltimore Orioles swept LA in the World Series, allowing just two runs and 17 hits over the four games. Wills hit a woeful .077 (1-for-13). LA infielder Jim Lefebvre said, "We couldn't do anything right."[29] Wills said, "I'm embarrassed, but I'm not ashamed."[30]

To make matters worse, Dodgers owner Walter O'Malley had organized a postseason goodwill trip to Japan. The Dodgers would play a series of exhibition games against Japanese teams. Several players, including Wills, asked for permission to skip the event. O'Malley told the shortstop that he had to go. Wills played a few games and then went AWOL. His right knee ached, and he wanted doctors in Los Angeles to check it out. First, though, he stopped off in Hawaii and played his banjo at a couple of shows starring Don Ho and Sammy Davis Jr. He said, "I've been relaxing here. Right now, I don't know when I will return to the mainland."[31] He added, rather brazenly, "The Japanese trip was important to Mr. O'Malley, and I suppose he's rather bitter about me leaving."[32]

O'Malley, probably already in a foul mood after Koufax announced his retirement on November 18, ordered Bavasi to ship Wills out of Los Angeles.[33] Bavasi wrote that O'Malley told him, "Not only did he embarrass the Dodgers, but he embarrassed the nation of Japan."[34] Bavasi sent Wills to the Pirates in exchange for Bob Bailey and Gene Michael. Wills couldn't believe it. He had found a home in LA, and now he had to leave. "I don't want to be traded," he said. "I've spent all my life playing for the Dodgers. The Dodgers are my life."[35]

Wills spent two seasons in Pittsburgh. He tied a career high by batting .302 in 1967, but stole only 29 bases, his lowest figure as a major leaguer. The Pirates, a team that featured standout players including Willie Stargell, Roberto Clemente, Felipe Alou, and Donn Clendenon in addition to Wills, finished the year 81-81, in sixth place. Wills swiped 52 bases the following year, but the Bucs dropped to 80-82, ending up again in sixth place.

That fall, baseball held an expansion draft to fill rosters for two new National League teams, the Montreal Expos and San Diego Padres. Montreal took Wills with its 11th pick, the 21st overall selection. The infielder lasted 47 games north of the border. He batted a lowly .222, although he did steal 15 bases. Expos owner Charles Bronfman lit into the shortstop. Wills had gone from the Dodgers to the Pirates and then to the Expos. And, he didn't enjoy life in Montreal. "He played like he didn't give a damn, and he didn't," Bronfman said.[36] Wills even retired from the team for a short time. Expos general manager Jim Fanning said that Wills requested on June 2 to be placed on the voluntarily retired list. "We had a nice visit and there is no doubt in my mind that he is sincere," Fanning said.[37] Wills said, "I'm not bitter. ... I just feel it's time for Maury Wills to retire."[38]

Wills sat idle for only a few days. "I informed the Montreal club that I realized they had a great investment in me, and after thinking it over I knew I didn't want to walk out on my obligation," Wills said in a June 7 newspaper article.[39] Exasperated, the Expos traded him back to the Dodgers, along with Manny Mota, in exchange for Ron Fairly and Paul Popovich. Team executive Al Campanis had lobbied to bring Wills back. O'Malley was less certain.

No one was happier than Wills. He heard about the deal while the Expos were on the road in San Diego. Wills hopped into his car and headed up to LA for a Dodgers game that evening. Apparently, all was forgiven. O'Malley sent a note down to the Dodgers clubhouse: "Welcome back, Maury."[40]

Dodgers pitcher Don Sutton also welcomed Wills back. "The first time Maury Wills walked into our dressing room, there was a different air in the clubhouse," Sutton said. "We knew we had someone to take charge ... to bust his tail for us."[41] Back in his baseball comfort zone, Wills hit .297 in 104 games in LA and stole 25 bases to give him 40 for the season.

He explained the situation in Montreal. "The (Los Angeles) pitching helps my game a lot. Good pitching keeps the score close enough that my type of game has more impact."[42]

191

Wills played another two seasons with the Dodgers. He hit .270 with 28 steals in 1970 and .281 with 15 thefts in 1971. The Dodgers finished in second place both years. Sutton, Claude Osteen, Willie Davis, and Wes Parker led the way. The oft-traded Dick Allen enjoyed a big year in 1971, his only year with the Dodgers. He hit .295 with 23 homers and 90 RBIs, big numbers for the LA teams of that era. The Dodgers also called up a talented player out of Kansas named Bill Russell. The Dodgers were grooming the former outfielder to take over at shortstop. Wills, 38 years old in 1971, knew it. The team held a Maury Wills Day at Dodger Stadium late in the season, But, Wills told the crowd, he didn't plan on retiring.

In 1972, "They just put me on the bench, and paid me," he said. "Bill Russell was the new shortstop."[43] Wills played in only 71 games and went to bat just 132 times. He hit a woeful .129, stole one base, and knew the end was near. He got the bad news while playing golf at Yorba Linda Country Club in Orange County, California. A TV reporter with a camera crew walked up to Wills and told him that he had been released. A shocked Wills fought to find the right words. "These things happen," he said. "I've had a fine career. I'm happy to have been a Dodger."[44] He told Los Angeles Times writer Ross Newhan that he wanted to play another season. "I simply believe that 1972 was not a true indication of what I can still do if I am in shape and active," Wills said.[45]

Instead, he took a job broadcasting for the NBC Game of the Week. His son Bump Wills broke in as an infielder with the Texas Rangers in 1977 and played six seasons in the big leagues. Maury made it known that he wanted to manage in the major leagues. Bavasi encouraged him to take a minor-league managing job before accepting a major-league gig.

The Seattle Mariners thought Wills was ready. They hired him as skipper on August 4, 1980, to replace the fired Darrell Johnson. Mariners President Dan O'Brien said, "I think (Wills) was the best baseball man available."[46] The Mariners were mired in last place and had lost 20 of their last 24 games when Wills stepped into the dugout. The 47-year-old skipper felt confident that he could turn things around in the Pacific Northwest. "It shouldn't take longer than a week or 10 days to know what every player can do," he said.[47] But the losing continued. Seattle went 20-38 to wrap up the campaign. That included a seven-game winning streak in September.

Managing didn't get any easier in 1981. The players lacked

speed and didn't play sound baseball, Wills complained. "I lost my patience," he wrote in On the Run. "It was a lousy team. It was the Mariners."[48]

O'Brien let Wills go after the Mariners suffered through a 6-18 start in 1981. Some players felt relieved. Designated hitter Richie Zisk said, "Something had to be done on a positive note. (The firing) will change the atmosphere here. It was depressing."[49] Reporters hammered Wills for his curious decision-making. Among his list of supposed blunders: He called for a relief pitcher but had forgotten to tell anyone to warm up. He said outfielder Leon Roberts would be his starting center fielder. The problem? The Mariners had traded Roberts more than a month earlier. Another time, he called infielder Dave Edler into the manager's office and demoted him to Triple A. Then catcher Brad Gulden walked by. On a dime, Wills demoted Gulden instead of Edler.[50] Steve Rudman of the Seattle Post-Intelligencer wrote that Wills made "unconscionable strategic mistakes, third-grade, sandlot mistakes. And he compounded his mistakes by claiming to know all or by blaming somebody else."[51]

Later, Wills reconsidered Bavazi's recommendation. "Contrary to what I thought," he wrote, "I really needed managing experience below the major-league level, to learn how to organize, how to delegate responsibility, and how to deal with the press."[52]

Wills needed to address a much bigger problem. His life had descended into a fury of drug and alcohol abuse. He battled addiction for several years. "He spent more than $1 million on cocaine, sometimes, staying high for 10 days at a time, locking himself in his home alone for months," according to a Los Angeles Times article.[53] Los Angeles police arrested him in December 1983 on suspicion of car theft and cocaine possession.[54] Wills went into and out of rehab. He wrote in one of his books, "I didn't care if I died."[55] Former Dodgers Tommy Davis and Don Newcombe and team executive Fred Claire encouraged him to get sober.

The Dodgers invited Wills to spring training as a base-running and bunting instructor in 2001. He served in that capacity, first at the team's facility in Vero Beach, Florida, and then in Glendale, Arizona, for about 15 years. He also coached and served as a broadcast analyst for the Fargo-Moorhead RedHawks, an independent team. The Washington, D.C., Sports Hall of Fame honored Wills in 2013, and a youth baseball field in his hometown was named after him. The Country Music Hall of Fame in

Nashville even put one of his banjos on display.

Wills said he no longer worries about getting into the Baseball Hall of Fame in Cooperstown, New York. He stayed on the Hall of Fame ballot for 15 seasons and never earned more than 40.6 percent of the vote. (75 percent is needed for induction.) In 2014, he missed out on induction by the Hall of Fame Golden Era Committee, the revamped Veterans Committee.

As of 2018 the former speedster lived in Sedona, Arizona, apparently at peace after all the turmoil that plagued him for decades. In January 2016, Wills told a *Los Angeles Times* writer, "Through my program of recovery, I've learned to be grateful for where I am, and how wonderful my life is."[56]

## Sources

In addition to the sources cited in the Notes, the author also consulted baseball-reference.com.

## Notes

1 George Vescey, *Baseball's Most Valuable Players* (New York: Random House, 1966), 146.

2 Maury Wills and Steve Gardner, *It Pays to Steal* (New York: Prentice-Hall, 1963), 30.

3 Buzzie Bavasi and John Strege, *Off the Record* (New York: Contemporary Books, 1987), 91.

4 Maury Wills and Mike Celizic, *On the Run: The Never Dull and Often Shocking Life of Maury Wills* (New York: Carroll and Graf, 1991), 61.

5 Ibid.

6 *It Pays to Steal*, 35.

7 *It Pays to Steal*, 36.

8 *It Pays to Steal*, 27.

9 *On the Run*, 82.

10 *On the Run*, 89.

11 *On the Run*, 92.

12 Frank Finch, "Maury Wills from Spokane Joins LA," *Los Angeles Times*, June 6, 1959: 16.

13 *It Pays to Steal*, 54.

14 Zane Chastain, "Maury Wills Gallops on His Own, Claims He Has No Fear of Failure," *Daily Herald* (Provo, Utah), June 29, 1962: 12.

15 Associated Press, "Fabulous Maury Wills Stages Great Base-Running Display to Steal Show for Dodgers," *Standard Speaker* (Hazelton, Pennsylvania), August 27, 1962: 16.

16 *On the Run*, 198.

17 Michael Leahy, *The Last Innocents: The Collision of the Turbulent Sixties and the Los Angeles Dodgers* (New York: HarperCollins, 2016), 50.

18 A.E. Hotchner, *Doris Day: Her Own Story* (New York: William Morrow and Co.), 203.

19 Associated Press, "Maury Right 'On Schedule,'" *Hobbs* (New Mexico) *Daily News-Sun*, September 24, 1962: 6.

20 Milt Richman, Associated Press, "Wills Sets Steal Mark, Yanks Edge Near Flag," *Tyrone* (Pennsylvania) *Daily Herald*, September 24, 1962: 8.

21 Charles Maher, Associated Press, "It Wasn't Easy; But They Did It," *Index-Journal* (Greenwood, South Carolina), October 4, 1962: 8.

22 The St. Louis Cardinals' Lou Brock broke Wills' single-season mark in 1974 with 118 steals. Rickey Henderson as of 2018 was the single-season stolen base leader. He swiped 130 bases for the Oakland A's in 1982.

23 Joe Reichler, Associated Press, "Maury Wills Named NL Most Valuable Player," *Bakersfield Californian*, November 23, 1962: 27.

24 Jim Murray, "Thief of Bags, Dad," *Los Angeles Times*, September 10, 1962: 41.

25 *It Pays to Steal*, 73.

26 Steve Delsohn, *True Blue: The Dramatic History of the Los Angeles Dodgers, Told by the Men Who Lived It* (New York: William Morrow, 2001), 50.

27 Jim Murray, *Los Angeles Times* News Service, "Maury Wills' Destination: The Hall of Fame," *Honolulu Star-Bulletin*, September 12, 1965: 40.

28 Tom Adelman, *Black and Blue: The Golden Arm, the Robinson Boys, and the 1966 World Series That Stunned America* (New York: Little, Brown and Company, 2006), 87.

29 *Black and Blue*, 206.

30 Milton Richman, United Press International, "Alston Proud of Defeated LA Dodgers," *Deadwood* (South Dakota) *Pioneer-Times*, October 19, 1966: 4.

31 Associated Press, "Maury Wills Seen in Hawaii," *Santa Cruz* (California) *Sentinel*, November 8, 1966: 11.

32 Associated Press, "Maury Wills Returns Home After Leaving Dodger Tour," *Fort Myers* (Florida) *News-Press*, November 12, 1966: 11.

33 *Black and Blue*, 225.

34 *On the Record*, 99.

35 *Black and Blue*, 225.

36 Jonah Keri, *Up, Up, and Away: The Kid, the Hawk, Rock, Vladi, Pedro, le Grand Orange, Youppi!, the Crazy Business of Baseball, and the Ill-fated but Unforgettable Montreal Expos* (Toronto: Random House Canada, 2014),

32.

37 Associated Press, "Maury Wills Quits Expos," *Palm Beach Post* (West Palm Beach, Florida), June 4, 1969: 19.

38 Joseph Durso (*New York Times*), "Maury Explains," *Battle Creek* (Michigan) *Enquirer,* June 5. 1969: 21.

39 United Press International, "Maury Wills Rejoins Expos after Three-Day Retirement," *Ogden* (Utah) *Standard-Examiner*, June 7, 1969.

40 *On the Run*, 231.

41 Associate Press, "Maury Wills Makes Dodgers Go-Go," *McComb* (Mississippi) *Enterprise-Journal*, June 24, 1969: 6.

42 Dan Foster, "Mysterious Maury Wills," *Greenville* (South Carolina) *News*, June 27, 1969: 50.

43 *On the Run*, 234.

44 *On the Run*, 236.

45 Ross Newhan, "Maury Wills Put on Waivers, Wants One More Season," *Los Angeles Times*, October 26, 1972: 55.

46 Republic News Service, "Mariners Give Wills Long-Awaited Chance to Manage," *Arizona Republic*, August 5, 1980: 32.

47 Associated Press, "Johnson Fired; Maury Wills Named Mariners' Manager," *Hartford Courant,* August 5, 1980: 64.

48 *On the Run*, 279.

49 Associated Press, "Seattle Players Agree It Was Time for Change," *Elmira* (New York) *Star-Gazette*, May 7, 1981: 20.

50 Associated Press, "Maury Wills May Not Have Been Ready to be Major-League Manager," *Greenville News,* May 11, 1981: 15.

51 Steve Rudman, *Seattle Post-Intelligencer*, "A Comical Trip Through Wills' Seattle Command," as printed in the *News-Press* (Fort Myers, Florida), May 17, 1981: 53.

52 *On the Run*, 281.

53 David Shaw, "High and Away, Up and In," *Los Angeles Times*, April 7, 1991: 266.

54 Associated Press, "Friends Say That Maury Wills Is a Man in Trouble," *Ithaca* (New York) *Journal*, December 29, 1983: 13.

55 *On the Run*, 288.

56 Bill Shaikin, "Justice for Hall," *Los Angeles Times*, January 15, 2015: 41.

# IT'S A MAJOR LEAGUE CITY OR IT ISN'T:
# SAN DIEGO'S PADRES STEP UP TO THE BIG LEAGUES

BY JOHN BAUER

San Diego's quest for major-league baseball began in the mid- to late 1950s, around the time Los Angeles and San Francisco ascended to "the bigs." Home of the Pacific Coast League Padres since 1936 and backed by banker and businessman C. Arnholt Smith, San Diego looked for an opportunity to obtain major-league baseball. The local Chamber of Commerce and the Greater San Diego Sports Association had been sending a representative to baseball's winter meetings to lobby quietly on behalf of the city.[1] Smith had been part of the Hank Greenberg-Ralph Kiner group that sought the American League expansion team for Los Angeles that was ultimately awarded to Gene Autry for the 1961 season.[2] A man with a penchant for beige suits, Smith was characterized as something of a mystery man despite heading a diverse portfolio of business interests.[3] He headed the U.S. National Bank as well as the Westgate-California Tuna Packing Corporation, which was a business conglomerate with seafood, ground transport, aviation, hotel, and insurance interests.

To complement his bid, Smith teamed up with Los Angeles general manager Buzzie Bavasi. An executive with the Dodgers for almost two decades, Bavasi saw his chance to achieve an ownership role by partnering with Smith. Together, the Smith-Bavasi team provided a formidable combination of financial strength and baseball experience. San Diego itself seemed ripe for big-league ball. Noting the area population of one million (and growing), Bavasi saw the potential for success: "If everybody in the city of San Diego attends one game, we'll do all right."[4] In

addition, community support for major-league sports was evidenced in November 1965, when 72 percent of those voting approved city bonds that would finance construction of the 50,000-seat San Diego Stadium. While the stadium would also house the American Football League's Chargers, baseball officialdom took notice that the multipurpose facility could also accommodate a baseball team.

## The National League expands

The National League had not been seeking to expand in the late 1960s, but the senior circuit's hand had been forced by the American League. Attempting to assuage Missouri Sen. Stuart Symington over Kansas City's loss of the Athletics to Oakland (and to head off potential antitrust issues that an angry US senator might cause),

The 1969 Padres' coaches gather around manager Preston Gomez at their spring training site in Yuma, Arizona. Left to right are coaches Sparky Anderson, Wally Moon, Roger Craig, and Whitey Wietelmann. (Courtesy of Tom Larwin)

the American League elected to expand. On October 18, 1967, the junior circuit agreed to admit Kansas City and Seattle for the 1969 season. Although the move caught the National League by surprise, it agreed in principle in November to expand similarly without establishing a date for doing so. Mets chairman Donald Grant stated, "The question no longer is whether the National League expands – but when."[5] The NL formally agreed to do so on December 1, 1967, during the winter meetings in Mexico City.

In voting to expand, the National League left open the possibility that its expansion might not occur in concert with the American League; that is, the National League seemed poised to wait as late as the 1971 season before increasing its membership. The uncertainty did not dissuade cities from preparing their pitches as San Diego, Dallas-Fort Worth, Buffalo, Milwaukee, and Montreal emerged as the serious contenders. To evaluate the applicants, the National League appointed an expansion committee of Walter O'Malley (Los Angeles), John Galbreath (Pittsburgh), and Roy Hofheinz (Houston). The composition of the committee was important in two respects. Not only did Bavasi have a close ally on the committee in O'Malley, but it was assumed Hofheinz would block Dallas-Fort Worth in order to keep the Texas market to himself and the Astros. During a league meeting on April 19, 1968, the National League agreed not only that it would expand for the 1969 season but that a unanimous vote of an applicant city would be required for entry, with each city to be considered individually.

The National League convened in Chicago on May 27 with increasing expectations that the two expansion cities would be chosen. Eddie Leishman, general manager of

At the annual San Diego sports writers' dinner artist Eric Poulson shows off the 1969 Padres' scorecard design while team president E. J. "Buzzie" Bavasi looks on with a copy of the special newspaper page recognizing what will be San Diego's inaugural major league baseball Opening Day. (Courtesy of Tom Larwin)

the Padres of the Pacific Coast League, observed, "This just isn't going to be another meeting where they postpone a decision until the next meeting."[6] After 10 hours of deliberations, a likely consequence of the unanimity requirement, NL President Warren Giles announced that San Diego and Montreal were accepted into the league. Although it was assumed Bavasi's status as a baseball insider would assist the city's bid, it was revealed later how close the Padres came to missing out. To some surprise, the National League accepted Montreal unanimously early in the voting. Buffalo clinched nine votes with San Francisco's Horace Stoneham holding out for San Diego.[7] At one point, San Diego had the support of only four owners as some Eastern owners lobbied colleagues for two Eastern cities. After 18 ballots, momentum shifted away from Buffalo with San Diego's bid the beneficiary. When the contenders were called into the meeting room, O'Malley tipped off Bavasi as to the result with a smile followed by the question, "You got your ulcer yet?"[8] Indeed, Bavasi acknowledged a debt to O'Malley and Stoneham, "We owe a lot to Walter and Horace, they were for us all the way."[9] Smith had not accompanied Bavasi to Chicago but sent his attorney, Douglas Giddings. After speaking with Smith, Giddings reported, "He was happy but he wondered why the meeting lasted so long."[10] Smith confirmed his appreciation later: "I am gratified that years of planning and dreaming have come to reality today. ... The action in Chicago by the National League owners is another expression of confidence in the great future that lies ahead for San Diego."[11]

### The business side of becoming a big-league team

In the aftermath of the National League meeting, attention shifted to assembling San Diego's major-league organization. At the executive level, Smith was named chairman of the board, Bavasi would serve as president, and Leishman was elevated from the general-manager position of the Pacific Coast League Padres to the same spot with San Diego's new National League club. Additionally, the National League set the expansion fee at $10 million, the first $1 million of which was due on August 15. Of the $10 million aggregate, $6 million would be allocated to compensate the other National League clubs for each of the 30 players to be taken during the expansion draft to the tune of $200,000 each with the other $4 million constituting the actual expansion fee. Moreover, an additional $2.5 million would have to be placed in escrow as working capital. Bavasi delivered the first million on time, flying to New York on August 15 with 10 checks, each for

$100,000 and all signed by Smith. The Padres officially joined the National League with a $6 million payment on January 28, 1969, with the remaining $3 million to be paid over the next three years.

With the franchise in hand, the Padres turned to the business issues of negotiating contracts for local radio and television rights and a lease for San Diego Stadium. The Padres hoped to maximize local radio and television in light of the condition that neither expansion club would receive a share of national television revenue until the 1972 season. However, the fact that San Diego was hemmed in by the two-club Los Angeles market to the north and the Mexican border to the south caused some concern that the Padres would be hampered in their local negotiations. The team and local station KOGO announced an agreement at the end of July for both radio and television rights. Under the agreement, KOGO would broadcast all regular-season and some preseason games over the radio and telecast selected road games on its KOGO-TV station. Home telecasts were not anticipated. While the two sides did not announce financial terms, they represented that the deal would compare "favorably" with those of the majority of major-league clubs.[12] In September, the Padres broadcast team was in place: Jerry Gross and Frank Sims, formerly with the Cardinals and Phillies, respectively, would handle play-by-play, with Duke Snider doubling as color commentator and Padres scout.

Although the Pacific Coast League iteration of the Padres was already playing at San Diego Stadium, a new lease was required for the expansion team. San Diego City Manager Walter Hahn led negotiations on behalf of the city, with Giddings handling the matter on behalf of the ballclub. The two sides reached a tentative agreement on June 13 with agreement on a 20-year term and a rental payment of 7.5 percent of gross ticket sales. The parties became stuck on the issue of an approximate $2 million subsidy from the city to the club and the terms of its repayment. The subsidy was intended to defray some of the costs to obtain the franchise. Accordingly, the city would pay the Padres $285,000 per year for seven years, but the two sides reached an impasse over how it would repaid. After weeks of additional negotiations, Hahn delivered two tentative agreements to the city council on August 1. The parties to the first agreement were the city and the Padres, under which the club would pay a rental fee of 8 percent of ticket sales revenue over the 20-year term. The Padres would keep concessions revenue, but the city would receive the parking fees. The agreement also accounted for the Char-

National League president Warren Giles was in San Diego for Opening Day, April 8, 1969, and here joins Buzzie Bavasi holding an aerial photograph of the Padres' new ballpark, San Diego Stadium. (Courtesy of Tom Larwin)

gers, with Hahn stating that the football team would have "fair and equitable scheduling priority" when baseball and football season overlapped.[13] The second agreement was between the city and San Diego Stadium Management Co., the latter entity formed by the Padres to manage, operate, and promote the stadium. The city would pay the management company the actual costs to maintain and operate the stadium on an agreed annual budget plus a 10 percent management fee. Additional financial terms were intended to address the subsidy and repayment issue. The city would pay $306,420 annually for the first seven years of the agreement from local hotel-room taxes, payments that were to be reimbursed to the city over the final 13 years of the agreement based on a formula connected to Padres attendance.

The Board of Governors of the San Diego Stadium Authority approved the agreements on August 5, but the Chargers objected to the agreements during the city council meeting on the same day. Chargers attorney J. Stacey Sullivan argued that the agreements favored the Padres in a way that violated the Chargers' lease with the city. In particular, Sullivan asserted that the Chargers had scheduling priority over the Padres and also wanted equal treatment in light of the city's subsidy to the Padres. City attorney Ed Butler objected to Sullivan's characterization and suggested that if the Padres and Chargers could not work through any potential scheduling issues, then "I suppose a jury of 12 housewives will make a determination that the businessmen can't make."[14] When the Padres raised last-minute concerns that the lease would not guarantee them at least four weekend playing dates during August and September, Mayor Frank Curran snapped, "If the children can't play nicely together, perhaps a divorce is in order. ... I'm getting very tired and very disturbed by these two organizations." After an additional week of ne-

On the eve of the 1969 Opening Day are (left to right) Dr. Albert Anderson, a member of the San Diego Stadium Board of Directors; Bowie Kuhn Commissioner of Major League Baseball; and Padres' president E. J. "Buzzie" Bavasi. (Courtesy of Tom Larwin)

gotiations, the city council approved revised agreements that acknowledged the Chargers' scheduling priority and required the Padres to consult with the Chargers before scheduling. If the Padres were forced to reschedule any games, the city would reimburse the team for any losses sustained up to a maximum of eight games. Butler did not foresee a problem if the two teams worked together in good faith, and Bavasi offered that "[w]e're delighted with the way things worked out. The city is satisfied, we're satisfied and the Chargers should be satisfied."[15] As it turned out, there would be two conflicts during the 1969 season and the Chargers were definitely not satisfied. After withholding rent payments and demanding a revised rent-free lease agreement, the Chargers litigated their dispute with the city into the spring.

### Assembling the on-field product

Early speculation on the managerial appointment focused on Dodgers third-base coach Preston Gomez and then-Pacific Coast League Padres' manager Bob Skinner. The Padres were then the Triple-A affiliate of the Phillies, and the parent club tapped Skinner in mid-June 1968 to replace Gene Mauch in the Philadelphia dugout. While Mauch was believed to have interest in managing the National League Padres, Bavasi hired Gomez on August 29 on a one-year contract. The Cuban-born Gomez would be the first Latino hired to manage in the major leagues. Prior to his coaching stint in Los Angeles, Gomez managed successfully in Mexico, Havana, Spokane, and Richmond. O'Malley delivered the news to Gomez, telling him, "Buzzie has asked us to release you, and of course we will cooperate. We hate to lose you, but you go with our blessing."[16] At the introductory press conference, Leishman commented, "There were other people

we considered, but Preston is the man we wanted most."[17] Leishman also viewed Gomez's reputation as a teacher to be an important asset in assembling a new, young team to compete in the National League.[18]

For his part, Gomez characterized himself as being a gambler in his management style. Gomez cautioned, "But you cannot gamble without speed and speed is something we'll need in this big ballpark."[19] Gomez assembled his staff over the next month. His first coaching hires were made on September 12, with Wally Moon hired to be the batting and first-base coach and Pacific Coast League Padres coach Whitey Wietelmann to oversee the bullpen. Roger Craig, who managed Los Angeles' Albuquerque affiliate in 1968, received the pitching-coach job the following week, and successful minor-league manager George "Sparky" Anderson rounded out the staff as third-base coach. Bavasi said, "Now we can get down to work and on with the building of a ballclub."[20]

The expansion draft provided the main opportunity to harvest a roster capable to compete at the major-league level. Bavasi lured 20-year scouting veteran Bob Fontaine away from Pittsburgh to run San Diego's scouting operation. Bavasi nonetheless had his own idea of the team he hoped to assemble: "The thing we have in mind is to concentrate on good fielders, ballplayers who can run and control a bat. Naturally, we'll be after strength down the middle. ... The ground is hard at [San Diego Stadium] and we must have a good center fielder."[21] Prior to the expansion draft, San Diego participated in baseball's free-agent draft on June 6 in New York. Leishman selected 16 players, with pitcher-outfielder Luciano "Lou" Hernandez the prize of the bunch. Hernandez attended high school in Solana Beach, 30 miles north of San Diego, and Leishman was pleased to draft him.[22] The Padres general manager said of Hernandez, "We didn't think he would be around by the time we got our pick. He's a real strong kid and we're high on him."[23]

The National League expansion-draft rules mirrored those for the American League. Each existing club would submit a list of 15 protected players by October 1, with the World Series representative permitted a delay. San Diego and Montreal would both select 30 players, meaning that the 10 National League clubs would lose six players each. After each of six rounds, the existing teams could add three more players to their protected lists, which were kept confidential. In fact, only San Diego and Montreal would be able to see the lists, the secrecy intended to protect trade values. With the Royals and Pilots having a seven-month head start in preparing for the American League expansion draft, the Padres and Expos scrambled to obtain player information. The Giants and Cardinals made available personnel data as a courtesy to the new clubs, and Fontaine set about reviewing that information.[24]

The draft occurred on October 14, 1968, in the Versailles Room of Montreal's Windsor Hotel, the same location as the National Hockey League's "Second Six" expansion draft ahead of the 1967-68 season. San Diego won a coin flip with Montreal for the right to pick first, and the Padres used that choice to select "Downtown" Ollie Brown from the Giants. Brown, a 24-year-old outfielder with a strong throwing arm, slumped in 1968 after hitting .267 with 13 home runs in 1967. His 1968 misery was compounded by a six-week suspension after clashing with Giants manager Herman Franks and refusing to report for a minor-league assignment in Phoenix. With its second pick, San Diego chose pitcher Dave Giusti from St. Louis. Giusti had been traded from Houston after an 11-14 season to the National League champions the week before the draft, and made no attempt to hide his feelings. He complained, "I'm very disappointed. Nobody in St. Louis told me this was going to happen. I wanted to work for a championship club."[25] The Padres rounded out their first batch of selections with Dick Selma, 9-10, 2.75 ERA with the Mets, Al Santorini, a 20-year-old right-hander from the Braves organization, and Jose Arcia a "good glove, weak bat" second baseman from the Cubs.

The Padres brass drafted decidedly for youth with their next round of selections: Clay Kirby, a 20-year-old right-hander from the Cardinals organization; Fred Kendall, 19-year-old catcher from the Reds system; Julio Morales, an outfielder and another 19-year-old; and Nate Colbert, a 22-year-old first baseman-outfielder who hit .264 in 1968 for the Astros' Triple-A club in Oklahoma City. Craig became especially high on Kirby as he worked with his new pitcher, stating, "Kirby is a bulldog – he has determination as well as good stuff."[26] Of the second-round choices, only former American League Most Valuable Player Zoilo Versalles held veteran status and observers expected him to be flipped to another club. In the third round, the Padres took Jerry DaVanon with the 12th pick. DaVanon, a 23-year-old shortstop from the Cardinals organization, was a native San Diegan. Unlike Giusti, he was excited to join the Padres. "Being picked by San Diego was the nicest surprise I've ever had," he said.[27] Braves reliever

Dick Kelley was chosen 14th, and Dodgers outfielder Al Ferrara, who missed almost all of the 1968 season with a broken ankle, was taken with the 15th pick.

With their final 15 picks, the Padres continued to target youth but also grabbed established players who might have something to prove or provide trade value. From the Phillies, the Padres took outfielder Tony Gonzalez, a 32-year-old left-handed hitter, and infielder Roberto Pena, a 28-year-old who spent 1968 with the Pacific Coast League Padres. Pitcher Billy McCool, a left-handed reliever, went 3-4 with Cincinnati before military duty halted his season. The Pirates left 30-year-old pitcher Al McBean unprotected after a 9-12 season, but the former Buc departed with the endorsement of Pittsburgh GM Joe Brown. Squeezed out by Pittsburgh's plan to protect its younger hurlers, Brown foresaw a big season for McBean in stating, "He still has a great arm and knows how to pitch."[28]

After the draft, the differing strategies between the Padres and Expos became readily apparent. Expos GM Jim Fanning gloated that Montreal outperformed its mock drafts.[29] The Expos certainly had more familiar names in veterans Maury Wills, Donn Clendenon, Manny Mota, and Jesus Alou. Bavasi mused, "We drafted players who are on the verge of becoming real big leaguers and Montreal drafted a bunch of players who are trying to stay in the majors."[30] Bavasi explained the club's expansion draft strategy to San Diego Union columnist Jack Murphy: "Our job is to give fans a good show, and I don't think you can do it with veterans."[31] To hear Leishman comment, it appeared that San Diego got exactly the club it wanted. The Padres general manager said, "The club is tailored to fit a big park such as San Diego Stadium. We wanted speed, pitching, and defense."[32]

Notwithstanding the optimism for having executed their draft strategy, Bavasi knew the Padres had holes that required filling. The need for catching experience was particularly acute. In addition to Kendall, the Padres selected "defensive demon"[33] Ron Slocum from the Pirates organization. Despite the potential, neither Kendall nor Slocum possessed experience above the Double-A level. Bavasi also specified center field as another spot where the talent level required improvement. Other clubs inquired about the Padres veterans, with Giusti, Selma, Gonzalez, and McBean attracting interest. Leishman started making deals quickly and he acquired first baseman Bill Davis from Cleveland on October 21. Davis had shown power potential with Portland in 1965 and 1966 before an Achilles injury ended his 1967 season. Satisfied with scouting reports over his comeback in 1968, Leishman made the move.[34] Weeks later during the winter meetings, the Padres sent Versalles the other way to complete the deal.

Bavasi attended those same winter meetings in San Francisco with a mission. He stated, "We'll do something before we leave here ... because we have to have a catcher and another infielder."[35] Before striking a trade, the Padres claimed Bobby Klaus through the minor-league draft; Klaus served as the Pacific Coast League Padres' player-manager after Skinner joined the Phillies. The discontented Giusti served as the primary trade bait, and on December 3, Bavasi and Giusti both got what they wanted. The Padres sent Giusti back to the Cardinals with four players coming the other way: infielder Ed Spiezio, outfielder Ron Davis, catcher Danny Breeden, and pitcher Phil Knuckles. Spiezio and Davis spent time in St. Louis in 1968 although neither batted exceptionally well. Spiezio arrived, however, with the endorsement of pitching great Bob Gibson, who opined, "All Ed needs to do is play regularly and he'll be a dangerous hitter. He didn't get to play much for us."[36] Breeden played 118 games for Tulsa of the Pacific Coast League, "regarded as expert receiver and thrower."[37] Knuckles went 13-6 with a 2.93 ERA with Arkansas of the Double-A Texas League. In a sign that he had achieved his goals, Bavasi claimed, "Now we're respectable – we could open the season tomorrow with what we have."[38] He rejected Houston's offer of five players for Ron Davis, who started the 1968 season with the Astros. Bavasi asserted, "Davis is a great center fielder and we needed him."[39]

### Getting the fans to the ballpark

The Padres waited for the Chargers to conclude their 1968 American Football League season before making a concerted push for season-ticket sales. In that department, the Padres were lagging behind their Montreal expansion brethren. Having focused almost exclusively on business clients, they had sold only 1,500 season tickets, well short of the club's goal of 4,000. During the launch of the public sales drive, Bavasi pointed out that the Padres' break-even mark was total attendance of 800,000. He explained, "We can do it because we're an expansion team, but an established team would need to draw more, because it would have higher-salaried players."[40] He also worked out the math required to make that goal: Average 22,000 in the 18 games against the Dodgers and Giants

and attract around 7,000 for each of the other 60 dates on the schedule.[41] The Dodgers' Don Drysdale and the Giants' Willie Mays assisted the Padres' efforts by recording radio spots to let San Diegans know they would be visiting during the upcoming season.[42]

There was some concern that the decision to keep the Padres moniker contributed to tepid ticket sales. Bavasi favored dropping the name, but was overridden by both Smith and apparent fan sentiment.[43] Smith's influence brought around Bavasi as the latter declared, "It's a beautiful name, very apt and descriptive."[44] The swinging friar logo as well as the brown and gold color scheme debuted in November, and the club unveiled its on-field look in December with DaVanon and Klaus modeling the uniforms. As the 1969 season approached, Bavasi's initial concerns appeared to be manifested in still disappointing ticket sales. Bavasi explained, "When people see or hear the name Padres they still think of minor-league baseball."[45] He hoped the name would become an asset in time, but for now it seemed like a source of confusion.[46] Ticket manager Joe Sullivan would take delivery of 2.8 million tickets ahead of the March 28 opening of the San Diego Stadium box office; as it turned out, the vast majority of the Globe Ticket Company's output would go to waste.[47]

### Minor-league matters, past and future

As the Padres transitioned from a minor-league club into a major-league organization, there remained past and future minor-league issues requiring attention. To develop players for the National League club, the organization assembled a development structure during the fall of 1968. On October 31 Leishman announced an agreement with Key West of the Class-A Florida State League. One week later, the Padres agreed to share the new Triple-A team in Omaha with Kansas City; the Royals would operate the club with the Padres supplying a handful of players. Adding an affiliation with Salt Lake City of the rookie Pioneer League and working agreements with Elmira and Waterbury from the Eastern League, the Padres had their farm system for 1969 in place.

Shedding their Pacific Coast League identity would require costly and drawn-out negotiations. The Coast League sought a total indemnity of $1.2 million for the loss of its San Diego and Seattle clubs, with the league apparently using the 1958 indemnity for the losses of Los Angeles and San Francisco as its template. The league was remodeled further during the course of an offseason restructuring that increased the number of Triple-A leagues from two to three. In addition to losing two cities through major-league expansion, the Pacific Coast League's Easternmost outposts were incorporated into the revived American Association. The financial dispute lingered throughout the offseason. In January 1969, the Pacific Coast League requested the intervention of outgoing Commissioner William Eckert. Leishman noted that the realigned league would have the advantage of reduced travel costs among member clubs. The Padres and Pilots offered only $30,000 each. The Pilots eventually agreed to a $300,000 indemnity payment on March 25 and, days later, incoming Commissioner Bowie Kuhn ordered the Padres to pay $240,000 to the Pacific Coast League.

## Yuma

For their first spring training, the Padres selected Yuma, Arizona, over Mesa-Tempe, Arizona and Imperial Valley, California. The Cactus League seemed a natural fit for the Padres, and the circuit would include seven teams for 1969: San Diego, San Francisco, Oakland, Seattle, California, Cleveland, and the Chicago Cubs. For their first spring training, scheduled to begin on February 22, the Padres used temporary facilities and a remodeled Keegan Field while the City of Yuma built a permanent complex with four fields in time for 1970. The Padres' spring schedule was supposed to begin in Mexico City, as the club had agreed to be a last-minute substitute for the Chicago White Sox for three exhibition games against the Tigers and Reds of the Mexican League. The inability to secure visas forced cancellation of the games, but the club agreed to play four games in Mexico City the following spring. Instead, several days of intrasquad games provided the preparation for the opening of the spring season on March 7 against California. With 2,500 in attendance at Keegan Field, the Padres won their spring debut behind a Bill Davis grand slam and three no-hit innings from the recently signed Johnny Podres.

The dominant theme through spring training became the search for a dependable, major-league-ready catcher. The Padres purchased Jerry Zimmerman's contract from Minnesota but he ultimately decided to end his playing career and pursue the coaching path. The team even extended an invite to Chris Krug, a catcher formerly of the Cubs' and Angels' organizations who had been out of baseball for a year and a half. San Francisco's Bob Barton, Cincinnati's Pat Corrales, and Pittsburgh's Manny Sanguillen were also considered. Ultimately, the club found

their man in the form of a different Pirates catcher. On March 28, San Diego acquired Chris Cannizzaro and pitcher Tommie Sisk from the Steel City in exchange for the previously untradeable Ron Davis as well as the recently acquired Klaus. Bavasi noted that Cannizzaro knew National League hitters, and Sisk would fill the final spot in a rotation currently composed of Selma, Podres, McBean, and Kelley. "We got two things we needed badly," said Bavasi.[48] Bavasi made one final deal before the start of the season, adding reliever Jack Baldschun after his release from Cincinnati.

## The big-league Padres take the field

The new San Diego Padres made their National League debut at San Diego Stadium on April 8 against the Houston Astros. Bavasi maintained his optimism about the new venture despite having to revise downward his hopes for a bumper crowd on Opening Day. He commented, "San Diego is either a major-league city or it isn't. I think it is and I believe I made the right decision."[49] Although the attendance of 23,370 fell short of expectations, the on-field result did not disappoint. At a sportswriters dinner the previous evening, an interaction with Astros starter Don Wilson left Padres starter Selma annoyed. Wilson told Selma, "You know, don't you, that you're going to lose tomorrow night?"[50] Although Selma allowed the Astros a run in the opening frame, that run was Houston's last. Scattering five hits and backed by Spiezio's line-drive home run in the fifth and an RBI double by Brown that scored Pena in the sixth, Selma secured the first win in Padres history, 2-1. In fact, all four expansion teams won their opening games but all predictably struggled during their maiden seasons.

The Padres struggled on and off the field. The final season attendance barely topped a half-million; at 512,970, the Padres drew about 160,000 fewer fans than the Pilots, who moved to Milwaukee in April 1970 after the bankruptcy of the team. Cash flow became an issue as Bavasi admitted later, "There was never a lot of money from the start."[51] On the field, the Padres completed the opening series sweep of the Astros, but finished April at 9-14. During April, inaugural-game winner Selma was traded to the Cubs for pitchers Joe Niekro and Gary Ross and shortstop Francisco Libran. In May, the Padres took a series from the Cardinals at Busch Stadium, and also traded Bill Davis and local boy DaVanon to St. Louis for pitcher John Sipin and catcher Sonny Ruberto. The move cleared first base for Colbert, who would pace the club in home runs and RBIs. Back-to-back road sweeps in Montreal and Philadelphia took the Padres to 24-30 on June 4, but the team proceeded to drop 31 of its next 36 games to establish a firm hold on the National League West Division cellar. Podres retired on June 27 to become a minor-league pitching coach. Cannizzaro became the first Padre selected for the All-Star Game, although he did not play. With the team collapsing on the field, attendance followed suit; Buffalo and New Orleans inquired about relocation in July.[52] Gomez kept a brave face on results, and his patience was rewarded as the club played spoiler for other divisional contenders. The Padres swept the Dodgers in early September, but drew only 35,000 for the four-game series at San Diego Stadium. Later in the month, the Padres took crucial games from the Astros and Reds, and won a three-game series against the Giants that cleared the path for the Braves to take the division crown. The Padres finished the season at 52-110, the same record as the Expos. In a debut season filled with ups and (a lot of) downs, on and off the field, San Diego was now a major-league city. Questions about that status would persist, but San Diego continues to answer Bavasi's comment in the affirmative. It's a major-league city.

**Notes**

1  "City Made Its First Move For Majors 10 Years Ago," *San Diego Union*, April 7, 1969: X3.

2  Bill Swank, *Baseball in San Diego: From the Padres to Petco* (Charleston, South Carolina: Arcadia Publishing, 2004), 49.

3  Bob Ortman, "Scouts Are No. 1 on Bavasi's List of Musts," *The Sporting News*, June 22, 1968: 9.

4  David Porter and Joe Naiman, *The San Diego Padres Encyclopedia* (Champaign, Illinois: Sports Publishing, 2002), 6.

5  Jerome Holtzman, "A.L. Vote to Expand Marks 1967 History," *The Sporting News Official 1968 Baseball Guide* (St. Louis: The Sporting News, 2002), 167, 169.

6  Dick Kaegel, "Sweating, Waiting ... As N.L. Debated," *The Sporting News*, June 8, 1968: 5.

7  Ibid.

8  Collier, "Montreal Gets Second Franchise," *San Diego Union*, May 28, 1968: C1.

9  Collier, "Whew! S.D. Nearly Missed," *San Diego Union*, May 29, 1968: C1.

10  Jack Murphy, "Phone's Ring Starts Tense Final Hours," *San Diego Union*, May 28, 1968: C1.

11  Collier, "Montreal Gets."

12  "KOGO Will Air Padre NL Games for Next 3 Years," *San Diego Union*, July 31, 1968: C1.

13  Frank Exarhos, "Padres, Hahn Reach Stadium Use Accord," *San Diego Union*, August 2, 1968: B1.

14  Exarhos, "Board OKs Padre Pacts for Stadium," *San Diego Union*, August 6, 1968: B1.

15  Murphy, "That $1 Million Isn't Bavasi's But He Feels Quite Prosperous," *San Diego Union*, August 15, 1968: C1.

16  Murphy, "The Long Wait Is Over – Gomez Is Bavasi's Man," *San Diego Union*, August 30, 1968: C1.

17  Collier, "Padres Name Preston Gomez to Manage 1969 NL Team," *San Diego Union*, August 30, 1968: C1.

18  Ibid.

19  Ibid.

20  "Signing of Anderson Completes Pad Staff," *San Diego Union*, September 27, 1968: C1.

21  Murphy, "Buzzie Buys Name Padres After Hearing From a Certain Source," *San Diego Union*, September 29, 1968: H1.

22  Hernandez's page on baseball-reference.com includes only a single at-bat in 1969 for Salt Lake City of the Pioneer League.

23  "San Dieguito High Star Padres' First Major Draft Choice," *San Diego Union*, June 7, 1968: C1.

24  Murphy, "Buzzie Buys Name."

25  Paul Cour, "Padres Placing High Hopes on Big Bill Davis," *The Sporting News*, November 9, 1968: 51.

26  Collier, "Padres Launch."

27  Cour, "Padres' Plum Is Homegrown DaVanon," *The Sporting News*, November 30, 1968: 51.

28  Collier, "Expos' Warm Draft Leaves Bavasi Cold," *San Diego Union*, October 15, 1968: C4.

29  Ibid.

30  Ibid.

31  Porter and Naiman, 6.

32  Collier, "Padres Stress Youth, Speed; Avoid Older Stars in Draft," *San Diego Union*, October 15, 1968: C1, C4.

33  Ibid.

34  Collier, "Padres Get Cleveland's Davis in Delayed Swap for Versalles," *San Diego Union*, October 22, 1968: C3.

35  Collier, "Padres Weighing Trade Possibilities as Winter Meetings Get Underway," *San Diego Union*, December 2, 1968: C2.

36  Howard Hagen, "22-Foot Putt On Playoff Hole Does It," *San Diego Union*, February 17, 1969: C1, C4.

37  Collier, "Padres Deal Giusti for 4 Young Cards," *San Diego Union*, December 4, 1968: C1.

38  Ibid.

39  Collier, "Padres Reject Astros' Offer for Ron Davis," *San Diego Union*, December 6, 1968: C1.

40  Collier, "Padres Launch Season Ticket Drive," *San Diego Union*, January 21, 1969: C1.

41  Ibid.

42  Ibid.

43  Murphy, "Buzzie Buys Name."

44  Ibid.

45  Murphy, "San Diego Has Disbelievers but Bavasi Isn't Among Them," *San Diego Union*, March 28, 1969: C1.

46  Ibid.

47  "Padre Ducats Arrive in Big Bundle," *San Diego Union*, March 13, 1969: E4.

48  Collier, "Pads Bolster Catching, Mound," *San Diego Union*, March 29, 1969: C1.

49  Murphy, "San Diego Has Disbelievers."

50  Collier, "Padres Sparkle in Debut, Selma Beats Astros, 2-1," *San Diego Union*, April 9, 1969: C1.

51  Porter and Naiman, 9.

52  Porter and Naiman, 14.

## SAN DIEGO PADRES EXPANSION DRAFT

| PICK | PLAYER | POSITION | FORMER TEAM |
|---|---|---|---|
| 1 | Ollie Brown | of | San Francisco Giants |
| 2 | Dave Giusti | p | St. Louis Cardinals |
| 3 | Dick Selma | p | New York Mets |
| 4 | Al Santorini | p | Atlanta Braves |
| 5 | Jose Arcia | ss | Chicago Cubs |
| 6 | Clay Kirby | p | St. Louis Cardinals |
| 7 | Fred Kendall | c | Cincinnati Reds |
| 8 | Jerry Morales | of | New York Mets |
| 9 | Nate Colbert | 1b | Houston Astros |
| 10 | Zoilo Versalles | ss | Los Angeles Dodgers |
| 11 | Frank Reberger | p | Chicago Cubs |
| 12 | Jerry DaVanon | 3b | St. Louis Cardinals |
| 13 | Larry Stahl | of | New York Mets |
| 14 | Dick Kelley | p | Atlanta Braves |
| 15 | Al Ferrara | of | Los Angeles Dodgers |
| 16 | Mike Corkins | p | San Francisco Giants |
| 17 | Tom Dukes | p | Houston Astros |
| 18 | Rick James | p | Chicago Cubs |
| 19 | Tony Gonzalez | of | Philadelphia Phillies |
| 20 | Dave Roberts | p | Pittsburgh Pirates |
| 21 | Ivan Murrell | of | Houston Astros |
| 22 | Jim Williams | of | Los Angeles Dodgers |
| 23 | Billy McCool | p | Cincinnati Reds |
| 24 | Roberto Pena | 2b | Philadelphia Phillies |
| 25 | Al McBean | p | Pittsburgh Pirates |
| 26 | Rafael Robles | ss | San Francisco Giants |
| 27 | Fred Katawczik | p | Cincinnati Reds |
| 28 | Ron Slocum | 3b | Pittsburgh Pirates |
| 29 | Steve Arlin | p | Philadelphia Phillies |
| 30 | Cito Gaston | of | Atlanta Braves |

# NATE COLBERT

## BY GREGORY H. WOLF

Nate Colbert wasn't supposed to play on August 1, 1972. The San Diego slugger had injured his knee in a collision at home plate the night before and was listed as doubtful against the Atlanta Braves. Looking forward to hitting in Atlanta Stadium, known as the Launching Pad, Colbert decided to tough out the pain. He responded by belting a record-tying five home runs and driving in a record-setting 13 runs in a doubleheader. Colbert, an often-overlooked power hitter, averaged 30 home runs and 85 RBIs over a five-year stretch (1969-1973), becoming the expansion Padres' first bona-fide star. Chronic back problems prematurely ended Colbert's budding career after just 1,004 games and he retired after the 1976 season.

Born on April 9, 1946, in St. Louis, Nathan Colbert Jr. grew up in a predominantly African-American community on the city's north side. His father, Nate Sr., was a former semipro Negro League catcher and occasional pitcher who instilled in Junior, his two brothers, and his three sisters an uncompromising work ethic and passion for sports. "I just loved baseball," said Nate, whose fondest childhood memories included playing ball with his father and regularly seeing the Cardinals play.[1] Young Nate enjoyed going to Sportsman's Park, just about 10 minutes from his home, and marveled at his favorite players, among them Jackie Robinson, who once signed his glove, and Stan Musial. Nate was in the stands when Stan the Man belted five home runs in a doubleheader on May 2, 1954, a feat the youngster would duplicate some 18 years later.

Nate played baseball whenever he could, on nearby sandlots, and in the afternoons after attending Cole School. Nate Sr., who worked in a local mill, also coached baseball in a boys' club and taught his son the fundamentals. "I was a little bigger than a lot of the kids," Colbert told Wayne McBrayer of Padres360.com, "so baseball, it became easy to me."[2] At Charles H. Sumner High School, Nate dabbled in some football, but a knee injury convinced him to stay on the diamond. Tall and lithe, Nate seemingly glided in the outfield and on the basepaths and attracted major-league scouts who followed his progress in prep, summer, and local semipro leagues. According to Bruce Markusen, the New York Yankees were in hot pursuit and promised to double offers from any team;[3] however, Colbert could only think of Cardinal red. Tracked by George Hasser, an area bird-dog scout for the Cardinals, Colbert was invited by Redbirds scouting director George Silvey to Busch Stadium (the official name of Sportsman's Park since 1953) to hit a few balls for skipper Johnny Keane, who was impressed with the skinny kid's power.[4] Upon graduation in 1964, one year before the inauguration of the amateur draft, Colbert signed with the hometown team on scout Joe Monahan's recommendation for a reported $20,000 bonus.

Colbert's professional baseball career commenced just months later. The Cardinals assigned him to the Sarasota Rookie League, where the right-handed hitter split his time at first and in the outfield. His stint in the Redbirds organization was short. A fractured left hand in July ended his 1965 season with Cedar Rapids in the Class-A Midwest League.[5] Colbert got some additional experience in the Florida Instructional League, but just weeks after that season concluded, he was selected by the Houston Astros in the Rule 5 Draft on November 29.

To call Colbert's tenure with the Astros a disappointment is an understatement. Under Rule 5 stipulations, the Astros were required to keep him on their roster the entire season or risk losing him if they optioned him to the minors. The 20-year-old Colbert had just 504 minor-league at-bats and was completely unprepared to hit major-league pitching. After participating in the Astros spring training at Cocoa Beach, Florida, Colbert bided his time on skipper Grady Hatton's bench. He made just 19 appearances (12 as a pinch-runner and 7 as a pinch-hitter) and did not play in the field, not even an inning. He went hitless, though he scored three times. "It was just a year lost as far as playing is concerned," said Colbert bluntly.[6] The highlight of Colbert's season took place on July 27 when he married Carol Ann Allensworth, whom he had met while completing three weeks' training in the Army National Guard in Oklahoma City.

Colbert worked the rust off his atrophied skills in another stint in the Florida Instructional League, then faced major leaguers in the Venezuelan League with Caracas. More than anything, the 6-foot-2, 200-pound Colbert needed at-bats, and was consequently assigned following another spring training with the Astros to the Amarillo Sonics in the Double-A Texas League. Colbert showcased his power and speed, pacing the circuit in home runs (28) and stolen bases (26). He was the league's MVP, a unanimous All-Star, and was named to the Double-A Topps-National Association All-Star team. The young slugger was fully aware that he was still learning how to hit. "When I started, I didn't know much, and swung hard. Now I don't swing as hard, but hit the ball just as far," he said in 1967. "I use my wrists and reflexes more now to give me power."[7]

Assigned to the Triple-A Oklahoma City 89ers to start the 1968 season, Colbert was moved to center field to take advantage of his speed. A two-week call-up in July to the Astros proved disastrous (3-for-22). His first major-league hit was a single off fireballer Jim Maloney of the Cincinnati Reds. He was returned to the PCL, but broke his hand and played in just 92 games. He was healed enough for another two-week look-see with the Astros in September. The results weren't much better than his first stint (5-for-31) and he was still homerless in the majors.

"You can destroy a man's confidence," said Colbert, recalling his struggles with the Astros. "[Manager] Harry Walker almost destroyed mine."[8] Walker was determined to mold Colbert into his own image, a spray hitter to all fields, and constantly tinkered with his swing. A natural pull hitter, Colbert was told to wait longer for the ball, and his timing suffered, as did his power. "I got so confused, I began to doubt myself. I thought I'd never find myself again. I was terrified. Here I was 22 years old and I was being told I couldn't hit big-league ball."[9]

Colbert's stock had dropped so dramatically that the Astros made him available in the expansion draft. The San Diego Padres selected him with their 18th pick on October 14, 1968. "I had no way of checking to see if I had been drafted," explained Colbert about the days before access to around-the-clock sports news via Internet and social media. "So, I stayed up and I kept calling the newspaper. I was in Oklahoma City. And they said, 'Well, we've got nothing yet.' And I was like, 'Oh, come on.' So, the next morning, [GM] Eddie Leishman from the Padres called me to welcome me. ... And I just let out a yell because I wanted to go to the San Diego Padres."[10] Leishman, who had been GM of the PCL San Diego Padres in 1968, was well acquainted with Colbert ("Nate used to hurt us.") and was convinced that he would blossom into a star if he had a chance to play.[11]

After playing with Estrellas in the Dominican Winter League, Colbert reported to the Padres camp in Yuma, Arizona, relishing the opportunity to reset his career. "[T]he first spring training was really a unique experience, because I was with 30 or more players, most of whom I did not know," recalled Colbert.[12] The spring facilities at Keegan Field on 24th Street in Yuma were primitive. A former youth baseball field in shabby condition, the entire infield and outfield needed to be leveled and the mound elevated to major-league standards. It also lacked basic amenities, such as bleachers, dugouts, showers, locker rooms, a press box, a PA system, and concession stands.[13] "We showered in a city gym, in a recreation center," recalled Colbert.[14] The 23-year-old slugger probably wondered what he had gotten himself into, but noted that "we survived." Padres players dressed and showered at the Kennedy Swimming Pool, while visiting players traveled across town to do the same in Municipal Stadium, the former spring home of the Baltimore Orioles, which was in even worse shape than Keegan.

Skipper Preston Gomez took a decidedly hands-off approach to Colbert's swing and gave the youngster the freedom to rediscover his stroke. "Colbert has a quick bat," said Gomez, "probably the quickest on the club."[15] Nonetheless, Colbert began the season as the backup first baseman to the Jolly Green Giant, 6-foot-7 Bill Davis. About two weeks into the season, Colbert took over for the slumping Davis and held down the first-base bag for the next five seasons. His breakout game had an air of revenge. On April 24 in the Astrodome, Colbert blasted his first career home run, a game-winning three-run shot in the eighth off Jack Billingham. The next day he whacked his first home run in San Diego Stadium, a solo shot off Reds fireballer Jim Maloney, and he clouted his third home run in as many days when he connected off the Reds' Jim Merritt for a three-run dinger which also proved to be the game winner, in the eighth. Those contests inaugurated an eight-game stretch in which Colbert went 11-for-30, hit five home runs, and drove in 12 runs, becoming the Padres' first star and fan favorite. Colbert was having the time of his life playing for the Padres in what he called "big, but beautiful" San Diego Stadium. "I kept saying, 'It's the big leagues. It's the big leagues.' You know, I know we don't have a lot fans or a lot of money, but this is major league baseball. This is my goal."[16]

He was also reaching some home-run milestones. In the first game of a twin bill on May 25, in front of 13,115 hometown fans, almost twice the Padres' major-league-low 6,333 average, Colbert took the Chicago Cubs' Don Nottebart deep for his first of six career grand slams. Six days later, against the Expos in Montreal, he belted two home runs in a game for the first of 14 times in his career and seemed destined for a berth on the All-Star squad. On June 11 he was batting .299 with 12 home runs and slugging .588 (fourth best in the NL), then reported to Oklahoma City for three weeks of service in the National Guard. A weekend pass enabled to him join the Padres for a four-game series in Houston, but Colbert didn't rejoin the team permanently until June 30 and subsequently

struggled mightily. In his next 25 games he batted just .180 with a sole home run in 100 at-bats. "My timing was off and I started to pull everything," said Colbert.[17] He rediscovered his stroke, slugging .516 from August 1 through the rest of the season to lead the offensively challenged team with 24 home runs, 9 triples, and 66 RBIs. The Padres finished with the worst record in baseball (52-110) and ranked last in majors in runs scored (averaging just 2.89 per game), batting average (.225), and on-base percentage (.285).

After another year of winter ball, earning all-league honors with Caguas in Puerto Rico, Colbert arrived at the Padres' brand-new training facility in Yuma with heightened expectations. His spring-training performance foreshadowed his season: He knocked in 21 runs in 60 at-bats and hit a 500-foot home run that Oakland A's coach Bobby Hofman called the longest he had ever seen.[18] On Opening Day, the 24-year-old walloped a monstrous three-run blast off Phil Niekro in the Padres' 8-3 victory against the Atlanta Braves. "If I stay healthy, I have a chance to hit 30," said Colbert, who doubted he could reach the 35 mark his skipper Gomez predicted.[19] The round-trippers kept coming. He whacked four in 17 at-bats in a three-day, four-game stretch on the road on May 6-8, including two in one game against the Phillies in the City of Brotherly Love. "[Colbert can] hit a ball as far as anyone," gushed Gomez, who compared his slugger to the hardest hitters in the game, such as Willie McCovey and Willie Stargell. "The ball just jumps off his bat."[20] Colbert blasted his former team on May 15, reaching two more milestones, by cranking his first extra-inning and first-walk-off home run, a two-run blast in the 10th to give the Padres a 10-8 victory.

Despite Colbert's success (he was tied with Hank Aaron, Dick Allen, and Tony Perez for the major-league lead with 16 home runs after hitting two against the San Francisco Giants in the first game of a twin bill on May 26), Colbert's name barely registered on the national radar. He was even left off the All-Star ballot (fans were given the right to vote in 1970 for the first time since the Cincinnati Reds ballot-box-stuffing scandal in 1957). "I could be leading the league in home runs and runs batted in and hitting .300 and people wouldn't know who I am," Colbert complained.[21] A 21-game homerless streak to begin June dropped him well off the NL lead, and his name further receded from national attention. After spending the All-Star break at home in San Diego, Colbert equaled his home-run output from the first half by belting 19 as the Padres kept losing, finishing with the league's worst record (63-99). In a strange statistical anomaly, the Padres ranked third in the league in home runs (172), easily led the majors with 104 on the road, yet ranked 11th of 12 NL teams in scoring. Colbert (38-86-.259 and .509 slugging) formed with his roommate Cito Gaston (29-93-.318, .543) and Ollie Brown (23-89-.292 .489) one of the most potent trios in baseball. A free swinger, Colbert finished in the NL's top nine in strikeouts in all six of his full seasons in the majors, including third in 1970 with 150 punchouts. On August 12, he became part of strikeout history when the St. Louis Cardinals Bob Gibson fanned him for the hurler's 200th K of the season to become the first major-league pitcher to reach the 200-strikeout mark in eight seasons.

Considered among the toughest parks for home-run hitters, San Diego Stadium had a deep 420-foot center field, with 375-foot power alleys, all of which were made even more imposing by a 17-foot outfield wall. "Whitey Wietelmann, one of our coaches, drew an imaginary line on his scorebook on what the dimensions were in most of the other ballparks," recalled Colbert. "And then he took where I hit every ball and he said every year routinely, I would hit 15 to 20 balls that would be off the walls, on the warning track in deep center, that would have been home runs in another ballpark."[22]

Colbert achieved success despite cognitive degeneration of his vertebrae which caused chronic lower back pain throughout his baseball career. "I have trouble getting loose," he explained, adding that he acclimated himself to the discomfort. "I feel tight a lot at the start of games and I try to compensate and wind up swinging at bad pitches. I'll have this problem all my life."[23]

Colbert's ailing back limited his participation in spring training in 1971 and raised concerns about the long-term effectiveness of the 25-year-old. Nonetheless big Nate was ready when the season commenced and he slammed two home runs against the San Francisco Giants in his second game of the season. Four days later he victimized Don Sutton of the Los Angeles Dodgers for two home runs in his first two at-bats en route to six RBIs in the Padres' 9-7 victory on April 11, leading sportswriter Ross Newhan of the *Los Angeles Times* to declare him "baseball's best young slugger."[24] Shrugging off those lofty pronouncements, Colbert developed a reputation as an emotionally charged team player who vented his frustrations after his strikeouts, but also at Padres fans, whom he

once described as "impatient" and chided them for the "empty seats" in San Diego Stadium.[25] The club finished last in the majors in attendance in 1971 for the second time in three years, averaging 6,883 per game. "I just want the team to be recognized," Colbert said. "If the team gets recognition, I will, too. Recognition is tough when you play for a last-place team."[26] The club extended its cellar-dwelling streak in the NL West to three years; however, Colbert earned a berth on the All-Star team (selected by skipper Sparky Anderson of the Reds) and struck out against the Baltimore Orioles' Mike Cuellar in his only plate appearance. Suffering through severe bouts of back pain, Colbert saw his power numbers drop, though he still led the team in home runs (27), RBIs (84), and slugging (.462), while batting .264 for the lowest-scoring team in baseball (3.02 runs per game).

Colbert enjoyed a magical 1972 season even while the Padres finished in the NL West cellar yet again with the league's lowest-scoring offense (3.19 runs per game). He arrived at spring training at a chiseled 215 pounds, having dropped about 25 pounds by "taking shots," reported sportswriter Phil Collier.[27] Eleven games into the season, delayed by 13 days because of the first players strike in major-league history, Don Zimmer replaced Gomez as skipper. Soon thereafter Colbert commenced one of his patented tears by hitting a home run and driving in a pair of runs on May 5 against the Mets, who had tried to pry the slugger away from the lowly Padres in the offseason. Eight days later, Colbert concluded a seven-game stretch on the road with five home runs and 12 RBIs and was leading the majors with nine round-trippers. He began one of the worst slumps of his career the next day, managing just 14 hits in his next 107 at-bats as his averaged plummeted to .194. A surge in July (8 home runs and 19 RBIs in 20 games) catapulted Colbert back among the league leaders in those categories and garnered him another berth on the NL All-Star squad. In the bottom of the 10th, Colbert, pinch-hitting for pitcher Tug McGraw, drew a walk off Dave McNally. Two batters later he scored the dramatic winning run in his home-away-from home, Atlanta Stadium, on Joe Morgan's single. After gaining some national recognition with that game-deciding tally, Colbert continued his July hot streak by homering in his first game after the All-Star Game, and then adding two more and knocking in all three Padres runs in a loss to the Astros at the Astrodome, setting up his fateful afternoon against the Braves in Atlanta on August 1.

Ever since Colbert was a minor leaguer with Amarillo, in

1967, he had a routine when he stepped into the batter's box. "As I walk up to the plate," he said, "I automatically touch my helmet. It gets me thinking about what I want to hit. Then I draw a Roman numeral seven in the dirt, backwards, with the end of the bat. I don't know why I do it. It just do it. It clears my mind."[28] Leading the majors with 25 round-trippers, Colbert wielded his 35-inch, 36-ounce bat to go 4-for-5, belting two homers and driving in five runs in the Padres' 9-0 laugher in the first game. Colbert recalled that he had felt exceptionally tired when the club arrived in Atlanta from Houston late the night before. "I didn't sleep well," he said. "I knew there was no way I could play both games. My back hurt, I felt down."[29] After his performance in the first game, there was no question he'd back in the field in the nightcap. He torched three different Braves hurlers to cap the best game of his life, clubbing three home runs for the first and only time and knocking in a career-high eight runs in the Padres' 11-7 victory for the twin-bill sweep. Colbert's five home runs tied Musial's record for the most in a doubleheader and his 13 RBIs set a new record, breaking the mark of 11, held jointly by Earl Averill (1930), Jim Tabor (1939), and Boog Powell (1966). Colbert's 22 total bases broke Musial's record of 21. Given the Padres' lack of home-run threats (Leron Lee was the only other player to have double-digit round-trippers that season with 12), it's a wonder that opposing pitchers even threw to Colbert. He finished the season by tying his own club record with 38 home runs (finishing in second place in the majors, two behind Johnny Bench). Colbert's 111 runs batted in set an intriguing major-league record, which still stood as of 2018, and might be among the baseball records least likely to be broken. His RBI total accounted for 22.75 percent of all the Padres' runs, breaking the mark set by the Boston Braves' Wally Berger (130 RBIs, 22.61 percent) in 1930.[30]

No one could have imagined that Colbert would go from one of the game's most feared sluggers in 1972 to out of baseball four years later at the age of 30. The initial signs of Colbert's alarming decline came in the first three months of the 1973 season, when he managed just seven home runs through June. A hot streak to start July (18 hits in 36 at-bats in nine games) helped salvage his season and earned him another berth on the All-Star squad. (He fouled out in his only appearance.) Once again the biggest offensive threat on the NL's worst team and the lowest-scoring (3.38 runs per game) club in the majors, Colbert posted career bests in batting average (.270) and on-base-percentage (.343), though he slipped to 22 home

runs and 80 runs batted in.

In his final three campaigns (1974-1976), Colbert batted an anemic .186 with a .346 slugging percentage and hit only 24 home runs. After three consecutive All-Star Game appearances at first base, Colbert was moved by the Padres to left field in 1974 to accommodate the acquisition of Willie McCovey. Colbert never acclimated himself to the new position, struggled at the plate, drew the ire of the fans, and was ultimately benched by skipper John McNamara. In the offseason he was traded to the Detroit Tigers. A short, disastrous stint in the Motor City was followed by a similar one with the Montreal Expos, who released him on June 2, 1976. Signed by the Oakland A's, Colbert attempted to revive his career in the minors with the Tucson Toros of the Pacific Coast League. He was called up by the A's in September and went hitless in two games. Granted free agency on November 1, 1976, Colbert was not selected in the inaugural free-agent re-entry draft, effectively ending his career. He participated in the Toronto Blue Jays spring training in 1977, but was jettisoned well before camp ended.

The Padres' first star and multiple All-Star, Colbert finished his career with 173 home runs, 520 RBIs, and a .243 batting average. As of 2018, he still held the Padres' career record for home runs (163) and ranked among the club's top 10 in numerous offensive categories.

Like many ballplayers, Colbert's transition into life after baseball was initially rocky. After holding down a few odd jobs and divorcing in 1979, Colbert married Kathrien (Kasey) Louis Barlow and became an ordained minister. He also gradually found his way back to the Padres, serving as an instructor during spring training and later as hitting coach for several seasons with the Riverside Red Wave in the Class-A California League. In October 1990, the day Colbert lost his job with the Padres, he was also indicted on 12 felony counts of fraudulent loan applications.[31] He eventually pleaded guilty to one count and served a six-month sentence in Lompoc, a medium-security penitentiary in California.[32] After his incarceration, Nate rededicated his life to his ministry and operated various baseball schools and camps in which youngsters learned about the sports and Christian values. He managed in two short-season independent leagues (Western Baseball League and Big South League) in 1995 and 1996, though he preferred to spend his time working with disadvantaged youths and combining his two passions, baseball and ministry. In 1999 Colbert, 1976 Cy Young Award winner Randy Jones, and former Padres owner Ray Kroc were the inaugural inductees into the Padres Hall of Fame, founded in 1999 on the team's 30th anniversary. Colbert continued his ministry work into the new millennium. As of 2018, he lived in the San Diego area and occasionally made appearances with the Padres.

"I never had a bad day in baseball," said the soft-spoken Colbert decades after retiring. "It was, I woke up, I wanted to go to the ballpark. I liked playing every day. I didn't need an offday. I played with a bad back, broken toe, fractured wrist, and concussion. I played. I just played, because I figured I'm going to hurt anyway, so I might as well play."[33]

## Sources

In addition to the sources noted in this biography, the author also accessed Colbert's player file and player questionnaire from the National Baseball Hall of Fame, the *Encyclopedia of Minor League Baseball*, Retrosheet.org, Baseball-Reference.com, the SABR Minor Leagues Database, accessed online at Baseball-Reference.com, and *The Sporting News* archive via Paper of Record.

## Notes

1  "The Padres First Star -- #17 –Nate Colbert," *Padres360.com*, August 21, 2014. padres360.com/2014/08/21/the-padres-first-star-17-nate-colbert/.

2  Ibid.

3  Bruce Markusen, "#Card Corner: 1969 Topps Nate Colbert," baseballhall.org. baseballhall.org/discover-more/stories/card-corner/nate-colbert.

4  Arnold Hano, "Nate Colbert Is Definitely Accident Prone," *Sport Magazine*, May 1973: 50. Neal Russo, "Colbert's Brother Says Father Inspired Nate," *St. Louis Post-Dispatch*, February 8, 1971: 29.

5  Jim Sims, "Shaking Foes Hear the High Sonic Boom – It's in Colbert's Bat," *The Sporting News*, June 3, 1967: 39.

6  John Wilson, "Astros See Bright Future for Bench Kid, Colbert," *The Sporting News*, November 26, 1966: 37.

7  Sims.

8  Hano.

9  Hano.

10  Padres360.

11  Paul Cour, 'Big Colbert Booster: G.M. Leishman," *The Sporting*

News, June 27, 1970: 11.

12  Padres360.

13  Sarah Wisdom, "San Diego Padres in Yuma – Spring Training 1969," Yuma County District Library, February 8, 2016. yumalibrary.org/san-diego-padres-in-yuma-spring-training-1969/.

14  Padres360.

15  Paul Cour, "Colbert New Power Man for Padres," *The Sporting News*, May 17, 1969: 18.

16  Padres360.

17  Paul Cour, "Army Chilled Nate's Bat," *The Sporting News*, October 18, 1969: 35.

18  Paul Cour, "Corkins Winning Battle With Batters and Ulcers," *The Sporting News*, April 18, 1970: 28.

19  Paul Cour, "New Padres 'Snake' Brings Foes to Knees," *The Sporting News*, April 25, 1970: 20.

20  Paul Cour, "Colbert's Cannon Shots Jolt Padre Foes," *The Sporting News*, May 9, 1970: 10.

21  Paul Cour, "Herby Proves Answer to Padre Prayers," *The Sporting News*, June 20, 1970: 21.

22  Padres360.

23  Allen Lewis, "Colbert Slams 2 Homers as Padres Best Phils, 8-2," *Philadelphia Inquirer*, May 8, 1970: 25.

24  Ross Newhan, "Nate Colbert: Name to Remember," *Los Angeles Times*, April 12, 1971: 1.

25  Paul Cour, "Barton Relaxes, Starts Belting the Ball," *The Sporting News*, May 22, 1971: 16.

26  Newhan.

27  Phil Collier, "Fewer Pounds Lift Colbert's Stock as Pounder," *The Sporting News*, May 27, 1972: 23.

28  Hano.

29  Ibid.

30  Bob Carroll, "Nate Colbert's Unknown RBI Record," *National Pastime* (2014 reissue), 1982. SABR.

31  Michael Granberry, "Ex-Padre Slugger Nate Colbert Indicted," *Los Angeles Times*, October 24, 1990: B2.

32  Alan Abrahamson, "Colbert Pleads Guilty," *Los Angeles Times*, March 31, 1991: C9.

33  Padres360.

# FRED KENDALL

## By Brian Geller

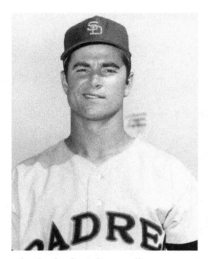

Twelve seasons in the major leagues. That's quite a run at that level of baseball. Let's face it, how many people get to live their dream of being a major-league baseball player?

Looking back throughout the history of major league baseball, Fred Kendall will be looked at as an average catcher who had a less than stellar career on a lot of bad teams. But he made it to "The Show." Not only did he make it, he will forever be part of a unique club in the history of baseball, father-and-son combinations who have played or managed at the big-league level.

After being released by the San Diego Padres, instead of continuing his career, Kendall retired after the 1980 season to spend more time with his family. During retirement Kendall worked as an assistant coach of the Torrance (California) High football team and a volunteer assistant coach for the baseball team. His oldest son, Mike, pitched for San Diego State while his younger son, Jason, a catcher like his father, went on to have an impressive 15-year career. "Jason did a lot more than I did, but I played in era that I thought was a bit tougher than my son," said Fred. "There's more teams now and back then we had to contend with four-man rotations and pitchers like Juan Marichal, Gaylord Perry, Tom Seaver, and Bob Gibson."[1] Torrance High baseball coach Jeff Phillips said the elder Kendall was a great help to the program. "Fred would come out to the practices and pitch a little batting practice or just come out and talk with the kids," Phillips said. "That's just the type of guy that Fred is. He's not out there to try and impress anybody. He just comes out and helps them because he wants to them improve."[2]

Fred Lyn Kendall was born on January 31, 1949, in Torrance. Besides playing for Torrance High, he played Little League, Babe Ruth League, American Legion, and Connie Mack ball. In 1967, his senior year, the right-handed batter hit .425 with 22 RBIs, was named All-Bay League and All-California Interscholastic Federation Class AAA first team and was voted the school's Athlete of the Year and shared the league's Baseball Player of the Year honors. The catcher was part of an impressive crop of talented baseball players in the South Bay (the southwest corner of Los Angeles County) who went on to the major leagues. "The Bretts (Ken and George) were in the league at the time over at El Segundo, pitcher Dave LaRoche was at West (Torrance High), and George Foster at Leuzinger," Kendall said. "With Bobby Grich at Long Beach (Wilson), we were able to put together an American Legion team that had nine future major leaguers."[3] Like Kendall, LaRoche was part of a father-and-son combination; two sons, Adam and Andy, played in the major leagues.

On June 6, 1967, the 6-foot-1, 185-pound Kendall, was drafted in the second round by the Cincinnati Reds. Other catchers in that draft who made it to the major leagues were Ted Simmons, Steve Yeager, and Rick Dempsey, and others who played in the majors were Grich, Jon Matlock, Vida Blue, Dave Kingman, Jerry Reuss, Ralph Garr, and Richie Zisk. Kendall was drafted ahead of Steve Busby, Al "The Mad Hungarian" Hrabosky, Dusty Baker, Chris Chambliss, Steve Rogers, and two future National Football League quarterbacks, Dan Pastorini (New York Mets) and Archie Manning (Atlanta Braves).

Kendall quickly learned that there was a roadblock on his way to being the Cincinnati Reds starting catcher: Johnny Bench then making his way through the Reds farm system.

Kendall made his professional debut with the Sioux Falls Packers of the Class-A Northern League. The 18-year-old catcher led the team in batting at .301, and was second in hits and RBIs. Behind the plate though, his 8 errors and 22 passed balls in 61 games were less than impressive.

After the season Kendall headed to the Florida Instruction League where he had the opportunity to play alongside with future star Hal McRae (another teammate who would have a son make it to the majors) as well as Bernie Carbo, Frank Duffy, and Tommy Helms. His catching skills improved as both his errors and passed balls declined dramatically.

In 1968 Kendall was one of seven nonroster players invited to spring training with the Reds and for the season was promoted to Double-A Asheville, managed by Sparky Anderson. (Kendall called him "an intense manager."[4]) The Tourists won the Southern League championship and Kendall's .291 batting average was among the league's top 10. He caught five future major-league players, including high-school rival Wayne Simpson, with whom he roomed in spring training. "Wayne and I played on the same semi-pro team before we signed with the Reds," said Kendall.[5] When the season ended Anderson tapped Kendall along with Simpson and two other Tourists as "Reds of the future." With the impending expansion draft coming, would Kendall be one of the 15 Cincinnati Reds on the coveted frozen list?[6]

In the draft, on October 14, 1968, four new teams, the San Diego Padres, Montreal Expos, Seattle Pilots, and Kansas City Royals, drafted players left unprotected by the existing major-league teams. With their seventh choice, the Padres tabbed Kendall as their future catcher, giving the hot prospect a clear path to the major leagues. Many in the Reds organization figured Kendall, who was just 19 and unproven, to be safe from selection, but in a twist of fate, Sparky Anderson was hired by San Diego to be a part of manager Preston Gomez's coaching staff and recommended Kendall to the Padres.[7] (Anderson found his way back to Cincinnati 12 months later when he was hired as skipper of the future Big Red Machine.) Cincinnati general manager Bob Howsam admitted that the loss of Kendall, rated one of the Reds' top farmhands, hurt but the price tag placed on the draftees and the knowledge that young Johnny Bench would be around for years eased the pain. "It's a great opportunity going to San Diego," said Kendall.[8] In 2017 Kendall recalled, "I knew I didn't have much of a future with the Reds with Bench around. I could throw with Bench and I could hit, loved the fastball but they wouldn't play me. I was just 19 and Bench was already at Triple A. I look at it this way: If it wasn't for Sparky I would have been backing up Bench for years."[9]

At the end of the Padres' spring training, Kendall was optioned to the Elmira Pioneers of the Double-A Eastern League, a minor-league affiliate the Padres shared with the Kansas City Royals. Switching franchises did not slow down the catcher; Kendall picked up where he left off the previous season. He again found himself among the top players in multiple offensive categories, enjoyed a 14-game hitting streak, and was named to the Eastern League All-Star game. At season's end the Padres recalled Kendall, and he made his major-league debut on September 8, 1969, Kendall made his major-league debut, as the starting catcher in a losing game against the Houston Astros in Houston. He went 0-for-3. A week later, after going hitless in his first 11 at-bats, Kendall picked up his first major-league hit, against Scipio Spinks, helping San Diego seal a two-game sweep of Houston.

In 1970, Kendall caught in 65 games and played first base in 44 contests for the Salt Lake City Bees of the Triple-A Pacific Coast League, managed by Don Zimmer. The Bees finished a dismal 44-99 and it was the start of one losing season after another for the young catcher. Kendall said Zimmer, like Anderson, "was equally as intense and if you made a mistake both skippers were going to tell you."[10] The highlight Kendall's season came when he came within one at-bat of tying a league record of 12 consecutive hits. For the second consecutive September, the Padres called up Kendall. He played in four games at three different positions, catcher, first base, and left field.

In 1971 Kendall split time between Triple-A Hawaii and San Diego with Bob Barton doing most of the catching for the Padres. On a cool July evening at San Diego Stadium, Kendall hit his first major-league home run, on a slider thrown by future Hall of Famer Bob Gibson.

The Padres dealt Barton in June of 1972 for another catcher, Pat Corrales, but by August the newly acquired Corrales was shelved with a glandular problem and the door was opened for Kendall. "I've always hit well in the minors, but this is the first real chance I've ever had to play in the majors," he told an interviewer in 1972.[11] The backstop, who had seen playing time at both first and third base, was finally gaining notoriety for skillfully calling a game. His biggest problem was a below-average throwing arm that he injured in the Arizona Instructional League in 1968. He told "I think I've improved my throwing," Kendall told the interviewer, "by getting rid of the ball sooner than I used to."[12]

Although the Padres handed rookie Bob Davis the starting catcher job to start the 1973 season, things were finally coming together for Kendall. By the sixth game of the season, Kendall had regained the starting job. Critics continued to say he couldn't throw well enough or hit for a high-enough average to play regularly. But after a hot start, the critics were silenced when the Cincinnati Reds came to town. At the time, second baseman Joe Morgan had stolen eight bases in eight attempts and Kendall was the first to cut him down. Besides Morgan, other Reds tried to steal twice more in the series and both times were gunned down by Kendall. As Kendall finished April 10-for-23 in batting during a six-game stretch, general manager Peter Bavasi took some of the credit for the up-and-coming catcher. "He came into my office to negotiate his contract before spring training and I noticed him squinting when he was reading. I talked him into having an eye examination and he was surprised to learn he needed glasses," said Bavasi.[13]

A number of San Diego pitchers were making it no secret that they preferred Kendall behind the plate. Pitcher Bill Grief said, "Fred calls a perfect game – pitching in and out, out and in, keeping the hitters honest."[14] In a span of six games in mid-September, Kendall went on a hitting spree with 12 hits in 24 at-bats to raise his average to .283.[15] At the end of the season, Kendall was named the club's most valuable player, finishing the campaign batting

.282 with 10 home runs and 59 RBIs in 145 games.

Uncertainty greeted Kendall and the rest of Padres prior to the 1974 season; the team was in discussions to move to Washington. San Diego's relocation was put to rest when the majority stockholder in McDonald's, Ray Kroc, purchased the Padres. "I think we can win 20 games more than we did last year," predicted Kendall, "and if we can do that, we can play .500 ball and get out of last place."[16] But the season proved to be disappointing; the Padres finished in last place once again, with a 60-102 record.

The most interesting thing about San Diego that summer may have been their Topps baseball trading cards. To meet distribution demands, the printing of the cards began the previous November. At the time, Topps and most others were certain that Washington would replace San Diego in the National League. So the trading card company printed Washington-National League on the face side of the Padres players' cards. Kendall was one of 14 to have his card released that year with the Washington name, ultimately a costly and embarrassing mistake for Topps. On a positive note, during a game on August 29, Kendall saved the Padres from being no-hit by St. Louis Cardinals southpaw John Curtis when he delivered a two-out single in the eighth.

At the end of 1975 spring training, Kroc hinted that the club was looking for someone who was stronger behind the plate. Both 1975 and 1976 proved to be subpar years for both Kendall and the Padres. Kendall, hit just two home runs but caught a career-high 146 games in 1976 (more games started that season than Johnny Bench or Thurman Munson). "I'm proud of the fact that I played more games than any other catcher in the big leagues. I'm especially proud I was able to prove I'm both capable and durable," Kendall said.[17]

On December 8, 1976, Kendall, outfielder Johnny Grubb, and infielder Hector Torres were dealt to the Cleveland Indians in exchange for outfielder George Hendrick. Kendall, the last of the original Padres who were born of expansion, joined old high-school rival and ace reliever Dave LaRoche. "When I was traded by the Padres, I was disappointed because I like them so much, especially the manager, John McNamara, and the San Diego area," Kendall said.[18] With the Indians, Kendall shared the catching job with Ray Fosse until mid-August, when he was named the first-string catcher. Indians manager Jeff Torborg, a catcher himself in 10 major-league seasons, held Kendall in high regard. "Behind the plate we are solid with Fred

Kendall, a pitchers' catcher who handles a staff superbly and is a hard-nosed, play-at-any-cost guy who gets some big hits," Torborg said.[19] In 103 games, Kendall hit .249.

Although he was being tabbed as Cleveland's Opening Day starter, on the eve of the 1978 campaign Kendall found himself once again traded. This time it was to a legitimate pennant contender, the Boston Red Sox. Kendall was dealt along with pitcher and future Hall of Famer Dennis Eckersley for Rick Wise, Bo Diaz, Ted Cox, and Mike Paxton. Originally Kendall was not part of the deal but on the eve of the trade, Boston manager Don Zimmer insisted that his old backstop be included in the deal. It was déjà vu for Kendall. Just as in Cincinnati earlier in his career, he was being blocked by a future Hall of Fame catcher, Carlton Fisk. "Zim told me to just be ready," Kendall said. "I just sat there and watched, it was a shock, he never played me but you know what, he never played anybody off the bench, we had guys with 8 or 12 years experience waiting to get a chance to play and it was that club's ultimate downfall. Zim played the horses until they ran out of gas."[20] That season, Kendall joined Bob Montgomery as a backup to Fisk and periodically filled in as a defensive replacement for George Scott at first base, his first time playing first base since 1972. In one start at first, against the Toronto Blue Jays, Kendall went 3-for-4 with two runs scored and one RBI. Earlier in that season, in a twist of fate, Kendall became first player in 18 years to pinch-hit (in a clutch situation) for future Hall of Famer Carl Yastrzemski. Yaz was hit on the right forearm by a pitch from Milwaukee southpaw Bob McClure and could not proceed with his at-bat.[21] Boston did not tender a contract to Kendall for the 1979 season. Kendall later reminisced about the '78 season, "It was great, we won every day, 99 wins and we came in second. I watched Jim Rice have an MVP season, the lineup was ungodly, Fisk, Scott, Fred Lynn, Yaz, Dwight Evans, where was I going to play?"[22]

Kendall finished his career back where it started: with San Diego. The Padres, who had catcher Gene Tenace locked in as their starter, took a flyer on Kendall for 1979. In hindsight, Kendall said going back to the Padres was likely a mistake,[23] but that he was glad to be back home. He played in only 65 games his final two seasons before being given his unconditional release on August 11, 1980. Three days before his release, his final hit came against the Houston Astros, who had given up his first. Kendall, pinch-hitting for Tim Flannery, singled to left field against Joe Sambito, helping San Di-

ego score three runs in top of the ninth in a 5-3 comeback victory. He finished his major-league career with a batting average of .234, 31 home runs, and 244 RBIs.

In 1992, the Chicago White Sox' director of minor-league instruction, Buddy Bell, Kendall's roommate with the Indians in 1977, offered the former catcher the opportunity to manage Utica. "I always planned on going back into baseball," Kendall said. "I wanted to spend more time with my family, but I felt the time was right to get back into the game."[24]

"I was one happy guy," Jason Kendall said of his father's hiring. "That's where he belongs. He quit baseball to spend time with his family, and I'm happy that he's getting back into it."[25] Kendall managed the next four seasons in the White Sox organization at the Class-A level, managing future major-league players including Mike Cameron, Greg Norton, Magglio Ordonez, Scott Radinsky, and Mike LaValliere.

Kendall then worked for Buddy Bell as the bullpen coach for the Detroit Tigers from 1996 to 1998, and for the Colorado Rockies from 2000 to 2002. The next three seasons, 2003-2005, he was a Rockies minor-league catching instructor. In 2006 Kendall joined Bell for the third time, as bullpen coach with the Kansas City Royals. "He's an exceptional catching instructor who understands calling a game," Bell said. "He's just a good baseball guy."[26]

Among Kendall's achievements, he hit a home run against Bob Gibson, and was the primary catcher for Randy Jones during his Cy Young Award-winning 1976 season. He caught Hall of Famers Dennis Eckersley, Gaylord Perry, and Rollie Fingers. Sparky Anderson thought Kendall, not Johnny Bench, was the future in Cincinnati. He was a part of the original expansion San Diego Padres and was the last player to leave from the original roster. He even had a front-row seat for the Red Sox/Yankees rivalry in 1978. Later in his life he instructed, coached, and managed a new crop of players. As of 2018, Kendall was enjoying retirement, and lived a quiet, private life raising horses with his wife.

**Sources**

In addition to the sources noted in this biography, the author also accessed Kendall's player file from the National Baseball Hall of Fame, Retrosheet.org, and Baseball-Referece.com.

## Notes

1  Fred Kendall, telephone interview with author, July 5, 2017.

2  Cap Carey, "He's Stepping Up to Management Level: Baseball: Twelve Years After His Major League Career Ended, Fred Kendall Gets Back Into the Game as a Minor League Manager," *Los Angeles Times*, March 6, 1992: SBC10.

3  Carey.

4  Fred Kendall interview.

5  Earl Lawson, "Second Gary Nolan, Reds May Have One in Greenie Simpson," *The Sporting News*, March 9, 1968: 14.

6  Ibid.

7  Earl Lawson, "Draft Blows Fog Over Cardenas' Future," *The Sporting News*, November 2, 1968: 34.

8  Paul Cour, "Padres Present a Big Chance for Catcher Kendall," *The Sporting News*, November 23, 1968: 42.

9  Fred Kendall interview.

10 Fred Kendall interview.

11 Phil Collier, "Kendall of Padres Delivers Sermon: 'We Have Catcher,'" *The Sporting News*, September 9, 1972: 23.

12 Ibid.

13 Phil Collier, "Padres Approve Cheaters – If They're on Kendall," *The Sporting News*, May 12, 1973: 28.

14 Ibid.

15 Phil Collier, "Further Padre Harvest Likely in Norman Deal," *The Sporting News*, October 6, 1973: 10.

16 Phil Collier, "Padres Get Break They Deserve, From Big Mac," *The Sporting News*, February 9, 1974: 29.

17 Russell Schneider, "Hard-Working Kendall Bids for Indians' Caching Job," *The Sporting News*, March 26, 1977: 10.

18 Ibid.

19 Russell Schneider, "Indians 'Set' Everywhere but Shortstop: Torborg," *The Sporting News*, March 4, 1978: 12.

20 Fred Kendall interview.

21 Larry Whiteside, "Hobson Bats Ninth – And Bombs Pitchers," *The Sporting News*, May 13, 1978: 5.

22 Fred Kendall interview.

23 Fred Kendall interview.

24 Carey.

25 Ibid.

26 Bob Dutton, "Royals Hire Pitching and Bullpen Coaches," *Kansas City Star*, October 12, 2005.

# JERRY MORALES

## BY RICHARD BOGOVICH

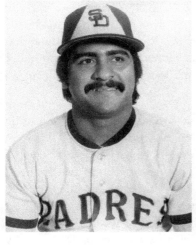

"WHO'S Jerry Morales?"

This question began an article in the *Chicago Tribune* on November 13, 1973, about the previous day's trade by the Cubs of four-time All-Star Glenn Beckert to the San Diego Padres for Morales. That simple inquiry "was the prevalent reaction" as word of the trade spread, according to influential *Trib* sportswriter Richard Dozer. Dozer characterized Beckert's roommate on road trips, nine-time All-Star Ron Santo, as being disappointed. "They're breaking up that ol' gang of ours," Santo said.[1]

That old gang was beloved, and the low expectations of the Padres during their first five years of existence couldn't have prepared Morales for becoming one of the substitutes in Chicago. Soon after their loss in the 1945 World Series, the Cubs barely managed one winning season in a 20-year span, but from 1967 to 1972 they were contenders and finished in either second or third place. Their manager was quotable Hall of Famer Leo Durocher and Santo was one of four future Hall of Famers in the field.

Beckert was one of four other players to represent the Cubs at All-Star Games during that era.

The Cubs didn't overhaul their team in a single offseason, and more than a year after the Beckert trade, their manager still felt there was too much pressure on Morales and other recent arrivals. "This is a new beginning, not an extension of the past," said Jim Marshall, who took the reins from Whitey Lockman in mid-1974. "I want Cub fans to know these young men for who they are ... not as replacements for stars of the past." *Tribune* sportswriter Rick Talley said Marshall had chosen his words carefully, and that they were "directed toward the press and fans of Chicago. He wants us, finally, to forget about Ferguson Jenkins, Ernie Banks, Ron Santo, Ken Holtzman, Glenn Beckert, Bill Hands, Billy Williams, Randy Hundley and all the others."[2]

Before reviewing how Jerry Morales responded as a Cub, it seems fitting at this point to first answer that initial question: Who's Jerry Morales?

Julio Rubén Morales y Torres was born on February 18, 1949, on Calle Cristobal Colon (Christopher Columbus Street) in Yabucoa, Puerto Rico, a city of about 30,000 near the island's southeastern coast. Yabucoa is nicknamed the City of Sugar because its valley was known for growing sugar cane, and that inspired the name of the local amateur baseball team on which Jerry eventually played. He spent his early years living in public housing named after a Dr. Victor Berrios.[3] Morales' father was a government health inspector, and Jerry was the third oldest of four children.[4]

Jerry played Little League baseball growing up, and on his way to graduating from Yabucoa's Teodoro Aguilar Mora High School he ran track and captained the school's baseball team.[5] In 1963 he had the opportunity to see the AL pennant winners, the New York Yankees, play an exhibition game in Puerto Rico.[6] When Jerry was 14 or 15 he received important instruction from a legendary major leaguer from Puerto Rico. Roberto Clemente "came to my hometown for a clinic. I remember everything, particularly the things he taught me about playing the outfield. It helped me my whole career," Morales recalled more than two decades later. "He showed me the way to throw the ball, and the way to catch it, and the best way to hit the cutoff man, and he taught me how to learn to anticipate where the ball would come."[7]

At the age of 16 Jerry played amateur baseball for the Yabucoa Azucareros.[8] Around that time he also played in Cidra, a city west of Yabucoa and south of San Juan. He and future major leaguer Ed Figueroa were on a Cidra squad that won the championship in a league named for Hiram Bithorn, the first Puerto Rican to play in the majors.[9]

A very momentous month for Morales was June of 1966, when he was 17 years old. He and Figueroa were on the Puerto Rican national team that won a silver medal at the 10th quadrennial Central American and Caribbean Games, held in San Juan. Puerto Rico lost only to Cuba, the gold medal winner in baseball.[10] Morales made quite an impression in the games, because scout Nino Escalera swiftly signed him to a contract with the New York Mets.[11] He reportedly received a signing bonus of $21,000 and used it to buy his mother a house.[12]

Morales made an immediate impact for the rookie league Mets in tiny Marion, Virginia. On July 24 he was leading the Appalachian League in batting with a .446 average, far above the .400 mark of runner-up Richie Hebner of the Salem Pirates[13] (for whom Morales would be traded after the 1979 season). Morales soon won a gold wristwatch from the Topps Chewing Gum Company when the baseball-card company named him the Appalachian League Player of the Month for July. He finished the month with an average of .414 and 21 RBIs in 21 games.[14] Hebner ended the season with the league's highest batting average but Morales was the only regular who reached base more

than half the time (.527 on-base percentage), and it was Morales who was chosen by the league's managers and sportswriters as the most outstanding player.[15]

During the subsequent offseason Morales played in Puerto Rico's winter league on the Caguas Criollos. His manager was former Milwaukee Brave John "Red" Murff, and coaching was the aforementioned Nino Escalera. Teammates included Félix Millán (also from Yabucoa), Willie Montañez, and Ron Swoboda.[16] As much as Morales learned at age 15 from Roberto Clemente, it was Vic Power whom Morales credited with helping him develop the most, as his manager in a later winter-league season.[17] Morales ultimately played in the league for 18 winters.[18]

In 1977 Morales explained why he returned to Puerto Rico regularly in the fall. "I wanted to be with my people, and to speak Spanish and not have any trouble and know what places I can go," he said. When he played for Marion, he knew almost no English. "I knew what was a hamburger and a hot dog, but I wanted something else," he recalled. "My roommate and I finally learned how to order liver and onions." They ate liver for several consecutive days. Strongly missing Puerto Rico wasn't something that subsided quickly. "My first three, four years in pro ball, I was always looking for the last day of the season to go home," he admitted.[19]

At least he had frequent contact with Figueroa during his second and third years as a pro up north. They were teammates briefly with Marion, which employed Figueroa as a starting pitcher for two games, but the two spent all of 1967 together with the Winter Haven Mets of the Class-A Florida State League. "Jerry Morales was my best friend on the team," Figueroa said. "We had a nice apartment by a lake and it was a good place to live."[20] They were teammates one more time with Raleigh-Durham for part of 1968.

Morales played in 139 out of Winter Haven's 140 games. His batting average plunged almost 100 points from a year earlier, to .248, but he demonstrated considerable speed with 14 triples plus 27 stolen bases in 31 attempts. Despite Morales' mediocre batting average, he was one of seven Winter Haven players promoted to New York's 40-man roster on October 20.[21] As a result, he spent spring training in 1968 with big leaguers, and a four-day stretch was probably most memorable: On March 8 he saw Tom Seaver hit in the head by a line drive during practice, on March 9 he saw Tommie Agee hit in the head by a pitch from Bob Gibson, and on March 10 his clutch eighth-inning hit drove in Bud Harrelson for his team's only run in a 14-inning tie against the Cardinals.[22] On March 11 his walk with the bases loaded in the 11th inning won a game against the Astros.

For the regular season, however, it was back to Class-A baseball for Morales. He split the year between Raleigh-Durham in the Carolina League and Visalia in the California League. His statistics weren't much different than in 1967, and the Mets left him unprotected for the expansion draft on October 14, 1968. The Padres made him their eighth selection.

Morales spent most of 1969 with the Padres' Elmira, New York, team in the Double-A Eastern League. He had a particularly memorable game on May 6, when his speed kept him from hitting for the cycle: Instead of a homer, triple, double, and single, he had a homer, two triples, and a single.[23] In 127 games he reached new heights in home runs, RBIs, and total bases while batting .272. He was promoted to the parent club, and made his major-league debut in San Diego on September 5, 1969.

In that game, the Padres were leading the Dodgers by three runs in the bottom of the eighth inning. Left fielder Al Ferrara singled with one out, and Morales ran for him. He was soon erased on an inning-ending double play. Morales took over in left field but the Dodgers were retired quietly in the ninth inning without a ball hit to him. The next day he entered the game under similar circumstances except that he was put out trying to steal, and he at least got to touch the ball in the ninth inning when he fielded a Dodger single. In his third consecutive game against LA, he ran for Ferrara in the seventh inning and scored his first run as a major leaguer, then recorded his first putout in the eighth. He didn't play on September 8 but the next day he batted second in the starting lineup, in Houston. He played center field and enjoyed his first major-league hit, a single, in the top of the ninth inning. In Cincinnati on September 10, he batted third and played right field. In the fourth inning he homered for the first run of the game, and the Padres ended up winning, 2-1. All told, Morales played in 19 games for the Padres that month and hit .195.

Morales was the Opening Day left fielder in 1970 for the Padres and played in 28 games during the season's first five weeks. He batted only .155 and on May 12 was shipped to Triple-A Salt Lake City for the remainder of the season. In 1971 Morales played for Triple-A Hawaii until early September, and was then called up for 12 games by the

Padres. His big-league batting average declined again, to .118. His 1974 Topps baseball card noted that he led PCL outfielders in fielding percentage in 1970 and 1971, but his minor-league batting stats weren't exactly impressive. Still, he didn't play in the minors again for more than a decade.

In 1972 Morales was the Opening Day center fielder for the Padres and throughout the season was one of five San Diego outfielders who played regularly. He wasn't in San Diego's starting lineup on Opening Day in 1973 but during the course of the season he was one of four regular outfielders. The one constant during his five seasons with the Padres was that the team finished last in the six-team NL West. At least things started clicking for Morales personally in 1973, at age 24, when he hit .281 in 122 games. Thus, the Cubs offered Beckert (plus minor leaguer Bobby Fenwick) to the Padres in trade for Morales after that season.

About six weeks into the 1974 season, Morales made a big splash against the team that drafted him with a six-RBI game in New York on May 22. He homered off Tom Seaver in the fourth inning and collected a two-run single as well. After eight innings the score was tied, 6-6. With a Cub on third base and one out in the ninth inning, the Mets elected to walk Rick Monday intentionally to bring up Morales. His homer into the left-field bullpen produced the final score, 9-6. "This had to be my biggest game of my major-league career," Morales said at the time.[24] Morales batted .273, and though his 15 homers were only third highest among Cubs that season, his 82 RBIs topped the team. Morales scored 70 runs, the highest total of his major-league career. On the downside was a particularly ugly pair of numbers: Morales had two stolen bases but was caught stealing 12 times.

Jerry Morales was still only 26 years old at the start of the 1975 season. "Morales has the marking of a future star and maybe even a super star," wrote Ulish Carter in the spring of 1975 in the *New Pittsburgh Courier*.[25] Morales' production that year didn't contradict such optimism: He hit .270 and drove in 91 runs, the best mark of his career. The second highest total by a Cub that year was 70, by Manny Trillo. What's more, no other Cub had that many RBIs during the six seasons from 1973 through 1978.

During the first half of 1976, Morales was in the headlines for an unusual reason. On the last weekend of May he and a friend, off-duty Chicago police officer Frank Ramirez, paid a late-night visit to a taco stand on Chicago's northwest side, and as Ramirez drove Morales back to the latter's apartment building, four young men followed them after having felt that Ramirez cut them off in traffic at some point. The four men attacked Ramirez and Morales when they saw their chance but the doorman at Morales' building summoned on-duty officers, who arrested the quartet. Both victims suffered back injuries and Morales (whose weight on Topps cards had been listed as just 165 pounds as recently as 1974) also was cut on the head. He missed a few games as a result.[26] In August Morales was hospitalized with muscle spasms in his back,[27] which caused him to miss 13 games, and the team's media guide for the next season said this was one reason his total RBIs declined to 67.[28] Nevertheless, his total of 16 homers was his personal best as a pro.

Relative to other outfielders, Morales' defensive performance peaked during 1975 and 1976. His 11 assists in 1975 were second best among NL right fielders, and his 12 in 1976 were third best. In 1975 he had the fifth best range factor among NL right fielders. In 1976 he initiated the most double plays among NL outfielders, with six. His .980 fielding percentage in 1975 was fourth best among NL right fielders and his .982 mark in 1976 was third.

Morales was known for preferring to make basket-style catches of fly balls, with both hands at his waist, and once dispensed detailed advice on how to break in a new glove. He needed to do that before the 1977 season because he and a few teammates had their gloves stolen during spring training. (Bill Buckner lost five.) "I take a new glove and beat it with a bat until I get it the way I like it," said Morales. "Then I tie it up with string and soak it in water for a day or two. I'll put a little oil on it, but not too much, because I don't want to make it too heavy." (He admitted that he wasn't using gloves made by the company with which he was under contract but added, "As long as they don't find out I think I'll be okay.")[29]

By 1977, Morales had developed a reputation as a clutch hitter. "This is our best man in the clutch," José Cardenal said of Morales about two months into the season.[30] Sportswriter Jerome Holtzman generalized later that season in *The Sporting News* that "so far as the Cub players are concerned Morales is Mr. Clutch."[31] Stats for the previous year back up this assessment: The baseball-reference.com "Splits" web page for Morales shows that in "late and close" situations Morales batted .360 and had an on-base percentage of .400.[32]

By the 1977 All-Star break, Morales was hitting .331, best in the NL. This happened in the midst of an impressive first half for Chicago. On June 28 they peaked at 47-22 with a lead of 8½ games in the National League East. NL All-Star manager Sparky Anderson chose Morales and three other Cubs as All-Stars, and that was the only time he received that honor.

The game was played in Yankee Stadium on July 19. Morales entered the game in the bottom of the sixth inning replacing starting center fielder George Foster. An inning later he made his only putout, and in the top of the eighth he batted against Sparky Lyle with a teammate on second base. Lyle hit him on the left knee.

"I was lucky," Morales said shortly afterward. "If Lyle's pitch had hit the kneecap, forget it! It'd have been busted." Bob Kennedy, general manager of the Cubs, said he "almost had a heart attack" when he saw where the stray pitch landed.[33] Lyle then threw a wild pitch to Dave Winfield. Morales' knee must not have been bothering him too much because he remained in the game and scored from second base when Winfield singled.

Robert Markus of the *Chicago Tribune* grumbled after the game that Cub All-Stars Morales, Manny Trillo, and Rick Reuschel were mostly ignored by sportswriters, who "hovered about Tom Seaver, Joe Morgan, and Steve Garvey." Markus was particularly defensive of Morales, who he said wasn't "an effusive talker."[34] Holtzman, of the *Chicago Sun-Times,* was of like mind, and took advantage of an opportunity early the next month to talk up Morales in *The Sporting News.*

Holtzman implied that fans may have noticed Morales on television even if they didn't know his name. "Morales has an unmistakable batting stance. He keeps his feet wide apart and holds the bat over his head," Holtzman wrote. "This unusual stance, he insists, enables him to wait longer on the pitch."[35]

The Cubs collapsed during the second half of the 1977 season and finished 81-81. Meanwhile, Morales' batting average regressed somewhat and he finished at .290, but that was the highest mark of his career. He also finished with 34 doubles, the most of his big-league career by far.

GM Kennedy presumably felt that Morales' trade value would never be higher, and on December 8, 1977, he sent Morales, catcher Steve Swisher, and cash to the Cardinals for catcher Dave Rader and outfielder Héctor "Heity"

Cruz. This occurred about six weeks after the Cubs traded the very popular Cardenal to the Phillies. Chicago's Latino community was very upset by the two trades, according to Julio Montoya, associate editor of the Chicago weekly newspaper *La Raza*. "The reputation of the Cubs was very bad in the community," he said in 1980. "But, at first, it seemed like they still kept going out to the ballpark, to see if the Cubs could win without Morales and Cardenal."[36]

Morales played in 130 games for the Cardinals but his batting average slumped to .239. About a year after they traded for him, St. Louis dealt Morales and pitcher Aurelio Lopez to the Tigers for pitchers Bob Sykes and career minor leaguer John Murphy. In Morales' 15 years as a major leaguer, 1979 was the only time he played for a winning team. Still, Detroit's record of 85-76 was only good enough to finish fifth in the AL East. His batting average slipped even more, to .211, and on October 31 he and Phil Mankowski were traded to the Mets for Richie Hebner. Morales played only one season for the team that originally drafted him. His batting average rebounded somewhat, to .254, but he was now a part-timer. He returned to the Cubs for three more seasons, 1981-1983, and in the first two of those seasons of limited duty his average returned to his peak levels, at .286 and .284.

Morales was single when he first became a Cub but by the time he ended his playing career with them he was married to the former Carmen Lourdes Hernández.[37] His last game in the majors was a loss at home to the Phillies on September 28, 1983. As a pinch-hitter, he lined out. Morales concluded his major-league career with a .259 batting average.

The Cubs kept Morales in their organization through 1986 as minor-league hitting coordinator and a roving instructor for outfielders. He then served as a Puerto Rican scout for the Dodgers from 1987 through 1990. During the winter from 1986 to 2002 he was a fixture as a coach in the Puerto Rican league. He was elevated to San Juan's manager for 1999-2000.[38]

The strike by major-league players in August of 1994, which ended up canceling the World Series, motivated many Puerto Rican major leaguers to play in their native island's winter league season. As a result, San Juan Senadores manager Luis "Torito" Melendez had an incredibly difficult time choosing among many worthy candidates to represent Puerto Rico on its 1995 Caribbean Series team. Morales was one of four coaches who helped

Melendez make those choices. The resulting "Dream Team," which won the Series, included Hall of Famer Roberto Alomar, Edgar Martinez, Juan Gonzalez, Bernie Williams, Ruben Sierra, Carlos Baerga, and Carmelo Martinez.[39]

Morales limited his baseball work to Puerto Rico through early 2002 in order to raise his children but then took a coaching job with the Montreal Expos because making a living through the winter league was proving to be difficult, and he felt his children were old enough to cope with their father being away for long periods.[40] For three years Morales coached first base for the Expos and also coordinated the defensive positioning of their outfielders. He was with the Expos until 2004, the franchise's final season before it relocated to Washington.[41] He resigned so that he could spend much more time with his wife, who was battling lupus.[42] He returned to the mainland as a minor-league instructor for the Mets in 2006,[43] and was the first-base coach for the Washington Nationals in 2007 and 2008.

In early 2009 the Mets signed Morales as a coach for their St. Lucie team in the Florida State League,[44] but first he was committed to helping coach the Puerto Rican team in the 2009 World Baseball Classic in March.[45]

Things came full circle for Jerry Morales in the spring of 2015, when his hometown of Yabucoa named its municipal gymnasium after him, and he took part in a ceremony that made the new name official.[46] The facility includes a large sign with biographical information about him, along with many life-size photos spanning his life in baseball. He can rest assured that plenty of residents can easily answer the question, "Who's Jerry Morales?"

**Notes**

1 Richard Dozer, "Beckert Goes to San Diego," *Chicago Tribune*, November 13, 1973: Section 3, Page 1. Dozer had chaired the Chicago Baseball Writers Association three years earlier and became president of the Baseball Writers Association of America three years later.

2 Rick Talley, "Marshall Asks Cub Fans to Forget 'Stars of Past,'" *Chicago Tribune*, January 17, 1975: Section 4, Page 3.

3 The street of his birth and early home are identified on a public plaque honoring him in Yabucoa, visible in several sources, including "Bautizan con el nombre Julio Rubén 'Jerry' Morales Gimnasio Municipal de Yabucoa," *La Esquina* (Maunabo, Puerto Rico), May 2015: 36.

4 Walter L. Johns, "San Diego's Jerry Morales," *Cumberland* (Maryland) *News*, March 28, 1970: 12.

5 *1977 Chicago Cubs News Media Guide*, 20.

6 Robert Markus, "He's Top NL Hitter, but Morales Still Ignored," *Chicago Tribune*, July 21, 1977: Section 4, Page 3.

7 Pohla Smith, "Clemente Sons Choose Non-Baseball Careers," *Los Angeles Times*, March 29, 1987; 15. Morales told Pohla Smith that he was 15 at the time, but a decade earlier he said that happened when he was "about 14." See Jerome Holtzman, "Bat Speaks Volumes for Quiet Morales," The Sporting News, August 6, 1977: 5.

8 "Bautizan con el nombre."

9 "Breve historia del béisbol en Cidra 1962-1968," *Periódico La Cordillera* (Cidra, Puerto Rico), August 27, 2009; see lacordillera.net/index.php?option=com_content&view=article&id=288:breve-historia-del-beisbol-en-cidra-1962-1968&catid=43:columnistas&Itemid=110.

10 See baseball-reference.com/bullpen/1966_Central_American_and_Caribbean_Games_(Rosters) and baseball-reference.com/bullpen/1966_Central_American_and_Caribbean_Games.

11 "Young Outfielder Contracted by Mets," *Schenectady* (New York) *Gazette*, June 28, 1966: 24.

12 Johns.

13 "Morales Holds Appy Lead," *Bluefield* (West Virginia) *Daily Telegraph*, July 31, 1966: 12.

14 "Stroud, Pepper Capture Third Topps Citation," *The Sporting News*, August 20, 1966: 33.

15 "Morales Named Top Player in Appalachian's Balloting," *The Sporting News*, September 24, 1966: 36.

16 "Puerto Rican Squads," *The Sporting News*, October 29, 1966: 41.

17 Johns.

18 Thomas E. Van Hyning, *Puerto Rico's Winter League: A History of Major League Baseball's Launching Pad* (Jefferson, North Carolina: McFarland & Company, Inc., 1995), 105.

19 "Quicksand of Anonymity Bothering Jerry Morales," *Independent Record* (Helena, Montana), June 2, 1977: 17.

20 Dave Klein, *On the Way Up: What It's Like in the Minor Leagues* (New York: Julian Messner, 1977), 89.

21 "Mets Send 6 Players to Farm," *Troy* (New York) *Record*, October 21, 1967: 17.

22 "Mets, Cards Knot, 1-1," *Playground Daily News* (Fort Walton Beach, Florida), March 11, 1968: 7.

23 Ken Rappoport, "York's Angel Bedevils Yankees, 8-5," *Nashua* (New Hampshire) *Telegraph*, May 7, 1969: 18.

24 "Morales Slaps Six RBIs in Cub Win over Mets," *Freeport* (Illinois) *Journal Standard,* May 23, 1974: 15.

25 Ulish Carter, "Cubs No Longer Floor Mats," *New Pittsburgh Courier*, May 3, 1975: 9.

26 "Hearing Set in Morales Case," *Arlington Heights* (Illinois) *Herald*, June 3, 1976: Section 2, Page 2.

27 "Bench, Foster 'Solos' Rock Burris, Cubs 4-3," *Chicago Tribune,*

August 21, 1976: Section 2, Page 1.

28 *1977 Chicago Cubs News Media Guide*, 20.

29 Roger Farrell "Breaking in That Glove? Give These Methods a Try," *Daily Chronicle* (De Kalb, Illinois), April 30, 1977: 7.

30 "Quicksand of Anonymity."

31 Holtzman.

32 See baseball-reference.com/players/split.fcgi?id=moralje01&t=b&year=1976. The *1977 Chicago Cubs News Media Guide* (Page 5) stated that "Jerry had a .322 on-base percentage, seventh on the team. However, in a clutch situation, this intelligence stat soars to a .469 which is by far the best for the Cubs." It is unclear how the media guide defined "a clutch situation."

33 David Condon, "Morales Glows in Cub Sky," *Chicago Tribune*, July 23, 1977: Section 2, Page 1.

34 Markus.

35 Holtzman.

36 "¡Béisbol!," Fred Mitchell, *Chicago Tribune*, July 11, 1980: Section 6, Page 1.

37 Ned Colletti, Sharon Pannozzo, and Bob Ibach, *1983 Chicago Cubs Media Guide* (Chicago National League Ball Club Inc.), 54.

38 "Nationals Manager Manny Acta Names 2007 Coaching Staff," MLB.com, November 21, 2006; washington.nationals.mlb.com/content/printer_friendly/was/y2006/m11/d21/c1744911.jsp.

39 Gabrielle Paese, "Remembering the '95 'Dream Team,'" ESPN.com, February 1, 2015; espn.com/mlb/story/_/id/12263157/remembering-puerto-rico-1995-caribbean-series-dream-team.

40 Harvey Araton, "Puerto Rico: No Longer an Island of Dreams," *New York Times*, April 13, 2003: SP7.

41 "Nationals Manager Manny Acta."

42 Bill Ladson, "Nationals to Interview Coaches," MLB.com, December 10, 2004; washington.nationals.mlb.com/content/printer_friendly/was/y2004/m12/d10/c920268.jsp.

43 Barry Svrluga, "Acta Fills Out Nationals' Staff," *Winchester* (Virginia) *Star*, November 22, 2006: C2.

44 "Transactions," *Northwest Florida Daily News* (Fort Walton Beach, Florida), February 4, 2009: C2.

45 "World Baseball Classic," *The Sun* (Yuma, Arizona), March 3, 2009; D3. See also asapsports.com/show_interview.php?id=54816, March 9, 2009.

46 "Bautizan con el nombre."

# THE FLIGHT OF THE SEATTLE PILOTS

## BILL MULLINS

"Dewey was in a dream world. He had no money. I swear to God, the whole franchise was being run on a Visa card." The *Seattle Times's* Dick Rockne was exaggerating, but he caught the essence of the Pilots' precarious situation at the end of 1969, their first and only season in Seattle.[1] Dewey was Dewey Soriano, one of the principal co-owners of the team whose boyhood dream of bringing major-league baseball to the Pacific Northwest had turned into a nightmare. The Pilots became the second team in major-league history to last only a single year in its original city. Ironically, given the ultimate landing spot of the Pilots, the other instance of a one-year sojourn was the 1901 Milwaukee Brewers, who moved to St. Louis in 1902 to become the Browns.

Despite a nucleus of enthusiastic fans, overall passion for baseball in Seattle in the late 1960s was lukewarm at best. Between 1919 and 1968, attendance for the minor-league Rainiers, and later the Seattle Angels, had been steady, even robust. The Pacific Coast League team led the circuit in ticket sales for several years after World War II, but by the 1960s, attendance was slumping.[2] Several local entrepreneurs, such as Dewey Soriano and his brother Max, were eager to bring major-league baseball to Seattle. Chief among these boosters was Joe Gandy, a local Ford dealer, who was indefatigable in his efforts to build a ballpark to attract a team. And, of course, the entire contingent of sportswriters at the two local daily newspapers, the *Post-Intelligencer* and the *Times*, beat the drum enthusiastically. In an era when one might speak of "City Fathers," there were

civic leaders, usually not politicians, who set the course for the city behind the scenes. Ed Carlson, the president of Western International Hotels, was one of them. Carlson provided the impetus for the Seattle World's Fair in 1962. Attorney James Ellis was another municipal visionary. He worked to prepare Seattle for growth, cleaning up the polluted Lake Washington to the east of the city, while successfully urging citizens to modernize infrastructure for future economic development. His multifaceted Forward Thrust election campaign to approve construction bonds included a domed stadium. These men smiled upon the idea of big-league sports in their city, but, unlike the boosters, did little in the beginning to facilitate a team. It was not until Seattle battled to preserve major-league baseball for their city that the civic leaders took a real interest in the Pilots.

The front cover of a 1965 brochure by the Seattle Chamber of Commerce urging fans to support the Seattle Rainiers to demonstrate that Seattle is committed to support a major league team (Courtesy of David S. Eskenazi)

Opening Day at Sicks Stadium, April 11, 1969 (Courtesy of David S. Eskenazi)

The third group of decision makers in the city was the politicians; some were uninterested in sports while others incorporated campaign promises to build a stadium. Mayor James D'Orma "Dorm" Braman was of the former group. He and his successor, Floyd Miller, had little interest in advancing sports in the city and no desire to finance a playing venue. At the other end of the spectrum sat John Spellman, the King County executive (something like the mayor of Seattle's home county) and County Commissioner turned Councilman John O'Brien. O'Brien had been a star basketball player at Seattle University and an infielder and pitcher for the Pittsburgh Pirates, while his twin brother, Eddie O'Brien, became the bullpen coach for the Pilots. With his pedigree, John O'Brien could also be included in the circle of boosters.

Today there is serious debate about who bears responsibility to build a ballpark in order to lure a new team or perpetuate an established club. Historians of sports business have argued that construction is surely a losing economic proposition for the local government. In the mid- to late twentieth century the economics might have been debated, but a city without a new venue would be a city without a franchise.[3] The attempts undertaken by the City of Seattle and King County to build a major-league ballpark followed an exceptionally bumpy road. The first effort was clearly premature. As early as 1957, Dewey Soriano suggested that a stadium with a plastic dome could serve as a multisport and convention building in order to circumvent Seattle's rainy climate. In 1960, stimulated by support from Washington Governor Albert Rosellini, the city and county hired Stanford Research Institute to conduct an economic study of the region and the feasibility of building a stadium. SRI concluded that a stadium could be built for $15 million; baseball would almost surely plant a franchise in the Northwest to furnish nearby playmates for the Giants and Dodgers.[4] Stadium

bonds were placed on the November 1960 ballot. A tepid campaign consisting of fliers and bumper stickers was launched and encouraged by the local media. A 60 percent supermajority was required. The campaign garnered less than 48 percent of the vote.[5]

After the surprise success of the Century 21 Exposition (Seattle World's Fair), the boosters were ready to attempt another public stadium campaign. Joe Gandy had assumed the leadership of the Fair from Ed Carlson midway through the project and brought it to fruition. He later proclaimed, "The Fair was a dying dog. And a lot of people thought I'd be the one to bury it."[6] His next project oversaw the construction of a ballpark to lure a team. The vote, originally scheduled for 1964, was delayed until 1966. In the meantime, something stoked the boosters' fire. Gabe Paul and William Daley, owners of the Cleveland Indians, examined Seattle as a possible target to move their team. Mayor Braman met with the two and effectively dissuaded them from coming to Seattle. When Paul asked Braman when Seattle would be ready for major-league baseball, the mayor responded, "Oh, in about five years." The mayor's assistant helpfully added, "Seattle is not panting with excitement, mind you, but is in favor of [a franchise]."[7] To be fair, Braman's lack of optimism was not misplaced. A ticket sale to lure the Indians fell well short; and Seattle did not boast a truly established team until the Mariners years later. The Indians remained in Cleveland.

Nonetheless, Gandy and his crew persevered. When the National Football League deliberated expansion in 1966, it dropped broad hints that Seattle would be considered with an appropriate stadium. The drive for stadium bonds gained momentum. This time, the venue in question would be a $38 million domed stadium. Gandy went into overdrive. An array of civic leaders enthusiastically endorsed the bond issue.[8] The sportswriters spilled gallons of ink in support.[9] Even Braman agreed to follow the will of the public.[10] In a televised debate, when two of Gandy's opponents questioned why the public had to finance the stadium for a private ownership, his response was unconvincing. Consequently, the wind seemed to blow out of the sails.[11] The voters endorsed the bonds by 52.5 percent – but 60 percent was required.[12] Once again the stadium and the possibility of an NFL franchise and a major-league baseball team went a-glimmering.

Charlie Finley accomplished what Joe Gandy, the other boosters, and the sportswriters failed to do: He won a baseball franchise for Seattle, and made possible a domed stadium in the city. Finley did not do this wittingly, but he turned out to be the essential catalyst for Seattle's entrance into the major leagues. The owner of the Kansas City A's was certainly aware of Seattle. Finley had visited the city in 1967 with an eye to moving his team to the Puget Sound region. He and Mayor Braman had more encouraging conversations than were held with the Cleveland ownership, but any agreement foundered on the terms of use for the city's minor-league field, Sicks' Stadium, and Finley's freedom to move if the third time of approving stadium bonds was not the charm.

Finley's dalliance with Seattle may have been a ploy to leverage the best deal he could from Oakland. In any case, Finley moved his team to the Bay Area in 1968, leaving Missouri Senator Stuart Symington furious. Symington, like any US senator spurned, attacked baseball's Achilles heel, its antitrust exemption. Not only did he demand a replacement team but he demanded that it begin play in 1969 rather than 1971. Those were two years of preparation lost to Pilots ownership. The American League quickly complied, approving an expansion team for Kansas City. And the AL decided to beat the National League to the unoccupied Pacific Northwest by granting Seattle a team.[13] The boosters who attended the American League meeting were not caught unprepared. They presented a film of the Great Northwest and then detailed the economic strength of the region. But to even the most optimistic Seattleites, winning a franchise at the October 1967 League meeting was a surprise, and the city had done little to earn it.

Ownership was not contested. Shortly before the meeting, American League President Joe Cronin contacted Dewey Soriano to form a partnership in case Finley's demands toppled the dominoes toward Seattle. Soriano was a baseball insider and a logical choice. Born in Prince Rupert, British Columbia, he grew up in Seattle constantly involved with local baseball. He had served as general manager of the Rainiers and had risen to the presidency of the Pacific Coast League when Cronin called. Soriano assured Cronin that he could form a local ownership syndicate.[14] The promise did not hold. Though Dewey and brother Max, PCL counsel, were the local face of the team, they held only 33 percent of the franchise shares. The primary owner was William Daley, with 47 percent of the stock.[15] The former Indians owner must have been impressed with Seattle's potential when he visited in 1964. He proclaimed, that he "would enjoy the opportunity of getting in bed" with the Sorianos.[16] The consortium became known as Pacific Northwest Sports, Incorporated. Daley verbally guaranteed the $8 million that the league required to capitalize the team, but only in the event of a cash shortage.[17] In the meantime, the Bank of California issued a $4 million loan. In May 1969, two months into the season, concessionaire Sportservice provided an additional $2 million loan in return for a 20-year "follow the team" contract.[18] That meant Sportservice was the team's concessionaire no matter where it played. As the American League approved the new owners, Jerold Hoffberger of the Orioles fretted, "We are actually convinced there is no other group in Seattle, they have been scared off for some reason." Later he regretted not having examined the ownership more carefully.[19] The leveraged arrangement and Daley's $8 million promise loomed large in the ultimate fate of Seattle's new baseball team.

Staffing a front office, assembling a team, assuring an adequate temporary place to play, and building a permanent domed stadium were pressing priorities for Dewey Soriano. The most important front-office hire was general manager Marvin Milkes. Milkes started in the Cardinals organization and won his credentials with the Los Angeles/California Angels. To say he was intense is an understatement. As he described himself, "I'm very candid. I get a little impatient sometimes and I don't smile all the time when we lose. ... This is not a buddy-buddy organization. I believe in results."[20] Sportswriter Hy Zimmerman observed, "[Milkes] has splendid mental furniture, but it may need re-arranging."[21] The intense will to win while overseeing an expansion team resulted in 53 different players on its 25-man roster.[22]

The front office consisted of a capable collection of professionals who were knowledgeable about the local market along with experienced baseball hands. Bill Sears,

Pilots' president Dewey Soriano and general manager Marvin Milkes (Courtesy of David S. Eskenazi)

A press conference held in Berkeley, California to discuss efforts to keep the Pilots in Seattle, January 27, 1970. From left: John Spellman, Dan Evans, Eddie Carlson, Wes Uhlman, Slade Gorton, and Fred Danz (Courtesy of David S. Eskenazi)

erstwhile public-relations director for the Rainiers, held the same role for the Pilots. Harry McCarthy came from the San Francisco Giants as ticket manager. Ray Swallow and Art Parrack, both from the A's, headed scouting and the farm system, respectively. Harold Parrott, longtime Dodgers official, and most recently with the Angels, was hired at twice his Dodgers salary to oversee promotions and sales. He was gone by the first of June, a cost-cutting casualty, and an indication of apprehension over cash flow.

Bringing together a team also signaled some early financial concerns. The team purchased the contracts of outfielder Mike Hegan and pitcher Jim Bouton from the Yankees in June 1968, almost a year before the team's debut. (Bouton, of course, became famous as the chronicler of the Pilots' one and only season with his tell-all book *Ball Four*.) The expansion draft occurred in October 1968. Initially, the Pilots decided to build for the future, selecting promising players left unprotected from the draft. The day before the draft, Dewey Soriano had a change of heart. Season-ticket sales, which had been running for two or three months, were lagging. A member of the front office told the *New York Times*, "We felt we needed a product someone could understand right now."[23] So it would be veterans, not emerging major leaguers. Many had been stars, but now were aging, injured, or both. Don Mincher, drafted from the Angels, was beaned in 1968; Tommy Davis (White Sox) never fully recovered from a broken ankle in 1965; Rich Rollins (Twins) had sore knees; Steve Barber (Yankees), a sore arm. Tommy Harper from the Indians was probably the best draftee. As a Pilot, he led the American League with 73 stolen bases. Others were typical expansion picks: Ray Oyler (Detroit) hit under .200, Marty Pattin (Angels) had his moments, but finished 7-12, and

catcher Jerry McNertney (White Sox) was steady but unspectacular. Milkes hired Joe Schultz, St. Louis third-base coach, to manage the team. The easygoing, affable Schultz was a good buffer between the players and the hard-driving Milkes. The former catcher was a baseball man, but ill at ease with reporters. "He was as rough as his gnarled fingers," his press liaison remembered.[24] Schultz was able to select one of his coaches, conditioning coach Ron Plaza. Pitching coach Sal Maglie and third-base coach Frankie Crosetti were probably chosen for name recognition.

The Pilots' publicity crew devised several engaging ideas. There was a name-the-team contest. Few were surprised that Dewey Soriano, part-time harbor pilot, declared that Pilots was the winning name. The logo was both nautical and aeronautical, featuring a ship's wheel around a baseball, with wings attached. A catchy song was written for the team: "Go, Go, You Pilots." The uniforms sported a cap with a naval officer's "scrambled eggs" on the bill. The radio deal was probably the Pilots' greatest business accomplishment. The team signed a deal with Golden West Broadcasting for $850,000 a year. The network ranged from Alaska to North Dakota and south to Elko, Nevada. (This hinterland proved to be more supportive of baseball in the Northwest than the locals. Numerous families planned their vacations to Seattle when the Pilots were at home.) Jimmy Dudley, whose soft Southern drawl was reminiscent of Red Barber, came from Cleveland to anchor the broadcasts.[25] A TV contract never materialized. Soriano reportedly asked for $20,000 per game, then lowered it to $10,000, but could not strike a deal.[26]

But the crucial negative decision involved ticket prices. Soriano believed that a new major-league market would pay for the privilege to watch the team; prices ranged from $6 box seats to $2.50 for backless bleacher seats. Only the San Francisco Giants sold tickets priced that high; and a number of clubs charged as little as 75 cents.[27] The reaction was immediate. The *Seattle Times* sports editor exclaimed in print, "Great Soriano! Where are the cheap seats?"[28] Season-ticket sales lagged from the beginning. At the end of the 1969 season, Pilots attendance stood fifth lowest among major-league clubs at 677,944, some 150,000 below break-even.[29] Could layoffs at Boeing have restrained fan enthusiasm? It's possible. The Boeing recession that crested in 1971 was just getting started in 1969. Unemployment in Seattle was steady at 3.6 percent in the Pilots' only season, but some Boeing families might have decided that a brace of high-priced baseball tickets was not the wisest choice in the shadow of increasing layoffs at the city's largest employer.[30] But premium prices for expansion baseball were a more likely culprit. The quality of play outpaced expectations for over half the season. Although they were 16 games under .500, the Pilots were in third place among six teams in the American League West by the end of July. Then age and ability began to show. Injuries and losses multiplied. At the end of the 1969 season the record was 64 wins and 98 losses. That landed them in last place in the division. Only Cleveland suffered more losses in the American League.

If there was a worse plague than a lagging box office for the Pilots, it was a ramshackle playing field. They were scheduled to play in an upgraded minor-league ballpark, Sicks' Stadium, for four years, then move into a new domed stadium. The American League granted Seattle a franchise on the condition that voters approve the King County Multipurpose Domed Stadium. The ballot to ratify stadium construction bonds passed with 62 percent in a February 1968 election.[31] The success of that vote was the good news. Virtually all of the other stadium stories were bad news. Sicks' was a model minor-league park when it opened in 1938, but work was required to bring the city-owned facility up to the undefined major-league standards. Negotiations to use the ballpark continued until the early fall of 1968. The city was determined for rental fees to pay for all remodeling costs. Braman was all but immune to any threats to withdraw the franchise. The final agreement settled for a five-year lease at $165,000 per year, though the Pilots fully expected to move to a new building in four. The city promised $1.75 million to refurbish Sicks' and expand it to 28,000 seats.[32] The timing of the September 1968 agreement left seven rainy months to remodel the stadium. Initial bids came in 65 percent over budget.[33] Corners were cut and seating scaled down to 25,000. The ballpark never reached major-league quality, according to Charlie Berry (Joe Cronin's man in the field), Commissioner Bowie Kuhn, and several American League owners who visited Sicks'.[34] Fans filing into the gates on Opening Day, April 11, could hear hammers ringing as workmen continued to install seats. *Post-Intelligencer* sportswriter John Owen captured it best, commenting, "Not bad for a bunch of brash amateurs. Even if they did get caught with a few of their bleachers down."[35] An estimated 19,000 seats were completed by Opening Day and capacity probably never reached 25,000.

Problems with Sicks' vexed the Pilots ownership throughout the season. The sound system failed, the bench seats warped, and a short circuit in an electrical vault almost burned down the ballpark. Worst of all, there was no water pressure in the ballpark after the seventh inning if attendance rose above the season's average level of 8,370.[36] Soriano complained to the press about these shortcomings, hardly an ideal strategy to advertise his product to a less than passionate fan base. Pacific Northwest Sports then withheld a promised surety bond, demanding repairs and upgrades. In March 1969, Floyd Miller replaced Braman as mayor and was no more enamored of baseball than his predecessor. By August 1969 Miller threatened to evict the Pilots. Daley and Cronin came to Seattle and smoothed things over.

The great hope amid this wrangling was the promise of the brand-new domed stadium. After the successful ballot initiative in February 1968, things bogged down. A squabble over the ballpark's location erupted. The Stadium Commission's consulting firm recommended a spot at the southern edge of Seattle. Meanwhile, civic leaders lobbied hard for Seattle Center, the site of the World's Fair. Though closer to downtown, it was a more expensive location. When the commission bowed to the downtown pressure, a successful petition was circulated for an initiative vote. In January 1970 voters rejected the Seattle Center site. A new Stadium Commission would have to start all over. Pacific Northwest Sports understood the ramifications of the siting controversy: The ballpark might not be under construction by the December 1970 deadline imposed by the American League. The situation in Seattle had become bleak. The region was not excited about the team. The current ballpark was inadequate. Relations with the city were strained at best. Moving to the new venue was becoming a steadily more distant prospect. Daley made his displeasure known. "We don't seem to be getting support from the Seattle business people," he groused at the end of August 1969, "If I continue to get the brush-off I'm going to lose interest too."[37] Hy

Seattle Pilots spring training program from 1970. The franchise began spring training as the Pilots but officially became the Milwaukee Brewers on April 1 (Courtesy of David S. Eskenazi)

Zimmerman, rebutted in a *Seattle Times* column entitled "Won't You Go Home Bill Daley?"[38] This may not have been the final straw. However, by early September, Pacific Northwest Sports had begun to negotiate with the Milwaukee Brewers, a civic group led by Allan H. "Bud" Selig, to move the Pilots to Wisconsin.[39] Unlike Daley's group, Selig's partners were well-heeled. Firms such as Schlitz, Evinrude, Northwest Mutual Life, and Oscar Meyer were represented. Also, they had Milwaukee County Stadium, and it was in good shape.[40] A deal was struck at the 1969 World Series in Baltimore to sell the Pilots to the Milwaukee consortium, and it quickly became an open secret in Seattle. Although that is what ultimately happened, the Pilots had not yet become the Brewers.

Persuaded by obvious comments about baseball's antitrust exemption from Washington's two U.S. senators, Warren Magnuson and Henry Jackson, Cronin gave Seattle about a month to devise a competing offer for the Pilots. Ed Carlson spearheaded the effort, mainly to preserve Seattle's esteem. Fred Danz, a local theater owner, was the face of the undertaking. Carlson appealed to his fellow city fathers' sense of civic pride and rounded up a bevy of Seattleites to pledge $100,000 or more. Daley would become a 25 percent owner and the Sorianos, at Cronin's insistence, would be cashed out. The goal was to add $4.8 million to the $4 million Bank of California loan and the $2 million advanced by Sportservice to cover the purchase price and furnish operating capital of $1.7 million.[41] On November 18, 1969 the *Post-Intelligencer's* front page proclaimed, "It's the SEATTLE Pilots."[42] But a month later, Danz announced, "I felt I should tell the public there is trouble in Paradise." The Bank of California had informed the Sorianos in September that if the team was transferred, its loan would be due and payable.[43] After a futile appeal to Seattle banks for loans to replace the Bank of California financing and an unsuccessful ticket drive, the Danz initiative was done.

Now Ed Carlson openly took up the reins. The Pilots would become a publicly held nonprofit organization. Here was civic leadership at its purest. Hundreds of community leaders invested what they could afford to keep the team and keep egg off the public face of Seattle. Any profits that were not reinvested into the organization would go to city charities and amateur sports.[44] When Carlson issued his proposal at the American League meeting that was supposed to approve the Danz ownership, the owners were dumbfounded. Cronin observed, "I think we are dealing with a different breed of cat."[45] Some

owners saw it as a threat, fearing they would have to follow suit and distribute their profits to their communities. The American League owners gave Carlson permission to try to create a viable ownership team, but privately expected – hoped – he would fail. Behind closed doors the Orioles' Frank Cashen commented, "By going along with them, all we are doing is giving them enough rope to hang themselves because they just can't make it."[46]

The next meeting was in 15 days, in early February 1970. More than 60 businesses, labor organizations, and individuals agreed to assist Carlson. He persuaded Bank of California and Sportservice to perpetuate their loans and for Daley to remain a partner. When Carlson and his allies met in Chicago on February 6, everything was in place (although it is questionable whether the prospective ownership team was sufficiently capitalized). The American League owners were nervous about the funding, but could not accept the nonprofit. They wondered who would be in charge of a public-ownership syndicate. After questioning Carlson, the owners tried to make a decision. Cronin announced to the press that "We took nine million votes." (Actually, it was nine.) The Carlson plan fell one vote short.[47] The owners then voted to keep the Pilots in Seattle, retain Pacific Northwest Sports Incorporated as owners, and lend them $650,000.[48] The American League understood that moving the team would awaken the wrath of two powerful senators. Consequently, the league scrambled to find a buyer to save the team. Bowie Kuhn even sounded out Carlson to see if he would try again. The answer was a firm "No."[49] The league owners' decision proved to be no more than a liferaft. The Seattle press was incredulous.

Wisely, the Sorianos stepped aside from active participation to leave Roy Hamey and Marvin Milkes to run the team. There was some shuffling. Dave Bristol and a new group of coaches replaced Joe Schultz. Milkes, as was his wont, traded several players, including Don Mincher, mainstay pitcher Diego Segui, and fan favorite Ray Oyler. There was some attempted civic fence-mending, but ticket sales were slipping.

The team was collapsing financially and the league, fearful of having baseball's antitrust exemption questioned, had no remedies. The state of Washington let Cronin know it would file an $82.5 million lawsuit for breach of promise, financial damage, and fraud if the team moved, and had obtained a court restraining order against relocation.[50] Pacific Northwest Sports Incorporated was not going to continue in Seattle and the only solution was to declare bankruptcy. Everyone knew that if the declaration was approved, the sale to the Milwaukee group would be the bankruptcy court's remedy.

The deal to sell the team to the Milwaukee Brewers group became official on March 8, 1970. All that was lacking was American League approval. The last days of the Pilots were spent in court. In the morning, there were hearings in King County Superior Court over the restraining order. In the afternoon, the federal bankruptcy court heard arguments. Pacific Northwest Sports asserted that it had lost $2.3 million in 1969 and was unable to pay its debts. The accounting firm Peat Marwick later estimated losses at about $630,000. Most importantly, Pacific Northwest Sports could not repay its loans from Bank of California and Sportservice. Moreover, if player salaries were deferred by 10 days, the players would become free agents.[51] Not mentioned was Daley's crucial written promise of $5 million to $8 million in the event of insolvency.[52] In addition, bankruptcy judge Sidney Volinn overlooked the clause that the American League by its own constitution was responsible for the club if it became insolvent.[53] With the regular season just days away, the $10 million deal offered by the Milwaukee syndicate was too attractive a solution to ignore. Volinn declared Pacific Northwest Sports Incorporated bankrupt. The injunction against moving the team to Milwaukee had already been stayed. On April 2, 1970, the formal papers were signed.[54] With "Brewers" newly stitched on their uniform tops, the team opened the season in Milwaukee County Stadium against the California Angels on April 7.

Volinn's ruling protected Pacific Northwest Sports from any lawsuits. But since the American League was liable, the State of Washington sued the circuit. After six years of litigation, the league settled out of court in January 1976, granting Seattle a new franchise that would become the Mariners.

The Seattle Pilots story is one of more errors than hits. The American League was eager to stake out a new territory. The AL owners' enthusiasm probably outpaced that of most Seattleites. Attendance was not the worst in the league, but it fell short of reasonable expectations. Charging the highest prices in the league did little to kindle enthusiasm among the fans. Ownership, including those who scrambled to save the team at the last minute, was undercapitalized. William Daley is the only figure who could have afforded to absorb even moderate loss-

es and he reneged on his $8 million pledge to shore up the franchise. The ballpark situations – both Sicks' and the squabbles over the new domed stadium – burdened an already struggling franchise. For the boosters it was a bittersweet experience. For the civic leaders the Pilots brought more embarrassment than pride. And for most of the politicians the whole situation was an annoying distraction. In short, Seattle was not ready in 1969 for a major-league team. Groundbreaking on the Kingdome did not take place until December 1972, nearly three years after the Pilots departed Seattle for greener pastures in Milwaukee.

## Notes

1 Rockne quoted in Nick Russo, "An Exhilarating Big League Bust: The Seattle Pilots," in Mark Armour, ed., *Rain Check: Baseball in the Pacific Northwest* (Cleveland: Society for American Baseball Research, 2006), 121.

2 Carson van Lindt, *The Seattle Pilots Story* (New York: Marabou Publishing, 1993), 26.

3 See Rodney Fort, *Sports Economics* (Upper Saddle River, New Jersey: Prentice-Hall, 2003), 300-301 and Michael Danielson, *Home Team: Professional Sports and the American Metropolis* (Princeton: Princeton University Press, 1997), 225.

4 *Seattle Times,* September 13, 1960 and Eric Duckstad and Bruce Waybur, *Feasibility of a Major League Sports Stadium for King County, Washington* (Menlo Park: Stanford Research Institute, 1960), 59.

5 Folder 1, box 4, Series 261 Bond Files, Record Group 102 Commissioners, King County, Washington Archives.

6 Gandy quoted in *Seattle Post-Intelligencer,* February 5, 1966.

7 Paul, Braman, and Devine quoted in Sam Angelhoff, "Are We Ready for the Big Leagues?" *Seattle: the Pacific Northwest Magazine,* January 1965, 10, 14-15.

8 See *Seattle Post-Intelligencer*, September 20, 1966; *Seattle Post-Intelligencer*, August 31, 1966; *Seattle Post-Intelligencer*, August 24, 1966; and *Seattle Times,* September 14, 1966.

9 For example, see Georg Meyers in the *Seattle Times,* May 11, 1966.

10 Braman quoted in *Seattle Post-Intelligencer,* September 7, 1966.

11 Folder 18, box 20 and folder 3, box 22, Gandy Collection, University of Washington Libraries Special Collections.

12 Folder 10, box 8, Series 261 Bond Files, Record Group 102 Commissioners Washington State Archives Puget Sound Branch, Bellevue, Washington.

13 Plaintiffs' Brief Opposing New Motion from Washington v. American League, folder 9, box 5, Seattle Municipal Archives, City of Seattle Law Department Baseball Litigation Files.

14 Max Soriano, interview by Mike Fuller, January 1994, http://

www.seattlepilots.com/msoriano_int.html and *Tacoma News Tribune*, October 31, 1967.

15  Max Soriano, interview by Mike Fuller, January 1994, http://www.seattlepilots.com/msoriano_int.html.

16  Daley quoted in deposition of Charles Finley, folder 5, box 3 Washington v. American League, Washington State Archives, Northwest Branch, Bellingham, Washington.

17  Folder 26, box D-1, Series 491 Director's Files, Record Group 502 Stadium Administration, King County Washington Archives.

18  Affidavit of William Daley, folder 1, box 6, Seattle Municipal Archives, City of Seattle Law Department Baseball Litigation Files.

19  Hoffberger in transcript of American League meeting, December 1967 in deposition of Charles Finley, folder 5, box 3 Washington v. American League, Washington State Archives, Northwest Branch, Bellingham.

20  Milkes quoted in *Milwaukee Journal*, April 5, 1970.

21  *Seattle Times*, December 20, 1970.

22  Nick Russo, "An Exhilarating Big League Bust: The Seattle Pilots," in Mark Armour, ed., *Rain Check: Baseball in the Pacific Northwest*, 117.

23  *New York Times*, April 13, 1969.

24  Author's interview with Rod Belcher, January 8, 2008.

25  http://seattlepilots.com; *Seattle Post-Intelligencer*, April 11, 1969; and *Pilots Scorebook*, April 1969, Private Collection of David Eskenazi.

26  *Seattle Post-Intelligencer*, March 21, 1969.

27  *Seattle Times*, July 21, 1968.

28  Ibid.

29  Bill Mullins, *Becoming Big League: Seattle, the Pilots, and Stadium Politics* (Seattle: University of Washington Press, 2013), 152.

30  Robert Gladstone and Associates, "Basic Economic Indicators and Development Problems and Potentials for Seattle Model Cities Program: Final Report," Vol 2 (Seattle: 1970), 43, 57.

31  Susanne Elaine Vandenbosch, "The 1968 Seattle Forward Thrust Election: An Analysis of Voting on an Ad Hoc Effort to Solve Metropolitan Problems without Metropolitan Government" (Ph.D. dissertation, University of Washington, 1974), 85, 92.

32  *Seattle Times*, September 4, 1968 and Concession Agreement [Stadium Lease], file 1, Pacific Northwest Sports, Inc., Debtor, Case File 6682, United States District Court for the Western District of Washington, Northern Division (Seattle), Records of the District Courts of the United States, Record Group 21, National Archives and Records Administration--Pacific Alaska Region (Seattle).

33  *Seattle Times*, September 19, 1968.

34  Owners' complaints: *Seattle Times*, March 26-27, 1969, *Seattle Post-Intelligencer* February 7, 1976,, and deposition of Robert Short,

folder 10, box 3, Washington v. American League, Washington State Archives, Northwest Branch, Bellingham, Washington; Kuhn's comment: Bowie Kuhn, *Hardball: The Education of a Baseball Commissioner* (New York: Random House, 1987), 91; reference to Charlie Berry: deposition of Joe Cronin, folder 4, box 3, Washington v. American League, Washington State Archives, Northwest Branch, Bellingham, Washington.

35  *Seattle Post-Intelligencer*, April 11, 1969.

36  Henry Berg to Staff, June 27, 1969, folder 11, box 2, Henry Berg, handwritten report, August 3, 1969, folder 1, box 16, and Bouillon, Christofferson, and Schairer Report, August 8, 1969, folder 21, box 1, all from Seattle Municipal Archives, City of Seattle Law Department Baseball Litigation Files.

37  Quoted in *Seattle Post-Intelligencer*, August 31, 1969.

38  *Seattle Times*, October 2, 1969.

39  Deposition of Allan Selig, folder 9, box 3 in Washington v. American League, Washington State Archives, Northwest Branch, Bellingham, Washington.

40  *Milwaukee Journal*, April 1, 1970.

41  Carlson to supporters, November 10, 1969, Notes of contributions, November 29, 1969, and deposition of Edward Carlson, folder 3, box 3, Washington v. American League, Washington State Archives, Northwest Branch, Bellingham, Washington; and "Pilot Purchase Activities," folder 5, box 7, Seattle Municipal Archives, City of Seattle Law Department Baseball Litigation Files.

42  *Seattle Post-Intelligencer*, November 18, 1969.

43  Danz quoted in *Seattle Times*, December 17, 1969; "Pilot Purchase Activities," folder 5, box 7 and "Pacific Northwest Sports, Inc. Loan," folder 14, box 6, Seattle Municipal Archives, City of Seattle Law Department Baseball Litigation Files.

44  *Seattle Times*, January 27, 1970.

45  *Seattle Times*, January 28, 1970.

46  Cashen in meeting transcripts, Washington v. American League in folder 9, box 5, Seattle Municipal Archives, City of Seattle Law Department Baseball Litigation Files.

47  Cronin quoted in *Seattle Post-Intelligencer*, February 11, 1970 and brief in support of renewed motion of baseball defendants, folder 10, box 5, Seattle Municipal Archives, City of Seattle Law Department Baseball Litigation Files.

48  Deposition of Joe Cronin, Pacific Northwest Sports, Inc., Debtor, case 6682, United States District Court for the Western District of Washington, Northern Division (Seattle), Records of the District Courts of the United States, Record Group 21, National Archives and Records Administration--Pacific Alaska Region (Seattle).

49  *Seattle Post-Intelligencer*, March 14, 1970 and Bowie Kuhn, *Hardball: The Education of a Baseball Commissioner* (New York: Random House, 1987), 92.

50 *Seattle Times*, March 16, 1970.

51 *Seattle Times*, March 24, 1970.

52 Folder 26, box D-1, Series 491 Director's Files, Record Group 502 Stadium Administration, King County Washington Archives.

53 Carson van Lindt, *The Seattle Pilots Story* (New York: Marabou Publishing, 1993), 205.

54 There is an unverified story which Steve Hovley related at the Seattle SABR Convention, June 30, 2006. The truck carrying the Pilots' equipment was said to have awaited word in Provo, Utah whether to turn left or turn right. When the bankruptcy court's decision became official, the truck veered towards Wisconsin.

## SEATTLE PILOTS EXPANSION DRAFT

| PICK | PLAYER | POSITION | FORMER TEAM |
|---|---|---|---|
| 1 | Don Mincher | 1b | California Angels |
| 2 | Tommy Harper | of | Cleveland Indians |
| 3 | Ray Oyler | ss | Detroit Tigers |
| 4 | Jerry McNertney | c | Chicago White Sox |
| 5 | Buzz Stephen | p | Minnesota Twins |
| 6 | Chico Salmon | 2b | Cleveland Indians |
| 7 | Diego Segui | p | Oakland A's |
| 8 | Tommy Davis | of | Chicago White Sox |
| 9 | Marty Pattin | p | California Angels |
| 10 | Gerry Schoen | p | Washington Senators |
| 11 | Gary Bell | p | Boston Red Sox |
| 12 | Jack Aker | p | Oakland A's |
| 13 | Rich Rollins | 3b | Minnesota Twins |
| 14 | Lou Piniella | of | Cleveland Indians |
| 15 | Dick Bates | p | Washington Senators |
| 16 | Larry Haney | c | Baltimore Orioles |
| 17 | Dick Baney | p | Boston Red Sox |
| 18 | Steve Hovley | of | California Angels |
| 19 | Steve Barber | p | New York Yankees |
| 20 | John Miklos | p | Washington Senators |
| 21 | Wayne Comer | of | Detroit Tigers |
| 22 | Darrell Brandon | p | Boston Red Sox |
| 23 | Skip Lockwood | p | Oakland A's |
| 24 | Gary Timberlake | p | New York Yankees |
| 25 | Bob Richmond | p | Washington Senators |
| 26 | John Morris | p | Baltimore Orioles |
| 27 | Mike Marshall | p | Detroit Tigers |
| 28 | Jim Gosger | of | Oakland A's |
| 29 | Mike Ferrero | 2b | New York Yankees |
| 30 | Paul Click | p | California Angels |

# TOMMY HARPER

## BY BILL NOWLIN

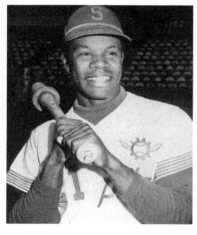

In 1970, Tommy Harper became a member of what was once among the most exclusive "clubs" in baseball. That year, his first with the Milwaukee Brewers, he hit 31 homers and stole 38 bases, thereby joining the "30-30 Club." At the time, the only other members of the club were Hank Aaron, Bobby Bonds, Willie Mays, and Ken Williams of the 1922 St. Louis Browns.[1] *Baseball Digest* once called the accomplishment "the most celebrated feat that can be achieved by a player who has both power and speed."[2] Harper was, not surprisingly, the MVP for the Brewers that year. Three years later, he was Boston Red Sox MVP, a year in which he stole 54 bases. His season high for stolen bases was in 1969, when he led the majors with 73 for the Seattle Pilots.

Harper's athleticism saw him excel in many sports. He was an all-league quarterback while in high school, and was named as a guard on the All-Northern California basketball team. He ran the 100-yard dash and played baseball.[3] As a student at Santa Rosa Junior College, he was all-league in three sports before he enrolled at San Fran-

cisco State. He'd turned down scholarship offers at Utah State and Washington State because he didn't want to play football in college.[4]

Scout Bobby Mattick of the Cincinnati Reds signed Harper on May 28, 1960. Mattick urged him to convert from outfielder to infielder. The Reds assigned him to the Topeka Reds, their affiliate in the Class-B Three-I League.

Tommy Harper was born in Oak Grove, Louisiana, on October 14, 1940. When he was 4 years old, the family moved to Alameda, California. His father was a carpenter who gained employment in an industrial mill after the move. His mother worked at the naval air station in Alameda.

Tommy attended the public schools there, graduating from the city's Encinal High School. He was captain of the baseball team in his senior year, captain of the football team, and captain of the basketball team for two years. He ran the 100-yard dash in 10.2 seconds. After his first year at San Francisco State, striving for a degree in physical education, Mattick signed him for Cincinnati.

After joining Topeka in 1960, Harper appeared in 79 games. He hit .254 in his first pro season, stealing 26 bases, and showed a good eye at the plate, drawing 76 walks and bumping up his on-base percentage to .429. The team, managed by Johnny Vander Meer, finished in last place.

Under Dave Bristol, Topeka finished first in 1961. Harper hit .324, with 136 bases on balls and an impressive .488 on-base percentage. Harper stole 31 bases. He led the league in runs scored with 131 and was named all-star second baseman and Three-I League MVP.

Harper made the majors in 1962, debuting at Crosley Field at third base on April 9, batting eighth in the order. He had a 1-for-4 day, his first big-league base hit coming his second time up, a single to right field on a check swing.[5] Harper was right-handed, listed at 5-feet-9 and 165 pounds. He played the very next day, in Los Angeles against the Dodgers and had a 3-for-4 day with his sixth-inning single providing his first RBI and tying the game, 2-2. Over his next 16 plate appearances, Harper failed to reach base and struck out six times. "Pressure caught up with the kid," said manager Fred Hutchinson. "He'll find himself down at San Diego. He's a helluva prospect."[6]

On April 15, the Reds recommended that Harper spend the rest of the year in Triple-A ball with the Pacific Coast League San Diego Padres. He was among the league leaders all season long and there was some thought of bringing him up to the big-league club at the end of July, but Padres manager Don Heffner said he felt Harper would benefit from a full season at Triple A and the Reds brass concurred.[7] The Padres won the PCL pennant by 12 games.

In 144 games, Harper hit for a .333 average (105 walks helped earn him a .450 on-base percentage) with 26 homers, 84 RBIs, and 120 runs scored. At the time, Regis Philbin had his own local TV show on station KOGO and Harper was his guest on the 11 P.M. show on July 14, 1962, sharing the limelight with "Giselle MacKenzie, star of Gypsy at the Circle Arts; George Pernicano, the pizza king; [and] Judi Henske folk singer."[8]

Come 1963, Harper was in the majors to stay. When he returned, though, he was played in the outfield alongside Frank Robinson and Vada Pinson.[9] There was anticipation and Fred Hutchinson said, "[H]e could well be our top rookie this spring."[10]

Before the season began, Harper married Bonnie Jean Williams of Topeka, Kansas. Receptions were held both in Topeka and Oakland.[11]

He got in a pretty full season's work, appearing in 129 games. He hit his first big-league home run on June 11 and added nine more before the season was done. He was more adept at scoring runs (67) than at driving them in (37), in part a function of leading off. With a .260 batting average and 44 walks, he had an on-base percentage of .335. Both his average and his OBP were very similar to his career finals: .257 and .338. The year 1963 was also his teammate Pete Rose's debut year; Rose hit .273. Harper was named to the Topps Rookie All-Star Team, as was Rose.[12]

In 1963 Harper played right field more and in 1964 most of his games were in left, though he played in only 102 games in 1964 (.243 with an OBP of .326). Basically, he said, he was platooned, "hit mainly against left-handed pitchers who I hated to hit against. I would rather bat against right-handers any day."[13]

After the 1964 season, he did a tour of reserve duty at Wright-Patterson Air Force Base.

When Harper finally became an everyday player, starting in 1965, he produced. He played in 159 games in 1965, almost all in left, and led the major leagues in runs scored (126, tied with Zoilo Versalles of the Twins). He hit for a .257 average, with 18 homers, and drove in 64 runs. His 35 stolen bases led the Reds. "That year was the first chance I had to play every day. I did well in '65 and the next year I was back on the bench platooning again. It was kind of frustrating."[14]

Harper must have been thinking of 1967. In 1966, reunited with Dave Bristol, who'd been his manager in Topeka, he appeared in 149 games with 621 plate appearances.[15] Harper hit .278, got on base 34.8 percent of the time, and scored 85 runs. He played all three outfield positions, often moving fields during the course of the game – 92 games in right, 77 in left, and 26 in center. During the offseason, he remained in Ohio, working in Dayton's Montgomery County Family Court Center with boys in detention aged 8-17. He taught them sports, at the same time serving as a role model.[16]

He'd hit four homers in 1964, 18 in 1965, and five in 1966. In mid-September of the 1965 season, Harper pleaded with a reporter not to call him a slugger. "Write about me stealing bases, or write about me beating out bunts. But, please, don't write about me being a home-run hitter. That's just not me...My job is to score runs, not hit home runs."[17]

In 1967 Harper was in just 103 games, batting .225. He

would have played more but missed two months, from May 29 to July 26. He'd suffered a fractured right wrist on May 28 crashing into the outfield wall when chasing a foul fly in Pittsburgh. The Reds still got value for him after the season, when they traded him to the Cleveland Indians for three players – George Culver, Bob Raudman, and Fred Whitfield. It was Cleveland club President and GM Gabe Paul who acquired Harper; Paul had been Reds GM when Cincinnati first signed Harper.

Harper had already proved himself to be an excellent leadoff man, and strong on defense at more than one position – he'd been the best second baseman in the Three-I League in 1961 and the best third baseman in the PCL in 1962. He was solid as an outfielder; looking back on his career as a whole, he had a .986 fielding percentage when playing outfield. One self-criticism he voiced over the wintertime of 1967 was in regard to his throwing: "My arm isn't as strong as maybe It should be. But I try to make up for it by getting to the ball quicker."[18]

In the American League, Harper was used more often in 1968, appearing in 130 games, but batting only .217. Once more he was critical of the way he was platooned, this time by manager Al Dark.[19] "It's no secret I was unhappy in Cleveland. I was platooned too much. I don't want to be in the lineup just because the pitcher is a lefthander. If you're going to bench me, bench me."[20]

In early October, the Indians offered Harper and four other players to the Washington Senators, hoping to acquire Frank Howard. It wasn't enough. The Tribe left him unprotected in the 1968 expansion draft. The Seattle Pilots had first pick and selected Don Mincher. After the Kansas City Royals picked pitcher Roger Nelson, Seattle used its next pick to take Tommy Harper. Bobby Mattick, the scout who had first signed Harper, was involved in the draft, working at the time as a special assistant to Pilots GM Marvin Milkes.[21]

Manager Joe Schultz believed Harper had not been used to best advantage. "Under happier circumstances," he said, "Tommy could lead the American League. Harper said that coming to Seattle was like getting a new life. He's raring to go."[22]

Schultz initially penciled in Harper to play second base for Seattle, and indeed he appeared in as many games there as he did at any other position, but he played 59 games at second and also 59 games at third base. He also played 26 games in the outfield, mostly in center.

The first game in the Pilots' history was played in Anaheim Stadium on April 8. The first Pilot to perform for the team was their leadoff batter in the top of the first inning. Tommy Harper doubled to left field. Next up was Mike Hegan, who homered. Harper thus scored the first run in franchise history. The team's first home game was on April 11 at Sick's Stadium, Seattle. The first Pilot to bat in front of the home crowd was Harper, who singled to the shortstop – and then stole second base, the first home theft in franchise history. He scored later in the inning.

There were a lot of stolen bases for Harper in 1969. He stole 73 bases, 11 more than anyone else in the major leagues. It was more than double his total in any prior season. "Joe [Schultz] just told me I would run when I wanted to. It was the first time I was able to run on my own without any signs."[23] The confidence Schultz showed in him bred self-confidence in Harper.[24] On May 24, he stole home. The next day, he stole three bases. "Tailwind Tommy" went on to credit Maury Wills and Lou Brock as players from whom he had learned, adding, "I was quicker than most, but I wasn't blinding fast. The thing that helped me the most was being quick and then learning the pitchers."[25]

For the only time in his career, Harper drew more walks than he struck out. He hit .235 (the Pilots' team average was .234), with an on-base percentage of .349. He drove in 41 runs and scored 78.

Harper never played for the Pilots again. Neither did anyone else. After just one season of existence, and in financial difficulty, the team was declared bankrupt on April 1, 1970. The team relocated to Milwaukee and were named the Brewers. Harper played for the Brewers in 1970 and 1971, and the 1970 season was "my best year in baseball."[26]

Dave Bristol was Harper's manager yet again, for the Brewers in 1970 and 1971. Harper truly excelled in 1970. He hit for a .296 batting average, leading the Brewers. He led as well in home runs (31), RBIs (82), runs scored (104), and of course in stolen bases (38). There were, naturally, fewer opportunities to steal bases when one hits home runs, or for that matter, extra-base hits (Harper hit 35 doubles, up from 10 the year before.) He ranked fifth in the league in slugging. This was his 30/30 year, and he was not only named team MVP but placed sixth in league MVP balloting. He was a reserve on the American League All-Star team and entered the game as a pinch-runner for Harmon Killebrew, but was cut down trying to steal second base.

Harper said that he'd simply worked harder to prepare for the season, staying late after every game in spring training to get extra batting practice. He was learning the pitchers better, Bristol said, and become more confident. Harper said that in getting a chance to play every day he felt "more involved with the team. ... I feel that winning and losing falls on me and I like that feeling."[27]

In 1971, Harper struggled to get going, and as late as June 20 had rarely even reached .200 in batting average. After being moved from third base to left field, he hit .317 in July and .343 in August, winding up the '71 season at .258. In midseason, on July 24, Rev. Jesse Jackson presented Harper with the Martin Luther King Jr. Sports Medallion co-sponsored by Coca-Cola and the local chapter of Operation Breadbasket.

The Brewers felt they needed more hitting, and worked out a 10-player trade with the Boston Red Sox, with George Scott and Billy Conigliaro as their primary targets. The October 10, 1971, deal netted Milwaukee Scott, Conigliaro, Ken Brett, Joe Lahoud, Jim Lonborg, and Don Pavletich for Harper, minor-leaguer Pat Skrable, Lew Krausse, and Marty Pattin. Harper had always hit well at Fenway, which was part of the thought process. One unnamed Red Sox official said, "We got rid of all our headaches."[28] Sox executive Dick O'Connell was quoted on the record, regarding some of the malcontents, "I'm sick of listening to some of these people."[29]

More than one newspaper article said that Harper "has a reputation at a brooder."[30] And yet, it was agreed near the end of spring training, "Harper is well-liked by his new teammates."[31] *Milwaukee Journal* sportswriter Larry Whiteside said, "Few people know the real Tommy Harper. He's the strong silent type, except when pressed, and prefers to let his bat and his feet do his talking."[32] Manager Eddie Kasko, who had been a teammate of Harper's in Cincinnati, was more interested in his baseball talent. "I'm going to play him at left, center and third in spring training. If I move Yaz to first, Tommy will be my left fielder."[33] Where he played in 1972 was center field, for 143 games. Yaz stayed in left and Reggie Smith played right field. Harper roomed with Luis Tiant (15-6) when the team was on the road. Sportswriter Fred Ciampa called Harper "the most exciting player to come to the Red Sox in years."[34]

Harper hit .254, with a .341 on-base percentage, and scored a team-leading 92 runs. He drove in 49. His 25 stolen bases placed him sixth in the American League. He might have attempted more steals, but Luis Aparicio batted second in the order and the pair worked on the hit-and-run more than just the straight steal. Harper also missed time to a hamstring injury in late June and a balky knee later in the season. Rick Miller often filled in for Harper in late innings.

And Harper came very close to seeing the Red Sox win the pennant. The year 1972 started late due to a work stoppage. The agreement was that when the season began belatedly, teams would play the remaining games on the schedule but not make up the games that had been lost. The Red Sox played 155 games and finished with a record of 85-70. They finished in second place, a half-game behind the 86-70 Detroit Tigers. Had the Red Sox played one more game (so that the two teams played the same number of games), and had they won that game, there would have been a tie. As it was, Detroit advanced to the playoffs. The Red Sox went home.

If 1970 was Harper's best year, 1973 ranks second. Yaz moved to play first base, and Harper took over left field. He played in 147 games, 140 in left field. And he got in his time at the plate; only Yaz had more plate appearances. It was the first year of the designated hitter. Orlando Cepeda was Boston's first DH and he acquitted himself very well, second only to Yastrzemski in runs batted in. It might have seemed like a role Harper, age 32, could envision for himself in 1973 or in the future. He took a wait-and-see attitude, to see how the new experiment worked out, but didn't see it as likely to be in his future. "I do know I hit better when I'm in the ball game all the way. I've never been much of a pinch hitter."[35]

Harper had a subpar first half, batting .216 in May and .180 in June, but then caught fire with .342 in July and .320 in August. By season's end, he had a .281 average (.351 OBP) with 17 homers and 71 RBIs, and — most notably — 54 stolen bases. That set a Red Sox team record, not surpassed until Jacoby Ellsbury stole 70 in 2009 (with Harper's encouragement all season long).

The Red Sox finished second yet again. After the season, Tommy Harper was named Red Sox MVP.

What might explain the ups and downs of the yearly stolen-base totals throughout his career? Or, for that matter, his home-run totals? It had to do with his approach to the game, he told the *Boston Herald's* Bill Liston before the 1973 season began. Every player has a particular job to do. "When I was with Seattle, they wanted me to run. So, I ran. That's what I was supposed to do. ... I can run when I feel like it on this club. I don't have to wait for a signal. But last year we (the Red Sox) were going more with the hit-and-run play and it was working pretty good, especially early in the season before Luis (Aparicio) got hurt. If you're effective that way, there's no sense in stealing." He added, "Three years ago in Milwaukee when I hit 31 homers a lot of things just fell into place for me. I was batting third or fourth in the lineup in those days and I was expected to try to drive in a lot of runs. But that's not my job any more. I'm just supposed to get on base and that's all I think about now. ... I just want to make a contribution. Like I said everybody has a special job to do and I'll bust my hump doing whatever that job turns out to be."[36]

In 1974, it was pretty clear that Cecil Cooper was going to make the big-league team. Where would he fit in? Would he dislodge Harper? Harper said he wished he were Pete Rose with the Reds because Rose had built a consistent record and knew where he'd be playing. "But every year I have to guess where I'll be playing." Red Sox manager Darrell Johnson said he'd be playing, for sure.[37] But as the headline of a Peter Gammons column asked, "Yaz, Harper Sign – But to Play Where?"[38] There was some thought of Harper becoming designated hitter and after Cepeda was released outright at the end of March, that's how Harper began the season.

He got off to a bad start, hampered by a number of minor injuries and performing significantly worse than the slow start of 1973: He hit .180 in April but only .109 in the month of May. He was still under .200 when June ended. Until mid-July, Harper was indeed the team's DH. From then on, he primarily played left field. Without a doubt, it was a down year. appeared in only 118 games, and hit .237 (though he had a .312 on-base percentage).

The Red Sox had a number of very talented outfielders on the way up – witness the home-grown outfield they fielded in 1975: Jim Rice, Fred Lynn, and Dwight Evans. They felt they no longer needed Harper and so traded him to the California Angels on December 2 for utilityman Bob Heise, getting such value as they could. In retrospect, one can see that the Sox were well set. At the time, though, the deal prompted "derision" – trading the very popular Harper for someone most fans "had never heard of."[39]

Harper had the opportunity to reinvent himself with Dick Williams's Angels. Williams wasn't sure at first whether he would use him as DH or outfielder.

Harper hadn't been surprised to be traded, but it was portrayed that he'd been dumped. He didn't want to demean Heise, but he asked, "How can you be a club's MVP one year and not make the lineup the next?"[40] Ross Newhan wrote that it was a jolt to his pride and that he resented the way the Red Sox had used him. "I don't know why they got rid of me," he told Dick Miller. "They could have gotten more, Evidently, I was the only one who lost it last year. I was the only one they sent away. I must have blown a seven-game lead."[41] Clearly, he was bitter. He was also ready to prove himself.

He hit consistently in 1975, starting stronger than usual but then dropping a few points each month as the season progressed. He DH'ed most of the time, but played 19 games at first base and only nine in the outfield. Harper was batting .239 on August 13, with 40 runs scored and 19 stolen bases, when the Oakland Athletics purchased his contract from the Angels. The deal was reported as being in excess of the $25,000 waiver price, but it clearly was a relatively small sum. The A's let pitcher Jim Perry go to make room on the roster for Harper.

For Harper, it was a move to a contending club. Oakland was leading its division at the time. In a classy move, the Angels' Mickey Rivers – who led the league with 70 stolen bases – credited Harper with helping him hone his craft.[42]

Harper contributed some to the A's, and indeed saw his team go into the American League Championship Series against the Red Sox. Harper appeared only once, in Game Two. Boston had a 4-3 lead and Harper pinch-hit to lead off the top of the seventh and drew a walk, but was held to the bag, unable to steal, and then was doubled off first base on a fly ball to center field.

Harper's last year as a player was 1976. The Athletics released him in November 1975. He got an invite from the Baltimore Orioles to spring training and made the team, signing as a free agent just as the season began, on April 9, 1976. Primarily he pinch-hit or pinch-ran, while DH'ing in 27 games. Once he played first base and once he played left field. He appeared in 46 games in all, batting .234 (.318 OBP). He stole four more bases, for a total of 408 in his career.

Harper's last major-league game was on September 29, and he enjoyed a 3-for-5 game with two doubles and two runs batted in.

There was another expansion draft and the Seattle Mariners were one of the teams being staffed. It would have been interesting had the Mariners selected Harper as the Seattle Pilots had years earlier, but it was not to be. He was not protected by the Orioles, but he was also not selected in the draft. On December 21, the O's placed Harper on waivers for the purpose of releasing him.

Harper was invited to join the A's in 1977 spring training, and hit .400, but was released on March 25, a casualty of a trade that Oakland had to make involving other players.[43] He took a position as a minor-league instructor and scout with the New York Yankees. That November, it was announced that Harper would take a position in the Red Sox front office working with Johnny Pesky and trainer Charley Moss selling advertising.[44] In February 1978, the Red Sox announced that he would work as an administrative assistant and minor-league instructor, in uniform during spring training and then working with their farm clubs during the season and in public relations during the offseason.[45] As Harper learned from a newspaper reporter, sometime after arriving to take his job, the team had listed him as their affirmative-action officer. He had no idea, and later told writer Bob Hohler, "Had I known my job would include that title, I would have stayed in New York."[46]

The Massachusetts Commission Against Discrimination had its eye on the Red Sox and had termed the team's efforts in hiring women and minorities to have been "minimal" in 1977. In May 1978, it was publicly announced that the team had assigned Harper to "oversee compliance by the team with affirmative action."[47] He had the title of assistant director of marketing and promotions and player coordinator for special events. Harper said that, as part of his job, "I deal a lot with the players and I make it my business to talk to all of them, especially the black ones. They tell me they've never had anybody they could sit down and talk to before."[48] Harper could share that very experience; in Winter Haven for spring training in 1972, he had found the region "so intimidating that he seldom ventured far from his room."[49] At some point, an MCAD investigator paid an unannounced compliance visit and, Harper said years later, "I told them the Red Sox were ignoring everything in the settlement. I told them it was business as usual and the Red Sox didn't intend on hiring anyone [of color]. It was all a charade." Though it was said to have not been known until Hohler's article in 2014, the Sox relieved him of his affirmative-action position – but kept him on the masthead as such.[50]

In October 1979, the Red Sox asked Harper to join the uniformed team as first-base coach. He served in that capacity for five years, through the 1984 season, under Don Zimmer in 1980 and then Ralph Houk for the next four years.

When John McNamara was hired as Red Sox skipper to begin in 1985, Harper was brought back in to the front office and named a special assistant to new GM Lou Gorman.

In February 1985, Peter Gammons wrote that "the local Elks Club in Winter Haven gives privilege cards to the Red Sox delegation – except those who are black. Believe it or not, there is still a segregated institution in this country, so Rice, Mike Easler, Tommy Harper and others can't eat there."[51] Harper acknowledged he'd been aware of this since 1972 when he asked Reggie Smith about the cards that the white players received but black players did not. Michael Madden said that some on the Red Sox saw this as "much ado about nothing," quoting Haywood Sullivan as saying, "There's nothing wrong, and there has been nothing wrong." Lou Gorman, however, promptly said the Red Sox would have "no further connection with the Elks Lodge and that he would personally rip up all the Elks passes on the team's premises."[52]

Harper recalled an incident when he was with the Brewers in 1970; at that time, the team as a whole decided not to attend a welcoming luncheon to which the team's black players had not been invited. That had not happened with the Red Sox – and Jim Rice was quoted as saying it didn't really bother him because he didn't want to go there anyhow. Harper said it was a matter of principle.[53]

That December, Harper lost his job. Madden basically blamed Haywood Sullivan, noting that Gorman worked for Sullivan. He wrote, "Harper spoke out only because he was most loyal to the Boston Red Sox, he was so loyal that he would risk his own career so that perhaps the Red Sox might see the light. Harper's loyalty was most basic, that no organization could ever succeed if it treats white people with more preference than blacks or Hispanics."[54]

On January 30, Harper filed a formal complaint of race discrimination with the US Equal Employment Opportunity Commission. "I'm not here to be a hero," he said. "I'm not out to get the Red Sox. What the Red Sox did was wrong and demeaning. ... The only reason I'm here is to retain my job, maintain my dignity and end all the whispering and reasons the Red Sox had given for my firing."[55]

He said he'd been ostracized by the team after the newspaper articles in March and given no work assignments.

*Globe* columnist Will McDonough, often seen as a mouthpiece for management, suggested in an aggressive column that perhaps it was that Harper had been brought into the organization by Buddy LeRoux, and now found himself on the outs due to the political infighting that had pushed out LeRoux.[56]

Harper sat at home in Stoughton, Massachusetts, for a half a year without a job until he found a position working at an auto-body shop just 200 yards from Fenway Park. In July 1986, the EEOC found that the Red Sox "committed unlawful employment practices" by firing Harper – and went further, saying that the team had "created and perpetuated a working environment that was hostile to minorities."[57]

In December, the two parties reached a settlement that forestalled a federal lawsuit against the Red Sox. The financial terms were, of course, confidential, and there was no admission of liability on either side, but the agreement was accompanied by public covenants that the Red Sox would undergo semiannual review of their employment practices to ensure nondiscriminatory employment practices.[58]

Harper also began to work for UPS and in the summer of 1987 worked running a summer baseball program for the City of Boston Parks Department. That November, the Montreal Expos hired him to become the team's minor-league baserunning instructor.[59]

A bit of an olive branch was extended when Harper was included in the 1989 Old-Timer's Game at Fenway Park in May 1989.

He was promoted to Montreal's major-league staff in late 1989 and served as Montreal's first-base coach from 1990 through 1992 and their hitting coach from 1993 through 1999.

In January 2000, Harper was hired to coach for the Red Sox under manager Jimy Williams. He coached for the next three seasons, through 2002. "This is like night and day," he said in February 2000. "This is a different atmosphere altogether. It's refreshing. It's not the same as it was. It's a lot better, and the Red Sox as an organization have done it quietly."

As Grady Little began his second year as Red Sox manager, he moved to bring in his own coaches, and the Red Sox fired both hitting instructor Dwight Evans and Harper in October 2002. Harper said, "I'm not in any way upset. I had three wonderful years here."[60]

A significant change had occurred under new ownership, Harper felt. "When John Henry, Tom Werner, Larry Lucchino bought the team, yes, there was a definite change," he said. "There are changes that maybe you can't see, but I see. There's a different attitude. There's a feeling of genuineness. … As a black person, yes, I do feel a difference. I can't put a finger on it. But it's not because they hired this guy or that guy. No, it's not that. It's not numbers. It's how well you're treated."[61]

After being relieved of his position as coach, Harper was named a special assignment instructor with the Red Sox, appearing in the *2003 Media Guide* as such, along with Dwight Evans, Johnny Pesky, and Charlie Wagner. He thus earned his first world-championship ring in 2004, and has since earned two more, in 2007 and 2013, though his title became player development consultant along the way.

Tommy and his wife, Bonnie, have lived in the Greater Boston area for many years.

In 2009, Harper worked closely with Jacoby Ellsbury on basestealing and saw Ellsbury surpass his franchise mark for stolen bases. Just a couple of days before Ellsbury broke the record, Harper approached him in the clubhouse, and playfully said, " 'I'm going to kick you in the knee,' … faking an assault on Ellsbury's leg. Ellsbury laughed as he feigned collapsing on the bench. Both knew how Harper really felt. They faced the field, and Harper placed his hand on Ellsbury's shoulder. 'I'm here,' Harper told him. 'Do it tonight.'"[62]

In 2010, Tommy Harper was named to the Red Sox Hall of Fame. As 2017 closed, he remained a Player Development Consultant for the team.

**Notes**

1  A considerable number of other players have since joined the 30-30 Club, including Bobby Bonds' son Barry Bonds.

2  Bill Deane, "Here Are Top Candidates to Join Elite '30–30' Club," *Baseball Digest,* May 1987.

3  Rich Marazzi, "Tommy Harper," *Sports Collectors Digest,* February 27, 1998: 80.

4  Earl Lawson, "Harper Is 3-Sport Athlete," *Cincinnati Post and Times Star*, March 2, 1962.

5  As sportswriter Billy Reed put it, he got his first major-league hit "even though he didn't mean to. Harper started to swing at [an Art] Mahaffey pitch, but tried to hold back. The ball hit his bat and looped into right field for a single." See Billy Reed, "Reds, Phils Switch Roles for Opener," *Lexington* (Kentucky) *Leader,* April 10, 1962: 8.

6  "Reds Ship Harper to S.D.," *San Diego Union*, April 16, 1962: 25. Harper agreed: "The pressure got me," he said a year later. Earl Lawson, "Harper's Record Rips No-Hit, No-Field Tag Off Reds' New Rookie," *The Sporting News*, March 9, 1963.

7  Jack Murphy, "Speaking of Gilman, Harper, Littler and Assorted Topics," *San Diego Union*, July 29, 1962: 147.

8  Steven S. Scheuer, "Beauties Parade Tonight," *San Diego Union*, July 14, 1962: 27.

9  Coincidentally, all three players completed high school near one another. Both Pinson and Robinson were graduates of Oakland's McClymonds High.

10  Associated Press, "Hutch: Reds Looking for Men to Push Regulars Out of Job," *Lexington Leader,* February 21, 1963: 18.

11  "Weddings," *Jet*, April 11, 1963: 39.

12  "Jesse Gonder, Tommy Harper on All-Star Rookie Team," *Atlanta Daily World*, September 25, 1963: 7.

13  Marazzi.

14  Ibid.

15  Harper told Rich Marazzi that Bristol was his favorite manager.

16  Associated Press, "Locked Up Red Pays Debt," *Charleston* (South Carolina) *News and Courier,* January 20, 1967: 17.

17  Earl Lawson, "Harper Power Secret Weapon; 'Call Me Bunter,' He Requests," *The Sporting News*, September 11, 1965.

18  Russell Schneider, "More Tribe Deals Due," *Plain Dealer* (Cleveland), November 22, 1967: 25.

19  "Tommy Harper Restless, Hits Dark's Platooning," *Chicago Daily Defender*, May 18, 1968: 16.

20  Hy Zimmerman, "Base-Burglar Harper Says His Bat Calls Tune," *The Sporting News*, July 5, 1969: 5.

21  Georg N. Myers, "The Sporting Thing," *Seattle Daily Times*, April 13, 1969: 29.

22  Lee D. Jenkins, "Schultz Lauds 2," *Chicago Daily Defender*, March 1, 1969: 16.

23  Marazzi. Ed Rumill picked up on this early in the season, quoting Schultz in May as saying, "I've turned him loose. … It gave him confidence." Ed Rumill, "'Go' Sign Sparks Harper," *Christian Science Monitor*, May 24, 1969: 11.

24  See Rumill.

25  August 22 was Tommy Harper Night at Sick's Stadium and every fan attending the game was given a color photograph of "Tailwind Tommy." See advertisement on page 75 of the August 21 *Seattle Daily Times*. Harper had two singles and a walk, but the Pilots lost, 9-8.

26  Ibid.

27  "Brewer's *(sic)* Tommy Harper Having Great Year," *Milwaukee Star*, August 8, 1970: 17. With the Reds, he said, the winning and losing tended to rest on the shoulders of Pinson and Robinson.

28  Tim Horgan, "Which Was Worse – The Ball Game or Sox Trade? Weaver Likes Both," *Boston Herald*, October 12, 1971: 33.

29  Clif Keane, "Sox Brass Sing No Sad So-longs," *Boston Globe*, October 12, 1971: 25.

30  Tim Horgan, "Harper Answers All Questions," *Boston Herald*, October 20, 1971: 44. The headline was meant to be ironic; to every question that Harper was asked, he replied, "No comment."

31  Larry Claflin, "Moret Top Disappointment on Sox," *Boston Record American*, March 25, 1972: 33.

32  Larry Whiteside, "Milwaukee Baseball Writer: 'Red Sox Getting 3 Real Pros,'" *Boston Globe*, October 12, 1971: 25.

33  Fred Ciampa, "First Things First! Yaz Belongs in LF," *Boston Record American*, January 12, 1972: 54.

34  "A Message from the Publisher," *Boston Herald*, June 24, 1972: 2.

35  Tim Horgan, "DH Rule Splits Sox Camp," *Boston Herald*, March 4, 1973: 38.

36  Bill Liston, "Harper Using Speed in New Fashion," *Boston Herald*, March 5, 1973: 24. Harper said that stealing bases works best when the baserunner sees the opportunity, not when he gets the nod from the dugout. Phil Elderkin, "Red Sox Harper – He Runs to Steal," *Christian Science Monitor*, April 10, 1974: F3.

37  Tim Horgan, "Gas Shortage to Curb Red Sox Crowds," *Boston Herald*, March 2, 1974: 17.

38  *Boston Globe*, February 16, 1974: 21.

39  Larry Claflin, "The Pressure's on Johnson," *Boston Herald,* March 3, 1975: 26.

40  Ross Newhan, "Harper's Out to Prove the Angels Got a Steal," *Los Angeles Times*, March 30, 1975: C9.

41  Dick Miller, "Angels Strumming Their Harps Over Harper," *The Sporting News*, March 29, 1975: 33.

42  "Rivers Credits His Thievery to Harper," *Boston Globe*, August 24, 1975: 80.

43  Owen Canfield, "Harper Accepts New Role," *Hartford Courant*, May 21, 1978: 4C.

44  Bill Liston, "Dodgers Pondering Tigers' John Hiller," *Boston Herald*, November 12, 1977: 8.

45  United Press International, "New Role for Harper," *Springfield*

(Massachusetts) *Union,* March 1, 1978: 50.

46   Bob Hohler, "Memories Still Haunt Harper," *Boston Globe*, September 21, 2014:  C1.

47   "Harper Heads Hiring Plan," *Boston Herald*, May 18, 1978: 48.

48   Larry Whiteside, "Harper Has a Mission for Sox, Blacks," *Boston Globe*, July 29, 1979: 77.

49   Larry Whiteside, "Jim Rice's Dilemma," *Boston Globe*, March 9, 1980: 66.

50   Bob Hohler.

51   Peter Gammons, "Ready or Not? Stapleton's Pact Poses Problems," *Boston Globe*, February 25, 1985: 32.

52   Michael Madden, "Tacit Complicity?" *Boston Globe*, March 15, 1985: 23. Harper later said he had tried to work things out quietly with the Red Sox the year before the story surfaced in the press. See Dan Shaughnessy, "Harper Sign of Red Sox' Redemption," *Boston Globe*, February 28, 2000: D1.

53   Ibid. Madden's story goes into considerable detail on the history. Harper also noted that Frank Robinson had quietly resolved a racial discrimination issue during the season the two were teammates in Cincinnati. See Gordon Edes, "Harper Finally at Home," *Boston Globe*, February 1, 2006: D2.

54   Michael Madden, "Harper's Firing" Sox Dishonor," *Boston Globe*, December 28, 1985: 29. Peter Gammons followed with a January 5, 1986, article entitled, "It's Time for Sox to Turn a New Leaf" in which he stepped back and looked at the bigger picture on the Red Sox. See also David Margolick, "Boston Case Revives Past and Passions," *New York Times*, March 23,1986: S1.

55   Michael Madden, "Harper: Sox Are Racist," *Boston Globe*, January 31, 1986: 39.

56   Will McDonough, "Sox Racist? Says Who?" *Boston Globe*, April 17, 1986: 51.

57   Michael Madden, "Harper's Charges Against Sox Upheld," *Boston Globe*, July 2, 1986: 67. Harper said the Red Sox had twice tried to reach a settlement with him, but that he had rejected their offers out of principle.

58   Larry Whiteside, "Sox, Harper Settle," *Boston Globe*, December 6, 1986: 21.

59   Dan Shaughnessy, "Harper Sign of Red Sox' Redemption."

60   Bob Hohler, "Evans, Harper Fired; Sox Moves Signal Little Is Secure" *Boston Globe*, October 5, 2002: G1.

61   Gordon Edes, "Harper Finally at Home."

62   Adam Kilgore, "Harper Waits to Pass Baton," *Boston Globe*, August 24, 2009: C7.

# MARTY PATTIN

### BY RICHARD BOGOVICH

"Being the best is great, it means you're number one. But being unique is greater, because you're the only one." This quote, which can be found all over the internet (reportedly anonymous, a bit ironically), applies to Marty Pattin in at least one regard: On April 8, 1969, he became the only Opening Day starting pitcher in major-league history to sport a Seattle Pilots uniform.

He was reportedly relaxed as that milestone in Anaheim approached, despite his general manager, Marvin Milkes, adding some pressure by declaring, "Beating the Angels will be my pennant."[1] Milkes had been executive vice president of the Angels. Regardless, Pattin rose to the occasion against California, the club with which he'd made his major-league debut the previous season. Pattin allowed two earned runs in five innings and the Pilots hung on to win, 4-3. It's no surprise that he seemed relaxed, because his nickname of "Duck" stems from his uncanny impersonations of a humorous Disney character. Yet it was his other nickname, "Bulldog," that reflected his tenacity and hinted at his ability to perform under pressure.[2]

Martin William Pattin was born on April 6, 1943, in Charleston, Illinois, home to what is now called Eastern Illinois University.[3] The city's population was about 8,000 then. He was the youngest child born to Clifton Wayne Pattin and Velda (Roberts) Pattin.[4] Wayne was a tailor, and during World War II he was a Navy Seabee.[5] Martin had an older sister, Charlotte, and an older brother, Jerry.[6] Wayne and Velda divorced about five years after Marty was born, and the three children were raised by relatives.[7] Mostly that fell to their grandparents, whose small home and family apple orchard sat next to Illinois Central Railroad tracks.

Marty demonstrated great throwing ability at a young age. "Nobody in the neighborhood messed with me because if they got me mad, I was deadly from a block away with a rock," he said in 2011.[8] His brother was among early athletic role models; Jerry was an offensive contributor on both football and basketball teams in grade school during the early 1950s.[9]

It was in baseball later in the '50s that Marty started making a big name for himself locally. However, an actual career in baseball didn't seem likely until a fateful day in May of 1953, when he was barely 10 years old. Marty was pitching for the fifth-grade boys at Charleston's Washington Elementary, and his team had lost all 12 of its softball games against the fifth-grade girls. Almost 20 years later, he told a local sportswriter that he had become so obsessed with developing his Donald Duck voice around classmates that he neglected his pitching. The writer's account reported the turning point on that warm afternoon:

> This day was no different. The score was 2-0 in favor of the girls. The bases were loaded and no one was out.
>
> "Please talk like a duck, Marty," the girls at bat shouted. Pattin looked around suddenly and caught his outfield sneering at him.
>
> He realized for the first time that he had to choose ... pitcher or duck, which would it be?
>
> Pattin flipped a coin to decide his fate. Heads, it would be pitcher and tails, duck. The coin read heads and Pattin went on to win the game.
>
> This columnist still has the two-headed coin he let Pattin use.[10]

Pattin's 1970 Topps baseball card noted that he went on to throw three no-hitters during his high-school years. One was as a sophomore for the Charleston High School Trojans three days after his 16th birthday. He struck out 15 on the Martinsville, Indiana, team in the process. A walk and two teammate errors kept him from a perfect game.[11] He also hurled a no-hitter in late June of 1960 for an American Legion team in Mattoon.[12] Just a week later he hurled another.[13]

During Pattin's junior year, Charleston High School coach Merv Baker arranged for him to work for a local philanthropist and restaurant owner, Walt Warmoth. Marty was employed 30 to 40 hours a week at Walt's Café, and Warmoth became a father figure to the rising star. Warmoth eventually told him not to worry about paying college tuition, and the Charleston native chose to enroll in town at Eastern Illinois University. Pattin continued to work at Walt's all through college, and the two remained close for many years afterward.[14]

One collegiate highlight for Pattin occurred with the Champaign-Urbana team in the new Central Illinois Collegiate League during the summer of 1963, after his sophomore year at EIU. Champaign-Urbana won the championship, and Pattin notched three one-hitters.[15] At the end of the season he was named a First Team All-Star of the league.[16]

In April of 1964, toward the end of his junior year at Eastern, Pattin married Vera Replogle of Charleston, and the couple received a memorable surprise when Pattin's

EIU baseball teammates stood in two rows outside the church and formed a long archway by holding baseball bats aloft. At the time he had a 4-0 record for Eastern's team, and he had made clear his desire to play pro ball as his career.[17] By season's end he ran that record to 10-3, and his 130 strikeouts were the most among all smaller colleges in the National Intercollegiate Athletic Association.[18] He helped his cause further that summer by earning mentions in The Sporting News for nine consecutive weeks. Reasons included winning three complete games in eight days,[19] stretching his Central Illinois Collegiate League career total of one-hitters to five,[20] and earning a First Team All-Star spot again, this time unanimously.[21]

The high point of Pattin's senior season with EIU came early, on April 23, 1965, in Normal against Illinois State. He struck out 22 of the 27 batters he retired.[22] Pattin's 1970 Topps card states that he graduated with a bachelor's degree in education. He eventually earned a master's degree from EIU as well, but he kept the big leagues squarely in his sights as life after college loomed. But despite Pattin's consistent success, major-league scouts were reportedly skeptical that he had the physical tools to reach the majors. "It made me more determined to make it to the big leagues and to stay there," Pattin said in 2012.[23] In particular, he never forgot a scout for the Phillies telling him that, at 5-feet-11, he was too short to be taken seriously as a major-league prospect.[24]

That kind of thinking didn't stop the Los Angeles Angels from selecting Pattin in the seventh round of the June 1965 amateur draft. After signing with the Angels, he made his first professional start on July 11 for the Double-A El Paso Sun Kings against the Dallas-Fort Worth Spurs. El Paso lost, 6-5. Pattin gave up four runs on 10 hits in six innings, but he wasn't the losing pitcher.[25] Manager Chuck Tanner was pleased, saying, "I think Marty Pattin did well in his first start in pro ball. ..."[26] It ended up being a very unfamiliar summer for Pattin. Though his 4.70 earned-run average was lower than the team mark of 5.19, his record was 0 wins, 6 losses.

In the aftermath of that rude awakening, it's understandable that during the subsequent winter a newspaper back home might have implied that he was developing a contingency plan for his career. "Marty Pattin, holder of almost every pitching record at Charleston High School and Eastern Illinois University, has evidently checked professional baseball out of his life for a while," reported the *Mattoon Journal Gazette*. "Pattin this week signed a con-

tract to teach industrial arts and physical education at Stewardson-Strasburg High School this coming semester."[27]

Be that as it may, by the end of April Pattin had accepted a demotion to the Angels' Class-A team across Illinois in the Quad Cities. In five starts, four of which he completed and three of which were shutouts, he bounced back with a record of 4-1 and a 1.26 earned-run average. He was soon promoted to Triple-A Seattle (Pacific Coast League), and experienced the minor-league high point featured on his first Topps baseball card in 1969: He won his first six games for Seattle, on his way to a 9-2 record.

As the following winter drew to a close, Pattin found himself facing two future Hall of Famers who'd each already appeared in multiple All-Star Games. He apparently couldn't wait to write home about it: "Palm Springs is great! We won our first exhibition game Saturday, March 11 against the Cubs in 11 innings. I came in and pitched the eleventh inning and got the win," he wrote on a postcard to Mattoon's daily newspaper. "Sure felt good pitching against Billy Williams and Ron Santo. Eisenhower was at the game."[28]

Pattin had a very different reason to be excited during the regular season: On May 29, 1967, he and Vera became parents with the birth of their son Jon.[29] As for baseball, Pattin spent the entire 1967 season with Seattle. Though his record for the 69-79 Rainiers was 12 wins and 11 losses, his ERA was 2.69, versus 3.01 for the staff as a whole, and his 140 strikeouts in 184 innings easily topped all Seattle pitchers. After 1967, he played only 10 more games in the minor leagues.

The first of those 10 was on April 20, 1968, against Spokane, and served notice that Pattin belonged in the majors. He gave up single with two outs in the first inning, after which he pitched hitless ball and struck out 11 batters, 10 in the first five innings.[30] He pitched well in three more starts, and then the Mattoon newspaper, under a very large photo of him wearing a California Angels cap, was delighted to announce that he would join the Angels.

The paper also noted that the team would be in Chicago, about three hours north, for the start of a two-game series with the White Sox. The paper also noted, for any fans looking to make the trip, that the second game would be played in Milwaukee's County Stadium instead of Chicago's Comiskey Park.[31]

California manager Bill Rigney was kind enough to accommodate travelers from Mattoon and Charleston by making the date of Pattin's major-league debut Tuesday, May 14, in Chicago before 8,708 people in the seats. Pattin became the Angels' sixth pitcher of the contest, won by the White Sox, 7-6, and held the home team in check in the eighth inning. His very first pitch was a called strike, thrown to second baseman Tim Cullen. Pattin's second pitch was a ball, and then he induced Cullen to foul out to third. Pattin then struck out pitcher Wilbur Wood. Shortstop Luis Aparicio, a future Hall of Famer, singled to center, but he was soon thrown out trying to steal.[32]

Three months later, on August 13, in Anaheim, Pattin experienced a top highlight of his debut season: pitching against Mickey Mantle. "I worked him to 3-and-2 and then my knees actually started shaking," Pattin recalled a few years ago. "I said to myself, 'Mick, it's either you or me. My best pitch is a fastball, so here it comes.' So I reared back and I threw him a high fastball as hard as I could throw it. He swung and missed it. Man, I could have floated off that mound. That was the greatest thrill. As a kid, I dreamed about that so many times and then to actually do it. ..."[33]

Pattin stuck with the Angels for the rest of the 1968 season. All but four of his 52 appearances were in relief, and though he had a 4-4 record, his 2.79 earned-run average compared favorably with the staff's 3.43. Nevertheless, he didn't remain an Angel for much longer: On October 15, was selected by the brand-new Seattle Pilots in the expansion draft.

The Mattoon newspaper printed a long article about Pattin's thoughts on the switch. For one, he looked forward to having a much better chance of being a starting pitcher, partly because bullpen duty proved to be pretty taxing on his arm, but also for financial gain. "You can't make any money relieving," he said, "unless you're a Hoyt Wilhelm." To make ends meet that winter, he had already started working as a substitute teacher at Charleston's Jefferson Junior High School. That was scheduled to last until December, at which point Pattin would continue pursuing his master's degree at EIU.[34]

It wasn't all downhill for Pattin in 1969 after that one-of-a-kind starting assignment on April 8. Toward the end of April he came within four outs of no-hitting the Angels on his way to a two-hit shutout – but his ERA of 5.62 was the worst of his entire career by more than a full run. He finished with a record of 7-12, and he had only two other losing seasons in his major-league career.

In 1970 Pattin had a solid season for the team after its sudden move to Milwaukee, posting a 14-12 record, completing 11 starts, and lowering his earned-run average by more than two runs. His winning record looks even better when one considers that the Brewers won only 65 games and lost 97. Though his record the next year was 14-14, he reduced his ERA a little more, to 3.13, thanks to five shutouts. One big highlight of the 1971 season came off the field, when his and Vera's second son, Jeff, was born on May 10.[35] His baseball high point was being named as the only Brewer on the American League All-Star team. He didn't get in the game, as manager Earl Weaver used only three relievers after starter Vida Blue went three innings. It was the only time Pattin was named a league All-Star.

In a major trade on October 10, 1971, Milwaukee sent Pattin and outfielder Tommy Harper, along with Lew Krausse and minor-leaguer Patrick Skrable, to the Boston Red Sox for a boatload of talent: Jim Lonborg, Ken Brett, George Scott, Billy Conigliaro, Joe Lahoud, and Don Pavletich.

Pattin joined a team that had a winning record. Boston's record in 1971 was 85-77 and they finished third in their division, far behind the pennant-winning Orioles. In 1972, the Red Sox were serious playoff contenders. Boston was in first place for more than 20 days and entered October with a narrow lead over the Tigers, whom they happened to play the final three games of the season. Boston lost to the Orioles on October 1 and then the next two games against Detroit, and the latter clinched the divisional crown in the process.

Still, Pattin helped considerably with a record of 17-13, four shutouts, and an ERA of 3.24. The 17 wins proved to be his career best. Along the way, he almost made history: On July 11, 1972, he took a no-hitter against the Oakland Athletics into the ninth inning. After he retired the first batter, Reggie Jackson singled. Pattin completed a 4-0 one-hitter.

In 1972, he hit the only two home runs of his major-league career. They were hit three months apart, both at Fenway Park against Milwaukee, both off former Brewers teammate Bill Parsons, and both were hit with a runner on base after two outs in the bottom of the second inning.

In 1973 the Red Sox improved their winning percentage again but finished eight games behind the Orioles in the division. Pattin split 30 decisions and had an ERA a run higher than in 1972, though his 11 complete games matched the second highest total of his career. After the season, the Red Sox traded him to the Kansas City Royals for Dick Drago. Pattin spent the rest of his major-league career, seven seasons, as a Royal. The location was fine with him.

"Coming from a small town and growing up there, I got used to the Midwest," Pattin said of this particular trade. "The first time I experienced going to a big city was in 1968 with the Angels in the Anaheim-Los Angeles area. It was a lot easier to get used to an area like Kansas City. I enjoyed playing everywhere but I was more comfortable in Kansas City and Milwaukee."[36]

Pattin's first season with the Royals was far from comfortable. He started only 11 games and made only 14 more appearances out of the bullpen throughout all of 1974. He won only three games, the fewest of his major-league career, and with seven losses his .300 winning percentage was his worst. His ERA of 3.99 was above his career figure, though the staff's was 3.51 so his wasn't too much worse. In the offseason he and his family still lived in Charleston, and shortly before her husband's move back home, Vera told his hometown newspaper that Marty was very deep in manager Jack McKeon's doghouse.

"Marty doesn't know why either. He really doesn't," Vera said. "I know Marty has even asked McKeon and still can't get a straight answer as to why he's not pitching." She was aware that her husband had struggled during April and May but said that happened to him almost every season. "I just can't help but feel McKeon has a personal dislike for some reason and neither one of us really can figure out why," she concluded.[37]

McKeon remained KC's manager for 1975 but Pattin also remained with the club. McKeon was fired shortly after the All-Star break and replaced by Whitey Herzog. Pattin continued to make most of his appearances out of the bullpen, which remained true for the rest of his career, but he completed five of his 15 starts on his way to rebounding with a 10-10 record and an ERA of 3.25. He had five saves.[38]

In 1976 Pattin had the last losing record of his career, 8-14, despite his best ERA ever, 2.49. Most importantly, he had his first experience in the playoffs. The Royals finished the season atop the AL West and Pattin pitched in relief in two of the five games of the American League Championship Series against the Yankees, both in New York. In Game Three, on October 12, he entered in the decisive sixth inning. Starter Andy Hassler left two runners on and none out. Due up was DH Lou Piniella, a right-handed batter, so Pattin, a righty, was brought in. Yankees manager Billy Martin countered by having left-handed batter Carlos May replace Piniella. Pattin was directed to issue an intentional walk to May to load the bases. With two more lefties batting next, Pattin was in turn replaced. All three runners soon scored, and it took the fifth pitcher of the inning, Mark Littell, to retire the side without further damage. A 3-2 Kansas City lead had turned into a 5-3 deficit, which also became the final score. Two days later, Pattin pitched in the final game. He relieved the second Kansas City pitcher, Paul Splittorff, with the bases loaded and two outs in the bottom of the fourth. Pattin faced Thurman Munson, who flied out to left field to end the threat.

In 1977 Pattin recorded the best winning percentage at that point in his career, .769, by winning 10 games and losing 3. He had eight straight wins from June 26 to September 9, including a nine-inning scoreless relief outing versus the Cleveland Indians on July 1. The Royals again topped the AL West. Pattin's lone appearance in the ALCS lasted six innings. It was at home on October 8, during the fourth game, against the Yankees. He replaced Larry Gura with two on and none out in the top of the third inning. Though one of those runners ended up scoring, and the Yankees already had the lead and never yielded it. Pattin faced 24 batters and was touched for two runs, one unearned. The next night the Yankees won the finale as well.

Each season from 1978 through 1980 Pattin pitched fewer than 100 innings, as he was shifted to more relief work, but in 1978 he had the chance to face the Yankees one last time in the ALCS. That was at home in October 4. After six innings the Royals led 5-0 but in the top of the seventh starting pitcher Larry Gura gave up two runs. Pattin took over with two runners on base and coaxed a popout to short by Thurman Munson. The inning ended when the

next batter, Piniella, lined out to center. Pattin, in turn, left the game with two on and none out in the eighth. Al Hrabosky allowed both inherited runners to score but the Royals still won by a final score of 10-4. It was their only win of that ALCS.

The 1980 season was Pattin's last in the majors. He made no starts and won four relief appearances without a loss. His final regular-season appearance came on October 1 versus Seattle. He gave up one earned run in four innings. Over his big-league career, Pattin compiled a record of 114-109 with 25 saves. He completed 64 of his 224 starts and had an ERA of 3.62.

Dan Quisenberry provided what little relief pitching the Royals required in sweeping the Yankees from the 1980 ALCS, and that resulted in Pattin finishing his career on a World Series team. The Royals lost to the Phillies in six games. Pattin pitched in the finale at home on October 21. In the seventh inning Kansas City's third pitcher, Splittorff, gave up a leadoff single to Pete Rose. Pattin came in to face future Hall of Famer Mike Schmidt. Rose was caught stealing, and Pattin struck out Schmidt looking. Bake McBride reached on an error, but Pattin ended the inning by striking out four-time All-Star Greg Luzinski.

Pattin was granted free agency three days later, and in the mid-November free-agent draft he was selected by California, Oakland, and Seattle, but ultimately nothing came of that.[39] When it was clear that he had retired, Walt Warmoth and his wife, Donna, gave Pattin the scrapbooks they'd kept of his mentions in newspapers over the years. Their effort filled 16 volumes.[40] And Walt's Café, where Pattin worked so many hours? In 1972 it had been renamed Marty's.[41]

In August 1981, the University of Kansas signed Pattin as head baseball coach for the 1982 season.[42] Pattin held that job through the 1987 season and, as of early 2018, continued to live in the area.

From 1989 to 1991 Pattin had the pleasure of following his son Jon as a first baseman and catcher for Class-A teams of the San Francisco Giants. Meanwhile, Marty pursued other baseball activities. Soon after leaving the Kansas position, he coached for two years in the minor leagues for the Toronto Blue Jays and then spent two years coaching for the Lucky Gold Star Twins in Seoul, South Korea. Vera died of cancer in early 1996. He remarried a few years later, but his second wife, Joy, died in 2009, also of cancer.[43]

Pattin had extra incentive to root for the Royals in their march toward the 2014 World Series. The Royals' Mike Moustakas had made headlines the previous year for calling 911 to report a hit-and-run accident. The pedestrian who was struck was taken to a hospital, and it turned out to be Pattin's step-grandson. The next time Pattin attended a Royals home game, George Brett made sure Pattin and Moustakas spoke.

"I said, 'Moose, man, I don't know what to say, but I thank you from the bottom of my heart,'" Pattin said. "I remember putting my hands on his shoulders and telling him, 'Moose, good things are going to happen for you. Just be patient.'"[44] And as many fans know, though the Royals lost the 2014 World Series, they were world champions a year later.

Marty Pattin died on October 3, 2018.

### Notes

1 "Marty Pattin to Pitch Pilot Opener," *Union Bulletin* (Walla Walla, Washington), April 8, 1969: 6.

2 Don Zminda, *From Abba-Dabba to Zorro: The World of Baseball Nicknames* (Chicago: STATS Publishing, 1999), 116.

3 At the time of Pattin's birth it was called Eastern Illinois State Teachers College.

4 Her first name was given as Velda in the 1920, 1930, and 1940 censuses, as well as in September of 1937 in the US Social Security Applications and Claims Index entry for her, but updates in April of 1949 and shortly after her death in March of 1993 indicate that her first name was Mary and that Velda was her middle name.

5 "Wayne Pattin," *Mattoon* (Illinois) *Journal Gazette*, May 30, 1998: 6.

6 Charlotte was born in Charleston on born May 18, 1938, according to her Montana Marriage Application dated August 9, 1976. The census taker visited the Pattins on April 4, 1940, and Jerry was listed as three months old, but the precise date of his birth was December 12, 1939, according to newspaperarchive.com/jerry-pattin-obituary-244765693/.

7 Tom Keegan, "Duck Tales: Ex-MLB Pitcher, KU Coach Pattin Recalls Playing Days," *Lawrence* (Kansas) *Journal-World*, June 28, 2011: 1B.

8 Keegan: 12B.

9 For example, see "Lincoln Plays Bennett Today for Grade Title," *Daily Journal-Gazette* (Mattoon, Illinois), November 16, 1951: 11; "Lincoln Gridders Cop Tournament," *Daily Journal-Gazette*, November 17, 1951: 5; and "Washington Defeats Lowell, 38-18, to Win Grade Tournament Crown," *Daily Journal-Gazette*, March 21, 1952: 5.

10 Harry Reynolds, "To Duck or to Pitch," *Daily Journal-Gazette*,

November 29, 1972: 4.

11 "Charlton Soph Pitches No-Hitter," *Daily Journal-Gazette*, April 11, 1959: 5.

12 "Pattin Twirls No-Hitter for Legion Nine," *Daily Journal-Gazette*, June 27, 1960: 5.

13 "Pattin Hurls No-Hitter in Legion Play," *Daily Journal-Gazette*, July 5, 1960: 5.

14 Keegan, 12B, blending in additional details from Bill Lair, "Field of Dreams: Panther Style," *Eastern Illinois Alumni*, Summer 2012, 6.

15 Ed Alsene, "Champaign-Urbana Cops College League's Title," *The Sporting News*, August 24, 1963: 41.

16 Ed Alsene, "Unanimous Four Top CIC Loop's All-Stars," *The Sporting News*, August 31, 1963: 37.

17 Jerry Parsons, "Sports Stop," *Daily Journal-Gazette*, April 15, 1964: 6.

18 Jerry Parsons, "Sports Stop," *Daily Journal-Gazette*, June 20, 1964: 5.

19 Ed Alsene, "Hanssen Hurls 2nd No-Hitter; Urbana Champ," *The Sporting News*, July 25, 1964: 40.

20 Ed Alsene, "Another One-Hit Game for Pattin, Fifth in 2 Years," *The Sporting News*, August 1, 1964: 40.

21 Ed Alsene, "Champ Urbana Grabs 5 Spots on Star Squad," *The Sporting News*, September 5, 1964: 18.

22 "EU Meets Illinois State in IIAC Twin Bill Today," *Mattoon Journal Gazette*, April 24, 1965: 5.

23 Bill Lair, "Field of Dreams: Panther Style," *Eastern Illinois Alumni*, Summer 2012, 6.

24 Keegan, 12B.

25 *El Paso* (Texas) *Herald-Post* box score.

26 Don Sanders, "El Paso Hustles but Sees Sixth Consecutive Loss," *El Paso Herald-Post*, July 12, 1965: A9.

27 Tom Hoppin, "Hoppin' Around Sports," *Mattoon Journal Gazette*, January 20, 1966: 7.

28 Marty Pattin, "Postcard from Marty," *Mattoon Journal Gazette*, March 17, 1967: 6.

29 Jon's birth date is specified at baseball-reference.com/register/player.fcgi?id=pattin001jon.

30 Hy Zimmerman, "Goose Eggs, Goose Pimples in PCL," *The Sporting News*, May 4, 1968: 33.

31 "Marty Pattin Is an Angel!" *Mattoon Journal-Gazette*, May 9, 1968: 13.

32 "White Sox Whip California, 7-6; Marty Pattin Pitches in Relief," *Mattoon Journal Gazette*, May 15, 1968: 6.

33  Keegan, 12B.

34  Jim Kimball, "'Glad to Leave Rigney Bullpen'," *Mattoon Journal Gazette*, October 17, 1968: 13.

35  "Marty Pattin Becomes Father a Second Time," *Mattoon Journal Gazette*, May 12, 1971: 13.

36  Lair, 6.

37  Jim Kimball, "On the Ball: Pattin in Doghouse, Wants to Be Traded," *Mattoon Journal Gazette*, September 17, 1974: 6.

38  Pattin "was named American League pitcher of the month twice during the 1975 campaign, in June as a starter and in September as a reliever," according to his Wikipedia entry, but numerous sources indicate that only the NL started issuing that award in 1975 and that the AL didn't follow suit until 1979.  For example, see baseball-alma-nac.com/awards/pitcher_of_the_month_award.shtml.

39  "Royals Inactive in Draft; No One Picks La Cock," *Sedalia* (Missouri) *Democrat*, November 14, 1980: 11. A special draft was held on January 20, 1981, for three remaining free agents who were still unsigned, namely Pattin, Bill Travers, and Bill Castro, but only Travers was selected by anyone. See, for example, "Sports Digest," *Wisconsin State Journal* (Madison), January 22, 1981, section 2, page 2.

40  Brian Nielsen, " 'Too Small to Make It' Pattin to Have Jersey Retired at EIU," *Mattoon Journal Gazette*, April 17, 2009: 13.

41  Tom Keegan, "Pattin Bleeds Blue," *Lawrence Journal-World*, October 13, 2014: 1B.  Pattin is mentioned after the article continues on page 3B.

42  Gary Bedore, "Jayhawks Sign Pattin for Baseball," *Lawrence Daily Journal-World*, August 4, 1981: 11.

43  Eileen Roddy, "Slice of Life: Former Royal Marty Pattin Gets Start Pitching Apples," *Lawrence Journal-World,* May 2, 2011; apparently not published in a print edition of this daily newspaper. See 2.ljworld.com/news/2011/may/02/slice-life-former-royal-marty-pattin-gets-start-pi/.

44  Keegan, October 13, 2014: 3B.

# LOU PINIELLA

## BY JOHN DIFONZO

Lou Piniella was a key member of the expansion franchise Kansas City Royals. Piniella earned the nicknamed "Sweet Lou" because of his sweet swing and (facetiously) his temper tantrums. As a member of the Yankees of the 1970s, Piniella was never the best player on a team of superstars, but he was always a fan favorite for his style of play, his clutch play, and his passion for the game. He was always greeted with a chorus of "Loooooou." Though he had low walk and home-run totals, Piniella had a reputation as one of the game's best pure hitters with a career batting average of .291. He was a student of the game and hitting. Though not the most gifted fielder, through hard work, Piniella proved to be a steady performer.

Piniella learned the game from every manager he played for. "Earl Weaver taught me some important lessons about winning when I played for him as a kid, and now Billy (Martin) taught me about team chemistry."[1] Piniella transmitted his desire and will to win to his players. He turned three struggling franchises into contenders.

He liked players who were like him, who had a fire in their bellies, cared deeply about the game and who could back it up. He took indifference and lack of emotion as not caring. He has been described by his players as tough but fair. "I hated to lose as a player," Piniella said. "As a manager, I hate it even more."[2] Piniella was named Manager of the Year three times, led seven teams to the postseason, winning one World Series, and won 1,835 games, 16th all-time.[3]

Piniella had a quick temper that he inherited from his parents. His mother once came onto the basketball court in a high-school game to argue a call. His father fought his own catcher during a baseball game. When his mother was interviewed by a local newspaper and the reporter mentioned that Lou was a wonderful "fella" except for his temper, his mother responded, "Temper, what temper?"[4] Early on in his career, Piniella referred to himself as a "red ass," a slang term meaning someone who is so intense in his or her competitive spirit that they are constantly on the verge of boiling over. As a player, he broke helmets and bats, damaged water coolers, and broke lights in the runway. As a manager, he kicked dirt and threw bases. His tantrums are legendary; they were sometimes used to motivate his players but sometimes embarrassed his family. He led the league in ejections three times as a player and three times as a manager. A Piniella childhood friend said, "Piniella would never be mad at you, he was always mad at himself. All the kids would tell you he would throw his glove, swing his bat. There are guys who are bullies and hotheads but he was just tough on himself, he never took it out on others. His teammates loved him."[5]

Piniella was a natural-born leader, as described by a childhood friend: "He had a magnetism. He was a down-to-earth guy, but certain people have that magnetism where they can get people to do things and energize people around him."[6]

Louis Victor Piniella (pronounced Peen-YAY-ah) was born on August 28, 1943, to Louis Piniella Sr. and Margaret (Magadan) Piniella in Tampa, Florida. Margaret's parents, Marcelino and Benina, had emigrated from Spain and Spanish was spoken at home. Piniella was taught English by nuns in kindergarten. He grew up in a close-knit Spanish and Italian neighborhood where neighbors relied on each other and made lifelong friends. Both his parents were accomplished athletes. Margaret was tall and strong, was an All-State center from 1936 to 1939, and played softball on the boys' team in grammar school and played volleyball. Louis Piniella was a star pitcher in the highly competitive semipro Intersocial League in West Tampa with his brothers-in-law Joe and Mac. Uncle Joe's son and Lou's first cousin is Dave Magadan. When Piniella was old enough, he served as the team's batboy. The Piniella family were baseball fanatics, discussing every nuance of the game, and this included Margaret.

Cigar making was a dominant industry in Tampa until the Cuban tobacco embargo in the 1960s. Piniella's parents both worked in the industry. Margaret worked as a secretary for the Morgan Cigar Company. Lou Sr. was a salesman of cigars, cigarettes, candy, and household drugs. When he bought his own distributorship, Margaret went to work for him, handling the bookkeeping.

Piniella demonstrated his athletic ability as young as 3 years old; he would hit tennis balls with a bat made from a broomstick and his mother would marvel at how hard he hit them. At age 13 in 1956, Piniella suffered a broken ankle hiking in California while representing West Tampa in the Pony League national baseball championship. Piniella played basketball – some say his it was first love and the sport in which he had the greatest talent; he was an All-American in high school. He held the single-game Tampa scoring record – 54 points – for nearly 40 years. Piniella was so good that opposing teams would foul him and try to provoke his temper into retaliation, perhaps to get thrown out of the game. His mother would not allow him to play contact football because her brother Joe lost a kidney while playing football in college.

One of Piniella's early influences was Jesuit High School basketball coach Paul Straub. Straub was a World War II veteran who had lost both his legs and had his right hand permanently disabled. Straub noticed Piniella's talent, saying, "He was one of the best athletes to come out of Tampa. I really wanted to make him a quarterback, but his mother wouldn't let him play."[7] Piniella said of Straub, "In sports, the will to win, to compete, it all starts early in life. And he was tough on me, which was good because I had a hot temper. He started to try to change that process."[8]

In Piniella's senior year he did not play baseball for Jesuit High School because of a dispute he had with the baseball coach on how he was being used as a pitcher. Piniella was not drafted and he went to the University of Tampa on a basketball scholarship. His basketball career was cut short when he reinjured his ankle jumping off a roof while avoiding police who were looking for underage drinkers.

Piniella had a solid freshman year in baseball and was signed by the Cleveland Indians on June 9, 1962, for a $25,000 bonus. He started his professional career playing for the Class-D Selma Cloverleafs of the Alabama-Florida League. Piniella started out poorly. His manager, former major-leaguer Pinky May, suggested that he worry about the fastball first and pull the ball. Piniella broke out of his slump and ended the season batting .270 with 8 home runs and 44 RBIs.

After the season Piniella was grabbed by the Washington Senators in the first-year draft. In 1963, he played for the Peninsula Senators of Hampton, Virginia, in the Class-A Carolina League, batting .310 with 77 RBIs and clubbing 16 home runs.

During the 1964 season, Piniella served in the National Guard at the beginning of the year and did not play for the Senators. He was traded to the Baltimore Orioles on August 4. He was assigned to the Aberdeen (South Dakota) Pheasants of the Class-A Northern League. Piniella was managed by Cal Ripken Sr. and among his teammates were future major leaguers Jim Palmer and Mark Belanger. The manager's 4-year-old son, Cal Ripken Jr., was the team's batboy. Piniella also played for the Orioles' Florida Instruction League team and got a September call-up. In his only plate appearance, he pinch-hit for Robin Roberts and grounded out Roberts told him, "Young man, I could have done that."[9]

In 1965 Piniella was promoted to the Elmira Pioneers of

the Double-A Eastern League, managed by Earl Weaver. Piniella said that Weaver was "the first manager who really intimidated me."[10] But he said Weaver was a great manager who instilled in him a passion for winning. Although they feuded in the majors, Weaver said of Piniella, "He was my kind of ballplayer, he got the job done. You can count on him to play every day, and you could count on him in the clutch, especially in the clutch."[11]

The following season, 1966, the Indians reacquired Piniella and promoted him to the Triple-A Portland Beavers. Piniella slumped early in the season, but finished the season batting .289 with 7 home runs and 52 RBIs. In the offseason he met Anita Garcia, a college student majoring in art and education, who had been Miss Tampa in 1962. It was a quick courtship and the couple married in the spring of 1968; they raised three children, Lou Jr., Kristi, and Derek.

In 1967, Piniella spent another season at Portland, batting .308. He spent a third season with Portland in 1968, again with improved stats (.317 and 62 RBIs) and this time got a September call-up. He played in six games for the 1968 Indians, but did not get a hit.

At the end of the 1968 season, Piniella had spent seven years in the minors and was 25 years old. In 1969 he was chosen by the Seattle Pilots in the expansion draft and felt this would be his last chance. That year there was talk of a players' strike. Jim Bouton was on the team and Piniella told Bouton he would stand behind the players. "That impressed the hell out of me," Bouton wrote in *Ball Four*. "Here's a kid with a lot more at stake than I, a kid risking a once-in a-lifetime shot. And suddenly I felt a moral obligation to the players. I decided not to go down."[12]

During spring training Piniella was dealt to another expansion team, the Kansas City Royals. On Opening Day, April 8, 1969, at Kansas City's Municipal Stadium, Piniella led off the bottom of the first with a double to left. This was the first hit of his major-league career and both the first at-bat and base hit for the Royals. When Jerry Adair singled to left, Piniella scored the franchise's first run. Piniella hit safely the next three times to start the season with four hits in a row, 4-for-5 for the game. The next game he drove in the winning run in the 17th inning.

Piniella credited manager Joe Gordon with helping him become a better hitter and being more selective. Piniella batted .282 and was named the American League Rookie of the Year, the first player to win the award playing with

an expansion team in its inaugural season.

In 1970 Piniella missed 24 games with a foot injury, but he adjusted to the abundance of sliders he was getting and improved his average to .301, tied for eighth in the American League, and had a career-high 88 RBIs.

In 1971 Piniella injured his thumb and missed 30 games, but came back to hit .304 in the second half of the season to raise his average to .279.

Always the student of hitting, after the 1971 season Piniella played six weeks of winter ball in Venezuela and was coached by Charlie Lau. Lau had Piniella crouch more and abandon his stiff "telephone booth" stance. Piniella said it helped him see outside pitches and breaking balls better. It seemed to work in 1972: On June 8 he was leading the American League in hits and batting .341, and by midseason was named to his only All-Star Game. Piniella led the league in doubles (33) and was second in batting average (.312), only 6 points behind Rod Carew.

In 1973 Piniella had a down year at the plate, batting only .250. He made a bad impression with new manager Jack McKeon when he arrived late and out of shape for spring training. Piniella was also unhappy with his contract and lost his outfield job to Jim Wohlford, a McKeon favorite. Now expendable, Piniella was traded with pitcher Ken Wright to the New York Yankees for Lindy McDaniel.

Piniella had a solid first year with the Yankees in 1975 and led the team in batting (.305), slugging (.407), and doubles (26). The following season he punctured his eardrum while bodysurfing in Puerto Rico during spring training. He had an inner-ear infection, suffered from dizziness and headaches, and was limited to 74 games and a career-low .196 batting average. He received a 20 percent pay cut the next season.

In 1976 Yankees manager Billy Martin employed a more aggressive style, which suited Piniella. In a game against their arch-rival Boston Red Sox on May 20, Piniella collided with catcher Carlton Fisk at home plate in an attempt to dislodge the ball, which touched off a benches-clearing brawl. Piniella badly bruised his right hand in the fight and later reinjured it punching a wall after making an out. That season he platooned with Roy White as DH but was limited to 100 games and batted .281.

The Yankees won the American League East and defeated the Kansas City Royals in the ALCS on Chris Chambliss's dramatic Game Five walk-off home run. The Cincinnati Reds swept the Yankees in the World Series.

In 1977 the Yankees added veteran Jimmy Wynn to be the team's DH. Piniella was retained as an insurance policy in case Wynn didn't work out, and he requested a trade. When Wynn was released, Piniella made the most of the opportunity and hit .330, a career best.

The Yankees clubhouse was divided into three cliques, headed by Reggie Jackson, Martin, and Thurman Munson. Piniella skillfully managed to get along with all groups. Adding to the tension was team owner George Steinbrenner, who would criticize the manager in public and would often make his own lineup requests. This era of Yankee teams would be dubbed "The Bronx Zoo" by the media. Tensions boiled over on June 18, 1977, in a nationally televised game. Martin removed Jackson in the middle of an inning, feeling Jackson had loafed on a double by Jim Rice. Martin and Jackson argued in the dugout and had to be separated. Jackson asked for advice from Piniella. Jackson felt that Martin had humiliated him. Piniella advised him to go to the hotel and to not fight Martin.

In midseason Munson and Piniella met with Steinbrenner and told the owner that the situation on the club was intolerable, that Steinbrenner should stop ripping Martin in the papers, let him manage as he saw fit, and let Jackson bat cleanup.

Soon after, Jackson was moved to the cleanup spot and the Yankees went on a winning streak and won the AL East. They met the Royals in the ALCS. Down two games to one, facing elimination in Kansas City, the players were told to leave their bags in the lobby in case they lost. Piniella objected to the implied defeatism and Steinbrenner agreed. The Yankees won the next two games in Kansas City to win the pennant. Piniella batted .333 in the series.

The Yankees faced the Los Angeles Dodgers in the World Series. With the Yankees leading, two games to one, in Game Four in Los Angeles, Piniella drove in a run and robbed Ron Cey of a home run that would have tied the game. The Yankees won in six games, punctuated by Reggie Jackson's three home runs in the finale. Piniella was relieved, "I don't think this club could take another week of this," he said.[13]

On July 19, 1978, the Yankees were in fourth place, 14 games behind the Red Sox. The clubhouse infighting got so bad that Piniella complained to the press that he did not want to be there. On July 24 Martin resigned and the tensions subsided. Around this time, Piniella stood up in the clubhouse and said, "Play like we know we can and we'll catch the Red Sox or be awfully close."[14] Piniella had one of his best seasons, batting .314, playing in 130 games at the age of 34.

The Yankees staged one of the greatest comebacks in history and tied the Red Sox for the American League East title to force a one-game tiebreaker at Fenway Park. In a classic game, the Yankees led, 5-4, in the bottom of ninth inning. By this time, the sun was setting and impairing Piniella's vision in right field. Goose Gossage walked Rick Burleson with one out. Jerry Remy hit a line drive right at Piniella. "I saw the ball leave the bat," he said, "and that was the last time I saw it. I knew if the ball got by me, the runner would go to third or maybe score the tying run. I couldn't allow Burleson see that I had lost it in the sun. I kept my composure as I searched for the ball backtracking as hard as I could. I wanted to give myself more room to find it. Out of the corner of my eye, I saw the ball landing a few feet to my left on the grass."[15] Piniella's decoy prevented Burleson from reaching third. The next batter, Jim Rice, hit a drive to deep right that probably would have scored Burleson from third. Carl Yastrzemski popped out and the Yankees won the AL East.

Piniella pointed to another defensive play in the sixth inning with the Red Sox up, 2-0. Fred Lynn was up with runners on first and second. The count was 3-and-2. Piniella figured that Ron Guidry did not have his best stuff and Lynn was a dead pull hitter, so he moved 15 feet to his left. On the next pitch Lynn hit a deep fly ball to the right-field corner where the perfectly positioned Piniella was waiting for it to end the inning.

The Yankees went on to beat the Royals three games to one in the League Championship Series. They met the Los Angeles Dodgers again in the World Series. In Game Four, with two outs in the bottom of the 10th, Piniella singled home the winning run to tie the Series at two games apiece. The Yankees won the next two games and repeated as champions.

Tragedy struck the Yankees in 1979 when Thurman Munson died in an airplane accident. Piniella gave a eulogy at his friend's funeral. In 1981 the Yankees again faced the Dodgers in the World Series; this time the Dodgers prevailed in six games. Piniella batted .438 in his last World Series, but he would blame himself for the loss because in his first at-bat in Game Three, with two runners on in the first inning, he pulled the ball and hit into a double play instead of going to the opposite field.

In August 1982,[16] Piniella became a part-time player and was named the Yankees' batting coach. In June 1984, battling a torn rotator cuff, the 40-year-old Piniella retired. The news broke in Boston, where the Yankees were playing the Red Sox. When it was flashed on the scoreboard, Piniella received a standing ovation.

His last game was on June 16 at Yankee Stadium. August 5 was Lou Piniella Day at the ballpark. He was presented with many gifts, including a bashed-in water cooler and two replacement fluorescent light tubes to symbolize the many he had broken in the tunnel at Yankee Stadium. Piniella remained with the club as first-base coach and hitting instructor.

George Steinbrenner signed his management team to personal services contracts so he could fire and bring them back in various capacities, and Piniella was no exception. Steinbrenner made him the manager in 1986. He promised Piniella that he would not meddle in his decisions, but that did not last. After two seasons as manager, Piniella became GM, chief evaluator of talent, manager again, then spent a year in the broadcast booth. Steinbrenner offered Piniella the manager's job for a third time but Piniella turned it down. He was interested in several American League jobs, but Steinbrenner blocked the moves by demanding compensation.

Steinbrenner let Piniella out of his personal-services contract without compensation to manage the Cincinnati Reds. Piniella effectively replaced Pete Rose after the gambling scandal. The Reds had some good young talent and Piniella felt they could win in 1990. Piniella surrounded himself with veteran NL coaches to help him make the league transition. The Reds led the National League West wire-to-wire for the first time in National League history.

After defeating the Pittsburgh Pirates in the NLCS, the Reds met the heavily favored 103-win Oakland A's in the World Series. The A's were managed by childhood friend and Tampa native Tony La Russa.

The Reds upset the A's. They started out fast in Game One with Eric Davis's two-run home run in the first inning and won easily, 7-0. In Game Two they scored the winning run off Dennis Eckersley in the bottom of the 10th inning, prevailing, 5-4. In Game Four, Piniella trusted his gut and made all the right moves. The A's led 1-0

late in the game, Piniella kept the bunt sign on with two strikes, and Herm Winningham delivered a single. The Reds eventually scored two runs to take the lead. In the bottom of the ninth, with his ace, Jose Rijo, working on a two-hitter, Piniella replaced him with Randy Myers, who got the final two outs to win the Series. Piniella was credited for getting the Reds over the top by the sheer force of his personality, his unwillingness to let up on his players, and his passion for winning.[17]

While the Boss [Steinbrenner] was hosting *Saturday Night Live*, Piniella was addressing the media. He felt he had proved to himself that he could win when given a chance. "I was a little bitter when I left (New York)," he said. "I carried a grudge for a while because of what happened. I knew I could do the job if I was afforded the chance to do it on fair terms. They let me do it here. In New York, we had a team in position every year I managed but there were always problems that were the fault of the players or the manager. When things got tough this summer, I got calls from the owner saying, 'Keep your chin up, you're in first place. Everything will be all right.' I'm not accustomed to those types of calls."[18]

Piniella added, "To win this thing is a great feeling. It's much more meaningful to me as a manager than as a player. You're more involved, more responsible. It's the total picture. You got to make decisions. Because of the hard work and responsibility, you appreciate it more."[19]

In 1991 the injury-plagued Reds regressed. They won 90 games in 1992 but finished in second place. Piniella wrestled Rob Dibble in the locker room when Dibble disagreed with the manager's assessment of his shoulder in a postgame interview. The whole incident happened in front of reporters and the camera. Dibble apologized and Piniella forgave him. The next night Dibble saved the game and Piniella came onto the field, threw some fake punches at Dibble, and then gave him a big hug. The crowd went wild.

When Piniella's contract was up in 1993, he did not want to return. Piniella had been sued by umpire Gary Darling in 1991 after accusing Darling of bias. Piniella felt that he did not get support from the organization, either publicly or behind the scenes. He had not been offered a contract for 1993 and owner Marge Schott was talking about cutting payroll.

The Seattle Mariners wanted Piniella, but he had concerns about the position. He had had financial problems from bad investments and needed the income. Piniella agreed to manage the Mariners and negotiated an unlimited travel budget for his wife. The Mariners were 64-98 in 1992, the worst record in the American League, but had a nucleus of good young talent. Piniella said, "Winning is an attitude just like losing is. We plan on bringing in a winning attitude and have it permeate the clubhouse."[20] In 1993 the Mariners finished 82-80, their second winning season in franchise history.

In 1995 the Mariners overcame a 13-game deficit on August 2 to tie the California Angels and force a one game tiebreaker. (This was the third in AL history and Piniella participated in two of them.) The Mariners won, 9-1, behind the pitching of Randy Johnson. In the best-of-five Division Series, the Yankees jumped out to a commanding 2-0 lead in games. Piniella remained positive and declared, "We are going to win this thing." The Mariners won the next two games, setting up the deciding game in the Kingdome. The Yankees took a 5-4 lead in the top of the 11th inning, but the Mariners won on a walk-off two-run double by Edgar Martinez in the bottom of the inning. Ken Griffey Jr. slid into home plate to score the winning run. The Mariners lost the ALCS to the Cleveland Indians, four games to two; Cleveland had swept the Red Sox in their previous series and their pitchers were well rested.

The Mariners remained competitive the next five years, winning the AL West in 1997 and the wild card in 2000. They lost core talent including Alex Rodriguez, Randy Johnson, and Ken Griffey Jr., but in 2001, they signed Ichiro Suzuki as a free agent from Japan and employed a small-ball offense. The Mariners won an AL record 116 games, topping the 1998 New York Yankees (114) and tying the major-league mark set by the 1906 Chicago Cubs.[21] The Mariners defeated the Cleveland Indians in the Division Series but lost to the Yankees in the ALCS, four games to one.

Although the Mariners won 93 games in 2002, they finished third in the AL West and Piniella needed a change. He was under contract and the Mariners wanted compensation if he departed. Eventually the Mariners worked out a trade of Piniella to the Tampa Bay Devil Rays for Randy Winn.

Piniella went to Tampa in part to be close to his family. His father was in ill health and his daughter was going through a divorce. The club also promised to increase payroll. Piniella's pitching coach, Stan Williams, warned him that he would be jeopardizing his Hall of Fame managerial career. The team was below .500 in each of Piniella's three years there, the first teams he managed that had sub-.500 records. Piniella hated losing and what made matters worse was that it was in his hometown. Piniella was frustrated that ownership did not increase payroll, and he and the club agreed to a $2.2 million buyout of the last year on his contract.

Piniella took 2006 off from managing and became a broadcaster for Fox. In 2007 he became the manager of the Chicago Cubs, a team with the worst record in the National League, the second-worst-scoring offense and third-worst ERA. But GM Jim Hendry was impatient like Piniella and the Cubs were willing to spend on free agents. The team started out 22-29. They were described as an "overpriced, slapped together mess" in the media.[22] Piniella seemed to take the pressure off the team by getting himself ejected during the team's sixth straight loss. Michael Barrett was traded shortly after a fight with Carlos Zambrano. But the team turned it around and won the division. They were swept by the Arizona Diamondbacks in the Division Series.

In 2008 the Cubs finished with the best record in the National League, the first Cubs team to make back-to-back postseason appearances since 1908. In the Division Series they were swept by the Los Angeles Dodgers.

The Cubs' high-priced stars underperformed their contracts and the Cubs struggled in both 2009 and 2010. The 66-year-old Piniella had planned to retire at the end of the season, but his 90-year-old mother was ailing. August 22, 2010, was Piniella's last game. He and Braves manager Bobby Cox exchanged lineup cards in a pregame meeting. It was Cox's last game at Wrigley Field; he was retiring at the end of the season. The two shared an embrace. Piniella said, "I cried a little bit before the game. This will be the last time I put on a uniform."[23]

Piniella remained active in baseball as a consultant and broadcaster. In 2013, the Mariners even tried to coax him out of retirement at the age of 70, but he declined. Piniella was on the Hall of Fame ballot for 2017 for the veterans committee and received 43.8 percent of the vote.

## Sources

In addition to the sources cited in the Notes, the author also consulted various articles in *The Sporting News*. Retrosheet.org, Baseball-Reference.com, and the National Baseball Hall of Fame clipping file.

## Notes

1  Melissa Isaacson, *Sweet Lou: Lou Piniella A Life in Baseball* (Chicago: Triumph Books, 2009), 50.

2  Hank Hersch, "Sweet Start for Lou's Crew," *Sports Illustrated*, May 5, 1986, si.com/vault/1986/05/05/629517/sweet-start-for-lous-crew, accessed May 1, 2018.

3  Piniella was named AL Manager of the Year in 1995 and 2001 with the Seattle Mariners and NL Manager of the Year in 2008 with the Chicago Cubs.

4  Isaacson, 24.

5  Isaacson, 25.

6  Isaacson, 11.

7  Isaacson, 13.

8  Isaacson, 14.

9  Isaacson, 19.

10  Ibid.

11  Ibid.

12  Frank Deford, "Sweet & Lou. Age, Success and a Good Woman Have Mellowed Mariners Manager Lou Piniella. So Whom Can We Rely on Now to Storm Out of the Dugout in a Righteous Rage?" *Sports Illustrated*, March 19, 2001. si.com/vault/2001/03/19/8094038/sweet-lou-age-success-and-a-good-woman-have-mellowed-mariners-manager-lou-piniella-so-whom-can-we-rely-on-now-to-storm-out-of-the-dugout-in-a-righteous-rage, accessed April 26, 2018.

13  Isaacson, 58.

14  Isaacson, 62.

15  Isaacson, 64.

16  Phil Pepe, "Piniella Preaches What He Teaches, and Then Delivers," *New York Daily News*, September 8, 1982: C29.

17  John Harper, "Lou Savors Sweet Taste of Vindication," *New York Post,* October 22, 1990: 48.

18  Ibid.

19  Mark Newman, "When Piniella Took Charge, the Reds' Charge Began," *San Jose Mercury News*, undated 1990 clipping from Piniella's file at the National Baseball Hall of Fame

20  Mel Antonen, "Piniella Likes Seattle's Talent: Priority No. 1 Pitching Staff," *USA Today*, November 10, 1992.

21  The Cubs' record came in a 154-game schedule, the Mariners' in a 162-game schedule.

22  Isaacson, 197. This was written by *Chicago Tribune* scribe Phil Rogers.

23  Gabe Laques, "Outgoing Cubs Manager Lou Piniella: This Will Be the Last Time I Put On a Uniform," *USA Today*, August 22, 2010. content.usatoday.com/communities/dailypitch/post/2010/08/cubs-manager-lou-piniella-wont-wait-for-october-to-retire-after-todays-game/1#.WuOHSUxFzkc , Accessed April 26, 2010.

# MAJOR-LEAGUE BASEBALL RETURNS TO THE PACIFIC NORTHWEST

## By Steve Friedman

When considering the formation of the Seattle Mariners, one should look to two key developments. The first was the long-term task of building a major-league-appropriate stadium in Seattle. The second was the departure of the Seattle Pilots, prior to the 1970 season, and the lawsuit it generated. The State of Washington and King County sued the American League for breach of contract and antitrust violations.

Talk of a domed stadium had begun in the 1950s. In 1957, Washington Governor Albert Rosellini said, "We in this area must have the facilities to accommodate big-time sports events, whether they be major-league baseball, professional football or championship boxing." He added, "I immediately will explore the possibilities of what this office can do to hasten the day when such facilities can be available."[1]

Dave Cohn, chairman of the board of Consolidated Restaurants and a major player in downtown politics, first proposed the idea of a domed stadium in 1950. For several years, Cohn's idea gained little or no traction. Seattle and King County officials were acquainted with the pitfalls of asking taxpayers to underwrite the construction of a multimillion-dollar stadium. The potential of luring a major-league team to the new ballpark might not be sufficient to draw voter support. In 1960, despite a hurried and somewhat ramshackle campaign, an omnibus bill that included a $15 million stadium bond proposal almost got over the hump. More than 146,000 voters, 48.3 percent of the voting electorate, favored the measure, but 60 percent was required for approval.[2]

Despite this early failure at the ballot box, the need for a domed stadium had become apparent. However, local officials were focused to prepare for another major project, the Seattle World's Fair of 1962. Any serious discussion of a domed stadium was deferred until after the fair.

By the mid-1960s, ongoing debate about the stadium had resumed, especially on its location and funding. With the success of the World's Fair and the region's ensuing economic boom, led by Boeing, the interest in bringing major-league sports to Seattle continued to amplify. Ongoing stadium proposals suggested multiple locations in Seattle,

American League President Leland S. MacPhail (l.) awards the Seattle Mariners' charter to co-owners Danny Kaye (c.) and Lester Smith. In addition to being a Hollywood star, Kaye co-owned a California-based radio network with Smith. (Courtesy of David S. Eskenazi)

A 'First Nighter' certificate from the Mariners' inaugural game at the Kingdome on April 6, 1977. A sellout crowd of 57,762 watched as the Mariners behind Diego Segui lost 7-0 to Frank Tanana and the California Angels. (Courtesy of David S. Eskenazi)

along with outlying cities including Tukwila and Bellevue. There even were proposals for a floating stadium situated on Elliott Bay.[3] Ultimately, however, the Seattle Center location won out, primarily due to its centrality. The State Stadium Commission endorsed it in December 1968.[4]

By 1967, the stadium budget had risen to $40 million. To finance its construction, public funding was included under the auspices of a set of ambitious urban infrastructure and growth proposals by King County. Known as the Forward Thrust package, it consisted of sweeping locally funded improvements encompassing multiple bond proposals totaling $815.2 million that embodied transportation, community housing, water issues, and other publicly financed capital improvements, including a proposition for a multipurpose stadium.[5] Voters approved a portion of the proposals, authorizing $334 million in bonds on February 13, 1968, including $40 million earmarked for the stadium.[6]

Despite financing approvals and the award of an expansion franchise, actual construction was delayed, as cost increases and the stadium site met public pressure. A new vote was necessary in 1970 to approve the location, which was soundly defeated.[7] With the project now in jeopardy, King County Commissioners stepped up and approved an alternate King Street site, near the International District and the eventual Kingdome location.[8] Finally, on November 2, 1972, King County commissioners, led by County Executive John Spellman, initiated the construction at groundbreaking ceremonies.[9]

The 1967 American League plan to expand was driven by its decision to let Charlie Finley's Kansas City A's to move to Oakland. The move left Stuart Symington, a US sena-

tor from Missouri, furious. Only after Symington threatened to attack baseball's antitrust exemption was Kansas City awarded a replacement club. In order to maintain an even number of teams, a second franchise was added in Seattle.[10] A key problem with this plan was that the new teams would begin play in 1969. This created an unrealistic timetable to prepare the team for success in Seattle.[11]

Knowing that this stadium funding measure was prepared for approval, the American League in 1967 awarded an expansion franchise to Seattle. As a condition, the city and county were expected to build a ballpark within three years. With the approval of the funding, via Forward Thrust, it appeared that they would meet this stipulation.

The new team, the Seattle Pilots, was underfunded and undercapitalized. Significant local support failed to materialize and the owners had to borrow heavily to keep the team afloat.[12]

These financial problems of the Pilots were, in many ways, the beginning of the history of the Seattle Mariners. On April 1, 1970, Federal Bankruptcy Referee Sidney Volinn declared the Pilots insolvent, just six days before Opening Day. They were free to move to Milwaukee, where a group led by automobile dealer Allan H. "Bud" Selig had become their suitor.

A few months before the Pilots departed, Washington Attorney General Slade Gorton and King County Executive John Spellman assessed Seattle's dire baseball situation. They retained Seattle attorney William Dwyer to represent the state and county in a legal effort to keep the Pilots in Seattle.[13] In creating his claim, Dwyer argued that a contract was created between the American League, on one side, and the state, county, and city – in effect, the people – on the other. He contended that the American League had violated this contract.

Dwyer further argued that the implied contract called for the American League to place and keep an expansion franchise in Seattle. In return, citizens, through their government, would fund the renovation of the aging Sicks Stadium, home of Seattle's Pacific Coast League teams, before supporting a $40 million bond issue to fund a domed stadium. When new facility was completed, the team would move from Sicks Stadium, to become the new ballpark's prime tenant.

In the fall of 1970, Dwyer filed a $32 million antitrust lawsuit against the American League on behalf of Washington citizens. He alleged breach of contract, fraud, and antitrust violations, even though baseball was exempt from prosecution under antitrust law.

The case did not go to trial until January of 1976. The court date was prolonged in order to afford the American League and Washington's government entities the opportunity to reach a settlement aimed at securing a new major-league team. In 1975, a plan was hatched to move the Chicago White Sox to Seattle. The plan assumed that the White Sox' owner, John Allyn, would sell the team to a group in Seattle, who would relocate to play in the multipurpose domed stadium under construction. To replace the White Sox, Charlie Finley would move the Oakland A's closer to his insurance interests in Chicago.[14]

This prospect looked encouraging until Bill Veeck offered to purchase the White Sox to keep the team in Chicago. After the American League initially vetoed his offer, it relented and approved the purchase in December 1975.[15]

With confidence that major-league baseball would return to Seattle within a few years, King County continued to build the multipurpose Kingdome. However, it was not without construction woes. In January 1973, steel towers that formed the core of the stadium's concrete piers fell on a workman and toppled other standing towers like dominoes.[16] Donald M. Drake Co., the original contractor, fell behind schedule and then walked away from the project in late 1974. They claimed they weren't being paid by King County for work beyond the original scope. The parties sued each other. Four years later, after the Kingdome had opened for events, a federal court ruled against Drake and ordered it to pony up $13 million. Despite financial relief for the Kingdome, the judgment did not cover the increased $27 million tab over its original $40 million budget.[17] Throughout the construction, local and project officials hailed the stadium for being economically sound, making it possible that corners were cut during construction to keep the project closer to budget. In the end, it is possible that this contributed to many of the later issues with the ballpark, such as roof leaks and tiles falling.[18]

The stadium was ready for major-league sports by 1976 and celebrated its opening on March 27. In addition to housing the Mariners, it became the home to the NFL expansion Seattle Seahawks and even hosted the NBA's Seattle SuperSonics from 1978 through 1985.

For baseball, the Kingdome, named for the stadium's lo-

cation in King County, Washington, was an early domed stadium built with multipurpose use in mind. The publicly funded stadium ultimately cost $67 million. In the future, repairs would exceed the original construction cost.[19]

The ballpark offered some unique features.[20] A large American flag was flown above the concrete dome. The AstroTurf carpet was rolled out by a "Rhinoceros" machine and smoothed by the "Grasshopper" machine after it had been zipped together. The stadium displayed home plate from Sicks Stadium in its Royal Brougham trophy case. For fan comfort, the stadium contained 42 air-conditioning units, 16 in fair territory and 26 in foul territory, with eight ducts in each unit. The units would blow air in toward the field, which meant fewer home runs in what would normally be a home-run hitter's park because of its short 357-foot power alleys. For speakers located within the field of play, a ball that hit a speaker would be considered in play.

When the lawsuit commenced in 1976, the American League awarded Seattle an expansion baseball franchise in return for dropping the suit. To maintain an even number of teams, a formal expansion proceeding resulted in a second team awarded to Toronto.[21]

The expansion vote by the American League, conducted in advance of any settlement, was held on January 14, 1976. American League owners voted 11 to 1 to place an expansion franchise in Seattle for the 1977 season. There were two conditions: sustainable ownership and a suitable ballpark.

The formal settlement of the antitrust lawsuit, however, was not reached until February 14. The Seattle legal team argued that the plaintiffs were entitled to damages, including reimbursement of legal fees. Considering

James G. "Lou" Gorman: from the Royals to the first general manager of the Mariners. (Courtesy of David S. Eskenazi)

Dave Niehaus: from broadcaster of the Angels to mikeman of the Mariners - "My oh my!" (Courtesy of David S. Eskenazi)

Dwyer's success in presenting his case and the overall damages to the American League if it lost, the league caved. It agreed to pay damages to the State of Washington, King County and the City of Seattle. It marked the first time a major-league franchise had been secured through litigation.[22] Sportswriter Emmett Watson of the *Seattle Post-Intelligencer* commented that the team should be named the Litigants instead of the Mariners.[23]

After the Kingdome was approved as a host venue, the American League awarded the Seattle franchise to a group of investors for $6.5 million.[24] The ownership group was led by entertainer Danny Kaye, who provided most of the initial financing, and Lester Smith. Kaye and Smith had built a radio network, Kaye-Smith Enterprises. Their ventures also included a concert promotion company (Concerts West), a recording studio, a film-production company (Kaye-Smith Productions), and a radio syndication company.[25] The syndicate owned several major radio stations in the Pacific Northwest, including KJR-AM in Seattle and KXL-AM in Portland.[26]

Other owners included Stanley Golub, a local jewelry wholesaler; Walter Schoenfeld, founder of the designer jeans company Brittania Sportswear and a founding partner of the Seattle Supersonics and the original Seattle Sounders soccer team; and James Stillwell, owner of Stillwell Construction, which was active in highway construction in the Pacific Northwest.

The formation of the Seattle Mariners was the beginning of a franchise whose general lack of success on the field has not necessarily matched its historical accomplishments. Despite never playing in a World Series, the franchise eventually generated interest beyond its accomplishments on the field. From unique plays to special players to a few exceptional seasons, the Mariners have earned attention beyond their on-field success, or lack thereof.

After the American League awarded the franchise, the ownership group set about setting up its initial management team in preparation for its first season, which was to begin in April 1977. On April 18, 1976, the team hired Lou Gorman away from the Kansas City Royals, to become its first director of baseball operations. Gorman held numerous roles with Kansas City dating back to 1968, when he served as their first scouting director. Gorman brought to the Mariners experience in building an organization from scratch.[27]

On June 2, the team named Dick Vertlieb as its first executive director. Vertlieb had been instrumental in the early development of the NBA's Seattle SuperSonics and NFL's Seattle Seahawks.

The lack of a nickname was resolved on August 24, 1976. "Mariners" was selected as the winning entry from more than 600 suggestions in a name-the-team contest. Multiple fans submitted the nickname, but the team determined that Roger Szmodis of Bellevue provided the best reason. "I've selected Mariners because of the natural association between the sea and Seattle and her people, who have been challenged and rewarded by it," said Szmodis, who received two season tickets and an all-expenses-paid trip to an American League city on the West Coast.[28]

With their executive team hired, and a team name selected, the Mariners began to prepare their product on the field. On September 3, they hired Darrell Johnson as their first manager from a candidate pool that included Bob Lemon, Joe Altobelli, and Vern Rapp. Johnson had been fired earlier in the 1976 season after 86 games with the Boston Red Sox. His real success, however, was in leading the Red Sox to the pennant in 1975 and an exciting seven-game World Series. Despite losing to the Cincinnati Reds, Johnson was named Manager of the Year by *The Sporting News*.

On November 5, 1976, the Seattle Mariners and the Toronto Blue Jays held their expansion draft. Each team drafted 30 players from the other American League teams, paying a fee of $175,000 for each player drafted. Existing American League teams were allowed to protect 15 players in the first round, plus three more after each of the first three rounds (and two more players after the fourth round).[29] Highlighting the Mariners selections was their first pick, outfielder Ruppert Jones of Kansas City. The Mariners began to develop their minor-league system by participating in the 1977 amateur draft. With their first pick, they selected Dave Henderson. "Hendu" became a popular player in Seattle, playing in parts of six seasons with the Mariners before settling in Seattle after his retirement.[30] Their sole minor-league franchise that year was the Bellingham Mariners of the short-season Northwest League. By 1978, their farm system had expanded to include the San Jose Missions of the Pacific Coast League and the Stockton Ports of the California League.[31]

Before the two drafts, the Mariners had already begun building their team as they purchased the contracts of seven players, including Dave Johnson, Jose Baez, and former Seattle Pilot Diego Segui.[32]

Spring-training games were played in Tempe Diablo Stadium, the same Arizona site used by the short-lived Seattle Pilots. It remained the Mariners' site through 1993, when they moved to Peoria, Arizona, where as of 2018 they continued to conduct spring training in a facility shared with the San Diego Padres.

On April 6, 1977, the Seattle Mariners played their inaugural game in the Kingdome before a sellout crowd of 57,762. The opposing team was the California Angels. The Mariners' starting pitcher was veteran Diego Segui, who, ironically, had pitched the final inning of the final game in Pilots history.[33] Segui allowed six runs in the first 3⅔ innings, and the Mariners went on to lose 7-0, the mirror-image of the Pilots' home-debut win against Chicago eight years earlier. Despite the team's struggles on the field, it was, at least and at last, baseball.

Leading off for the Mariners was the designated hitter Dave Collins. He was followed by Jose Baez at second base, left fielder Steve Braun, and cleanup hitter and right fielder Leroy Stanton. Bill Stein and Danny Meyer played each of the corner infield positions. Batting seventh was center fielder Ruppert Jones, followed by catcher Bob Stinson and shortstop Craig Reynolds.[34]

Jose Baez connected for the first hit, a single in the first inning off Frank Tanana. It was not until April 10, their fifth game, that designated hitter Juan Bernhardt hit the team's first home run.[35] The team was shut out in its first two games, but finally earned a win on April 8, defeating the Angels 7-6. For the season, the team finished 64-98. Thanks to a late-season collapse by the Oakland A's, the Mariners finished one-half game ahead of Oakland. They drew 1,338,511 fans, an attendance total they would not exceed until 1990.

That season, the team's offense was led by Leroy Stanton, who hit .275 with 27 home runs and 90 RBIs. The pitching was led by Glenn Abbott, who threw 204⅓ innings and posted a 12-13 record with an ERA of 4.45.

Newsletter about the King County Domed Stadium from 1973. (Courtesy of David S Eskenazi)

The Mariners struggled in their early years to build a successful product. After a relatively successful first year at the gate, attendance dwindled each year under the initial ownership group and never topped 900,000 after the first year. By the end of 1980, the team was cash-strapped and weary. While accepting a 1981 award from the National Conference of Christians and Jews, Stanley Golub quipped, "When Danny Kaye and Lester Smith came to ask me to become involved in the Mariners, they said it would be a new chapter in my life. Little did I know it would be Chapter 11."[36]

On January 14, 1981, California real-estate developer George Argyros agreed to purchase 90 percent of the Mariners for $10.2 million from the original ownership group. Argyros subsequently bought the other 10 percent for $2.9 million. Argyros, who had also just purchased Richard Nixon's former Western White House in San Clemente, California, assumed the Kingdome lease after negotiating a provision that removed his personal liability for bankruptcy.[37]

Thus continued a period in which the Mariners struggled both on the field and at the gate. They did not post a winning season until 1991. Highly leveraged and arguably inept owners failed to build a quality organization. Only in 1992 were the Mariners sold to a strong ownership group, which consisted of Nintendo and local prominent business owners. The group saved the team from a potential relocation and eventually created a stable and strong franchise with a lasting and positive effect on the community.

## Notes

1  Georg N. Meyers, "Build New Park or Lose out – Soriano," *Seattle Times*, May 29, 1957.

2  David Eskenazi and Steve Rudman, "Wayback Machine: The Floater That Didn't Fly," SportspressNW.com, May 6, 2014, sportspressnw.com/2184239/2014/wayback-machine-the-floater-that-didnt-fly.

3  Heather MacIntosh, "Kingdome: The Controversial Birth of a Seattle Icon (1959-1976)," HistoryLink.org, March 1, 2000, historylink.org/File/2164.

4  Ibid.

5  Ibid.

6  Ibid.

7  Associated Press, "Voters in Seattle Reject Proposal," *Spokane Spokesman-Review*, May 20, 1970.

8  Heather MacIntosh.

9  "Kingdome Groundbreaking and Construction," *Seattle Post-Intelligencer*, December 31, 2009.

10  Maury Brown, "The Team That Nearly Wasn't: The Montreal Expos," *The Hardball Times*, January 16, 2006, fangraphs.com/tht/the-team-that-nearly-wasnt-the-montreal-expos/.

11  Matt Blitz, "The Only Major League Baseball Team to Go Bankrupt: The Story of the Seattle Pilots," Today I Found Out, September 5, 2014, todayifoundout.com/index.php/2014/09/happened-seattle-pilots/.

12  Kenneth Hogan, *The 1969 Seattle Pilots: Major League Baseball's One-Year Team* (Jefferson, North Carolina: McFarland, 2006).

13  David Eskanazi and Steve Rudman, "Wayback Machine: Dwyer KO's American League," SportspressNW sportspressNW.com /2124781/2011, October 25, 2011.

14  John Owens, "Bill Veeck, Baseball's Barnum," *Chicago Tribune*, February 9, 2014.

15  Rob Hart, "Switching Sox: When the A's Almost Move In," SB Nation, November 16, 2012, southsidesox.com/2012/11/16/3649842/switching-sox.

16  Heather MacIntosh.

17  Seattle Kingdome, thisgreatgame.com/ballparks-kingdome.html.

18  Jordan Miller, "King Dome – Roof Performance Failures and Ceiling Collapse," Pennsylvania State University 2014. failures.wikispaces.com/King+Dome+-+Roof+Performance+Failures+and+-Ceiling+Collapse.

19  Ballparks.com, ballparks.com/baseball/american/kingdo.htm.

20  Ibid.

21  David Eskanazi and Steve Rudman, "Wayback Machine: Dwyer KO's American League."

22  Steven A. Riess, *Encyclopedia of Major League Baseball Clubs* (Westport, Connecticut: Greenwood Publishing Group, 2006), 802.

23  Ibid.

24  Baseball Club of Seattle LP, *International Directory of Company Histories*, Vol. 50. (Detroit: St. James Press, 2003).

25  "Lester M. Smith Obituary," *Seattle Times*, October 27, 2012.

26  History of Kaye-Smith Enterprises, kayesmith.com/about-us/history/.

27  Larry Stone and Associated Press, "Obituary/Former Mariners GM Lou Gorman," *Seattle Times* April 1, 2011.

28  Associated Press, "The Mariners Chosen as Name for New Team, *Eugene* (Oregon) *Register-Guard*, August 26, 1976.

29  MLB Expansion Drafts History, baseball-reference.com/draft/1976-expansion-draft.shtml.

30  Baseball Draft Research, thebaseballcube.com/draft/research.asp.

31  Baseball Reference, baseball-reference.com/register/affiliate.cgi?id=SEA.

32  1977 Seattle Mariners Trades and Transactions, Baseball reference, baseball-reference.com/teams/SEA/1977-transactions.shtml.

33  Seattle Mariners Baseball Information Department, From the Corner of Edgar & Dave, marinersblog.mlblogs.com/on-this-date-mariners-play-inaugural-game-4984af8e53e3.

34  Seattle Mariners Baseball Information Department, On This Date: Mariners Play Inaugural Game, From the Corner of Edgar & Dave, marinersblog.mlblogs.com/on-this-date-mariners-play-inaugural-game-4984af8e53e3.

35  Seattle Mariners, Mariner Firsts. seattle.mariners.mlb.com/sea/history/club_firsts.jsp.

36  Carol Beers, "Stanley Golub, 85; Jeweler Was Part Owner of Mariners," *Seattle Times*, October 10, 1998.

37  SPNW Staff, Mariners: Ownership, Organizational Timeline, sportspressnw.com/2163322/2013/mariners-ownership-organizational-timeline 9/26/13.

## SEATTLE MARINERS EXPANSION DRAFT

| PICK | PLAYER | POSITION | FORMER TEAM |
|------|--------|----------|-------------|
| 1 | Ollie Brown | of | San Francisco Giants |
| 2 | Dave Giusti | p | St. Louis Cardinals |
| 3 | Dick Selma | p | New York Mets |
| 4 | Al Santorini | p | Atlanta Braves |
| 5 | Jose Arcia | ss | Chicago Cubs |
| 6 | Clay Kirby | p | St. Louis Cardinals |
| 7 | Fred Kendall | c | Cincinnati Reds |
| 8 | Jerry Morales | of | New York Mets |
| 9 | Nate Colbert | 1b | Houston Astros |
| 10 | Zoilo Versalles | ss | Los Angeles Dodgers |
| 11 | Frank Reberger | p | Chicago Cubs |
| 12 | Jerry DaVanon | 3b | St. Louis Cardinals |
| 13 | Larry Stahl | of | New York Mets |
| 14 | Dick Kelley | p | Atlanta Braves |
| 15 | Al Ferrara | of | Los Angeles Dodgers |
| 16 | Mike Corkins | p | San Francisco Giants |
| 17 | Tom Dukes | p | Houston Astros |
| 18 | Rick James | p | Chicago Cubs |
| 19 | Tony Gonzalez | of | Philadelphia Phillies |
| 20 | Dave Roberts | p | Pittsburgh Pirates |
| 21 | Ivan Murrell | of | Houston Astros |
| 22 | Jim Williams | of | Los Angeles Dodgers |
| 23 | Billy McCool | p | Cincinnati Reds |
| 24 | Roberto Pena | 2b | Philadelphia Phillies |
| 25 | Al McBean | p | Pittsburgh Pirates |
| 26 | Rafael Robles | ss | San Francisco Giants |
| 27 | Fred Katawczik | p | Cincinnati Reds |
| 28 | Ron Slocum | 3b | Pittsburgh Pirates |
| 29 | Steve Arlin | p | Philadelphia Phillies |
| 30 | Cito Gaston | of | Atlanta Braves |

# JULIO CRUZ

## By Michael Marsh

Julio Cruz made a strong statement about his value during a Seattle Mariners home game against the Cleveland Indians on June 7, 1981. Cruz's glove and legs sparked Seattle in a 5-4 victory in 11 innings.[1] He tied a major-league record for second basemen when he handled 18 chances without an error in nine innings.[2] Cruz's speed helped seal the win. With one out in the bottom of the 11th and the score tied, 4-4, he singled, stole second base, and scored the winning run on a single. After the game, Cruz told a reporter a player does not have to be a superstar to help his team.[3]

Julio Cruz never reached superstar status, but he enjoyed a notable career. The 5-foot-9, 160-pound second baseman spent 10 seasons in the major leagues, earning the nicknames "Cruzer" and "Juice." Although Cruz exhibited weak hitting during his career, his rangy, acrobatic fielding and basestealing prowess helped him rise from undrafted free agent to steady major-league starter. He joined the Mariners midway through their inaugural season in 1977

and eventually emerged as a fan favorite because of his play and affable manner. He later helped spark the Chicago White Sox to a division title. Although a toe injury derailed his career, he had earned a place in baseball history. He joined a small group of players who achieved a career stolen-base percentage of at least 80 percent and at least 300 bases.

Julio Luis Cruz, of Puerto Rican descent, was born in Brooklyn, New York, on December 2, 1954, to Julio Luis Cruz and Lydia (Vargas) Cruz. He told the Chicago Tribune his father had left his mother during the eighth month she was pregnant with him. Cruz lived with his maternal grandparents, Raphael and Soledad Vargas, because his mother had to work.[4] She found employment slipping bubble gum into Topps baseball-card packs. His mother eventually remarried, but Cruz's grandparents insisted on keeping him.[5]

Cruz has several half-siblings. One, Ivan Cruz, played in the major leagues. An outfielder and first baseman, Ivan played 41 games for the New York Yankees, Pittsburgh Pirates, and St. Louis Cardinals between 1997 and 2002.

Julio Cruz's love for sports started while he grew up in the Williamsburg section of Brooklyn. An uncle, Ralph Vargas, taught a 10-year-old Cruz the fundamentals of softball and took him to his softball games at a park near Cruz's home. Vargas played in the outfield. Cruz played third base and struggled to lift a heavy bat.[6] Away from the park, he listened to radio broadcasts of Yankees and Mets games, collected baseball cards and played ballgames with friends.[7] His favorite baseball players included Pittsburgh Pirates great Roberto Clemente. Cruz especially liked Clemente because of his Puerto Rican heritage and generous nature. Clemente died on New Year's Eve 1972 when his plane crashed en route to Managua, Nicaragua, carrying supplies for the victims of an earthquake. Cruz carried Clemente's card in his wallet while he played in the minor leagues.[8]

Williamsburg, with plentiful factory jobs, attracted many Puerto Rican migrants. During the 1960s, however, job losses led to an increase in poverty, crime, and drug usage. The quality of life in the neighborhood sharply declined.

"I had two things to choose between in my life, hanging around on the streets or getting into trouble," Cruz recalled. "A lot of kids thought I was chicken for playing baseball, but they changed their minds when they heard I was good at stealing bases. I wasn't the best player in the neighborhood. I wasn't even the best player on my block. But some of the better players hung out with the wrong group, and I never heard about them again. ... We played a lot of stickball, that's where you try to hit a rubber ball with a broomstick, and stoopball, where you throw the ball against the point of a stoop, and running bases, where you run between two bases."[9]

His family, including extended relatives, fled the adverse conditions in Williamsburg. They flew to California in 1968 and settled in unincorporated Loma Linda, 60 miles east of Los Angeles in the San Bernardino Valley. Loma Linda is known for its high percentage of residents who are Seventh-day Adventists. Cruz's maternal grandparents practiced the faith. Loma Linda was incorporated as a city in 1970. At the time, it had approximately 10,000 residents.[10]

Cruz attended Cope Junior High School (now Cope Middle School) in nearby Redlands, California, during the 1968-1969 school year. He played on a Senior Little League team called the Orioles, earning all-star honors in 1969. Between 1969 and 1972, he attended Redlands High School. He earned all-Citrus Belt League honors in both basketball and baseball.

Cruz played guard on the basketball court for the Terriers. Despite his short stature, he developed good passing skills and scored with drives to the basket and shots from long distance.

Another future sports star, Brian Billick, played forward on the same basketball team. Billick later played tight end at Brigham Young University and coached the Baltimore Ravens to victory in Super Bowl XXXV.

Cruz played shortstop and second base for the baseball team. Redlands baseball coach Joe DeMaggio (no relation to the New York Yankees legend) recalled that Cruz displayed special qualities during his high-school career. "We played him at short in his sophomore year," DeMaggio said. "But I found out when I put him on second base that he had great natural talent, quickness, coordination, and leaping ability, all of which he developed through basketball. He was one of the best base stealers I've had."[11]

No major-league team drafted Cruz after he graduated in 1972. Instead, he played for the Redlands American Legion Post 106 baseball team for two consecutive summers. He displayed his speed during a home game at Community Field against Apple Valley in June 1972. The score was tied, 6-6, in the bottom of the 10th inning. Cruz batted with two outs. He hit a slow groundball to second and sped to first base. A teammate scored the winning run on the play.[12]

That fall, Cruz attended San Bernardino Valley College. He played on the basketball team during his freshman year. He eventually graduated with an associate's degree in liberal arts.

In January 1974, the California Angels drafted Redlands alumnus Juan Delgado. Delgado, an outfielder, had played with Cruz on the Little League, high-school, and American Legion baseball teams. He took Cruz to pickup games conducted by the California Angels on Sundays at the University of California at Los Angeles's Sawtelle Field.[13] After games, Angels scout Lou Cohenour treated him to hamburgers. Cohenour eventually offered to sign Cruz as an undrafted free agent.

Cruz hesitated to sign. He lived with his grandparents, who spoke only Spanish. He served as their translator. He worried about leaving them alone, but they gave him their blessing. He signed with the Angels.[14]

Afterward, Cohenour took Cruz to a sporting-goods store and bought him a glove and a pair of spikes as a bonus. Cruz later learned that draftees had received financial bonuses. The revelation foreshadowed his future salary battles with the Mariners and White Sox.

Cruz's undrafted status motivated him to succeed. He started his professional career in Idaho Falls (Idaho), a rookie-level team in the Pioneer League managed by Larry Himes. Himes played a key role in Cruz's career years later. The team paid Cruz $500 per month and provided $5 per day for meals. Cruz phoned his grandparents every day, racking up huge long-distance bills. Cruz batted .241 in 72 games and stole 34 bases.

Cruz liked to earn money while he played baseball, but he disliked other aspects of life in the Pioneer League. "I thought I'd get lost in the shuffle for a while," he said. "You got paid $500 a month at the start and you spent most of your time on buses. The cities you were at weren't too good and the fields you played on weren't too good either. "Thank God I had the ability to get ahead."[15]

The natural right-hander began to switch-hit after coaches told him it would help him advance to the major leagues. Cruz, however, struggled during the learning process. During his first attempt to bat left-handed, Cruz didn't know how to handle the bat when coaches took him to a cage and tossed balls to him. Cruz also had trouble during games. He was hit by pitches seven times. "The toughest part was the ball being thrown at you," he said. "I had nowhere to go. I got hit in the numbers, busted ribs. I took it personally after a while."[16]

The next year, Cruz advanced to Quad Cities in the Class-A Midwest League. He improved to .261 and stole 60 bases. Only three pitches struck Cruz that season.

Playing for three minor-league teams in 1976, Cruz showed significant progress. He started the summer with Salinas (California) of the Class-A California League, and batted .307 with 68 stolen bases in 96 games. His 41 consecutive errorless games set a league record. Afterward, the Angels bumped Cruz up to El Paso (Texas) of the Double-A Texas League, for whom he batted .327 in 13 games with three stolen bases. Toward the end of the season, Cruz played 20 games with Triple-A Salt Lake City (Pacific Coast League). He batted .246 and stole 12 bases. Altogether, Cruz stole 83 bases.

Cruz displayed feisty behavior on the field during his time with Salt Lake City. The club hosted a best-of-five championship series against Hawaii, a San Diego Padres affiliate. In the fifth and deciding game, Honolulu's Dave Hilton charged the pitcher's mound after he struck out in the third inning. Both benches cleared and a brawl ensued. The *Honolulu Advertiser* said Cruz gave Hilton a cheap shot

and was ejected from the game. Before he left the field, Cruz argued with opposing pitcher Mike DuPree. DuPree invited him to settle the dispute. Cruz accepted the invite. Both benches cleared again. Umpires restored order. Honolulu won the game, 3-2, and took the series.[17]

Though Cruz had emerged as one of the top prospects in the Angels farm system, the club left him unprotected in the November 1976 expansion draft. That decision helped Cruz because Jerry Remy had established himself as a solid starting second baseman for the parent club. The newly formed Mariners chose Cruz in the fifth round. They signed him to a one-year contract a month later.

Instead of competing with Remy, Cruz got a chance to shine for a brand-new team. He played well during spring training in 1977. The club, however, thought he needed more seasoning at Triple A, choosing Jose Baez to start at second base and trading for Larry Milbourne, a utility player. Because the organization did not have a Triple-A affiliate yet, it sent Cruz to Honolulu.

Cruz worried that the fans in Hawaii would boo him because of the rhubarb the previous season. His fear proved correct. The fans booed him on Opening Day.[18] Cruz eventually won them over with a .366 batting average and 47 stolen bases in 75 games.

He found another benefit to playing in Hawaii. He met Rebecca Nickerson there. They married several years later. Three sons were born to the union: Austin, Alexander, and Jourdan. Rebecca died in 2007.[19]

Cruz's statistics proved irresistible for the Mariners. While Hawaii was playing in Phoenix, the Mariners called up Cruz on July 4, 1977. The next night the Mariners hosted the Chicago White Sox in the Kingdome. The Mariners put Cruz in the leadoff spot for his debut. He hit two singles and scored a run as the Mariners lost, 6-2.

On July 14 Cruz's mother and 35 other relatives and friends traveled from Loma Linda to Anaheim Stadium to see the Mariners play the Angels. Cruz asked teammates for extra passes in order to accommodate the group. He rewarded the travelers when he hit a single and triple and scored twice to help the Mariners win, 4-1.[20]

Cruz finished the 1977 season with a .256 batting average and 15 stolen bases in 60 games. Early in the next season, he beat out Baez for the starting job. Cruz slumped to .235, but stole a career-high 59 bases, second in the American League behind Ron LeFlore's 68 for the Detroit Tigers. Cruz also led major-league second basemen with a .987 fielding percentage.

During the early years of the Mariners, Cruz and center fielder Rupert Jones helped each other on offense. Cruz most often batted leadoff and Jones batted fourth or fifth. When Cruz reached base, he signaled to Jones to indicate when he would run. "I would put a finger in my ear hole, and that meant I would go on that pitch," Cruz said. "He would take the pitch or fake a bunt, just to give me that little edge. But it gave him a little edge, too, because the other teams all knew I was going to run and they would throw him fastballs."[21]

In 1979, Cruz achieved two additional career highs: a .271 batting average and a .363 on-base percentage, but missed 54 games after tearing ligaments near his left thumb. He tripped while running to first base in a game against the visiting Tigers on June 4. Playing in only 107 games, Cruz still stole 49 bases.

In an assessment of Cruz printed in *The Sporting News* at the beginning of the 1979 season, Seattle sportswriter Hy Zimmerman acknowledged that Cruz occasionally got picked off first and thrown out on steal attempts, but praised him anyway. "In trade talks, his name crops up quickly," Zimmerman wrote. "But were the M's to trade him, there's a chance they might have to close the Kingdome's doors. For Julio not only swipes bases, he steals hits from the enemy. His specialty is the diving stop on a sure hit and an almost simultaneous leap to his feet for the throw. Whereas Rupe Jones was the instant hero of the fans in 1977, that mantle now belongs to Julio, a bubbling, dynamic young man."[22]

After the 1979 season Cruz filed for an arbitration hearing. He requested $130,000. The Mariners offered $95,000. The arbitrator sided with the Mariners. Cruz also filed for arbitration after the next three seasons, winning only once. The hearings, which occasionally became contentious, helped poison his relationship with the team's management.

In 1980 Cruz batted an anemic .209. He still stole 45 bases. During the season, Steve Wulf described Cruz in an article for *Sports Illustrated*: "He is a great lover of basketball – he says he can dunk even though he's 5'9" – so he likes to take a jumping pivot at second base even when it's not necessary. That's given him a hot-dog reputation he doesn't mind. … When he first came up, Julio had a

tendency to take out his frustrations by swinging his bat at defenseless sinks and batting helmets. He has since calmed down. He is also one of the more popular Mariners, especially with children. 'No child within reach of Julio escapes being swept into his arms,' says Jack Carvalho, Seattle's promotion director."[23]

Cruz had established himself as a solid big-league player. Although he never won a Gold Glove, he ranked among the best-fielding second basemen in the majors. His inconsistent hitting, however, hampered his career. He explained the batting issues. "I was a good hitter in the minor leagues; twice I hit .300. I didn't have any theories about hitting or anything, I just got up to bat and hit the ball. But when I got to the big leagues with the Mariners, they had instructors for everything. They had an infield instructor, a base-running instructor, a hitting instructor, and they all wanted me to do things differently than I had been doing. What I had been doing had gotten me to the big leagues, but I figured since they were already in the big leagues, they must know what they're doing. I tried doing things their way.

"If I had been smarter, I would have told them to let me hit my way instead of changing, but I was really intimidated. I tried to do everything everybody told me to. I got very confused. I had no consistent way of hitting. I would change stances for different pitchers. I even wanted to change bats for different pitchers. I figured, if the pitcher can change baseballs because one didn't feel good, I should change bats."[24]

Meanwhile, the Mariners generated woeful records during their first several years. They finished the 1977 season under manager Darrell Johnson with a 64-98 record. From 1978 to 1980, they finished 56-104, 67-95, and 59-103.

Johnson was fired in August 1980, and was replaced by Maury Wills, the majors' third African-American manager. The club hoped Wills, formerly an outstanding basestealer for the Los Angeles Dodgers, would provide a spark for the team. The opposite took place. Wills alienated nearly everyone on the team with his erratic behavior and incompetent leadership. In one awkward episode during a game against the Oakland A's, Wills ordered Cruz to hold Rickey Henderson on second like a first baseman. Henderson stole third anyway.[25] The Mariners fired Wills in May 1981 and replaced him with Rene Lachemann.

Despite Wills' conduct, Cruz liked him. Wills had taken an interest in Cruz, teaching him how to steal against left-handed pitchers. Wills told him: "When they look at you and turn away, their next move is to go to first base. When they are looking straight at you, they are going to pitch."[26]

In 1981 Cruz rebounded by batting .256 and stealing 43 bases in a season shortened by a players' strike. On June 11 he tied the American League record for consecutive steals without being thrown out, getting number 32 in an 8-2 Mariners victory over the visiting Baltimore Orioles.[27] The players strike began the next day.

The strike ended on August 9. The next day Cruz tried for number 33 in a row, but Angels catcher Ed Ott gunned him down to end the streak.

Cruz batted .242, notched a .316 on-base percentage, and stole 46 bases in 1982. He tied for second among American League second basemen with a .987 fielding average, just .001 under Detroit's Lou Whitaker. On May 6 he helped Mariners pitcher Gaylord Perry defeat the visiting New York Yankees, 7-3, and earn his 300th career win. Cruz scooped up a grounder by Willie Randolph and fired to first for the final out. "The biggest thrill I had when I was playing with the Mariners was being on the field when Gaylord Perry, the greatest spitball pitcher of all time, won his three-hundredth game. Man, when there were two outs, I was really nervous. I kept reminding myself, Cruiser, if the batter hits it to you, make sure you grab the ball on the dry side."[28]

Cruz and shortstop Todd Cruz (no relation) earned plaudits in the New York Times for a spectacular game-ending double play on July 21, 1982, against the Yankees at Yankee Stadium. The Mariners led 6-5 in the bottom of the 12th inning. With one out and runners on first and second, Dave Winfield hit a sharp grounder up the middle. Cruz was playing toward the right side, but scurried to his left. He dived, backhanded the ball, and tossed it to the shortstop, who got the force out and threw out Winfield on a very close play to end the game.[29]

That season Cruz also displayed kindness off the field. A woman told Cruz that she had cancer during their chat at the Seattle-Tacoma International Airport. Cruz came to the hospital for her next chemotherapy session, brought her a Julio Cruz baseball shirt and tickets for her family to attend a Mariners game. Years later, the woman's son, Skip Kulle, wrote about Cruz's kindness for the *Seattle Times*. "Julio became a regular visitor to my mother's bedside until she succumbed to cancer in December of that

year. Sitting amidst our family at her memorial service was Julio Cruz."[30]

On May 24, 1983, Cruz swiped a team-record four bases against the visiting Indians.[31] The Mariners, however, figured the team would lose Cruz in free agency without compensation after the season. They traded Cruz to the White Sox for second baseman Tony Bernazard on June 15. Cruz had finalized the purchase of a home in Bellevue, Washington, on the same day. He left with a then club-record 290 steals. (That record has since broken by Ichiro Suzuki, who stole 438 during his first stint with the Mariners, from 2001 to 2012.)

The White Sox announced the trade on the Comiskey Park scoreboard during their game against the California Angels. Bernazard was a fan favorite, and White Sox fans in the crowd of 24,561 booed at the news. The White Sox had a 28-32 record at the time of the trade. Cruz helped spark the team to a 71-31 record after the trade. The White Sox won the American League West championship by 20 games over Kansas City. Cruz played in 99 games, batting .251 with 40 RBIs and 24 stolen bases. He scored the winning run in the clinching game against the visiting Mariners at Comiskey Park on September 17, on a sacrifice fly by Harold Baines.

"As I scored, everyone broke out of the dugout and ran onto the field to celebrate," Cruz recalled. "Before I joined that celebration, I looked into the Mariner dugout. Everybody was sitting on the top step watching the Chicago players jumping up and down. At that moment, when I was so happy, I was also sad for them. I had played with those guys for six years, and I wished very much that they could all experience the same feelings I had running through my body."[32]

The White Sox lost the American League Championship Series, three games to one, to the eventual World Series winner Baltimore Orioles. Todd Cruz, who had moved on from Seattle to Baltimore in June, started at third base for the Orioles. The Orioles pitchers stifled the Sox bats, but Julio Cruz batted .333 and reached base three times on walks for a .467 on-base percentage.

After the season, Cruz filed for free agency. Tense negotiations with the White Sox dragged on for two months. Cruz ended talks with the team and negotiated with the Angels. After White Sox broadcaster Hawk Harrelson talked to Cruz, the latter signed a six-year contract with Chicago worth between an estimated $3.6 million and

$4.8 million.

Cruz received a big payday. After he signed the contract, however, his career declined. In 1984 he slumped to .222 with 14 stolen bases. He made a career-high 18 errors. Fans booed Cruz.[33] The White Sox finished the season 74-88.

In 1985 Cruz slipped even further as an injured right big toe affected his play. He could not push off his right foot. He batted only .197 and stole 8 bases in 91 games. The team shifted him to platoon status with Scott Fletcher.

Cruz gave one of his final great plays early in the season against the Yankees' Dave Winfield at Comiskey Park. Cruz dived behind second base to grab a groundball by Winfield, and flipped the ball out of his mitt to short-stop Ozzie Guillen. Guillen caught the ball barehanded, tagged second for the force and gunned the ball to first to beat Winfield. The White Sox won, 5-4, in 11 innings.[34]

Cruz showed promise in 1986 when he hit .359 during spring training, but he suffered a leg injury early in the season and landed on the disabled list.[35] He batted only .215 and stole seven bases in 81 games.

From 1984 through 1986 Cruz played in only 315 of a possible 486 games. In 1985 and 1986 he landed on the disabled list three times. After three toe operations, he had lost his speed.[36]

By October 1986, Larry Himes, who had managed Cruz at Idaho Falls was the White Sox general manager. He traded for second baseman Donnie Hill, intending him to take the starting sport. Himes also traded for two back-ups.[37]

The team had hoped Cruz would play well and attract interest from other teams during spring training in 1987. Cruz, however, hit only .200. Himes told him the White Sox would release him. Cruz said: "If there's one thing I have a chip on my shoulder about, it's that I couldn't contribute like in '83. Because of the foot, I wasn't able to be myself. In the back of my mind, I wonder what if I had never sustained the foot injury. There are a lot of 'what ifs.'"[38]

Cruz finished his major-league career with a batting average of .237 and 343 stolen bases, a success rate of 81.5 percent. Only 28 players with at least 300 stolen bases have a higher percentage.

After his release, Cruz had a brief stint with Albuquerque, the Los Angeles Dodgers' team in the Pacific Coast League. The Kansas City Royals invited Cruz to spring training in 1988, but he rejected their request that he join their Triple-A team. Cruz retired, then changed his mind.[39] He briefly played for the Fresno Suns of the Class-A California League, then retired for good.

The game took a physical toll on Cruz. He spent much of his major-league career playing on Astroturf in Seattle. He said playing on the surface had hurt his right toe. Since retirement, he has endured eight operations on his knees. He has an artificial left knee. As of 2018, his right toe still hurt.[40]

After retiring, Cruz coached in the Mariners and Milwaukee Brewers organizations. In 1997 he led Pulaski, a Texas Rangers farm club, to a first-place finish in the West Division of the rookie-level Appalachian League and was named Manager of the Year. Cruz left after the one season because he wanted to work closer to his family. He and Bill Caudill coached the baseball team at Eastside Catholic High School in Sammamish, Washington. All three of Cruz's sons played for the squad. Cruz has conducted youth baseball clinics. He has served as a color commentator for broadcasts of Mariners home games on the team's Spanish-language network. He has represented the Mariners at community events.[41]

In 2002, Cruz was inducted into the Redlands High School Hall of Fame. In 2004 Cruz was inducted into the San Francisco-based Hispanic Heritage Baseball Hall of Fame. In 2016 he was honored by SEAT 21, an MLB program that recognizes people who emulate Roberto Clemente's humanitarian spirit. Cruz supports Toys for Kids, which raises money to buy holiday gifts for homeless and hospitalized children.[42] In 2017 he was recognized at Julio Cruz Day hosted by the Chelan County Public Utility District in Wenatchee, Washington.[43]

Cruz settled in Redmond, Washington, with his second wife, Mojgan Moini. He spends time with his grand-daughter. He does Mariners Spanish-language broadcasts on Fridays and Saturdays. He occasionally gives baseball clinics at high schools.

Cruz maintains his love of basestealing. Shortly before he received the SEAT 21 honor, he visited Auburn High School in Kent, Washington. Cruz had intended to stay about 20 minutes. Instead, he talked for close to an hour. He discussed stealing with the school's baseball team. He emphasized that successful baserunning partially results from observation. To prove his point, he stood on the pitcher's mound and showed how a right-hander might relax his shoulders and release air before he delivers the ball. "Once you see the lean," Cruz told the players, "you must get going."[44]

The author wants to thank Julio Cruz for sharing his story. The author also would like to thank the following for their assistance: Jim Corcoran, co-owner/general manager Wenatchee AppleSox Baseball Club; Rebecca Hale, director of public information, Seattle Mariners; Suzanne Hartman, communications manager, Chelan Public Utility; Tim Herlich, treasurer, Northwest SABR chapter; Cassidy Lent, reference librarian, National Baseball Hall of Fame and Museum; and William Wade Norris, San Bernardino Valley College.

## Sources

In addition to the sources cited in the Notes, the author also consulted Baseball-almanac.com,

Baseball-reference.com, Bklynlibrary.org, Newspapers. com, Retrosheet.org, Paperofrecord.com, Julio Cruz's player file at the National Baseball Hall of Fame Library, and the following:

Anderson, Claude. "Area Players Sparkle in Minors," *San Bernardino County Sun-Telegram,* November 6, 1975: E-3.

Anderson, Claude. "Page's Latest Chapter on Bicycle Trek Proves It's Not a Dog's Life," *San Bernardino County Sun-Telegram*, July 12, 1977: B7, B8.

Buchan, Jim. "Baseball Hunch – Bet on the American League," *Walla Walla* (Washington) *Union-Bulletin*, June 30, 1983: 17.

Dilbeck, Steve. "Cruz One of Best Ballpark Hot Dogs," *San Bernardino County Sun*, March 14, 1979: D-1, 4.

Feinstein, John. "Happiest Mariner Is the Manager," *Washington Post*, August 9, 1980. Retrieved October 26, 2017.

Holtzman, Jerome. "LaRussa May Be Next to Go," *Chicago Tribune*, June 19, 1983: B3.

Hulse, Gilbert. "Julio Cruz Wants to Improve His Staying Power," *San Bernardino County Sun-Telegram*, March 14, 1978: B-7, 10.

Lane, Jeff. "Cruz Leads Mariners to Win Over Angels," *Redlands* (California) *Daily Facts*, July 15, 1977: 7.

Ringolsby, Tracy. "M's Certain They Picked a Gem in Moore," *The Sporting News*, June 27, 1981: 39.

Ringolsby, Tracy. "'Secure' Zisk Feels Obligation to Strike," *The Sporting News*, July 4, 1981: 39.

Schulian, John. "Brooklyn Stickball Groomed Cruz for Sox," *Palm Beach Post*, May 30, 1984: D2.

Stone, Larry. "Cruz Just the Hombre for M's Spanish Radio Cast," *Seattle Times*, February 7, 2003. Source: National Baseball Hall of Fame.

Wigge, Larry, ed. *The Sporting News Official Baseball Guide 1983* (St. Louis: The Sporting News Publishing Company, 1983).

"Ryan Ties Strikeout Mark in Win Over A's," *Redlands Daily Facts*, July 5, 1977: 9.

*The Sporting News* March 7, 1988: 21.

## Notes

1 Kirby Arnold, *Tales from the Seattle Mariners Dugout: A Collection of the Greatest Mariners Stories Ever Told* (New York: Sports Publishing, Inc., 2007, 2014), 18.

2 The Philadelphia Phillies' Terry Harmon set the record in 1971.

3 "The Seattle Mariners' Julio Cruz says you don't have…," United Press International, June 7, 1981.

4 Mike Kiley, "Both Love and Money Kept Cruz with the Sox," *Chicago Tribune*, March 1, 1984: 4, 1 and 2.

5 Phone interview with Julio Cruz, April 9, 2018.

6 Phone interview with Julio Cruz, April 17, 2018.

7 Bill Virgin, "In Spanish Broadcasts, Cruz Has Bases Covered," *Seattle Post-Intelligencer*, April 5, 2004. Retrieved October 22, 2017; Ross Foreman, "Julio Cruz," *Sports Collector's Digest*, February 9, 1996: 130-131; Ron Luciano and David Fisher, *The Fall of the Roman Umpire*, (New York: Bantam Books, 1986), 299.

8 Phone interview with Julio Cruz, April 17, 2018.

9 Ron Luciano and David Fisher, 297-299.

10 "Voters Approve City of Loma Linda," *San Bernardino County Sun*,

September 23, 1970: B-1.

11  Joyce Hall, "Go-Go Cruz Has Finally Found a Stopping Place," *San Bernardino County Sun-Telegram*, July 5, 1977: B-8.

12  George Andrews, "Redlands Legion Wins in Extra-Inning Game," *Redlands Daily Facts*, June 5, 1972: 15.

13  UCLA built Jackie Robinson Stadium on the site of Sawtelle Field. The stadium was dedicated in 1991.

14  Phil Fuhrer, "Julio Cruz Translates Baseball Talent," *San Bernardino County Sun-Telegram*, November 3, 1974: E-4.

15  Paul Oberjuerge, "Clearly, Julio Is Cruzin' in the Majors," *San Bernardino County Sun-Telegram*, July 17, 1977, E-1, E-7.

16  Larry Stone, "The Art of Baseball: Flipping the Switch," *Seattle Times*, July 16, 2006. Retrieved October 26, 2017.

17  "They Won When They Had To," *Honolulu Advertiser*, September 13, 1976: D-1, D-3.

18  Rod Ohira, "Islander Gem," *Honolulu Star-Bulletin*, May 3, 1977: C-2.

19  Phone interview with Julio Cruz, April 17, 2018.

20  Terry Greenberg, "Cruz' Fan Club Lives It Up," *Redlands Daily Facts*, July 15, 1977: 7.

21  Kirby Arnold, 16.

22  Hy Zimmerman, "Julio Cruz to Run for More Money from M's," *The Sporting News* April 14, 1979: 51.

23  Steve Wulf, "Choose Which Cruz Is Whose," *Sports Illustrated* May 5, 1980. Retrieved October 15, 2017.

24  Ron Luciano and David Fisher, 302-303.

25  Michael Emmerich, *100 Things Mariners Fan Should Know & Do Before They Die* (Chicago: Triumph Books LLC, 2015), 252.

26  Phone interview with Julio Cruz, April 17, 2018.

27  Vince Coleman of the Cardinals set the record with 50 consecutive steals in 1988. Ichiro Suzuki of the Seattle Mariners set the American League record of 45 consecutive steals in 2007.

28  Ron Luciano and David Fisher, 306.

29  Joseph Durso, "Plays; Double Play Executed with Flair," *New York Times*, July 23, 1982. Retrieved January 31, 2018.

30  "Thanks for the Memories," *Seattle Times*, June 27, 1999. Retrieved November 26, 2017.

31  Since then, Henry Cotto, Mark McLemore, Harold Reynolds, and Ichiro Suzuki (twice) have tied the team record.

32  Ron Luciano and David Fisher, 307.

33  Mike Kiley, "Cruz's Bubble Punctured by Fan Reaction," *Chicago Tribune*, September 14, 1984: D3.

34  Mike Kiley, "Sox Just Too Tough to Lose," *Chicago Tribune*, April 28, 1985: Section 4, 1 and 14.

35  Ed Sherman, "Cruz Eager to Test Leg, Bat in Detroit on Weekend," *Chicago Tribune,* April 24, 1986: C6.

36  Dave van Dyck, "Cruz Primed to Fight for Job," *Chicago Sun-Times*, February 10, 1987: 92.

37  Ibid.

38  Dave van Dyck, "Cruz Sent Packing by Sox," *Chicago Sun-Times*, March 24, 1987: 96.

39  David T. Bristow, "New Beginning for an Old Ballplayer," *San Bernardino County Sun,* May 20, 1988: C2.

40  Phone interview with Julio Cruz, April 17, 2018.

41  Larry Stone, "Cruz Just the Hombre."

42  "Robinson Cano and Julio Cruz Honored on Roberto Clemente Day," Seattle Mariners Baseball Information Department, September 6, 2016. Retrieved October 15, 2017.

43  E-Mail correspondence with Suzanne Hartman, April 5, 2018.

44  Chris Chancellor, "Trojans Ride Around Diamond with Mariners' Legend," *Auburn Reporter*, April 20, 2016. Retrieved October 15, 2017.

# RICK JONES

## BY JEFF FINDLEY

When the Boston Red Sox broke camp in 1976 after winning the American League pennant the previous year, a young and relatively unknown left-hander claimed a spot on a roster that included future Hall of Famers Carlton Fisk, Fergie Jenkins, Jim Rice, and Carl Yastrzemski. The expectations weren't high at such a young age, but Rick Jones, a lanky 6-foot-5, 190-pound pitcher from Jacksonville, Florida, who was the Red Sox fifth pick in the June 1973 draft found himself on a major-league roster before he had celebrated his 21st birthday.

As a prep, Jones held promise, having been named to the Florida All-State Baseball third team by the Florida Sports Writers Association,[1] and earning a selection to play for the North squad of the state high school all-star baseball game at Lakeland's Marchant Stadium.[2]

"I didn't play in the game," Jones said. "I was at practice with my Legion baseball team when I found out I had been drafted by the Red Sox. Two days later, I was on a plane."[3]

Jones's first stop was Elmira of the New York-Pennsylvania League. A short-season Class-A team, Elmira was 32-37 in 1973, with future major-league pitchers Luis Aponte and Allen Ripley joining Jones on the staff. At 18 years old, Jones appeared in 17 games, with 13 starts, and registered a 5-3 record with a 2.39 earned-run average and seven strikeouts per game. He pitched 98 innings, second most on the team.

In 1974, his first full season in professional baseball, Jones was assigned to Winter Haven of the Class-A Florida State League. Jones was 6-12 in 24 games (23 starts) for his 59-71 team, with a 3.65 ERA.

Jones began the 1975 season at Winston-Salem of the Class-A Carolina League, and it was the first step of a rapid ascent to the majors. Barely 20 years old when the season began, Jones posted a 13-3 record with 14 complete games and a 2.11 ERA. Considered the ace of the staff, he was promoted to Bristol of the Double-A Eastern League on July 2. He was named the Carolina League's Topps Player of the Month award for June,[4] and later was named the league's Pitcher of the Year by league managers. For Bristol (81-57), Jones threw nine complete games in 12 starts and posted a 7-4 record.

Meanwhile the Red Sox won the American League pennant before losing the World Series to the Cincinnati Reds in seven games.

"In 1975, I had a good year," Jones said. "After the season, I went to instructional league in Sarasota. Red Sox manager Darrell Johnson had a winter home in Sarasota, so he would come around occasionally and knew who we all were."[5]

Spawned in part by judicial rulings regarding the reserve clause and the expiration of the collective-bargaining agreement, the owners announced on February 23, 1976, that spring-training camps would not open until a new agreement was finalized. With no place to report, Jones continued to work out with the Jacksonville State and University of North Florida college baseball teams, as he had most of that winter.

"The lockout delayed spring training," Jones said. "I had been working out with the local college teams, so the delay didn't hurt me at all. When spring training finally started, I was ready to go."[6]

Jones pitched in three exhibition games that spring, tossing 4⅔ innings, allowing two hits, two walks, and no runs.[7]

"On the final day of spring training, it came down to me, Jim Burton, and Diego Segui," said Jones. "We were told whoever pitched the best would get the last spot on the roster. Segui was average that day, Burton gave up back-to-back home runs against the White Sox, and I pitched well. When the game was over I was asked if my bags were packed. They weren't – I figured I was just going to the minor-league camp, so when I found out I made the roster, I had an hour to get my stuff and get on the plane to travel north since I had made the team."[8]

The first stop for the Red Sox was Baltimore, but Jones didn't see any action in that series or the following two-game set with Cleveland. He finally saw mop-up action against the Chicago White Sox on April 18, 1976, two days after his 21st birthday, entering the game with the Red Sox trailing 8-2. He gave up four hits and two earned runs in two innings pitched.

His next outing didn't occur for another 11 games, again wrapping up a lopsided loss, to the Texas Rangers after Luis Tiant surrendered nine unearned runs in the second inning. Jones faced 19 batters in four innings, again allowing two earned runs. His next six appearances followed a similar script: He pitched no more than two innings at a time without registering a win or save.

On June 13 Jones got his first major-league start, and he responded with a complete-game performance against the Twins at Metropolitan Stadium in Minneapolis. The Red Sox staked him to an early lead with a seven-run third, and although Jones surrendered two runs in a three-hit fourth inning, and by his own admission sported just a "mediocre fastball,"[9] the Red Sox won, 10-2.

"I can't think of any other pitcher like him," said catcher Carlton Fisk about Jones's performance that day. "Changeups starting hitters off, breaking balls, then he pops the fastball in pretty well."[10]

With this performance, Jones became a regular starter in the Boston rotation. After 10 additional starts, he was 4-1 with a 2.34 earned-run average.

In an August 5 start at Detroit, Jones lasted just 2⅓ innings in a 5-4 Boston victory. Despite the win, the defending American League champions were a distant fourth place in the AL East with a 50-55 record, 14 games behind the division-leading Yankees.

Boston's longtime owner Tom Yawkey had died on July 9, and just 10 days later, Johnson was fired as manager and replaced by Don Zimmer. The move was unpopular with a faction of the players, including Bill "Spaceman" Lee, who was the de-facto leader of the Buffalo Heads, an anti-Zimmer clique of players that included Fergie Jenkins, Lee, Rick Wise, Jim Willoughby, and Bernie Carbo.[11]

Jones's association with this group of players wasn't popular with Zimmer. When he missed a flight to California on August 9, he was demoted to the Triple-A Rhode Island Red Sox, in Pawtucket. With his steady performance up to this point, the move came as a surprise.

Peter Gammons, who often traveled with the Red Sox, accounted for the surprise demotion in his book *Beyond the Sixth Game*:

"When he missed a curfew or two, management blamed older players, particularly [Jim] Willoughby and Bill Lee, citing their wilder influences on this hayseed. But no one had to lead Tall Boy – so named by Willoughby after the Schlitz 16-ounce Tall Boy can and the fact that Jones was 6-foot-5 – astray. His high school buddies were three members of the rock band Lynard Skynard *[sic]*; the band was named after principal Leonard Skinner, their high school athletic director and football coach, who had suspended the band members and Jones from the athletic program. Tall Boy unfortunately was ahead of his time as far as getting himself into trouble, and while he would return in September [1976] for a brief stay before going to Seattle in the expansion draft, he threw away what appeared to be a promising career."[12]

Jones's account differs slightly. "I had car problems driving to the ballpark to catch the bus that took us to the airport to fly to California. Right fielder Dewey Evans also missed his flight. I flew out later that day to California, and when I got to the hotel I called Zimmer's room, no answer, and left a message. Also left a message in his box with the front office hotel clerk. I didn't hear back from him until the next morning, when he told me I was being taken out of starting rotation and sent to bullpen.

"When I found out Dewey Evans was still going to start that night I was ticked and told Zimmer I didn't know if I would be going to the game. I showed up late, and after the game was demoted to Pawtucket, they already had an airline ticket for me to fly that same night, and I arrived in Pawtucket the following morning. I pitched that night (Jones was the pitcher of record in a 7-4 loss to Rochester). Not going to game in California was the biggest mistake of my life. I found out later Zimmer was at a horse track when I first tried to contact him in California. Also found out later I probably got blackballed after that and probably cost me my big-league career, but it was my mistake."

"I don't know where that Lynyrd Skynyrd story came from, some band members did go to my high school, but they were older than me. I was in junior high when they were in high school."[13]

While with the Rhode Island Red Sox, Jones was 0-3 with a 9.90 ERA. He was recalled in September, and his initial start was a Monday Night Baseball game in Yankee Stadium on September 6. Jones surrendered five hits and three earned runs in 2 ⅔ innings, with the Red Sox losing 6-5.

He subsequently didn't get out of the first inning in a loss to Cleveland on September 11 but posted his fifth win of the season in a 12-6 victory over Detroit on September 20.

Jones's final appearance for the Red Sox was a no-decision stint in relief of Tiant in a September 29 loss to the Yankees in Fenway Park. With the Red Sox, he won five games, lost three, and posted a 3.36 ERA.

Whether through rumored off-the-field troubles or sim-

ply a baseball decision, Jones was left unprotected by the Red Sox in the 1976 expansion draft. Seattle selected him as its 11th pick, reuniting him with Darrell Johnson, who was now managing the Mariners. He anticipated going to Seattle for Opening Day, but he didn't initially make the roster out of spring training, instead being optioned to the Wichita Aeros of the Triple-A American Association.

As a first-year expansion team, the Mariners didn't have a Triple-A franchise in 1977. (The Aeros were a Chicago Cubs farm team.) Jones was 0-2 in five appearances (one start) at Wichita before being recalled by the Mariners in early May.[14] Although Jones was back in the majors, he wasn't enamored with his surroundings.

"I had shipped my car from Phoenix to Seattle, and catcher Larry Cox drove it until I got called back from Wichita," Jones said. "I loved Boston," he continued. "To this day, I'm still a big fan of the Patriots and Celtics. Going to Seattle was tough – the fans were great, but the Kingdome was dark, and it just wasn't the same."[15]

Jones's first start with the Mariners was a 4-2 loss at Baltimore, in which he allowed six hits and two earned runs in 4 ⅓ innings. In the next seven outings, he failed to register a win, although he didn't allow an earned run in 5 ⅔ innings, during stints against Detroit (June 9) and Oakland (June 14). Both were wins for Seattle, but Jones didn't figure in either decision.

On June 18 Jones had his longest outing with the Mariners, tossing 9 ⅓ innings and earning his only major-league victory with the expansion club, a 6-1 win at Texas. Jones faced 42 batters, giving way to Enrique Romo who faced one batter, inducing a double-play grounder from Ken Henderson. Jones walked 11 batters in the win, a Mariners record for most walks in a victory that still existed in 2018.[16]

Five days later, Jones surrendered three earned runs in three innings at Kansas City, but injured himself warming up for the fourth and couldn't continue.

"I threw a curveball that went about 10 feet," Jones said. "My arm felt like I was shot with a .22. At the time, everything had to go through the team doctor, and they decided to operate on my ulnar nerve. Today, I believe that's considered Tommy John surgery.

"I was told I would be okay in about 30 days (he was placed on the 21-day disabled list), but two months later I still couldn't brush my teeth. To this day, my left arm has a 30-degree bend in it."[17]

Done for the season, Jones rehabbed and returned to Triple A in 1978, this time with the San Jose Missions, a Mariners affiliate in the Pacific Coast League. He started 20 games, posting a record of 7-8 and an ERA of 3.87.

A late season call-up to Seattle resulted in one relief appearance and two starts, both losses.

"After the injury, my control was okay, but I never got my speed back," Jones said. "I never could get my fastball back."[18]

After two seasons and minimal impact, Jones was traded to Pittsburgh on December 5, 1978, along with Enrique Romo and Tom McMillian, in exchange for Odell Jones, Rafael Vasquez, and Mario Mendoza. He left Seattle having won only one game in two seasons, the record-breaker in which he walked 11. He was now a member of the Pittsburgh Pirates, the soon-to-be 1979 World Series winner.

"In spring training with the Pirates in 1979, Harvey Haddix, my pitching coach, told me I had a good chance to make the team," Jones said. "About two days before we broke camp, the Pirates signed Andy Hassler, and I was sent to the Portland Beavers of the Pacific Coast League."[19]

"I actually loved the Pacific Coast League," Jones said. "We flew everywhere except Tacoma – it wasn't like the other minor leagues."[20]

Jones had solid seasons in Portland in 1979 (12-8, 3.59 ERA) and 1980 (10-11, 4.67 ERA) but he never made another appearance in the majors.

In 1981, his final year in Organized Baseball, Jones led the Mexico City Tigres to first place in the Southwest Division of the Mexican League. The Tigres lost to the Campeche Piratas in the playoffs, four games to one.

"I was invited to spring training with St. Louis as a nonroster player in 1982, but by then, I had kids and decided to hang it up," Jones said. "The final player I faced in Mexico was Bill Buckner's brother (Jim). I always thought that was interesting since I started with Boston and considering Buckner's history with the franchise."[21]

Thomas Frederick Jones was born on April 16, 1955, in Jacksonville, Florida, the youngest of five children of Marion F. "Dixie" Jones and Betty Bennett Jones. Known as Rick or Ricky, he attended Nathan Bedford Forrest High School in Jacksonville, a school that was renamed Westside High School in 2014 by the Duval County School Board in response to public outcry over the namesake, a Confederate general and first grand wizard of the Ku Klux Klan.[22]

Jones's father was a Navy veteran who served in the Pacific during World War II, had a short stint in professional baseball, and later became a longtime teacher at Forrest High School. He died in 2007.

His mother, who died in 2005, was a kindergarten teacher. She was married to Marion for 62 years before her death.

Kenneth Jones, Rick's older brother, was drafted by the Washington Senators in 1965, but chose to attend Stetson University rather than sign with the Senators. He graduated from Stetson with honors in 1969 with a major in economics. He received a law degree from the University of Florida Law School in 1972.

Three sisters (Bette, Susan, and Rebecca) were born between Kenneth and Ricky.

When his baseball career ended, Jones returned to Florida. "I did different things, spent some time in sales, and worked for one company for over 20 years before they went out of business," he said.[23]

"I coached my boys in Little League and Senior League. I never had a job I liked as much as playing baseball."[24]

Jones said he continued to watch baseball on a regular basis, cheering for the Atlanta Braves. "Growing up in northern Florida, I've been a fan of the Braves my entire life," he said.[25]

As of 2018, Jones was retired and lived in his native Jacksonville.

## Sources

In addition to the sources cited in the Notes, the author also consulted Retrosheet, Baseball-Reference.com, and SABR.org.

**Notes**

1  "All-State Baseball: Four Central Floridians Named to High School Team," *Orlando Sentinel*, July 1, 1973: 65.

2  "MI's Williams on 'Star Team,'" *Florida Today* (Cocoa, Florida), May 22, 1973: 2C.

3  Rick Jones, telephone interview with author, May 6, 2018 (May 6 interview).

4  "Jones Is Named CL Player of Year," *Rocky Mount* (North Carolina) *Telegram,* August 21, 1975:15.

5  May 6 interview.

6  Ibid.

7  United Press International, "Red Sox Drop Segui, Reach 25-Man Roster," *Berkshire Eagle* (Pittsfield, Massachusetts), April 7, 1976: 32.

8  May 6 interview.

9  UPI, "Rookie Jones Says He Had No Fast Ball in First Major-League Win Yesterday," *Berkshire Eagle,* June 14, 1976: 26.

10  Ibid.

11  David Laurila, "Bill Lee Interview," Baseball Almanac, baseball-almanac.com/players/bill_lee_interview.shtml.

12  Peter Gammons, *Beyond the Sixth Game* (Boston: Houghton Mifflin Company, 1985), 78.

13  Rick Jones, email exchange with author, May 7, 2018.

14  "Seattle Mariners Recall Rick Jones," *Miami* (Oklahoma) *News Record*, May 16, 1977: 4.

15  May 6 interview.

16  Steve Rudman, "Pitching Improbables from Mariners History, *Seattle Post-Intelligencer,* May 11, 2006. seattlepi.com/sports/baseball/article/Pitching-improbables-from-Mariners-history-1203352.php.

17  May 6 interview.

18  Ibid.

19  Ibid.

20  Ibid.

21  Ibid.

22  Denise Smith Amos, "Duval School Board Backs Westside High School as New Name for Forrest High," *Florida Times-Union*, January 7, 2014. jacksonville.com/news/2014-01-07/story/duval-school-board-backs-westside-new-name-forrest-high-school.

23  Rick Jones, telephone interview with author, May 18, 2018.

24  Ibid.

25  Ibid

# DANNY MEYER

## BY PAUL HOFMANN

Life isn't always a fastball down the middle. Sometimes it is unpredictable, with all the ups and downs and erratic sharp curves of a Wiffle Ball thrown into a still breeze. An original Seattle Mariner, Danny Meyer experienced the full gamut of life's changes both on and off the field. Through it all, Meyer adjusted, even if it meant traveling a different road than the one he imagined.

Daniel Thomas Meyer was born on August 3, 1952, in Hamilton, Ohio, a suburb of Cincinnati. He was the only child of Thomas and Judy (Nichting) Meyer.[1] Tom was a US Navy officer and later worked as an electrical engineer with Beckman Instruments in Fullerton, California. Judy was a stay-at-home mother while Dan was growing up. Like many military families, the Meyers moved frequently when Dan was very young. The family spent time in Florida, Tennessee, and San Diego before settling in Santa Ana, California, after Thomas left the Navy.

Meyer credited his father with getting him interested in

baseball and having a profound impact on his hitting. From an early age the senior Meyer would come home from work and take his son out to hit. "My dad wasn't the type of guy who came home from work and read the paper with a martini. He would take me out to hit," he said. When they didn't have time to go to the park to hit, Meyer's father would throw Wiffle Balls to him on the sun-soaked driveway swept by the warm Santa Ana winds. "When you can learn to hit a Wiffle Ball fluttering in the wind, you can hit anything," Meyer said. Dan demonstrated an uncanny ability to hit the ball at an early age and went on to star in the Sunset Little League in Santa Ana.

Meyer attended Mater Dei High School in Santa Ana, where he was a standout third baseman. He graduated in 1970 and was inducted into the school's athletic hall of fame that same year.[2] Tom was adamant that his son would attend college. Despite his desire to stay close to home to be near his girlfriend, Meyer accepted a baseball scholarship at the University of Arizona, where he majored in business. According to Meyer, it was a bit of an "ill-fated arrangement."[3] He wasn't very interested in business and he became disillusioned when he was put on the freshman team in the spring of 1971 and decided to go home.

Meyer announced the decision to his father when the latter came to pick him up at the end of the spring semester. Meyer remembered that his father was none too happy about the decision and he described the drive home as the "least pleasant 7-hour experience of my life."[4]

Roger Wilson, the Santa Ana College baseball coach, invited Meyer to play on a summer-league team. After the season, Wilson persuaded Meyer to enroll at Santa Ana and in 1972 he was the Dons' starting second baseman. Meyer had a solid year and attracted the attention of California Angels and Los Angeles Dodgers scouts, as well as other teams.

The right-handed-throwing, left-handed-hitting Meyer was selected in the fourth round of the June 1972 amateur draft by the Detroit Tigers. He was signed by Tigers scouts John Deutsch and John Hockenberry for $12,500, with the standard $7,500 progression bonuses he would receive as he was promoted through the system.[5] After signing, he was assigned to the Bristol (Virginia) Tigers of the Appalachian League. That year, he enjoyed the best offensive season of his professional career.

Meyer played in 65 games for the rookie-league Tigers. Defensively he appeared in 49 games at third base and 13 at second. He was hitting over .400 late in the season and flirted with the league record of .410 established by Tony Oliva in 1961, finally capturing the circuit's batting title with a .396 mark.[6] The effort earned Meyer the 1972 Silver Bat Award, given to the player with the highest batting average in Organized Baseball.[7] He led Tigers in hits (93), home runs (14), RBIs (46), and stolen bases (13). Meyer was named the Topps George M. Trautman Player of the Year for the Appalachian League.[8]

Meyer's success was somewhat unexpected. In fact, he was nearly finished before the season started. "I struggled during the second spring training and about got released," he said.[9] He wasn't in the starting lineup on Opening Day and was inserted at third base in the second game of a doubleheader due to a rainout. He collected three hits that game and was a mainstay in the Tigers lineup for the rest of the season. Reflecting back on the season, Meyer remembered Hoot Evers, the Tigers' director of player development, apologizing to him late in the season for almost releasing him. Evers was a mentor of Meyer's throughout his time in the Tigers organization.

Tigers executives had trouble believing the .396 and sent Meyer to Dunedin, Florida, to see if he could handle advanced pitching in the Florida Instructional League.[10] Meyer had little difficulty with the league's pitchers. He captured his second batting title of the year with a .409 average.[11] His Instructional League season ended prema-

turely when he suffered a sprained ankle in November. Collectively he finished the year 131-for-328 for a combined .399 average.

After the Instructional League season, Meyer returned to Southern California and on November 25, 1972, married Eugenia Maria Formolo, the high-school sweetheart he reluctantly left behind two years earlier to attend the University of Arizona.[12]

There was a great deal of buzz about Meyer after his unexpected success. His seeming out of nowhere success resulted in his being dubbed a "novice of promise" by one national magazine.[13] The Tigers assigned him to the minor-league camp at Tigertown to start spring training in 1973. General manager Jim Campbell attempted to quell speculation that Meyer would be rushed up to the majors, saying, "We won't let him get too excited. But everyone says he is some kind of hitter. First base might be his best position, although he plays second and third base as well."[14]

After spring training Meyer was assigned to the Lakeland Tigers of the Class-A Florida State League. He played in 133 games, all at second base, and hit .241 with 10 home runs and a team-leading 59 RBIs. Meyer had a simple explanation for the drop in average: "I was a dead pull hitter at the time and by my second year they had figured it out and started to defend me with a slight shift."[15] After the season, Meyer returned to the Instructional League and bounced back with a .330 average.[16]

The 5-foot-11-inch, 180-pound Meyer started the 1974 season with the Evansville Triplets of the Triple-A American Association. He played first, third, and some outfield during a bounceback year at the plate. He finished the season with a .302 average, 9 home runs, and 57 RBIs, and was rewarded with a September call-up to the Tigers.

Meyer made his major-league debut on September 14, 1974, in a game against the New York Yankees at Tiger Stadium. It was the *Game of the Week,* televised nationally on NBC. Meyer entered the game in the bottom of the eighth inning as a pinch-hitter for third baseman Aurelio Rodriguez. With a runner on first and one down, he grounded into a fielder's choice against Dick Tidrow.

Meyer made his first start for the Tigers on September 20 and collected his first major-league hit when he singled off Brewers right-hander Bill Champion in the top of the first at Milwaukee's County Stadium. Two innings later he hit his first major-league home run, a one-out, bases-empty line drive to right-center off Champion. He hit another home run, also a solo shot to right-center, in the bottom of the seventh inning off left-hander Bill Travers. The Tigers left fielder finished the day 3-for-5 with two runs scored and two RBIs. In 13 games with the Tigers that fall, Meyer batted .200, with three home runs, and seven RBIs.

Three years removed from their 1972 AL East Division championship, the Tigers were faced with the need to begin rebuilding an aging roster. Meyer was a key piece, if not the centerpiece, of this youth movement.[17] *The Sporting News* hailed the young outfielder as "the best pure hitter the Tigers have had since Al Kaline joined Detroit fresh out of high school in 1953."[18]

The Tigers broke spring training in 1975 with Meyer as the everyday left fielder. He played the position in 73 of the Tigers' first 82 games and was hitting .267 with 5 home runs and 31 RBIs before being sidelined with a fractured foot, suffered while he scaled the left-field wall of Tiger Stadium in an attempt to catch a drive off the bat of the White Sox' Bill Stein. When he returned to the lineup after a nearly four-week absence, the Tigers were in the midst of a 10-game losing streak.

The return of Meyer, who was moved to first base, did little to bring the Tigers out of their funk: They went on to lose nine more games and establish a team-record 19-game losing streak. Reflecting on the team's slide, Meyer said, "For us it wasn't any big thing. Sure, we wanted to win. But we didn't sit around each day wondering how many we had lost. We'd just go out and play. It's the press that worried about numbers."[19] He hit only .191 the remainder of the season and finished at .236 with 8 home runs and 47 RBIs, as the Tigers wound up in last place in the AL East with a dismal 57-102 record.

Despite his injury-plagued tail-off at the end of the season, Meyer was the toughest player in the American League to strike out in 1975. He led the league with 18.8 at-bats per strikeout. Throughout his career, Meyer had a reputation as a tough strikeout and was known for his ability to make contact. He ranks high on the all-time list with 13.48 at-bats per strikeout, much better than a host of Hall of Famers.

After the season, the Meyers welcomed the birth of a son.[20] (The couple had no other children and divorced in 1978.)

**DAN MEYER**

Meyer began the 1976 season as the Tigers' starting first baseman. He struggled during the first few weeks of the season, and the Tigers called up first baseman Jason Thompson from Evansville.[21] Meyer spent the rest of the season in a part-time role, backing up Alex Johnson in left field and Thompson at first, and pinch-hitting. In 105 games he hit .252 with 2 home runs and 16 RBIs.

Despite the reduced playing time and the Tigers growing stable of young left-handed sluggers, including University of Southern California superstar Steve Kemp, whom they selected with the first overall pick of the 1976 draft, Meyer was assured by manager Ralph Houk that he would be back with the Tigers the next year. "Ralph told me, 'Don't worry. You're one of our guys,'" Meyer said.[22]

While he was not among the 15 players the Tigers were able to protect in the November 1976 expansion draft, the Tigers were confident that one of the expansion teams, the Seattle Mariners and Toronto Blue Jays, would select 21-year-old right-handed pitcher Frank MacCormack, allowing the Tigers to protect Meyer after the first round. The draft did not play out that way. The Mariners selected Meyer with the ninth overall pick in the first round. (Seattle also grabbed MacCormack, with the 16th overall pick.)

Given what he had been told, Meyer had moved his family to Ypsilanti, Michigan, outside Detroit, and found an offseason job. He was surprised when he learned he was no longer a Tiger. He heard the news while listening to the radio on the drive home from playing racquetball with Tigers teammates Chuck Scrivener and Vern Ruhle. Meyer epitomized the Mariners' drafting strategy, which produced a first-year team with the ability to hit home runs with some frequency but was short on pitching.

Meyer was hitless in eight at-bats during the Mariners' first two games, a pair of shutouts tossed by Angels Frank Tanana and Nolan Ryan.[23] After 21 scoreless innings, Meyer recorded the franchise's first RBI on April 8 with a fourth-inning double off Angels starter Gary Ross that drove in Dave Collins. The Mariners won the seesaw affair in dramatic fashion by scoring two runs in the ninth inning for a 7-6 walk-off victory at the Kingdome, the team's first regular-season victory.

On May 3, in a 10-8 Mariners victory over the Boston Red Sox at Fenway Park, Meyer had the rare distinction of reaching first base on catcher's interference twice in one game when Carlton Fisk's mitt made contact with his bat in the fifth and ninth innings. The next day Fisk claimed that Meyer had intentionally hit his glove, to which Meyer responded, "I'm hitting .179. I couldn't hit it twice if I was trying."[24] Meyer was just the third player and as of 2018 was one of only six to have reached on catcher's interference twice in the same game. [25]

Meyer played in a career-high 159 games in 1977 and proved to be a major contributor during the Mariners' in-augural season. The team's everyday first baseman, he batted .273 with career highs in runs scored (75), home runs (24), RBIs (90), and stolen bases (11). His 90 RBIs tied for the team lead with left fielder Leroy Stanton. Though he was only 25 years old when the season ended, the 1977 season was the best of Meyer's career.

Meyer got off to a slow start in 1978. He was hitting .179 with 4 home runs and 15 RBIs when he went on the disabled list with an abdominal strain suffered during batting practice in Cleveland in early May. The injury periodically resurfaced and hampered Meyer throughout his career. After his return, he hit only .245 the rest of the season. Meyer summed up his frustrations in mid-August when he commented, "Every time I'm at the plate it seems there are 40 fielders out there to keep me from getting a hit."[26] In 123 games, he batted .227 with 8 home runs, 56 RBIs, and 7 stolen bases.

After the 1978 season, Meyer married Laura Hilger. The couple had three children and divorced in 1989.

Meyer started the 1979 season in left field before settling in at third base when Bruce Bochte was moved from the outfield to first base. Despite struggling defensively at third, Meyer enjoyed a solid season at the plate. From June 9 to 30, he had a career-high 21-game hitting streak in which he hit .412 with 7 home runs and 16 RBIs. He captured AL Player-of-the-Month honors in June with a .369 average, 9 home runs, and 23 RBIs. Meyer's average remained over .300 until he slumped at the end of the season. He hit .209 during the last seven weeks of the season and finished with a .278 average, 72 runs scored, 20 home runs, and 74 RBIs in 144 games.

Meyer was a fan favorite in the early years of the Mariners franchise. He was captain of the Pepsi Jr. Mariners Fan Club and was actively involved in United Way charities in the Greater Seattle area. Along the way, he acquired the nickname Disco Danny for his unique mannerisms during his routine to prepare to hit. The moniker was used in a 1980 promotional piece for the Mariners in which coaches, teammates, and fans mimicked Meyer's neck-loosening movements and upper-body gyrations.[27]

Back in left field, Meyer got off to one of the best starts of his career in 1980. He hit safely in the first 10 games and finished April with a .324 average and 11 RBIs. While his power numbers were down, he was hitting .306 with 34 RBIs at the All-Star break. After the break, his average dropped to .242 with 8 home runs and 37 RBIs. He finished the season with a .275 average, 11 home runs, and 71 RBIs.

The strike-shortened season of 1981 was Meyer's last with the Mariners. He started the season on the disabled list after tearing an abdominal muscle during spring training and missed the team's first 11 games. He returned to pinch-hitting duty in late April before getting back into the lineup in left field and eventually migrating back to third base. The injury, coupled with the strike, limited Meyer to 83 games. He finished the year with a .262 average, 3 home runs, and 22 RBIs.

After the season Meyer's five-year tenure with the Mariners ended when he was traded to the Oakland Athletics for 21-year-old right-handed pitching prospect Rich Bordi. Years later he reflected on his years with the Mariners. Meyer described the first year as hopeful, but said malaise that would affect the franchise for years quickly set in. "It got to the point where you just knew you were going to end up in the cellar or close to it, because we hadn't done anything to make ourselves better," Meyer said.[28] The Mariners were 290-465 (.384) during Meyer's five years with the club.

Meyer attributed some of his late-season slumps to the revolving-door nature of expansion team rosters and the annual late-summer realization that the team would finish at or near the bottom of the standings. "It was tough to stay up mentally," he said.[29]

The A's acquired Meyer in the hope he would be a left-handed power hitter off the bench, a void manager Billy Martin thought the A's needed to fill if they were to improve on the team's AL Championship Series appearance the year before. While Meyer joined the A's logjam of position players in left field and at first base, A's President Roy Eisenhardt was confident that the acquisition strengthened the bench. "We felt we really needed bench strength. We got that with Meyer and Joe Rudi," he said.[30] The A's had signed Rudi as a free agent. For his part, Meyer was excited to be joining a contending team, or at least he thought so.

The A's emerged from spring training in 1982 with Meyer as their primary left-handed designated hitter. By early July, he returned to the infield and played first base. In 120 games, he batted .240 with 8 home runs and 59 RBIs.

The A's finished 1982 with a disappointing 68-94 record and a fifth-place finish in the AL West. Still, Meyer said the season was enjoyable in one respect. Acknowledging that Billy Martin had a tendency to self-destruct, Meyer said he had a great baseball mind. "It was very interesting watching Billy operate that year," he said.[31]

Meyer played a part-time role for the A's in 1983. In May and early June, he filled in for Wayne Gross, who had moved from first base to third when Carney Lansford went on the disabled list. Meyer endured a 0-for-37 stretch while Lansford was out. In a self-deprecating moment during the swoon, Meyer told teammates, "It's all Carney Lansford's fault. If he had been playing, I never would have been out there."[32] He finished the year with a .189 average, one home run, and 13 RBIs.

When the A's broke camp in 1984, Meyer was the odd man out and was assigned to the Tacoma Tigers of the Triple-A Pacific Coast League. He played in 124 games, at first base, third base, and a few games in the outfield. He finished the season with a .293 average, 7 home runs, and 57 RBIs before being called up to the A's in September. In 20 games with A's, 18 as a pinch-hitter, he hit .318 with 4 RBIs.

Meyer started the 1985 season with A's in a pinch-hitting role. In 14 games he went 0-for-12 before being released on May 26. That brought an end to his 12-year major-league career. In 1,118 games he batted .253 with 86 home runs and 459 RBIs. Defensively, he never found a permanent spot on the field. He played 469 games at first base, 314 in left, and 157 at third base.

Not quite ready to call it a career, Meyer signed a minor-league contract with the Tigers' American Association affiliate Nashville Sounds. Tigers general manager Bill Lajoie wanted Meyer to go to Nashville to get his swing back before calling him up to DH and pinch-hit for the defending World Series Champions. Meyer suffered another abdominal injury when he volunteered to throw batting practice and a liner off the bat of Dwight Lowry found its way through a hole in the protective screen and into Meyer's rib cage. The injury caused Meyer to miss three weeks and hampered his ability to find his stroke. In 51 games with the Sounds, he hit .225 with one home run and 13 RBIs.

The Tigers released Meyer during spring training of 1986. Meyer, who always believed he had the skills and the temperament to be a coach or manager, turned down a coaching position with the Tigers.[33] Still only 33 years old, he believed he could make it back to the majors as a role player. With no offers from major-league clubs, Meyer signed with the Mexico City Reds and spent 2½ months of the 1986 season playing in the Mexican League. When he returned to Northern California he purchased and operated the Dog House Restaurant in San Ramon, California.

Former A's teammate Steve McCatty, who was attempting a comeback and playing for the Class-A San Jose Giants, enticed Meyer to come back for a few games in 1987. He played three games with the Giants and went 3-for-12 with one RBI.

Meyer later worked for AT&T as an account representative in Pleasanton, California. When AT&T closed its facility in Pleasanton, he was offered a position with the company in Utah. Rather than uproot his family, Meyer decided to stay in California.

The Meyers divorced in 1989 and sold their restaurant. Meyer was granted custody of the couple's three children and became a single father. He took a series of graveyard-hour jobs that allowed his family to stay in California and be available during the day to coach Little League and be an active in his children's other activities.

Meyer also worked as a private hitting coach for Wellman Sports, a baseball training facility in San Ramon, California. He married Linda Peters in 2013 and as of early 2018 the couple resided in a retirement community in Rio Vista, California. The Meyers enjoyed playing tennis and pickle ball, a hybrid of tennis, badminton, and table tennis played with a plastic ball, similar to a Wiffle Ball, still proving that if you can hit a Wiffle Ball fluttering in the wind, you can hit anything.

## Sources

In addition to the sources cited in the Notes, the author also relied on Baseball-reference.com and Retrosheet.org.

### Notes

1 Dan Meyer, personal communication, March 9, 2018.

2 "Hall of Fame," materdeiathletics.org/apps/pages/index.jsp?u-REC_ID=452859&type=d&pREC_ID=1045476.

3 Dan Meyer, personal communication.

4 Dan Meyer, personal communication, March 14, 2018.

5 Dan Meyer, personal communication, March 9, 2018.

6 "Topps Player of the Month: Appalachian League," *The Sporting News*, September 23, 1972: 5.

7 *Detroit Tigers 1975 Media Guide*, 41.

8 "Meet the Winners of the Topps George M. Trautman Minor League Player-of-the-Year Awards," *The Sporting News*, December 9, 1972: 39.

9 Dan Meyer, personal communication, March 9, 2018.

10 William Leggett, "The Phenoms That Bloom in the Fall," *Sports Illustrated*, December 4, 1972: 70.

11 "FIL Frontrunners," *The Sporting News*, November 18, 1972: 55.

12 "California Marriage Index, 1960-1985," database, FamilySearch (familysearch.org/ark:/61903/1:1:V6JJ-4Z6: 27 November 2014), Daniel T Meyer and Eugenia M Formolo, 25 Nov 1972; from "California, Marriage Index, 1960-1985," database and images, *Ancestry* (ancestry.com : 2007); citing Orange, California, Center of Health Statistics, California Department of Health Services, Sacramento.

13 *Tigers 1975 Baseball Yearbook*, 41.

14 Watson Spoelstra, "Campbell Facing Pay Assault by Tiger Players," *The Sporting News*, January 13, 1973: 45.

15 Dan Meyer, personal communication, March 9, 2018.

16 *Detroit Tigers 1975 Media Guide*.

17 Dan Holmes, "Willie Horton," sabr.org/bioproj/person/e320ca42.

18 "A.L. Flashes," *The Sporting News*, June 14, 1975: 22.

19 Art Spander, "Tigers Victims of Numbers Game," *The Sporting*

*News*, September 6, 1975: 25.

20 *Detroit Tigers 1976 Media Guide*, 47.

21 Dan Holmes, "40 Years Ago: Thompson Was the 'Other' Tiger Rookie in 1976," Detroit Athletic Co., February 3, 2016. detroitathletic.com/blog/2016/02/03/40-years-ago-thompson-was-the-other-tiger-rookie-in-1976/.

22 Dan Meyer, personal correspondence, March 9, 2018.

23 Bob Dutton, "Mariners Notebook: Altavilla Provides Bullpen with Another Benoit Dividend," *Tacoma* (Washington) *News Tribune*, April 7, 2017. thenewstribune.com/sports/mlb/seattle-mariners/mariners-insider-blog/article143457834.html.

24 Dan Meyer, personal communication, March 14, 2018. He was actually hitting .233 at the time.

25 Pat Corrales is the only player to have reached base on catcher's interference twice in the same game more than once. He did it twice in 1965.

26 Hy Zimmerman, "Mariners," *The Sporting News*, August 19, 1978: 16.

27 "1980 – Disco Danny," youtube.com/watch?v=1Kfst1oBrWI.

28 Dick Rockne, "Memories – 20 Years of Mariners – Meyer's Life Revolves Around His Children," *Seattle Times*, April 13, 1997. community.seattletimes.nwsource.com/archive/?date=19970413&slug=2533738.

29 Dan Meyer, personal communication, March 9, 2018.

30 Kit Stier, "Meyer Provides A's With Lefty Power," *The Sporting News*, January 2, 1983: 43.

31 Dan Meyer, personal communication, March 9, 2018.

32 Stan Isle, "Caught on the Fly," *The Sporting News*, July 4, 1983: 14.

33 Dick Rockne.

# BIRTH OF THE BLUE JAYS

## By Maxwell Kates

The date was September 4, 1967. As Canada's centennial summer drew to a close, a sparse crowd of 802 gathered at Maple Leaf Stadium to watch the hometown Leafs of the International League host the Syracuse Chiefs.[1] A ninth-inning home run by Syd O'Brien could not overcome a 7-2 loss to Stan Bahnsen and the Chiefs. The once-proud Maple Leafs franchise drew an aggregate total for the year of only 67,216 spectators and was teetering on bankruptcy.[2] After the season, Toronto Community Baseball Ltd. sold the franchise and its debts to Indiana developer Walter Dilbeck for $65,000. The Leafs were moved immediately to Louisville, Kentucky.[3] Baseball, a summer tradition in Toronto since 1886, had "crept out ... without a whimper of public protest."[4]

Baseball was not absent from the Toronto sports scene for long. In 1969, boxing promoter Jack Dominico was awarded an expansion team, also called the Maple Leafs, in the Ontario Inter-County League. However, municipal leaders like Paul Godfrey were not satisfied. Up the Macdonald-Cartier Freeway in Montreal, the Expos set an attendance record for expansion teams as 1.2 million flocked to Jarry Park. Godfrey surmised that if Montreal was major league, then Toronto should be as well.

"It disturbed me that Montreal was given a franchise," Godfrey told Bob Elliott of the *Toronto Sun* in 1993. "I made up my mind that now was the time to champion baseball for Toronto."[5] The alderman from North York received a terse response from Commissioner Bowie Kuhn

in 1969 when he approached Kuhn without a venue:

"Son, here's the way baseball works. You get a stadium to play in and baseball will decide whether we'll come."[6] According to Louis Cauz of the (Toronto) *Globe and Mail*, "Downsview Airport [in North York] and the Woodbine Racetrack in Etobicoke were bandied about as possible locations, but those sites would involve many more millions to develop than [was cost feasible]."[7]

The question of a proper venue was addressed in 1973 when Godfrey, now Metro Toronto Chairman, met Ontario Premier William Davis prior to the Grey Cup finals

A photo of the Toronto Blue Jays' front office in 1977. Some of the notable club employees included (back row left) Gord Ash, (back row 2nd right) Elliott Wahle, (back row right) Bob Prentice, (3rd row left) Paul Beeston, (3rd row 2nd left) Pat Gillick), (3rd row right) Howard Starkman, and (2nd row left) Peter Bavasi. (Courtesy of Elliott and Helene Wahle)

A 'Smile Toronto' button. These buttons were used as part of the lobbying effort in 1976 to convince the American League and the Municipality of Metropolitan Toronto to award a baseball team to the city. (Courtesy of Elliott and Helene Wahle)

at Exhibition Stadium. Davis asked, "Where can we put it?" Godfrey replied "Why not here?"[8] The two Conservative politicians agreed to split the costs to expand and upgrade Exhibition Stadium to meet the standards of major-league baseball.

Amid double-digit inflation and a global energy crisis, Metro Toronto taxpayers demanded to know that any proposed renovation would be profitable. Although Godfrey estimated a $15 million investment, a *Globe and Mail* editorial rebutted by asking, "Should be we satisfied with 'ballpark figures' just because the topic under discussion is a stadium?"[9] Metro aldermen approved the project in 1974 by a vote of 23 to 6; it would serve only as a temporary facility until a domed stadium was ready. The capacity for baseball was estimated at 40,000.[10]

As is often the case with municipal projects, the Exhibition Stadium budget was a gross underestimate. Once the renovation was ratified, the budget was closer to $17.8 million, not including the scoreboard, private boxes, and concessions. The dressing rooms required additional renovation, adding another $2 million. Several corporations agreed to absorb construction costs and receive advertising rights and a share of the profits once a team began to play."[11] Also in 1974, former Boston Red Sox executive John Alevizos sought to purchase the Cleveland Indians and move them to Toronto.[12] Upon approaching Davis for partners, Alevizos was advised to get in touch with local construction magnate Sydney Cooper.[13] Meanwhile, in London, Labatt's Breweries executives Donald McDougall and Ed Bradley brainstormed marketing ideas to improve the popularity of their product in Ontario.

"We were the number-3 market share in Ontario behind Molson and Carling O'Keefe and we knew that professional sports were a positive way to brand our product. We had recently become the sponsor of the Winnipeg Blue Bombers [of the Canadian Football League] and the product was so successful that we changed the name from Labatt Pilsener to Labatt's Blue," McDougall said. "Being on the ground floor [to sponsor] a major-league baseball franchise was a good place to solve the Toronto problem."[14] Although Labatt's had sponsored local sporting events in Ontario like golf and curling, the brewery could not make inroads with any hockey or football teams in the province. In September, McDougall and his adviser, Alan Eagleson, met with Cooper to discuss a strategic alliance to bring baseball to Toronto. Cooper, who died in 2018, appreciated their interest but rejected their offer. He thought that asking a brewer to sponsor a baseball team would send the wrong message to the "Tory blue" Toronto of 1974. McDougall remembered:

"We got out on the street and Eagleson said, 'I've never heard such [nonsense] in my life. You should be competing with them, not going with them.'"[15] Thus, the idea of owning a team, rather than merely sponsoring one, was planted in McDougall's mind. The next step was to speak to league presidents Lee MacPhail and Chub Feeney at the 1974 World Series. A third consortium spearheaded by Lorne Duguid and Harold Ballard joined the baseball sweepstakes.[16] As McDougall recalled, "the Duguid group [jovially] handed out brochures at the World Series. By contrast, we went to every place National League and American League owners met. Our market share responded positively to our effort to bring a team to Toronto, even if we hadn't achieved it yet."[17] McDougall's next hurdle was to convince his fellow executives at Labatt's that owning a baseball team was a good business venture.

"They took the position that we shouldn't own the team [outright]," he said. "We could associate ourselves with the team ... as long as we didn't own more than 45 percent of the shares."[18] By the end of 1975, a partnership was cobbled out. Montreal financier R. Howard Webster pledged to finance an additional 45 percent, with Page Wadsworth of the Canadian Imperial Bank of Commerce contributing the remaining 10 percent."[19]

This was not the first attempt to bring a major-league baseball franchise to Toronto. In the 1950s, when Jack Kent Cooke owned the Maple Leafs, he initiated unsuccessful attempts to persuade the Boston Braves, the Detroit Tigers, the Philadelphia Athletics, and the St. Louis Browns to relocate from their respective cities."[20] In 1959, Cooke became a catalyst for the Continental League to emerge as a third major league. When the American League voted to expand for 1961, thereby crushing the Continental League, Cooke abandoned the Leafs.[21]

In addition to the Indians, the city of Toronto also entered preliminary talks with the San Diego Padres and the Baltimore Orioles to move their teams north of the border. However, these discussions all occurred before the stadium renovation was complete in August 1975.[22] Solway and his associates tried to purchase an existing team and move it to Toronto. The San Francisco Giants, owned by Horace Stoneham, became their test case.

"It was common knowledge [Stoneham] was trying to sell," recalled Solway. "If he had been able to find a buyer in San Francisco, we wouldn't ever have been involved."[23] The 72-year-old owner was nearly bankrupt and suffering from a chronic heart ailment.[24] Once a perennial contender in the National League, as recently as 1971, the Giants struggled under baseball's new economic structure. The team was $4.5 million in debt, compounded by massive losses for 1974 and 1975.[25] The league recalled a $500,000 loan on December 1, 1975.[26] As the club was saddled with a municipal lease through 1994, Stoneham decided to clot the red ink. The Giants were officially for sale. John D'Acquisto, a pitcher for the Giants, remembered:

"They were talking about the National League taking over the official business of the team but had to cut salaries to make it affordable. Just a bad situation for a team. We didn't know if we were going to Tampa or Toronto ... or if we were staying home in San Francisco."[27]

To compound matters, the Giants had become accustomed to playing their home games before a sea of empty bleachers. Having inherited the team in 1936, Stoneham was "oblivious to modern marketing methods."[28] Fans who continued to purchase overpriced tickets could expect to eat rotten food at the concessions before returning to slashed tires in the parking lot.[29] Though they finished a respectable third in 1975, the Giants drew a paltry 522,919. That attendance figure was actually an improvement over 1974!

Giants vice president Charles Rupert and solicitor Jim Hunt met with McDougall and Solway at the winter meetings in Hollywood, Florida, to negotiate the sale of the team. The parties agreed on $13.25 million: $8 million for the team and $5.25 million to finance litigation costs associated with breaking the municipal lease.[30] After both ownership groups received approval from their boards, Stoneham made the announcement official on January 9, 1976.[31]

This was not how George Moscone envisioned spending his first day as mayor of San Francisco. Almost immediately, he filed an injunction with Superior Court to prevent the Giants from moving. One of Stoneham's directors, real-estate magnate Bob Lurie, formed a partnership with Minnesota hotelier Bob Short to purchase the Giants and keep them in San Francisco. Feeney insisted that he was through granting loans to float the franchise.[32] Lurie had until noon on February 11 to find appropriate financing.[33] With one day to spare, Short backed out.[34] McDougall remained hopeful that the Giants would play the 1976 season in Toronto.

"Logic is still on our side," said McDougall. "Changing ownership is not going to put people in the ballpark and it's not going to pay the bills."[35] Lurie asked the National League for an extension to find a partner. The league gave him five hours! At 2:45 P.M. on February 11, Lurie took a long-distance call from Arizona. It was meatpacker Arthur Herseth, offering to invest the funds required to keep the Giants in San Francisco. An agreement in principle on a deal was reached, and the offer to purchase was approved by Feeney with only minutes to spare.[36] Judge John Benson ruled that the Giants were remaining in ... "Baghdad by the Bay." Godfrey described the ensuing atmosphere in Toronto as "letting a ground ball go through your legs."[37]

Assistant general manager Elliott Wahle and his prize pupils at the Canadian Baseball Hall of Fame induction, June 2018; (from left) Paul Hodgson, Lloyd Moseby, Wahle, and Willie Upshaw. (Courtesy of Lisa Chisholm)

Opening Day in Toronto, April 7, 1977, as a snowstorm blankets the field at Exhibition Stadium. (Courtesy of Elliott and Helene Wahle)

Although Toronto struck out in San Francisco, a white knight appeared on the horizon in Seattle. After the city lost the Pilots in 1970, the State of Washington filed a $32 million antitrust lawsuit against the American League.[38] The suit was dropped when the junior circuit agreed to expand to Seattle and one additional city. Godfrey recalled that "all the time we spent ... trying to focus on buying a National League team, Lee MacPhail would tell us, 'Don't be surprised if you wind up in our league.'"[39]

MacPhail was not wrong. On March 20, 1976, the American League voted 11 to 1 to award its second expansion franchise to Toronto."[40] In the words of Bob Elliott, "Irish wakes lasted longer than the [city's] mourning period."[41] After establishing a $7 million entrance fee, McDougall exclaimed that "we are very pleased, needless to say."[42]

Charles Bronfman, the owner of the Montreal Expos, and John McHale, the club president, began to campaign among their fellow National League owners to expand to Toronto. As McDougall assessed, "They knew they didn't have a successful product on the field and that a team in Toronto would help them at the gate."[43] A preliminary vote showed 8 in favor and 4 against but league rules required unanimity. As long as August A. Busch of the Cardinals remained resolute in his opposition to expansion, it was not going to happen. Don McDougall said he could still hear the words of his fellow brewer from St. Louis:

"I have no problem with Labatt's, I have no problem with Toronto, but I do have a problem with watering down our product. That's what I fear expansion is going to do."[44] A second vote was taken, 9 in favor and 3 against. When the Reds and Phillies echoed Busch's concerns, Commissioner Kuhn advised Toronto officials to refrain from signing any paperwork with the American League, as he envi-

sioned that the strategy would generate enough time for National League owners to arrive at a consensus.[45] The American League remained prepared to expand to Toronto, but not until the National League had committed not to do so. Somehow, the Cardinals had switched their bias and after a third vote, the score was now 10 to 2. Kuhn told Godfrey to "give me a couple of weeks and I'll work on the two votes."[46] The final vote was 7 to 5; Toronto was going to the American League.

Although the league issue had been resolved, McDougall now had competition from a second ownership group, headed by Philip and Irving Granovsky of Atlantic Packaging. Their presence posed a problem for the Labatt's consortium. The brothers were friends of Jerold Hoffberger, owner of the Orioles and former president of the National Breweries in Baltimore. In 1975, Hoffberger had sold National to none other than Carling O'Keefe. As per Louis Cauz, "[he] was against the Labatt's group, which needed at least nine of twelve votes to be awarded a franchise. Hoffberger had control of three votes and needed one more owner to side with him at league meetings."[47] The Labatt's people hatched a plan to convince the American League to award the franchise to them.

"Lee MacPhail was flying to Toronto to meet with [Phil and Irving]," Don McDougall remembered. "I had a guy meet him at the airport and said, 'After you meet with him, come downtown and meet with us.' We entertained MacPhail for the rest of the day."[48] The ploy worked and the American League voted 11 to 1 to award the franchise to Labatt's as Hoffberger cast the dissenting ballot. Webster was named chairman of the board of Metro Baseball Ltd. while Labatt's vice president Peter Hardy became vice chairman. Rounding out the Board of Directors were CIBC vice president David Lewis and former Premier of Ontario John P. Robarts. Toronto's membership in the American League became official on April 27, 1976."[49]

The first employee of Metro Baseball Ltd. was Paul Beeston, a chartered accountant from Welland appointed to oversee business operations. After initially considering Frank Cashen, the club hired Peter Bavasi away from the Padres to become general manager.[50]

"What an opportunity!" recalled Bavasi. "At age 34, to have a chance to build a club from scratch for a wealthy and detached ownership group didn't take much thought on my part. Padres owner Ray Kroc and my father [Buzzie Bavasi] both said, 'You've been in training for this job since you were a kid. Go do it!'"[51]

Pat Gillick soon followed from the Yankees to serve as vice president, bringing his assistant Elliott Wahle with him. Gillick's mentor with the Astros and the Yankees, Tal Smith, encouraged him to accept the Toronto position: "Pat has been a dear friend ever since we worked together with the Houston Colt .45s, when he joined us in 1963. When I went to New York I was able to encourage Pat to join us there. I had a hand in recommending him to Don McDougall to head up their operation."[52]

Beeston was not the only Canadian hired by the original Blue Jays. Scarborough's Bob Prentice was hired from the Detroit Tigers to become the director of Canadian scouting. Barrie's Ken Carson left the Pittsburgh Penguins to become the trainer while Howard Starkman moved across town from the hockey Toronto Maple Leafs to become the director of public relations.[53] Whom would Bavasi hire to manage the team? What nobody realized is that the position was preordained as far back as 1964.

"During that first year at Albuquerque, I was so grateful to Roy Hartsfield for having been such a big part of my baseball education, that I said to him, 'Skip, if I ever get a big-league club of my very own, I hope you'll consider being my manager,'" Bavasi said. "I was, what, 22? The chance of me making it out of the Texas League was a distant thought back then."[54] In 1976, Hartsfield led the Hawaii Islanders to their second consecutive Pacific Coast League championship.[55] The Georgia native was as famous for his unintelligible homespun expressions as his exceptional ability to mold young players with patience and understanding.[56]

Rod Gaspar, who played four years for Hartsfield, retains fond memories of his manager: "Roy was a good man and I enjoyed playing for him in Hawaii. Of course, I enjoyed any manager who played me regularly."[57]

Bavasi made the unilateral decision on Father's Day to hire Hartsfield. "I called Roy at his hotel in Honolulu and told him I was making good on my promise. He'd be the team's manager if he wanted the job. Roy accepted. I told him we'd wait to announce his appointment until later September, so as to milk the story of who might manage the club."[58] Names like Yogi Berra, Elston Howard, and Dick Williams were all linked as potential managers.[59]

In hindsight, Bavasi was amazed that in a city with three daily newspapers, the story never leaked. He said, "Neil MacCarl [of the *Toronto Star*] came knocking on my door at 4 A.M., yelling, 'We know it's Joe Altobelli! We're going

with it.' But now someone said Walter Alston is considering your offer.' I would call Roy often, warning him that no matter what he read on the wire, he was our manager."[60]

Torontonians submitted more than 30,000 entries in a "name the team" contest and the results were announced on August 12. Metro Baseball Ltd. was now officially known the Toronto Blue Jays.[61] According to the press release, "The blue jay is a North American bird. ... [I]t is strong, aggressive, and inquisitive. It dares to take on all comers yet is down-to-earth, gutsy, and good looking."[62] Initial reaction to the name was lukewarm if not cynical. Harvey Sahker, then a high-school sophomore, said he did not "remember what I suggested but it was not Blue Jays."[63] Budding sports author Eric Zweig added, "[T]o be honest, 'Blue Jays' seemed a little wimpy as a name but I think it was the logo that won us all over."[64]

Bavasi aimed to introduce a logo that was "as easily recognizable as [Ray] Kroc's golden arches."[65] He argued that "the logo did three important things: it said who we are, what we do, and where we're from."[66] Though the logo was popular with the fans, it was not approved immediately. American League rules prohibited the image of a baseball on any logo because the graphic hindered the hitter's ability to follow the trajectory of the actual horsehide. As Bavasi recalled, "[F]ortunately for us, no one complained."[67] Forty years later, Howard Starkman observed that "the logo was ranked among the best in baseball."[68]

This photo representing the death of the Seattle Pilots was taken at Sicks Stadium in March 1970, one month before the franchise expired in bankruptcy court. The threat of an antitrust lawsuit by the State of Washington against the American League prompted the circuit to expand to Seattle and Toronto. (Courtesy of David S. Eskenazi)

Once the regular season had concluded, the Blue Jays hired their coaching and broadcasting staff. Bob Miller, Hartsfield's pitching coach in Hawaii, followed him to Toronto. Other coaches included Don Leppert, Harry Warner, Jackie Moore, along with former Red Sox All-Star second baseman Bobby Doerr. Two Southerners, Tom Cheek and Early Wynn, were hired to broadcast baseball on the radio to millions of Canadians.

With a coaching staff in order, it was time to assemble the team. On October 21, 1976, Phil Roof became the first Blue Jay when the club acquired the former Leafs catcher from the Chicago White Sox. The following day, the team purchased the contracts of Dave Hilton, Dave Roberts, and John Scott from the Padres and Chuck Hartenstein from Hawaii – all disciples of Bavasi and Hartsfield.

The Plaza Hotel in New York played host to the expansion draft on November 5. With their first pick, the Blue Jays selected Bob Bailor. A star prospect in the Orioles farm system, Bailor was unable to displace Mark Belanger at shortstop in Baltimore. On Gillick's advice, the club drafted Otto Velez and Garth Iorg from the Yankees. Meanwhile, Bill Singer, who had pitched a no-hitter for the Dodgers, was drafted from the Twins. Former Leaf Rico Carty was drafted from the Indians. Other notable names included Jim Clancy, Pete Vuckovich, and Ernie Whitt – all of whom continued to play well into the 1980s. The one Canadian Blue Jay, Dave McKay, was at home in Vancouver when he was drafted from the Twins: "I found out watching the late-night news. We turned our phone off having put the baby [Cody McKay] down that afternoon, and forgot to turn it back on. Friends and family were calling all evening.[69]

In a pre-orchestrated deal with the Indians, the Blue Jays sent drafted pitcher Al Fitzmorris to Cleveland for Alan Ashby and Doug Howard. A month later, Carty was traded back to the Indians for John Lowenstein and Rick Cerone. Dave Roberts and Mike Weathers were soon traded for two more Bavasi players, Jerry Johnson and Ron Fairly, respectively.

The best trade of all, as it were, was the one that was never executed. Here is how Elliott Wahle recalled what transpired: "At the very end of spring training, sitting in an office with one desk and two telephones. We sat with the polyester uniforms drying over our heads with the heat on. The phone rang and it was Gabe Paul with the Yankees. He offered us Ron Guidry for Bill Singer, straight up. Peter says, 'We're not making the trade because Singer

is the marketing face of the new Blue Jays.' Gillick says, 'I can put the uniform on and people will think I'm Singer.' Peter was unmoved."[70]

As training camp broke in Dunedin, Florida, in 1977, the Blue Jays estimated their payroll budget at $5.2 million.[71] Although Singer had pitched well, the fledgling franchise experienced growth pains in many other areas. While watching Bob Bailor play shortstop, Pat Gillick noted "questions about his arm," and the prospect was moved to the outfield.[72] The top-rated hitter, John Lowenstein, batted .222 and butted heads with the manager, prompting a trade back to Cleveland for Hector Torres.[73] Even a man of Hartsfield's optimism could not hide his low expectations, offering that "the guys I managed in Hawaii were probably a better team."[74]

Ultimately, the Blue Jays posted a Grapefruit League record of 8-16. Errors were commonplace both on and off the field. One game in Sarasota, Starkman neglected to bring a tape of "O Canada" from Dunedin. After "The Star Spangled Banner" concluded, the numerous Canadians in the crowd began to sing their anthem in unison. Home-plate umpire Jim McKean, a Montrealer, halted the first pitch until "O Canada" had concluded.[75] Tom Cheek recalled the cramped quarters of the broadcast booth in Dunedin that forced the engineer to sit in the stands adjacent to the players' wives. One game, the sound of a baby crying was being carried by a microphone on the field; it belonged to Ashley Whitt, Ernie's infant daughter.[76]

Moving north to Toronto, the Blue Jays faced additional obstacles as they prepared to host the White Sox on April 7. As the team was celebrated by a civic parade the day before, Ed Roete of Environment Canada forecast, "[T]he weather isn't going to be terrific for baseball, but there will be no snow or rain."[77] Louis Cauz recalls that at 10:00 A.M. on the morning of the game, he "didn't think it would be possible to play because of a swirling snowstorm [just west of Toronto]."[78]

As the scheduled 1:30 start time approached, Eric Zweig was eating lunch at a restaurant near Exhibition Stadium: "At some point, standing in the buffet line, someone said, "It's snowing!" We looked out the window and it was really coming down!"[79] White Sox infielder Jack Brohamer strapped on a pair of shin pads to be used as cross-country skis as the teams waited for a Zamboni to arrive. Would the weather postpone or cancel the game? For 44,649 fans, the climate hardly seemed to matter. Louis Cauz observed the pregame atmosphere as follows:

"Earlier, when I arrived at the stadium and saw the field, I had my doubts that a game would be played. But knowing the importance of the historic moment, and witnessing other snow-plagued fields on Opening Day in places like Cincinnati. ... I hoped the Zamboni could do the job of clearing the field."[80] He added, "[P]late umpire Nestor Chylak joked about his crew, saying that third-base rookie umpire Steve Palermo had never seen snow before." Although no fans were brave enough to streak across the frigid field, Cauz can still picture "one group of fans behind home plate, from Quebec, removed their sweaters and shirts and was bare-breasted for a few innings."[81]

Toronto industrialist Harvey Wagman, who died in 2003, described the crowd passing his factory on Dufferin Street as "a parade of people wearing their parkas and carrying coolers."[82] In times of less restrictive security and archaic blue laws, the coolers were required to sneak beer into Exhibition Stadium. Even though the Blue Jays were owned by Labatt's, "Prohibition Stadium" could not legally sell alcoholic beverages.

Despite the awful weather, Chylak insisted that the game go on. Anne Murray sang the national anthems and was accompanied by the 48th Highlanders. Robin Godfrey, Paul's son, threw out the ceremonial first ball as chants of "We want beer!" could be heard throughout the stadium.[83]

Finally, at 1:48 P.M., Bill Singer delivered the first pitch of the game to Chicago leadoff hitter Ralph Garr. It was a strike. Baseball was back in town.

## Epilogue

The Blue Jays defeated the White Sox, 9-5, in their inaugural game despite the frigid temperatures. After posting a record of 10-11 in April, the wheels fell off the engine. The Blue Jays completed the 1977 season with a record of 54-107. Failing to crack even the 60-win barrier, the club fired Roy Hartsfield as manager in 1979. Pat Gillick estimated that it would take a decade for the team to contend and he was not far off. The Blue Jays won 99 games and their first division title in 1985, their ninth American League campaign, before falling one game short of the World Series to the Kansas City Royals.

*Acknowledgements*

Marty Appel, Alan Ashby, Peter Bavasi, Louis Cauz, Scott Crawford, John D'Acquisto, Alan Eagleson, Bob Elliott, Dan Epstein, Marsha Franty, Rod Gaspar, Pat Gillick, Jerry Howarth, Donald McDougall, Dave McKay, Jim Prime, Harvey Sahker, Robin Silverberg, Tal Smith, Howard Starkman, Harvey Wagman (1919-2003), Elliott Wahle, Sam Zeifman, and Eric Zweig.

**Notes**

1 Louis E. Cauz, *Baseball's Back in Town* (Toronto: Controlled Media Corporation, 1977), 143.

2 Lloyd Johnson and Miles Wolff, *The Encyclopedia of Minor League Baseball*, 2nd edition (Asheville, North Carolina: Baseball America Inc., 1997), 496.

3 Jane Finnan Dorward, "The Fleet Street Flats," in *Dominionball: Baseball Above the 49th* (Cleveland: Society for American Baseball Research, 2005), 68.

4 Interview with Louis Cauz, January 5, 2018 (Hereafter Cauz interview).

5 Bob Elliott, *Canada's World Champions: Blue Jays Trivia Quiz Book* (Toronto: McClelland & Stewart Inc., 1993), 24.

6 Elliott, 24.

7 Cauz interview.

8 Elliott, 25.

9 Dorward, 94.

10 Cauz, 185.

11 Dorward, 95.

12 Neil MacCarl, „In the Beginning..." in Eric Zweig, ed., *Toronto Blue Jays Official 25th Anniversary Commemorative Book* (Toronto: Dan Diamond and Associates Inc., 2001), 10.

13 Helena Moncrieff, "Sydney Cooper, P.Eng. (ON), M.E.I.C., Athlete and Family Man, Shares Talent, Time and Treasures," *Canadian Jewish News*: October 12, 2017: B7.

14 Interview with Don McDougall, January 13, 2018 (Hereafter McDougall interview).

15 Ibid.

16 Cauz, 187

17 McDougall interview.

18 Ibid.

19 Elliott, 27.

20 Cauz, 102.

21  Dorward, 94.

22  Ibid.

23  Elliott, 28.

24  Dan Epstein, *Stars and Strikes: Baseball and America in the Bicentennial Summer of '76* (New York: St. Martin's Press, 2014), 36.

25  Ron Fimrite, "A Giant Step in the Right Direction," *Sports Illustrated*, April 19, 1976: 19.

26  Steve Clarke. "The San Toronto Giants," in Keith McArthur, ed., *Bat Flip: The Greatest Toronto Blue Jays Stories Ever Told* (Toronto: FanReads Inc., 2016), 2.

27  Interview with John D'Acquisto, December 27, 2017.

28  Epstein, 36.

29  Ibid.

30  Elliott, 29.

31  Clarke, 3.

32  Epstein, 50.

33  Elliott, 32.

34  Cauz, 189.

35  Epstein, 50.

36  Fimrite: 19.

37  Elliott, 32.

38  Ken Hogan, *The 1969 Seattle Pilots: Major League Baseball's One-Year Wonders* (Jefferson, North Carolina: McFarland & Company Inc., 2006), 139.

39  Elliott, 46-47.

40  Cauz interview.

41  Elliott, 32.

42  Epstein, 83.

43  McDougall interview.

44  Ibid.

45  Epstein, 84.

46  Elliott, 48.

47  Cauz interview.

48  McDougall interview.

49  Cauz, 189.

50  Stephen Brunt, *Diamond Dreams: 20 Years of Blue Jays Baseball* (Toronto: Viking Canada AHC, 1996), 69.

51  Interview with Peter Bavasi, December 30, 2017 (Bavasi interview).

52  Interview with Tal Smith, November 7, 2017.

53  MacCarl, 11.

54  Bavasi interview.

55  Maxwell Kates, "Rod Gaspar," in Matthew Silverman and Ken Samelson, eds., *The Miracle Has Landed* (Hanover, Massachusetts: Maple Street Press LLC, 2009), 75.

56  Jim Prime, *Tales from the Toronto Blue Jays Dugout* (New York: Sports Publishing, 2014), 116.

57  Interview with Rod Gaspar, December 2, 2017.

58  Bavasi interview.

59  Elliott, 59.

60  Bavasi interview.

61  MacCarl, 10.

62  Epstein, 252.

63  Interview with Harvey Sahker, December 29, 2017.

64  Interview with Eric Zweig, December 28, 2017 (Zweig interview).

65  David H. Flaherty and Frank E. Manning, *The Beaver Bites Back: American Popular Culture in Canada* (Kingston, Ontario: McGill-Queen's University Press, 1993), 159.

66  Bavasi interview.

67  Elliott, 58.

68  Interview with Howard Starkman, January 10, 2018.

69  Interview with Dave McKay, January 3, 2018.

70  Interview with Elliott Wahle, January 17, 2018.

71  Elliott, 59.

72  Interview with Pat Gillick, January 20, 2018.

73  Interview with Louis Cauz, January 5, 2018 (Cauz interview).

74  Prime, 116.

75  MacCarl, 12.

76  Ibid.

77  Elliott, 41.

78  Cauz interview.

79  Zweig interview.

80  Cauz interview.

81  Ibid.

82  Conversation with Harvey Wagman, June 15, 2003.

83  Cauz interview.

## TORONTO BLUE JAYS EXPANSION DRAFT

| PICK | PLAYER | POSITION | FORMER TEAM |
|------|--------|----------|-------------|
| 1 | Bob Bailor | ss | Baltimore Orioles |
| 2 | Jerry Garvin | p | Minnesota Twins |
| 3 | Jim Clancy | p | Texas Rangers |
| 4 | Gary Woods | of | Oakland Athletics |
| 5 | Rico Carty | dh | Cleveland Indians |
| 6 | Butch Edge | p | Milwaukee Brewers |
| 7 | Al Fitzmorris | p | Kansas City Royals |
| 8 | Alvis Woods | of | Minnesota Twins |
| 9 | Mike Darr | p | Baltimore Orioles |
| 10 | Pete Vuckovich | p | Chicago White Sox |
| 11 | Jeff Byrd | p | Texas Rangers |
| 12 | Steve Bowling | of | Milwaukee Brewers |
| 13 | Dennis DeBarr | p | Detroit Tigers |
| 14 | Bill Singer | p | Minnesota Twins |
| 15 | Jim Mason | ss | New York Yankees |
| 16 | Doug Ault | 1b | Texas Rangers |
| 17 | Ernie Whitt | c | Boston Red Sox |
| 18 | Mike Weathers | 2b | Oakland Athletics |
| 19 | Steve Staggs | 2b | Kansas City Royals |
| 20 | Steve Hargan | p | Texas Rangers |
| 21 | Garth Iorg | 3b | New York Yankees |
| 22 | Dave Lemanczyk | p | Detroit Tigers |
| 23 | Larry Anderson | p | Milwaukee Brewers |
| 24 | Jesse Jefferson | p | Chicago White Sox |
| 25 | Dave McKay | 3b | Minnesota Twins |
| 26 | Tom Bruno | p | Kansas City Royals |
| 27 | Otto Velez | of | New York Yankees |
| 28 | Mike Willis | p | Baltimore Orioles |
| 29 | Sam Ewing | of | Chicago White Sox |
| 30 | Leon Hooten | p | Oakland Athletics |

# BILL SINGER

## BY JOEL RIPPEL

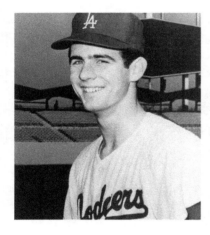

Late in his major-league career, Bill Singer pitched a complete-game victory despite throwing in pain the entire game. His postgame comments accurately described much of his career.

"It was so bad when I was warming up that I almost quit," said Singer. "It was killing me. But then it's easy to quit. Too easy. I wanted to give it a try."[1]

In a career plagued by injuries and illness, Singer never stopped trying and when healthy, he was a quality pitcher – throwing a no-hitter, finishing among league leaders in complete games and strikeouts, and winning 20 games in a season in both the American League and National League.

Singer, born William Robert Singer, was born on April 24, 1944, to Robert and Margaret Singer in Los Angeles. Singer and his sister were raised 30 miles east of Los Angeles in the suburb of Pomona. His father worked for General Dynamics in Pomona. In high school he played basketball and baseball. He was on the varsity baseball squad three years. He caught the attention of major-league scouts as a Pomona High School senior in 1961. (He had skipped a grade to graduate a year early.[2])

In September of 1961, the Los Angeles Dodgers outbid 14 other major-league teams for Singer with a signing bonus of $50,000. After signing, Singer reported to the Dodgers team in the Arizona Winter Instructional League.

He began his minor-league career in 1962 with Reno of the Class-C California League. His season got off to slow start, but he showed glimpses of his potential. On June 25 he improved to 5-2 with a 9-0 shutout of Visalia. "(The Los Angeles Dodgers') investment has started paying off," *The Sporting News* wrote. "The righthander, who was handicapped by a sore arm early in the season, gave up eight hits and struck out 14 batters."[3]

Singer finished the season with a 9-3 record, a 4.32 ERA and seven complete games. In 127 innings pitched, he struck out 136.

After the season Singer returned to the Arizona Instructional League and was added to the Dodgers' 40-man roster. He was one of "nine youngsters included on the 40-man roster … to help the club force-feed its youth movement."[4]

Singer spent the 1963 season with Albuquerque of the Double-A Texas League. Early in the season, in a 4-3 victory in Tulsa in which he struck out 14, he caused a commotion.

In the seventh inning, Tulsa manager Grover Resinger argued with umpire Gene Haack that Singer had been pitching illegally the entire game by starting his motion before he stepped on the rubber. Haack disagreed and ejected Resinger after he continued the debate.

In his next start, Singer hit San Antonio's Jim Wynn in the head with a pitch. Wynn was uninjured but was taken to a hospital as a precaution.

Later in May, Singer was sidelined with a sore arm. On July 6, he pitched five shutout innings against Tulsa but had to leave because of a sore arm. On August 30, he tossed his second shutout of the year, a 2-0 victory over San Antonio.

For the season Singer was 6-7 with a 5.78 ERA in 17 starts. He struck out 90 in 95 innings.

The 1964 season was a busy one for Singer. It included a no-hitter, a wedding, and his major-league debut. On April 23, the day before his 20th birthday, Singer pitched the no-hitter for Spokane in the first game of a Pacific Coast League doubleheader at Dallas. He walked two and struck out three in the 3-0 victory.

On September 11 Singer married Virginia Goodson, the sister-in-law of Marv Breeding, who had spent most of the season with Spokane before being sold to Rochester of the International League. Two days later – the final day of the PCL regular season – Singer was outdueled by Seattle's Wilbur Wood. After the game both pitchers earned promotions – Wood to the Pittsburgh Pirates and Singer to the Dodgers. For the season, Singer was 11-10 with a 4.16 ERA.

Singer made his major-league debut on September 24, 1964, in Chicago. He started and went 6 1/3 innings, allowing just one run, but got no decision in the 4-3 loss to the Cubs. In his first major-league at-bat, in the third inning against Cubs starter Dick Ellsworth, he singled.

Five days later, the 6-foot-4, 184-pound Singer started against the Cubs in LA. He went 7 2/3 innings and was the losing pitcher in the Cubs' 4-3 victory.

Singer returned to Spokane in 1965, and his season included several gems. On May 9 he had a one-hitter in the eighth inning before finishing with a four-hitter in a 3-1 victory over Vancouver. On July 6 he took a no-hitter into

the eighth inning before settling for a two-hitter in a 5-0 victory over San Diego. His bid for a perfect game was ended by Mel Queen's single with two out in the eighth.

A low point to season occurred before the Spokane Indians' 6-4 victory over visiting Vancouver on August 2. Singer and teammate Larry Staab got into a dispute and teammate Joe Moeller injured his left (nonpitching) shoulder trying to break up the dispute. The Indians announced that Singer and Staab would be "fined an undisclosed amount for each day Moeller is sidelined."[5] (Moeller, who had suffered a mild separation of his left shoulder, returned to action on August 18.) For the season Singer was 14-15 (Spokane was 57-90) with a 4.52 ERA.

Singer joined the Dodgers in early September, but he made just two short relief appearances for Los Angeles, which was en route to the National League pennant. On September 15 in Chicago, he faced two hitters, allowing a hit and a walk (neither scored), in the Dodgers' 8-6 loss to the Cubs. On October 3, the Dodgers' regular-season finale and the day after they clinched the pennant, Singer pitched one shutout inning in the Dodgers' 3-0 victory over Atlanta. After the season he pitched for San Juan in the Puerto Rico League.

In 1966, for the third consecutive year, Singer began the season with Spokane and finished it with the Dodgers. It would be his final season in the minor leagues. In 33 appearances with Spokane, he was 13-11 with a 3.48 ERA and 217 strikeouts in 233 innings pitched. In September, he made three relief appearances for the Dodgers, pitching four scoreless innings.

In 1967 Singer made the Dodgers' Opening Day roster for the first time. But he made just two relief appearances – pitching 3 2/3 innings – in the first month of the season.

He made his first start on May 14, in the second game of a doubleheader against the Cubs in Los Angeles, allowed two runs in five innings in the Cubs' 6-3, 11-inning victory. He earned his first major-league victory on May 29, when he went seven innings in a 7-2 victory over the New York Mets in Los Angeles. His next victory – and first shutout– was a 2-0 eight-hitter over San Francisco (and Juan Marichal) in Los Angeles on June 24. He struck out 10. Singer finished the season 12-8 with a 2.64 ERA in 32 appearances.

Over the next two seasons, Singer would live up to his nickname, "The Singer Throwing Machine." In 1968 he was 13-17 with a 2.88 ERA in 37 appearances. His 36 starts ranked fourth in the National League and he had six shutouts.

From start to finish in 1969, Singer was outstanding. On Opening Day, in Cincinnati, he made his only relief appearance of the season and pitched three shutout innings in relief of starter Don Drysdale to save the Dodgers' 3-2 victory over the Reds. The first save of Singer's career was also the first official save in major-league history. (That season saves became an official statistic.)

On July 23, Singer, who was 13-7 at the All-Star break, made his first All-Star Game appearance, pitching two perfect innings in the National League's 9-3 victory over the American League at RFK Stadium in Washington.

On October 2, the final day of the regular season, Singer went the distance in a 5-4 victory over Houston in Los Angeles for his 20th victory. He lost 12 games and had a career-best 2.34 ERA. He was third in the National League in innings pitched (315 $\frac{2}{3}$) and strikeouts (247).

Singer's 1970 season got off to a slow start. After allowing four earned runs in four innings in the Dodgers' 12-2 loss on April 16 at Cincinnati, he was 1-2. On April 22, two days before his 26th birthday, Singer was diagnosed with hepatitis. He spent three weeks in the hospital and was sidelined for nearly two months.

He returned to the mound on June 14 with a two-inning stint against the Cubs in Los Angeles. On June 19, he earned his second victory of the season by pitching five scoreless innings in a 6-1 victory over the Reds in Cincinnati. In his next start, on June 23 in Atlanta, he took a no-hitter into the eighth inning before it was broken up by Clete Boyer's single with two outs. The Dodgers won 7-0.

On July 20 Singer threw a no-hitter in a 5-0 victory over the Phillies at Dodger Stadium. He didn't walk anyone and struck out a season-high 10. "It's really fantastic. I'm so happy I could cry. I'm so thrilled and excited it's hard to explain," Singer said.[6]

Singer's season came to an abrupt finish on August 12. He suffered a fractured right index finger when he was struck by a pitch by the Pirates' Bob Moose. He finished the season with an 8-5 record and 3.13 ERA.

The next two seasons were a struggle for Singer. In 1971, he was 10-17 with a 4.16 ERA in 31 starts. In 1972 he was

a tough-luck pitcher. In his first 11 starts, he allowed just 32 runs (29 earned). But on June 24, in the second game of a doubleheader against Atlanta at Dodger Stadium, he suffered a broken middle finger on his left (nonpitching) hand during an at-bat. He was sidelined for three weeks. He finished the season with a 6-16 record and 3.67 ERA.

On November 28, 1972, Singer was part of a seven-player trade between the Dodgers and California Angels. Singer, Frank Robinson, Mike Strahler, Billy Grabarkewitz, and Bobby Valentine were sent to the Angels in exchange for Andy Messersmith and Ken McMullen.

After going 16-33 the previous two seasons with the Dodgers, Singer regained his 1969 form in the 1973 season. At the All-Star break, he was 15-5. He made his second All-Star Game appearance, pitching two innings (allowing three runs) in the National League's 7-1 victory on July 24 in Kansas City.

Singer got his 20th victory on the next-to-last day (September 29) of the regular season, pitching a complete-game 4-3 victory in 11 innings over the Twins in Anaheim. For the season, he was 20-14 with a 3.22 ERA. He made an Angels team-record 40 starts.

In 1974 Singer took a 7-3 record into his start against the Brewers on June 4 in Milwaukee. He pitched eight innings and took the 4-3 loss. It was Singer's last decision of the season.

After Milwaukee, the Angels went to Detroit for a three-game series. During the weekend, Singer returned to Southern California to have his back examined. He had first complained about lower back pain on May 22 after pitching a complete-game 6-1 victory over the Royals in Kansas City. On June 9, Singer was placed in traction and five days later, he underwent surgery to repair a ruptured lumbar disc. He was sidelined the rest of the season.

Singer recovered from the back surgery and returned to the Angels starting rotation in 1975. His season started off with promise. On April 30 in Kansas City, he earned the second and final save of his career by getting the final two outs in the Angels' 7-6 victory. On May 22 he pitched a complete-game, 6-3 victory over the Red Sox in Boston. After the game, Singer told reporters he had "worked the entire game with a pain behind his right shoulder."[7]

Singer said he thought the issue was tendinitis, which was a relief to him.

"When I pitched against Boston on the last homestand," he said, "I had my worst stuff in years. I've been concerned all season about my velocity and I went to the hospital for a checkup on the last day before we left on this trip. My mother and grandfather had diabetes and I had been showing some of the symptoms. The hospital has become my home away from home and I spent four hours there going through all kinds of tests. Fortunately, they were all negative."[8]

For the next month Singer made his scheduled starts. On May 31 at Anaheim Stadium, he lost a pitcher's duel with Baltimore's Mike Cuellar. Singer allowed just three hits and one walk while striking out 10, but Cuellar allowed just one hit in the Orioles' 1-0 victory.

On June 5 at Anaheim Stadium, Singer needed just 93 pitches in a complete-game 8-3 victory over Detroit, improving his record to 5-7. He would win just two more games the rest of the season.

After allowing eight runs in a 10-4 loss to Oakland on June 28, Singer pitched just two innings over the next three weeks. On August 14, he went 6 $\frac{1}{3}$ innings and was the winning pitcher over the Red Sox in Anaheim. It was his final victory of the season. He made his final appearance of the season on September 12, taking the loss in the first game of a doubleheader in Kansas City. For the season, he was 7-15 with a 4.98 ERA.

The 1975-76 offseason was eventful for Singer. He was mentioned in several proposed Angels trades, and on October 8 he underwent surgery on his elbow. Singer was optimistic after the surgery.

"If the elbow is in as good condition as they say it is, I should win a lot of games wherever I am," said Singer. "Dr. (Frank) Jobe says he did a little housework on the elbow and smoothed down the spurs. He said the elbow was in remarkably good condition for pitching as many years as I have."[9]

After the surgery, Singer was expected to resume throwing in mid-December. A week before his return to the mound, he was traded. On December 10 the Angels sent him to the Texas Rangers in exchange for first baseman Jim Spencer and $100,000. The trade was expected to set up another deal by the Angels.

When he announced the trade at baseball's winter meetings in Hollywood, Florida, Angels general manager Harry Dalton said, "The addition of Spencer gives greater depth and opens up an opportunity to put together a package for another trade."[10]

Singer told reporters, "I can't remember the last time I entered a season in which I wasn't attempting a comeback. But I definitely feel I can be a winning pitcher again. If I didn't feel that way, I wouldn't play. I realize that the operation may have diminished my trading value, but apparently Harry Dalton just wanted to get rid of me. I think Texas got the best of the deal by far. I want to play on a contender and I'm hopeful Texas can be one. The Angels treated me fairly but they certainly aren't going to win a pennant next year."[11]

The next day the Angels traded Spencer and Morris Nettles to Chicago White Sox in exchange for Bill Melton and Steve Dunning.

Singer was healthy again in 1976, making 36 starts — for two teams. He got off to a good start with the Rangers, going 4-1 with a 3.48 ERA in 10 starts. On June 1 he was traded to the Minnesota Twins, which sparked a controversy.

On the day of the trade, Singer started for the Rangers against the White Sox in Chicago. He went 5 $\frac{1}{3}$ innings in the Rangers' 6-5 victory in 16 innings. While the game was still in progress — but after Singer had been replaced on the mound — the trade of Singer, pitcher Jim Gideon, and infielders Roy Smalley and Mike Cubbage to the Twins in exchange for Bert Blyleven and shortstop Danny Thompson was announced.

After the announcement of the trade, the White Sox played the rest of the game under protest, claiming the Rangers had used an ineligible player. Three days later, American League President Lee MacPhail turned down the protest but criticized the Rangers for the way they handled the deal.

"The manner in which this transaction was handled by the Texas club could properly be questioned," MacPhail said in a statement. "Although on occasion it may be necessary to play a player after a trade has been agreed upon but before it takes effect, such a practice should be avoided whenever possible.

"This is especially true of a starting pitcher. There is the danger of injury and there is also the danger of premature publicity and knowledge by the player that he is playing for a team of which, in a few hours, he will no longer be a member. Potentially this could create a problem involving the integrity of the game."[12]

Singer pitched effectively for the Twins, going 9-9 with a 3.77 ERA. For the season, he was 13-10 with a 3.69 ERA.

There would be another uniform change for Singer after the season. In November the Twins left him unprotected and he was taken by the Toronto Blue Jays in the expansion draft.

Singer, who had signed a three-year contract with Texas for approximately $100,000 per season before the trade to the Twins, was apparently too expensive for Twins owner Calvin Griffith. "I don't believe," Griffith said, "that you should guarantee anybody three years' salary. A Rod Carew, or somebody like that, you can guarantee them. But a pitcher can go out there and throw one ball and be through for the rest of his life."[13]

Singer was expected to be a leader on the Blue Jays pitching staff. In *The Sporting News,* Neal MacCarl wrote, "The pitching starts with veteran Bill Singer, 32, who had his normal unimpressive spring because of the usual shoulder problems, but he will be okay."[14]

Singer was the Blue Jays' Opening Day pitcher on April 7 against the Chicago White Sox in Toronto. He allowed four runs (three earned) and 11 hits in 4 $\frac{1}{3}$ innings in the Blue Jays' 9-5 victory. The playing conditions were less than ideal – snow before the game and near-freezing temperatures.

MacCarl wrote, "(Singer) had trouble with a slippery mound on the snow-covered field. ..."[15]

After going 0-4 in April, Singer earned his first victory of the season on May 4, allowing two runs and five hits in six innings in a 10-3 victory over Milwaukee in Toronto. In his next start, on May 9, he went seven innings, his longest outing of the season, in defeating Seattle, 10-4 for his second victory. It was his final victory of the season.

Singer was still being bothered by pain in his shoulder. He had a cortisone injection in mid-May. After a start on June 1, when he allowed four earned runs in 4 $\frac{1}{3}$ innings in an 11-3 loss to Milwaukee in Toronto, he missed his next scheduled start because of the pain. He was placed on the disabled list on June 7. He came off the disabled list on July 13 and pitched 2 $\frac{1}{3}$ innings of relief (allowing four runs) in an 11-3 loss to Detroit in Toronto on July

16. He returned to the disabled list on July 22 because of back pain.

On August 3 Singer underwent surgery in California to repair a damaged disc. For the season he was 2-8 with 6.79 ERA in just 13 appearances.

Singer spent the 1978 season on the disabled list and on December 2, the Blue Jays released him. For his career, he was 118-127 with a 3.39 ERA in 322 appearances. He had 94 complete games and 24 shutouts.

After retirement, Singer transitioned to the real-estate business. The *Los Angeles Times* wrote, "Former Los Angeles Dodger pitcher Bill Singer has joined Coldwell Banker in Newport Beach as a commercial real estate salesman. … [H]e has been interested in real estate for some time. In 1961, when the Dodgers signed him up at the age of 17, he invested a bonus in a duplex on the Balboa peninsula."[16]

Besides running Bill Singer & Associates, an industrial and commercial real-estate company, Singer devoted a lot of time to youth baseball in Southern California. In 1983, he organized the Newport Beach Little League, which as of 2018 operated on 10 fields and included more than 1,000 players. He also had a hand in forming a PONY League in Newport Beach and a Winter League for 8- to 18-year-olds. He became commissioner of Orange County's first Connie Mack League, for players 18 and under.[17]

Singer helped organize the Newport Beach Little League because there was no place for his young sons, Randy and Jason, to play.

"There are a lot of kids who want to learn the game," Singer said. "I'm just glad I can help in some way. Baseball was really good to me, and I guess you can say I'm giving back to the game. But I really just enjoy doing it. It's fun to see kids given a chance to learn."[18]

Singer also worked with American League President Bobby Brown to develop a program to alleviate the fear factor for young players. He also helped create the Greater Los Angeles Basin Collegiate League, an eight-team wood-bat league.

He also held various scouting and consulting positions with several major-league organizations.

## Sources

In addition to the sources cited in the Notes, the author also consulted Baseball-Reference.com, Newspapers. com, and Retrosheet.org.

## Notes

1 Ross Newhan, "Singer Pitches in Pain, Red Sox Do Suffering," *Los Angeles Times*, May 23, 1975: III, 1.

2 Author interview with Bill Singer on May 24, 2018.

3 "Minor League Highlights, Class C," *The Sporting News*, July 7, 1962: 53.

4 Bob Hunter, "Dodgers Sort Chaff from Wheat – Load Roster with Kiddies," *The Sporting News*, November 24, 1962: 9.

5 "Players to Be Fined Until Peacemaker Pal Recovers," *The Sporting News*, August 14, 1965: 32.

6 Bill Langley, "Singer Gains 'The Hall' by No-Hitting Phillies," *Pomona* (California) *Progress-Bulletin*, July 21, 1970: B6.

7 Ross Newhan, "Singer Pitches in Pain."

8 Ibid.

9 Dick Miller, "More Surgery Clouds Singer's Future," *The Sporting News*, November 1, 1975: 19.

10 Ross Newhan, "Angels Trade Singer to Set Up New Deal," *Los Angeles Times*, December 11, 1975: III, 1.

11 Ibid.

12 "MacPhail Nixes Protest, Raps Texas," *Chicago Daily Herald*, June 5, 1976: 14.

13 Gary Libman, "Twins' Singer, Braun drafted," *Minneapolis Tribune*, November 5, 1976: 1B.

14 Neal MacCarl, "Jays Opting for Experience," *The Sporting News*, April 9, 1977: 28.

15 Neil MacCarl, "Only Beer Is Missing at Blue Jays' Heady Bow," *The Sporting News*, April 23, 1977: 16.

16 "People on the Move," *Los Angeles Times*, November 5, 1978: IX, 11.

17 Chris Foster, "Pitching in to Promote His Passion," *Los Angeles Times*, August 2, 1990: C12.

18 Ibid.

# PETE VUCKOVICH

## BY RORY COSTELLO

Pete Vuckovich was a menacing figure. He was big: 6-feet-4 and 220 pounds (or more). He glowered over a Fu Manchu mustache and often had a few days' growth elsewhere to go with his long, unkempt hair. While pitching, he had "a streak of calculated weirdness."[1] Rasputin comparisons arose, and he encouraged them, applauding the Mad Monk's "extreme mental energy and intense concentration."[2] To those who knew him, Vuckovich was funny and friendly – but his on-field demeanor was just right for his small yet memorable role as the unpleasant, tobacco-spitting "Clu Haywood" in the 1989 cult classic *Major League*.

As a player, the combative Vuckovich combined mound psychology with a very wide repertoire. It made the righty effective for several years in the late 1970s and early '80s. With the Milwaukee Brewers, he led the American League in winning percentage in both 1981 and 1982. He won the AL Cy Young Award in 1982, helping the Brewers to the pennant.

Arm problems then curtailed Vuckovich's career. He pitched in just three games in 1983 and missed all of '84. He retired as a player after spring training 1987. Vuckovich soon came back to baseball, though, as a color commentator for Brewers telecasts. He went on to serve the Pittsburgh Pirates, Seattle Mariners, and Arizona Diamondbacks in various capacities for more than 20 years.

Peter Dennis Vuckovich was born on October 27, 1952, in Johnstown, Pennsylvania. "Having a life at all was his biggest victory – actually a series of victories," said St. Louis sportswriter Mike Eisenbath. "He had many brushes with death. Vuke was born with the umbilical cord wrapped around his neck; he suffered undiagnosed appendicitis that led to peritonitis when he was 1½; he had a benign tumor removed from his head a year later."[3]

The close calls didn't end there. As a high-school sophomore, complications from his appendicitis episode led to emergency surgery. "I almost cashed it in right there," he said in 1982. At age 21, he drove over an 80-foot embankment at 105 miles per hour. The car rolled over several times, yet somehow he walked out of it. After that he was installing a 15,000-volt reactor, which shorted. "Six more inches and I'd have been fried like a piece of bacon."[4]

Vuckovich's parents were both of Serbian descent. His father was Lazo Vuckovich, a steel-mill worker. His mother, Bosiljka (née Gjurich), was a homemaker known for her baked goods, especially orehnjača, or Serbian nut roll. They were fondly known as "Laze" and "Bossie" or "Bosa" – but they also went by the Americanized names Louis and Betty. Pete was the only boy among five children. His sisters were named Dianne, Karyn, Melanie, and Maryann.[5]

Vuckovich's childhood baseball heroes were Roberto Clemente, Bob Gibson, and Juan Marichal.[6] He was later compared to "The Dominican Dandy" for using varied arm angles. Pete knew he wanted to be a pitcher when he was 8 years old.[7] He inherited some ability from his father, a noted pitcher in fast softball circles around Johnstown. He was largely a self-made player, though, because "Dad was too busy earning a living in the steel mills."[8]

At Conemaugh Valley High School in Johnstown, Vuckovich stood out in three sports, also including football (as a receiver) and basketball (as a forward).[9] The school's baseball field was later named in his honor.

After graduating in 1970, Vuckovich turned down football scholarships from Navy, Pitt, Michigan State, and other major schools. Instead, he attended Clarion State College in northwestern Pennsylvania – mainly because his wife-to-be, Anna Kuzak, was going there.[10]

Staying in school also kept Vuckovich out of the Vietnam War. Of this, he later remarked, "I've taken a lot of guff along the way but that's politics and I don't want to get into politics."[11] He aimed to become a schoolteacher.[12]

Though Vuckovich had mainly been a pitcher in high school, he had filled in across the infield, so he told Clarion baseball coach Joe Knowles that he could play anywhere but catcher. "Maybe I shouldn't have said that," Vuckovich recalled, "but I was cocky back then. Coach Knowles said I'd play second base – the position I had probably the least experience with." However, he proved more valuable as a pitcher.[13] He was All-Conference in the Pennsylvania State Athletics Conference from 1972 through 1974 and an NAIA All-American in 1974.[14]

While in high school and college, Vuckovich also played with the All American Amateur Baseball Association. Johnstown has hosted the AAABA's annual tournament since 1945. Vuckovich became the first player from his hometown to appear in that tourney for four consecutive years (1969-72).

On the recommendation of scout Fred Shaffer, the Chicago White Sox selected Vuckovich in the third round of the June 1974 amateur draft.[15] He split that summer between Appleton (Class-A Midwest League) and Knoxville (Double-A Southern League).

Vuckovich then jumped to Triple A in 1975. With Denver of the American Association, he went 11-4 with a 4.34 ERA in 19 games. That May he thanked White Sox pitching coach Johnny Sain, saying, "He taught me all my breaking pitches in spring training – I mean everything – curve, slider, how to make the fastball sink, how to throw a changeup."[16]

Vuckovich got his first call to the majors that August, appearing twice before going back to Denver as Terry Forster came off the disabled list. As he later told it, Chicago manager Chuck Tanner had scouted him, liked what he'd seen, and said, "You're coming with me." To Tanner's great surprise, Vuckovich said that he didn't want to go, but explained that he wanted to be with Denver because he thought the Bears could win the Triple-A championship. Tanner agreed to send Vuckovich back for the league playoffs, which Denver lost in six games.[17] Vuckovich returned to the big club in September and got into two more games. He would not hurl again in the minors until 1986.

Also in 1975, Vuckovich married Anna. They had three sons: Lazo (like his grandfather, also known as Louis), Peter, and Damian.[18] Pete Jr. was also drafted by the White Sox out of Clarion (48th round, 2004) but injury cut his career short. In 2017, he became a scout for the Brewers.[19]

Vuckovich pitched in Puerto Rico for the Ponce Leones during the winter of 1975-76 and "showed well."[20] His manager was Ken Boyer, later his skipper with St. Louis. "Ken's the man who got me thinking like a big leaguer," Vuckovich later remarked. "He said to give it my best and not to let the little things bother me. He taught me the importance of concentration."[21]

For the White Sox in 1976, Vuckovich started seven times in 33 appearances, posting marks of 7-4, 4.65. He later took a swipe at manager Paul Richards (who'd succeeded Tanner) about how he was used. "I'll tell you what [Richards] knew about pitching. He made me a reliever, and he made Goose Gossage a starter."[22]

The AL added two new franchises – Seattle and the Toronto Blue Jays – for the 1977 season. In November 1976, the Blue Jays took Vuckovich as the 19th pick in the expansion draft. "To be truthful," he said the next year, "I didn't think that much about whether or not I would be protected. If I got drafted, I figured it was because somebody wanted me and I'd still be in the big leagues."[23]

Five years later, though, he thought differently. "It was a stupid decision for the White Sox to make. I had a pretty good idea even at 23, and I cared a lot. But I suppose it was all business for them. Maybe they spent $50,000 developing me, and they got $150,000 for me in the draft [actually $175,000]. So, they made $100,000 off the whole thing."[24] The team did run on a shoestring budget under Bill Veeck's ownership then.

Vuckovich was the first player to report to spring training for the Blue Jays. Manager Roy Hartsfield promptly told him, "We will not have any long hair or beards. Mustaches on the upper lip are OK, but that's all." Vuckovich, who said he'd had a mustache since he was 17, was already sporting his Fu Manchu.[25]

Vuckovich remained a swingman for Toronto, going 7-7, starting eight times in 53 games with a team-leading 3.47 ERA. He recorded the franchise's first save (on the frigid Opening Day at Exhibition Stadium) and its first shutout (as he outdueled Jim Palmer in Baltimore on June 26). However, that was his only season with the Jays. In December, he and a player to be named later (John Scott) went to the St. Louis Cardinals for Victor Cruz and Tom Underwood. Two days later, the Cardinals dealt away another pitcher known for his Fu Manchu and ferocity: Al Hrabosky. Earlier in 1977, "The Mad Hungarian" had clashed with manager Vern Rapp and owner Gussie Busch over Rapp's ban on facial hair.

St. Louis beat writer Neal Russo called Vuckovich a good prospect after the trade.[26] He was right. During his first season with the Cardinals, Vuckovich posted a 12-12 record, but his ERA was a career-best 2.54, third in the National League behind Craig Swan and Steve Rogers. He was a reliever to begin the year, but Ken Boyer – who'd replaced Rapp as manager in April – put him in the rotation in early June.

Vuckovich blossomed immediately as a starter. In late July, Cardinals pitching coach Claude Osteen – who'd helped Vuke as a teammate in 1975 – said, "He's a master at changing speeds, and he does it with total command of three or four basic pitches, with quite a few variations of each kind of pitch. He's deceptive, too."[27]

On August 8, after a complete-game win over the Philadel-

phia Phillies, Vuckovich credited much of his success to his ability to remain calm and collected under pressure. That game report noted the "sometimes strange behavior" that inspired another nickname – "Vuke the Spook" – and that he worked more quickly than most pitchers.[28] A few weeks later, the great Bob Gibson – also noted for his brisk pace – said, "I've watched him on television and like his tenacity and the rapidity with which he works. He's already found that the quicker you pitch, the more your defense is likely to be on its toes to make the good plays behind you."[29]

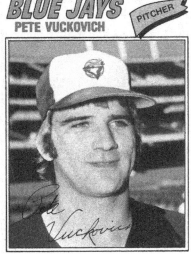

Vuckovich remained a capable starter for the Cardinals in 1979-80, winning 27, losing 19, and posting a 3.50 ERA. Mike Eisenbath cited Vuckovich's variety of pitches and arm slots – and, in particular, his fiercely competitive nature. Vuke later said, "I really hate hitters. They're goofy. They're trying to get me, to ruin my career, so I hate them. That's the way it has to be – them or me. I want it to be me."[30] Yet his free spirit was also visible as he belly-flopped through puddles in the outfield and hung an "out to lunch" sign over his locker.[31]

On December 12, 1980, St. Louis and Milwaukee – who would face each other in the 1982 World Series – swung a seven-player deal. The Cardinals traded Rollie Fingers, Ted Simmons, and Vuckovich for pitchers Dave LaPoint and Lary Sorensen, outfielder Sixto Lezcano, and another outfielder, touted prospect David Green. It started off in October with an even-up swap proposal from St. Louis: Vuckovich for Sorensen.[32] But it developed into a blockbuster, with many moving parts before everything fell into place. In the final analysis, both sides benefited.[33]

Vuckovich could be droll. When asked why he thought Cardinals manager/general manager Whitey Herzog traded him, he replied, "Whitey wanted to build a team on speed and I never really ran that well."[34]

In Milwaukee, Vuckovich struggled early in 1981 but turned his season around after coach Cal McLish suggested using a no-windup delivery even with no one on base.[35] Vuke went on to lead the AL with 14 wins during the strike-interrupted season; he lost just four. He came in fourth in the AL Cy Young Award voting – the winner was Fingers.

The Brewers also made it to the postseason for the first time. They faced the New York Yankees in the AL Division Series, and Vuckovich appeared in two games. He started and won Game Four, allowing one unearned run in five innings. In Game Five at Yankee Stadium, he faced the Yankees' final batter; New York eventually won the pennant.

The 1982 Brewers were called "Harvey's Wallbangers" because manager Harvey Kuenn had such a potent batting order. Yet they wouldn't have won the AL pennant without respectable pitching. The team ERA of 3.98 was sixth in the AL, but not far behind the league-best 3.80. There were no dominant starters – but they got the job done.

Vuckovich led the staff with 18 wins against 6 losses. He was in hot water often – his WHIP in 1982 was 1.5. Yet more often than not, he got himself out of the jams; his ERA was just 3.34. "He gets further behind, works deeper in counts, throws more pitches and generally contradicts more canons of pitching with more success than anybody else in baseball," said sportswriter Tom Boswell.[36]

Interesting observations of Vuckovich in '82 come from Daniel Okrent's book *Nine Innings*, which focused on a game between the Brewers and Baltimore Orioles on June 10 of that season. For example, "If considered looniness won ball games, the eccentric Vuckovich would forever be a success." Okrent also noted the hurler's habits of crossing his eyes as he stared in for the sign and (while holding runners on) "twitching his head rapidly ... again and again, as if he had a violent tic." Catcher Simmons, Vuckovich's closest friend on the team, thought it helped the pitcher as much as his strange delivery did.[37]

Center fielder Gorman Thomas (who looked like a brother to Vuke) expanded. "You could look past the goofy hair and the growth on the face. He'd go out there and pitch with two different brands of shoes on. He'd have Puma on one foot and Adidas on the other. It was almost like he was semi-clownish. Yet he knew what he was doing and he'd get other people to focus more on his man-

nerisms than on what they're supposed to be doing."[38]

Beneath the quirky trappings, though, Vuckovich's intensity was unrivaled. Thomas added, "I don't think I ever saw anybody who would be so competitive when it was time to pitch. It's hard to stay 100 percent, 100 miles per hour, 24 hours a day. But when it was Pete's day to pitch, it was more than tunnel vision. It was straw vision. That's how finely tuned he was. He was that way every time I saw him pitch."[39]

Vuckovich started twice in the 1982 ALCS against the California Angels. In Game Two, he gave up four runs in an eight-inning complete game, losing to Bruce Kison, who went all the way. In Game Five, he allowed three runs in 6⅓ innings and left the game as the pitcher of record on the losing side. But the Brewers took the lead with two in the seventh and held on to win the pennant.

Vuckovich also started twice in the World Series. In Game Three, he allowed six runs (four earned) in 8⅓ innings and took the loss. In Game Seven, he took a 3-1 lead into the sixth inning but put the tying runs on base and was pulled. The bullpen couldn't hold the lead, and though Vuckovich got no decision, the Cardinals won the championship.

Vuke had been pitching while hurt.[40] As Roger Angell later wrote, he was "in great pain during the final stages of the pennant race. ... In late September, two days after receiving a cortisone shot in his shoulder, he somehow went 11 full innings against the Red Sox, throwing 173 pitches, and won the game."[41] After his first outing against St. Louis, Vuckovich was stoic: "I get paid to take the ball when they give it to me, and I get paid to give it back when they ask for it."[42] When he retired, he said that he carried on because the pennant race would have been a bad time to "walk."[43]

A few weeks later, the Cy Young Award was announced. Five pitchers got first-place votes, but Vuckovich got 14 of the 28 and outdistanced runner-up Jim Palmer. "I feel great about it, but I can't take full credit for it," he said. "I just happen to be lucky enough to be out there on the days the team's playing well enough to be a winner."[44]

Indeed, "He Doesn't Look Pretty, but He Wins," proclaimed *Baseball Digest*'s cover story in May 1983. By the time it appeared, though, Vuckovich was on the disabled list. In March, an arthrogram revealed a tear in his rotator cuff. He put the downtime to good use, though, gaining his first experience as a cable TV commentator for the Brewers. He also filled in for Bob Uecker on the radio when Ueck was calling games for ABC-TV.[45]

Vuckovich started throwing gingerly on the sidelines in May.[46] His progress continued, and he made it back at the end of August. He pitched well in his first two starts, going five innings in each and surprising Simmons with his velocity. In the third, however, he was hit hard and pulled a hamstring. The Brewers kept him sidelined after that for fear that he might reinjure his arm.[47]

Before the 1984 season, Vuckovich was cautiously optimistic after a busy offseason continuing his exercise program. However, he wasn't ready for Opening Day because of pain from a bone spur in his right shoulder.[48] The resulting surgery included muscle repair as well as removal of the spur. It kept him out for the whole season. Yet again, he wasn't idle – he charted pitches, worked the radar gun, and studied hitters' tendencies. This too laid the foundation for his future career.[49]

Vuckovich was back in action in 1985 but was largely ineffective in 22 starts (6-10, 5.51). A shoulder strain landed him on the DL in May and June, and he underwent surgery for a large calcium deposit and another small bone spur in mid-September. That November, he became a free agent after refusing a minor-league assignment.[50]

Milwaukee invited Vuckovich to spring training in 1986 as a nonroster player. At the end of camp, he announced his retirement and went to work for the Brewers as a scout and minor-league instructor. In August, however, he wanted to see if he could still pitch. He joined Milwaukee's Triple-A club in Vancouver.[51] He did well (2-1, 1.26 in six games) and got back to the majors in September, going 2-4, 3.06 in six starts.

Vuckovich was a nonroster invitee again in 1987, but he retired for good on April 1, saying, "I'm a realist. I have an awareness of myself."[52] He finished with a lifetime record in the majors of 93-69 and an ERA of 3.66. Charlie O'Brien, who caught Vuckovich during that last spring training, summed up his career nicely. "He had a great feel for pitching. … [T]he word that comes to mind is guile. … He marched to his own drummer. … He liked a cold beer and a good time, and he liked to play baseball. He was willing to do whatever it took to win."[53]

Vuckovich, who then lived in the Milwaukee suburb of Hales Corners, tended bar at "Stormin' and Vuke's,"

the joint he co-owned with Gorman Thomas.[54] He was also involved in local civic affairs. At the opening of the Samson Jewish Community Center in Whitefish Bay in September 1987, he helped teach youngsters how to play baseball along with Sal Bando and Bill Castro.[55]

*Major League* was filmed at Milwaukee's County Stadium in the summer of 1988. The project – like many Hollywood movie properties – had been in gestation for years. But when it finally got the green light, the cast included many inspired choices, and Vuckovich was one of them. Originally he was to play opposing closer Duke Simpson, but writer/director David S. Ward liked Vuckovich's look so much that he was given a slightly bigger role. Vuke then brought in his old Brewers teammate Willie Mueller to take over as Simpson.[56]

The new part was well suited to Vuckovich's image. In April 1989, shortly after the film was released, *Sports Illustrated* wrote, "Former Brewers pitcher and dirtball Pete Vuckovich plays Yankee slugger and dirtball Clu Haywood." The article quoted Bob Uecker's line as announcer Harry Doyle: "He [Haywood] leads the majors in most offensive categories, including nose hair."[57] A 2016 article described the character as "awesomely gross," noting that his "favorite pastime, apart from hitting dingers, is to call rookies Hayes and Vaughn 'meat' whenever he gets the chance."[58]

Vuckovich made another juicy little contribution to the film. In one scene, Haywood approaches the plate and says to catcher Jake Taylor (played by Tom Berenger): 'How's your wife and my kids?' The line wasn't in Ward's script; he told Vuckovich to improvise something that major-leaguers would say. What's more, "Stormin' and Vuke's" was a regular off-hours hangout for the cast and crew while they were on location in Milwaukee.[59]

Vuckovich was an analyst on Brewers telecasts from 1989 through 1991. Then Ted Simmons, whom the Pirates had hired as GM in February 1992, invited his old friend and batterymate to join the Pittsburgh organization. It was ideal because no big-league franchise was closer to family in Johnstown. Vuke stayed with the Bucs for 20 seasons, through 2011. He was first a roving pitching instructor (1992-93) and then special assistant to GM Cam Bonifay (1994-95). In 1996 he was promoted to assistant GM/director of player personnel.[60]

Shortly after the '96 season ended, the Pirates made Vuckovich the big club's pitching coach, a longstanding goal of his. He replaced Ray Miller because "the club didn't feel Miller's methods were resulting in progress. Vuckovich will coach attitude and mental approach as much as mechanics." A subsequent report noted that he would "spend a lot of time getting to know young players, trying to determine the best way to tap their talents."[61]

Vuckovich held that position for four seasons (1997-2000). When the Pirates hired Lloyd McClendon as manager, he and Bonifay turned over the coaching staff.[62] As a result, bullpen coach Spin Williams moved up and Vuke returned to the front office. He continued to work as special assistant to Bonifay, and later to David Littlefield, then Neal Huntington.

Vuckovich joined the Mariners as a special assistant to GM Jack Zduriencik before the 2012 season. His job included much travel, scouting amateurs and pros, as well as visiting with minor-league teams. Zduriencik, who'd been scouting director for the Pirates from 1991 through 1993, respected his old colleague's baseball mind. In November 2013, Vuckovich was a candidate for pitching coach with the Phillies, but he removed his name from consideration.[63] The job went to his former Milwaukee teammate Bob McClure.

Seattle fired Zduriencik in August 2015, and that October Vuckovich was part of the ensuing organizational purge.[64] A few months later, he became a roving scout for the Diamondbacks. When asked what brings a scout the most satisfaction, Vuckovich said, "Being right on a player. … That's what you strive to do."[65]

In late 2017, Pete and Annie Vuckovich still called Johnstown home. "It's where I grew up, and where my wife and I met. Even when I was playing, in the offseason we always came home to Johnstown," he said just before taking the Diamondbacks job. Vuckovich is a member of the Sports Halls of Fame of Cambria County, Clarion University, the AAABA, Western Pennsylvania, and Pennsylvania. He remained happy and confident at work. "Baseball has been my whole life. It's what I know, and I know it better than most."[66]

## Sources

*Internet resources*

Cambria County Sports Hall of Fame (ccshof.org/member/pete-vuckovich/).

Official website of the AAABA Tournament (aaabajohnstown.org/).

Findagrave.com.

Betty Vuckovich funeral announcement (hindmanfuneralhomes.com/obituary/betty-bosa-j-vuckovich/).

newspapers.com.

## Notes

1  Daniel Okrent, *Nine Innings* (Boston: Houghton Mifflin Company, 1985), 237.

2  Neal Russo, "Vuckovich: Unusual Man With Some Evil Pitches," *St. Louis Post-Dispatch*, July 25, 1978: 36.

3  Mike Eisenbath, *The Cardinals Encyclopedia* (Philadelphia: Temple University Press, 1999), 300.

4  Bob Verdi, "Close Calls All Go Vuckovich's Way," *Chicago Tribune*, March 18, 1982. Tom Boswell, "Brewers' Vuckovich Becomes Off-the-Wall Force on the Mound," *Washington Post*, October 13, 1982.

5  David L. Porter, editor, *Biographical Dictionary of American Sports*, Volume 2, Q-Z (Westport, Connecticut: Greenwood Press, 2000), 1607. The Vuckovich parents' Serbian nicknames are visible on the pictures of their shared grave marker at findagrave.com. There are various references to Lazo Vuckovich as "Louis," including his 2005 obituary in the *Johnstown Tribune-Democrat*. The *Biographical Dictionary of Sports* entry gives Bossie's Americanized name as "Betty Jane." See also Betty Vuckovich funeral announcement.

6  "Life Inside the Diamond," Clarion University website, January 4, 2016.

7  Rick Hummel, "Birds V-Sign Stands for Vuke and Victory," *The Sporting News*, May 3, 1980: 13.

8  Neal Russo, "'Gimme the Ball, Often,' Vuckovich Tells Cards," *The Sporting News*, February 25, 1978: 54.

9  "Mariners Name Pete Vuckovich Special Assistant to the General Manager," MLB.com, September 16, 2011. Football position comes from *Indiana* (Pennsylvania) *Gazette*, accessed via newspapers.com. Basketball position comes from email to Rory Costello from Mike Mastovich of the *Johnstown Tribune-Democrat*, October 5, 2017.

10  Bob Broeg, "McBride Deal Wins Belated OK," *St. Louis Post-Dispatch*, September 3, 1978: 76.

11  Hummel, "Birds V-Sign Stands for Vuke and Victory."

12  Verdi, "Close Calls All Go Vuckovich's Way."

13  "Life Inside the Diamond."

14  "Mariners Name Pete Vuckovich Special Assistant to the General Manager."

15  Russo, "'Gimme the Ball, Often,' Vuckovich Tells Cards."

16  "Pitcher Credits Sain," *The Sporting News*, May 17, 1975: 38.

17  "Life Inside the Diamond."

18  Porter, op. cit., 1608. Front-office biographies, Pittsburgh Pirates, MLB.com. Date unknown, but could range from 2008 to 2011.

19  Pete Vuckovich Jr. profile on LinkedIn.com.

20  Jerome Holtzman, "Dent, Downing Only Chisox Certain of Regular Berths," *The Sporting News*, March 6, 1976: 11.

21  Russo, "'Gimme the Ball, Often,' Vuckovich Tells Cards."

22  Okrent, *Nine Innings*, 207. The original source of this quote is uncertain.

23  Neil MacCarl, "Shear Locks, Jays Order Vuckovich," *The Sporting News*, March 12, 1977: 43.

24  Verdi, "Close Calls All Go Vuckovich's Way."

25  MacCarl, "Shear Locks, Jays Order Vuckovich," 46.

26  Neal Russo, "Devine Gives Royal Look to New Card Hand," *The Sporting News*, December 24, 1977: 59.

27  Neal Russo, "Brother Vuckovich a Wheelhorse for Cards," *The Sporting News*, August 5, 1978: 20.

28  "Cards Spook Phillies," *Pittsburgh Press*, August 9, 1978: 56.

29  Broeg, "McBride Deal Wins Belated OK."

30  Eisenbath, op. cit., loc. cit. Original source of quote: "The Pete Vuckovich Story Is Filed Under 'Sci-Fi,'" *St. Louis Post-Dispatch*, February 8, 1983: 30.

31  Hummel, "Birds V-Sign Stands for Vuke and Victory."

32  Okrent, *Nine Innings*, 206.

33  Dave Anderson, "Trade That Brewed the 6-Pack Series," *New York Times*, October 12, 1982.

34  Boswell, "Brewers' Vuckovich Becomes Off-the-Wall Force on the Mound."

35  Tom Flaherty, "Vuckovich Brewers' Big Bargain," *The Sporting News*, June 27, 1981: 25.

36  Boswell, "Brewers' Vuckovich Becomes Off-the-Wall Force on the Mound."

37  Okrent, *Nine Innings*, 71, 237.

38  Mike Mastovich, "From AAABA to Cy Young, Vuckovich Made His Pitch," *Johnstown Tribune-Democrat*, August 5, 2007.

39  Mike Mastovich, "Competitiveness, Talent Took Vuckovich to the Top of Baseball," *Johnstown Tribune-Democrat*, October 8, 2016.

40  Tom Flaherty, "Vuke Shares Credit With Teammates," *The Sporting News*, November 15, 1982: 53.

41  Roger Angell, "The Arms Talks," *The New Yorker*, May 4, 1987.

42  Stan Hochman, "Life in the Fast Lane Doesn't Faze Vuckovich," *Philadelphia Daily News*, October 15, 1982.

43  Mike Mastovich, "Vuckovich Honored: Area Ex-Big-Leaguer to Take Spot With Pennsylvania's Best," *Johnstown Tribune-Democrat*, October 23, 2008.

44  "Vuckovich Says He's Happy," Associated Press, November 4, 1982.

45  Peter Gammons, "Brewers' First Three Rank with Best," *The Sporting News*, May 2, 1983: 14.

46  Tom Flaherty, "Outlook Bleak for Vuckovich," *The Sporting News*, March 28, 1983: 42. Flaherty, "Simmons Hits .300 Jackpot," *The Sporting News*, May 23, 1983: 22.

47  Tom Flaherty, "Vuckovich's Return Impresses Brewers," *The Sporting News*, September 19, 1983: 14; Flaherty, "Job in Jeopardy, but Kuenn's Secure," *The Sporting News*, October 3, 1983: 17.

48  Tom Flaherty, "Vuckovich Is Cautiously Optimistic," *The Sporting News*, February 27, 1984: 36. Flaherty, "Hurts Hamper Molitor, Vucko," *The Sporting News*, April 9, 1984: 15.

49  Mastovich, "Vuckovich honored: Area Ex-Big-Leaguer to Take Spot With Pennsylvania's Best."

50  Tom Flaherty, "As Vuckovich Exits, Porter Returns," *The Sporting News*, September 23, 1985: 20; Flaherty, "Yount Will Return to Center Field," *The Sporting News*, December 2, 1985: 48.

51  "A.L. Notebook: Brewers," *The Sporting News*, August 11, 1986: 17.

52  Tom Flaherty, "Facing the Inevitable," *The Sporting News*, April 13, 1987: 16.

53  Charlie O'Brien and Doug Wedge, *The Cy Young Catcher* (College Station, Texas: Texas A&M University Press: 2015), 18-19.

54  "Brewers' First Loss of Season Fails to Dampen Fan Enthusiasm," United Press International, April 22, 1987.

55  "Thousands Celebrate Opening of Sampson [sic] JCC," *Wisconsin Jewish Chronicle*, September 25, 1987: 3.

56  Jonathan Knight, *The Making of "Major League,"* (Cleveland: Gray & Company, 2015), exact page number unavailable online.

57  Steve Wulf, "Too Bush for the Bigs," *Sports Illustrated*, April 17, 1989. This article spelled the character's first name as "Klu," as have other sources over the years.

58  Danny Kelly, "'Major League' Is Baseball," *The Ringer*, July 22, 2016.

59  Knight, op. cit. Mike Oz, "'Major League' Turns 25 – Here Are 15 Things You Didn't Know About the Movie," Yahoo! Sports, April 7, 2014. Chris Nashawaty, "A League of Its Own," *Sports Illustrated*, July 4, 2011.

60  "Mariners Name Pete Vuckovich Special Assistant to the General

Manager." Mike Mastovich, "Johnstown native Pete Vuckovich Starts New Baseball Chapter as Diamondbacks Scout," *Johnstown Tribune-Democrat*, January 6, 2016.

61  John Mehno, "Pittsburgh Pirates," *The Sporting News*, October 21, 1996, 20. Mehno, "Pittsburgh Pirates," *The Sporting News*, November 11, 1996: 37.

62  John Mehno, "Pittsburgh," *The Sporting News*, November 6, 2000.

63  Jim Salisbury, "Phils Feel Rejection in Pitching Coach Search," NBC Sports Philadelphia, November 11, 2013.

64  "Sources: Mariners' Front Office Overhaul Begins With Four Changes," Foxsports.com, October 5, 2015.

65  Mastovich, "Johnstown Native Pete Vuckovich Starts New Baseball Chapter As Diamondbacks Scout."

66  "Life Inside the Diamond."

# ERNIE WHITT

## BY BOB LEMOINE

On November 25, 2017, thousands of Canadians turned to the streets of Windsor, Ontario, for the annual Winter Fest Holiday Parade, and many went on that chilly Saturday to see Santa Claus ring in the holiday season. Others, though, were there to see someone even more popular in their eyes: Ernie Whitt, who served as the grand marshal. Ernie Whitt is synonymous with the early history of the Toronto Blue Jays. They grew up together. Whitt was selected in the expansion draft and through the 1980s was the solid rock behind the plate as the Blue Jays emerged into a pennant contender. He was there to guide the young pitching staff and provide eight straight seasons of double-digit home runs with his left-handed power. He was the last of the original Blue Jays, and after retiring as a player he remained in the game, coaching in the Blue Jays and Phillies farm systems and putting Team Canada on the baseball map. "We're here, signing autographs and talking to people about the old days of baseball and the beauty of playing at Tiger Sta-

dium, playing at Exhibition Stadium," Whitt said. "Just talking baseball."[1] Even Santa couldn't top that.

Whitt grew up across the river in Detroit and became one of the most popular athletes in Canada. As of 2017, his 131 home runs as a Blue Jay ranked him 10th in team history, while his 19.2 WAR ranked him third. As of 2018, he was sixth (1,218) in games played. Bill James listed Whitt as the 72nd best catcher in baseball history in his *New Bill James Historical Baseball Abstract*:

"Whitt was never a hot prospect, never caught many breaks, didn't get a real look in the majors until he was 28, [and] didn't get 300 at-bats in a season until he was past 30. But he worked hard, stayed in shape, just kept doing his best, and wound up having a pretty decent career."[2]

Leo Ernest Whitt was born to Ernest and Dolly (Perrigan) Whitt on June 13, 1952, in Detroit, just a few blocks away from Tiger Stadium. Originally from the rolling hills of the Cumberland Gap in southwestern Virginia, Ernest and Dolly had relocated to Detroit in the early 1950s when Ernest sought work as a truck driver. The family, including brother Mike and sisters Melinda and Bernadine, often returned to visit the grandparents and take in the fresh air of farm life in Virginia. When Ernie was 3 years old, the family moved to a house in the Detroit suburb of Roseville. "The house looks pretty small now," Whitt wrote in his autobiography, *Catch: A Major League Life*, in 1989. "But when I was a kid I thought it was huge."[3]

# Time For Expansion Baseball

Roseville had a lot of young families with children who loved the open spaces to play baseball. "In our backyard, there were two trees that made great first and third bases, and we could always find something to throw out for second. We'd play baseball all day, run in for dinner and run back out to play until we couldn't see the ball anymore."[4]

"I started playing baseball with the VFW post when I was seven years old," Whitt remembered. They were supposed to be 8 years old, but brother Mike got Ernie in. "They needed a catcher and I basically lied and said I was a catcher," he said with a chuckle. "From the earliest grades that I can remember, whenever some school form came around asking what I wanted to be when I grew up, I'd always write 'professional baseball player.'" His Little League team often traveled to Tiger Stadium on Saturdays, where they saw stars Al Kaline, Norm Cash, and Willie Horton. Whitt's hero was Tigers catcher Bill Freehan.[5]

In his teen years, Whitt grabbed his glove on Saturday mornings, jumped on a bus and headed for sandlots where professional baseball scouts held clinics. "Kids used to come from all over the city," he remembered. "It was a bit of a madhouse and pretty hard to impress anyone. But if you were good and a particular scout liked the way you played, you would get invited back the next Saturday. I had one of their [Tigers] scouts following me. They told me they would draft me. They never did. I heard the general manager thought I'd never make it past Double-A ball."[6]

Whitt was an all-state quarterback at Carl Brablec High School, and also played baseball and basketball. He had the opportunity to play football in college, but changed his mind after visits to Central Michigan and Eastern Michigan Universities. "I saw guys who were bigger than me and faster than me. I knew if they hit me, it would hurt," Whitt joked.[7] Ernie also played baseball in the Adray League, named for an appliance dealer who sponsored local youth athletics. "I'd always be at their tryout camps at Butzel Field and they'd always tell me, 'You're our boy. We're gonna get you. Wait and see.' They'd pick all-star teams to represent Detroit in a series in Canada, and all I'd think about was the Tigers signing me up."[8]

After graduating from high school in 1970, Whitt enrolled at Macomb Community College in Warren, Michigan. "Playing at Macomb gave me an opportunity to play baseball and basketball," he said. "It got me seen." Major-league scouts had seen Whitt play, and Ernie hoped

to be drafted in June 1971 after hitting .324 in his first season at Macomb. As no calls came, he continued at the school for another year, batting .333 with 32 RBIs and was voted the baseball team's MVP and the college's most outstanding athlete.

Whitt waited by the phone on June 6, 1972, as baseball's amateur draft was taking place. "When the telephone rang, I said to myself, 'This might be it,'" he recalled of those anxious moments. "It was, but it was the wrong team." Whitt naturally hoped his hometown Tigers had selected him, but the voice on the other end belonged to Maurice DeLoof of the Boston Red Sox. "Would you like to play professional baseball?" DeLoof asked. "Are you kidding?" answered Whitt.[9] The Red Sox drafted him in the 15th round for $2,500 and an allowance for college.

Whitt arrived in Williamsport, Pennsylvania, to join the Red Sox affiliate in the rookie-oriented New York-Pennsylvania League. Sam Mele, an instructor with the club, was impressed with Whitt's hitting. After the 1972 floods postponed the season by a week. Ernie finally got into a game, playing first base, and collecting two hits. After the game, he was promoted to Winter Haven of the Class-A Florida State League.

Whitt had trouble adjusting to professional ball, as he batted only .183 in 31 games. Over the winter, Mele helped his swing in the Florida Instructional League, allowing him to bat .300. Ernie was promoted to Winston Salem of the Class-A Carolina League in 1973. He batted .290 in 130 games. In 1974 Whitt played for the Red Sox' Double-A affiliate in Bristol, helping them win the Eastern League's American Division title.

Ernie married Christine "Chris" Louise Jordan on June 19, 1974. Originally from Iowa, Christine met Ernie while visiting family in Michigan. The couple planned a fall wedding, but Ernie grew lonesome and suggested they marry during the season. The wedding was at 1:00 P.M. and Ernie was at the ballpark at 3:00. He went 2-for-3 in a 3-1 win. For the third consecutive year, Whitt returned to the Instructional League. Scouts were concerned that success would entice other scouts to select him in the Rule 5 Draft. "We don't want anyone to see you," Whitt was told. "We're not going to protect you on a major-league roster, but we're protecting you [in] Triple A and we're inviting you to spring training next year."[10]

Whitt was invited to the Red Sox' spring camp in 1975 but was ultimately returned to Bristol. Things deteriorated when he separated his shoulder, requiring an operation, during a home-plate collision. "The runner charged in, crashed into me and ripped my left shoulder apart," Whitt gruesomely recalled. "I could actually tilt my head and touch my ear to the bone sticking out. The Harvard doctor who looked at the tendons said it looked like an explosion in a meat factory."[11] Whitt was limited to 82 games at Bristol, where he batted .254 with only two home runs. However, during the postseason, Whitt laid down a squeeze bunt in the 17th inning of the deciding Game 3 to bring the Eastern League championship to Bristol.[12]

Frustrated by the numbers game, Whitt had to remain at Bristol for yet another year; he felt he deserved a shot at Triple A. "I went home and told Chris it was time to get out and get on with our lives. But she told me, 'I've always said that I'd live in a paper bag with you. But I won't live with you if you're going to be miserable. You know you can play in the big leagues. You just have to hang on. With your talent, there'll be an opportunity.'"[13]

Whitt played 26 games at Bristol in 1976, before his opportunity at Triple-A Rhode Island (Pawtucket) presented itself. A roster spot opened when Andy Merchant was recalled to replace an injured Carlton Fisk. Whitt shared catching duties with Bo Diaz. "I don't know what the organization's got planned for you," his new manager, Joe Morgan, stated honestly. "I don't know whether you'll go back to Double A when Fisk gets healthy or what. So I'm going to play you the way I think is best for this team, and you just have to go out and do the best you can."[14] Whitt had a strong season, batting .266 with 7 home runs in 90 games. Once Rhode Island's season was over, Whitt was promoted to Boston. He made his major-league debut on September 12, 1976. With the Red Sox ahead, 11-3, over Cleveland, manager Don Zimmer sent Whitt to pinch-hit for Carlton Fisk. Whitt grounded out to second, then remained in the game to catch.

Whitt had a homecoming when the Red Sox had a two-game series in Detroit. In the opener, Whitt replaced Fisk behind the plate in the ninth inning of an 8-3 Boston win. Fisk approached him after the game. "You're from this area, right? Go home and tell your family and friends that you are going to start tomorrow." The kid from Detroit was starry-eyed as he made his first at bat that day. "When I came up to hit, Bill Freehan was behind the plate for the Tigers and said 'Welcome to the big leagues.'"[15] Whitt went 0-for-2 before being replaced by Bob Montgom-

ery in a 5-4 win. Whitt's first major-league hit was a solo home run off Milwaukee's Jim Colborn that clanged off the right-field foul pole in a 3-1 loss on September 21.[16] He finished the season batting .222 in eight games.

Boston left Whitt unprotected in the expansion draft, and he was selected by Toronto in the third round. But there were no guarantees of a spot on Toronto's roster, since the team had three experienced catchers in Alan Ashby, Rick Cerone, and Phil Roof. "I was depressed for a while the first few weeks of training," Whitt admitted to Bill Newell of the *Hartford Courant*, "but lately I've been feeling great because I'm getting some opportunities to play. The first game manager [Roy] Hartsfield let me start I hit a home run and threw out five runners trying to steal. I think I made an impression that day, but, truthfully, I'm just not hitting."[17] On the final day of spring training, Whitt was sent to Charleston (West Virginia) of the International League, a Houston affiliate, because Toronto had no Triple-A team. "I was very disappointed I wasn't on the club," Whitt recalled.[18]

Whitt played in 29 games for Charleston and was recalled to Toronto at the end of May when Cerone was sent down. Ernie played in 23 games as Ashby's backup, starting 10 and batting only .171, but achieved a flawless fielding percentage. He was frustrated at being used strictly as a pinch-hitter, not starting a game behind the plate until late June. "Actually I don't have fond memories of those first few years in the Hartsfield regime," Whitt admitted late in his career.[19] Frustrations continued when his season was truncated in August after a home-plate collision with California's Andy Etchebarren, resulting in a dislocated tendon in his foot.[20]

Whitt spent most of 1978 with Triple-A Syracuse. Since the Blue Jays focused on developing Pat Kelly as a catcher, Whitt spent 20 games at first and a handful of games in the outfield, batting .246 with 12 home runs. He was recalled to Toronto for only two games in September.

Whitt spent all of 1979 with Syracuse, earning a Silver Glove Award for being the best defensive catcher in the International League, but still didn't seem to be in the Blue Jays' plans for the future. "I don't know why [Hartsfield] didn't care for me. It was a frustrating year."[21] Again he contemplated quitting. He admonished Hartsfield: "I don't think you can manage at the big-league level. You don't know talent." He asked Toronto GM Pat Gillick for a trade, which never happened. Chris once again motivated him to persevere: "You're in Triple A. You're one step away. You'll never know if you quit now. You'll go to bed every night and your head will hit the pillow and you'll lay there and think, 'I wonder if I could have made it if I'd just stayed in'"[22]

Time was on Whitt's side, as he was now out of minor-league options. He had to be called up or placed on waivers. But Ernie's perseverance paid off when Hartsfield was fired and replaced by Bobby Mattick as manager. Mattick had been impressed with Whitt's 1979 season, even trading Cerone to open a spot on the major-league roster for him. The first day Mattick was appointed, he called Whitt to say he would be the Blue Jays' starting catcher in 1980. "I've got to give [Mattick] credit for giving me the opportunity to play, and for sticking with me, when I was trying too hard," Whitt said. He platooned with Bob Davis, sitting against lefties. Although he continued to be platooned, he remained with Toronto for the entire decade. He finally made it.

Ernie struggled at the plate (.237-6-34) in 1980 but had a decent .986 fielding percentage and was fifth among catchers in the AL in assists (56). His second-half batting (.254) overshadowed his first-half slumps (.204), and the team had its first season with fewer than 100 losses (95). Whitt upped his fielding percentage to .991 in 1981 and was second in assists in the strike-shortened season. On a cold, damp May night in Cleveland, Ernie got a call while in the bullpen. He wasn't thrilled with the idea of pinch-hitting, but he trotted in to bat in the ninth inning. He flied out to center and was the last out of Len Barker's perfect game. "There were a lot of bad feelings around here at the time," Whitt said. "We were losing. We couldn't score any runs. Everybody was down, and then we were out of a job."[23] But the Jays, 16-42 before the strike, showed some spark and finished 21-27 in the second half, while Whitt, batting .232 before the strike, batted .286 from September on.

New manager Bobby Cox came aboard in 1982 and the team played near-.500 ball (78-84). Whitt had breakout numbers at the plate (.261-11-42), including a 4-for-4 game against Milwaukee on August 3. His 11 home runs began an eight-year streak of double-digit home-run totals. The 1983 season saw continued success for both Whitt and his team. Whitt started off hot, batting .308 at the end of April, and the Blue Jays were in first place in the AL East at 26-19 at the end of May. Cox's catching platoon of Whitt versus righties and Buck Martinez against lefties was also successful. Whitt batted .272 against right-

ies, with 17 home runs, while the veteran Martinez hit .270 versus southpaws.[24] Whitt's fielding percentage (.992) ranked fifth among catchers and he remained in the top five in that category in five of the next six years. The Blue Jays had their best season in franchise history yet (89-73) and finished in fourth place.

Whitt realized he was part of a rising team as the 1984 season dawned. "You could see the younger players developing," he said. "In '84 when the Tigers got out to such a great start (35-5), we were still right with them. I think if we would have had a closer that year, we could have competed with them and made it a lot closer." Toronto hung close to the surging Tigers through May, but by the end of June were 10 games behind despite a strong 45-31 record. The Tigers easily won the division by 15 games and rolled over all opponents on their way to a World Series title. But the Jays (89-73) were primed for a run of their own. Whitt had his usual consistent numbers at the plate (.238-15-46), and his .994 fielding percentage was third among AL catchers.

The 1985 season was a memorable one, as the Blue Jays won the AL East for the first time. Whitt helped guide Toronto's top four starting pitchers: Dave Stieb, Doyle Alexander, Jimmy Key, and Jim Clancy. Three of them had double-digit victories, and all four had ERAs under 3.78. The staff as a whole led the league in ERA (3.31), the fewest runs allowed per game (3.65), and WHIP (1.24). Stieb led the league with a 2.48 ERA, and Tom Henke arrived from Triple A to secure their need for a closer. Henke was unscored upon in his first 11 appearances, finishing with 13 saves down the stretch for a team that ranked second (47) in saves. On the batting side, their batting average (.269) and hits (1,482) were second only to Boston's. Despite the artificial turf at Exhibition Stadium, the Jays were first in defensive efficiency. Whitt's WAR value of 2.5 ranked him sixth on the team.

The Jays took over first place for good on May 20 and built their lead to 9½ games in early August. Defensively, Whitt (.245-19-64) ranked fifth in putouts (649), and third in games (134) as he joined five other Blue Jays with double-digit home runs. One of those home runs came in a memorable game on June 23. Earlier in the month, Boston pitcher Bruce Kison and Jays second baseman Damaso Garcia had words with each other and had to be restrained. On this day, Kison was facing the Blue Jays at Exhibition Stadium. He knocked Ernie down with a pitch and brushed back Rance Mulliniks. Then he hit George

Bell, who charged the mound and karate-kicked Kison, with both benches emptying. Whitt later knocked Kison out of the game with his bat: a grand slam in the sixth inning for an 8-1 Toronto win. Whitt, so steamed at Kison, didn't even realize it was a grand slam until he made it around the bases. "I was just yelling at Kison, calling him every nasty name I could think of," he remembered.[25]

Whitt was an All-Star in 1985, serving as a backup to Carlton Fisk, nine years after pinch-hitting for Pudge in his first at-bat. "For me, it's an honor to be here. I really didn't think it would happen. I'm having a good season offensively, and that helped me get here. But I think I can do better defensively."[26] He replaced Fisk in the sixth inning. He caught two innings and didn't bat in his only All-Star Game appearance.

Despite a seven-game lead in the division on September 24, the Jays slumped down the stretch. They lost four in a row and saw their lead dwindle to two games over the Yankees, who arrived for the final three-game series of the season. The champagne was ready to pop during the Friday night opener, but in heartbreaking fashion the Yankees stunned all of Toronto with a ninth-inning comeback. Now the pressure mounted on the Jays to win just one more game for the AL East title.

On Saturday, October 5, before 44,608 anxious fans, Whitt made sure the Jays got on top first by blasting a second-inning home run off Joe Cowley. "We thought it was very important for us to score first," Whitt said. The Blue Jays won, 5-1, and clinched the division. Whitt joined Jim Clancy and Garth Iorg as original Blue Jays who now celebrated a division title. "The first four years here seemed like a century," he said. "We've been able to put tough losses behind us. I don't think we've ever had a tougher one than Friday."[27]

The Blue Jays suffered more heartbreak, however, failing to reach the World Series. "For us to win the Eastern Division and to play in the Championship Series was nice," Whitt said. "It was disappointing, though, because we were up three games to one on Kansas City, but they came back to beat us."[28] Whitt batted a meager .190 in the ALCS against the eventual World Series champion Royals. Whitt later revealed he had played through a muscle tear in his shoulder after breaking up a double play in an early September game, which hampered his performance.[29]

Back trouble plagued Ernie during spring training in 1986, and he missed a couple of weeks in April. Injuries mounted for the Jays as well; they played sub-.500 ball through the end of May. Whitt and Martinez were batting a combined .175 at the end of May as the Jays found it a difficult road to repeat as division champions. But both player and team started to improve. Ernie's 11th-inning walk-off home run gave Toronto an 8-7 win over Texas on August 17 in a game that was going to be suspended within the hour because of a Bill Cosby concert. Had the suspended game resumed the following day, it would have interfered with Whitt's charity golf tournament. "I wanted to play golf tomorrow, not baseball," said Whitt.[30] The Jays had a strong August but couldn't overcome the Red Sox, who beat them, 12-3, on September 28 and clinched the AL East. Whitt batted .336 in August and September to finish with his usual dependable numbers (.268-16-56).

Whitt's contract expired after the season, during the era when the owners colluded not to sign free agents. Ernie felt he was worth $900,000 a year and a three-year contract, on par with other veteran catchers like Fisk, Rich Gedman, Lance Parrish, Ozzie Virgil, and Jody Davis. Settling for arbitration would give him only a one-year deal. Pat Gillick offered two years at $700,000 a year with an optional third year. The back-and-forth negotiations with the Jays resulted in an unsatisfactory deal in which Whitt felt he was not being paid what he was worth. "I feel like I've got a cauliflower ear from all the phone calls," he said after negotiations ended in the wee hours of the morning of January 9, 1987. "I'm glad I've got one of those call-waiting things on my phone. It paid for itself this week," he said. The contract was reported to be a two-year deal for $2.3 million with a third-year option. "I don't think I got what was my worth, I feel, in today's market," he said. "Definitely the swing is on the owners' sides and your hands are tied. I felt I gave up an awful lot."[31]

Whitt had consistent numbers at the plate again in 1987 (.269-19-75) for what he considered the best team he ever played on. Blue Jays pitchers again led the league in ERA (3.74) and WHIP (1.30). Whitt ranked second in the AL in games as a catcher (131), first in putouts (803), second in throwing out basestealers (46) and second in fielding percentage (.994). The Jays spent much of the season in second place, within a handful of games of the division lead. Witt's two-run ninth-inning double in Chicago on August 5 gave Toronto a dramatic 3-2 win to stay one-half game behind the Yankees. Whitt batted .344 in August to help the Jays' cause.

His bat cooled in September, however, as the Blue Jays made their move toward their second division title in three years. Mired in a 3-for-29 slump on September 11, Whitt came through against one of the toughest lefties in the game. With the winning run on second in the bottom of the 10th of a 5-5 game, Whitt, who batted only .238 against lefties all year, lined a single to right off Dave Righetti to win the game and keep Toronto tied with Detroit for first place. On September 14 he had a career night and was part of baseball history in an 18-3 mauling of the Orioles. Whitt smashed three home runs off three Orioles pitchers and the Jays hit 10 home runs in the game, still a major-league record through 2017. "I don't know. I've never been on a streak like this before," Whitt said after the game. "I can't deny I wasn't thinking home run that last time. I'll never forget this night, but this is no time for celebration. It'll be something I can, one day, tell my grandkids but, let's face it, tonight means nothing if we don't win this thing."[32] The win kept the Blue Jays tied with Detroit at 86-57.

Whitt was involved in a controversial play on September 17 that cost the Blue Jays a win in the heat of the pennant race. With the Blue Jays leading the Yankees, 5-4, in the eighth inning at New York, Toronto's David Wells fanned right-handed hitter Phil Lombardi on a pitch down and in. Home-plate umpire Larry Young was blocked from seeing the pitch, so first-base umpire Joe Brinkman raised his hands indicating a strikeout. Whitt, the out recorded, threw the ball to third so it would go "around the horn." But while he was doing so, Yankees manager Lou Piniella thought Whitt had not fielded the ball cleanly and yelled at Lombardi to take off for first, where he stood. Piniella stormed out of the dugout to plead his case. Third-base umpire Tim Welke agreed with Piniella that Whitt had not caught the ball cleanly. The umpires decided Lombardi was safe. Toronto manager Jimy Williams went on a tirade and was ejected. Whitt was irate. "It's the first time I've ever heard of a guy [Welke] who was in the worst position to see a play overruling the guy [Brinkman] who was in the best position. He [Lombardi] didn't take off right away. He knew he was out so he went to the dugout. He didn't run to first until Lou started shouting at him." The Yankees wound up tying the score and winning that game. It was a costly loss which may have changed the entire season. Williams called Brinkman "gutless." "If he saw the play and he called it a catch, why is he running around getting dissenting opinions?" wrote Al Strachan of the *Globe and Mail*. "Once he has decreed that Whitt caught the ball, how can he expect Whitt to make the play

to first? The batter has been called out. The play is over. End of chapter. Get another hitter up."[33]

Whitt didn't mince any words in his autobiography concerning Brinkman. "Joe Brinkman hates our ballclub," he wrote, creating national headlines when the book was published. "I used to talk to Joe all the time until 1987. Now we don't speak at all. He's one of the few I purposely won't speak to because I think he's gone downhill as an umpire. He's incompetent. And the scary part is he runs an umpiring school." In remembering the call, Whitt wrote, "(Brinkman) let a rookie umpire (Welke) from the opposite side overrule him, and that should never have happened."[34]

After a thrilling, 10-9 walk-off win over Detroit on September 26, the Blue Jays led Detroit by 3½ games with just seven games to play. The season unraveled for the Blue Jays and Whitt from that point on. After a loss to Detroit, the Jays had a series against the Milwaukee Brewers. They would drop the opener, but still held a 2½-game lead with five games left. On September 29, Whitt collided with Paul Molitor at second base and broke two ribs. "I felt the knee go directly into my ribs," he said. "I had trouble breathing. It was pain I'd never experienced before."[35] He watched the Blue Jays lose that and the following game to the Brewers, and the Tigers cut the lead to one game. Motown now anticipated the closing-weekend three-game series between the two clubs at Tiger Stadium while Whitt hoped to get back on the field.

Whitt dominated his hometown Tigers throughout his career, slamming 23 home runs, or 17 percent of his career total. Eleven of those homers came at Tiger Stadium. His 73 RBIs against them also proved headaches for Tiger pitchers. "I just really enjoyed hitting at Tiger Stadium," Whitt said. "A lot of teams you play, [pitchers] make a mistake and you foul it off. It seemed with the Tigers, I was always able to hit their mistake pitches."[36] This series would not be a celebratory homecoming for Whitt, however.

"I remember going through all types of hell, basically trying to get in there to play," Whitt recalled. "I had shots to numb the area, flak jackets, the whole nine yards. I never got in. There was no way Friday." The Jays lost the opener, 4-3, and now the two clubs were tied for first with two games remaining. Whitt was available for pinch-hitting, but even that was a stretch. On Saturday he sat on the bench in stunned silence as Alan Trammell's bases-loaded single in the 12th inning gave the Tigers a 3-2 win. The

Blue Jays now needed to win the season finale to force a one-game playoff. Whitt sat out Sunday as the Jays faced tough lefty Frank Tanana, who threw a complete-game six-hit shutout in the 1-0 victory. The Jays had an epic collapse. "I was more than a little pissed off that I had gone through all the agony of trying to numb the pain, getting myself ready to pinch hit, showing (Williams) in batting practice that I could swing the bat and then not get used in a situation where I could have helped," Whitt said.[37]

The 1988 Blue Jays started a sluggish 21-29 and were 12 games out of first to start the season. Whitt struggled too, as he allowed the most stolen bases in the AL (90) and was second in passed balls (10) but was also was fourth in throwing out basestealers (34) and second in putouts (643) and fielding percentage (.994). He batted .251 with 16 home runs and 70 RBIs and played 123 games behind the plate. The team came alive in September, going 20-7 and cutting a 9½-game deficit to two at the end of the season, but had still too many games to overcome. Yet they were resilient to the end. On September 27 Boston was a win away from clinching the AL East, but Whitt tied his career best with six RBIs to go with two home runs as Toronto blasted Boston, 15-9.

At the end of the season, the Jays exercised their $850,000 option on Whitt for 1989. He had been granted free agency by an arbitrator in the Collusion II case but preferred to stay in Toronto. Now 37, he hit 11 home runs, his fewest in seven years, and his RBIs (53) were his lowest in five years. But one of those home runs was a memorable one in Boston on June 4. The Red Sox led 10-0 in the seventh when the Jays mounted a dramatic comeback. They scored two runs in the seventh, four in the eighth, and five in the ninth, highlighted by Whitt's grand slam against Lee Smith. Toronto prevailed, 13-11, in 12 innings.

The team flew back to Toronto and the next day played the inaugural game at SkyDome. Appropriately, Whitt, the last of the original Blue Jays, was the starting catcher. Two nights later he went 3-for-3 with three RBIs in the first baseball game played both indoors and outdoors, as SkyDome's retractable roof was closed during the game.[38]

The Blue Jays played poorly early in the 1989 season, costing manager Jimy Williams his job. He was replaced by Cito Gaston on May 15, and the Jays caught fire in the second half, playing .627 ball. After falling 10 games behind Baltimore in the AL East race on July 5, the Blue Jays were one game ahead on September 1 and survived

the division race by two games over Baltimore to reach the postseason for the second time. Whitt, who batted .300 in the first half of the season, hit only .220 in the second. He was platooned with Pat Borders. Whitt went 2-for-16 in the ALCS, his last appearance in the postseason, and the Jays lost the series to the Oakland A's, four games to one. Whitt's last at-bat in a Blue Jays uniform was a groundout in the ninth inning of Game Five, a 4-3 loss that ended Whitt's season and lengthy playing tenure in Toronto.

The Blue Jays planned their future catching core around Borders and Greg Myers, but wanted to keep Whitt as a third-string catcher and DH. That was not the direction Whitt wanted to go in. "I wasn't ready to accept being a third-string catcher," he said. "I'll always cherish my time in Toronto – I'll miss the city, the fans, my teammates – but this, apparently, was something that had to be done. It was tough but, because I wanted to keep playing, I felt it was the only decision I had." Whitt, as a 10-year veteran with five consecutive years at Toronto, could veto any trade. He agreed to be traded to Atlanta (where his former manager Bobby Cox was the GM) on December 17, when he was sent with outfielder Kevin Batiste for reliever Ricky Trlicek. "Negotiating with Bobby was the easy part. Basically, I got an offer I couldn't refuse, but the tough part was accepting … actually saying, 'Yes, we have a deal.' I'm leaving with good feelings and I hope the Jays feel the same way about me," Whitt said.[39]

The trade meant the Braves picked up the remaining year left on Whitt's contract, which paid him $1.15 million and included an option year with a buyout clause. "We got a catcher that can hit," said Cox. "He's so much better than the other guys who are available. He's an outstanding competitor. All Ernie wants is to play."[40]

At 37, Ernie was surrounded by young stars who made the Braves the celebrated "team of the '90s." But they were still a year away, and the Braves of 1990 would have their sixth straight season of at least 89 losses. Manager Russ Nixon planned to platoon Whitt with veteran Jody Davis, who had hit a meager .169 as the Braves starter in 1989.

Whitt started the first game of an Opening Day doubleheader and went 0-for-1 before being pinch-hit for in an 8-0 loss to San Francisco. His only season in the National League was a lost one, as he batted a weak .171 at the end of May when he injured his thumb making a tag at the plate against Montreal. He did not return until the end of July. Rookie Greg Olson batted a hot .308 in June, was selected as an All-Star reserve, and all but secured the Braves starting catcher's job.

By the time Whitt returned, Nixon was gone and Cox became the manager, where he would stay for the next 21 years of his Hall of Fame managerial career. But Whitt (.172-2-10 in 180 at-bats) had a disastrous season and the Braves bought out his contract for $475,000.[41] "I just stunk the place out," he admitted, conceding that his thumb injury contributed. "I don't know whether the switch of leagues affected me, but I know the injury had a lot to do with it."[42]

Whitt was given one final chance to extend his career. The Baltimore Orioles invited the veteran to spring training as a nonroster player for 1991. He was solely a backup to Bob Melvin and Chris Hoiles. He impressed the Orioles with his bat, batting .333 in his first 12 at-bats in spring training with two home runs. One was against Toronto at their spring park in Dunedin, Florida, where the crowd showed their appreciation for him with a standing ovation. "It's nice when people respect you for what you have done," Whitt said. "I was actually embarrassed a little bit."[43] Whitt made the club, receiving a $300,000 incentive-laden contract from Baltimore.[44] He had a frustrating debut for the Orioles on April 14 when he struck out four times, three against Nolan Ryan. That is understandable against the future Hall of Famer, but for Whitt it ended his career against the Ryan Express: 0-for-10 with nine strikeouts.

The 1991 season was just as forgettable as 1990 had been. Whitt was batting .222 and starting only his 11th game of the season when he came up to bat in Toronto on June 14 for the first time since being traded. "Ern-nie, Ern-nie!" chanted the 50,000 fans who gave him a 40-second standing ovation at SkyDome as he came to bat. Whitt struck out and went 1-for-4 as his days were winding down. "It was really nice; the fans were great," Whitt said. "I'm kind of excited, coming back home and all. I still consider this home. The fans here have been very supportive."[45] The end of the road came on July 5 when Baltimore released him. "I wasn't surprised," Whitt said. "If you look at it, I hadn't started a game in 18 days. The writing was on the wall. Surprised, no. Disappointed, yes. I'd like to have finished the year with them, and I'm disappointed that I didn't get to play more."[46]

After 15 seasons, Whitt took off his catcher's gear for the final time. "I wasn't having fun," he later said of his final

season. "I told myself a long time ago that I'd get out of the game if it wasn't fun anymore." He stayed away from the game for the first couple of years to concentrate on having fun again: spending time with his family, golfing, and boating. But the game soon lured him back. In 1994, he and two groups of Canadian businessmen acquired the Blue Jays' Class-A St. Catharines club. In 1996 he returned to his alma mater and coached the Macomb baseball team. "I'm doing something that I enjoy," he told Bill Roose of the *Detroit Free Press*. "I guess I'm very fortunate because there are so many people out there that are doing what they don't want to do out of necessity." He also ran the Ernie Whitt Baseball Academy, which caused a public embarrassment to him in 1997 when the program suddenly closed due to mismanagement. Whitt had no ownership stake in the organization but approved instructors for the program. "It's unfortunate what's happened and I feel terrible about it," Whitt said. "I feel like there's egg on my face. I've worked too hard to have something like this blow up. The last thing I'd want to do is take advantage of any child, parent, or person. I'm going to do everything I can do from my end to get the money back to all the people." He also shared a percentage of ownership of a golf and ski resort in Ontario. His tenure at Macomb lasted just the one season and in 1997 he was a roving catching instructor for the Blue Jays and also managed their Dunedin Class-A club for part of the season.[47]

Beginning in 1999, Whitt began managing Team Canada, which won its first-ever baseball medal (Bronze) at the Pan Am Games. The team placed fourth in the 2004 Olympic Games, won Bronze at the 2011 Baseball World Cup, and Gold at the 2011 and 2015 Pan Am Games. The team also participated in the 2006, 2009, and 2013 World Baseball Classics.

Whitt was a catching instructor in the Blue Jays organization until 2004. He then served as the Blue Jays bench coach from 2005 to 2007, then became their first-base coach in 2008. On June 20, 2008, manager John Gibbons and his entire coaching staff were fired, ending Whitt's nearly two decades with the organization. He was hired by the Philadelphia Phillies in 2009 and spent a season as the manager of Clearwater of the Class-A Florida State League. After the season, Whitt became a roving catching instructor in the Phillies organization, where he continued into the 2018 season.

During his playing days in Toronto, Whitt gave back to his community, serving as chairman of the Canadian Cancer

Society, and was actively involved in fundraising for the Special Olympics. Whitt was inducted into the Canadian Baseball Hall of Fame in 2009. The Whitts have three grown children: Ashley, EJ, and Taylor.

## Sources

In addition to the sources listed in the Notes, the author was assisted by the following:

Cassidy Lent, Reference Librarian at the Giamatti Research Center at the Baseball Hall of Fame, who provided copies of Whitt's file and questionnaire.

"Ernest H. Whitt. Supervisor, Was Ballplayer's Dad," *Detroit News*, September 25, 2002.

"Ernie, Ernie!" *Toronto Sun*, June 19, 1989: A20.

## Notes

1 Julie Kotsos, "Winter Fest Parade Draws Thousands to Downtown Windsor to See Santa," *Windsor Star*, November 25, 2017. windsorstar.com/news/local-news/winter-fest-parade.

2 Bill James, *The New Bill James Historical Baseball Abstract* (New York: Simon & Schuster, 2010), 416.

3 Ernie Whitt and Greg Cable, *Catch: A Major League Life* (Toronto: McGraw-Hill Ryerson, 1989), 10.

4 Ibid.

5 Whitt and Cable, 12.

6 Joe Sexton, "Blue Jays' Catcher Rooted for the Tigers," *New York Times*, September 28, 1987: C3.

7 Jim Evans, "The Whitt and Wisdom of Roseville High's Athletic Hall of Fame," *Macomb Daily* (Macomb County, Michigan), January 22, 2018. macombdaily.com/article/MD/20180122/SPORTS/180129897.

8 Mike Downey, "At Whitt's End: A Position as Budding Big League Star," *Detroit Free Press*, April 15, 1982: F1.

9 Bill L. Roose, "Ex-Major Leaguer Whitt Back in the Game as Macomb Coach," *Detroit Free Press*, April 4, 1996: 6D.

10 Whitt and Cable, 41.

11 Whitt and Cable, 42.

12 "Six Players Sent Down; Tony Idle," *Boston Globe*, March 24, 1975: 19; Peter Gammons, "Red Sox Cut 3; Guerrero Still Waits,"

*Boston Globe*, April 3, 1975: 32; "Bristol Defeats Reading in 17th," *Hartford Courant*, September 5, 1975: 58.

13 Whitt and Cable, 45.

14 Whitt and Cable, 47.

15 Evans.

16 Whitt and Cable, 50.

17 Bill Newell, "Whitt Living Baseball's Highs and Lows," *Hartford Courant*, March 31, 1977: 61.

18 Cathal Kelly, "Whitt, Ashby Share History: Ex-Jays Catchers Recall Excitement About April 7, 1977." *Toronto Star*, April 10, 2007: C2.

19 Neil MacCarl, "Whitt and Jays Have Grown up Together; Veteran Catcher a 'Father Figure' Now," *Toronto Star*, February 7, 1988: F11.

20 "Winfield Remembers Being Poor," *Detroit Free Press*, August 18, 1977: 2D.

21 MacCarl.

22 Whitt and Cable, 69-71.

23 Downey.

24 Kevin Boland, "Witt's Hit Testimony for Platoon System," *Globe and Mail* (Toronto), June 22, 1983: S2.

25 Whitt and Cable, 2.

26 Larry Whiteside, "Catching the Fever; All-Stars Fisk, Whitt, Gedman of Same Mold," *Boston Globe*, July 16, 1985: 33.

27 Bob Elliott, "Jays Finally Clinch It; Scoring First Run Was Crucial; Blue Jays 5, Yankees 1," *Ottawa Citizen*, October 7, 1985: B1.

28 Roose: 6D.

29 "Whitt Wounded, Not Weary," *Globe & Mail*, October 18, 1985: D14.

30 "Whitt Whacks Winner as Jays Jolt Rangers; Jays 8, Rangers 7," *Ottawa Citizen*, August 18, 1986: B3.

31 Neil MacCarl, "A Look at Whitt's Longest Day: Marathon Negotiations Result in $2.3 Million for Jay," *Toronto Star*, January 10, 1987: D1.

32 Allan Ryan, "Home Run Kings Whitt, 3; Bell, 2; Mulliniks, 2, etc. etc. etc." *Toronto Star*, September 15, 1987: E1.

33 Al Strachan, "Anatomy of a Controversial Call," *Globe and Mail*, September 19, 1987: E5.

34 Whitt and Cable, 87-88.

35 Charlie Vincent, "Pain Sabotages Whitt's Dream Night," *Detroit Free Press*, October 3, 1987: 5D.

36 Roose: 1D.

37  Whitt and Cable, 243.

38  "Today in Baseball," *Baltimore Sun*, June 7, 1991: 33.

39  Allan Ryan, "So Long, Ernie! Last of Original Jays Traded to Braves for a Minor-Leaguer," *Toronto Star*, December 18, 1989: D1.

40  Joe Strauss, "Braves Acquire Whitt to Fill Need at Catcher," *Atlanta Journal-Constitution*, December 18, 1989: E1.

41  Joe Strauss, "Braves Will Buy Out Whitt for $475,000," *Atlanta Journal-Constitution*, October 12, 1990: D1.

42  Kent Baker, "Whitt OKs Invitation From Orioles," *Baltimore Sun*, January 29, 1991: C1.

43  Kent Baker, "Whitt's Hitting Gives Him Solid Chance to Catch On," *Baltimore Sun*, March 19, 1991: 6D.

44  Kent Baker, "Orioles Complete Roster, Sending Milacki to Suns," *Baltimore Sun*, April 8, 1991: B1.

45  "Whitt Still a Fan Favorite with Blue Jay Fans," *Edmonton Journal*, June 16, 1991: D5; Neil A. Campbell, "Whitt Returns to Glory; Warm Reception Greets Former Jay," *Globe and Mail*, June 15, 1991: A12.

46  Peter Schmuck, "Team Reaches Whitt's End; Chito Martinez Brought Up," *Baltimore Sun*, July 6, 1991: 23.

47  Roose: 1D; "Former Jay Catcher Whitt to Buy St. Catharines Team," *Toronto Star*, November 10, 1994: B8; Randy Starkman, "Kids Feel 'Ripped Off' as Baseball School Closes; Ex-Blue Jay Embarrassed as Owners Tell 200 Cheques in Mail," *Toronto Star*, February 15, 1997: A3; Jim Byers, "Moseby Back with Jays," *Toronto Star*, October 18, 1996: C5; John Lowe, "Slumping Boggs, O'Neil Benched," *Detroit Free Press*, October 12, 1996: 3B.

# WELCOME TO THE TIME ZONE WITH A TEAM

## By Roger L. Kinney

The year 1959 was a good one– a very important year for baseball in Colorado. It was the first time a formidable, well-assembled plan was presented for bringing major-league baseball to Denver.

During the late '50s, the Denver Bears were the Triple-A farm team of the New York Yankees. The team was loaded with future major-league stars including Bobby Richardson, Tony Kubek, Ryne Duren, Mark Freeman, and Marv Throneberry. Ralph Houk was the manager. Denver fans loved their baseball and they supported the team with record attendance among minor-league cities.

Denver was emerging as a major transportation hub as well as a leading financial center in the Rocky Mountain area. Enthusiastic fans in the Denver area were eager to welcome and support major-league professional sports. The Denver Broncos began play in the American Football League in 1960 and the fans hoped a major-league baseball team would soon follow.

Bob Howsam, president of Rocky Mountain Sports, and US Senator Edwin "Big Ed" Johnson, his father-in-law, created a plan to bring major-league baseball to Colorado. Actually, they began to formulate the plan in the early '50s while the Howsam family was building a successful leadership team, both on and off the field. They met with Branch Rickey, who agreed that there was a need throughout the country for more major-league teams. While Howsam discussed plans with representatives of other major- and minor-league cities, Senator Johnson met with colleagues and friends in Congress. They made lasting friendships and paved the way for future alliances.

In 1958, the city of New York lost the Dodgers and Giants when they moved to California. New York Mayor Robert Wagner and Bill Shea formed a committee to attract another team for the city. They were unable to attract an existing

The National League Expansion Committee visited Denver Mile High Stadium after a tour of the metropolitan area in several helicopters. Here, they huddle on the infield grass to exchange information. (Courtesy of Roger Kinney)

franchise to move to New York. Once they considered an expansion team, they joined forces with Howsam and potential candidates from seven other cities for gaining major-league status. Thereafter, with extensive study and faced with rejection from the existing major-league teams, the eight cities gave their support to the formation of a new major league.

Unveiling of the Colorado Rockies logo (Courtesy of Koi Drummond-Gehrig)

The Continental League was officially organized on July 27, 1959.[1] The original members of the league were: Denver, Houston, New York, Buffalo, Dallas-Fort Worth, Toronto, Minneapolis-St. Paul, and Atlanta. The new league appeared to be formidable, especially with some wealthy and determined owners and the abundance of talented players in the minor leagues who were capable of playing at the major-league level. But the announcement of the new league was met with strong opposition from the existing major-league teams. National League and American League owners united in opposition and directed Commissioner Ford Frick to appeal to Congress for support. With a negative vote from the Senate, the new league was derailed and eventually terminated. However, with the threat of the new league, the existing major-league teams responded with a promise that eventually all of the cities from the Continental League would someday have major-league baseball.[2]

Denver's presentation was important because it set the stage. From then on, Denver became a player in the ongoing game whenever a new city was considered for a major-league franchise. Although it took 33 years, Denver became the seventh city of the original Continental League to have major-league baseball when the Colorado Rockies began play in 1993. What happened during those 33 years of knocking on the door and waiting for a team is a fascinating story, filled with great expectations, some sad and disappointing setbacks, and wild jubilation when the team finally arrived.

### The Early Years

The first recorded game of "base ball" in Denver was played on April 26, 1862, when the McNeils Side defeated the Hulls Side, 20-7.[3] After the Civil War, as settlers moved west, baseball grew in popularity throughout the mining towns, the farming communities, and Denver, the Queen City of the Plains. Common rivalries grew in popularity as baseball outings became the social and family entertainment throughout the summer. George "Patsy" Tebeau (December 26, 1861- February 4, 1923) and David Rowe (October 9, 1854 - December 9, 1930), who both played major-league baseball, are referred to as the "fathers of Colorado baseball."[4] They were instrumental in developing amateur teams and bringing barnstorming teams to play in Denver. The first professional team was the Denver Browns in 1879 and the first team to play in the Western Baseball League was the Denvers in 1886.[5]

As Denver's population increased and the economy grew stronger, youth baseball programs flourished throughout the state. As baseball grew in popularity, there were many sandlot fields and ballparks where the games were played. In Denver, Merchants Park was built in 1922 and provided the site for Denver Post Tournaments and exhibition games involving barnstorming teams. Babe Ruth and Lou Gehrig played in Denver in 1927 on a barnstorming tour. Baseball in Denver gradually developed a strong grassroots following and a reputation as a good baseball town as local players developed and the visiting players, who had favorable experiences in Denver, traveled about the country.

### Professional Baseball

After World War II, the Western League was reorganized and began play with eight teams: Denver (farm team of the New York Yankees), Pueblo (Brooklyn Dodgers), Omaha (St. Louis Cardinals), Des Moines (Chicago Cubs), Sioux City (New York Giants), and Lincoln (Philadelphia A's). The country was in a rebuilding period; the success and the fortunes of all the professional baseball teams rested heavily with the ownership of the local minor-league teams.

The owner of the Denver Bears was a group headed by former Mayor Will Nicholson, his brother Eddie Nicholson, and Colorado financial magnate Charles Boettcher.[6] In 1948, Bob Howsam and his family purchased the Bears and moved to a new location in central Denver where they built Bears Stadium.[7] Howsam proved to be a knowledgeable baseball entrepreneur as well as a popular and successful businessman. He made friends and loyal supporters throughout the country, and he never lost his zeal or support for Denver's bid for a major-league team. After the demise of the Continental League, on May 26, 1961, Howsam sold the Denver Bears to Rocky Mountain Sports, Inc., headed by Gerald and Allan Phipps. Shortly thereafter, Howsam moved to St. Louis and later, to Cincinnati, where he was the general manager of the Cardinals and then the Reds. His teams won four World Series before he returned with his family to Colorado.

Gerald "Jerry" Phipps, a legend in his own right, had a genuine love for baseball, the Denver Bears, the Denver Broncos, and his beloved state of Colorado. He hired Jim Burris, former general secretary of the American Association, to be the general manager of the Bears. Burris, a baseball loyalist, became the leader of Denver's ongoing campaign to attain a major-league team. Whenever an opportunity occurred, he would trumpet the favorable attributes of Colorado for a big-league team. Burris attended major-league baseball meetings every year. While other prospective cities were often represented with elaborate displays and well-organized promotional teams, Denver's presence was sometimes a lonely affair. Burris, who had a charming sense of humor, used to tell friends that he held the meetings for the Denver delegation in a telephone booth.

Over time, Denver's presence began to change, and in 1974, the Denver Chamber of Commerce sent four members, Jim Burris, Larry Varnell, Rex Jennings, and Dale Mitchell (a former player with the Cleveland Indians), to New Orleans with a model of Mile High Stadium (formerly Bears Stadium) and a presentation promoting the attractions of Denver.[8] For 21 years, Burris continued to "carry the torch" for Denver at the major-league meetings, often escorting supporting members of the Denver delegation.

**Destination Denver**

In the early 1970s, a formal bid was made to hold the Winter Olympics in Colorado. The International Olympic Committee approved the bid and the Winter Olympics were scheduled to be held in Colorado in 1976. But there was strong opposition to the organizers' plan. After a heated campaign, the voters rejected the plan and the Colorado Olympics were canceled. (The 1976 Winter Games were instead held in Innsbruck, Austria .)

The Colorado sports scene was shaken for several years. Some people called it a black eye for the state. Promoters were hesitant to submit bids to attract other sporting events. Some hostelries said tourism suffered with Denver becoming known as an airport city on the way to the mountains. In time, the city rebounded and its desire to attract major sporting events was renewed. Denver Conven-

tion and Visitors Bureau president Roger Smith vowed to attract major events, including national conventions and sporting events. This eventually led to a successful vote to finance a new Denver Convention Center. Presidents Rex Jennings and Shelby Harper of the Denver Chamber of Commerce created the Denver Metro Sports Committee. This eventually led to support for the Denver Nuggets of the NBA and for the NBA All-Star Game, which was held in Denver in 1984. This in turn led to the NCAA Final Four basketball tournament. held in Denver in 1990. With these successes and the improving economy, sports fans again set their sights on a major-league baseball franchise.

**High Hopes – Disappointing Results**

When Marvin Davis, a wealthy oil investor, expressed an interest in owning a big-league team and bringing it to Denver, the fans were hopeful for success. There were reports that Davis tried to purchase the Chicago White Sox in 1976 and the Baltimore Orioles in 1977.[9] Larry Varnell, past president of the Colorado Sports Hall of Fame, became the public spokesman for Davis as he made numerous attempts to purchase a team. Varnell said, "One year when I went to the winter (baseball) meetings, Davis said, you find the team, I'll write the check."[10] In 1985, there were reports that the San Francisco Giants might make a temporary move to Denver to facilitate the construction of a new stadium in San Francisco. There were other rumors involving the Pittsburgh Pirates, the Cleveland Indians, and the Minnesota Twins.

Perhaps the closest possibility for a sale came in two stages. First, in 1977-78 when Marvin Davis was negotiating with Charlie Finley to move the Oakland A's to Denver, Varnell reported that the American League owners were agreeable to a sale to Davis if a settlement could be made

When Don Baylor was selected to be the Colorado Rockies' first manager, Mrs. Jackie (Rachel) Robinson came to Denver to celebrate the inaugural season for the Rockies. Here she is shown with Rockies president Jerry McMorris and Don Baylor. (Courtesy of Roger Kinney)

Baseball legend John Jordan "Buck" O'Neil visited Denver in support of the new franchise for the Colorado Rockies. Here he previews the initial model of the new stadium, Coors Field, with Rockies staff members Roger Kinney and Paula Colorosa. (Courtesy of Roger Kinney)

with the Oakland Coliseum Authority. After extensive negotiations, the parties could not reach a settlement and the sale was canceled. The second proposal come in 1979-80 when "an official of the Oakland Coliseum made a public disclosure that the Oakland Coliseum would consider a cash offer to allow Finley to break his lease and sell the team to Davis."[11] Rumors circulated that a deal was close to completion. But Marvin Davis denied the rumors and a sale was never completed.

The Denver Baseball Commission, created by Mayor Federico Pena and led by executive director Steve Katich and City Attorney Steve Kaplan, worked in support of Marvin Davis. To gain fans' support, the commission held a Baseball Symposium and sponsored exhibition games played by visiting major-league teams. In 1984, the commission hosted a display booth at the winter baseball meetings and distributed a daily newspaper extolling Denver's worthiness for a major-league team.

Marvin Davis eventually lost interest in bringing a team to Denver, and the Denver Baseball Commission shifted support to John Dikeou and his family. The Dikeous had purchased the Denver Bears from Gerald and Allan Phipps in 1984 and renamed the team the Zephyrs. A popular Denver native and a successful businessman, Dikeou assembled a strong management team led by Robert Howsam Jr. and Tom Maloney. The team won the Triple-A championship in 1991. The fans responded, and as the Zephyrs prospered, the momentum for a major-league team gained strength. John Dikeou became the likely and assumed new owner of an expansion team.

## Congress and the Commissioner

In 1985, Peter Ueberroth became commissioner of base-

ball, succeeding Bowie Kuhn. At that time, baseball owners were dealing with a wide range of financial problems involving the players' salaries, free agency, and the wide disparity of economic interests among the owners. In 1986 Tim Wirth of Colorado was elected to the US Senate. In the spring of 1987, Wirth suggested to Ueberroth that, "Major League Baseball and the Senate could talk to each other about expansion."[12] Extolling the attractions of Denver for a new franchise, Wirth continued to attempt to convince Ueberroth that expansion would be good for baseball and the country. Wirth gained support from other members of Congress, and on November 4, 1987, they formed a Senate Task Force on Expansion of Major League Baseball. Their goal was to have six new major-league teams by 2000.[13]

For the next two years, Wirth and his colleagues made a persistent campaign for expansion. Commissioner Ueberroth resisted any public commitments to expansion and continued to deal primarily with the financial concerns of the major-league owners, the players, and their union. But in the summer of 1988, while announcing that he planned to step down, he indicated that "expansion was coming in the not too distant future."[14]

A. Bartlett Giamatti was selected to succeed Ueberroth in the spring of 1989. Giamatti was popular, dedicated, and a forceful advocate for the traditional values associated with the national pastime. In the summer of 1989, at the owners' quarterly meeting, they agreed to expand by two teams in the National League.[15] Giamatti died of a heart attack on September 1, 1989, just five months after becoming commissioner. Fay Vincent succeeded him.

## The Invitation

Shortly after a contract agreement was signed with the Players Association on June 16, 1990, Vincent presented a timeline for all prospective new owners.[16] The owners' Expansion Committee would receive presentations from the applicants by September 30, and the finalists would be announced by the end of the year. The committee would make its recommendation to the major-league owners and the final selection would be made by September 30, 1991.

It soon became apparent that the application would have four major requirements. First, the owners of a new franchise (preferably local people) must be acceptable to the current owners. "This is the fundamental thing to remember in expansion. Cities are never awarded franchises. Owners are rewarded franchises."[17] Second, there must be a new, baseball-only stadium that is first class in all respects. Third, there must be sufficient support from the fans and general public. This meant a support base of at least 20,000 season-ticket holders. Fourth, the entry fee would be $95 million. The applicants needed to agree to all the accompanying conditions regarding the expansion process, including the draft of eligible players, the finance schedule, and the nonparticipation in television revenue for the initial season.

## Colorado's Response – House Bill 1351

In 1988, Pat Grant, a Colorado legislator, had been instrumental in creating a successful district taxing authority to support the cultural arts in the Denver area. Faced with a stalemate over the financing of a new ballpark, Neil Macey, a Denver real-estate entrepreneur and avid baseball fan, envisioned a similar plan as a practical way to finance the planning and construction. Macey envisioned the creation of a five-county authority that would expand the tax base, oversee the project, and impose a 0.01 percent sales tax. Macey took his plan to John Dikeou and Kathi Williams, a member of the Colorado House of Representatives from Adams County. They took the plan to Governor Roy Romer, and after considerable negotiating, they presented Colorado House Bill 1351. With an appeal to all the state legislators who supported major-league baseball, the bill passed the Colorado legislature and sent the measure to the electorate in August 1990.[18]

The bill created a Colorado Baseball Stadium Authority with a seven-member board responsible for site selection, financial planning, construction, and the ongoing operation of the ballpark. The bill also created an 18-member Colorado Baseball Commission tasked to conduct the election campaign and any activities necessary to support the prospective owners and meet the requirements set by the major leagues' expansion committee. The commission would go out of existence once its mission was completed.

## The Colorado Baseball Stadium Authority

After House Bill 1351 was passed, Governor Romer, with input from Neil Macey and Kathi Williams, began to make appointments to the Stadium Authority and the Baseball Commission.[19] All appointments were subject to approval by a committee of the Colorado Senate. Senator Claire Taylor conducted many of the appointment hearings and passed along the recommendations to the governor. Once the seven members were selected and approved, the

Stadium Authority began meeting on a regular basis.

At the first meeting, John McHale Jr. was elected chairman. Shortly thereafter, Jack Sperling and Craig Umbaugh of the legal firm Fairfield and Woods were named legal counsel. Lee White, an investment banker, was chosen to be the financial adviser. Since there were minimal funds available for the operations of the authority, in-kind contributions were solicited. Many supporters responded, including Dave Herlinger, president of the Colorado Housing Authority, who provided office and meeting space for the authority.

Under McHale and Ray Baker (who succeeded McHale as chairman), the board began seeking a site for the new stadium. Many sites were considered. With recognition of the large amount of land along the Amtrak rail lines, the site at 20th and Blake was selected on March 13, 1991.[20] In addition to the availability of the land for parking, the site had other attractive features: The site was above the flood plain, which would facilitate building the playing field at the lower level, and it was within walking distance of the downtown area and Union Station, the transportation center for the metropolitan area. Shortly thereafter, HOK Sports was selected to be the architectural firm for the stadium.

Once the site was selected and the election neared, the Stadium Authority created an ambitious schedule, making public presentations to all five of the counties in the voting district. The presentations included a display of the plans for the stadium, followed by a "no holds barred" question-and-answer session with the board members. The response throughout the five-county area from those attending was positive and they were asked to seek the support of their neighbors and friends, especially those who would vote in the election slated for August 1990.

As the time neared for the National League expansion committee to visit Denver, the Stadium Authority Board turned its attention to the lease of the new stadium to the owners. John McHale, as chairman of the MLB Stadium District and Steve Ehrhart, then president of the Colorado Baseball Partnership, signed a memorandum of agreement for the lease of the new stadium on March 14, 1991.[21] The lease caught the immediate attention of major-league owners and the expansion committee. Carl Barger, president of the Florida Marlins, said, "It's a great lease. I gotta hand it to those people who negotiated it."[22] With the site and the lease in place, the Stadium Authority prepared to meet with the expansion committee, who were planning to be in Denver in March 1991.

## The Colorado Baseball Commission

The Colorado Baseball Commission was created with 15 members representing all of the five counties in the district. John Dikeou was named chairman and Neil Macey was the executive director. After a difficult start to raise money for its operational needs, cable magnate Bill Daniels and the Greater Denver Chamber of Commerce made substantial contributions to set the campaign on a winning track. United Airlines made a generous contribution to facilitate goodwill visits to six National League teams, the Dodgers, Padres, Giants, Cardinals, Reds, and Cubs. Many supporting companies and loyal fans made monetary and in-kind contributions. A record number of volunteers donated their time and talents to the campaign.

The commission had a wide range of projects to address. One of the first was to create a plan for the sale of season tickets. With help from the accounting firm of Deloitte Touche and the legal firm of Holme, Roberts and Owen, who donated office space and telephone service, they began the season-ticket drive in early May 1990. The conditions for a commitment were well publicized by the media, including a deposit for obtaining a priority number on a first-come (via a telephone call), first-served basis. Priority would be given to season-ticket holders of the Denver Zephyrs, the Triple-A farm team. A team of volunteers would man the telephones, ready to take orders. When the switchboard opened, the telephone calls (including those for the law firm) overwhelmed the system. Callers were desperate in their attempts to make a deposit and obtain a low priority number. Carolyn "Skinny" Writer, a supervisor for the event, said, "It was the most frantic, and the most gratifying experience I could possibly imagine."[23] It took several days to properly record the initial ticket requests and return the telephone system to normal operation. The season-ticket campaign was off to a great start.

At that time, the Denver Broncos had a huge following in the area and dominated the sports pages. Some avid baseball fans were concerned that the Broncos not support the drive for a baseball team. Just the opposite was true. The Broncos were very supportive, and when the season-ticket drive was close to reaching its goal, Rod Buscher, president of John Elway Motors, committed to purchase enough season tickets to surpass the goal of 20,000, putting the drive over the top. Eventually, the sale of season tickets reached 28,250. The success of the drive had a positive impact as the election for the stadium bond issue approached.

The vote was scheduled for August 14, 1990. The campaign theme was simple: The cost of the ballpark would be "a penny on a purchase of ten dollars." The bonds would be paid off within 20 years. (Actually they were paid off in about eight years.) With the leadership of co-chairmen Larry Varnell and Sam Suplizio, the Colorado Baseball Commission campaigned with public appearances, media coverage, and personal calls to sports fans in the area. The early polls were discouraging because they predicted defeat. Since the election would be held as a primary, not a general election, a smaller than average turnout was expected. Rick Reiter, the campaign adviser, developed a selective plan to target key areas.

As the voting results came in, the celebration party at the downtown Radisson Hotel grew with optimism and excitement as it became apparent that the bond issue would pass. The votes in favor were 187,539, about 54 percent, and the opposing votes were 157,954, about 46 percent.

The votes in Arapahoe and Jefferson Counties were so overwhelmingly favorable that they overshadowed the negative votes in Denver and Adams County. The election was a big step forward. It meant that if Colorado were awarded a franchise, the plan was in place, approved by the electorate, to build a new, first-class ballpark.

The next step was to solidify the ownership and support their presentation to the expansion committee. When John Dikeou withdrew his ownership interest, there was widespread uncertainty about finding a new owner. Several potential ownership groups expressed an interest. The Colorado Baseball Commission informed Governor Romer of the potential problems. He quickly responded, drawing on business leaders, involving Dick Robinson, Jim Baldwin, and Tryg Myhren, to conduct a search and identify the best qualified ownership group. Romer identified the "Ehrhart-Nicklaus" group as the local ownership official leaders on August 23, 1990.[24]

Paul Jacobs, a Denver lawyer and sports enthusiast, became the driving force to assemble the new ownership group. As potential owners moved in and out of the picture, Jacobs worked night and day to assemble an ownership group with sufficient investment to pay the franchise fee of $95 million and the initial startup costs. The ownership group gained strength and momentum when Peter Coors, representing the Coors Brewery, made a major commitment of $25 million, part of which would be allocated to the naming rights of the new stadium. Several very important commitments followed, including those from Cary Teraji, Linda Alvarado, Bill Fletcher, representing the *Rocky Mountain News,* Lee Larson, representing radio station KOA, and the Beverage Distributing Company.

Jacobs established a good relationship with National League President Bill White and members of the expansion committee, Doug Danforth, Fred Wilpon, and Bill Giles. Jacobs later became executive vice president and general counsel of the Rockies, instrumental in creating the partnership agreements, the leases, and other initial legal documents.

### The Visit

The National League expansion committee visited Denver on March 26, 1991.[25] It was billed as "the biggest day in Denver's baseball history."[26] Before making the trip, the committee had requested that there be no elaborate displays, wining, or dining. They simply wanted it to be a business trip. But the CBC, with the agreement of business leaders, disagreed. This was Denver's biggest chance and they were going to make the most of it.

Shortly after the arrival at Stapleton Airport, the eight members of the expansion committee were taken on a helicopter tour of the Denver area with a landing on the outfield grass at Mile High Stadium. It was anticipated that the new team would play one or two years at Mile High while the new ballpark was being built. Next the committee went to the governor's mansion for a festive lunch and a visit with the governor and other dignitaries. As the committee traveled throughout the city, baseball fans, all volunteers, lined the streets with welcome signs and a mile-long petition supporting the campaign for a big-league team.

After lunch, the committee went to the United Bank Center, where about 5,000 baseball fans had gathered to welcome them. As scheduled by Don Hinchey, director of the event, when the committee arrived, the crowd sang "Take Me Out to the Ball Game," followed by cheers and applause for the visitors. Sportscaster Norm Jones gave a short welcoming address, several of the guests responded, and the crowd continued to sing and cheer for the distinguished visitors. The committee was visibly moved by the enthusiastic reception. "That visit, highlighted by the forbidden rally, sealed the deal."[27] On the way to the business meeting, Doug Danforth of the Pittsburgh Pi-

rates said, "I never get an ovation like this back in Pittsburgh."[28]

While the warm reception set a positive stage, the committee still wanted to know the financial condition of the owners. Jerry McMorris, Steve Ehrhart, and Paul Jacobs led their presentations, providing updated information about the ownership and their ability to meet the required financial investment. The meeting lasted about 2½ hours. At the press conference after the meeting, the mood was upbeat with favorable comments from the committee about the owners' presentation. The expansion committee would continue to evaluate the applicants and a decision would be anticipated later in the spring.

### The Announcement

Bill White, president of the National League, came to Denver on July 5, 1991. A crowd of fans, dignitaries and the media gathered at the Denver Hyatt Hotel. White spoke directly: "I am here to tell you that at 10:40 A.M., you officially became a member of the National League."[29] The audience reacted with a boisterous standing ovation. When the celebration calmed, White continued his remarks, indicating that Miami and Denver would be the new franchises, and that he anticipated both teams would be competitive much sooner than expansion teams in the past. Players from the National and American Leagues would be available to the expansion teams and both leagues would participate in the distribution of the funds from the expansion fees. White spoke with confidence that Denver and Miami had the potential to be very successful franchises for the long term.

Shortly after the announcement, John Antonucci, the chairman of the new team, and Steve Ehrhart, the president, set up offices in the United Bank Center and began to hire key personnel for the business operations. Michael Kent, formerly with the Philadelphia Phillies, and Sue Ann McClaren, formerly with the St. Louis Cardinals, joined the organization. Paul Egins, from the Atlanta Braves, was named assistant director of scouting and player development. They announced that purple would be one of the colors for the team, with reference to "the purple mountain majesties" as written by Katharine Lee Bates in the song "America the Beautiful."

With an effort to reach out to the entire state and the Rocky Mountain areas, they introduced the logo and announced that the team would be called the Colorado Rockies.[30] Governor Romer gave special recognition to the governors of Wyoming, New Mexico, Nebraska, Oklahoma, and Kansas for their support in bringing major-league baseball to the region, at that time America's only time zone without a team.

The first Rockies banquet, billed as "Colorado Welcomes Major League Baseball," was held on September 25, 1991, at the Denver Marriott Hotel.[31] Jim Wilkins was the general chairman and Commissioner Fay Vincent and Bill White were the honored guests.

In September, Bob Gebhard was selected to be the general manager for the Rockies. At the time, Gebhard was working for the soon-to-be American League champion Minnesota Twins, and it was agreed that he would not come to Denver until after the World Series. The Twins won the World Series and Gebhard arrived one day later, ready to begin a new career in Denver. It did not take long for everyone in the organization to recognize his devotion and commitment to building a championship organization.

### New Leadership

Jerry McMorris became the chairman, president, and CEO of the Colorado Rockies on January 26, 1992.[32] He assumed the leadership position after he, Oren Benton, and Charlie Monfort purchased the stock in a buyout agreement from Steven Kurtz and Paul Jacobs. Confronted with extensive legal problems, Michael "Mickey" Monus and Antonucci left the team after Monus was charged with embezzlement and fraud at Phar Mor. Kurtz and Jacobs purchased the stock from Monus and Antonucci, and held it during the interim period.

As the transition of ownership moved forward, McMorris set his sights on selecting key personnel, commencing business operations, and making preparations for the selection of coaches and players. General manager Bob Gebhard hired Pat Daugherty to head the scouting department and veterans Larry Bearnarth and Dick Balderson joined the staff.

Gebhard drew up elaborate plans for himself and his scouting staff to cover the entire country in preparation for the draft of players and the formation of the Rockies' farm teams. It was reported that "Pat Daugherty's 15 scouts traveled 198,105 miles by car and watched 2,250 high school and college games in the continental 48 states and Puerto Rico."[33]

In February, KOA Radio was selected to be the flagship station for the Rockies. Jeff Kingery and Wayne Hagin would cover the play-by-play. KWGN Channel 2 was chosen to be the television station with veteran announcer Charley Jones. Alan Roach was selected to be the public-address announcer. Frank Haraway, with over 50 years' experience, was selected to be the official scorer.

In March, the Rockies announced that they would hold spring training in Tucson, Arizona. Their home field there would be Hi Corbett Field, former home of the Cleveland Indians. The Pima County Sports Authority agreed to make major improvements to the field and the supporting facilities.

In the June major-league draft, the Rockies chose John Burke, a Colorado native and pitcher for the University of Florida, to be their number-one draft selection.[34] He would eventually join the other Rockies rookies to play for the Bend Rockies in the first organized game, June 16, against the Boise Hawks in the Class-A Northwest League. The Bend Rockies won the game, 6-4, with a grand slam by catcher Will Scalzitti.

In June, the Rockies held a tryout camp at the University of Denver. With the Rockies coaches and staff participating, the tryout camp was very popular with the local fans and participants. On July 4 the Rockies introduced their home and away uniforms. With purple pinstripes, the home uniforms were distinctive. The away uniforms were gray and black.

On October 27, Gebhard named Don Baylor to be the Rockies' first manager. Baylor was quickly put to work preparing for the expansion draft. The draft was held on November 17. Denver's Currigan Hall, site of many conventions and public events, was packed with an estimated 10,000 fans who came to watch the event, taking place in New York, Miami, and Denver. Alan Bossart of the Rockies staff created an elaborate venue, complete with a stage, numerous TV screens, and Rockies decorations throughout the hall. Secrecy and security surrounded the preparations before the announcement of the player selections.

Denver won the coin-flip and would select first. General manager Bob Gebhard selected David Nied, pitcher from the Atlanta Braves.[35] Marlins general manager Dave Dombrowski selected Nigel Wilson from the Toronto Blue Jays. Gebhard also announced the signing of Andres Galarraga as a free agent. In a surprise announcement,

Galarraga and Nied, who were kept in hiding prior to the announcement, appeared on stage for their introductions. The crowd went wild and shouted for joy as the players were surrounded by fans and members of the media. Throughout the evening, as additional players were selected, the fans continued to welcome the new team with wild enthusiasm.[36]

## Spring Training

After the players, coaches, and managers were selected, Gebhard and the staff turned their attention to spring training. Major improvements at Hi Corbett field were underway, including additional seating, improved clubhouse facilities, extended practice fields, and improved media facilities.

Several weeks before spring training, manager Don Baylor and players David Nied and Eric Wedge went on the first Caravan trip throughout the Mountain Time zone. They visited Wyoming, Utah, New Mexico, and many cities in Colorado. It was a promotional trip for the coming season and a time to thank the fans for their support in attracting a franchise. Many people had moved to the region from throughout the country where they had previously enjoyed major-league baseball. They knew what they were missing. Now it was time for them to change their allegiance and become fans of the Rockies. The annual Caravans proved to be a big success and have continued over the years.

The pitchers reported to Tucson about February 22 and the position players reported by February 27. The players needed to become acquainted with their teammates and coaches. To add a little levity to the situation, pitcher Bryn Smith handed out name tags to his teammates. The players responded with clever additions and exchanges, which confused some unsuspecting fans and media writers.

Once the team began practicing, the focus turned to preparation for the coming exhibition games. Veteran Don Zimmer was hired as bench coach and veteran Larry Bearnarth became the pitching coach, giving the team confidence that they would be ready to play at the major-league level.

The first exhibition game was played on March 6 against the San Francisco Giants. The opening game ceremony began with a flyby performed by the Davis-Monthan Air Force Base aerial team. The Sons of the Pioneers sang the national anthem. A crowd of 7,726 was on hand to see the Rockies win, 7-2.

The first regular-season game was played on April 5 in New York against the New York Mets. The first home game followed on April 9 at Mile High Stadium against the Montreal Expos before a record crowd of 80,227.[37]

The founding of the Colorado Rockies is a unique story involving many people from all walks of life, uniting and working together to enrich the quality of life with the major-league baseball experience. Colorado Rockies baseball is a game for all ages, all nationalities, and all creeds. It is a reflection of our national heritage, the bedrock of our common values, and involves the constant struggle to play the game, win or lose, to the best of one's ability. And now, throughout the Rocky Mountain area, it is a cherished part of our history - and our future lives, to be shared throughout the ages.

*Appendix*

## Metropolitan Stadium Authority Board Members

*(who served prior to April 1, 1993)*

| | |
|---|---|
| Ray Baker, Chairman | Dan Muse |
| John McHale, Past Chairman | Jack Shapiro |
| Debra Brody | Joe Talarico |
| Steve DelCastillo | Penfield Tate |
| Edmundo Gonzales | Dean Quamme |
| Josie Heath | Max Wiley |
| Roger Kinney | |

## Colorado Baseball Commission Board Members

Sam Suplizio, Co-Chairman

Larry Varnell, Co-Chairman

Neil Macey, Past Director

Roger Kinney, Director

Helen Anderson          Bob Howsam,

# Time For Expansion Baseball

Gary Antonoff

Odell Barry

John Benitez

Joe Blake

Robert Bows

Irv Brown

Chris Christiansen

John Dikeou

Jim Harrington

Don Hinchey

Robert Howsam Jr.

James Murray

Trygve Myhren

Sue O'Brien

Chris Paulson

Jim Turner

Gil Whiteley

Kathi Williams

Zee Ferrufino

Steve Kaplan

Willie Kellum

Elena Metro Kroll

Dan Kubby

Bob Litchard

Larry Varnell

Steve Welchert

## Denver Baseball Commission Members

Federico Pena, Mayor

Steve Katich, Chairman

Dean Bonham, Vice Chairman

Jerry Arca

Jim Burris |

Forrest Cason

Don Carlsen

Craig Caukin

Deb Dowling

Richard Fleming

John Gawaluck

Tom Grimshaw

Bruce Hellerstein

Dave Herlinger

Don Hinchey

Neil Hinchman

Eloy Mares

John McHale

Bill Michaels

Sherm Miller

Dan Muse

Mike Raabe

Bob Russo

Elwyn Schaefer

Carl Scheer

Rob Simon

Steve Stern

Irv Sternberg

Ruben Valdez

## MLB Visitation Team Members

Don Hinchey, Chairman

Carolyn Writer, Vice Chairman

Alan Bossart

Lew Cady

Tom Clark

Butch Cosby

Mike Flaherty

Lana Fry

Kevin Hannon

Linda Hantman

Ed Henderson

Robert Howsam Jr.

Chuck Javernick

Doug Kinney

Ken Reed

Roger Smith

Michelle Strauss

Joe Talty

Howard Weese

Nancy Holst

## Notes

1   Robert Lee Howsam, *My Life In Sports* (Denver: Bob Jones, 1999), 44.

2   Howsam, 46.

3   Jay Sanford, *Before the Rockies* (Denver: KEM Publishing, 2016), introduction page.

4   Sanford, 1.

5   Matthew Kasper Repplinger II, *Baseball in Denver* (Charleston, South Carolina: Arcadia Publishing, 2013), 7.

6   Alan Gottlieb, *In the Shadow of the Rockies* (Niwot, Colorado: Roberts, Rinehart Publishing, 1994), 12.

7   Gottlieb, 13.

8   Mary Kay Connor, *Dick Connor Remembered* (Golden, Colorado: Fulcrum Publishing, 1995), 122.

9 David Whitford, *Playing Hardball* (New York: Doubleday Press, 1993), 26.

10 Whitford, 26.

11 Irv Moss and Mark Foster, *Home Run in the Rockies, The History of Baseball in Colorado* (Denver: Publication Design, Inc., 1995), 26.

12 Whitford, 58.

13 Whitford, 59.

14 Whitford, 70.

15 Moss, 41.

16 Whitford, 77.

17 Whitford, 84.

18 Whitford, 51.

19 See Appendix for a full list of appointments.

20 "Rockies Timeline," Rockies.com, accessed April 23, 2017, colorado.rockies.mlb.com/col/history/timeline2jsp.

21 Whitford, 124.

22 Whitford, 87.

23 Personal interview with Carolyn Writer, June 12, 1990.

24 Moss, 51.

25 Norm Clarke, *High Hard Ones* (Denver: Phoenix Press, 1993), 151.

26 Clark, 151.

27 Gottlieb, 23.

28 Clarke, 154.

29 Moss, 62.

30 Benjamin M. Leroy, *Colorado Rockies* (Madison, Wisconsin: Quiz Master Books, 2008), 8.

31 Carolyn Writer, *Colorado Welcomes Major League Baseball, Banquet Program* (Denver: Hirschfeld Press, 1991), 1.

32 *Colorado Rockies Inaugural Media Guide*, 1993, 3.

33 Moss, 70.

34 Leroy, 8.

35 Leroy, 12.

36 Leroy, 13.

37 Leroy, 13.

## TORONTO BLUE JAYS EXPANSION DRAFT

| PICK | PLAYER | POSITION | FORMER TEAM |
|---|---|---|---|

### ROUND 1

| PICK | PLAYER | POSITION | FORMER TEAM |
|---|---|---|---|
| 1 | David Nied | p | Atlanta Braves |
| 2 | Charlie Hayes | 3b | New York Yankees |
| 3 | Darren Holmes | p | Milwaukee Brewers |
| 4 | Jerald Clark | of | San Diego Padres |
| 5 | Kevin Reimer | of | Texas Rangers |
| 6 | Eric Young | 2b | Los Angeles Dodgers |
| 7 | Jody Reed | 2b | Boston Red Sox |
| 8 | Scott Aldred | p | Detroit Tigers |
| 9 | Alex Cole | of | Pittsburgh Pirates |
| 10 | Joe Girardi | c | Chicago Cubs |
| 11 | Willie Blair | p | Houston Astros |
| 12 | Jayhawk Owens | c | Minnesota Twins |
| 13 | Andy Ashby | p | Philadelphia Phillies |

### ROUND 2

| PICK | PLAYER | POSITION | FORMER TEAM |
|---|---|---|---|
| 14 | Freddie Benavides | ss | Cincinnati Reds |
| 15 | Roberto Mejia | 2b | Los Angeles Dodgers |
| 16 | Doug Bochtler | p | Montreal Expos |
| 17 | Lance Painter | p | San Diego Padres |
| 18 | Butch Henry | p | Houston Astros |
| 19 | Ryan Hawblitzel | p | Chicago Cubs |
| 20 | Vinny Castilla | ss | Atlanta Braaves |
| 21 | Brett Merriman | p | California Angels |
| 22 | Jim Tatum | 3b | Milwaukee Brewers |
| 23 | Kevin Ritz | p | Detroit Tigers |
| 24 | Eric Wedge | c | Boston Red Sox |
| 25 | Keith Shepherd | p | Philadelphia Phillies |
| 26 | Calvin Jones | p | Seattle Mariners |

## ROUND 3

| | | | |
|----|----|----|----|
| 27 | Brad Ausmus | c | New York Yankees |
| 28 | Marcus Moore | p | Toronto Blue Jays |
| 29 | Armando Reynoso | p | Atlanta Braves |
| 30 | Steve Reed | p | San Francisco Giants |
| 31 | Mo Sanford | p | Cincinnati Reds |
| 32 | Pedro Castellano | ss | Chicago Cubs |
| 33 | Curtis Leskanic | p | Minnesota Twins |
| 34 | Scott Fredrickson | p | San Diego Padres |
| 35 | Braulio Castillo | of | Philadelphia Phillies |
| 36 | Denis Boucher | p | Cleveland Indians |

# BRAD AUSMUS

## By Thomas J. Brown Jr.

Bradley David Ausmus enjoyed a prosperous career in baseball after he took a circuitous road to get to the major leagues. Although it took more than five years for him to reach the majors, his path to being a major-league manager was much shorter. Ausmus became manager of the Detroit Tigers after a brief managing stint in the 2013 World Baseball Classic.

Ausmus was born on April 14, 1969, in New Haven, Connecticut. His father, Harry Jack Ausmus, a Protestant, retired from a long career as professor of European history at Southern Connecticut State University. His mother, Linda, is Jewish. While growing up in Connecticut, Ausmus didn't have a strong connection with his Jewish roots. He would occasionally celebrate the high holidays with his mother's family but it never went further than that.[1]

When Ausmus was 5 years old, he told his father that "when he grew up he wanted to go to Dartmouth and he wanted to play baseball." Harry Ausmus gave his son a lecture about having to work hard and told him if he

did, he could do both.[2] Little did father and son know at the time that both of these dreams would eventually come true.

Ausmus attended Cheshire High School in Cheshire, Connecticut. He played several sports there but excelled in baseball. As a sophomore he played shortstop and batted .327. Ausmus became a catcher as a junior, hit .436 and was chosen for the All-State team. He hit .411 during his senior year and was named the Cheshire Area High School Player of the Year.[3] His leadership skills were evident to those who coached and played with him.

"Looking back now, we all realized how confident Brad was, and how intelligent he was. And if any of us forgot, he wasn't bashful about reminding us," recalled Nick Carparelli Jr., a teammate on the Cheshire High baseball team.[4] When Ausmus became the Tigers manager in 2013, he credited his Cheshire High coach, Nick Carparelli Sr., for helping him to learn how to coach.

"He was a huge influence," Ausmus said of his coach. "Not so much from the baseball perspective, but more on how to treat human beings and how to work hard." Carparelli was also complimentary of Ausmus: "He was always the type of kid in control of things – in control of the game, of a pitcher. I think he always knew he wanted to stay in the game [after he stopped playing], whether on the administrative end or as an on-field manager."[5]

By the time Ausmus graduated from high school, recruiters from Dartmouth, Harvard, and Princeton pursued him as a catcher. Also, the New York Yankees selected him in the 48th round of the June 1987 amateur draft. Ausmus initially refused to sign with the Yankees. His parents were adamant that he pursue a college degree. They eventually agreed that he could play baseball as long as it didn't interfere with school.[6] Ausmus signed with the Yankees after they agreed that he could attend classes and play in the minors when school ended.

After his freshman year Ausmus adjusted his schedule to spend the fall and winter terms at Dartmouth, taking four courses each term to keep up with his classmates. This left him free to go to spring training and play baseball during the season. Ausmus graduated from Dartmouth with a degree in government in 1991.[7]

In the summer of 1988 the Yankees sent Ausmus to their rookie-league team, the Gulf Coast Yankees. He spent most of the season there before getting a promotion to the low Class-A Oneonta Yankees (New York-Pennsylvania League) for two games. In the rookie league he had 15 RBIs and a .255 batting average before returning to classes in the fall of 1988. In the summer of 1989 Ausmus played in 52 games at Oneonta; in 1990 he played in 107 games for the high Class-A Prince William Cannons (Carolina League). Ausmus started the 1991 season in Double A, with the Albany-Colonie Yankees of the Eastern League, but the Yankees sent him back to Prince William for the second half of the season, and he raised his batting average to 304.

After graduating from Dartmouth in the winter of 1991, Ausmus spent most of the 1992 season with the Triple-A Columbus Clippers (International League), with a brief stay at Albany-Colonie.

The major leagues were expanding and one of the new teams, the Colorado Rockies, drafted Ausmus from the Yankees in the expansion draft after the 1992 season. He spent the first part of the 1993 season with the Colorado Springs Sky Sox (Pacific Coast League), batting .270 in 76 games. On July 26, Ausmus was traded by the Rockies with Doug Bochtler and a player to be named to the San Diego Padres for Greg Harris and Bruce Hurst. ( Andy Ashby was the player to be named.)

Ausmus finally reached the majors with the Padres. He played in his first major-league game two days after the trade, on July 28, starting against the Chicago Cubs at Wrigley Field. Ausmus got his first major-league hit in the fourth inning, a single off starter Greg Hibbard. He threw out speedster Willie Wilson trying to steal second in the eighth inning, a sign of his excellent defensive skills.

By the time Ausmus reached the majors, he had spent more than five years in the minors. He reflected on those years later: "I was naïve. In my mind, I was going to make it eventually and I just kept slogging away. My first year, I think I got paid $700 a month. I didn't know any better. I just assumed the best and that eventually I would make it. I didn't realize how stacked the odds were against me."[8]

Ausmus became the Padres' full-time catcher in 1994 when he started 94 games. He batted .251 with 7 home runs, a career best to that point. But his importance to the Padres was not his offense but his defensive skills. He led the league in putouts by a catcher when he had 683 putouts that year. The Padres were pleased with Ausmus and he remained their starting catcher in 1995. He batted .293 that year, a career best, and stole 16 bases, the most by a major-league catcher since Craig Biggio stole 19 in 1991. Defensively, Ausmus led the league in assists (63) and double plays by a catcher (14).

Ausmus married Elizabeth Ann "Liz" Selfridge in 1995. They had two daughters, Sophie, born in 1998, and Abigail, born in 1999.

Ausmus got off to a shaky start offensively in 1996. By mid-June, hitting just .181 in 149 at-bats, Ausmus was traded to the Tigers with Andujar Cedeno and minor leaguer Russ Spear for John Flaherty and Chris Gomez.

The Tigers made Ausmus their full-time catcher. He played in 75 Detroit games, improving his batting average to .248, and continued to be an asset defensively.

Yet Ausmus was traded by the Tigers in the offseason. He went to the Houston Astros along with José Lima, Trever Miller, C.J. Nitkowski, and Daryle Ward, for Doug Brocail, Brian Hunter, Todd Jones, Orlando Miller, and cash. (This was the first of three consecutive deals over a four-year span inn which Ausmus was exchanged between the two teams.)

Ausmus spent 1997 and 1998 as the Astros starting catcher, batting a cumulative .268. He had 25 doubles in 1998 and averaged 44 RBIs during the two seasons, both offensive improvements for him. He continued to an excellent defensive catcher.

By this time, Ausmus was considered a weak hitter but an excellent defensive player. On January 14, 1999, the Astros sent Ausmus back to the Tigers along with minor-leaguer C.J. Nitkowski for Paul Bako, Dean Crow, and Brian Powell and minor-league players Mark Persails and Carlos Villalobos.

Ausmus had his best offensive season in 1999. He batted .275 and set career highs in on-base percentage (.365) and slugging percentage (.415). He was chosen for his only All-Star game appearance, as the backup catcher for Ivan Rodriguez. After replacing Rodriguez in the sixth inning, Ausmus showed his defensive prowess when he threw out Brian Jordan trying to steal second in the seventh. He got one at-bat in the game and grounded out to second.

Ausmus had another solid year defensively in 2000. He was recognized for his ability to block pitches at the plate. Pitchers regarded him highly for identifying their strengths and weaknesses and using that knowledge to guide them through a game.[9]

The Tigers were looking for a catcher who might help them offensively so Ausmus was traded back to the Astros on December 11, 2000. With Doug Brocail and Nelson Cruz, he went to Houston in exchange for Roger Cedeno, Chris Holt, and Mitch Meluskey.

By the time Ausmus returned to Houston, he had fully established his reputation as a defensive asset and was acknowledged as one of the tops at bringing out the best in pitchers. Timothy de Block reflected on his defensive prowess in 2012: "My lasting imagery of Ausmus is his ability to block any and every ball in the dirt. Jason Castro's inability to do so this season reminds me how good Ausmus was at it, and listening to various announcers tell kids that's the way to do it."[10]

Upon his return to the Astros, Ausmus began the most productive period of his career. He became Houston's starting catcher, a position he held through 2007. He never became a consistently solid hitting threat during those years although he did improve offensively. In 2004, he batted .308 against left-handers, and was .302 in situations that were "late and close," meaning in the seventh inning or later, with the score tied or the tying run on base, at the plate, or on deck. These were significant improvements from the previous year and helped the Astros as they made the postseason run.

Ausmus had more walks than strikeouts for the only time

in his career in 2005. In 2007, he batted .235 but tied for second among National League catchers with six stolen bases. He recorded his 100th career stolen base on July 27.[11]

Even though he never became a solid hitter, Ausmus was valuable to the Astros for his work behind the plate. He earned his first Gold Glove Award in 2001, and followed it up with a second in 2002. His fielding percentage both years was .997. In many ways, Ausmus's leadership gave the Astros another manager on the field.

"I'm thinking what's the score, what inning are we in, how many outs, what's this hitter's weakness, what's this pitcher's strengths, who's on deck, who could pinch-hit, who is up after the hitter on deck and you kind of go through all of these things in an instant. And then you make a decision and put down the next signal."[12]

The Astros pitchers relied on Ausmus and respected his hard work to prepare them for the game. He prepared graphs for his pitchers before every series showing the strengths and weaknesses of every player on the opposing team.

The Astros made the playoffs in 2001, losing the National League Division Series in three games to the Atlanta Braves. Ausmus contributed a two-run home run off Greg Maddux in the first game. He finished the series with a .625 slugging percentage.

In 2004, the Astros reached the NLCS, falling to the St. Louis Cardinals in seven games. Ausmus felt he let his teammates down in the series when he called for one too many sliders from closer Dan Miceli. That misstep led to a tie-breaking home run by Albert Pujols The Cardinals took a two-games-to-none lead in the series and the Astros never caught up afterward.[13]

In the 2005 NL Division Series, against Atlanta, Ausmus hit a home run that Tal Smith, a longtime Astros executive, called "one of the greatest hits in Astros history." The homer, off Kyle Farnsworth with two outs in the bottom of the ninth inning of Game Four, tied the game, 6-6, and the Astros got a walk-off victory in the 18th inning. Smith, the Astros' president of baseball operations at the time, said the homer was "[a]bsolutely critical."[14] Ausmus caught the first 12 innings of the game, played first base from the 13th inning to the 15th, then returned to catch the 16th through 18th for Roger Clemens.

The Astros defeated the Cardinals for the National League pennant in the NCLS. Ausmus was 7-for-22 during the series, including three hits in the sixth and final game, a 5-1 Astros win.

Tal Smith said Ausmus "was invaluable" during the Astros' playoff run, adding, "He deserves an awful lot of credit for our success. It was like having another manager on the field. He was very active with the pitching staff. He was so knowledgeable, so savvy. I thought he was instrumental with our success."[15]

The Astros were swept in the World Series by the Chicago White Sox. Ausmus started all four games behind the plate and collected four hits. Even with the disappointing loss in the World Series, Ausmus said he had many fond memories of those winning years in Houston. "It was fun. Baseball was the sport in Houston and it had been historically a football town," he said.[16]

During his years with Astros, Ausmus began to be recognized as a possible manager after he finished playing. Astros manager Phil Garner quipped, "I have to keep him playing, because if he starts managing, he'll be better than me."[17]

During Ausmus's tenure with the Astros, the team granted him free agency every other year. The first two times Ausmus signed a two-year contract shortly after entering the free-agent market. He signed his last contract, a one-year pact, with the Astros on October 30, 2007. The Astros were planning for J.R. Towles to become their starting catcher in 2008. They felt that the 23-year-old rookie would need some help in adjusting to the majors so they signed Ausmus to be Towles' mentor as well as the backup catcher.

At the time, Houston general manager Ed Wade said: "Brad is an established veteran catcher with the ability to play a lot. The [team's] mindset is if we can get 20 more points on the batting average [from Towles] or get a guy to knock in 20 more runs, and we have [Ausmus], who has a great presence behind the plate and who handles pitchers so well, we think we've got a pretty complete package going at that particular position."[18]

On May 12, 2008, Ausmus got his 1,500th career hit. As of 2018 he was one of only eight major-league catchers to get 1,500 hits and steal at least 100 bases. Although Ausmus mentored Towles, the young catcher struggled.

By June, Towles was hitting only .145 and the Astros optioned him to the minors. Ausmus became the starting catcher until Towles returned later in the season.

Ausmus scored his 700th career run on August 12, 2008, in a 12-4 Astros win over the Giants. He became the 25th catcher to reach that mark.[19]

Toward the end of the 2008 season, Ausmus said it would be his final year in Houston. He said that he wanted to be closer to his family in San Diego, commenting, "Large chunks of time away from home is not in the best interest of my family." When the season ended, Ausmus had become Houston's all-time leader for catchers with 1,259 games, 1,119 starts, 970 hits, and 415 runs. The Astros released him on October 31, 2008.

Although he had contemplated retiring, Ausmus signed a one-year contract with the Los Angeles Dodgers on January 21, 2009. He would be the backup to Russell Martin. Dodgers manager Joe Torre was impressed with Ausmus and his leadership, and said, "There's no question he can manage. He's a smart cookie, everybody knows that, and he has an engaging personality."[20]

Ausmus even managed the Dodgers in the final game of the season. Torre had a tradition of letting one player manage the last game of the year if it had no bearing on the standings. Ausmus stood by Torre throughout the game and made all the decisions. When he was asked about it before the game, he said, "I'll let you know if it was still a good idea in about five hours." He called on acting hitting coach Jim Thome to pinch-hit in the eighth and after Thome hit a single, he replaced Thome with himself as a pinch-runner.[21]

The Dodgers released Ausmus after the 2009 season but he signed another one-year contract with the team on January 26, 2010. On April 10, 2010, he was placed on the disabled list for the first time in his 18-year career in the majors. He missed most of the season after having surgery in April to repair a lower-back herniated disc. Ausmus played in only 21 games, the last one on October 3, after which he announced his retirement as a player.

Ausmus finished his career ranked third in major-league history with 12,839 putouts as a catcher, trailing only Iván Rodríguez and Jason Kendall; seventh in games caught with 1,938; and 15th in fielding percentage (.994).

A month after he retired, the San Diego Padres hired

Ausmus as a special assistant in baseball operations. "He brings a tremendous amount of experience from his long and successful playing career. We look forward to having him help with the development of catchers throughout our system," Padres general manager Jed Hoyer said.[22]

Ausmus was also one of the several Jewish players in major-league baseball when he played. His Jewish background eventually led to his first managing job, with Team Israel in the 2013 World Baseball Classic. Ausmus's team won its first two games before being eliminated by Spain in a 10-inning loss.

Ausmus used many of the same skills he had developed during his years as a catcher. As he assembled the club, he compiled information about prospective players on his iPad and index cards. "He told me he felt that he was not just the manager, but the general manager. [T]hat it was a lot of fun choosing his own players. It gave him the feeling he could [manage the team]," said Peter Kurz, president of the Israel Association of Baseball.[23]

The job of managing the Israeli national team gave Ausmus the opportunity to put into place what he had observed during his playing days. "The best baseball managers I've been around have been very good communicators and they understand that in baseball, unlike maybe football or basketball, it's not so much the "x's" and "o's" that you're managing but [its] people," he said.[24]

On November 3, 2013, Ausmus was named the 38th manager of the Detroit Tigers, succeeding Jim Leyland. He had gone right to the majors without any managerial experience in the minors. Tigers general manager Dave Dombrowski said Ausmus was chosen because "[we] received positive feedback on Brad from players, managers, and baseball executives. Brad had a long-standing career as a player and we feel that he will relate well with the current players. We were most impressed with Brad's preparation and leadership, which are among his many quality attributes."[25]

Although many were surprised by Ausmus's selection because of his lack of managing experience, Dombrowski said: "Everybody's different, but playing 18 years at the major-league level would prepare him much more than managing one year at the Double-A level, because the problems he encounters in the major leagues now are so different than what they are at Double A."[26]

Ausmus briefly faced controversy in his first season when

he responded to a question from a reporter in the middle of a losing streak. After being asked, "How are you when you go home?" Ausmus replied, "I beat my wife." After a few moments of silence, he quickly apologized. "I shouldn't say — listen, I didn't want to make light of battered women. I didn't mean to make light of that, so I apologize for that if that offended anyone."[27] Although he faced a storm of criticism, Ausmus weathered it and the Tigers soon began to win again.

In his first year as manager, Ausmus led the Tigers to a 90-72 record, winning the American League Central Division title. The Tigers were swept in the Division Series by the Baltimore Orioles. In his second year as manager, the Tigers had a disappointing 74-87 record, finishing in last place in their division.

In his third season as manager, 2016, the Tigers finished in second place in the division with an 86-75 record, 2½ games out of the second postseason wild-card spot. At one point during the season, Ausmus made news when he pulled off his jersey and covered home plate with it. The umpire had ejected him before he'd even stepped out of the dugout but Ausmus still let his frustrations out on the arbiter. He later explained: "There comes a point when you get seven or eight guys coming back from home plate complaining about the strike zone, they can't all be wrong, I understand sometimes hitters have a skewed view of something, but when you've got that many guys coming back, they can't all be wrong."[28]

Ausmus returned as Tigers manager in 2017. The team finished with a 64-98 record, in last place in the division. It was their worst finish since 2003. At the end of the season, the Tigers fired Ausmus. General manager Al Avila explained the team's decision: "[W]e needed change on the field, we needed change in the roster, and that's when we started trading players. Let's just take a whole brand-new road and open up to new things. We felt it's a new beginning, a fresh start, and we'll have fresh leadership, new leadership, as we move forward."[29]

After the season, Ausmus was reported to be a candidate for several managing positions but got no offers. On November 22, 2017, he was hired as a special assistant to Los Angeles Angels general manager Billy Eppler to help with scouting and evaluations.

Ausmus was inducted into the National Jewish Sports Hall of Fame in 2004. He has embraced his Jewish heritage and is proud to have used it to inspire others. "I have had quite a few young Jewish boys who will tell me that I am their favorite player, or they love watching me play or they feel like baseball is a good fit for them because it worked for me. It has been a sense of pride. If you can have a positive impact on a kid, I'm all for it," he said.[30]

## Sources

In addition to the sources cited in the Notes, the author also used the Baseball-Reference.com, Baseball-Almanac.com, and Retrosheet.org websites for box-score, player, team, and season pages, pitching and batting game logs, and other pertinent material.

## Notes

1 David Borges, "Brad Ausmus Connects with Jewish Roots as Manager of Team Israel for the WBC," *New Haven Register*, July 22, 2012.

2 Matthew Mosk, "The Rookie," Dartmouth Alumni Magazine.com, September-October 2014.

3 John Petit, "Astros Ausmus Sky High on Shot at Series," *Meriden* (Connecticut) *Record-Journal*, October 21, 2005.

4 "Tigers Manager Brad Ausmus Learned from Carparelli at Cheshire," *New Haven Register*, August 5, 2014.

5 Ibid.

6 Matthew Mosk, "The Rookie."

7 "Brad Ausmus" Baseball Library.com, bit.ly/2DnqFis.

8 Bob McManaman, "Most Minor-League MLB Players Below Poverty Level," AZ Central.com, August 16, 2014.

9 "Covering The Plate: A Baseball Catcher Tells All," NPR.org, August 11, 2011.

10 Timothy De Block, "Astros History: Brad Ausmus," Crawfishboxes.com, April 17, 2012.

11 Alyson Footer, "Astros Ink Ausmus to One-Year Contract," MLB.com, October 30, 2007.

12 Dave Davies, "Behind the Plate, a Baseball Catcher Tells All," WBUR.org, April 6, 2012.

13 Anthony French, "Tigers' Brad Ausmus Recalls Run with Successful Astros," *Detroit Free Press*, August 15, 2015.

14 Maxwell Kates interview with Tal Smith, November 18, 2017.

15 Ibid.

16 Anthony French, "Tigers' Brad Ausmus Recalls Run."

17 Pat Cooke, "Who Is Brad Ausmus?," TheSportsCol.com, November 5, 2013.

18 Alyson Footer, "Astros Ink Ausmus."

19 Brian McTaggart, "ASTROS NOTES: Brother of Pitcher Wolf Umps Game," Chron.com, August 13, 2008.

20 "Ausmus Headed to Padres' Front Office," Jewish Baseball News.com, November 17, 2010.

21 "Dodgers Catcher Ausmus Is Manager for a Day," Redlands Daily Facts.com, October 5, 2009.

22 "Brad Ausmus Joins Padres Front Office," San Diego Padres MLB.com, November 26, 2010.

23 Hillel Kuttler, "On Way to Tigers Post, Ausmus Earned His Managing Stripes in Israel," Jewish Telegraphic Agency, November 7, 2013.

24 Sara Appel-Lemon, "Del Mar Resident Brad Ausmus Hired as Team Israel Manager," *Del Mar Times*, September 3, 2012.

25 David Solano, "Detroit Tigers Introduce Brad Ausmus as Team's New Manager," WXYZ.com, November 3, 2013.

26 Tyler Kepner, "Fitting the New Managerial Mold," *New York Times*, March 7, 2014.

27 Christy Strawser, "Brad Ausmus Misses With Joke About Beating Wife After Loss," Detroit.CBSlocal.com, June 14, 2014.

28 Jason Beck, "Ausmus Drapes Hoodie on Plate After Ejection," MLB.com, May 17, 2016.

29 Jason Beck, "Ausmus' Contract Won't Be Extended Past '17," MLB.com, September 22, 2017.

30 Brad Greenberg, "There's a New Jew in Dodger Blue," *Washington Jewish Week*, July 1, 2009.

# JOE GIRARDI

## By Mark S. Sternman

Joe Girardi had the big hit in the deciding game of the 1996 World Series, caught a perfect game, won a Manager of the Year Award with one team, and skippered another to a World Series win. An above-average major leaguer for 15 seasons, Girardi will be remembered most for his time helming the post-Joe Torre Yankees. As one observer put it, "Girardi was often a proxy for the Yankees' ideals. There he was, year after year: jaw squared, hair closely cropped, relentless pursuing championships, no matter how broken down or unproven the roster would become."[1]

Girardi inherited his determination from his father. Born on October 14, 1964, the fourth of five children, he grew up in Peoria, Illinois. "His father ... was ... a salesman, but ... [Gerald Girardi] ran a restaurant, tended bar, even laid bricks. ... [Mother] Angela Girardi ... work[ed] full-time as a child psychologist."[2] After long battles, his mother died of ovarian cancer, and his father of Alzheimer's. Of his father, Girardi reminisced, "I think about all the things

he taught me about hard work, and fighting through adversity, and toughness. I carry all the things that he taught me as a little boy growing up."[3]

Joe Girardi started catching at 12, "because they didn't have anybody else," he said. "I tried to go back to being a shortstop when I was 13 but they didn't let me."[4] Girardi had three brothers, two of whom played baseball. "[I]f you're a ballplayer, it's great to have older brothers," Girardi said. "My brothers always brought me to play with the older kids. Any time you play at a level that's higher than your level, you're going to get better."[5]

At Spalding Institute, a Catholic high school in Peoria, Girardi, Class of 1982, was an All-State selection in baseball.[6] He attended Northwestern University before the Cubs drafted him in 1986 and sent him to Single-A Peoria. He got off to a hot start "hitting near .330 ... despite an air splint on his ankle from a hairline fracture suffered at Northwestern ..."[7]

Girardi's bat cooled as he advanced through the minors. He hit .309 with Peoria, .280 with Carolina in 1987, and .272 with Double-A Pittsfield in 1988. Going into the 1989 season, Cubs manager Don Zimmer considered keeping Girardi with the team to spell Damon Berryhill. "We're not talking about a kid here," Zimmer said. "He came out of college ... at 22 and has played a few years."[8]

Girardi debuted on April 4, 1989, against the Philadelphia

Phillies in the season opener for both teams. In his first plate appearance, he singled off Floyd Youmans. A single by Jerome Walton scored Girardi with the first run of the Chicago campaign. Girardi finished 2-for-3 with a walk, made an error, but also threw out the only runner (Bob Dernier) attempting to steal as the Cubs won, 5-4.

Chicago won the NL East in 1989. Girardi played 59 games in the regular season and four NLCS games. He also authored an article for his hometown paper during the playoffs, writing, "It's great to be on a winning club, especially to be a part of the club you always dreamed about playing on as a little kid. I worshipped the Cubs as a little kid, I followed them very closely and whenever you're winning it's a lot of fun."[9]

Bill James thought little of Girardi's prospects after his rookie year: "Looked solid as an emergency call-up. There are worse catchers in the majors; could platoon with Berryhill. No star potential."[10]

In fact, Girardi beat out Berryhill in 1990, a year in which Girardi established career highs in games (133), doubles (24), and defensive Wins Above Replacement (1.5). He led the NL in throwing out base stealers with 47, but tied for the league lead in passed balls with 16. Zimmer praised his receiver, stating, "When it comes to throwing, I rate Girardi No. 1 or No. 2 with (San Diego's) Benito Santiago."[11]

Girardi played less in his next two seasons in Chicago than he had in 1990 alone. Staggered by a bulging back disc and a broken nose, he played in only 21 games in 1991 and in 91 games in 1992 before leaving Chicago, where he developed a sense of professionalism that would lead to a lengthy career. In 1998, *New York Times* columnist Claire Smith opined, "Joe Girardi was reared right, by his parents, by ... Zimmer, by his former teammates Andre Dawson, Rick Sutcliffe, Scott Sanderson, Vance Law and Greg Maddux."[12]

The Colorado Rockies selected Girardi in the fall 1992 expansion draft. He started the first game in franchise history and batted seventh. Moving from a friendly hitters' park to the friendliest one, Girardi set career highs in triples (5), slugging (.397), and OPS (.743) in his first campaign with the Rockies.

Bill James remained unimpressed: "A pretty awful player, even for an expansion team. He hit .290, but that's .266 if you adjust for the park, and there was ... no power, no

walks, no runs, no RBI. His defense isn't anything special, and ... he's not likely to get any better. He missed two months in mid-season following surgery on his right hand, which kept him from driving in 40 or even 45 runs."[13]

Girardi's offense worsened during his subsequent years in Denver even as the Rockies improved each season. *Denver Post* columnist Mark Kiszla castigated Girardi as "a non-essential part ... a player so expendable even the Chicago Cubs didn't want him.... Baseball goes on strike almost as often as he gets an extra-base hit. ... Girardi is a defensive specialist who allows approximately 70 percent of base-runners to steal him blind."[14]

But Colorado manager Don Baylor appreciated his skills. "Baylor knew what he had in Girardi, a catcher who would guide a questionable pitching staff. 'Guys had 5.00 ERAs and high 4.00s, and you have to try to talk them through that,' Baylor explained. 'Joe really worked on the mental part of the game.'"[15]

After the 1995 season, the Rockies, clearing payroll to pursue free agent Craig Biggio,[16] sent Girardi to the Yankees for reliever Mike DeJean. Girardi had enjoyed Denver. "Those three years in Colorado were magnificent," Girardi said. "We played at Mile High Stadium, and you'd have seventy thousand people there. It was loud, it was exciting, people loved baseball."[17]

One reporter writing at the end of Girardi's career saw another motivation for the transaction. "Girardi earned his teammates' respect during the labor conflict that erased the 1994 season and delayed the 1995 campaign, when he served as the Rockies' player representative. Girardi's stance against management helped instigate his trade. ... The Rockies missed Girardi more than he missed them."[18]

With the transaction, New York bade farewell to free agent Mike Stanley and announced that Girardi would start in 1996. "To me, Joe Girardi is one of the best catchers in the game," Yankees manager Joe Torre said. "Mike Stanley did a heck of a job offensively for this ballclub. But the defensive part we improved."[19]

New Yorkers viewed the transition from Stanley to Girardi skeptically. "I know some people are very, very unhappy over what happened," Girardi said. ... "I know I've taken heat on the radio and in some articles. But to me, that will make the rewards at the end all the more special."[20]

Girardi proved prescient. "I'm not going there to replace Mike Stanley," he said. "We're two different types of catchers. ... I think what it really comes down to is winning ballgames."[21]

In 1996, New York won the AL East and then its first World Series title since 1978. Over a year, Girardi had improbably transformed himself from the discard pile of a third-year expansion team to the backstop of a championship edition of the game's most storied franchise.

The '96 Yanks got unexpected boosts from a pair of declining ex-Mets in Dwight Gooden and Darryl Strawberry. Girardi particularly helped Gooden. "We're already on the same page," Gooden said in spring training. "The thing I like is that he communicates with us. He's constantly talking strategy. ... I talked to (Bret Saberhagen) recently and he said he loved pitching to Joe (in Colorado)."[22]

A little more than two months after Gooden praised Girardi, the two teamed up on a no-hitter, the first for both pitcher and catcher. "Moments after throwing the 135th pitch of his gem, Gooden ... said, 'Joe Girardi is the best catcher I've ever thrown to.'"[23]

Girardi praised his pitcher. "He was able to place it wherever he wanted to," Girardi said. "So we were able to throw his slider and a few changeups at any time. ... There's only one more thing for me to do in my career and that's play in a World Series."[24]

Girardi got his wish during his first season in the Bronx. After losing the first two games of the Series at home, the Yankees won all three in Atlanta. New York would have to break through at home to take the title.

In the top of the third of Game Six, Girardi kept the contest scoreless. "Leadoff-hitter Terry Pendleton skimmed a grounder ... that Mariano Duncan ... bobbled for an error. On the next pitch, Pendleton took off for second, but Jeff Blauser failed to swing ... and Pendleton was easily tagged out despite Girardi's double pump."[25] The caught-stealing proved critical after Blauser doubled.

Batting ninth, Girardi came to the plate with a career postseason record of no RBIs and only 8 singles in 54 at-bats, including an 0-for-7 mark in the 1996 Series. Maddux, the Cy Young Award winner each season from 1992 through 1995, faced Girardi with one out in the bottom of the third inning and Paul O'Neill on third base.

Girardi smashed Maddux's high pitch to deep center, just

out of the reach of speedy center fielder Marquis Grissom, who, understandably, had played the weak-hitting Girardi shallow.[26] Girardi had an RBI triple ("I felt like I was running on air. It was the biggest hit in my career in the biggest game in my career"[27]), his lone career playoff RBI in 127 postseason plate appearances.

Jeter singled in Girardi, and later in the frame Bernie Williams drove in Jeter with another single, giving the Yankees a 3-0 lead in a game that ended 3-2. After John Wetteland induced a foul out to Charlie Hayes to end the Series, Girardi embraced his closer.

A free agent after the World Series, Girardi hoped to remain in New York[28] and did so with diminishing playing time due to the emergence of Jorge Posada.[29] Girardi hit less well in 1997, a season highlighted by an eighth-inning homer on April 28 to give the Yankees a 6-5 comeback win over the Seattle Mariners. "I'm surprised," Girardi said of his first homer of the year. "It took me until August last year to get my first home run. I don't hit homers."[30]

Girardi did not hit another home run for more than 13 months (off Pedro Martinez of the Red Sox on May 31, 1998).

Girardi suffered personal tragedy in 1997 when his wife, Kim, miscarried. Girardi later revealed, "She took it a lot harder than I did. We went through a tough period until like a year later. It was much tougher for her because it was part of her. I just told her it wasn't her fault. It was God's will."[31] Two years later, Kim gave birth to a daughter named Serena. Son Dante (named after Girardi's Colorado teammate Dante Bichette) and daughter Lena followed.

New York secured the AL wild card in 1997. The Indians eliminated the Yankees in five games. Girardi had 17 postseason plate appearances with more grounded-into-double-plays (3) than hits (two singles).

With Girardi playing in his fewest games since 1991, New York featured one of the best teams ever in 1998. A minor contributor to the superb squad, Girardi again caught the championship clincher.

Surprisingly, New York exercised its $3.4 million option on its 34-year-old backup backstop for 1999. In spite of a career-high seven-RBI game on August 23 when he went 4-for-6, Girardi still struggled to a career-low .271 OBP in

1999. Nevertheless, he contributed defensively,[32] caught seven postseason games, and won his third World Series ring.

Girardi caught David Cone's perfect game against Montreal. "He always knows how to say the right thing at the right time," Cone said. "Maybe a younger catcher or a different catcher might get a little angry with me because I have a tendency to show some emotions on a mound that a catcher might interpret as showing him up. But Joe has a great personality."[33]

As in 1996, New York faced Atlanta in the 1999 World Series. Girardi starred in Game Three, the closest contest. The Braves led 4-1 in the third with Bret Boone on second and one out. Girardi threw out Boone trying to steal third, a critical play that saved a run as Chipper Jones followed with a single. The Yanks trailed 5-3 in the bottom of the eighth. Girardi led off with a single and scored on Chuck Knoblauch's game-tying homer.

Boone singled off Mariano Rivera to start the ninth. Otis Nixon, with 29 steals in 36 attempts in the 1999 regular season and playoffs combined, ran for Boone, but Girardi threw out Nixon attempting to swipe second. In the bottom of the 10th with the scored tied and Girardi on deck, Chad Curtis hit a walk-off homer to give New York the win on its way to a Series sweep.

"When Girardi went home that night, the first thing he said to his wife, Kim, was, 'Honey, I think I just played my last game for the Yankees.' He was right."[34] Girardi wanted to play more for another team that did not have a catcher like Posada. "Obviously, it's been a great four years here for me, winning three championships. But I want to play every day and I have to see what's out there," Girardi said.[35]

Spurning bigger offers from St. Louis and San Francisco,[36] Girardi returned to the Cubs. He made the All-Star team for the only time in his career in 2000 as an injury replacement for Mike Piazza but did not play. In Girardi's second Chicago go-round, the Cubs never made the postseason.

Girardi's old-school ways occasionally grated on his younger teammates, a foreshadowing of his fate as Yankee manager. After a loss to Pittsburgh near the end of the dismal 2002 season, Girardi lowered Sammy Sosa's clubhouse music. "I just said, 'I'm a little older and I don't like the [loud] music,'" he told a sportswriter. "'I have

nothing against you playing it when you're in here. … He didn't realize that I turned it down because I thought he went outside.'"[37]

Chicago declined to keep Girardi, but St. Louis inked him to a one-year contract. After moving on from Girardi, Cubs general manager Jim Hendry said, "It was a baseball decision, not a personal decision, and he has a great future … as a manager or a front-office guy."[38]

Girardi hurt his back in spring training[39] with the Cardinals and played in only 16 games in 2003, his last season as a player. In his final plate appearance, he singled off Arizona's Edgar Gonzalez on September 28.

The Yankees invited Girardi to spring training in 2004. Saying "players don't realize how fortunate they are to play for the Yankees," Girardi battled to back up Posada and had a backup plan of his own to join the YES Network as a broadcaster.[40]

Girardi failed to make the team and chose a different post-playing career than the one he had foreseen in 1998. "When I retire, I think I'd have to go and work in a front office at some level," Girardi said, "scouting or maybe, if you got real lucky, an assistant's job."[41]

In 2005, he served as Torre's bench coach. Florida hired Girardi as manager for 2006 and then traded away most of its front-line talent for prospects.[42] "In May, the team tied a franchise record with 11 consecutive home losses. After [a road loss in the middle of the streak], a beat writer asked Girardi if it would be hard for him to sleep that night. 'No harder than when I was a player,' he said. 'I didn't sleep too good after losses then, either.'"[43]

By August, Girardi faced rumors of troubles with the front office as a result of his declining to argue against the call by a home-plate umpire that resulted in a walk by a Florida pitcher in a game attended by the Florida owner.[44] "There's no rift; there never was a rift," Girardi said. "There's always tension when I lose."[45]

Girardi kept his job after he "agreed to apologize to the owner [Jeffrey Loria] in front of the team"[46] but was fired in October. Florida GM Larry Beinfest did his best to justify the decision, explaining, "This team exceeded everybody's expectations in terms of wins, and Joe…played an integral role in the team's success. Joe is not returning because he was not a good fit. … We felt that Joe was not able to integrate himself into the workings of our organization."[47]

In November, the Baseball Writers Association of America named Girardi NL Manager of the Year. "It's nice that people who watched the games every day understood what we accomplished," Girardi said. "I don't know if vindicated is a good word, just because as a manager you want to manage. Whether you are Manager of the Year or not, it's not going to put you in that seat."[48]

Girardi returned to YES for the 2007 season to broadcast games and co-host a show with former catcher John Flaherty,[49] an ironic pairing given that Flaherty had held off Girardi in 2004 to back up Posada. Few thought Girardi would remain off the field for long. As *Sports Illustrated*'s Tom Verducci observed, "Girardi is the rare manager who emerged from a firing – and a first-year firing at that – without his reputation diminished. The hottest managerial candidate of last winter is the hottest managerial candidate of this season."[50]

Indeed, Girardi sat out a single season before beating out Yankees legend Don Mattingly to replace Torre as New York manager. Replacing the popular Stanley as catcher in 1996 represented a serious challenge for Girardi; beating out a former Yankee MVP in Mattingly and stepping in for the beloved Torre represented monumental hurdles for Girardi to overcome. "I can't be Joe Torre, because I'm made up different," said Girardi … "I'm a different character."[51]

By wearing a uniform with the number 27 (the Yankees at the time of Girardi's hiring had won 26 titles), Girardi sent a signal that in the Bronx, "This team's ultimate goal is to win the World Series," he said. "It's not going to change."[52]

In 2008, New York won 89 games but missed the playoffs for the first time in 14 seasons. In contrast to what happened in Florida, Girardi survived because Yankees management realized that he helmed a flawed team. Jose Molina caught most of the games; Darrell Rasner and Sidney Ponson made 35 ineffective starts.

With better talent, New York made the playoffs for the next four years. During the first half of his managerial tenure with the Yankees, Girardi won few plaudits; rather, as Will Leitch concluded in a *New York Magazine* analysis, "He has done what a manager is supposed to do: put his players in the best mental position to succeed and then stay out of the way."[53]

New York reloaded for 2009 by signing three big-name free agents in A.J. Burnett, CC Sabathia, and Mark Teixeira. The Yankees also made a terrific trade for Nick Swisher. After hitting only three homers in an injury-plagued 2008 campaign, Posada juked 22 in 2009.

Nevertheless, New York started slowly in 2009 and did not move into first place for good until July 20. The Yankees struggled against the Red Sox, losing their first eight games against Boston before winning nine of their final 10 versus their arch-rivals. Girardi deftly handled players in a high-pressure atmosphere. In 2008, Girardi had benched Robinson Cano for not hustling. In 2009, Cano credited Girardi for his tough love. "He's been the same as last year," Cano said. "Always talks to everybody."[54] Future Yankees would not appreciate Girardi's consistency.

A good regular-season club that got 130 starts from Burnett, Joba Chamberlain, Andy Pettitte, and Sabathia, New York became a great postseason squad by returning Chamberlain to the bullpen and taking advantage of off-days to use three starters.

The Yankees returned to the World Series and beat the defending champion Phillies to make Girardi's uniform number prophetic. Making for an even bigger storybook ending, Girardi, heading home after the final game, assisted a stranded driver who had a car accident. "Obviously, there's a lot of joy in what we do, but we can't forget that we're human beings where we help others out," Girardi said. "I think that's the most important thing that we can do in life."[55]

Although he swapped his number-27 jersey for number 28, Girardi never managed the Yanks to another World Series. In 2010, the Yanks fell in six games to the Rangers in the ALCS. In 2011, New York lost to Detroit in the AL Division Series. The Yanks took the division title again in 2012 and opened the playoffs against Baltimore. Girardi had weightier matters to consider due to his father's passing during the ALDS and attended the funeral on an off-day. With the teams tied at a game apiece, "Girardi made the toughest decision of his six years as a major league manager"[56] by pinch-hitting Raul Ibanez for Alex Rodriguez in the ninth inning of Game Three with New York down a run. Ibanez homered to tie the game and homered again in the 12th to win it. "Asked what his father would have thought of this decision, Girardi replied, 'He would have been extremely proud and probably told all his buddies.'"[57]

The Yankees outlasted the Orioles in five games before

getting swept by the Tigers in the ALCS.

New York had a trio of unsuccessful seasons in 2013, 2014, and 2016 that nevertheless showcased Girardi's managerial skills. While the 2015 Yankees outscored opponents by 66 runs en route to an 87-75 record and a wild-card loss to the Astros, the other three clubs all yielded more runs than they scored but nevertheless had three winning records:

| YEAR | SCORED | ALLOWED | MARGIN | W-L |
|------|--------|---------|--------|-------|
| 2013 | 650 | 671 | -21 | 85-77 |
| 2014 | 633 | 664 | -31 | 84-78 |
| 2016 | 680 | 702 | -22 | 84-78 |

Teams that get outscored usually have losing marks. Teams that get outscored but still win more games do so due to strong bullpens, good luck, and capable managers.

In 2013, New York went 85-77 despite a starting lineup with a single star in Cano and one accomplished player in Brett Gardner. The other seven regulars were past their primes (34-year-old Vernon Wells, 36-year-olds Travis Hafner and Lyle Overbay, and 39-year-old Ichiro Suzuki) and career backups (Jayson Nix, Eduardo Nunez, and Chris Stewart). A *Boston Globe* Red Sox beat writer lauded Girardi as "one of the top managers in baseball this [2013] season. You normally can't have that many injuries – lose that much payroll – and survive. The Yankees not only survived, they took their quest for a playoff spot into the final week of the season."[58]

Likewise, the 2014 Yanks went 84-78 with a lackluster starting rotation featuring a future star in Masahiro Tanaka who pitched in just 20 games due to injury and a steady pitcher in Hiroki Kuroda. But Girardi mixed and matched 85 starts among eight fringe hurlers (Chris Capuano, Shane Greene, Brandon McCarthy, Bryan Mitchell, Vidal Nuno, David Phelps, Esmil Rogers, and Chase Whitley).

In 2016, New York had big names who failed to produce. All nine offensive regulars had OPS+ figures below 100, meaning the Yankees did not have a single league-average hitter in the batting order. GM Brian Cashman traded the present for the future by swapping veterans for prospects. The young players returned New York to the playoffs in 2017 but also paved the way for Girardi's departure from the Bronx.

A pair of youngsters led the 2017 Yankees. Aaron Judge hit 52 homers, and Luis Severino went 14-6. As in 2015, New York won the wild card and opened the playoffs at home, this time against Minnesota. Severino faced only six batters, who homered, fouled out, walked, homered, singled, and doubled to put the Twins up 3-0. Managing aggressively, Girardi yanked Severino in favor of the fireballing Chad Green, who, along with his bullpen mates and the Yankee bats, rallied New York to an 8-4 win that advanced the Yankees to face the Indians in the ALDS.

After losing the first game of the ALDS, New York led the second one, 8-3, in the sixth inning, a disastrous frame during which Girardi arguably overmanaged and assuredly undermanaged. With one out and one on, and CC Sabathia throwing well at just 77 pitches, Girardi again went to Green, who got an out and gave up a double to put two on with two outs. Green then hit Lonnie Chisenhall to load the bases. Replays showed that the ball had in fact hit the bat rather than the batter, but Girardi failed to ask for a review, "an all-time mess-up … easily the lowest point of his managerial career."[59] Francisco Lindor followed with a grand slam to make the score 8-7. Cleveland tied the game in the eighth and won it in the 13th to take a commanding 2-0 series lead.

Surprisingly, New York won all three straight elimination games to win the ALDS and, seemingly, minimize the meaningfulness of Girardi's miscues. The manager expressed relief after the comeback. "I've been carrying this burden for five or six days," Girardi said. … "It's hard. … So for me, what these guys did for me, I'll never forget."[60]

As in 2015, the Astros ended the playoff run of the Yanks, this time by taking the ALCS in seven games. With an expired contract, Girardi "had an almost fatalistic tone as he discussed his baseball future. 'I've had 10 great years here,' he said. 'I feel extremely blessed. God has been good to me, and we'll see what the future holds.'"[61]

As New York had gone 910-710 under Girardi, *Washington Post* columnist Barry Svrluga urged the Nationals to hire him: "He dealt with the Yankees' aging, expensive and inflexible roster, and then managed the transition … to this new, athletic, powerful core that looks like it will restore order in the Bronx for years to come," wrote Svrluga.[62]

But New York declined to retain Girardi amid accusations that younger players disdained him. "He just wears you down," one of his players said when Girardi's fate was still not public. "Nobody hates him, everybody respects the work ethic, but there is no real connection. He wears his tension … and it is too long a season for that style all the time."[63]

GM Cashman questioned Girardi's "ability to fully engage, communicate and connect with the playing personnel."[64] Understandably, Girardi expressed surprise at Cashman's judging him on style over results especially after "the year we had and the progress the team had made … I thought I'd be back."[65]

The Yankees replaced Girardi, who returned to television, with Aaron Boone. Staying classy, Girardi praised Boone as "a bright man [who] understands the game and has been around it a long time."[66]

Tyler Kepner, baseball columnist for the *New York Times*, summed up Girardi's legacy, opining, "Girardi was an excellent manager – driven, prepared, caring – and he shepherded a young clubhouse into a new era."[67] Girardi seems likely to manage again; when Cincinnati made the first managerial firing of 2018 by canning Bryan Price, Girardi's name surfaced as a potential successor.[68]

Regardless, Girardi's legacy remains secure as the first catcher of the Rockies, and as a champion player and manager of the Yankees.

## Notes

1 Billy Witz, "The Yankees' New Manager Takes a Number, and Decides Not to Use Girardi's," *New York Times*, February 25, 2018.

2 Nancy Armour (Associated Press), "Girardi's Leadership Stems from His Parents' Hard Work." This undated article comes from the National Baseball Hall of Fame and Museum's file on Girardi. Thanks to Reference Librarian Cassidy Lent for scanning the Girardi file.

3 Bryan Hoch, "Girardi Cherishes Talks with Father," MLB.com, June 19, 2009.

4 Vic Ziegel, "Girardi Only Thinks Deep; with Pitchers, He's a Hit," *New York Daily News*, March 17, 1998.

5 Jack Curry, "Girardi Gets Turn to Play Big Brother," *New York Times*, March 27, 1997.

6 "About Joe Girardi," joegirardi.com/about-joe/ (accessed March 12, 2018).

7 "Cubs," *The Sporting News*, August 18, 1986: 25.

8 "Cubs," *The Sporting News*, January 2, 1989: 52.

9 "Joe Girardi, 'Always Ready to Go,'" *Peoria Journal Star,* October 7, 1989: C1. As a kid, Girardi had "two idols … Ron Santo and Jose

Cardenal." Chuck McAnulla, "Joe Girardi," *Sports Collectors Digest*, February 14, 1997: 161.

10 Bill James, *The Baseball Book 1990* (New York: Villard Books, 1990), 286.

11 "Girardi, Berryhill Give Cubs Catching Depth," *The Sporting News*, August 13, 1990: 13.

12 Claire Smith, "Yanks' Girardi Leaves His Ego in the Clubhouse," *New York Times*, May 12, 1998.

13 Bill James, *The Bill James Player Ratings Book 1994* (New York: Collier Books, 1994), 90.

14 Mark Kiszla, "Show Girardi the Door as Antidote for His Venom," *Denver Post*, February 28, 1995: D1.

15 Kevin Kernan, *Girardi: Passion in Pinstripes* (Chicago: Triumph Books, 2012), 159-160.

16 John Harper, "Rockies High on Biggio; Yanks' Deal for Girardi Frees Up Colorado Cash," *New York Daily News*, December 5, 1995.

17 Gay Talese, "The Crisis Manager," *The New Yorker*, September 24, 2012: 45.

18 Unattributed and undated article in the Hall of Fame's file on Girardi.

19 John Harper, "Yanks Get Rockie, Throw Out Stanley," *New York Daily News*, November 21, 1995.

20 John Giannone, "Girardi's Catching Heck," *New York Daily News*, February 5, 1996.

21 Don Burke, "A Case for the Defense," *Newark Star-Ledger*, December 10, 1995.

22 John Giannone, "Seems Girardi Is Catching On," *New York Daily News*, March 8, 1996.

23 Jim Salisbury, "One Lucky Joe," *New York Post*, May 22, 1996.

24 D.L. Cummings, "Joe Catches Bit of History," *New York Daily News*, May 15, 1996.

25 John Giannone, "Yanks Rule the World; Key, Girardi Spark Bombers to Title," *New York Daily News*, October 27, 1996.

26 youtube.com/watch?time_continue=17&v=YCSnK_ctjdk (accessed April 4, 2018).

27 Steve Serby, "Serby's Sunday Q&A with Joe Girardi," *New York Post*, November 4, 2007: 105.

28 John Giannone, "With Wells in Waiting, Yanks Pitch to Girardi," *New York Daily News*, November 19, 1996.

29 In 1996, Girardi by his own subsequent account said of Posada, "This is a scary situation. He's young, he's got a tremendous arm, he's a good receiver and hits for power on both sides." 1998 World Series program article by Joe Girardi with Pat McEvoy, "What Ceiling?"

30 Luke Cyphers, "For Yanks, '96 Déjà vu; Girardi HR in 8th Caps

Comeback over M's," *New York Daily News*, April 29, 1997.

31  Jack Curry, "Throughout Life's Travails, Girardi Is Keeping the Faith," *New York Times*, February 28, 1999.

32  With the Yankees suffering through a five-game losing streak but leading 2-1 in the sixth inning of a May game, the White Sox had runners on the corners with none out. "Darrin Jackson topped the ball … and Girardi bolted … to field it.  Magglio Ordonez broke for the plate and Girardi quickly turned back toward home, forcing Ordonez to reverse direction.  Girardi ran him toward third and flipped the ball to Scott Brosius, who tagged Ordonez." Anthony McCarron, "Girardi Catches Falling Yankees 'D,'" *New York Daily News*, May 17, 1999.

33  Ralph Vacchiano, "Girardi's Perfect for Cone," *New York Daily News*, July 21, 1999.

34  Tom Verducci, "New York Yankees:  They May Be Getting Long in the Tooth, but These Bombers Still Have Their Bite," *Sports Illustrated*, March 27, 2000.

35  Peter Botte, "Girardi May Catch on Elsewhere," *New York Daily News*, October 29, 1999.

36  "Girardi Catches On with the Cubs," *Albany Times Union*, December 16, 1999.

37  Teddy Greenstein, "Looney Tunes at Wrigley," *Chicago Tribune*, September 28, 2002.

38  Teddy Greenstein, "Girardi Move 'Part Of Game,'" *Chicago Tribune*, December 20, 2002.

39  Dan O'Neill, "Girardi Sets Up Behind the Mike," *St. Louis Post-Dispatch*, September 29, 2003.

40  Mark Feinsand, "Girardi Invited to Spring Training," MLB.com, February 4, 2004.

41  Buster Olney, "Girardi Sees His Future as a General Manager," *New York Times*, March 19, 1998.

42  "According to reports, Girardi was blindsided by the Marlins' massive youth movement after he was hired." Mike Berardino, "Points of Conflict," *Sun Sentinel* (Fort Lauderdale, Florida), October 4, 2006.

43  Michael Sokolove, "Happy Just to Be here," *Play*, June 2006: 84.

44  Kevin Baxter, "Anger Management," *Miami Herald*, August 8, 2006. "Loria was upset when Girardi asked him from the dugout not to yell at the umpires. But … Girardi's bench lieutenant, Gary Tuck … caused all the clubhouse commotion afterward. 'If you don't f----- like it, get someone else,' Tuck shouted from the dugout to Loria." Dave Hyde, "Firing Unfair but Necessary for Everyone," *Sun Sentinel*, September 22, 2006.

45  Mel Antonen, "Inside the NL," *USA Today*, August 9, 2006.

46  Greg Cote, "A Loria Apology to Girardi Would Be the Right Thing to Do," *Miami Herald*, August 19, 2006.

47  Clark Spencer, "Beinfest:  Girardi 'Was Not a Good Fit,'" *Miami Herald*, October 3, 2006.

48  Juan C. Rodriguez, "Girardi Gets His Due as Top Manager," *Sun Sentinel*, November 16, 2006.

49  Jack Curry, "Girardi Says Broadcasting Is Best for Now," *New York Times*, November 14, 2006.

50  Tom Verducci, "Fish Out of Water," *Sports Illustrated*, February 19, 2007.

51  Bob Nightengale, "Girardi Replaces Torre, Who May Join Dodgers," *USA Today*, October 31, 2007.

52  Harvey Araton, "Girardi's Introduction Starts the Clock Ticking," *New York Times*, November 2, 2007: D4.

53  Will Leitch, "Joe Cool," *New York Magazine*, September 16, 2011.

54  Tyler Kepner, "The Taskmaster Loosens Up," *New York Times*, September 25, 2009: B13.

55  Jon Fogg, "Girardi's Selfless Act," *Washington Times*, November 7, 2009: 2.

56  Ronald Blum (Associated Press), "Joe Girardi's Father, Jerry, Dies at 81," October 11, 2012.

57  Mike Bauman, "Girardi Does His Best Through Triumph, Tragedy," MLB.com, October 12, 2012.

58  Nick Cafardo, "Girardi Couldn't Have Managed to Time It Better," *Boston Globe*, October 6, 2013.

59  Andrew Marchand, "The Simple Truth in the Bronx:  It Was Time For Joe to Go," ESPN, October 26, 2017.

60  Billy Witz, "For Girardi and Judge, Game 5 Became the Great Escape," *New York Times*, October 13, 2017: B11.

61  Billy Witz, "After 10 Seasons and a Title, Girardi Is Done as Yanks Manager," *New York Times*, October 27, 2017: B10.

62  Barry Svrluga, "If Nationals Are Serious About a World Series, They Should Make Joe Girardi an Offer," *Washington Post*, October 25, 2017.

63  Joel Sherman, "What Made Girardi a Success Cost Him His Job," *New York Post*, October 26, 2017.

64  Billy Witz, "Girardi Didn't Connect With Players, Cashman Says," *New York Times*, November 7, 2017.

65  Ken Rosenthal, "Q&A with Joe Girardi:  How He Feels About Being Let Go By the Yankees And Whether He Will Manage Again," *The Athletic*, October 31, 2017.

66  Billy Witz, "Girardi Joins MLB Network as an Analyst," *New York Times*, February 8, 2018.

67  Tyler Kepner, "Boone on Day 1: 'How Stable Everything Is,'" *New York Times*, February 14, 2018.

68  John Fay, "Cincinnati Reds 2018:  Barry Larkin, John Farrell, Buddy Bell or Jim Riggleman May Be Next," *Cincinnati Enquirer*, April 19, 2018.

# CHARLIE HAYES

## By Rory Costello

Third baseman Charlie Hayes was a solid journeyman. He played for seven teams over 14 years in the majors from 1988 through 2001. He had a good glove, a strong arm, and some pop in his bat. His best offensive numbers came in 1993 with an expansion club, the Colorado Rockies. Yet the moment for which he is best remembered came as he caught a foul pop to end the 1996 World Series.

"I walk around and people still talk about that catch," said Hayes during a visit to Yankee Stadium on Old-Timers' Day 2013. "You'd think it would go away, but it hasn't happened yet. I'm honored to be part of that. Just being part of the Yankee tradition is unbelievable, and this is proof."[1]

Charles Dewayne Hayes was born on May 29, 1965, in Hattiesburg, Mississippi. He was the oldest of four children; his younger sisters were named Sabrina, Selina, and Bernilla. Their mother, Lutherea Hayes, was a cook in a nightclub. She was the one raising all four children; little Charlie was only 4 years old when his father died.[2]

Young Hayes' sports hero was the great basketball player Julius Erving. "I always wanted to play basketball, but baseball came easier," he said in 1993.[3] The previous year he noted, "It was baseball that worked out for me. My mother worked hard. But she helped me reach my dream. If I needed, say, a new glove, she went without things so I could have it."[4]

At age 12 in 1977, Hayes was a member of the Hub City team from Hattiesburg that represented the South Region of the United States in the Little League World Series.[5] Hattiesburg, with Hayes on the mound, lost to El Cajon, California, in the first round. It was a competitive game; the final score was 3-1. Hayes went all six innings, striking out six and allowing four hits while giving up a solo homer; runs also scored on his balk and wild pitch.[6] Hattiesburg eventually won the consolation bracket.

Hayes attended Forrest County Agricultural High School in Brooklyn, Mississippi. He was a two-sport star there; one may infer the other was basketball. In baseball, however, his feats led the school to retire his number.[7] As a senior, he hit .530 with 14 doubles and 4 homers; he was also 8-3 as a pitcher. He was named to Mississippi's All-State high school team, a squad that also included Marcus Lawton, who played 10 games for the Yankees in 1989 (younger brother Matt Lawton played in the majors from

1995 through 2006).[8]

The *Jackson Clarion-Ledger* noted that *Baseball America* had ranked Hayes among the top 25 high-school players in the nation. "He's probably the best athlete ever to come through Forrest County AHS," said his coach, Glen Dewease. "A lot of pro scouts are looking at him as a third baseman. If he really wants (a pro career), he can go." One scout said, "Most everybody likes him as a third baseman or possible outfielder. He's got good running speed and enough arm strength to play either spot. The big question is his bat, whether he'll hit. But his other tools measure up to major-league standards. He's got a chance of being drafted high."[9]

Indeed, the San Francisco Giants selected Hayes with their fourth-round pick in the June 1983 amateur draft. In the Pioneer Rookie League, he played both third base and outfield (he never pitched in a pro game).

Around that time, Hayes got married. He and his wife, Gelinda, had three sons: Charles Jr., Tyree, and Ke'Bryan. Charles Jr. grew to 6-feet-4 and 290 pounds – he preferred football to baseball.[10] The two younger brothers both became pro baseball players. Tyree was an eighth-round draft pick of the Tampa Bay Devil Rays in 2006. Ke'Bryan – whom Gelinda was expecting during the 1996 World Series – was a first-round pick of the Pittsburgh Pirates in 2015.

It took Charlie Hayes six seasons to climb the ladder to the majors. He wanted to give up baseball during the 1984 season, come home to Hattiesburg, and enroll in college – but his mother told him, "There are no quitters in this house."[11]

Hayes represented Fresno in the California League's 1985 All-Star Game. But as he recalled, "The turning point came when in 1987 I was sent back to Double A after spending spring training with the Triple-A team. I thought then there were other things I could do, and that it wasn't too late to go to college. I was doubting myself. Jack Mull, my manager, said, 'You're too hard on yourself. You're such a team player. Remember, sometimes you have to be selfish.' And my mother said, 'Give it your best shot. Something good will happen and other good things will follow.'"

"Jack Mull's support – and my mother's – helped me reach my dream. My mother matured me in a way that gave me that extra drive that I needed to make it."[12]

Hayes had not shown much power in his first four pro seasons, hitting just 11 homers in total. With Shreveport of the Texas League in 1987, though, he hit 14 and had 75 RBIs while also breaking the .300 mark for the first time. He thus earned promotion to Triple-A Phoenix in 1988 and had another good year (.307-7-71), though he played more outfield than third base that season.

When rosters expanded in September 1988, Hayes got his first call-up. His big-league debut came in left field. Hayes got into six more games over the rest of the season, appearing twice more in left and once in right. After that, he played just once more as an outfielder in the majors, for two innings in 1999.

Hayes returned to Triple A to start the 1989 season. The Giants continued to experiment with him as an outfielder. He was called up briefly in early May as Matt Williams was optioned to Phoenix. He appeared in three games at third base before being sent back.

On June 18, 1989, Hayes became part of a five-player trade with the Philadelphia Phillies that sent Steve Bedrosian and Rick Parker to San Francisco. Philadelphia also received lefty pitchers Terry Mulholland and Dennis Cook. Hayes reported to the Phillies' top farm club, Scranton/Wilkes-Barre, but at the end of the month Philadelphia brought him up after receiving glowing reports from special-assignment scout Jim Fregosi and Red Barons manager Bill Dancy.[13] Hayes never played again in the minors.

Hall of Fame third baseman Mike Schmidt had retired near the end of May, stating that he could no longer live up to the high standards he had set for himself as a player.[14] The Phillies tried outfielder Chris James at third for a little while. Then they used Randy Ready, a utilityman; Von Hayes, an outfielder/first baseman; and Steve Jeltz, a shortstop. Hayes got the job in large part because he was a true third baseman.

Shortly after the promotion, Philadelphia's general manager, Lee Thomas, remarked, "Charlie has been a good hitter at every level in the minor leagues. If he can hit a little up here, he'll be our third baseman. Defensively, he's got soft hands and a better than average arm. So far, we've been very impressed."[15] Indeed, Hayes started 79 of the Phillies' remaining games at third. His production with the bat was promising: 8 homers and 43 RBIs in 315 plate appearances, while batting .258.

Hayes made 11 errors in his first 23 games, including four in one game as the Phillies lost on July 15. Yet he was unfazed. "I heard some boos," he said, "but my job is to play as best I can. Errors are part of the game. I was going hard and it just happened."[16] Manager Nick Leyva added, "He's been pressing. I believe he's a better fielder than he's shown."[17] He wound up with 22 errors for the year and drew frequent criticism from Leyva.[18]

Hayes, who trimmed down from 223 pounds to 202 over the winter, remained the regular at third for the Phillies in 1990. "I think we've reached Charlie," said Leyva not long before Opening Day. "I believe he is totally committed and that we are going to see a different player this year."[19] Hayes again hit .258 in 1990, but his power totals were rather modest: 10 homers and 57 RBIs in 141 starts. He did, however, cut his errors down to 20. One of them represented the only baserunner that Terry Mulholland allowed in his no-hitter at Veterans Stadium on August 15. Oddly enough, it was Rick Parker of the Giants who reached base as Hayes' throw pulled John Kruk off the bag. Hayes atoned for it, however, by backhanding pinch-hitter Gary Carter's liner to end the game.

Hayes slumped in 1991 and lost playing time. He started just 109 games and posted a batting line of .230-12-53. In late July, the Phillies recalled third baseman Dave Hollins from Scranton/Wilkes-Barre and gave him an audition as the starter, followed by an extended trial in September and October. Hayes bounced back at the plate toward the end of the season, but he could tell that his days in Philadelphia were numbered. He said, "All I can do now is hope that I played well enough down the stretch to convince somebody that I'm an everyday player."[20]

Looking back in 2015, Hayes said, "I loved Philly. It was a tough situation for me, being the guy who was kind of the heir apparent to Mike Schmidt. But one thing that Philadelphia taught me was about being tough, being determined – a blue-collar work ethic." He noted how that helped him in his work as a youth baseball coach. "I instill those things in all my kids. Always told them there were never any excuses. You just pick yourself up and try to get better every day."

He added, "I'm sure there were probably some things I could have done better: dealing with the media, accepting failure. But there's no doubt that Philadelphia made me the player I was."[21]

The Yankees obtained Hayes for the first time in February 1992. He was the player to be named later in the trade that had sent pitcher Darrin Chapin to Philadelphia the previous month. Dave Hollins took over the Phillies' third-base job in 1992 and had his most productive year; he was also a key member of the 1993 NL pennant-winners.

Hayes beat out Hensley Meulens at third base and had a nice year for New York in 1992: .257-18-66 in 142 games. He started 137 times at third and three times at first base, a position he played with some frequency later in his career. After the season ended, The Sporting News called him "the most pleasant surprise of the season for the Yankees. He was dependable defensively and productive offensively."[22]

Nonetheless, the Yankees made Hayes available in the expansion draft that November, and Colorado selected him with the third pick overall. Yankees general manager Gene Michael admitted, "We gambled. I'd hoped they would take a young player, and Charlie would slip through."[23] Shortly after that, however, New York signed Wade Boggs as a free agent.

Hayes had expected to be a Yankee for the long term. At first, he was devastated by the move. Yet it became part of his ongoing learning experience in the majors. "I grew up a lot that day," he said. "But instead of feeling sorry for myself, I started thinking like a Rockie. I just try to make the best of the situation. What baseball does is this: No matter how good you are, there's no security. But I can control being mentally prepared to play; I can control giving 110 percent."[24]

Hayes' new team felt fortunate. "The Rockies believed from Day One of their existence that one of their best expansion-draft pickups was third baseman Charlie Hayes," said STATS Inc.'s Scouting Report for 1994. "They were not disappointed, as Hayes – next to Andrés Galarraga – was Colorado's most consistent player. He was everything the Rockies hoped he'd be, and more."[25]

Mile High Stadium, where the Rockies played their first two seasons, was a hitters' ballpark. It was particularly favorable for right-handed hitters like Galarraga, Dante Bichette – and Hayes, who posted the best offensive season of his career.[26] He had a team-high 25 homers, 98 RBIs (tied with Galarraga for tops on the club), and a .305 batting average in 157 games. He also led the National League with 45 doubles. His home-away splits were notable, though: .338-17-66 at Mile High vs. .271-8-32 on the road.

Hayes remained the Rockies' starting third baseman in 1994. Perhaps the most noteworthy thing from that season was visual. On June 25, pitcher Salomón Torres of San Francisco hit Hayes in the face with a pitch. It came right after Torres had opened the inning by hitting Galarraga in the left arm; Colorado manager Don Baylor had to restrain Hayes from charging the mound, and a brawl almost erupted. Hayes suffered a broken cheekbone and left the game, but missed only two games after that. When he returned to action, he experimented with a couple of kinds of clear mask attached to his helmet.[27]

Hayes' power numbers dipped to 10 homers and 50 RBIs in 113 games during the strike-shortened season. His $3 million salary was more than Colorado found palatable, and so they did not tender him a contract.[28] The Rockies turned third base over to Vinny Castilla, who gave them five big seasons in a row with the bat.

While spring training 1995 was conducted with replacement players, the Giants expressed interest in signing Hayes as a first baseman.[29] But when the strike ended in April 1995, Hayes returned to Philadelphia, which moved Dave Hollins to first. Hayes was happier in Philadelphia the second time around. That June, Lee Thomas said, "Charlie has smiled more times in the last couple of weeks than he did in the couple years he was here before."[30] He had a good year (.276-11-85); The Sporting News remarked, "Hayes did what he usually does: drove in runs and played sound defense."[31]

Even so, the Phillies – who had star prospect Scott Rolen ready to take over at third – had no interest in meeting Hayes' wish for a two-year contract.[32] Thus, he became a free agent again. The Pittsburgh Pirates signed him near the end of 1995.

Forrest County Agricultural High retired Hayes' number 1 in February 1996. Not normally an emotional man, Hayes was greatly moved by the ceremony.[33] It was an auspicious start to the season, but the Pirates were disappointing and began to turn over their roster toward the end of the summer. On August 30, the Yankees re-obtained Hayes for a player to be named later (Chris Corn, a pitcher who never reached the majors).

Wade Boggs was still New York's starting third baseman in 1996, but the team wanted to platoon him. Manager Joe Torre had said that Boggs was tired and his bat was slow at times, and that Hayes was added to provide some power.[34] Boggs felt slighted, but the depth proved valuable because he missed several games in September with back spasms.

"That team was a group of guys that came together," said Hayes in 2013. "While there were a lot of superstars on that team, the biggest thing is that Joe Torre got everybody to make sacrifices. I remember one game where I wasn't playing against a lefty, and thought I should've been. I walked out on the bench and I saw (Darryl) Strawberry to my left, Tim Raines to my right, and Tino (Martinez) behind me, and I said to myself, 'What could you be complaining about? These guys here have done way more in this game than you have!' From that day forward, I just approached every game like it was my last."[35]

The Yankees played 15 games in the 1996 postseason, and Hayes appeared in 12 of them, starting six times. His best outing was in Game Four of the World Series at Atlanta, when he went 3-for-5 with an RBI.

Three nights later, at Yankee Stadium, Hayes entered Game Six in the top of the seventh inning, replacing Boggs at third. He didn't handle any chances until pesky Mark Lemke came to the plate with two outs in the ninth, the tying run on second base, and the go-ahead run on first. The count ran full, and Lemke popped John Wetteland's next pitch toward the visitors' dugout. Hayes had a chance to make the play, but an Atlanta batboy got in his way. Hayes got clear and continued his pursuit of the ball, but it was out of reach as he tumbled into the dugout. Tim McCarver, calling the game for Fox TV, noted that interference could have been called.[36] Had the Yankees lost that game and the Series, that batboy could have become as notorious as Cubs fan Steve Bartman did for his action in the 2003 playoffs.

On the pitch after that, though, Lemke lifted another little foul pop. This one stayed in play, and as it settled into Hayes' glove, the Yankees were champions of baseball for the first time in 18 years.

In retrospect, Hayes offered another intriguing detail – he got hurt on Lemke's first foul. "I think I broke my finger and I didn't even know it until after the game," he said. "So it would have been very interesting to see what would have happened if that ball was hit on the ground and I would have had to throw it to first base."[37] Whatever happened to that ball? It and the glove Hayes used that night were sold at auction in 2014.

Hayes and Boggs remained in a platoon at third for Yankees in 1997, which didn't make either man happy. Hayes played about 55 percent of the innings there and Boggs played 42 percent. For about a month, from early July through early August, Boggs served mainly as the team's designated hitter. It came shortly after he proclaimed himself "mentally shot" and said "it'll help the team more if Charlie plays."[38] Hayes started four of the five games in the AL Division Series, which New York lost to the Cleveland Indians.

The major leagues then were about to add two more franchises (Arizona and Tampa Bay). Thus, the possibility arose that Hayes could have been chosen for the second time in an expansion draft. Before that draft, however, New York sent him (plus cash) back to his original organization, the Giants. "He's a very good defensive third baseman and can play first base," said Dusty Baker, then San Francisco's manager. "Plus, he's a clutch hitter and run-producer."[39] Replacing Hayes and Boggs at third for the Yankees was Scott Brosius, a key member of the teams that won three straight World Series and nearly a fourth.

Meanwhile, during 1998 and 1999, Hayes backed up Bill Mueller at third and J.T. Snow at first. In 1998, Snow – a switch-hitter for his first several years in the majors – had fallen off so badly swinging from the right side that Baker began to platoon him with Hayes.[40] From 1999 on, Snow batted only left-handed.

In the fall of 1999 Hayes became a free agent again; the New York Mets signed him in January 2000. That March he received the troubling news that his beloved mother had been diagnosed with breast cancer. Hayes experienced heart irregularities and cited the emotional stress, but an EKG showed that he was OK.[41]

The Mets released Hayes on March 20, but two days later, the Milwaukee Brewers picked him up. He spent the 2000 season as a reserve corner infielder, starting 48 games at third behind José Hernández and 46 at first (Richie Sexson got the most action there). He hit the last of his 144 major-league homers on September 11 off Rich Rodriguez of the Mets.

Entering free agency once more, Hayes signed with the Houston Astros in January 2001. He made the team but had to leave on April 27 to be with his ailing mother in her final days. The Astros placed him on the restricted list, which enabled the team to call up a replacement (Keith Ginter) during the time of bereavement. Hayes was activated on May 8.[42]

Serving mainly as a pinch-hitter, the veteran got into 31 games for Houston. He hit .200-0-4 and was released on July 9. He thereupon retired.

Hayes then got into coaching youth baseball in the Houston area. Two former pros named Ray and Robert DeLeon had a baseball school called Home Plate Inc. in The Woodlands, a community in the Houston area. The DeLeons sold it in 2002 and started a bigger facility called Future Baseball Stars Academy. Hayes was one of the instructors, along with his good friend and former teammate with the Phillies, Ron Jones.

Jones approached Hayes in 2005 about starting their own baseball school. Initially, Hayes was reluctant to get involved, but the tight bond between the two men convinced him to go ahead. They opened the Big League Baseball Academy in Tomball, Texas (also outside of Houston).[43] They worked together until Jones died suddenly at home in June 2006. One of the big clues that something was wrong was the lack of response from Jones when Tyree Hayes was drafted. It was out of character for him not even to call.

Hayes could not bring himself to go back to the academy for months. He initially wanted to close it down after the loss of his best friend. Yet he heard from his wife that because Jones talked him into doing it, he should keep it open – which it still is (as of 2018).[44]

Tyree Hayes pitched through 2011 in the minors with the Tampa Bay and Cincinnati chains. He played in the independent Frontier League in 2012. Ke'Bryan Hayes began his fourth pro season in 2018. The promising prospect played for the Altoona Curve in the Double-A Eastern League.

Charlie Hayes returned to pro ball in 2017 as bench coach of the Lehigh Valley IronPigs in the Triple-A International League. The IronPigs became the Phillies' top farm team in 2008. "The only difference is the kids here are older than those [at my academy]," said Hayes. "I'm still teaching kids the fundamentals of the game, stuff I learned along the way."[45] As the 2018 season began, he was serving as a rookie-ball coach for the Gulf Coast League Phillies.

## Sources

*Onlin*

bigleaguebaseballacademy.com.

YouTube.com.

ha.com (Heritage Auctions).

## Notes

1 Lou DiPietro, "Almost 20 Years Later, Charlie Hayes Still Fondly Remembered for 'The Catch,'" Yesnetwork.com, July 12, 2013.

2 "Lutherea Hayes," *Hattiesburg American*, May 4, 2001: 15. Owen Canfield, "Always Worth Singling Out," *Hartford Courant*, November 11, 1992. José de Jesús Ortiz, "Astros' Hayes Feels Void After Mother's Death," *Houston Chronicle*, May 13, 2001.

3 Tracy Ringolsby, "Colorado Rockies," *The Sporting News*, January 11, 1993: 31.

4 Canfield, "Always Worth Singling Out."

5 Tim Doherty, "Aggies Pay Tribute to Hayes," *Hattiesburg American*, February 13, 1996: 11.

6 "Hattiesburg Out in Series Play," *Monroe* (Louisiana) *News-Star*, August 24, 1977: 13. "Sports Wire Notes," *Galveston Daily News*, August 24, 1977: 6.

7 Doherty, "Aggies Pay Tribute to Hayes."

8 "All-State Team Heralds Year of Skilled Catchers," *Jackson Clarion-Ledger*, June 5, 1983: 48.

9 Ibid.

10 Jerry Crasnick, "Charlie Hayes, Mike Cameron Basking in the Success of Their Sons," ESPN.com, June 8, 2015.

11 de Jesús Ortiz, "Astros' Hayes Feels Void After Mother's Death."

12 Canfield, "Always Worth Singling Out."

13 "N.L. East: Phillies," *The Sporting News*, July 10, 1989: 39.

14 "Schmidt Retires after 17 Years and 548 Homers," *New York Times*, May 30, 1989.

15 "N.L. East: Phillies," *The Sporting News*, July 24, 1989: 30.

16 "Old Man Evans Climbs Past Duke on Homer List," *The Sporting News*, July 24, 1989: 27.

17 "N.L. East: Phillies," *The Sporting News*, August 7, 1989: 22.

18 "[Dickie] Thon Doesn't Want 'To Make a Mistake,'" *The Sporting News*, April 2, 1990: 37.

19 Bill Brown, "Will 1990 Campaign Be a Repeat of 1989?" *The Sporting News*, April 1, 1990: 28.

20 Bill Brown, "Philadelphia Phillies," *The Sporting News*, November 4, 1991: 16.

21 Paul Hagen, "Hayes Fond of Philly, Friendship with Jones," MLB.com, August 28, 2015.

22 Jack O'Connell, "New York Yankees," *The Sporting News*, October 19, 1992: 19.

23 Jack O'Connell, "New York Yankees," *The Sporting News*, November 30, 1992: 36.

24 William C. Rhoden, "Yankees Should Look to Their Journeyman, Hayes, as an Example," *New York Times*, July 28, 1997.

25 John Dewan and Don Zminda, editors, *The Scouting Report, 1994* (New York: HarperCollins Publishers: 1994), 433.

26 John Dewan and Don Zminda, editors, *STATS 1994 Baseball Scorecard* (New York: HarperCollins Publishers: 1994), 45.

27 "Controversy Follows Torres to the Mound," *Deseret News* (Salt Lake City), June 26, 1994. Dan Gutman and Tim McCarver, *The Way Baseball Works* (New York: Simon & Schuster, 1996), 37. Uni-watch.com shows pictures of Hayes in his different masks.

28 Tracy Ringolsby, "Colorado Rockies," *The Sporting News*, October 24, 1994: 37. Tracy Ringolsby, "Colorado Rockies," *The Sporting News*, January 2, 1995: 36.

29 Bob Nightengale, "Around the bases," *The Sporting News*, March 20, 1995: 14.

30 Jon Heyman, "Following the Phillies' Formula," *The Sporting News*, June 12, 1995: 16.

31 George A. King III, "Philadelphia Phillies," *The Sporting News*, October 16, 1995: 20.

32 George A. King III, "Philadelphia Phillies," *The Sporting News*, November 13, 1995: 43.

33 Doherty, "Aggies Pay Tribute to Hayes."

34 Jack Curry, "Boggs Feels Slighted as the Yankees Acquire Hayes," *New York Times*, August 31, 1996.

35 DiPietro, "Almost 20 Years Later, Charlie Hayes Still Fondly Remembered for 'The Catch.'"

36 A similar play took place in a game between the New York Mets and Milwaukee Brewers on June 1, 2017. A Brewers batboy got in the way of Mets third baseman Wilmer Flores as Flores tried to catch a bunt that had been popped up in foul territory. An umpire initially called batter Chase Anderson out, but after the umpires conferred, they reversed the call because it was deemed to be unintentional interference. See Rule 6.01(d) in the Major League Baseball rulebook.

37 Peter Schwartz, "Remembering The 1996 Yankees: Second Time Was the Charm For Hayes," CBS New York website (newyork.cbslocal.com), July 22, 2016.

38 John Giannone, "Wade Wants Ride Out of Town," *New York*

*Daily News*, July 6, 1997.

39  John Shea, "San Francisco Giants," *The Sporting News*, November 24, 1997: 28.

40  Henry Schulman, "Snow Makes a Choice: He'll Try to Hit Lefthanded," *The Sporting News*, October 5, 1998: 63.

41  David Lennon and Marty Noble, "Hayes OK After Tests, Says Stress to Blame," *Newsday*, March 14, 2000.

42  "News and Notes," *Pittsburgh Post-Gazette*, May 8, 2001: 25.

43  Hagen, "Hayes Fond of Philly, Friendship with Jones."

44  Ibid.

45  Tom Housenick, "IronPigs Bench Coach Hayes Just One of the Boys," *The Morning Call* (Allentown, Pennsylvania), September 3, 2017.

# THE MAKING OF THE MARLINS

### By Stephen R. Keeney

The National League expansion of 1993 was a long time coming. The 1991 decision to add the Colorado Rockies and the Florida Marlins to the major leagues was the end of "the road that began six years, three commissioners, and three league presidents ago."[1]

This road began in January of 1984, when Major League Baseball announced an eight-member committee to study the possibility another expansion after 1977. In the fall of 1985, twelve groups presented expansion proposals to a 14-owner committee. At that year's winter meetings, Commissioner Peter Ueberroth mentioned expansion in his "state of the game" speech

Over the next few years, the owners tabled expansion talks, focusing instead on clubs claiming to be in financial trouble and on fighting claims of collusion by the players union.

By 1987, the US Senate had formed a Task Force on Expansion. This bipartisan group was led by Senator Tim Wirth (D) of Colorado, and included senators from several states with cities that had expressed interest in a baseball franchise. These included Arizona (Phoenix), Tennessee (Nashville), Indiana (Indianapolis), Ohio (Columbus), Colorado (Denver), Florida (Miami, St. Petersburg), and the delegate from Washington, D.C. As other congressional groups had done in the past, this task force told MLB to either expand to more cities or lose its antitrust exemption, which protected it from being sued or broken

up as an illegal monopoly. The owners agreed to expand, at one point planning to increase each league to 16 teams, for a total of 32. But the owners continued to stall. They conducted studies and held various rounds of presentations by competing cities and ownership groups. Some owners wanted to stall until a new collective-bargaining agreement was negotiated with the players union in 1990, in order to use expansion to win other concessions. The threat of losing their monopoly was made slightly more real when a group calling itself the Professional Baseball Federation announced plans to start a new league with 8 to 10 teams and to lure current major-league stars away.

Having faced threats to its monopoly profits from upstart leagues and Congress several times before, the owners again relented. In June of 1990, the National League announced that it would expand by two teams. The cities

Joe Robbie Stadium on Opening Day, April 5, 1993.
(Courtesy of the Miami Marlins)

Marlins' manager Rene Lachemann (l.) on Opening Day 1993 as he is besieged by autograph seekers. (Courtesy of the Miami Marlins)

would be selected by September 1991 with play to begin in 1993. In December 1990 the six finalists for expansion were announced: Buffalo, Denver, Orlando, St. Petersburg/Tampa, Washington, and Miami. On June 10, 1991, the ownership groups from Denver and Miami were announced as the winners of the two new franchises. The additions still had to be approved by a vote of all the owners, which required approval of three-quarters (9 of 12) of the National League owners and a majority (8 of 14) American League owners. The decision became official on July 5, 1991, when the owners from both leagues unanimously approved the two new franchises.

But the four rejected cities still wanted baseball. They wanted an ownership group to purchase an existing team and move it to town. The Houston Astros, the Cleveland Indians, and especially the Seattle Mariners were seen as potential buy-and-move targets. This also failed, but at the time there was reason to hope. The Buffalo group – the Rich family – already owned the city's Triple-A Bisons and had tried the buy-and-move tactic with the Montreal Expos in 1990. Washington Mayor Sharon Pratt-Kelly told the Associated Press that she would "work with investors and other baseball boosters to pursue teams for sale in order to bring baseball to Washington."[2] The Tampa-St. Petersburg area was especially desperate to lure an existing team, since the city of St. Petersburg had just finished building a $110 million domed stadium. Since construction on what is today Tropicana Field began in the 1980s when the notion of baseball expansion was first being batted around, missing out on the 1993 expansion was particularly painful. However, the city would get a team in the next round of expansion.

The Miami franchise chose the name Florida Marlins. Marlins was chosen as an homage to a line of several minor-league baseball teams that had previously called Miami home. Major League Baseball hoped the ownership group would choose the alliterative Miami Marlins, which it thought was better for marketing and kept open the door for the next round of expansion to include another Florida city. But the ownership group wanted to appeal to as many potential customers in the state as possible, and thus decided on the Florida Marlins.

This homage came with its own complications. The original Miami Marlins were a minor-league team that began play in 1956 in the International League. Its first game ever saw an almost 50-year-old Satchel Paige come out of a helicopter that landed on the field, only to go straight to the bullpen and not pitch at all that day – although he did pitch that season. The team moved to San Juan, Puerto Rico, after the 1960 season.[3]

Another team called the Miami Marlins began play in the 1960s. This team – with a family tree going back to the 1920s – was not affiliated with the original Marlins, but adopted the mascot as an homage. As affiliations changed, this team went from the Miami Marlins to the Miami Orioles and back again, before becoming the Miami Miracle of the Florida State League, which was the name it played under when the Florida Marlins became a team. It was this team – the Miracle – that sued the new Florida Marlins in October of 1992. The Miracle argued that the Florida Marlins had refused to negotiate with the Miracle about the rights to the team name and the exclusive territorial rights for the Miami territory. The Miracle held exclusive rights to everything within 35 miles of their home plate – an expanse that encompassed the new home of the Marlins, Joe Robbie Stadium – and under the master agreement between the major and minor leagues, the new Florida Marlins were supposed to compensate the Miracle for the loss of those rights. At the time, the compensation for these rights was estimated to be between $1 million and $14 million.

Once the search for expansion cities became serious, Miami had been all but counted out. The rain, the heat, and the lack of fans turned off many baseball observers. The Miami Miracle had drawn fewer than 125 spectators per game in 1989.[4] But Miami became a frontrunner after the South Florida Big League Baseball bidding group was chosen to represent the city's bid. What brought on this change? The deep, deep pockets of the group's owner, H. Wayne Huizenga.

Huizenga agreed to pay the entire $95 million franchise fee himself. After that, everyone found reasons to support Miami's bid. The prospect of professional baseball seemed to excite the city, at least a little – the Miracle's attendance increased to 700 per game (still well below any measure of success) and 114,000 fans went out to Joe Robbie Stadium over two nights in March of 1991 to watch the Yankees and the Orioles play. Suddenly, the fact that Miami was one of the nation's 20 largest television markets was a major factor. And of course, if Huizenga built it, the city's "Latin and Caribbean population" would come, and "provide a wellspring of fans."[5] But there is little doubt that at least part of the allure of Miami's bid to the other owners was Huizenga's wealth – his net worth in the summer of 1991 was estimated to be between $500 million and $800 million.

In all, it was estimated that it would cost Huizenga between $131 million and $142 million before the Marlins could begin play, not including his partial purchase of Joe Robbie Stadium. This included the $95 million franchise fee, about $30 million or $40 million more in start-up costs (including salaries and equipment), and about $6 million or $7 million for renovations to Joe Robbie Stadium to make it baseball-friendly. Huizenga ended up spending $10 million to get the ballpark baseball-ready. Compared with these numbers, the $500,000 Huizenga spent promoting his bid to the other owners seemed paltry.

Huizenga was born in 1937 in Chicago, where his Dutch-born grandfather had founded a garbage-hauling company in 1894. His father was a cabinetmaker and home-builder. The family moved to Fort Lauderdale, Florida, when Huizenga was 15. After dropping out of college in Michigan, Huizenga ended up managing a family friend's three-truck garbage-hauling company. Huizenga eventually started his own trash-hauling service with just one truck, which he drove. In a few years, his Southern Sanitation Service was a 20-truck operation with routes in several major South Florida cities.

After starting and growing his own small business, Huizenga made his real money by buying out small businesses and aggregating them into progressively bigger conglomerates. He bought dozens of small garbage haulers and added them to his own company to create his first billion-dollar company, Waste Management. Under Huizenga's leadership, Waste Management was accused of everything from price fixing to violating environmental laws to making improper political contributions. Huizenga stepped down as vice chairman in 1984, and planned to retire. Instead, however, he began growing his fortune

by buying up "mom-and-pop" companies and consolidating them into larger entities.

At the time of the Marlins' expansion, Huizenga was best known for owning Blockbuster Video. Huizenga and other Waste Management executives had bought shares in the nascent enterprise in 1987. Once the original founder left the company, Huizenga's experience in consolidating small local businesses like those that comprised most of the video rental industry of the time really paid off.

During his ownership of the Marlins, Huizenga sold Blockbuster to Viacom for $8.4 billion and – again using his buy-small-and-consolidate model – created AutoNation, a Fortune 500 network of car dealerships. In 2017, Huizenga was ranked the 288th wealthiest American, with a net worth of $2.8 billion. He died on March 22, 2018, at the age of 80 in his Fort Lauderdale home.

Huizenga started building his front-office staff before the other owners had cast their final votes of approval. The first person Huizenga brought on board was Carl Barger as president. Formerly the president of the Pittsburgh Pirates and a longtime friend of Huizenga's, Barger was a member of the board of directors of Huizenga's Blockbuster Video.[6] Barger technically resigned from the Pirates on July 8, 1991. But while major-league rules barred one person from working for two clubs at once, Barger was allowed to begin staffing the front office of the Marlins while also running the Pirates until the owners selected a new president.

As it turned out, Barger would never see his new team play a single game. On December 9, 1992, during the annual Winter Meetings in Louisville, he collapsed from a ruptured abdominal aortic aneurysm. He was taken to a hospital in an ambulance but died before surgery could be performed. Barger's position remained vacant through the Marlins' first season.

Charlie Hough was the pitcher of record on Opening Day 1993, a 6-3 victory over the Los Angeles Dodgers. (Courtesy of the Miami Marlins)

Team President David Dombrowski (l.) on Opening Day 1993. Dombrowski remained-with the Marlins through 2001 before moving on to the Detroit Tigers and the BostonRed Sox. (Courtesy of the Miami Marlins)

Today, Carl F. Barger Boulevard sits just outside what is now Hard Rock stadium (formerly Joe Robbie Stadium, among other names), the first home of the Marlins.

The next move for the Marlins was to appoint a general manager In September of 1991, the Marlins hired Dave Dombrowski away from the Montreal Expos. Dombrowski in turn "lured virtually all the Expos' front-office executives to the expansion Marlins."[7] As Murray Chass of the *New York Times* put it:

Dombrowski was not bashful about raiding his former employer's cupboard. At last count, 12 other former Expo employees had migrated, including the scouting director, the assistant scouting director, the player development director, the senior consultant on player personnel, the special consultant to the vice president for player personnel, three scouts, three minor league coaches and a secretary.[8]

But one position that was not filled by a former Expo was manager. The job of managing an expansion team had never been easy. Out of 34 seasons coached by the 10 previous managers of major-league expansion teams, only three seasons, all from the same manager (Bill Rigney of the Angels), were winning seasons. For this daunting task, the Marlins chose Rene Lachemann. In 1992, when Lachemann was hired, he had not managed a baseball team for eight years. His last stop had been with the Milwaukee Brewers in 1984. And if expansion dilutes the talent level of the major-league player pool by promoting previously unqualified or unsuccessful players, the same could be said of the managerial pool. Despite being liked by his players, particularly in Seattle, Lachemann had only three winning records in 13 minor- and major-league seasons[9] – once in Class A, once in Double A, and once in Triple A, when his Spokane Indians were 11-9 in the Pacific Coast League before Lachemann was promoted

to manage the Seattle Mariners for the rest of the season. Lachemann never had a winning season with the Marlins, and his only managing job after that was one game as interim manager of the Chicago Cubs.

The Marlins even had a television broadcast team lined up before any players had been drafted. For play-by-play, they hired Jay Randolph. For analysis, they hired future-Hall of Fame catcher Gary Carter. Carter was an 11-time All-Star, with three Gold Gloves and five Silver Slugger Awards, who had also won the 1986 World Series with the Mets. Carter had spent most of his career, including his final season, with – no surprise – the Montreal Expos.

The next step for the new Marlins franchise was to stock its roster. To do this, the major leagues held an expansion draft. This draft was unique among expansion drafts; all major-league teams had been required by Commissioner Fay Vincent to make players available to the two new National League franchises, the Florida Marlins and the Colorado Rockies. (By the time of the draft, Vincent was a former commissioner.) Each team was allowed to protect 15 players before the draft started, and could lose up to three players in the draft. This also meant that it was the first time teams from both leagues split the expansion fees. Each new franchise paid a fee of $95 million to join, for a total of $190 million. Of this total, 22 percent ($42 million) went to the American League, $3 million per team. The remaining $148 million was divided among the National League teams, for $12.33 million each.

American League officials were understandably upset that they had to provide just as many players to the draft but received less than a quarter of the amount of the franchise fees that the National League teams received. Oakland Athletics general manager Sandy Alderson said that the American League teams would rather have received no money and not have to provide players, because three players were potentially more valuable than the $3 million.[10] Chicago White Sox owner Jerry Reinsdorf, one of the most vocal opponents of the plan, said the same. However, when asked if he would have taken $3 million for the three players the White Sox had actually lost in the 1976 expansion draft, when the Toronto Blue Jays and Seattle Mariners were added to the American League, he said he happily would.[11] Another American League owner who complained about the deal said that he would "be thrilled" to have gotten $3 million in exchange for the five players his club lost in the 1976 expansion draft.[12] Still, the owners knew there was nothing they could do but try to change Commissioner Vincent's mind. As a compromise to the American League owners, Vincent decided that all 12 National League teams would lose three players, and that only eight American League teams would lose three players, with the other six teams losing only two players. He also allowed each National League team to protect three additional players each time they lost a player to the draft, but allowed each American League team to protect four more players each time.

The day finally came on November 17, 1992. All current major-league teams had to deliver their list of 15 protected players by November 9. Both expansion teams focused on pitching and youth, particularly the Marlins. Of the Marlins' 36 draft picks, 21 were pitchers – the Rockies drafted 20. The Marlins' first pick was Nigel Wilson, a top young outfield prospect in the Blue Jays' system. Many in baseball were surprised that Toronto had left him unprotected. The average age of the Marlins' 13 first-round picks was 24.6, against 26.5 for the Rockies, and only two of the Marlins' picks had more than two years of major-league experience, compared with seven for the Rockies.

Several of the veterans the Marlins chose were used as trade bait. They drafted veterans Greg Hibbard and Bryan Harvey in the first round, and traded Hibbard to the Cubs for Gary Scott, a young but struggling third baseman, and shortstop Alex Arias. They also drafted veteran left-hander Danny Jackson from the Pirates, just to turn him around to the Phillies for two young pitchers, Joel Adamson and Matt Whisenant. Both of these deals had been all but made before the draft, and were contingent upon how the draft went. In another fascinating swap, the Marlins drafted Eric Helfand, a young catcher the Athletics had left unprotected, and traded him right back to Oakland for veteran shortstop Walt Weiss, whom the Athletics had protected.

By far the most notable player drafted by the Marlins was Jeff Conine, their 11th pick in the first round. Then 26, Conine would become the only player to play for both of the Marlins' World Series-winning teams. Conine was nicknamed "Mr. Marlin" for his role as both an inaugural member of, and two-time champion with, the team.

Now that the Marlins finally had players, they needed a place to play. That place was Joe Robbie Stadium, the home of the NFL's Miami Dolphins, named after their owner. After several failed attempts at getting a publicly financed stadium, Robbie used loan money to build the $115 million stadium, which opened in 1987. After Rob-

bie died in 1990, Huizenga bought 50 percent of the stadium for a reported $40 million from the Robbie family. Huizenga also bought 15 percent of the Dolphins.

In 1994 Huizenga purchased the other half of the stadium's ownership rights, and would continue to own the stadium (and the Dolphins), collecting rent, concessions money, and luxury and club-seat revenues until long after he sold the Marlins in 1998.

Major-league Opening Day finally came to Miami on April 5, 1993. Opening Day souvenirs were sold out an hour before game time. Clearly the excitement was there. The team honored its late president, Carl Barger, in a pregame ceremony. The first pitch was thrown out by 78-year-old Joe DiMaggio, who had lent his name to the Children's Hospital in neighboring Hollywood. The Marlins' Opening Day pitcher, 45-year-old knuckleballer Charlie Hough, joked that DiMaggio threw harder than he could. Despite fielding a team ESPN later described as "your usual array of expansion team washouts and hopefuls,"[13] the Marlins won the franchise's first game, 6-3, over the Dodgers. Hough outpitched Orel Hershiser, throwing to batterymate Benito Santiago, who had played for the minor-league Miami Marlins 10 years earlier as an 18-year-old. Mr. Marlin, Jeff Conine, went 4-for-4. The opening three-game series drew 126,575 spectators. Everything was off to a good start for the fans and the owner.

The rest of that first season ended the way most expansion seasons do. The Marlins finished next to last in the National League East (above the Mets), but avoided the 100-loss fate suffered by half of the previous expansion teams, ending the season at 64-98 (.395). Center fielder Chuck Carr led the National League with 58 stolen bases. Attendance remained strong that first season. A total of 3,064,847 attended home games, an average of 37,838, making the Marlins one of only seven major-league teams

Dodgers' manager Tommy Lasorda and Marlins' owner Wayne Huizenga. (Courtesy of the Miami Marlins)

to draw over 3 million fans in 1993.

In the first years after expansion, the Marlins seemed to have a clear plan: to draft and develop young players, with just enough veterans to help the development along. Of the 10 expansion teams between 1961 and 1991, the average team started out with a winning percentage of .365, building up to .491 by year eight. The Marlins were ahead of the curve, winning .395 of games the first year and .494 by year four. The process seemed to be working.

But the process was not working quickly enough for Huizenga. By 1997 he owned the Marlins, the Dolphins, and the NHL expansion Florida Panthers. The Panthers had lost the 1996 Stanley Cup finals to the Colorado Avalanche. After being so close, Huizenga wanted a championship. As the Marlins' steady improvement showed, they already had a promising young core, which included players like Edgar Renteria, Charles Johnson, Al Leiter, and Gary Sheffield.

However, in the offseason after the Panthers' runner-up finish, Huizenga and Dombrowski shocked the baseball world by spending a record-breaking $89 million on free agents. To the already promising core, the Marlins added pitcher Alex Fernandez, and boosted the offense with third baseman Bobby Bonilla and outfielder Moises Alou, who alone cost $25 million. They also added depth through a series of smaller but solid moves. The payroll for the 1996 season was $31 million, and by 1997 it was $52 million.

The spending spree paid off. The Marlins finished the 1996 season 80-82, almost reaching .500. They finished the 1997 season 92-70 – their first winning season. They went on to beat the Atlanta Braves in the NLCS and the Indians in the World Series.

The World Series championship was the peak before a deep valley for the Marlins under Huizenga. Championship in hand, he began the first Marlins fire sale, a process one writer dubbed "a textbook case in how to alienate a fan base."[14] The Marlins sold off big-money free agents from a year earlier – Bonilla, and Alou[15] – as well as some of its promising core, including Gary Sheffield and Robb Nen, who had both been with the Marlins since their first season. Fans and sportswriters across the country skewered Huizenga, some saying he was just throwing a "hissy fit"[16] over his failure to get a new taxpayer-funded, baseball-only ballpark.

Huizenga also complained that he was losing money. He said the Marlins had lost $34 million during the 1997 World Series season. While they may well have lost $34 million on paper, paper losses in professional sports – as with many large companies – are largely due to accounting practices. The former president of the Toronto Blue Jays, Paul Beeston, said, "Under current generally accepted accounting principles, I can turn a $4 million profit into a $2 million loss, and I can get every national accounting firm to agree with me."[17] Using a tax benefit known in the sports context as the roster depreciation allowance – whose benefits Huizenga had already exhausted – and other paper-only accounting maneuvers, teams often claimed large financial losses while also raking in huge profits.

And such claims of massive losses were nothing new in baseball. As former Players Association executive director Donald Fehr once told *Sports Illustrated*, "You go through *The Sporting News* for the last 100 years, and you will find two things are always true. You never have enough pitching, and nobody ever made money."[18]

Another thing that made Huizenga's claim more dubious was the way he structured the various entities he owned that were connected to the Marlins. Huizenga owned Joe Robbie Stadium – by now called Pro Player Stadium – and the team's cable broadcaster, Sportschannel Florida. Between owning these two entities and giving the Marlins favorable deals with them, Huizenga made about $40.1 million in revenue off the Marlins that were counted under those other entities instead of the Marlins.

Championship in hand and tax shelter exhausted, Huizenga tried to sell the Marlins. He may have been trying to sell the team as early as April 1997. If so, part of the impetus for the free-agent splash may have been the thought that a successful team would fetch a higher sale price. Whether the goal of Huizenga's spending spree was the personal goal of a winning a championship or the financial goal of making a higher profit by selling the team, what is certain is that, despite claiming that the team's finances were suffering, Huizenga almost sold the team to longtime business associate and then team President Don Smiley. Surely, if the finances were so bad, Smiley would have known, and would not have tried to buy the team for $169 million. Smiley's bid fell apart when his group of investors came up $50 million short of the sale price.

Huizenga eventually did sell the team, to another South Florida multimillionaire, John Henry. After long, contentious, and very public negotiations, Henry agreed to buy the team for $150 million and to pay $8 million for renovations at Pro Player (formerly Joe Robbie, in 2018 Hard Rock) Stadium. But Huizenga still owned the ballpark and the cable channel. He was able to negotiate a 10-year contract for his cable channel to broadcast the Marlins' games before selling the team, and by owning the ballpark he kept all the luxury-box and club-seat revenue, as well as a majority (62.5 percent) of the parking revenue and a portion (30 percent) of the concession profit from Marlins games. So even after selling the team, Huizenga continued to profit off the Marlins until at least 2012, when they moved to Marlins Park and changed their name to the Miami Marlins.

## Sources

In addition to the sources cited in the Notes, the author also consulted Baseball-Reference.com and the following:

"6 Cities Named Finalists for 2 NL Expansion Teams," *Wilmington* (North Carolina) *Morning Star,* December 18, 1990: C1.

"And Batting Second…," *Palm Beach Post*, January 24, 1994.

Berardino, Mike. "Lloyd's Balks at Marlins' Claim on Fernandez's Injury." *Sun-Sentinel.com*, April 26, 2001, available at articles.sun-sentinel.com/2001-04-26/sports/0104260199_1_marlins-alex-fernandez-fernandez-s-case.

Blum, Ronald. "Owners Approve Rockies, Marlins," *Kentucky New Era* (Hopkinsville, Kentucky), July 6, 1991: 1B.

Chass, Murray. "A Busy Day of Drafting and Dealing," *New York Times*, November 18, 1992.

Chass, Murray. "Baseball Destined to Grow, but Not Any Time Soon," *New York Times*, June 26, 1988.

Chass, Murray. "Barger Leaves Pirates," *New York Times*, July 9, 1991.

Chass, Murray. "Expansion Losers Turn to Unlikely Plan 2," *New York Times*, June 12, 1991.

Chass, Murray. "For the Rockies and Marlins: At Last, the Envelopes Please," *New York Times*, November 9, 1992.

Chass, Murray. "Lawsuit from Minors Seeks to Derail Marlin Expansion Draft," *New York Times*, October 20, 1992.

Chass, Murray. "Marlins Have Old Business to Finish," *New York Times,* October 29, 1992.

Chass, Murray. "No Party for Expansion Managers," *New York Times*, November 1, 1992.

Chass, Murray. "Vincent Splits Expansion Booty," *New York Times*, June 6, 1991.

Clarke, Norm. "Expansion Cities Play Hardball," *Chicago Tribune*, November 15, 1987. articles.chicagotribune.com/1987-11-15/sports/8703260355_1_antitrust-protection-major-league-baseball-antitrust-lawsuit.

Clary, Mike, Marcia Heroux Pounds, and Craig Davis. "H. Wayne Huizenga, South Florida Business Titan, Dead at 80," *South Florida Sun-Sentinel*, March 23, 2018. sun-sentinel.com/news/obituaries/fl-reg-h-wayne-huizenga-obituary-20180118-story.html.

"Dave Dombrowski," Baseball-Reference.com. baseball-reference.com/bullpen/Dave_Dombrowski#Record_as_a_General_Manager.

Donnelly, H. "High Stakes of Sports Economics," *Editorial Research Reports, 1988*. Washington, DC: CQ Press. library.cqpress.com/cqresearcher/document.php?id=cqresrre1988040800.

"Expansion of 1993 – BR Bullpen," Baseball-Reference.com. baseball-reference.com/bullpen/Expansion_of_1993.

"Fifteen U.S. Senators, Many Representing States Seeking Big-League Franchises…" UPI.com, November 3, 1987. upi.com/Archives/1987/11/03/Fifteen-US-senators-many-representing-states-seeking-big-league-franchises/8050562914000/.

Fisaro, Joe. "New Name, but Deep-Rooted Tradition in Miami," Marlins.mlb.com. web.archive.org/web/20141204133053/http://m.marlins.mlb.com/news/article/25948494/.

Hyde, Dave. "M's Would Be Great Consolation Prize." *Fort Lauderdale Sun-Sentinel*, republished in *The Spokesman-Review and Spokane Chronicle*, July 6, 1991: B2.

Keeney, Stephen. "The Roster Depreciation Allowance:

How Major League Baseball Teams Turn Profits Into Losses," *The Baseball Research Journal* 45, 1 (Spring 2016): 88-95.

Keri, Jonah. "Is Wayne Huizenga a Genius?" In Jonah Keri, ed., *Baseball Between the Numbers: Why Everything You Know About the Game is Wrong.* (New York: Basic Books (for Baseball Prospectus), 2006).

"Marlins to Rest Alex Fernandez." UPI.com., September 5, 1999. Available at upi.com/Archives/1999/09/05/Marlins-to-rest-Alex-Fernandez/6922936504000/ph.

Olney, Buster. "Marlins Lose Fernandez to Bad Shoulder Injury," *New York Times.* October 10, 1997.

Peterson, Iver. "Cities Spending Big for Shot at Baseball," *Lawrence* (Kansas) *Journal-World*, January 8, 1984, 4B.

Rader, Benjamin. "The Resurgence of America's Game," In *Baseball: A History of America's Game* (Champaign: University of Illinois Press, 2008).

"Rene Lachemann," Baseball-Reference.com. Available at baseball-reference.com/register/player.fcgi?id=lachem-001ren.

"Rene Lachemann – BR Bullpen," Baseball-Reference.com. Available at baseball-reference.com/bullpen/Rene_Lachemann.

Sandomir, Richard. "New Teams Need Players and Patience," *New York Times*, June 16, 1991.

Sandomir, Richard. "Wayne Huizenga's Growth Complex," *New York Times*, July 9, 1991.

Smith, Claire. "National League Expansion Vote Delayed," *New York Times*, June 6, 1991.

"Sold! John Henry Buys Marlins." CBS News.com. November 6, 1998. cbsnews.com/news/sold-john-henry-buys-marlins/.

Sullivan, Paul. "Huizenga's Big Splash Engulfs All of Baseball," *Chicago Tribune*, June 29, 1997. articles.chicagotribune.com/1997-06-29/sports/9706290424_1_florida-marlins-wayne-huizenga-million-by-financial-world.

"Transactions," *New York Times*, September 20, 1991.

Weingarden, Steve, and Bill Nowlin, eds., *Baseball's Business: The Winter Meetings, Volume 2 – 1956-2016* (Phoenix: Society for American Baseball Research, Inc., 2017).

Zimbalist, Andrew. "The Capitalist: A Miami Fish Story," *New York Times Magazine*, October 8, 1998.

**Notes**

1  Murray Chass, "The Marlins? The Rockies? Get Used to It. It's Official," *New York Times*, July 6, 1991.

2  Murray Chass, "Baseball Ready to Add Miami and Denver Teams," *New York Times*, June 11, 1991: A1.

3  The team then moved several times, changing names, cities, and league affiliations.

4  Different sources have put the number of spectators per game as 40 (Tim Golden, *supra*, Endnote 4) and 112 (Lloyd Johnson and Miles Wolff, *The Encyclopedia of Minor League Baseball*, 2nd Edition, Baseball America: April 1997).

5  Tim Golden, "Miami Still Has Heat and Rain, but Now It Has a Team," *New York Times*, June 11, 1991.

6  There was talk of a potential conflict of interest regarding Barger, largely because Pittsburgh's chairman, Douglas Danforth, was chairman of the National League Expansion Committee, which had made the decision to award the new franchises to Denver and Miami. See Murray Chass, "New Teams Expect Approval Today," *New York Times*, July 4, 1991.

7  Murray Chass, "Youthful Executive Rebuilding the Expos in Old-Fashioned Way," *New York Times,* March 4, 1992.

8  Ibid.

9  This count includes 12 seasons with one team only, and one season (1981) that was split between two teams, the Seattle Mariners and their Triple-A affiliate.

10  "Denver and Miami a Step Closer to Obtaining Expansion Teams," *New York Times*, June 13, 1991.

11  Murray Chass, "New Teams, Not Some Owners, May Be Getting the Raw Deal," *New York Times*, June 23, 1991."

12  Ibid.

13  David Schoenfield, "Marlins, Rockies Still Seeking Answers," ESPN.com, April 5, 2013. espn.com/blog/sweetspot/post/_/id/34431/marlins-rockies-still-seeking-answers.

14  Frank Jackson, "It Was Twenty Years Ago Today," *The Hardball Times*, Fangraphs.com, April 9, 2013. fangraphs.com/tht/it-was-20-years-ago-today/.

15  Alex Fernandez survived the fire sale, as he was injured in the 1997 NLCS, and was essentially untradeable. He missed the entire 1998 season. However, the Marlins did avoid paying most of Fernandez's 1998 salary. About 75 percent of it was covered by an insurance policy. See Buster Olney, "Marlins Lose Fernandez to Bad Shoulder Injury," *New York Times*, October 10, 1997, and Mike Berardino,

"Lloyd's Balks at Marlins' Claim on Fernandez's Injury," *Sun-Sentinel. com*, April 26, 2001, available at articles.sun-sentinel.com/2001-04-26/ sports/0104260199_1_marlins-alex-fernandez-fernandez-s-case.

16 Tom Verducci, "The Faux Classic," *Sports Illustrated*, October 27, 1997: 42.

17 Dan Alexander, "Can Houston Astros Really Be Losing Money Despite Rock-Bottom Payroll?" Forbes.com. August 29, 2013. forbes. com/sites/danalexander/2013/08/29/can-houston-astros-really-be-losing-money-despite-rock-bottom-payroll/.

18 Richard Hoffer, "The Bucks Stop Here," *Sports Illustrated*, July 29, 1991. si.com/vault/1991/07/29/124615/the-bucks-stop-here-spiral-ing-salaries-and-a-potential-loss-of-tv-loot-imperil-baseballs-prosperity.

## FLORIDA MARLINS EXPANSION DRAFT

PICK  PLAYER                    POSITION  FORMER TEAM

### ROUND 1

| 1  | Nigel Wilson      | of | Toronto Blue Jays     |
|----|-------------------|----|-----------------------|
| 2  | Jose Martinez     | p  | New York Mets         |
| 3  | Bret Barberie     | 2b | Montreal Expos        |
| 4  | Trevor Hoffman    | p  | Cincinnati Reds       |
| 5  | Pat Rapp          | p  | San Francisco Giants  |
| 6  | Greg Hibbard      | p  | Chicago White Sox     |
| 7  | Chuck Carr        | of | St. Louis Cardinals   |
| 8  | Darrell Whitmore  | of | Cleveland Indians     |
| 9  | Eric Helfand      | c  | Oakland A's           |
| 10 | Bryan Harvey      | p  | California Angels     |
| 11 | Jeff Conine       | 1b | Kansas City Royals    |
| 12 | Kip Yaughn        | p  | Baltimore Orioles     |
| 13 | Jesus Tavarez     | of | Seattle Mariners      |

### ROUND 2

| 14 | Carl Everett      | of | New York Yankees      |
|----|-------------------|----|-----------------------|
| 15 | David Weathers    | p  | Toronto Blue Jays     |
| 16 | John Johnstone    | p  | New York Mets         |
| 17 | Ramon Martinez    | ss | Pittsburgh Pirates    |
| 18 | Steve Decker      | c  | San Francisco Giants  |
| 19 | Cris Carpenter    | p  | St. Louis Cardinals   |
| 20 | Jack Armstrong    | p  | Cleveland Indians     |
| 21 | Scott Chiamparino | p  | Texas Rangers         |
| 22 | Tom Edens         | p  | Minnesota Twins       |
| 23 | Andres Berumen    | p  | Kansas City Royals    |
| 24 | Robert Person     | p  | Chicago White Sox     |
| 25 | Jim Corsi         | p  | Oakland A's           |
| 26 | Richie Lewis      | p  | Baltimore Orioles     |

### ROUND 3

| 27 | Brad Ausmus        | c  | New York Yankees      |
|----|--------------------|----|-----------------------|
| 28 | Marcus Moore       | p  | Toronto Blue Jays     |
| 29 | Armando Reynoso    | p  | Atlanta Braves        |
| 30 | Steve Reed         | p  | San Francisco Giants  |
| 31 | Mo Sanford         | p  | Cincinnati Reds       |
| 32 | Pedro Castellano   | ss | Chicago Cubs          |
| 33 | Curtis Leskanic    | p  | Minnesota Twins       |
| 34 | Scott Fredrickson  | p  | San Diego Padres      |
| 35 | Braulio Castillo   | of | Philadelphia Phillies |
| 36 | Denis Boucher      | p  | Cleveland Indians     |

# CHUCK CARR

## By Rory Costello

Entertaining and irritating by turns, outfielder Chuck Carr was known for his speed and cocky personality. Carr's running ability was what made him fun to watch. He made many circus catches and stole a lot of bases. That made him a fan favorite in Miami, where he enjoyed his best year in 1993 for the Florida Marlins, as the first-year expansion team was then known. "He was once the Marlins' first impression, their leadoff hitter, part cartoon and mostly character, the ego and image and swagger of a franchise that had little else."[1]

Carr went through four organizations, getting brief big-league trials with the New York Mets and St. Louis Cardinals before emerging in Florida. "Why did it take him a while to make it?" said Clint Hurdle, one of his minor-league managers with the Mets. "No. 1, he had to refine his baseball skills. And No. 2, it probably took him a while to refine his social skills, as far as maturing and taking responsibility. He's a free spirit, one with a high evaluation of himself."[2]

Carr played just 507 games in a major-league career that ended after spring training in 1998. The switch-hitter had little power, and as it had been during much of his minor-league career, getting on base enough to use his speed was a factor. Various reports also focused on perceptions of Carr's flamboyant antics. For example, he was named one of baseball's "top ten jerks" ahead of the 1996 season.[3]

Yet as much as "Chuckie" may have annoyed teammates, managers, and opponents, he was also likable. In particular, he was always fan-friendly. "It's out there that I have an attitude problem," the man himself acknowledged. "Then you hear fans say, 'He's a nice guy, he's down to earth.'"[4] Throughout his career, Carr was active in stay-in-school and antidrug programs aimed at children.[5] His desire to help others was also visible as he played ball off and on overseas and in independent leagues through 2003. He later became a minor-league coach.

Charles Lee Glenn Carr was born on August 10, 1967, in San Bernardino, California. His father, Charles Lee Carr, was an Air Force veteran who became a Baptist minister while also conducting vocational and rehabilitation work. The elder Carr was a fine athlete too, becoming a Junior Golden Gloves champion in boxing. Known as Charles Benson when younger, he had also hoped to make the Olympic track team in 1964 but tore a hamstring.[6]

Young Chuckie was a daredevil who enjoyed the sensation of flight. A 1994 feature on Carr described him as a 12-year-old, doing wheelies off the roof of his parents' house in Fontana, California. He also liked to jump off the same roof onto the diving board of the family's swimming pool. That article mentioned his mother's name, Charlene.[7] However, no other information is presently available about her or any other children in the Carr family.

Available articles about Carr also do not discuss any other sports he may have played, such as football, basketball, or track. He attended Fontana High School, where he was a year ahead of a future teammate with the Marlins, Greg Colbrunn. Fontana was known as a football school. "The football stadium holds 10,000. The baseball stadium holds a couple hundred," said the Steelers' baseball coach then, Steve Hernandez. "When it came to baseball, we didn't have a fancy operation. It was a rags-to-riches story. … When I got to the school the team had won something like two or three games the year before. But I inherited these two incredible athletes."

Hernandez added, "Carr thought he was a second baseman. As soon as I took over, I told him he was going to play center field. He told me I must be mistaken. I told him there was a new sheriff in town." Carr started working on the diving catches that became his trademark, and Hernandez said, "Once in a while I'd get the feeling that Chuck was waiting a second before he started for the ball so he'd have to make the spectacular catch. But I'll say this much, you haven't seen anything on ESPN that I didn't see in our little ball field."[8]

By Carr's senior year, 1986, Fontana was playing Esperanza High of Anaheim in Dodger Stadium for the championship of the California Interscholastic Federation's Southern Section, division 4-A.[9] Just a couple of days later, the Cincinnati Reds selected Carr in the ninth round of the amateur draft. The scout was former big-league reliever Ed Roebuck.

Carr's pro career got off to an uncertain start. In 44 games of rookie ball in the Gulf Coast League, he hit just .171 and the Cincinnati organization released him. By one report, it depressed the 18-year-old so much that he considered taking his own life.[10]

In 1987, however, Carr signed with the Seattle Mariners. Reporting to Bellingham of the Northwest League (short-season Class A), he did better with the bat: .242 with a homer and 11 RBIs in 44 games. Getting on base

more also enabled him to steal 20 bases. Carr's natural confidence had rebounded. Allegedly he told his teammate Ken Griffey Jr., then a first-year pro, to find a position other than center field.[11] Griffey was already a budding superstar, though; the M's experimented with Carr at shortstop and second base that season.

Carr also met his wife, Candace Gilbert, that summer on a road trip to Oregon. "We were staying at the same hotel," Candace (an Arizona native) remembered in 1993. "It was his first road trip, and he'd forgotten to bring underwear. I gave him a ride to the mall. I helped him buy his underwear, he bought me an ice-cream cone, and we`ve been together ever since."[12]

Carr lifted his steals total to 62 in 1988. He batted .299 and stole 41 bases in 52 attempts for Wausau of the Midwest League (Class A). That won him promotion to Vermont of the Eastern League (Double A), where he swiped 21 in 30 tries. He hit .281 overall with 7 homers and 43 RBIs. That August 18, he and Candace were married.[13]

The Mariners traded Carr to the Mets in November 1988 for Reggie Dobie, a pitcher then at Triple A who lasted just one more season in the pros. Carr spent all of 1989 in Double-A ball, posting a line of .241-0-22 in 116 games for Jackson in the Texas League. He stole 47 bases, tied for second in the league, but got caught 20 times.

Carr started 1990 with Jackson again. After batting .306 with six steals in 14 games, he got his feet wet in the majors that April. The Mets called him up to replace injured center fielder Keith Miller.[14] Carr pinch-hit in one game; he was returned to Jackson after the Mets acquired Daryl Boston and promoted Darren Reed.[15]

Carr made it up to Triple-A Tidewater that summer, and in August the Mets summoned him again after outfielder Mark Carreon got hurt.[16] The next day, Carr played in the field for the first time as a big leaguer. It was only for the last half-inning in a blowout loss. He appeared twice more in August and went back to Tidewater after the Mets acquired veteran Pat Tabler.[17]

Carr hit just .195-1-11 in 64 games for Tidewater in 1991, yet he still got some limited action with the Mets. He played in two games in June during a call-up that lasted less than a week. He returned in August when Vince Coleman reinjured a hamstring and landed on the disabled list for the second time that year. Carr appeared nine times and got his first base hit in the majors, a single off Pittsburgh's Bob Kipper, in a loss at Three Rivers Stadium.

Carr then went on the DL himself.[18] He wore the Mets uniform in one more game, on September 26. That November, New York sent him outright to Tidewater. The next month, they traded him to St. Louis for Clyde Keller, a pitcher who never got beyond the low minors and was finished after 1992. The Mets then had a very similar center fielder in their chain: Pat Howell, who also had blazing speed, made many dazzling outfield plays, but had an even harder time reaching base.

To start the 1992 season, Carr went back to Double-A ball. However, minor-league hitting instructor Johnny Lewis helped shorten his swing and he averaged .308 at Louisville after being promoted from Arkansas.[19] Between the two levels, he totaled 61 steals. When Ozzie Canseco injured a shoulder, St. Louis called Carr up. He hit .219 in 64 at-bats over 22 games. He also stole 10 more bases.

Reportedly, the Cardinals seriously considered protecting Carr from the expansion draft that November because of his speed.[20] That November, however, the Marlins selected him as the 14th pick. It was his big break.

Right around then, Chuck and Candace welcomed their first child, a boy named Sheldon. The blessings of parenthood were hard-won; Candace had had six miscarriages and a baby born prematurely who lived only a few days. "This was a great off-season," she said at the end of March 1993. "We had the baby, and then Chuck got his first major league chance."[21]

Scott Pose, a Rule 5 pickup, was Florida's starting center fielder and leadoff hitter to begin the 1993 season. By mid-April, however, Carr had taken both spots. In May, The Sporting News wrote, "Carr emerged as a genuine leadoff threat, stealing three bases twice in a game and 10 in April. Carr, who may be the fastest player in the league, is erratic in the outfield but gives the team its one disruptive force on the basepaths."[22]

Carr used his speed another way: He put 42 bunts in play that year, getting 17 base hits.[23] One notable example came on July 28 at Shea Stadium in New York. In the ninth inning of a 3-3 tie, acting on his own, he beat out a two-out drag bunt to bring in the go-ahead run.[24] Anthony Young stood to lose his 28th straight decision, but the Mets rallied for two in the bottom of the ninth against closer Bryan Harvey, finally snapping Young's record losing streak.

Carr led the National League in 1993 with 58 steals, although he got caught a league-high 22 times. In contrast to the earlier report, he was routinely making great catches. STATS Inc.'s Scouting Report for 1994 wrote, "With Andy Van Slyke out for half the season, Carr dominated the highlight shows; every other night, it seemed, he was making another spectacular diving catch."[25]

In September 1993, *Miami Herald* writer Dan Le Batard said, "Chuck Carr catches balls no one else touches." However, he quoted Van Slyke, who had won five straight Gold Gloves in the outfield, as predicting that Carr would not get one because the NL's coaches and managers wouldn't vote for a hot dog. While acknowledging Carr's range, Van Slyke said, "Coaches like guys who don't draw extra attention to themselves. Chuck gives them reasons not to vote for him. His whole package tends to offend." Darren Lewis (Van Slyke's pick) and Marquis Grissom (one of the eventual winners) were mentioned. Yet in Le Batard's view, while both were as worthy as Carr, neither was as wonderful. Marlins manager René Lachemann said flatly that Carr was the best center fielder he had ever had. "There is nobody who covers more ground than Chuck Carr," Lachemann said. "Nobody I've seen." [26]

Le Batard also observed, "Never mind that fans love Carr's flair, love the color he brings to a game that can be as black and white as its box scores. There is no one in the league who does what Carr does, no one who can make the home crowd rise on a ball the other team hits into the gap ... who plays with such reckless disregard for his health."[27] Around the same time, Carr won a "Your Favorite Marlin" contest conducted by the Fort Lauderdale Sun-Sentinel.[28]

After a contract holdout in the spring, Carr tempered his baserunning in 1994. He stole 32 bases in the strike-shortened season and got thrown out just eight times, but he had mixed feelings about it. That June, he said, "I feel like I'm learning and becoming a better ballplayer. At the same time, I kind of liked the old me, my wild style of play. I was real aggressive, real wild on the bases. I don't feel that wildness in me. It takes a little fun out of the game." That report also observed that the Marlins didn't like Carr's arrogance and independence, and that the team was likely to deal him as soon as Carl Everett was deemed ready.[29]

Carr's woofing, strutting, and taunting were the talk of the National League. Marlins first baseman Dave Magadan noted that when opposing players reached base, the "pedigree hot dog" was the primary topic of conversation. "They ask how we can stand being around that guy," said Magadan. "I just smile and shrug. Chuck's all right if you're playing on the same team. To the other team he's an irritant, because he's always jumping around, always has a big smile on his face, having fun at your expense."[30]

Whereas in 1993 Carr hit leadoff for all but two-at-bats, in 1994 René Lachemann used him in the number-two hole frequently and even dropped him down to eighth for several games. Carr's on-base percentage slipped from .327, already subpar, to .305. He wanted to be like Brett Butler, who also had little power yet was a consummate leadoff hitter (lifetime OBP .377). Butler was also a superior bunter, and shortly before the strike Carr noted that he'd been thinking about getting back to bunting more (though a later scouting report said he didn't do it particularly well).[31]

In the winter of 1994-95, the Marlins sent Carr to play in the Dominican Republic, challenging him to prove that he could be a good leadoff hitter – or plan to bat eighth in the order in 1995. Six games into the season, however, the Licey Tigres kicked Carr off the team after discovering that he had been banned for five years from playing in Latin American winter leagues. That stemmed from his decision to leave Hermosillo, in Mexico's Pacific League, in 1991.[32]

That same report noted that Carr sought permission from the players union to work with the Marlins' new hitting coach, José Morales. The potential job challenge from Carl Everett was mentioned again. In late November, however, Florida traded Everett to the Mets. Thus, Carr remained the team's primary center fielder in 1995. He played in 105 games, starting 77 and batting mainly in the number-two spot. Though his average slid to .227, he did draw more walks and got his on-base percentage up to a career-high .330. He stole 25 bases and was caught 11 times.

That November, the Marlins signed Devon White, a seven-time Gold Glover in center field, to a three-year contract worth $10 million. The Sporting News observed, "He not only gives them speed and defense in center, but also a legitimate bat that the enigmatic Chuck Carr could not provide in three seasons."[33] Florida also opted to keep Jesús Tavarez, a younger player who was out of options, as the backup center fielder.[34]

Soon thereafter, the long-awaited Carr trade finally took

place. Florida dealt him to the Milwaukee Brewers for a minor-league pitcher named Juan González. Brewers general manager Sal Bando said he wasn't worried about Carr's clubhouse reputation. "He rubs some people the wrong way, but fans love him and he plays hard. Do you want a bunch of nice guys that lose?"[35]

Carr started strongly for Milwaukee. He was "giving us an identity, a spark at the top of the lineup," said manager Phil Garner. "He got on and he made things happen and he was making great plays defensively."[36] However, Carr played just 27 games in 1996. First, he strained a hamstring in April and went on the 15-day disabled list. Then, on May 30, he tore up his right knee making a sensational catch on the warning track. He landed awkwardly and bent the knee backward. He underwent surgery to repair two major ligaments, a hamstring tendon that was ripped from the bone, and a deep bone bruise. "The only thing keeping the knee together was the skin," said Brewers trainer John Adam.[37]

The injury ended Carr's season, but his return after the gruesome blowout was remarkably swift. By October, he knew he'd be back because he could dunk a basketball.[38] He beat out Gerald Williams for the starting job in center field in 1997. But after getting just one hit in his first 16 at-bats, he was benched. Sal Bando later said that Carr's attitude became a distraction, and that the front office didn't think he looked the same as he had in 1996. According to Phil Garner, though Carr was playing the field with his usual abandon, the knee affected his swing from the left side.[39]

Carr started just six games from April 7 onward. His time in Milwaukee ended after one of those starts, on May 16. The story of his release has become a minor legend. As he led off the bottom of the eighth inning, the Brewers trailed the California Angels 4-1. Carr got the take sign with the count in his favor. Instead, he swung away and popped up. Garner, who'd already had a one-hour, closed-door talk with Carr that month, confronted him about it after the game. Carr's response (as reported in the press): "That ain't Chuckie's game. Chuckie hacks on 2 and 0!"[40]

"I swear to God, that's what he said," Garner remarked later that month. "The guy is always talking about himself in the third person, which often gets you one of those white jackets that ties in the back."[41]

However, Carr – whose average had dropped to .130 after that last hack – denied the quote. The following year, he said, "It was just time to leave. I wanted to get out of there. I still felt like I could be a spark somewhere. I could've kept my mouth shut and taken the money. That wasn't my role. I asked, can they release me." Indeed, the Brewers let him go after he refused an assignment to Triple A, forfeiting the rest of his $325,000 salary. "I had to put everything on the line," said Carr. "But I believed. I felt like there was a team out there that needed me."[42]

There was – at the beginning of June, he signed as a free agent with the Houston Astros. He played for a few weeks with Triple-A New Orleans, and then the Astros called him up. Carr got into 63 games over the remainder of the season, starting 48 of them, and hitting .276-4-17 while also playing his usual exciting style of center field. Early that August, he returned to Florida to play against the Marlins for the first time after they traded him. The fans received him warmly, and Carr also said that he'd grown up.

"I was still living that kid life when I was here," he remarked. "People wanted me to be an adult, but I wasn't ready for that. That's different now. Believe me, I'm not the same person I used to be." Nonetheless, he added, "I look back and don't have any regrets. None at all. I'm serious. People don't like the fact that I'm so positive. I have a lot of confidence and expect big things. That's just the way I am. I'll never change."[43]

Carr got his only taste of major-league postseason play in 1997. He appeared in two of three games in the National League Division Series and went 1-for-4 as Atlanta swept Houston. He started Game Three, hitting a solo homer off John Smoltz.

Although Carr had played reasonably well in Houston, he did not get a contract offer and was granted free agency on December 21. The very next day, the Astros obtained their new starting center fielder – Carl Everett. It was ironic because Everett's odd behavior made Carr's look mild.

Carr never played again in a regular-season big-league game. The Montreal Expos invited him to spring training in 1998 on a minor-league contract, but he did not win a job.[44] He then went to Taiwan, joining the Mercuries Tigers. In 36 games, he hit .308-3-12 and stole 15 bases.

That July, the Carrs' fourth child was born prematurely, and Chuck decided that he would rather be with his

family than continue playing in Taiwan. He told the story of the baby's fight for survival. "My oldest son, Sheldon, named him. He said, 'Mommy, let's call him Chance,' because all he had was a chance. It was iffy."[45] One of the two middle children was named Aeron; research has not turned up the name of the other.

Carr still wanted to keep his baseball dream alive, though, so in 1999 he joined the Atlantic City Surf of the independent Atlantic League. Eric Davis, an old friend from Southern California, told him to keep following his passion until someone came and snatched the uniform off his back. Carr also said that his kids were getting tired of having to share video games with him![46]

Carr hit .263-8-21 in 49 games for the Surf and was regarded as genial, self-effacing, and popular. The self-effacing part stood in contrast to the past, but late that season, he said, "Life is about making mistakes, correcting them and going on and learning."[47]

A different Atlantic League team, the Long Island Ducks, began operations in 2000. The team's manager and part-owner, Bud Harrelson, had been Carr's skipper with the Mets in 1990 and 1991. Carr became the first player to sign with the Ducks. He was there to help himself, saying, I really believe teams are going to see how much I've matured as a ballplayer and as a man." However, he also expressed a desire to mentor younger players, as veterans such as Garry Templeton and Hubie Brooks had helped him when he was breaking in.[48] Carr hit .253-10-48 with 28 steals in 73 games for the Ducks. It does not appear that he got any feelers about returning to the majors.

Carr was out of pro ball in 2001. He then went abroad again in 2002, joining Rimini of the Italian Baseball League.[49] Rimini won its fourth consecutive Serie A/1 pennant, and Carr played a key role as his team overtook Bologna, which led Rimini by two games with six to play. Rimini then swept a three-game series from Bologna, as Carr went 6-for-12 with two homers. Even though the teams finished with identical records, Rimini was awarded the pennant because its head-to-head record against Bologna was 4-2.[50]

Carr gave it a last shot in 2003 as a player-coach with the Bisbee-Douglas Copper Kings of another indie circuit, the Arizona-Mexico League. (The Carr family had made its residence in Mesa, Arizona.) "He's looking to get back into Organized Baseball as a running coach," said Bisbee-Douglas general manager John Guy. "He still thinks he can play."[51] Carr was the four-team league's biggest name. In 14 games, he hit .365-1-8. The Copper Kings and the Nogales Charros both ran out of money, though, and so the league folded in mid-June, just 16 games into its schedule.

Carr rejoined the Astros organization in 2004. He was a coach with one of Houston's farm teams, the Salem Avalanche (Carolina League, high Class A), from 2005-2007. Since then, he has been out of the public eye, although he does participate in private memorabilia signings. Nonetheless, his name still pops up now and again. In 2017, the *Miami New Times* ran a column called, "Twenty Ways to Tell if You're a True Miami Marlins Fan." Number 18 was "About every five seasons, you ask someone out of the blue: 'Hey, remember Chuck Carr?'"[52]

## Sources

*Online*

twbsball.dils.tku.edu.tw/wiki/ (Taiwanese baseball website).

## Notes

1 Jeff Miller, "Carr Still Drawing Crowds in Florida," *Fort Lauderdale Sun-Sentinel*, August 5, 1997.

2 Gordon Edes, "Carr Usually Flies in Steering Marlins," *Fort Lauderdale Sun-Sentinel*, April 3, 1994.

3 Steve Rushin, "Bad Behavior," *Sports Illustrated*, March 12, 1996. The others identified by a survey of baseball writers across the country were Albert Belle, Barry Bonds, Steve Howe, Kevin Brown, Lenny Dykstra, Will Clark, Eddie Murray, Danny Jackson, and Bip Roberts. See also "Belle, Bonds, Clark Make All-Jerk Team," *San Francisco Examiner*, March 9, 1996.

4 Mark Herrmann, "Ex-Met Carr to Become First to Sign with Ducks," *Newsday*, April 11, 2000.

5 "Brewers' Carr Is Going Full Speed Ahead," *Amarillo Globe-News*, March 11, 1997.

6 "Rehabilitation Service Opens Fontana Facilities," *San Bernardino County Sun*, April 28, 1974: 79. "Brewers' Carr Is Going Full Speed Ahead."

7 Edes, "Carr Usually Flies in Steering Marlins."

8 Geoff Calkins, "Carr, Colbrunn Revisit," *Fort Lauderdale Sun-Sentinel*, April 7, 1994.

9 Scott Howard-Cooper, "Southern Section Baseball Finals: Fontana Tries to Complete Improbable Finish Tonight," *Los Angeles Times*, May 31, 1986.

10 Herrmann, "Ex-Met Carr to Become First to Sign with Ducks."

11 Ibid.

12 John Hughes, "Years of Perseverance Pay Off in Big-league Debut for Parents," *Fort Lauderdale Sun-Sentinel*, March 31, 1993.

13 Trevor Jensen, "Carr's Wife Files for Support but Not Divorce," *Fort Lauderdale Sun-Sentinel*, April 7, 1994.

14 "Mets call up Carr, send [Jeff] Innis to minors," *White Plains* (New York) *Journal News*, April 26, 1990: 41.

15 "Transactions," *Decatur* (Illinois) *Herald and Review*, May 1, 1990, 14.

16 "Gooden's 10-1 Spurt: 'Right Now, I Stink,'" *The Sporting News*, September 3, 1990: 10.

17 "Mets Acquire Phillies' [Tom] Herr," *Asbury Park* (New Jersey) *Press*, September 1, 1990: 42.

18 "Transactions," *Port Huron* (Michigan) *Times Herald*, August 30, 1991: 14.

19 Rick Hummel, "St. Louis Cardinals," *The Sporting News*, September 28, 1992: 22.

20 Ibid.

21 Hughes, "Years of Perseverance Pay Off in Big-league Debut for Parents."

22 Gordon Edes, "Carr Gets Used to Leading Role," *The Sporting News*, May 10, 1993: 18.

23 "Opposite Attractions," *Palm Beach Post*, April 3, 1994. John Dewan and Don Zminda, editors, *The Scouting Report, 1994* (New York: HarperCollins Publishing), 450.

24 Ed Giuliotti, "Marlins Help Mets End Young's Slide," *Orlando Sentinel*, July 29, 1993: D3

25 Dewan and Zminda, *The Scouting Report, 1994*; Gordon Edes, "Florida Marlins: Analyzing 1993," *The Sporting News*, October 11, 1993: 16.

26 Dan Le Batard, "Marlins' Carr Is Gold Glove – with Flair," *Miami Herald*, September 5, 1993. It was not until 2011 that the Gold Gloves for outfielders again specified awards for left fielder, center fielder, and right fielder. From 1961 through 2010, three outfielders were selected irrespective of their specific position (see "Gold Glove History" at Rawlings.com). As it turned out, the 1993 NL Gold Glove outfielders actually did play separate positions: Grissom (CF), Barry Bonds (LF), and Larry Walker (RF).

27 Ibid.

28 Gordon Edes, "Smooth-Running Carr," *The Sporting News*, September 6, 1993: 20.

29  Amy Niedzielka, "[Jeff] Conine Cookin'," *The Sporting News*, June 20, 1994: 21.

30  Larry Guest, "Carr's Confidence Rises with Batting Average," *Orlando Sentinel*, June 12, 1994.

31  Dave Hyde, "To Avert Nightmare, Carr Better Wake Up," *Fort Lauderdale Sun-Sentinel*, July 31, 1994. Gary Gillette, Stuart Shea, and Pete Palmer, editors, *The Scouting Report: 1996* (New York: HarperCollins Publishing, 1996), 417.

32  Amy Niedzielka, "Carr Suspended," *The Sporting News*, November 21, 1994: 40.

33  Scott Tolley, "Devon Intervention," *The Sporting News*, December 4, 1995: 47.

34  Scott Tolley, "Carr Out, [Joe] Orsulak In," *The Sporting News*, December 18, 1995: 44.

35  Drew Olson, "Fast, New Carr," *The Sporting News*, December 18, 1995: 48.

36  "Indians 2, Brewers 0," United Press International archives, May 30, 1996.

37  "Brewers' Carr Is Going Full Speed Ahead."

38  Cheryl Rosenberg, "Carr Proved Doctors Wrong," *Palm Beach Post*, August 5, 1997: 29.

39  "Carr Refuses Triple-A, Gets Released," *South Florida Sun-Sentinel* (Fort Lauderdale), May 22, 1997.

40  Ibid.

41  "Carr Swerves Out of Job," *St. Louis Post-Dispatch*, May 28, 1997: 17.

42  Rosenberg, "Carr Proved Doctors Wrong." "Carr Refuses Triple-A, Gets Released."

43  Miller, "Carr Still Drawing Crowds in Florida."

44  "Transactions," *New York Times*, February 4 and March 31, 1998.

45  Mark Herrmann, "It's Looking Ducky," *Newsday*, April 22, 2000.

46  Mark Herrmann, "Ex-Met Carr to Become First to Sign with Ducks."

47  Ibid.

48  Herrmann, ""It's Looking Ducky."

49  Harvey Sahker, "Some Familiar Names," *Baseball America*, May 14, 2002.

50  Harvey Sahker, "Rimini Continues Dominance," *Baseball America*, September 27, 2002.

51  Ken Brazzle, "Arizona-Mexico League," *Tucson Citizen*, May 6, 2003.

52  Ryan Yousefi, "Twenty Ways to Tell if You're a True Miami Marlins Fan," *Miami New Times*, June 16, 2017.

# JEFF CONINE

## By Adam Foldes

All across the world, when it comes to moments in baseball there are various scenes that play out in the minds of boys and girls. Most will think of hitting a home run to win the World Series *a la* Bill Mazeroski off Ralph Terry or Joe Carter off Mitch Williams or even Warren Morris off Robbie Morrison. However, for a select few that moment in the World Series or on a grander scale in the playoffs can come on the defense, which would end the game and the Series itself.

On October 4, 2003, Jeff Conine lived that singular baseball dream. The 2003 season looked like another lost season for the Florida Marlins. On May 10, with a record of 16-22, they fired manager Jeff Torborg and hired 72-year-old baseball lifer Jack McKeon to be the manager.[1] After a six-game losing streak ended on May 23, the Marlins went an incredible 72-42 to finish 20 games over .500 at 91-71. Two moves the Marlins made helped them toward this magical season. The first was the acquisition on July 11 of Texas closer Ugueth Urbina to solidify the bullpen;[2] the second acquisition was Jeff Conine. His was something of an under-the-radar acquisition necessitated by an injury to starting third baseman Mike Lowell. It brought back one of the original Marlins and the starting first baseman of the 1997 World Champion team.

On October 4, 2003, in Game Four of the National League Division Series, Marlins manager McKeon put his faith in his closer Urbina to close out the game against the 100-win San Francisco Giants, after the Marlins had put together a two-out rally in the bottom of the eighth to take a 7-5 lead. A win would give them the series and they would advance to the National League Championship Series.

The Giants' Jeffrey Hammonds stepped to the plate with base runners on first and second and two outs. At this point the Pro Player Stadium crowd of 65,464 had cheered for over three hours and had their hearts in their throat as they had seen their team already blow a 5-1 lead and faced the prospect of having their team lose the game and then be forced to go back to San Francisco for a deciding Game Five.

On the first pitch of the at-bat, Hammond hit a blooper into left field, where Jeff Conine fielded the ball cleanly and in one motion threw home to try to cut down J.T. Snow at the plate. Conine's throw was up the left-field line but two factors were working in his favor. One was that Snow was not known as a particularly fast runner. And his catcher on the play was Ivan Rodriguez, who had won 10 consecutive Gold Gloves, arguably the premier defensive catcher in baseball. Rodriguez caught the ball and braced for impact as Snow, the son of Notre Dame All-American and longtime Los Angeles Rams wide receiver Jack Snow, was barreling down on him. In one motion Rodriguez tagged Snow with his glove and in the subsequent collision was able to hold onto the ball. The Marlins won the game (which was later voted as number 19 on a list of the 20 greatest games in major-league baseball playoff history[3]), then beat the Cubs in a memorable series in its own right, and then moved on to win the World Series over the New York Yankees in six games.

Jeffery Guy Conine was born on June 27, 1966, in Tacoma, Washington, to Pam and Gerald Guy Conine. Gerald was a trade-show installer, who had been a two-way football lineman for three years and a wrestler at Washington State.[4] After graduating from college, Jerry Conine qualified for the US team in the men's light heavyweight division in the 1964 Tokyo Olympics, where he placed sixth.[5] After finishing his wrestling career, Jerry Conine took up handball and by 1976 had placed second for the US handball championship, and competed in handball championships well into his 60s.[6]

Jeff Conine's brother Jerry was also a two-sport standout at Washington State in both wresting and football.[7] Jeff first showed a talent not in baseball but racquetball, and if not for racquetball he might have never gained the body and reflexes to play professional baseball.

When Jeff was 13 years old he was 5-feet-2 and weighed 190 pounds; as he would later say, "I wasn't chubby I was fat."[8] To get in shape, Jeff took up racquetball, and by July of 1980, he had lost 25 pounds and grown 6 inches. However, during this transformation, Conine had a severe health scare when he was diagnosed with a condition known as chondramalatia, also called runner's knee, which occurs when the undersurface of the patella deteriorates and softens.[9] Rehabilitating from this injury by playing racquetball, Conine became an expert at the angles, to the point where two years later, he was playing in open tournaments and beating players who had been playing racquetball for years.[10]

Conine was also a standout baseball player at Dwight D. Eisenhower High School in Rialto, California. His baseball prowess saw him recruited as a pitcher at the University of California Los Angeles. While at UCLA, Conine played baseball and racquetball. In 1985 as a sophomore,

he won the US Junior National Championships, and received a spot on the US National Racquetball Team.[11]

Conine had a difficult time adjusting to college baseball; in his first three seasons (1985-1987) he had an earned-run average of 6.06, and as his first pitching coach at UCLA, Guy Hansen, said, "he had limited potential & in fact probably had the straightest fastball that I had ever seen."[12] In the only at-bat Conine had at UCLA, he was hit by a pitch. However, Hansen recognized Conine's athleticism. He not only played racquetball, but also played beach volleyball and during batting practice Conine would hit long home runs out of Jackie Robinson Stadium. Hansen left UCLA for a scouting position with the Kansas City Royals and persuaded the Royals to draft Conine. The Royals selected Conine in the 58th round of the June 1987 draft – as a first baseman.

Another life-altering event happened in December that year. While playing in a professional racquetball tournament, he met a fellow competitor, Cindy Doyle. In October of 1993 they were married.[13]

During his first five years in professional baseball Conine not only played first base, but also third base and the outfield, a position that would later serve him well in the majors.

In 1988 and 1989, Conine played for the Royals' Class-A Florida State League team in Baseball City (Davenport, Florida), where in 1988 he hit .272 with 10 home runs, 59 RBIs, and 26 stolen bases, and a year later hit 14 homers and had 32 stolen bases. In 1990 he was advanced to the Double-A Memphis Chicks (Southern League), where he hit .320/15/95 with 21 stolen bases. Conine had established himself as the top prospect in the Royals organization. He earned a September call-up to the Royals and debuted on September 16, 1990, collecting his first base hit the next day. In nine games he hit .250.

In 1991, Conine spent the whole season with Triple-A Omaha, where in an injury-shortened year (he twice needed surgery on his left wrist), he played in 51 games and batted .257. Healthy again in 1992, Conine had a bounce-back season, hitting .302 with 20 home runs. He was called up to Kansas City in early August and batted .253 in 28 games.

After the 1992 season an expansion draft was held for the National League's Florida Marlins and Colorado Rockies. As Conine was effectively blocked as a first baseman by future Hall of Famer George Brett and former All-Star Wally Joyner, the Royals left him unprotected in the draft, With the 22nd pick of the first round he was chosen by the Florida Marlins.

In Florida, Conine switched from first base to left field to accommodate the arrival of slugger Orestes Destrade, a home-run slugger for the Seibu Lions of the Japanese Pacific League.[14] Conine etched himself in the minds of South Florida fans when in the Marlins inaugural game he went 4-for-4 against the Los Angeles Dodgers and helped lead his team to a 6-3 victory. (Before the game, ESPN sportscaster Chris Berman bestowed on Conine the nickname "Jeff Conine the Barbarian" – a play on the Arnold Schwarzenegger movie *Conan the Barbarian.*)

During the 1993 season Conine was the only Marlin to play all 162 games, and – with Gary Sheffield – one of the team's first stars. Conine hit .292 with 128 homers and 79 RBIs. He finished third in National League Rookie of the Year balloting behind Mike Piazza of the Dodgers and Greg McMichael of the Atlanta Braves.

After the season Jeff and Cindy were married, and as part of their honeymoon they competed in the 1993 mixed doubles of the US Racquetball Championships. During the tournament the Conines, unseeded, upset the second-seeded team en route to the semifinals, where they lost a close match.

Over the next three years, Conine was one of the constants on the Marlins, improving on his 1993 campaign by playing in all 115 games of the strike-shortened 1994 season and hitting .319 with 18 home runs and 82 runs batted in. In 1995 he hit .302 with 25 homers and 105 RBIs, and in 1996 he hit .293/26/95.

During the early years of the Marlins, Conine and Gary Sheffield were the most recognizable stars of the Marlins. In 1994 and 1995 Conine was a National League All-Star. In the 1995 All-Star Game, he created one of the first big moments in Marlins history. Pinch-hitting for Reds outfielder Ron Gant, he hit the game-winning home run off Oakland A's pitcher Steve Ontiveros. Conine was named the game's MVP.[15]

On December 21, 1995, Cindy gave birth to their daughter Sierra.[16]

In 1996 Marlins owner Wayne Huizenga issued an edict to team management: He wanted to the Marlins to start

winning. The Marlins had tried the free-agent route in 1995 with little success as the signings of Andre Dawson, John Burkett, Terry Pendleton, and Bobby Witt did not work out. However, before the 1996 season the Marlins signed two pitchers and an outfielder who would be keys to the team's immediate future: Devon White, Al Leiter, and Kevin Brown.

In 1996, in the middle of an 80-82 season, the Marlins fired the team's inaugural manager, Rene Lachemann, and replaced him with interim manager John Boles. This move set the wheels in motion for what would be the first great team in Marlins history. After the season the Marlins hired former Pittsburgh Pirates manager Jim Leyland. They also acquired a number of high-priced players with the singular goal of winning the World Series. Those players acquired included Bobby Bonilla, John Cangelosi, Jim Eisenreich, Alex Fernandez, and Moises Alou.

Alou had been an All-Star left fielder with the Montreal Expos. He took over left field for the 1997 Marlins, with Eisenreich as his backup, and Conine was moved to first base to replace Greg Colbrunn. Conine hit only .242/17/61. The Marlins finished the season 92-70, good enough to capture the National League wild card. They beat the Giants in the Division Series and the Braves in the NLCS. Conine hit .364 and .111 respectively. During the Marlins' World Series triumph over the Cleveland Indians, Conine played in six of the seven games and batted .231. Throughout the postseason, he was without a home run and drove in only three runs. One of them, however, was the game-winner in the 2-1 Game Five NLCS victory over the Braves.

On June 11, 1997, Cindy gave birth to a son, Griffin Riley Conine.[17]

After the Marlins' thrilling 1997 World Series win, club owner Wayne Huizenga, claiming financial losses, ordered the team dismantled. General manager Dave Dombrowski was to trade all of the high-priced players. Conine was not immune to this "fire sale" and the Marlins traded "Mr. Marlin" to the team that originally drafted him, the Royals, for minor-league pitcher Blaine Mull. At the time of the trade Conine was the Marlins franchise leader in games played, hits, and runs batted in.[18]

In 1998, Conine suffered through an injury-plagued year for the Royals and played in only 93 games, batting .256 with 8 home runs and 43 RBIs. After the season he was on the move again, traded from the Royals to the Baltimore Orioles for pitcher Chris Fussell.[19] In his first year with Baltimore, he enjoyed a bounce back season, batting .291 with 13 home runs and 75 RBIs, and followed up with three more fine offensive seasons.

On July 31, 2000, Cindy gave birth to a second son, Tucker.[20]

In 2003, the Marlins, under new owner Jeffrey Loria, were in the hunt for a wild-card spot. On August 31, the Marlins acquired Conine from the Orioles for pitchers Don Levinski and Denny Bautista.[21]

Over the last month of the season, Conine played in 25 games and took over in left field for Miguel Cabrera, who moved to third base for the injured Mike Lowell. Conine batted .238 with 5 home runs and had 15 runs batted in. He had key hits and RBIs in the Division Series, the Championship Series, and the World Series, in which the Marlins topped the New York Yankees in six games.[22]

Conine was a solid, steady offensive force for the Marlins in 2004 and 2005. But after the latter season, the Marlins began yet another market correction and traded their veteran free agents or let them sign with other teams. They traded Carlos Delgado, Paul Lo Duca, Josh Beckett, Mike Lowell, and Juan Pierre, and let A.J. Burnett and the 39-year-old Jeff Conine leave in free agency.

Over the last two years of his career Conine played for four teams. In 2006, at the age of 40, he played in 142 games, the first 114 with the Baltimore Orioles, batting .265, then after a trade, for the Philadelphia Phillies, for whom he hit .280 in 28 games.[23] After the season the Phillies signed Jayson Werth and traded Conine to the Cincinnati Reds. The Reds hoped he could provide veteran leadership as a backup first baseman. The Reds struggled, and after playing in 80 games, on August 20, the Reds traded Conine to the New York Mets for two minor leaguers. It was the second consecutive year and the third time in his career that Conine was traded after the nonwaiver trade deadline.[24] Conine played sporadically for the Mets, who lost the NL East crown to the Phillies on the last day of the season.

After the season, Conine was a free agent but remained unsigned. On March 28, 2008, he signed a one-day contract with the Marlins. With that he ended his playing career. Conine became a special assistant to Marlins President Dave Samson. In that capacity he traveled to Cuba, Japan, and elsewhere on behalf of the Marlins. Conine

spent time on Fox Sports Florida, filling in for Tommy Hutton along with Rich Waltz on the Marlins' television broadcasts in 2008. In 2016 he was a TV color commentator along with Eduardo Perez, Al Leiter, and Preston Wilson, alongside Rich Waltz.[25] From 2015 to 2017 he also helped host the Marlins pregame show with Carl Pavano, Preston Wilson, and Craig Minervini.

During the 2015 amateur draft, the Marlins drafted Conine's son Griffin in the 31st round out of the Pine Crest School in Weston, Florida. Griffin chose not to sign and accepted a baseball scholarship to Duke University, where he was tabbed as one of baseball's hottest prospects.[26] Daughter Sierra excelled in lacrosse at Pine Crest and Tucker in track and field at St. Thomas Aquinas.[27]

Outside of baseball, Conine began training to enter triathlons and in 2008 became the first major league player to compete in the Ironman World Championships in Kona, Hawaii.[28] In training for this Ironman competition, Conine competed in the St. Anthony Triathlon in St. Petersburg, Florida, and the Ford Ironman at Walt Disney World.[29] In 2014, Conine, his 18-year-old daughter, Sierra, and his friend Sean Swarner climbed Mount Kilimanjaro, the highest mountain in Africa.[30]

In 2017 Jeffrey Loria sold the Marlins to a group led by Bruce Sherman and Derek Jeter, and it appeared that Conine's long association with the Marlins might be over. The new ownership initially fired Conine and the other Marlins special assistants. In a sudden reversal the owners offered Conine a different job within the organization, with a pay cut and a lesser role. Conine rejected the offer.[31]

# Time For Expansion Baseball

## Notes

1  United Press International, "Marlins Replace Torberg *(sic)* with McKeon," May 11, 2003. upi.com/Marlins-replace-Torberg-with-McKeon/26451052696791/.

2  assets.espn.go.com/mlb/news/2003/0711/1579625.html, Associated Press, July 11, 2003; updated July 12, 2003.

3  mlb.com/video/20-greatest-games-19/c-13084227.

4  Joe Strauss, "Conine's Father Quite a Hitter, Too," *Baltimore Sun*, June 26, 1999. articles.baltimoresun.com/1999-06-26/sports/9906260064_1_jeff-conine-handball-racquetball.

5  sports-reference.com/olympics/athletes/co/gerald-conine-1.html.

6  Strauss.

7  sports-reference.com/olympics/athletes/co/jerry-conine-1.html.

8  Strauss.

9  "Runners' Knee – Chondromalatia Patellae" physiobook.com/disease/orthopedic-and-sports-injuries/runners-knee-chondromalatia-patellae.html.

10  Strauss.

11  Tom Verducci, "Jeff and Cindy Conine," *Sports Illustrated*, November 1, 1993. si.com/vault/1993/11/01/129726/jeff-and-cindy-conine.

12  Ibid.

13  Ibid.

14  Gordon Edes and Ed Giulotti, "Translating Success/Baseball Players Such as Orestes Destrade Rekindle Careers in Japan . But Not All Can Keep the Fire Going in the U.S." *Sun Sentinel* (Fort Lauderdale, Florida), March 17, 1993. articles.sun-sentinel.com/1993-03-17/sports/9301310189_1_orestes-destrade-japanese-teams-marlins.

15  baseball-reference.com/allstar/1995-allstar-game.shtml.

16  imdb.com/name/nm1246331/bio.

17  goduke.com/ViewArticle.dbml?ATCLID=210614961&DB_OEM_ID=4200.

18  "Marlins Unload Conine on Royals for Mull," *Buffalo News,* November 20, 1997. buffalonews.com/1997/11/20/marlins-unload-conine-on-royals-for-mull/.

19  Associated Press, "Baseball: Spring Training – Baltimore; Hoiles Dumped for Conine," *New York Times,* April 3, 1999. nytimes.com/1999/04/03/sports/baseball-spring-training-baltimore-hoiles-dumped-for-conine.html.

20  Joe Strauss, "O's Conine Acquires Proper Prospective," *Baltimore Sun,* March 19, 2001. articles.baltimoresun.com/2001-03-19/sports/0103190098_1_jeff-conine-cindy-fort-lauderdale.

21  CBC Sports, "Conine Traded Back to Marlins," September 1, 2003. cbc.ca/sports/baseball/conine-traded-back-to-marlins-1.389157.

22  baseball-reference.com/players/c/coninje01.shtml#all_batting_postseason.

23  "Phillies Get Conine from Orioles," *Lewiston* (Maine) *Sun Journal,* August 28, 2006; sunjournal.com/phillies-get-conine-orioles/.

24  Associated Press, "Conine Traded to Mets," August 21, 2007. tbo.com/sports/conine-traded-to-mets-168600.

25  Barry Jackson, "Fox Drops Marlins TV Play-by-Play Man Rich Waltz, Two Former Marlins," *Miami Herald,* November 22, 2017. miamiherald.com/sports/spt-columns-blogs/barry-jackson/article186032833.html.

26  "Griffin Conine #9 Outfielder"; goduke.com/ViewArticle.dbml?ATCLID=210614961.

27  Walter Villa, "Mr. Marlin's Son Was Not Recruited Locally. But Now He Projects as a First Round Pick," *Miami Herald.* March 15, 2018.

28  Pete Williams, "Starting his Retirement with a Splash," *New York Times,* April 23, 2008. nytimes.com/2008/04/23/sports/othersports/23conine.html?_r=1&sq=triathlon&st=nyt&oref=slogin&scp=4&pagewanted=print.

29  Brentley Romine, "Jeff Conine Goes from Major League Baseball to Triathlon Circuit," *Orlando Sentinel,* May 22, 2008. articles.orlandosentinel.com/2008-05-22/sports/adv-lead22_1_conine-ironman-world-championship-triathlon.

30  Juan C. Rodriguez, "Miami Marlins: Ironman Jeff Conine Now a Mountain Man as Well," *South Florida Sun Sentinel* (Fort Lauderdale, July 19, 2014. articles.sun-sentinel.com/2014-07-19/sports/sfl-marlins-jeff-conine-mountain-blog-20140719_1_mountain-man-mount-kilimanjaro-cancer-patients.

31  Barry Jackson and Clark Spencer, "Derek Jeter Offered Mr. Marlin Less Pay and a Diminished Role. He Said No Thanks," *Miami Herald,* October 26, 2017. miamiherald.com/sports/spt-columns-blogs/barry-jackson/article181131891.html.

# TREVOR HOFFMAN

## By Max Mannis

From 1993 through 2010, Trevor Hoffman recorded 601 career saves. That was briefly a major-league record until Mariano Rivera surpassed him in 2011. Heading into the 2016 season, nobody else had as many as 500 – or will get there soon.

It was enough to get Hoffman into the Hall of Fame in 2018, when he received more than 79 percent of the baseball writers' votes in this third year on the ballot.

There is something to be said for such a reliable closer. Hoffman converted nearly 89 percent of his saves over the course of his 18-year career, ranking third out of the 50 closers with the most saves, behind only Rivera and Joe Nathan.

Moreover, Hoffman's life story is truly an inspiring one. Trevor William Hoffman was born on October 13, 1967 in Bellflower, California. As an infant of only six weeks, he had to have a kidney removed because of an arterial blockage. Because of this, Hoffman was unable to partic-

ipate in certain sports that he was interested in as a kid, like wrestling and football. Now, Hoffman does a lot of charity work to help kids with similar kidney diseases. In 2005, these efforts were a big factor in winning the Hutch Award, presented annually to the baseball player best displaying "honor, courage and dedication to baseball both on and off the field."[1]

From the limited athletic options left available to him, Hoffman decided to try baseball. He was introduced to the game early by his father. In addition to working at the post office, Ed Hoffman was an usher at California Angels games, and he would often bring young Trevor along to see the team play. Trevor's mother, Mikki, was a ballerina. She and Ed met in her homeland, England. Ed was originally a singer, and he continued to pursue his musical career for some years until he decided to quit traveling and stay with his family. At Anaheim Stadium, he became known as "The Singing Usher" – he performed the national anthem before games on various occasions.[2]

Trevor was the third of three children in the family, all boys. The oldest was named Greg; middle brother Glenn was an infielder in the major leagues for nine seasons (1980-87; 1989). Glenn also managed the Los Angeles Dodgers for much of 1998 and has since been a coach for that team (1999-2005) and the club for which Trevor starred, the San Diego Padres (2006-15).

In 1986, Trevor Hoffman graduated from Savanna High

School in Anaheim, a 20-minute drive from Bellflower. He played shortstop, since his father had banned him from pitching for fear of injury to his arm. He was not offered a scholarship after high school, and so he went first to junior college – Cypress College, a short distance west of Anaheim. Undersized as a schoolboy, Hoffman eventually grew to 6-feet-1 and 200 pounds.

Hoffman went on to attend the University of Arizona, where he excelled as a shortstop. He played with future major leaguers J.T. Snow and Scott Erickson, along with future coach Kevin Long. Hoffman led the team with a .371 batting average in 1988, and showed off his strong throwing arm at short.

Upon his graduation from Arizona, he was drafted by the Cincinnati Reds in the 11th round (the 289th pick overall). He signed with the team for $3,000, a rather low amount, especially considering that he went on to be such a great player. Two years later, after watching him play shortstop for the Reds in the minors, team scout Jeff Barton told Hoffman that he felt that he could excel more as a pitcher than as a position player. Barton explained to Hoffman that while he was a relatively weak professional hitter, his ability to throw 95 miles per hour would guarantee him at least a part-time job as a pitcher with a major-league team. "He had the best arm I'd ever seen," Barton recalled more than 25 years later. "When you see someone with those kinds of tools, you don't go by them. Those are the tools that impact the game."[3]

Hoffman spent two years in the minors as a pitcher, developing his off-speed and breaking pitches. His fastball came easier to him because he had such a strong throwing arm. It was during these two years that Hoffman began to develop his changeup, his top pitch for years to come.

In August 1992, while he was pitching for Nashville (Class AAA), Hoffman first met Tracy Burke, the woman who would become his wife. She was a real estate agent who was also a cheerleader for the Buffalo Bills of the NFL. In the November after that season ended, the Florida Marlins picked up Hoffman through the expansion draft with their fourth pick (eighth overall).[4] A couple of months later, in January 1993, Hoffman proposed marriage to Tracy on the field of the Rose Bowl during Super Bowl XXVII.[5]

Hoffman finally reached his dream on April 6, 1993, when he made his major league debut with Florida. He kept the game close, striking out Eric Davis with the bas-es loaded to end the top of the ninth, but the Marlins could not score in their half of the inning and lost, 4-2. A big early moment in his career came eight days later at Candlestick Park in San Francisco. Pitching in the eighth inning as a setup man, Hoffman faced the very dangerous Barry Bonds. Bonds, pinch-hitting because he had a pulled hamstring, represented the tying run at the plate. Hoffman fooled Bonds and retired him on a little trickler to first base.

"I knew I needed to go right at him," Hoffman said. Marlins teammate Jeff Conine added, "The guy doesn't get intimated by anyone. . .he's going to be a great closer someday because he's got that mentality. He's not going to pick around. . .you could see what he was going to do just by his facial expression."[6]

In the middle of that season, Hoffman was traded to the Padres for slugger Gary Sheffield. This was part of San Diego's "Fire Sale" in which they traded many of their top players, such as Sheffield, for young talent. Fans disapproved of the trade, and Hoffman was booed during his first few appearances with the club. In his San Diego debut the day after he was acquired,[7] he gave up three runs in one inning; he allowed eight runs over his first three innings, covering three appearances. He also blew his first save opportunity of the season soon after, and he finished the season with only five saves and a 3.90 ERA.

In his first full season with San Diego, Hoffman began to show his true potential, recording 20 saves. He then began to prove himself as one of the top closers in the majors, recording 31 saves in 1995 and 42 in 1996. For all but one of the next 14 seasons, Hoffman recorded at least 30 saves. The exception was 2003, when he missed much of the season recovering from shoulder surgery.[8]

Hoffman lost his superior fastball after hurting his shoulder while playing football and volleyball during the 1994 strike. He needed surgery on his rotator cuff after the 1995 season.[9] Thus, he refined his changeup and used it to dominate hitters throughout his career. His changeup was his specialty pitch – he claims he started practicing with it as an eight-year old playing Wiffle ball in his backyard.[10] It became truly effective, though, after Padres teammate Donnie Elliott showed him a different grip.

After the bullpen doors opened, Hoffman was almost unstoppable. Intimidating hitters with his big windup, high kick, and long stare, he established himself as one of baseball's toughest pitchers to face, both physically and mentally. Starting on July 25, 1998, with AC/DC's "Hell's Bells" blasting through the PA system, Hoffman's entry gained an ominous extra dimension.

Hoffman had the opportunity to play in only one World Series during his career, in 1998, when his Padres played the powerhouse Yankees. The Yankees had 112 wins in the regular season that year, making them the heavy favorites. Hoffman was highly efficient that year, converting 41 straight saves over the course of 1997 to 1998.[11] Unfortunately for San Diego, the Yankees swept them easily. Hoffman's lone appearance in the series came in Game Three, during which he surrendered a go-ahead three-run home run to eventual World Series MVP Scott Brosius in the eighth inning. Despite the disappointing result, this World Series was one of Hoffman's most memorable experiences.

Since batting artist Tony Gwynn played on the Padres with him for many seasons, Hoffman was often overshadowed and considered the second-best player on the team despite how much he contributed to the team's success. When Gwynn retired following the 2001 season, Hoffman became the undisputed centerpiece of the franchise. He made the All-Star team again and broke Dennis Eckersley's record for most saves with one team.[12] *Sports Illustrated* even issued a May article titled: "The Secret of San Diego: Why Trevor Hoffman of the Padres is the best closer (ever)." Although he was not the main face of the Padres for much of his career, Hoffman still collected some prestigious awards. A seven-time All-Star, Hoffman led the National League in saves in 1998 and 2006. In addition, he captured the NL Rolaids Relief Man of the Year in both of these years, as well.

Following the 2003 season, Hoffman was a free agent for the first time. He had lengthy conversations with the Cleveland Indians, but even though Cleveland offered him more money,[13] Hoffman eventually ended up re-signing with the Padres.[14] San Diego's general manager at the time, Kevin Towers, said of the new deal: "This is probably the most significant signing that I've had. This guy is the face of our organization. I can't put into words what he means to our community."

In 2004, Hoffman passed Jeff Reardon and Eckersley on the all-time saves list, securing the #3 spot. In May of 2005, Hoffman became just the third pitcher to record 400 saves, alongside John Franco (424) and Lee Smith (478).[15] Hoffman took home the NL Pitcher of the Month and Delivery Man of the Month awards for his performance.

Partially due to Hoffman's success, the Padres went 22-6 that month, the best in franchise history. Hoffman finished that year 43 for 46 in save opportunities, the second-most saves in the National League. Unfortunately for the Padres, despite a successful 2005 season that brought them to the NLDS, they ended up being swept by the St. Louis Cardinals.

2006 was another eventful year for Hoffman. To start with, his brother Glenn joined the Padres as third-base coach. Trevor made the All-Star team, but he was the losing pitcher in the game. Perhaps rattled, two of Hoffman's five blown saves that year came in the week after his subpar performance in the All-Star Game. However, he recovered and later that year would pass Smith for the most saves in major-league history. In August of that same year, he appeared in his 776th game as a reliever for San Diego, breaking Elroy Face's record for most appearances by a reliever with one club. Face accomplished the feat with the Pittsburgh Pirates.

Hoffman helped the Padres clinch the NL West for the second straight season, recording his eighth career 40-save season along the way. However, the Padres again lost to St. Louis in the NLDS. Nonetheless, Hoffman was awarded The Sporting News NL Reliever of the Year for the third time in his career, and he finished as the runner-up for the Cy Young Award for the second time in his career (the other time was 1998).

In 2007, Hoffman continued to add to his already impressive collection of records and awards, but one blown save at the end of the year is what is sadly remembered from that year. In an April win over the Dodgers, Hoffman earned the save in his 803rd game pitched for the Padres, breaking the major-league record for games pitched for one team. The record was previously held by Walter Johnson of the Washington Senators and Face (it has also since been surpassed by Mariano Rivera). In June, Hoffman recorded his 500th career save, helping him to make the All-Star team again.[16] On September 8, Hoffman struck out the Colorado Rockies' Todd Helton for his 1,000th career strikeout, which was notable considering that Hoffman had only pitched 917 innings at the time.

Unfortunately for San Diego, Hoffman struggled toward the end of the year. One strike away from getting San Diego to the playoffs for the third straight year, Hoffman gave up a game-tying, two-out triple in the ninth inning to Tony Gwynn, Jr. of the Milwaukee Brewers – the son of his longtime teammate. The Padres went on to lose in the

11th inning, 4-3. Hoffman finished the year converting 42 of 49 save opportunities.

This left the Padres tied with Colorado for the NL wild-card spot. They played a one-game tiebreaker to decide who would get the final playoff spot. Hoffman blew his second consecutive save opportunity, an 8-6 lead in the 13th inning, ending on a controversial play at the plate. Matt Holliday tagged up for Colorado to score the winning run on a sacrifice fly, but to this day, it is extremely difficult to tell whether Holliday was out or safe. In the end, the only part that matters is that Holliday was called safe, putting a devastating end to San Diego's season. It was incredibly difficult for Hoffman to move past this huge blown save.[17]

Hoffman recorded 30 saves in 2008, his last season as a Padre. Unfortunately, despite Hoffman's continued excellence, the Padres struggled greatly that year. They won only 63 games, even though they were considered finally ready to be the clear top team in their division. Following that season, Hoffman – by then aged 41 – signed with the Milwaukee Brewers.[18] San Diego was in the process of rebuilding and saving money at the same time. However, it was still a surprising move; many had thought that Hoffman wanted to finish his career in San Diego.[19] Hoffman looked at the signing as a fresh start and a chance to prove that he belonged on a major-league team despite his age.[20]

Hoffman missed the first month of the 2009 season with a strained rib cage, which led to a brief injury-rehab assignment in the minors. He recovered well in May, as he was named NL Pitcher of the Month and MLB Delivery Man of the Month, recording 11 saves in 12 scoreless appearances. He made his seventh and last All-Star appearance that same year, filling in as a late replacement for the injured Jonathan Broxton of the Los Angeles Dodgers.

2010 was Hoffman's final year in the majors. Milwaukee re-signed him to a one-year deal with a mutual option for 2011.[21] After a rocky start, however, he lost his closer role to John Axford. He still got occasional chances to close, though – and on September 7, 2010, Hoffman recorded his 600th career save,[22] becoming the first major-leaguer to achieve this milestone.[23] He retired following that season,[24] after Milwaukee turned down his second-year option.[25] Hoffman felt that he could still pitch at the major league level, but with all the available closer spots filled, he was not interested in being a setup man. He retired with a 61-75 record, 601 saves, a 2.87 ERA, and 1,133 strikeouts.

Following his retirement, Hoffman joined the Padres' front office as a special assistant.[26] He also worked on both the pregame and postgame TV shows for Fox Sports San Diego. On August 21, 2011, his number 51 was retired by the team.[27] He was the ninth inductee into the Padres Hall of Fame.[28] He, his wife Tracy, and his sons Quinn, Wyatt, and Brody were all in attendance.

The Padres continued to value Hoffman, appointing him Upper Level Pitching Coordinator in September 2013.[29] He became a senior advisor for baseball operations in February 2015.[30]

Trevor Hoffman's career was filled with awards and recognition – and in 2018, he received the ultimate recognition when he was elected to the Hall of Fame.

"It's hard to describe the emotions that flood you right away," he said after receiving the call. "I know it's a very standard line, but so many things go through you. You think of your earl days in the game, you think of parts of your career, you understand what you put in on a daily basis. To be sitting there at this stage, seven years after you retire, it just comes full circle. It's kind of the cherry on top of a sundae."[31]

**Sources**

In addition to the sources cited in the Notes, the author also consulted Baseball-Reference.com and a number of articles including:

"Padres announce plans to retire Hoffman's No. 51," *Sports Illustrated* (online edition), June 16, 2011, http://www.si.com, accessed January 2, 2016.

Center, Bill. "The Ace of Saves: Padres' Hoffman Becomes No.1 Closer of All Time," *San Diego Union-Tribune*, September 26, 2006.

Center, Bill. "Hoffman joins alumni in Padres front office," SignOnSanDiego.com, January 12, 2011, http://www.sandiegouniontribune.com/news/2011/jan/12/hoffman-joins-alumni-padres-front-office/, accessed January 2, 2016.

Center, Bill. "Trevor Hoffman adds coaching duties," UTSanDiego.com, September 12, 2013, http://www.sandiegouniontribune.com/news/2013/sep/12/padres-mlb-trevor-hoffman-coaching/, accessed January 2, 2016.

Haudricourt, Tom. "Selig reflects on Hoffman's career," *Milwaukee Journal Sentinel,* January 12, 2011.

Lin, Dennis. "Now full-time, Hoffman tackles new job," *UTSanDiego.com,* February 15, 2014, http://www.sandiegouniontribune.com/news/2014/feb/15/trevor-hoffman-padres-upper-level-pitching-spring/, accessed January 2, 2016.

Olney, Buster. "Trevor Hoffman's dive into history," *espn. go.com,* September 8, 2010, http://espn.go.com/blog/buster-olney/insider/post?id=1227, accessed December 29, 2015.

**Notes**

1  Associated Press, "Hoffman helps kids with kidney problems," June 20, 2005.

2  Chris Foster, "His Father Was a Save Artist Too," *Los Angeles Times*, July 14, 1996.

3  C. T. Rosecrans, "Longtime Reds Scout, Cross-Checker Jeff Barton Dead at 50," Cincinnati Enquirer, November 13, 2015. https://www.cincinnati.com/story/sports/mlb/reds/2015/11/13/longtime-reds-scout-jeff-barton-dead-50/75701346/

4  "Marlins Surprise Hoffman," *Sarasota Herald-Tribune*, November 18, 1992: 5C.

5  Tom Cushman, "Deep in the Heart Hoffman," *San Diego Magazine*, November 11, 2006.

6  S.L. Price, "Reliever Hoffman has batters feeling the heat," *The News* (Boca Raton, Florida), April 16, 1993: 3B.

7  *Pepsi Max Field of Dreams Game Program*, Cooperstown, New York: Pepsi Corporation, 2013, Print.

8  Associated Press, "Padres' Hoffman to have Shoulder Surgery," Miami Herald online edition, http://www.miami.com/mld/miamiherald/sports/baseball/5259774, February 25, 2003, accessed December 29, 2015.

9  Buster Olney, "Change Artist," *ESPN the Magazine*, September 11, 2006.

10  Bill Center, "One Pitch Wound Up Changing Baseball History," *San Diego Union-Tribune*, http://www.sandiegouniontribune.com/uniontrib/20060926/news_lz1x26pitch.html, September 26, 2006, accessed February 16, 2016.

11  "Alou ends Hoffman's save streak at 41," *USA Today*, July 27, 1998, Print.

12  Bill Center, "No. 321 is Vintage Hoffman," *The San Diego Union-Tribune*, May 2, 2002, http://www.uniontrib.com/sports/padres/20020502-9999_1s2padres.html, accessed December 29, 2015.

13  Tom Krasovic, "Hoffman takes San Diego discount to remain a Padre," SignOnSanDiego.com, November 5, 2003, http://legacy.utsandiego.com/sports/padres/20031105-1703-trevorsigns.html , accessed December 30, 2015.

14  Chuck Crow, "All-time saves leader was almost an Indian," *The Plain Dealer*, September 12, 2010.

15  Jayson Stark, "Arizona not the apple of Vasquez's eye," espn.go.com, May 27, 2005, http://proxy.espn.go.com/espn/print?id=2068831&type=story, accessed December 30, 2015.

16  Associated Press, "Padres' Hoffman secures place in history with 500th save," espn.go.com, June 7, 2007, http://espn.go.com/mlb/recap?gameId=270606125, accessed December 30, 2015.

17  Bill Center, "No relief for Hoffman: 'It still hurts,'" UTSanDiego.com, January 25, 2008, http://legacy.utsandiego.com/uniontrib/20080125/news_1s25hoffman.html, accessed December 30, 2015.

18  "Sources: Hoffman, Brewers have deal," espn.go.com, January 8, 2009, http://espn.go.com/espn/print?id=3818472, accessed December 30, 2015.

19  Tim Sullivan, "Club and closer still need each other, but can they mend the fences?", UTSanDiego.com, December 11, 2008, http://www.sandiegouniontribune.com/news/2008/dec/11/1s11sullivan215146-club-closer-still-need-each-oth/, accessed February 16, 2016.

20  Jack Curry, "Hoffman Savoring Fresh Start With Brewers," NYTimes.com, May 28, 2009, http://www.nytimes.com/2009/05/29/sports/baseball/29hoffman.html, accessed February 16, 2016

21  Buster Olney, "Hoffman to re-sign with Brewers," espn.go.com, October 5, 2009, http://espn.go.com/espn/print?id=4533333, Accessed December 30, 2015.

22  Tom Haudricourt, "Hoffman hits 600 save mark as Brewers win," Milwaukee Journal Sentinel, September 8, 2010.

23  Adam McCalvy, "Call the Hall: Hoffman gets 600th save," MLB.com, September 8, 2010, http://m.mlb.com/news/article/14424616/, accessed December 29, 2015.

24  Associated Press, "Trevor Hoffman's option declined," espn.go.com, November 2, 2010, http://espn.go.com/espn/print?id=5757290, accessed January 2, 2016.

25  Bill Center, "Hoffman retires, will wear 'different hats' for the Padres," SignOnSanDiego.com, January 11, 2011, http://www.sandiegouniontribune.com/news/2011/jan/11/hoffman-retires-will-join-padres-front-office/, accessed January 2, 2016.

26  Matt Snyder, "Trevor Hoffman takes position with Padres' front office," CBSSports.com, September 12, 2013, http://www.cbssports.com/mlb/eye-on-baseball/23613251/trevor-hoffman-takes-position-with-padres-front-office, accessed January 2, 2016.

27  Tim Sullivan, "Grand gesture is prime Trevor Time for good reason," SignOnSanDiego.com, August 21, 2011, http://www.sandiegouniontribune.com/news/2011/aug/21/grand-gesture-prime-trevor-time-good-reason/, accessed January 2, 2016.

28   Dennis Lin, "Hoffman inducted into Padres Hall of Fame," UTSanDiego.com, August 30, 2014, http://www.sandiegouniontri-bune.com/news/2014/aug/30/trevor-hoffman-inducted-padres-hall-of-fame-petco/, accessed January 2, 2016.

29   "Padres appoint Trevor Hoffman as Upper Level Pitching Coordinator," MLB.com, September 12, 2013.

30   Dennis Lin, "Trevor Hoffman's new title," *San Diego Union-Tribune*, February 22, 2015.

31   A. J. Cassavel, "Hall's Bells: Cooperstown Rings for Hofmann," MLB.com, January 24, 2018. https://www.mlb.com/news/trevor-hoffman-elected-to-hall-of-fame/c-265259268.

# MAKING THE VALLEY MAJOR LEAGUE: AN OWNERSHIP HISTORY OF THE ARIZONA DIAMONDBACKS

## By Clayton Trutor

In the 21 years since major-league baseball granted an expansion bid to Arizona Baseball, Inc., the Arizona Diamondbacks franchise has been characterized by the stability of its leadership. The franchise has had two managing general partners, the term it uses for its chief executive officer: Jerry Colangelo (1995-2004) and Ken Kendrick (2004-). The actual ownership of the club has been far more divided. Dozens of investors backed Phoenix Suns executive Jerry Colangelo's original ownership group, Arizona Baseball, Inc., in 1995. Ken Kendrick leads a four-man ownership group that also includes Jeffrey Royer, Michael Chipman, and Dale Jensen, all of whom have owned at least a portion of the club since its inception.

In contrast, the Diamondbacks' on-the-field performance has been consistently inconsistent ever since those heady early years. The team was a near-immediate contender for a world championship. Despite the Diamondbacks' more recent struggles in the standings, the steadiness of its leadership transformed the franchise into one of the National League's most respected almost immediately.

### Metropolitan Phoenix's Path to the Major Leagues

The arrival of major-league baseball in metropolitan Phoenix in 1998 was preceded by a half-century of close ties between the Valley of the Sun, as Phoenix and 9,200-square-mile Maricopa County are widely known, and the big leagues. The Arizona State University baseball program has been a national collegiate power since

the mid-1960s. As of 2016 the Sun Devils have won five NCAA championships, appeared in 22 College World Series, and produced numerous major-league stars, including Reggie Jackson, Barry Bonds, Dustin Pedroia, and Bob Horner. Since 1992, metropolitan Phoenix has hosted the six-team Arizona Fall League, which provides outstanding minor-league prospects with the opportunity to play in a highly competitive atmosphere once their Double-A and Triple-A seasons have concluded.

Metropolitan Phoenix's most significant historical connection to the majors has been as the primary host of the Cactus League. Arizona has been home to major-league spring training since the immediate aftermath of World War II. In 1947, the Cleveland Indians began taking up preseason residence 120 miles southeast of Phoenix in

Construction workers level the playing surface at Bank One Ballpark in the fall of 1997, months before the Arizona Diamondbacks began their inaugural season in 1998. (Photo courtesy of Joel Zolondek)

# Time For Expansion Baseball

Tucson, the winter home of the club's new owner, Bill Veeck. Veeck persuaded New York Giants owner Horace Stoneham to join the Indians in Arizona. Stoneham placed his club's spring-training camp in Phoenix. In 1952 the Chicago Cubs, who had previously trained on owner Phil Wrigley's Catalina Island (California) estate, began training in Mesa, just to the east of Phoenix. The arrival of the Cubs and the off-and-on presence of other clubs helped to formalize the existence of the Cactus League, the Grand Canyon State's spring-training counterpart to Florida's Grapefruit League.[1]

Throughout the 1960s and 1970s, the Cactus League remained a small yet stable operation, growing slowly to an eight-team league as major-league baseball expanded rapidly from 16 to 26 teams. Several of the Midwestern clubs in the Cactus League, particularly the Cubs, turned their spring-training homes into popular winter tourist destinations for their fan bases as well as homes away from home for seasonal residents or permanent transplants to Arizona.[2]

In 1989 the eight-team Cactus League was in danger of losing one of its founding members. The Cleveland Indians announced plans to move their spring-training headquarters from Tucson to Homestead, Florida. The impending departure, which threatened the existence of the Cactus League, provoked immediate action from local political leaders, including US Senator John McCain, Governor Rose Mofford, and Maricopa County Supervisor Jim Bruner, who later played a major role in the arrival of the Diamondbacks in Arizona. In 1990 the Arizona Legislature passed legislation that created a Maricopa County stadium district governed by the county Board of Supervisors. The measure authorized the county to collect a $2.50 car-rental tax. The revenue from the tax helped revitalize existing spring-training facilities and build several new complexes, including one for the Indians, who chose to stay in Arizona, moving to the Phoenix suburb of Goodyear in 1993. Four of the publicly financed facilities created by the legislation are each shared by two major-league clubs, including the Indians' facility in Goodyear, which they share with the Cincinnati Reds. Arizona's significant public investment in spring-training baseball helped lure a number of franchises to the Cactus League. As of 2016, 15 of the 30 major-league teams belonged to the geographically compact (every team but one is in Maricopa County) and virtually rainout-free Cactus League.[3]

The Maricopa County Stadium Authority, which was created to save the Cactus League, played a similarly decisive role several years later in the arrival of the Diamondbacks by providing the region with a public institution capable of financing a ballpark costing several hundred million dollars.

## Making Phoenix Major League (1985-1995)

The first concerted civic effort to secure a major-league franchise began as metropolitan Phoenix, with almost 2 million residents, became the nation's 14th largest metropolitan area in the late 1980s. Martin Stone, the owner of the Phoenix Firebirds, the San Francisco Giants Triple-A affiliate, was the driving force behind the push. Beginning in the mid-1980s, he sought either an expansion team or a relocated franchise.

It was no secret that Bill Bidwill, owner of the NFL's St. Louis Cardinals, intended to move to Phoenix. Stone persuaded Bidwill to join him in building a stadium in the downtown area. In April 1987 the city agreed to secure $150 million in bonding to build a 70,000-seat domed stadium on a 66-acre parcel of land in the southern section of downtown Phoenix. The stadium was to serve as the springboard to a $500 million downtown redevelopment plan that would include public and private investments in commercial and retail space, hotels, and housing. To pay off the construction bonds, Stone or any other prospective tenant agreed to turn over to the city the proceeds from the sale of 212 luxury skyboxes and 10,800 club seats. All of these plans would be executed once a major professional sports franchise signed a lease to play in the stadium.[4]

In January 1988 Bidwill won approval from the NFL to move his franchise to Arizona. But instead of becoming a tenant of Stone and the city in the planned domed stadium, Bidwill signed a long-term lease with Arizona State University to play the Cardinals' games at the football-only Sun Devil Stadium in Tempe, just east of Phoenix. That brought Stone's plans for a domed stadium to an end. In May 1988 Stone backed out of his deal with Phoenix, arguing that he could no longer negotiate the terms of a stadium lease from a position of strength as he had neither a franchise in hand nor another tenant with whom to share the burden of selling premium seats to the public.[5]

Without Stone's backing for the deal, stadium plans languished. In October 1989, nearly 60 percent of Phoenix voters rejected a ballot initiative that would have allowed the issuance of $100 million of the previously authorized bonds for a domed ballpark. Big-league insiders had made it clear to Arizona leaders that public support for a stadium was a prerequisite for serious consideration for a franchise. After the initiative failed, the Legislature passed a law allowing the city to bypass a referendum in their push for big-league baseball. The Legislature also authorized the county Board of Supervisors to impose a 0.25 percent sales tax to help finance construction of a baseball stadium if one of the county's municipalities was awarded a franchise.[6]

Stone continued to pursue a major-league team for Phoenix into the early 1990s. Then in 1991, he abandoned his Arizona plans to become a partner in what turned out to be an unsuccessful effort to purchase the Montreal Expos. (There was little indication that Stone pursued a stake in the Expos to move the franchise. Montreal was less than a two-hour drive from his home in Lake Placid, New York.) Stone's decision to withdraw his Arizona bid brought a de-facto end to Phoenix's chances to get a team during that expansion cycle, when franchises were awarded to Denver and Miami.[7]

While Martin Stone spent a half-decade in single-minded pursuit of big-league baseball for the Phoenix area, the bid that actually brought a major-league team to Arizona came together more serendipitously. In early 1993, Maricopa County Supervisor and longtime baseball supporter Jim Bruner began discussing the idea of putting together a bid for a forthcoming new round of expansion with a friend, Phoenix sports attorney Joe Garagiola Jr., the son of the baseball personality, player, and commentator. Later in 1993, Bruner and Garagiola set up a meeting with Phoenix Suns owner Jerry Colangelo, one of the region's most popular public figures and fervent boosters, to discuss their idea.

Colangelo's Suns had engendered unprecedented enthusiasm in the region for professional sports with an exciting run to the NBA playoff finals that year. Bruner and Garagiola persuaded Colangelo to spearhead the effort to bring in a baseball team. Taking on this role required Colangelo to manage a $125 million fundraising drive to pay the anticipated franchise fee for the 1994 expansion. Moreover, Colangelo took on the responsibility of negotiating a public financing deal for a downtown baseball stadium.

Several years earlier, the Suns owner had experienced this process while seeking public funds in support of a new

venue for the Suns. Colangelo later said that taking the lead in the baseball expansion effort fulfilled his desire to play a more prominent role in increasing the national profile of the Valley of the Sun. He was also playing a central role in negotiating the deal that led to the relocation of the National Hockey League's Winnipeg Jets to Phoenix's America West Arena, where they were rechristened the Phoenix Coyotes in 1996.[8]

Colangelo's rags-to-riches story was well known to Arizonans with even a passing knowledge of professional sports. Born the son of Italian immigrants in a hardscrabble section of Chicago Heights, Illinois, Colangelo Colangelo made use of his athletic and intellectual abilities as well as his unparalleled work ethic to become a great success. A high-school basketball star, Colangelo gained an athletic scholarship to the University of Illinois, where he captained the basketball team and earned All Big-Ten status. After graduating in 1962 he eventually found work with the NBA's Chicago Bulls and rose quickly through front-office positions. By the time he left the Bulls six years later, Colangelo was the franchise's director of marketing and its chief scout.

In 1968, the expansion Phoenix Suns basketball franchise hired the 29-year-old Colangelo as their first general manager, making him the youngest in major professional sports. Colangelo transformed the Suns into one of professional basketball's best managed and most consistently successful franchises. During his 35 years as a Suns executive, the team was a fixture in the Western Conference playoffs and played to large, boisterous crowds, first at the Arizona Veterans Memorial Coliseum on the State Fairgrounds and then at the downtown America West Arena. Despite never winning the championship, Colangelo earned numerous NBA Executive of the Year Awards,

Arizona Diamondbacks owner Jerry Colangelo, right, is interviewed by broadcaster Thom Brennaman before the MLB expansion draft on November 18, 1997, at the Phoenix Civic Center in Phoenix, Arizona. (Photo courtesy of Joel Zolondek)

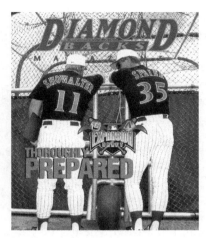

Cover of the Arizona Diamondbacks expansion draft program on November 18, 1998. (Photo courtesy of Joel Zolondek)

acknowledging both his franchise's success and his status as a mover and shaker in league circles.[9]

In 1987 Colangelo headed a 10-member limited partnership called JDM Partners LLC that purchased the Suns for $44.5 million. The move came soon after a drug scandal that threatened the franchise's squeaky-clean image. Colangelo cleaned house quickly and soon restored the Suns to on-court success; they put together a franchise-record streak of seven consecutive 50-win seasons between 1988-1989 and 1994-1995. Colangelo also negotiated a financing deal for a new arena to be built primarily with private money raised through JDM's limited partners and corporate sponsorship deals. America West Arena, the Suns' new downtown home, opened in June 1992. Bearing the name of a Phoenix-based airline, it was one of the earliest examples of stadium naming rights being sold to a corporation.[10]

In September 1993 Colangelo announced the formation of Arizona Baseball Inc., whose purpose was to bring a major-league baseball team to Phoenix. Colangelo's insider status made Arizona's bid an immediate frontrunner in the expansion chase. As an NBA executive, he ran in similar circles with major-league baseball executives. More than just a known commodity, Colangelo had the added advantage of being close personal friends with Chicago White Sox and Chicago Bulls owner Jerry Reinsdorf, who actively championed Arizona's bid. More than two dozen limited partners bought into Arizona Baseball Inc., including executives at Bank of America, Circle K, and Phoenix radio station KTAR, trucking magnate and future Phoenix Coyotes owner Jerry Moyes, comedian Billy Crystal, and Phoenix Suns All-Star Danny Manning.[11]

Colangelo set to work negotiating a financing deal for a downtown ballpark. His opposite number was Jim Bruner, a member of the Maricopa County Board of Supervisors, who also constituted the Maricopa County Stadium Authority. Despite his enthusiasm for bringing big-league baseball to the region, the fiscally conservative Bruner drove a hard bargain. He made it clear to Colangelo that there would be no increase in the 0.25 percent sales tax unless Maricopa County residents received a good deal on the facility. Colangelo agreed to a set of terms that saved Maricopa County taxpayers more than $40 million on the facility.[12]

The stadium financing deal Bruner and Colangelo worked out capped Maricopa County's sales tax contribution at $238 million. It gave ownership of the ballpark to the county and guaranteed the county one-third of the annual earnings from naming rights. (In 1998 Bank One acquired the naming rights for 10 years at a cost of $70 million.) The financing deal provided the county with an escalating annual revenue guarantee based on ticket sales while requiring the Diamondbacks to pay for the maintenance of the ballpark. In return, the county granted the baseball team a 30-year lease and primary-tenant status. Despite some misgivings, Colangelo agreed to the deal. He realized that if he alienated an ally like Bruner, the political pressure that other county supervisors would face from a public that less than five years earlier had turned down a stadium financing referendum would likely push their votes into the "no" column.[13]

Maricopa County tax assessors projected that revenue from the 0.25 percent sales tax would reach its $238 million target in approximately 2½ years, and the tax would end around the time the ballpark was slated to open in March 1998. In fact, the target was reached four months earlier than expected, in November 1997, two years after construction began on the 48,500-seat domed stadium and four months before the first pitch.[14]

But even with the taxpayer-friendly amendments to the deal, widespread opposition emerged almost immediately to the public financing of a ballpark without voter input. Many opponents decried what they perceived as collusion between the city's political and business elite. More than 800 residents, split roughly evenly between supporters and opponents, attended the February 1994 meeting at which the Board of Supervisors voted amid a heavy police presence on the stadium deal.[15]

After a contentious six-hour meeting, the Supervisors voted 3 to 1 with one recusal to impose the sales tax. Colangelo, the public face of the stadium project, skipped the meeting. His presence would likely have galvanized the already stinging criticism that he and pro-stadium legislators had already faced as a result of the deal. Long the darling of the Phoenix media, Colangelo had never experienced citizens referring to him in letters to the editor or public meetings as a "thief" or claiming that he was trying to "rape" the taxpayers. Jim Bruner, who both helped to develop the plan to pursue a baseball team and negotiated the terms of the financing deal with Colangelo, cast the deciding vote for the measure.[16]

The three supervisors who supported the tax faced serious consequences. After the vote, Bruner, as he had planned, resigned from the board to run for an open congressional seat. He lost in the Republican primary to attorney John Shadegg, who transformed the campaign into a virtual referendum on Bruner's support for the stadium tax. Pro-sales-tax Supervisor Ed King lost his bid for re-election in 1996 in a campaign that focused heavily on his support for the tax.[17]

More than three years after the vote, in August 1997, Supervisor Mary Rose Wilcox, the lone Democrat on the Board of Supervisors, who voted to impose the tax, was shot in the lower back after a Supervisors meeting by a man described as mentally deranged. The attacker told the press, "I shot Supervisor Mary Rose Wilcox to try to put a stop to the political dictatorship of Jerry Colangelo in pushing the baseball stadium tax." Wilcox survived the attack, which she blamed on the harsh opposition to the tax that remained a fixture of Phoenix talk radio.[18]

Ballpark deal in hand, Colangelo made his expansion pitch to major-league owners in February 1994. He emphasized the booming population of metropolitan Phoenix, the region's history of enthusiastic support for collegiate, spring-training, and Fall League baseball, and his history of managerial success with the Suns.[19] A few days later the owners awarded Arizona Baseball Inc. an expansion franchise. (They also awarded a franchise to a Tampa-St. Petersburg-based ownership group led by businessman Vincent J. Naimoli.) They were to begin playing in the 1998 season.

After a 1995 "name the team" contest conducted by the *Arizona Republic* in 1995, the nickname Diamondbacks was chosen for the team. The Diamondbacks adopted a quintessentially late 1990s palette of team colors: purple, turquoise, black, and copper. The colors were marketed as evocative of the region's cultural heritage. Collectively, the color scheme adopted by the Diamondbacks, or "DBacks," as they were soon dubbed by the local media, looked similar to the colors of Colangelo's other team, the Suns, whose stature in the region was then at its peak.

Colangelo persuaded the other partners in Arizona Baseball Inc. to call the team the Arizona Diamondbacks rather than the Phoenix Diamondbacks to cultivate a statewide sense of pride and ownership. Moreover, the "Arizona" branding of the Diamondbacks was in keeping with the previous round of baseball expansion, which brought the Florida Marlins and Colorado Rockies into existence.[20]

As general manager the Diamondbacks in June 1995 hired Joe Garagiola Jr., one of the founding fathers of big-league baseball in Phoenix. Later that year, Colangelo and Garagiola hired Buck Showalter as the club's first manager. Showalter came aboard just days after the New York Yankees fired him in the wake of the team's playoff loss in its first postseason appearance in 14 years. Like many of his predecessors in New York, the intense Showalter butted heads frequently with the club's domineering owner, George Steinbrenner. The Diamondbacks gave Showalter the additional responsibility to oversee the development of its minor-league system. The Diamondbacks fielded their first affiliated minor-league teams in 1996. In subsequent seasons Showalter clashed with Garagiola over the direction of the club. Showalter preferred a steady player-development program through a farm system while Garagiola adopted the "win-now" (meaning sign free agents) approach favored by Colangelo. As a result, Showalter was fired after the 2000 season.[21]

The "win-now" approach was clearly the governing ideology of the Diamondbacks by the time of the November 18, 1997, expansion draft. Colangelo believed that taxpayers deserved an immediately competitive club in return for the investment they had made in Bank One Ballpark. Moreover, he believed that unless the Diamondbacks fielded an immediately competitive team, they would not gain a foothold in the increasingly tight market for Ari-

This commemorative seat cushion, signed by Arizona Diamondbacks manager Buck Showalter, was available to fans on Opening Day, March 31, 1998, at Bank One Ballpark in Phoenix, Arizona. (Photo courtesy of Joel Zolondek)

zona sports fans' dollars. By the time the Diamondbacks played their first game at Bank One Ballpark, metropolitan Phoenix was home to teams in all four major professional leagues. In the expansion draft, the Diamondbacks scooped up veteran starting pitchers Brian Anderson and Jeff Suppan with their first two picks. After the draft they traded several of the prospects they had selected for veterans like Detroit Tigers third baseman Travis Fryman and Florida Marlins center fielder Devon White. During the 1997-1998 baseball offseason, the Diamondbacks acquired two of the most high-profile and high-priced players available, shortstop Jay Bell via free agency and third baseman Matt Williams via trade with the Indians.[22]

The Diamondbacks doubled down on the "win-now" approach in their early years, signing pitching aces Randy Johnson in 1999 and Curt Schilling in 2000 to long-term deals that deferred the big payments until the latter years of their contracts. The Diamondbacks' willingness to invest heavily in elite starting pitching put them on the fast track to the postseason. They finished first in the NL West in 1999, their second season in the major leagues. Never before had an expansion team reached the playoffs so quickly. Two years later, Johnson and Schilling anchored the team that won the 2001 World Series against the Yankees.[23]

The Diamondbacks' success helped them draw large crowds even after the honeymoon of their first season. More than 2.5 million people attended games at the Bank One Ballpark (nicknamed the BOB) in each of the franchise's first seven seasons. Initially, the BOB proved to be its own draw with an unprecedented array of amenities that appealed to spectators who were not especially interested in baseball: several playgrounds, a picnic pavilion, a day spa, and a swimming-pool party area (which could be rented for a group of up to 30 for $4,000 per game)

Pitcher Andy Benes throws out the first pitch in the history of the Arizona Diamondbacks franchise on Opening Day, March 31, 1998, at Bank One Ballpark in Phoenix, Arizona. (Photo courtesy of Joel Zolondek)

were among the most popular attractions. The ballpark's retractable roof allowed fans to enjoy the sun while sitting in air-conditioned comfort. Additionally, the BOB offered some of the most affordable prices in baseball. In the late 1990s, a family of four could attend a game for well under $50, including tickets, parking, and refreshments.[24]

On game days, thousands of suburbanites who would likely not have otherwise patronized downtown Phoenix brought their discretionary dollars to the BOB and its environs. The presence of the Diamondbacks hardly transformed commercial or residential patterns in Maricopa County. According to a 2015 study commissioned by the Diamondbacks, the franchise generated $8.2 billion in economic activity since it began in March 1998. This is less than 0.5 percent of the total economic activity in Maricopa County in that same time period. Nevertheless, Bank One Ballpark has contributed to the revitalization of downtown Phoenix. During the 1960s suburban shopping centers replaced downtown Phoenix as the region's retail center. But the downtown area slowly emerged from its doldrums, becoming a destination to visitors outside of banker's hours. The creation of a number of new institutions and attractions in downtown Phoenix added vibrancy to the once moribund area. In addition to the BOB, Maricopa County taxpayers subsidized municipal bonds that financed the construction of a number of other downtown attractions during the 1990s, including a new library, a science center, an art museum, and a museum of Arizona history.[25]

The success the Diamondbacks enjoyed during their early years came at a high price. In the late 1990s and early 2000s, the franchise signed high-priced free agents to large contracts that deferred large amounts of salary. Between 1998 and 2000, the Diamondbacks more than doubled their payroll from $32 million to $80 million. The 2001 World Series-winning team had an $84 million payroll, of which $46 million was deferred. To pay off the deferred salaries, the Diamondbacks raised ticket prices sharply in the early 2000s and eventually traded Schilling to the Boston Red Sox in November 2003 and Johnson to the New York Yankees in December 2004 for prospects and cash. By the end of the 2004 season, the club owed more than a quarter of a billion dollars in deferred salaries.[26]

Displeasure with the direction of the franchise led to Colangelo's ouster as managing general partner by the other four general partners in Arizona Baseball Inc. in August 2004. Garagiola followed Colangelo out the door in 2005.

Ken Kendrick, who had been a managing partner since the franchise's origins, took over as managing general partner. As of 2016 Jeffrey Royer, Michael Chipman, and Dale Jensen remained the other general partners.

A native of West Virginia, Kendrick made his fortune in the software business as the founder of Datatel Inc., a Virginia-based company that provided high-tech services and software to colleges and universities. He and his wife, Randy, have long been conservative political activists. In recent years, they have worked closely with the Koch political organization. During the 2016 Republican presidential primaries, the Kendricks made headlines in Arizona for their strident opposition to Donald Trump's bid for the nomination. Like Kendrick, Jensen and Chipman earned their fortunes in the software industry. Jensen is the co-founder of Information Technology, which develops software for the banking industry. Chipman was the creator and original owner of TurboTax. Royer was an executive in the cable television industry.[27]

Colangelo's tenure as managing general partner (1998-2004) coincided largely with Joe Garagiola Jr.'s term as general manager (1997-2005). Under Colangelo and Garagiola, the Diamondbacks won division titles in 1999 and 2001 as well as the pennant and World Series in 2001. Under Kendrick's leadership, the Diamondbacks have enjoyed significantly less success on the field. But the franchise did succeed in getting a handle on its salary situation, and from about 2005 it has ranked near the bottom of the league in payroll most years. Such austerity did not breed a great deal of on-the-field success. The Diamondbacks won the NL West in 2007 and 2011, but more often than not have finished well out of contention, including at least three last-place finishes since 2009. The "win-now" approach of the Colangelo-Garagiola era can take some of the blame for the diminishing returns. The franchise's financial situation and farm

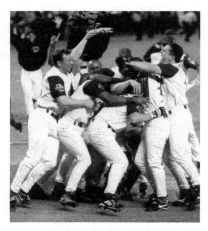

Randy Johnson, top, leaps onto the dogpile at home plate to celebrate the Arizona Diamondbacks' 3-2 win over the New York Yankees in Game 7 of the 2001 World Series on November 4, 2001, at Bank One Ballpark in Phoenix, Arizona. (Photo courtesy of Joel Zolondek)

system were in difficult straits at the time of the original regime's departure, but for for more than a decade this has been Kendrick's franchise. Since 2005 the Diamondbacks have gone through five general managers: Bob Gebhard (2005), Josh Byrnes, (2005-2010), Jerry Dipoto (2010), Kevin Towers (2010-2014), and Dave Stewart (2014-2016). The leadership of Mike Hazen

Arizona Diamondbacks catcher Damian Miller is shown during the 2001 season. (Photo courtesy of Joel Zolondek)

and Hall of Fame manager Tony LaRussa, through 2016 fell short of turning around the fortunes of the franchise, finishing well out of contention in all three seasons of their joint tenure.[28]

Since Kendrick became managing general partner, the Diamondbacks have moved into a new spring-training facility, the architecturally striking Salt River Fields at Talking Stick, an 11,000-seat facility in Scottsdale that they share with the Colorado Rockies. Opened in 2011, the facility ison land owned by the Salt River Pima-Maricopa Indian Community. Like Scottsdale itself, Talking Stick evokes the Old Southwest with its homages to mission revival architecture, sagebrush surroundings, and views of Camelback Mountain. Like other new spring-training facilities in Arizona, Talking Stick was subsidized in large part by the $2.50 rental-car tax that was put in place back in 1990 to revitalize the ballparks of the Cactus League.[29]

In 2005 Bank One merged with J.P. Morgan Chase, and Bank One Ballpark was renamed Chase Field. In 2016 Kendrick and the Diamondbacks organization were engaged in contentious negotiations with the Maricopa County Stadium Authority over the future of Chase Field. The Diamondbacks assert that Chase Field needs significant upgrades or replacement after nearly two decades of use. In March 2016 Kendrick made public his belief that the Diamondbacks needed a new ballpark, and presented a preliminary proposal to county officials. But the

Maricopa County Board of Supervisors made it evident that they had no interest in supporting any such municipal investments, particularly when Major League Baseball deemed Chase Field acceptable to host its All-Star Game as recently as 2011. In the summer of 2016 the Diamondbacks asked Maricopa County for help in subsidizing $65 million worth of renovations to Chase Field, which county officials have also rejected.[30]

## Notes

1  Rick Thompson, "A History of the Cactus League," *Spring Training Magazine*, March 1989. Accessed on June 17, 2016: springtrainingmagazine.com/history4.html#cactus; Gary Rausch, "The Cactus League Is a Major League Tourist Attraction in Arizona," *Chicago Tribune*, February 26, 1989, M23.

2  Ibid. Thompson, "A History of the Cactus League."

3  Rick Hummel, "Cactus League Is Coming on Strong," *St. Louis Post-Dispatch*, March 7, 2010, C1; Ron Fimrite, "The Selling of Spring," *Sports Illustrated*, March 27, 1989, 58-61.

4  Raymond Schultze, "Stadium Developer Quits Deal," *Phoenix Gazette*, May 27, 1988, A1, A11; David Schwartz, "Martin Stone Quits Pact for 'Dome'; Plan in Peril," *Arizona Republic*, May 27, 1988, A1, A8; Christopher Broderick, "Agreement Reached on Stadium," *Arizona Republic*, April 10, 1987, A1.

5  Martin Van Der Werf, "Martin Stone," *Arizona Republic*, March 12, 1995, BB2; "Stadium Developer Quits Deal"; "Martin Stone Quits Pact for 'Dome'; Plan in Peril"; "Agreement Reached on Stadium."

6  Robert Barrett, "Stadium Fails, Goddard Wins," *Arizona Republic*, October 4, 1989, A1.

7  "Martin Stone"; Bob Cohn, "Race for Big Leagues Begins," *Arizona Republic*, June 15, 1990, A1; Eric Miller, "Valley Strikes Out," *Arizona Republic*, December 19, 1990, A1.

8  John Walters, "Brazen Arizona," *Sports Illustrated*, January 29, 1996, 190-194.

9  Robert Logan, "Colangelo Quits Bulls to Take Phoenix Post," *Chicago Tribune*, February 29, 1968, C1; Bob Logan, "Colangelo Has Suns Climbing for Summit," *Chicago Tribune*, May 23, 1976, B3; Lee Shappell, "Jerry Colangelo," *Arizona Republic*, March 12, 1995, BB2; "Colangelo Took Bait All the Way to Finals"; Kevin Simpson, "The Place to Be," *The Sporting News*, November 7, 1994, S3; Jack McCallum, "Desert Heat," *Sports Illustrated*, May 28, 1990, 50-51; Joe Gilmartin, "Suns' Colangelo NBA Executive of the Year," *The Sporting News*, May 16, 1981, 46.

10  "NBA Notebook: Pacific," *The Sporting News*, October 26, 1987, 47; Steve Wilson, "When You're Colangelo, You Gotta Believe," *Arizona Republic*, January 16, 1994, 10; Norm Frauenheim, "Colangelo-Led Group Buys Phoenix Suns," *Arizona Republic*, October 13, 1987, A1, A2.

11  "Baseball Panel Backs Phoenix, Tampa Bay," *Arizona Republic*, March 8, 1995, A1, A16; "DBacks Ownership a Mixed Bag," *Arizona Republic*, March 30, 1998, C33; Richard Obert, "Floating on Air, Colangelo Readies Big Party Today," *Arizona Republic*, March 11, 1995, C1.

12  Mike Padgett, "Decision Cost Jim Bruner His Dream of Serving as U.S. Congressman," *Phoenix Business Journal*, March 26, 2008. Accessed June 10, 2016: bizjournals.com/phoenix/stories/2008/03/31/story7.html.

13  David Schwartz and Eric Miller, "County Close to Deal on Ballpark," *Arizona Republic*, January 9, 1994, A1; Frank Fitzpatrick, "Stadium Issues Can Explode: Take Phoenix," *Philadelphia Inquirer*, January 13, 1999, E1; "Decision Cost Jim Bruner His Dream of Serving as U.S. Congressman";

14  "Decision Cost Jim Bruner His Dream of Serving as U.S. Congressman."

15  "County Close to Deal on Ballpark." "Decision Cost Jim Bruner His Dream of Serving as U.S. Congressman."

16  David Fritze, David Schwartz, and Eric Miller, "Play Ball: Stadium Tax Wins OK," *Arizona Republic*, February 18, 1994; "Jerry Colangelo"; Bob McManaman, "Tax Foes' Name-Calling 'Hurt Deeply,'" *Arizona Republic*, February 19, 1994, A20.

17  "County Close to Deal on Ballpark"; *Arizona Republic*, January 9, 1994, A1; David Schwartz and Eric Miller, "Negotiators Strike Deal on Big-League Ballpark," *Arizona Republic*, January 15, 1994, A1; "Decision Cost Jim Bruner His Dream of Serving as U.S. Congressman."

18  Mike McCloy, "Supervisor Is Shot," *Arizona Republic*, August 14, 1997, A1, A12; William Hermann, Susie Steckner, and Mike McCloy, "Suspect: Tax Spurred Shooting," *Arizona Republic*, August 14, 1997, A1, A12; Mike McCloy, "Wilcox Snags 50 Tickets for Opening," *Arizona Republic*, March 31, 1998, A1; Mike McCloy, "'Guy has a Gun': Guard Acted Fast," *Arizona Republic*, August 15, 1997, A1; Frank Fitzpatrick, "Stadium Issues Can Explode: Take Phoenix," *Philadelphia Inquirer*, January 13, 1999, E1.

19  Bob McManaman, "Colangelo Winds Up to Make Big Pitch," *Arizona Republic*, February 19, 1994, A1, A20.

20  "Brazen Arizona."

21  Murray Chass, "Arizona Gets Set to Hire Showalter," *New York Times*, November 12, 1995, 42; Howard Fendrich, "Diamondbacks, Yankees Found Success After Showalter Left," *Seattle Post-Intelligencer*, October 25, 2001. Accessed June 10, 2016: seattlepi.com/sports/baseball/article/Diamondbacks-Yankees-found-success-after-1069899.php

22  Ken Rosenthal, "All Arizona Has to Do Now, Right Now, Is Win," *The Sporting News*, March 12, 2001, 49; Peter Schmuck, "In Hurry, a Trading Flurry After Draft," *Baltimore Sun*, November 19, 1997. Accessed June 10, 2016: articles.baltimoresun.com/1997-11-19/sports/1997323118_1_red-sox-pedro-martinez-rosters.

23  "Floating on Air, Colangelo Readies Big Party Today"; Pedro Gomez, "Tickled to Be in Arizona," *The Sporting News*, December 14, 1998, 80; "All Arizona Has to Do Now, Right Now, Is Win."

24  Mike McCloy, "Ballpark Looks Like a Million," *Arizona Republic*, October 13, 1996, B1; Don Ketchum, "In the Ballpark," *Arizona Republic*, November 16, 1995, D4; "Come Along on a BOB Tour," *Arizona Republic*, March 22, 1998, A1; Martin Van Der Wert, "1st Year Is a Tryout for Cooling System," *Arizona Republic*, March 22, 1998, BP6; "Family-Style Attractions Cover All the Bases," *Arizona Republic*, March 22, 1998, BP10; Bill Muller, Mark Shaffer, and Richard Ruelas, "BOB Takes a Bow," *Arizona Republic*, March 30, 1998, A1; Linda Helser, "Diamondbacks May Be Best Pro Sports Bargain in Valley," *Arizona Republic*, March 29, 1998, C37; Pedro Gomez and Mark Topkin, "Scouting the Expansion Cities," *The Sporting News*, March 30, 1998, 26; "Fans Guide: Ticket Prices," March 30, 1998, *Arizona Republic*, C41

25  "Arizona Diamondbacks Letter to Maricopa County Board of Supervisors, January 12, 2016," BallparkDigest.com, March 30, 2016. Accessed August 3, 2016: ballparkdigest.com/wp-content/uploads/2016/03/OriginalDbacksletterforChairmanSupervisors03242016.pdf ; "Maricopa County Stadium District: Comprehensive Annual Financial Report," Maricopa.gov, June 30, 2013. Accessed August 3, 2016: maricopa.gov/StadiumDistrict/pdf/MC-StadiumDistFY12AFR.pdf; David Fritze, "Boom! Downtown May Fully Awaken," *Arizona Republic*, March 12, 1995, BB7.

26  "All Arizona Has to Do Now, Right Now, Is Win"; Nick Piecoro, "Jerry Colangelo's Shadow Remains Prominent Over Diamondbacks," *azcentral.com*, September 27, 2014. Accessed June 3, 2016: azcentral.com/story/sports/mlb/diamondbacks/2014/09/27/jerry-colangelos-shadow-remains-prominent-diamondbacks/16344607/.

27  "Jerry Colangelo's Shadow Remains Prominent Over Diamondbacks."

28  Ibid.

29  "Cactus League Stadium Guide: Salt River Fields at Talking Stick," *FoxSports.com*, February 24, 2016. Accessed June 3, 2016: foxsports.com/arizona/story/cactus-league-stadium-guide-salt-river-fields-arizona-diamondbacks-colorado-rockies-022416; "Cactus League: Salt River Fields," azcentral.com, February 24, 2016. Accessed June 3, 2016: azcentral.com/story/entertainment/events/2015/02/25/cactus-league-stadium-guide-salt-river-fields-at-talking-stick/24009267/.

30  Rebekah L. Sanders, "Maricopa County Rejects Most of Arizona Diamondbacks' Requested $65M for Upgrades," *azcentral.com*, August 8, 2016. Accessed August 14, 2016: azcentral.com/story/news/local/phoenix/2016/08/08/maricopa-county-rejects-most-diamondbacks-request-65-million-chase-field-upgrades/88279408/.

## ARIZONA DIAMONDBACKS EXPANSION

| PICK | PLAYER | POSITION | FORMER TEAM |
|---|---|---|---|

### ROUND 1

| PICK | PLAYER | POSITION | FORMER TEAM |
|---|---|---|---|
| 1 | Brian Anderson | p | Cleveland Indians |
| 2 | Jeff Suppan | p | Boston Red Sox |
| 3 | Gabe Alvarez | 3b | San Diego Padres |
| 4 | Jorge Fabregas | c | Chicago White Sox |
| 5 | Karim Garcia | of | Los Angeles Dodgers |
| 6 | Edwin Diaz | ss | Texas Rangers |
| 7 | Cory Lidle | p | New York Mets |
| 8 | Joel Adamson | p | Milwaukee Brewers |
| 9 | Ben Ford | p | New York Yankees |
| 10 | Yamil Benitez | of | Kansas City Royals |
| 11 | Neil Weber | p | Montreal Expos |
| 12 | Jason Boyd | p | Philadelphia Phillies |
| 13 | Brent Brede | of | Minnesota Twins |
| 14 | Tony Batista | 3b | Oakland A's |

### ROUND 2

| PICK | PLAYER | POSITION | FORMER TEAM |
|---|---|---|---|
| 15 | Tom Martin | p | Houston Astros |
| 16 | Omar Daal | p | Toronto Blue Jays |
| 17 | Scott Winchester | p | Cincinnati Reds |
| 18 | Clint Sodowsky | p | Pittsburgh Pirates |
| 19 | Danny Klassen | ss | Milwaukee Brewers |
| 20 | Matt Drews | p | Detroit Tigers |
| 21 | Todd Erdos | p | San Diego Padres |
| 22 | Chris Clemons | p | Chicago White Sox |
| 23 | David Dellucci | of | Baltimore Orioles |
| 24 | Damian Miller | c | Minnesota Twins |
| 25 | Hector Carrasco | p | Kansas City Royals |
| 26 | Hanley Frias | ss | Texas Rangers |
| 27 | Bob Wolcott | p | Seattle Mariners |
| 28 | Mike Bell | 3b | Anaheim Angels |

**ROUND 3**

| 29 | Joe Randa | 3b | Pittsburgh Pirates |
|----|-----------|-----|---------------------|
| 30 | Jesus Martinez | p | Los Angeles Dodgers |
| 31 | Russ Springer | p | Houston Astros |
| 32 | Bryan Corey | p | Detroit Tigers |
| 33 | Kelly Stinnett | c | Milwaukee Brewers |
| 34 | Chuck McElroy | p | Chicago White Sox |
| 35 | Marty Janzen | p | Toronto Blue Jays |
| 34 | Scott Fredrickson | p | San Diego Padres |
| 35 | Braulio Castillo | of | Philadelphia Phillies |
| 36 | Denis Boucher | p | Cleveland Indians |

# CORY LIDLE

### BY JEB STEWART

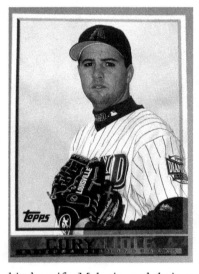

Cory Lidle pitched for seven teams in the major leagues, primarily as a starter, during nine seasons from 1997 to 2006. His life was cut short on October 11, 2006, when the Cirrus SR20 airplane he was piloting struck a building while attempting to make a turn over the East River in New York City.[1] He was 34 years old and left behind a wife, Melanie, and their young son, Christopher.

Lidle was the son of Doug and Rebecca Lidle; he and his fraternal twin brother, Kevin, were born in Hollywood, California on March 22, 1972. A descendent of the steam-engine inventor Robert Fulton, Lidle was given Fulton as his middle name.[2] He and his three siblings grew up in West Covina, California.[3] Lidle took an early interest in baseball, playing in the "West Covina American Little League, 1980-1984, West Covina Mustang Pony [League] 1985-1986, West Covina Mickey Mantle [League] 1987-1988, and West Covina Babe Ruth [League] 1989-1990."[4] In Senior Babe Ruth baseball, Lidle began to establish himself as a pitcher for the West Covina Wildcats in a competitive league in which future major leaguers Jason Giambi and Mark Loretta played, as he posted a 3.18 earned-run average.[5]

Giambi and his brother Jeremy, Shawn Wooten, and Aaron Small were Lidle's teammates at South Hills High School in West Covina.[6] Giambi, who was a senior when Lidle was a junior, occupied the last slot in the Huskies' rotation in 1989.[7] In his senior year, Lidle earned an opportunity to pitch and responded with an 11-2 record, with a 1.02 ERA and 100 strikeouts.[8] His brother Kevin played catcher on the squad; the duo made an effective battery.[9] Lidle was a First Team All-Star pitcher in the 4-A division.[10] He also batted .344 with 11 RBIs.[11] On a sour note, Lidle lost just his second game of the season as South Hills lost the Southern Section championship to the San Luis Obispo Tigers, 4-0.[12]

Despite his excellent performance as a high-school senior, Lidle went undrafted in the 1990 amateur draft. He blamed his stature, 5-feet-11 inches and 180 pounds, as the primary reason.[13] He signed a free-agent contract with the Minnesota Twins in August of 1990. In 1991 he appeared in a handful of games for the Twins in the rookie Gulf Coast League before an injury ended his season. The following year, Lidle pitched in Tennessee for the Elizabethton Twins in the Appalachian League; despite his respectable 3.71 ERA and six saves, the Twins were apparently unimpressed by his progress and released him.

Lidle was now 21 and his baseball career appeared to be over. Needing to make a living, he got a job working as a bartender.[14] The Pocatello Posse, an independent Idaho club in the Pioneer League, invited him for a pitching tryout, which Lidle missed after oversleeping.[15] "Given another chance, Lidle performed well and made the team."[16] He went 8-4 with a 4.13 ERA; perhaps more significantly, he threw over 100 innings for the first time. After the season the Milwaukee Brewers purchased his contract from Pocatello.

Lidle's control steadily progressed as he climbed each rung of the organizational ladder. In 1994 he pitched well for the Beloit Brewers in the low-A Midwest League and received a midseason promotion to the Stockton Ports (high A) of the California League. The following summer, he pitched well for the Double-A El Paso Diablos in the Texas League. However, a decision he made in the spring of 1995 reverberated negatively throughout the rest of his career.

In 1995, after the players strike that canceled the end of the 1994 season, the playoffs, and the World Series, the major-league owners decided not to take any chances on another lost campaign, and assembled replacement players for spring training.[17] Most of the players were not highly regarded prospects, and the striking major leaguers regarded them as "scabs." One of those replacement players was Cory Lidle. He pitched in just one inning; and although he later regretted the decision, he believed doing so kept him in the game.[18] Lidle explained:

> The reason I did it was because I was a released player. I was getting pressure from the [Brewers], otherwise, they said, I wouldn't have a job. At the same time, I told them I would not go into the season. There was a line that I wasn't going to cross. I tried to please both the owners and the players and there's no way to do that.[19]

At least one source corroborates Lidle's claim that he would not have been in the Brewers' rotation if the strike continued.[20] Lidle's transgression was somewhat mitigated because he had never been a member of the Major League Baseball Players Association, and was not violating any oath.[21] However, by appearing in a game in spring training, Lidle could never join the players' association. This meant he did not share in the licensing money, or "appear in any video games."[22] However, Topps included him on its baseball cards.

After a trade to the New York Mets in 1996, Lidle nearly made the organization's Triple-A roster in the spring,[23] but settled in as a regular starter for the Eastern League Double-A affiliate in Binghamton, going 14-10 with a 3.31 ERA in 190⅓ innings. His results justified climbing another rung in professional baseball, this time to the Triple-A Norfolk Tides in the International League in 1997.

His stay with Norfolk was brief. On May 7, 1997, Lidle's good control earned him a promotion to the New York Mets. At 2:30 A.M., the newlywed telephoned his wife to give her the good news, joking that he had been arrested when she asked why he was calling so late.[24] He appeared in his first game in Houston on May 8 where he immediately faced the heart of the Astros' lineup: Craig Biggio, Derek Bell, Jeff Bagwell, Luis Gonzalez, and Bobby Abreu; although he surrendered four hits, he pitched two scoreless innings in relief. Pitching mostly out of the bullpen, the rookie appeared in 54 games over 81⅔ innings, finishing with a 7-2 record and a 3.53 ERA, as the most reliable reliever on the Mets.[25]

In November, Lidle and his wife visited friends in Phoenix, Arizona.[26] The trip coincided with the expansion draft, when the Tampa Bay Devil Rays and Arizona Diamondbacks drafted major-league players who had been left unprotected on other rosters.[27] With the 13th overall selection in the draft, the Diamondbacks drafted Lidle, who was watching the draft on a television outside the Arizona Civic Center.[28] Lidle met his new manager, Buck Showalter, and offered him advice about members of the Mets who were available.[29]

Lidle happily remarked, "I wasn't protected and I didn't know I was going to get picked, but I did. This is one city that I do like and I'll be glad to play here."[30] The Diamondbacks wanted Lidle to compete for a role in the starting rotation.[31] Although he was "considered a steal in the expansion draft," he was not a member of the Diamondbacks for long.[32]

After a stress fracture in his shoulder, Lidle went on the disabled list; while rehabbing the injury in a minor-league game for the Tucson Sidewinders, Lidle injured his elbow, requiring season-ending Tommy John surgery.[33] He never appeared in a game for Arizona, which waived him; "the Devil Rays claimed him, making him the first player to be part of both 1998 expansion teams."[34] The Rays planned for Lidle to join the bullpen by the middle of 1999.

Like its namesake, Tampa Bay swam along the bottom of

the American League East in each of its first six seasons. Lidle spent most of 1999 recovering from elbow surgery. He finally appeared in minor-league games for the St. Petersburg Devil Rays (high A) and Durham Bulls (Triple A) in the second half. The Devil Rays promoted him in September and he pitched in a handful of games. However, when his new teammates learned he had been a replacement player they turned on him on the bus, prompting Lidle to challenge "the loudest and drunkest one to a fight."[35] Although the incident ended without a punch being thrown, Lidle received icy treatment from most of the Devil Rays during the rest of his stay with the team.[36]

In 2000, Lidle struggled and finished with a record of 4-6, but managed to have some highlights. In early June he struck out seven in seven innings in a win against the Phillies, but he experienced uncharacteristic control problems, walking five. His recovery from surgery began to manifest itself in box scores, as he rediscovered the strike zone and lowered his ERA from 6.23 to 5.03 from August 20 to September 27, and he finished 3-1, 2.22 in his final four starts.[37] In late August, nearing the end of a frustrating year, Lidle threw a ball behind the Boston Red Sox' Brian Daubach, himself a replacement player,[38] in retaliation for Pedro Martinez hitting Gerald Williams; he was ejected and suspended for three games.[39] After returning, he shut out the Oakland Athletics on two hits. He became the perfect target for A's general manager Billy Beane, who saw value in groundball pitchers with good control, like Lidle.[40]

On January 8, 2001, the A's acquired Lidle in a three-team deal, which also netted Johnny Damon for Oakland. Believing Beane had taken advantage of them in the trade, the Rays front office became wary of dealing with him.[41] In spring training, Lidle won the fifth spot in the starting rotation. *The Sporting News* reported he had developed "four pitches – fastball, curve, change, and split finger – and he is also developing a cutter. The split-finger tends to be Lidle's out pitch, and the other pitches set it up."[42] Because he threw in the high 80s/low 90s, keeping the ball down became his trademark when he was pitching well.[43]

Early in his career with the A's, Lidle also began to be known for being outspoken with the press; the reputation followed him for the rest of his career. When the Devil Rays visited Oakland for the first time in 2001, Lidle spoke his mind to reporters and criticized Tampa Bay's general manager, pitching coach, and veteran players for lacking leadership.[44] Rays pitcher Albie Lopez responded by calling Lidle "a scab" and "a replacement player."[45] The Rays got the last laugh as they defeated the A's, 5-1, scoring four earned runs off Lidle.[46] Greg Vaughn, a veteran who took the leadership remarks personally, homered off Lidle.[47]

Despite lingering issues with the Devil Rays, Lidle's 2001 campaign was the best of his big-league career. He found a home in Oakland and was popular with the media, who "appreciated his candor and good humor, and they enjoyed his world view – which extended significantly beyond an outfield fence in a ballpark."[48] Because Lidle often ate candy between innings during a start, his teammates playfully nicknamed him Snacks.[49]

The right-hander started 29 games and finished with a 13-6 record and an ERA of 3.59, striking out 118 batters. After a shaky start, he went 12-2 from July 4 to the end of the season, winning his last five starts; and during that three-month stretch his ERA was 2.74 and he was as effective as the more celebrated members of the A's staff, Tim Hudson, Barry Zito, and Mark Mulder. More importantly, the A's, who were 40-42 on the morning of July 4, finished with a 102-60 mark and qualified for the playoffs as a wild card.

Lidle appeared in only one game in the Division Series against the New York Yankees. Starting Game Four at home on 11 days' rest, he showed his rust as he surrendered six runs on five hits and three walks in $3\frac{1}{3}$ innings, as the Athletics unraveled and lost, 9-2. The next night the Yankees eliminated Oakland from the postseason.

Lidle remained hopeful that his good pitching would "secure him a place in the A's future and allow him to finally settle in one place for more than two seasons."[50] Although he pitched well the following year, he did not get his wish. In *Moneyball*, Michael Lewis chronicled GM Billy Beane's philosophy of obtaining undervalued players, allowing them to flourish with the A's, and then trading them at peak value; Cory Lidle would be no exception.

The A's lost established stars Jason Giambi, Johnny Damon, and Jason Isringhausen, among others, to free agency. In 2002, the A's started slowly once again. With a 29-30 record and a third-place start, Oakland trailed the first-place Seattle Mariners by eight games in the AL West. By the middle of June, Lidle's ERA ballooned to 6.16, and his season, like the A's, appeared to be wrecked.[51] A meeting with A's pitching coach Rick Peterson helped him change course. Lidle explained, "[Peterson] said you have to get back to what you did last year. It was then I really started working on my focus. Instead of 100 pitches, focusing on 70 of them, I'd focus 100 percent on every pitch. That's when it started to turn around."[52] He also modified the pitching angle in his shoulder to induce more groundballs.[53] On July 19 he pitched a one-hit shutout against the Texas Rangers. After the game, Lidle remarked, "Everything looks like it's going to turn around. ... I'm going to take this and roll with it."[54]

By the end of July, Lidle's ERA had decreased by over a run. From August 4 to August 31, he was the most efficient starter on the A's, winning five decisions in six starts; his 0.20 ERA for the month lowered his overall ERA to 3.74, as he won the AL Pitcher of the Month Award.[55] Lidle threw 43 consecutive innings without allowing an earned run, which as of 2018 stood as the record for the Athletics in Oakland.[56] On August 21 he threw another one-hit shutout, this time against the Cleveland Indians. After he finally allowed an earned run on August 31, the Oakland fans gave him a standing ovation. Lidle credited his streak on his preparation and his positive attitude.[57]

Like Lidle, the Athletics began to dominate the American League. On August 12, the A's were 68-51, but were still in third place, trailing Seattle by 4½ games. From August 13 to September 4, they won 20 straight games setting an American League record, which has since been surpassed by the Indians. On September 6, the A's finally faltered, as Lidle started and took the loss to the Minnesota Twins, 6-0. After the game, he reflected on the quiet excitement in the clubhouse over the accomplishment of such a long and improbable winning streak.[58] More importantly, the A's were then in first place with a two-game lead over the Angels.

The A's won the division with a 103-59 record, which was one game better than in 2001. In the playoffs, they went to a three-man starting rotation, and Lidle moved to the bullpen.[59] In the Division Series against the Minnesota Twins, the A's season again ended abruptly; they lost three games to two. Lidle pitched only one inning in the series, allowing a run on two hits in a 7-5 loss.

In November, in a move to avoid paying him a larger salary, Billy Beane traded the 30-year-old Lidle to the Toronto Blue Jays for minor-league prospects.[60] For the Athletics, Lidle had a 21-16 record pitching in 380 innings with a 3.74 ERA (116 ERA+), which was arguably his high-water mark for any team.

Lidle quickly signed to avoid salary arbitration.[61] The Jays expected him to be the number-two starting pitcher behind ace Roy Halladay.[62] Although he continued to "focus on every pitch," Lidle often left pitches up and over the plate; and even when groundballs were hit, more of them got through the infield because of the fast-artificial turf in Toronto.[63] In 31 starts in 2003, Lidle went 12-15 with a disappointing 5.75 ERA for the third-place Blue Jays. By October, he no longer fit in Toronto's plans and became a free agent.

In December 2003 Lidle signed a one-year deal with the Cincinnati Reds for $2.75 million. His 2003 struggles continued into 2004. In 24 starts, the 32-year-old went 7-10 with a 5.32 ERA. By August 9, the Reds were mired in fourth place in the NL Central, trailing the first-place Cardinals by 18½ games, and traded Lidle to the Phillies, who needed a starter for a playoff run.

Back on a contender, Lidle again proved to be a capable second-half starter as he went 5-2 for Philadelphia with a 3.90 ERA over 62⅓ innings. He also contributed his only big-league home run, in a 10-0 complete-game win on August 29 over the Brewers. The Phillies went 6-1 over Lidle's last seven starts as he won four games in September, including his final three starts, and tied for the league lead in shutouts with three. The Phillies finished second in the National League East with an 86-76 record, but missed the playoffs.

In 2005, the 33-year-old Lidle pitched the entire season in Philadelphia. Throwing 184⅔ innings, he went 13-11 with a 4.53 ERA, and won four of his last five decisions. The Phillies had an 88-74 record, narrowly finishing second behind the Braves by two games and only one game behind the wild-card qualifier, the Houston Astros.

In August Lidle sat down with a writer for *USA Today Sports Weekly* and talked about his career and his life outside of baseball. He discussed his passion for golf and playing in poker tournaments, which he compared to the strategy a pitcher needs on the mound. He said he wanted to get his pilot's license and buy a plane after his baseball career ended, adding, "I live in LA, so I'd like to be able to go to Vegas if I want, to Pebble Beach — out to Phoenix to golf. A nice plane would get me to any of those within an hour and a half."[64] Lidle decided not to wait and began working on his pilot's license the day after the 2005 campaign ended.[65]

Lidle's outspoken nature came out early in a 2006 interview as he questioned the legitimacy of Barry Bonds' chase of the career home-run record, which he related to Bonds' alleged use of performance-enhancing drugs.[66] On the field, the Phillies' own performance was suffering. Philadelphia had gotten off to a poor start, seemed to have righted the ship by mid-May, but scuffled from there until the end of July with a 49-55 record as the trade deadline approached. On July 8, Lidle's record stood at 5-7, but he had begun pitching with a more consistent focus, and was a dependable six-inning starter.[67] In keeping with his reputation as a second-half pitcher, Lidle won four starts in a row for the Phillies in July, and he drew Yankees GM Brian Cashman's interest.

In the American League East, New York and Boston were fighting tooth and nail for the division, and Boston held a half-game lead on July 30. Cashman knew the Red Sox were interested in obtaining Lidle for the stretch run; the Yankees also needed an outfielder due to injuries to Gary Sheffield and Hideki Matsui. He engineered a trade with the Phillies, sending marginal prospects for right fielder Bobby Abreu (along with his large contract) and Lidle. Although Abreu was clearly the headline of the trade, Lidle's inclusion was important to the Yankees, as Cashman explained:

> Yeah, I could use an extra starter. We valued Lidle. He has a history of strong second halves every year, his ERA is a huge drop every year. He's a different pitcher in the second half than the first half. We needed him. We could use him, and knowing that [Boston] needed him too, if we could take him for ourselves to our benefit, and at the same time keep him away from them, that was cooler.[68]

After the trade, Lidle wasted no time in criticizing the effort and focus of the Phillies.[69] Although he later apologized, the damage was done; Phillies reliever Arthur Rhodes called him a "scab," adding that Lidle was only interested in gambling, flying airplanes, and eating ice cream.[70] Mets closer Billy Wagner, himself a former Phillie who had also questioned the intensity of his ex-teammates, characterized the comments as being "kind of chicken that Cory said it out the door."[71]

In Lidle's first start after the trade, he went six innings, allowing one earned run, as the Yankees beat the Blue Jays, 8-1. Later in the month, the Yankees and Red Sox met in Boston for a pivotal five-game series with the potential to decide the East championship. Coming into the series, the Yankees clung to a 1½-game lead, and with the home

crowd at Fenway Park, the Red Sox figured to overtake them. However, the Yankees won the first four games of the series. Needing a win in the final game to send New York home with a 6½-game lead rather than 4½, the Yankees sent Lidle to the mound for his most important start for the ballclub.

Although Lidle walked five and allowed three hits in the Monday-afternoon game, none of Boston's baserunners managed to reach home, as he threw six shutout innings and struck out five. The bullpen allowed a run to score, but the Yankees finished off the sweep, winning 2-1. Bronx Banter blogger Alex Belth described the satisfaction of the final game:

> You just don't expect these kinds of things to happen. Yes, even if you are a Yankee fan, spoiled by winning and success, you don't necessarily plan for your wildest dreams to come true. But that is what happened late Monday afternoon as the Bombers' B-Squad, featuring a starting line-up which included the likes of Nick Green at short, Bernie Williams in center, and Sal Fasano behind the mask, edged by a flat Red Sox team, 2-1. It was the only briskly played game of the turgid, five-game sweep, which will go down as the sequel to the famous 1978 Boston Massacre. David Wells pitched well for Boston but his teammates were lifeless with the bats and were shut-down by Corey [sic] Lidle, Octavio Dotel, Mike Myers, Scott Proctor and Kyle Farnsworth.[72]

The five-game sweep all but clinched the Yankees' ninth straight AL East title. New York coasted through September and won the division by 10 games. Although Lidle finished with an ERA over 5, he went 4-3 for the Yankees and threw 45⅓ innings. However, in his first five weeks in New York, which was during the most critical part of the pennant race, Lidle's ERA was only 3.38.[73]

In the playoffs, the Detroit Tigers made short work of the Yankees. After losing the first game of the series, the Tigers rebounded to win the next three.[74] On October 7, Lidle entered the final game of the series in Detroit with the Yankees trailing 4-0. In what was be his only appearance of the series, Lidle pitched 1⅓ innings, allowing three runs on four hits. It would also be the final time he ever pitched. After the loss Lidle candidly leveled criticism at manager Joe Torre, claiming the Yankees were not as prepared as the Tigers for the series.[75] Four days later, Cory Lidle was dead.

Lidle was well aware of the dangers of flying small aircraft, which had taken the life of Yankees captain Thurman Munson in 1979.[76] He mitigated the risk by purchasing a plane with an Airframe Parachute System, which could deploy in the event of an engine failure and bring the plane safely to the ground.[77] He was also serious about developing his skills as a pilot; his instructor, Tyler Stanger, called Lidle his "best student," adding "[h]e learned very, very quickly, and a lot of it is desire. He had huge desire."[78]

Stanger was with Lidle on his fateful flight.[79] They were flying north above the East River; as they approached the Roosevelt Bridge on the east side of the river, they decided to do a U-turn and return to the south. Apparently misjudging both the wind and the turn distance, they began the turn over Roosevelt Island, instead of a few hundred feet to the east over Queens. Not having enough room to complete the maneuver, they flew into an apartment building on the Upper East Side of Manhattan; both men perished.[80] A Manhattan jury later found for the manufacturer in a civil case brought by the families of Lidle and Stanger.[81]

Across major-league baseball, former teammates and coaches expressed their shock and sympathy for the Lidle family. An emotional Rick Peterson, Lidle's former pitching coach, called the tragedy "horrific."[82] Billy Wagner penned an article about his grief for the *New York Post*.[83] Former Devil Ray Fred McGriff, recalled Lidle as being "a good guy."[84] In Oakland, Barry Zito found time to tell bittersweet stories about happier days with Lidle, including "a time when Lidle had his twin brother, Kevin, wear his uniform to the bullpen and start throwing off the mound as a prank on former A's pitching coach Rick Peterson."[85] Alex Belth summed up the feelings of Yankees fans everywhere:

> As I stared into space on the subway, I wondered why I was feeling so empty, so sad. I've never had any special affection for Lidle, a mouthy pitcher who seemed to have burned his fair share of bridges in different clubhouses across the big leagues. Nevertheless, he was a familiar face.

. . .

The first time I remember seeing my father cry when I was a boy was the day after Thurman Munson died. When they had a ceremony for Munson at Yankee Stadium, my father sat in his chair in the living room and sobbed. I was nine at the time and just couldn't understand why he was so upset. After all, he didn't even *like*

the Yankees. He explained to me that sometimes it is sad when a person dies, no matter who they are, even if they did play for the Yankees. When I got older, I *understood* what he was telling me. But it wasn't until my trip home on a chilly, wet, October night, that I really *felt* what he meant.[86]

Lidle was laid to rest on October 17 in West Covina, California, as many players assembled to pay their respects to the pitcher. Joe Torre reflected on Lidle's last appearance for the Yankees, which occurred just days before, adding, "[w]e play a game and we think how important it is until you face something like this."[87]

In 2007 the Yankees followed tradition and wore black armbands on their left sleeves to remember Cory Lidle.[88] Melanie Lidle and the couple's son, Christopher, threw out the first pitch at Yankee Stadium on Opening Day in 2007.[89]

Lidle pitched 1,322$\frac{2}{3}$ innings in the major leagues with a record of 82-72, 838 strikeouts, and an ERA of 4.57 (98 ERA+). In 2007, the City of West Covina erected a bronze statue of Lidle as a memorial to the fallen pitcher; he will forever wear the pinstripes of the New York Yankees.[90] Today, the Cory Lidle Foundation raises "money for the Make A Wish Foundation … contribute[s] to the Mt. San Antonio Cory Lidle Memorial Scholarship, the Tyler Stanger Memorial Scholarship and establish[ed] the Cory Lidle High School Baseball Scholarship."[91]

*Acknowledgments*

The author is indebted to Cassidy Lent, reference librarian at the National Baseball Hall of Fame and Museum, who provided him with a thick clip file on Cory Lidle only 45 minutes after he made the request. In addition, Mike Selleck, the baseball information manager for the Oakland Athletics, was very helpful in providing information about Lidle's streak of consecutive innings without an earned run; and generously mailed the author Jason Turnbow's *A's Magazine* article about Cory Lidle.

**Notes**

1 Tyler Kepner, "Lidle Had Passion for Flying, and for Speaking His Mind," *New York Times*, October 12, 2016: D1; Bill Sanderson, "Lidle's Bad Turn," *New York Post*, November 4, 2006: 9.

2 Jason Turnbow, "Making His Pitch: Opportunity Knocks for Cory

Lidle," *A's Magazine*, September 2001: 26.

3  Ibid.

4  corylidle.com/about-us.

5  "Senior Babe Ruth Baseball," *Los Angeles Times*, June 22, 1989: 12.

6  Michael Morrissey, *The Pride and the Pressure: A Season Inside the New York Yankee Fishbowl* (New York: Doubleday, 2007), 123; Turnbow: 27; Kepner: D1; "High School Baseball Honors," *Los Angeles Times*, June 19, 1990: 47.

7  Turnbow: 26.

8  "Six Troy Errors Don't Matter in Loss to South Hills," *Los Angeles Times*, May 30, 1990: C10; "High School Baseball," *Los Angeles Times*, June 19, 1990: C10

9  corylidle.com/about-us; South Hills/San Luis Obispo Box Score, *Los Angeles Times*: 126; Turnbow: 26.

10  "High School Baseball Honors," *Los Angeles Times*, June 19, 1990: 47.

11  "Valley Roundup," *Los Angeles Times*, June 21, 1990: J10.

12  Ian Jacquiss, "Lindsey's Hit Gives Marina 5-A Title," *Los Angeles Times*, June 3, 1990. Accessed from Newspapers.com on March 10, 2018 and showing as page 934.

13  Turnbow: 27.

14  Kepner: D1, Turnbow: 29.

15  Kepner, D1, Turnbow: 29.

16  Kepner, D1.

17  Tim Kurkjian, "Who's on First, Joe? The Cardinals' Joe Torre, Like Other Managers, Finds Replacement Players to Be Excess Baggage," *Sports Illustrated*, March 6, 1995: 44.

18  David Waldstein, "Lidle Regrets Bucking Union," *New York Post*, May 10, 1997; Richard Griffin, "Strike Memories Still Haunt: Lidle Lives with Crossing the Line," WAYMORESPORTS.COM, February 16, 2003; accessed from HOF Clip File.

19  Griffin.

20  Richard J. Pridge, "Ladies and Gentlemen, Your 1995 Replacement Milwaukee Brewers (Almost): The Opening Day Roster That Nearly Was," April 5, 2015, shepherdexpress.com/news/what-made-milwaukee-famous/ladies-gentlemen-1995-replacement-milwaukee-brewers-almost/.

21  David Waldstein, "Lidle Regrets Bucking Union."

22  Brian Costello, "Strike Against Them – Replacement Players Still Paying the Price," *New York Post*, August 13, 2006.

23  Rob Centorani, "Mets Notebook," *Binghamton Press and Sun-Bulletin*, September 5, 1996: 5D.

24  Ibid.

25  David Waldstein, "Lidle's Winning Mets' Respect," *New York Post*, September 13, 1997.

26  David Waldstein, "Stunned Lidle Finds Out Fate First-Hand," *New York Post*, November 19, 1997.

27  Ibid.

28  Ibid.

29  Tom Verducci, "Razing Arizona: SI Was Present at the Creation as the Diamondbacks Put Together Their Ball Club in Last Week's Expansion Draft," *Sports Illustrated*, December 1, 1997: 84-85.

30  Ibid.

31  Turnbow: 29.

32  "Baseball," *The Sporting News*, August 17, 1998: 47.

33  Turnbow: 29 "Baseball," *The Sporting News*, October 26, 1998: 60.

34  "Baseball," *The Sporting News*, October 26, 1998: 60.

35  John Romano, "Old Wounds," *Tampa Bay Times*, July 17, 2002: 1C.

36  Ibid.

37  Turnbow: 29.

38  Romano: 5C.

39  Fred Goodall, "Martinez Gets Nasty After Fight," *Indiana* (Pennsylvania) *Gazette*, August 31, 2000: 21; "Transactions," *Indiana Gazette*, September 6, 2000: 28.

40  Turnbow: 29.

41  Michael Lewis, *Moneyball: The Art of Winning an Unfair Game* (New York: W.W. Norton, 2001), 204.

42  "Baseball," *The Sporting News*, May 7, 2001: 21.

43  "Baseball," *The Sporting News*, November 25, 2002: 57; Jeff Pearlman, "Straighter A's: A Mid-May Housecleaning Toned Down the Club's Personality, and by Ignoring the Threat of a Strike, Oakland Played Its Way to the Top of the AL West," *Sports Illustrated*: 59.

44  Carter Gaddis, "Lidle's Statement May Motivate Rays," *Tampa Tribune*, May 30, 2001: 25.

45  Ibid.

46  Mark Topkin, "Lidle Bashes Rays; Then Rays Bash Back," *Tampa Bay Times*, May 30, 2001, 1C.

47  Mark Topkin, "Lidle Bashes Rays.": 3C.

48  Susan Slusser, "The A's Remember the Man They Fondly Called 'Snacks,'" October 12, 2006; Accessed from sfgate.com/sports/article/The-A-s-remember-the-man-they-fondly-called-2550143.php; and Morrissey, 248.

49  Ibid.

50  Turnbow: 29.

51  Pearlman: 56-59.

52  Griffin.

53  youtube.com/watch?v=mOhD9gVEylo

54  Ibid.

55  Ibid; /mlb.mlb.com/mlb/news/tributes/obit_cory_lidle.jsp.

56  mlb.mlb.com/mlb/news/tributes/obit_cory_lidle.jsp; Mike Selleck, baseball information manager, Oakland Athletics, email correspondence with author, February 20, 2018.

57  "Five Minutes With … Cory Lidle," *USA Today Sports Weekly*, August 24-30, 2005, Accessed from HOF Clip File.

58  Ben Walker, "Twins Stop Athletics' Win Streak at 20 Games," *Indiana Gazette*, September 7, 2002: 15.

59  "Baseball," *The Sporting News*, September 21, 2002: 54.

60  Laurence Miedema and Craig Lancaster, "A's Deal Lidle to Toronto," *San Jose Mercury News*, Bayarea.com, November 17, 2002.

61  "A's Transactions," *New York Daily News*, November 18, 2002.

62  "Baseball," *The Sporting News*, November 25, 2002: 57.

63  "Baseball," *The Sporting News*, April 14, 2003: 50.

64  "Five Minutes With … Cory Lidle," *USA Today Sports Weekly*, August 24-30, 2005, accessed from HOF Clip File.

65  Tyler Kepner, "In Lidle, Yankees Have Extra Pitcher and Backup Pilot," *New York Times*, September 8, 2006.

66  "Lidle: Bonds' Chase Not 'Legitimate,'" SI.Com, May 4, 2006, accessed from HOF Clip File.

67  Dan Gelson, "Luckless Lidle Stifles Pittsburgh," *Indiana* (Pennsylvania) *Gazette*, July 9, 2006: 17.

68  Morrissey, 155.

69  Jim Salisbury, "Sorry! Lidle Backs Down, but Rhodes Gets His Back Up," *Philadelphia Inquirer*, August 2, 2006: E1, E3.

70  Ibid.

71  Michael Morrissey, "Wagner: Lidle's 'Chicken,'" *New York Post*, August 5, 2006, accessed from HOF Clip File.

72  Alex Belth, "Slaughterhouse Five (Let the Good times Roll)," August 21, 2008, accessed at bronxbanter.baseballtoaster.com/archives/2006_08.html.

73  Tyler Kepner, "In Lidle, Yankees Have."

74  baseball-reference.com/postseason/2006_ALDS1.shtml.

75  Tyler Kepner, "Lidle Had Passion for Flying." *New York Times*, October 12, 2016: D1.

76  Ibid.

77  Tyler Kepner, "In Lidle, Yankees Have."

78  Ibid.

79  Bill Sanderson, "Lidle's Bad Turn," *New York Post*, November 4, 2006, accessed from HOF Clip File.

80  Ibid.

81  Associated Press, "Plane-Maker Cleared in Cory Lidle's Death," May 24, 2001, ESPN.Com, accessed from HOF Clip File.

82  Pete Iorizzo, "Seven Mets Were Former Teammates," *Albany Times Union*, October 12, 2006: C4.

83  Billy Wagner, "May God Help Cory's Family Get Well," *New York Post*, October 12, 2006, accessed from HOF Clip File.

84  Joe Henderson, "Lidle Remembered as Good Person," *Tampa Tribune*, October 12, 2006: 19.

85  Slusser, "The A's Remember."

86  Alex Belth, "A Sad Night in New York," October 11, 2006, Accessed at bronxbanterblog.com/2006/10/11/a-sad-night-in-new-york/.

87  Associated Press, "Family, Friends, Teammates Pay Tribute to Lidle," October 17, 2018, ESPN.Com, accessed from HOF Clip File.

88  "Honoring Lidle," *Oneonta* (New York) *Star*, February 16, 2007, accessed from HOF Clip File.

89  Cliff Corcoran, "Yankees 6 Blue Jays 3," bronxbanterblog.com/2007/03/.

90  Associated Press, "Council votes to create put statue of Cory Lidle in West Covina," April 5, 2007, accessed from HOF Clip File.

91  corylidle.com/about-us.

# DAMIAN MILLER

## By Joel Rippel

In 2002, in his sixth major-league season and 12th season of professional baseball, Damian Miller was named to the National League All-Star team.

His manager was happy his catcher received the recognition.

"I definitely have a soft spot for guys like Miller," Arizona Diamondbacks manager Bob Brenly said. "They're the guys who weren't drafted high but worked their way to the top. A lot of people don't realize how the odds are stacked against these guys. They don't get free passes like some bonus babies do."[1]

Miller was born on October 13, 1969, in La Crosse, Wisconsin. After graduating from West Salem High School, where he had been a three-sport athlete (football, basketball, and baseball), Miller enrolled at Viterbo University in La Crosse. Miller is the only major leaguer to be produced by the Catholic liberal-arts school (enrollment 2,700 in 2015), whose athletic teams competed at the NAIA level. The school has produced 11 professional baseball players.

As a freshman, Miller batted .312 with one home run and 19 RBIs in 26 games for the V-Hawks. As a sophomore, he hit .409 – the fourth-best single-season mark in school history – with 3 home runs and 22 RBIs in 34 games.

As a junior Miller batted .505 – the top single-season mark in school history – with 6 home runs and 46 RBIs (the RBIs were fourth-best in school history) in 36 games. He was named the NAIA District 14 Player of the Year after helping the V-Hawks get to within one game of the NAIA World Series. After the season he was selected in the 20th round of the 1990 amateur draft by the Minnesota Twins.

In his three seasons with the V-Hawks, the 6-foot-3, 200-pound Miller set school career records for batting average (.419), doubles (29), and RBIs (87). In 96 games he hit 10 home runs and had a .632 slugging percentage.

After signing with the Twins, Miller began his 18-year professional career with Elizabethton of the Appalachian League. He hit a home run in his first professional at-bat, going 2-for-3 with three RBIs against Johnson City on June 22. But his rookie season was cut short when he suffered a season-ending thumb injury in a collision at the plate on August 6.

While Miller recovered from the injury, he began the 1991 season at extended spring training. In the first week of May, he went 11-for-13 in five games to show that he was healthy. On May 10 he joined Kenosha (Wisconsin) of the Class-A Midwest League. He spent both the 1991 and 1992 seasons with Kenosha.

Miller, a right-handed batter, blossomed in his second season with Kenosha, hitting .292 with a .385 on-base percentage. Defensively, he threw out 38 percent of baserunners attempting to steal. He was named to the Midwest League All-Star team.

In 1993 Miller got his first taste of a big-league spring training by appearing in seven Twins exhibition games, going 0-for-4 as a nonroster player. He started the 1993 season at Fort Myers of the Class-A Florida State League. He hit just .212, but he was solid defensively as he threw out 33 percent of potential basestealers. His only home run was a grand slam on July 15 against Daytona. He finished the season in Double A after being promoted to Nashville on August 29. After another brief stint as a nonroster invitee in 1994, going 0-for-1 in two games, he spent the entire 1994 season with Nashville, rebounding with a .268 batting average in 103 games. He threw out 42 percent (third-best in the league) of potential basestealers.

Miller spent the entire 1995 and 1996 seasons with Triple-A Salt Lake City. In 1996 he hit .286 in 104 games and had a 15-game hitting streak (22-for-62, .355) from April 15 to May 5. His fielding percentage of .991 was tied for second-best in the league. He threw out 42 percent of potential basestealers.

In both seasons Miller again went to spring training with the Twins as a nonroster invitee. In late March of 1997 he was told that he would again start the season at Salt Lake. But he remained with the Twins until the end of spring training as an extra player and bullpen catcher.

"I never really was a candidate to make the team in training camp," said Miller. "It did give me enough of a taste of what [big-league] life might be like that I wanted it even more. I would say, 'Man, I don't want to go back to the minors,' but I always would."[2]

He put together solid numbers with Salt Lake in 1997. In 85 games, he hit 11 home runs and had 82 RBIs while batting a career-high .338. He was called up to the Twins on August 9 as a replacement for catcher Greg Myers, who was put on the disabled list with an ankle injury.

Miller made his major-league debut on August 10 against the New York Yankees as a pinch-hitter in the ninth in-

ning. The Twins, who were trailing 9-6, had runners at second and third with nobody out against reliever Mike Stanton. After Miller was announced as a pinch-hitter, the Yankees replaced the left-handed Stanton with closer Mariano Rivera. Miller popped out to right field.

After going 0-for-1 in each of the Twins' losses on August 11 and 12, Miller made his first big-league start on August 13 in Toronto. In his second at-bat of game, Miller singled to left field off Blue Jays starter Woody Williams for his first major-league hit.

On August 19, Miller hit his first major-league home run, in Detroit off Tigers starter Willie Blair. His two-run blast in the fifth inning was responsible for all of Minnesota's runs in an 8-2 loss to the Tigers.

Miller put together a seven-game hitting streak – going 10-for-25 – in mid-September. He punctuated the streak with his first major-league grand slam, off Milwaukee Brewers' starter Jeff D'Amico in a 5-2 victory in Minneapolis. In 25 games for the Twins in 1997, he hit .273 (18-for-66) with 2 home runs and 13 RBIs.

After the season, Miller was not among the 15 players protected by the Twins in the expansion draft to stock the rosters of the Tampa Bay Devil Rays and Arizona Diamondbacks. On draft day, November 18, he was taken by the Diamondbacks in the second round of the draft. Miller got an extended look in Arizona's first spring training.

The Arizona Republic's daily training camp log reported, "[Damian] Miller has been battling Kelly Stinnett for the No. 2 catching job behind Jorge Fabregas. Miller has struggled a bit [hitting .174 with one home run and two RBIs] while Stinnett has had a solid spring. But Manager Buck Showalter, not wanting to miss out on a chance to keep Miller on the squad because of his power as a right-handed hitter, has expanded Miller's horizons instead of limiting them. While some of the Diamondbacks traveled to Phoenix for a game against Oakland on Friday night, Miller stayed behind and took a bucketful of grounders at first base."[3]

The Diamondbacks decided to open their inaugural season with Fabregas and Stinnett, so Miller was optioned to Triple-A Tucson. He got off to a good start, hitting .349 with 11 RBIs in 18 games. He was recalled on May 6 and made his National League debut that night at New York's Shea Stadium in the Diamondbacks' 8-2 loss to the Mets. Miller entered the game in the ninth inning as a pinch-hitter for Brent Brede, who had also been selected from the Twins in the expansion draft. Facing Mets closer John Franco, Miller reached base on an error by second baseman Carlos Baerga.

Miller made his first start for the Diamondbacks on May 24 at home against the Los Angeles Dodgers, going 2-for-3 in Arizona's 8-5 victory.

Another highlight of the season for Miller was his first major-league appearances in his home state of Wisconsin. On July 31 he went 1-for-4 in the Diamondbacks' 8-2 victory over the Brewers in Milwaukee. Two days later, he went 3-for-3 with a solo home run in a 7-2 loss to the Brewers. For the season, he hit a team-leading .286 in 57 games with 3 home runs and 14 RBIs.

After hitting .264 in 53 at-bats in spring training in 1999, Miller began the season on an Opening Day roster for the first time. He and Stinnett split the catching duties for the Diamondbacks that season. Miller batted .270 with 11 home runs and 47 RBIs in 86 games. He missed the final two weeks of the regular season and the playoffs after a suffering a hairline fracture near his right thumb while blocking a pitch in the dirt in a game against the Rockies in Denver on September 21. Before he left the game in the ninth inning, he had homered twice – his first multiple-home-run game.

Miller participated in a defensive rarity in the Diamondbacks' 4-0 victory over visiting San Diego on May 25. He teamed with pitcher Randy Johnson for three strikeout/throw-out double plays. It was the first time a catcher had participated in three double plays of that nature since Shanty Hogan of the New York Giants in 1931.

The Diamondbacks went into the 2000 season with Miller and Stinnett again sharing the catching duties. On April 4 Miller made the first Opening Day start of his career and celebrated by hitting a three-run home run in his first at-bat in the Diamondbacks' 6-4 victory over the visiting Philadelphia Phillies.

On May 9 Miller hit a solo home run and a walk-off grand slam off Orel Hershiser in the 12th inning of Arizona's 11-7 victory over the Los Angeles Dodgers. The five RBIs were a career high. On August 16 he went 4-for-4 and drove in two runs in Arizona's 5-1 victory over the Phillies in Philadelphia, the first four-hit game of his career.

For the second time in as many years, Miller's season

came to end prematurely with an injury on September 21. He suffered a sprained right foot in the sixth inning of Arizona's 8-7 loss to the Giants in San Francisco. Miller had doubled in his final at-bat. For the season, Miller appeared in 100 games and batted .275 with 10 home runs and 44 RBIs.

Miller became the regular catcher for the Diamondbacks in 2001, playing in a career-high 123 games (111 starts). He got off to a slow start offensively. On May 29 he was hitting just .218. Over his next 48 appearances, between May 30 and August 11, he batted .335 with 12 doubles, 8 home runs, and 25 RBIs. In a six-game stretch in late July, he went 13-for-22 and had the second four-hit game of his career. Even though he was hampered late in the season by a strained right shoulder, he finished the regular season with a .271 batting average, a career-high 13 home runs, and 47 RBIs.

With 92 victories, the Diamondbacks earned their second National League West Division title. In the Division Series against St. Louis, Miller went 4-for-15 in the Diamondbacks' series victory in five games. In their conquest of Atlanta in five games in the National League Championship Series, he went 3-for-17. In the World Series against the New York Yankees, he went 4-for-21 with two doubles and two RBIs. In Game Seven the Diamondbacks went into the bottom of the ninth trailing 2-1 with Mariano Rivera on the mound for the Yankees. Mark Grace led off the inning with a single, bringing Miller to the plate. Miller bunted and Rivera threw wildly to second base trying to get pinch-runner David Dellucci at second. The Diamondbacks went on to score two runs to win the game, 3-2, and the World Series.

A controversy involving Miller developed after the Series. Miller, who had been a replacement player during spring training in 1995, was not a member of the Major League Baseball Players Association. Some of his teammates wanted Miller to be included in the royalties from World Series souvenirs. But they were voted down. Miller's name does not appear on any official commemorative merchandise from the 2001 World Series.

Miller started the 2002 season strong. After going hitless on Opening Day, he went 21-for-69 with 22 RBIs in his next 20 contests. His 22 RBIs in April were a monthly high for his career. During that stretch he had three four-RBI games and twice he was part of three consecutive home runs by the Diamondbacks – Steve Finley, Miller, and Grace on April 28, and Danny Bautista, Finley, and

Miller on May 3. On June 30, batting .285, he was named to the National League All-Star team as a reserve. In the All-Star Game, on July 9, at Milwaukee, he went 2-for-3 with two doubles and an RBI in the 11-inning, 7-7 tie.

After the All-Star break Miller was limited by a lower back strain and from July 24 to August 14 he was on the disabled list for the first time in his career. After playing in 71 of Arizona's 87 games before the All-Star Game, he started just 24 times in the second half. Four days after coming off the disabled list, Miller hit his first inside-the-park home run in a 3-2 loss to the Chicago Cubs at Wrigley Field.

The Diamondbacks earned their second consecutive division title with 98 victories, but they were swept in the Division Series by the St. Louis Cardinals. Miller was 1-for-2 against the Cardinals.

For the season, he batted .249 with 22 doubles, 11 homers, and 42 RBIs in 101 games. Defensively, he was the top catcher in the National League with a .997 fielding percentage, throwing out 38 percent of would-be basestealers. He did not make an error until August 31, and made only two all year.

Miller, who was paid $2.7 million in 2002, went into the offseason eligible for arbitration for the first time. On November 13, the Diamondbacks traded him to the Chicago Cubs for two minor leaguers, outfielder Gary Johnson and pitcher David Noyce.

The Cubs acquired Miller to be their regular catcher in 2003 and he played in 114 games. He hit a career low .233 with 9 home runs and 36 RBIs for the National League Central champion Cubs. In the postseason for the third consecutive year, Miller went 1-for-11 in the Cubs' 3-2 series victory over Atlanta in the National League Division Series and then went 2-for-10 in their loss to Florida in the Championship Series.

In December the Cubs traded Miller to the Oakland Athletics. It was reported that he was sent to the Athletics as a player to be named when the Cubs acquired catcher Michael Barrett. But it was technically a separate deal as the Cubs agreed to pay $800,000 of Miller's $3 million salary and the teams agreed to exchange minor leaguers before the 2004 season opener.

Miller rebounded to hit .272 in 2004 and reached career highs with 58 RBIs, 397 at-bats, 108 hits, and 25 doubles

while matching his career high with 39 walks. He hit five of his nine home runs and had 25 of his 58 RBIs in a 20-game stretch from June 6 to July 3. Between June 6 and June 11, he had five consecutive multiple-RBI games, driving in 16 runs total. In 19 games in June, he had 20 RBIs – the second-best month of his career. Between June 25 and July 8, Miller put together a career-high 10-game hitting streak (17-for-40).

Miller set an Oakland team record with a .999 fielding percentage with just one error. He began the season with 96 consecutive errorless games before committing his only error of the season on September 11. The error was his first since July 18, 2003, and ended a streak of 139 consecutive errorless games and 1,012 total chances without an error. That was the sixth-longest streak of consecutive errorless chances by a catcher in major-league history.

After the 2004 season, Miller became a free agent. On November 23, he and the Milwaukee Brewers reached agreement on a three-year contract worth a reported $8.75 million. The deal was held up briefly until team medical personnel could evaluate an MRI of Miller's right shoulder.

"Over the last three years, Damian has dealt with some great pitching staffs with the Cubs, Diamondbacks and Athletics and he's been in pennant races with all of them," Brewers' general manager Doug Melvin said. "This no doubt will bring a lot to this ballclub. Plus, we've scuffled for two years at the bottom of the lineup. We're hoping he can help out there too."[4]

Miller and Chad Moeller split the catching duties for the Brewers in 2005. Miller appeared in 114 games and ranked third among National League catchers with a .996 fielding percentage. He batted .273 with 25 doubles, 9 home runs and 43 RBIs. In 2006, Miller played in 101 games and batted .251 with a career-high 28 doubles, 6 home runs, and 38 RBIs. In the Brewers' 11-0 victory over the visiting Cincinnati Reds on April 22, he tied his career highs with four hits and five RBIs. He was one of five Brewers to hit a home run in their seven-run fourth inning. It was the fifth time in major-league history that a team hit five home runs in an inning. At the All-Star break, Miller was hitting .273 with 5 home runs and 28 RBIs. He batted just .207 after the break.

In 2007 Miller played in just 58 games, his fewest since 1998, and batted just .237 with 4 home runs and 24 RBIs. Despite his weakness at the plate, Miller had two offensive highlights. On June 27 against the Houston Astros on "La Crosse Day," Miller hit a walk-off, three-run home run in the 11th inning to give the Brewers a 6-3 victory. (It was the second walk-off home run of his career.) In his next start, on July 2, he enjoyed the best game of his career, going 4-for-5 with two home runs, including his sixth career grand slam, and driving in a career-high seven runs.

After the season, Miller filed for free agency but went unsigned. Early in the 2008 season, he drew interest from the New York Yankees after Jorge Posada was hurt and the San Diego Padres after Barrett was hurt. But Miller declined. "If I came back now, it would be only for the money and, if you play baseball, that's not why you should do it," Miller said on May 5 at a meeting of the Wisconsin State Associated Press sports editors. Miller told the group there was only one team that could convince him to play – the Brewers.[5]

In his 11-year major-league career, Miller batted .262 with 87 home runs and 406 RBIs in 989 games. He summed up his career by saying, "The most important thing for me was being a good teammate. Do the little things right, be respectful to your teammates, to the other team and the game."[6]

After retiring, Miller returned to his hometown, La Crosse, where he helped coach youth baseball teams, including West Salem's 16-and-under Legion team and the Coulee Christian High School team. After five seasons as an assistant at Coulee Christian, Miller took over as the head coach in 2017. As of 2018 he also coached basketball at the school.

Miller and his wife, Jeanne, have known each other since first grade. They started dating as high-school juniors and married shortly after graduating from high school. They have two children.

Miller was named to the Viterbo University Wall of Fame in 2001 and the La Crosse Area Baseball Hall of Fame in 2018.

## Sources

In addition to the sources cited in the Notes, the author also consulted Baseball-Reference.com, viterboathletics.com, Mlb.com, newspapers.com, and Retrosheet.org.

## Notes

1 Pedro Gomez: "Struggles Make Miller's All-Star Game Even Sweeter," *Arizona Republic* (Phoenix), July 8, 2002: C8.

2 Patrick Reusse, "Kelly: Twins Lack Makeup for Move to National League," *Minneapolis Star Tribune,* August 11, 1997: C7.

3 "Camp Log," *Arizona Republic*, March 22, 1998: C16.

4 Associated Press: "Brewers Finalize Deal with Miller," *Eau Claire* (Wisconsin) *Leader-Telegram*, November 30, 2004: 2D.

5 Brad Zimanek, "Miller Retired, Unless Brewers Call," *Appleton-Fox Cities* (Wisconsin) *Post Crescent*, May 6, 2008: D2.

6 Colten Bartholomew, "Miller Focused on Youth Coaching After MLB Career," *La Crosse Tribune*, March 15, 2016.

# JEFF SUPPAN

## By Dan Taylor

During the first seven seasons of the 2000s, no team in the National League won more games or enjoyed more success than the St. Louis Cardinals. Guided by Hall of Fame manager Tony La Russa, the Cardinals won 658 games, five division titles, and one World Series. During the 2004-2006 seasons, La Russa handed the ball in some of the team's biggest games to a determined, cunning pitcher, Jeff Suppan, who delivered some of the more memorable performances of that remarkable run.

The youngest of five children of Larry and Kathleen Suppan, Jeff was born on January 2, 1975, in Oklahoma City, Oklahoma. Larry Suppan was an air-traffic controller. His career had taken him from the nation's capital to Oklahoma, and by the time Jeff was six months old, the Suppans, their four boys, and their daughter were headed west to Southern California. "I was the only one of us who basically got to grow up in one place," Jeff Suppan said with a chuckle.[1] For Larry Suppan, the move began a 20-year stint in the control tower at Los Angeles International Airport.

The Suppans settled in the suburban community of West Hills, 35 miles northwest of Los Angeles in the burgeoning San Fernando Valley. Jeff became immersed in a variety of sports, but whether he joined others from the neighborhood in soccer, flag football, or basketball, it was baseball that captured most of his attention. He began playing the game as a 6-year-old in a T-ball league at Shadow Ranch Recreation Center. When Jeff was 10, his father arranged for him to receive pitching lessons from a Kansas City Royals minor-league pitcher, Guy Hansen. "I used the curveball he taught me my entire career," Suppan recalled. For the next six years, Hansen and the Suppans would get together once a year for a refresher session. The area was a youth-baseball hotbed that included future major leaguers Randy Wolf, Ryan McGuire, and Brad Fullmer.[2]

When Suppan was 13 his development expanded. His sister, Karen, had become involved in college athletics and shared what she learned. "She talked to me about mental preparation, about focus and concentration. Because of her, I read The Mental Game of Baseball," Jeff Suppan said. In 1987 Karen Suppan was a member of the Cal State Northridge volleyball team that won the NCAA Division II National Championship.

In the fall of 1989 Suppan enrolled at Crespi Carmelite High School in Encino. The school's baseball program had been made a Southern California power by its legendary coach, Scott Muckey. As a freshman, Suppan made the varsity. Muckey stressed throwing strikes and getting ahead in the count. "Pitchers had to have a two-to-one strikes-to-balls ratio in practice, or you didn't pitch in games," Suppan said. The young pitcher not only thrived, he rose above others in the region. The summer after his junior season placed a stamp of excellence on his reputation. The teen, who was as one scout described "a bit out of shape," had lost weight. In American Legion ball, Suppan, now in better physical condition, amassed an 8-1 record, an 0.93 earned-run average, and struck out 120 batters in 69 innings pitched.[3] At every game that Suppan pitched, his mother, Kathleen, was in the bleachers behind home plate keeping score. "It was a way to calm her nerves," the pitcher said.

Throughout the American Legion season, scouts and college recruiters began to come around. Most were impressed. "Puts the ball where he wants. Moves the ball around, changes speeds well," wrote Bob Bishop of the Kansas City Royals, who rated Suppan highly.[4] During the November signing period in 1992, Suppan inked a letter of intent to attend UCLA. "I feel Jeff is a high school pitcher who I could hand the ball to, and he could pitch against anybody we play right now and win," UCLA's coach, Gary Adams, told the *Los Angeles Times*.[5] The 17-year-old's choice of school closed an intense recruiting battle between the Bruins and their arch-rivals, USC.

Perhaps the most ardent of Suppan's followers was the legendary San Francisco Giants evaluator George Genovese. Genovese had Suppan rated high on his draft list. In March of 1993, just weeks into the high-school season, he asked the Giants director of scouting, Bob Hartsfield, to travel south to get a firsthand look at Suppan.

Crespi was to play Long Beach Millikan in the El Segundo Tournament. The day before the game a blood drive was held at Crespi High School. The organizer pressed Suppan to donate. "I can't. I'm pitching tomorrow," he said. The woman continued her persuasive efforts, finally telling the teenager that his body would replenish the blood in 24 hours. On her word, Suppan rolled up his sleeve and donated. That evening, when he informed his father what he had done, Larry Suppan became alarmed. "He ran out and bought a steak for me for dinner," Jeff recalled. The next afternoon with Genovese and Hartsfield in the stands, a weakened Suppan struggled on the mound. "I was terrible. I had nothing," Suppan said. Crespi lost, 3-1. "It was my only loss of my senior year."

In the stands, Hartsfield was so unimpressed that he burst into an expletive-filled tirade directed at Genovese.[6] After just two innings he shouted, "Take me back to the airport!"[7] Hartsfield insisted to Genovese that the Giants would not consider Jeff Suppan. The scout phoned Joe Stephenson, the Boston Red Sox area scout. "Joe lived 40 miles away in Anaheim and rarely traveled north to the San Fernando Valley. I thought he probably didn't know about Suppan but would like him once he saw him," Genovese said.[8]

Suppan bounced back from the defeat to throw a two-hitter and strike out 14 in a win over St. Paul and then followed it with a no-hitter and a 6-0 win over Harvard-Westlake. After throwing a three-hitter at Chaminade High, Suppan had compiled four consecutive shutouts, two shy of the area record held by Scott McGregor.[9] The pitcher had also amassed a string of 39 consecutive scoreless innings. Both streaks ended in Suppan's next start. By the time he concluded his senior season, Suppan had pitched Crespi to the semifinals of the area playoffs. He tallied 11 wins against just one defeat, sported an earned-run average of 0.92 and had struck out 127 batters in 91 innings.[10] He also batted .480 with 11 home runs. Suppan was named Mission League Player of the Year, San Fernando Valley Player of the Year, and Southern Section CIF Division I Player of the Year.[11]

When the first day of the major-league amateur draft arrived on June 3, 1993, Suppan did not know what to expect. "I was naïve to what was going on," he said. That evening he received a call from Joe Stephenson telling him Boston had selected Suppan in the draft's second round. He was the 49th overall pick and the first player chosen that year from Southern California.[12] "It's awesome, unbelievable. I don't know what else to say," Suppan told the *Los Angeles Times*.[13] For more than three weeks the Suppans and Red Sox negotiated before agreeing on a deal. The signing bonus was reported to be worth $240,000. "It's a substantial amount," Stephenson told the Los Angeles Times. "[The Suppans] are happy and I am happy."[14]

After taking a senior trip to Cancun, Mexico, then pitching in an area all-star game, Suppan signed and then began his professional career in Fort Myers, Florida, with the Red Sox farm club in the Rookie Gulf Coast League. The cross-country move and professional baseball lifestyle brought sharp change to a previously structured routine. "I was homesick for probably two years," the pitcher said. It was at Fort Myers that Suppan was introduced to a coach whose teaching and advocacy would put him on a fast track to the big leagues. "Al Nipper was an incredible developer. That's when I started learning." Nipper urged Suppan to keep a journal, and the young pitcher was soon filling pages with notes, scouting reports on opposing hitters, reminders about things he had done well as well as poorly, diagrams of arm angles and pitching mechanics, and advice about professional comportment, focus, and concentration. "Nip spoke a lot about the mental part of the game," Suppan said.

Suppan finished the short season campaign with a 4-3 won-lost record, an earned-run average of 2.18, and 64 strikeouts in 57⅔ innings pitched. The following spring, he was assigned to Sarasota of the Class-A Florida State League. Suppan lost his first five decisions and surrendered eight home runs. Nipper suggested he add a new pitch to his arsenal. He called the pitch the "fosh," a mixture of split-finger fastball and changeup. The repertoire addition helped Suppan go on a tear. He won 11 of his next 12 starts and ended the season with a 13-7 record.[15] "He's already learned what some pitchers in Triple A haven't, and that's to control the hitter's bat speed by changing speeds," Nipper explained.[16] The results got the attention of the Red Sox front office.

Suppan's results and Nipper's advocacy saw the young prospect begin the 1995 season with the Red Sox' Double-A team in Trenton, New Jersey. As Suppan shone for Trenton, starting pitching became a problem in Boston. The two hurlers that the Red Sox counted on the most couldn't be counted on. Roger Clemens had an earned-run average of 5.30 and a fast ball that was being clocked at 86 miles an hour. Aaron Sele was on the disabled list with shoulder tendinitis. Ideas for help were weighed. Trades and call-ups were debated. In mid-July it was decided that Jeff Suppan would be summoned. In only his second full season of professional baseball, Jeff Suppan was in the major leagues. He was the youngest pitcher in the majors. On July 17, 1995, the 20-year-old made his major-league debut. "I said to myself, This is real, not something you dream about," he recalled. Suppan was given a start against the Kansas City Royals. He was greeted by Keith Lockhart, who lined the sixth pitch Suppan threw in the big leagues over the right-field wall for a home run. Suppan was removed with two outs in the sixth inning. He had given up three runs, struck out four, and allowed nine hits. Boston lost, 4-3. Suppan made two more starts. The Red Sox were defeated in each. He acknowledged that he had let Fenway Park's Green Monster, the sometimes intimidating 37-foot-high wall that stands just 310 feet from

home plate, affect his style of pitching. At the close of July, the Red Sox returned Suppan to the minor leagues.

One month later he was back in the big leagues. He made five relief appearances as the Red Sox fought to catch the Yankees in the American League East pennant race. Suppan was especially stellar in a September 19 appearance against the Milwaukee Brewers. He faced seven batters and struck out five of them.

The young pitcher's performances raised eyebrows around baseball. In January, when Boston engaged in trade talks with Montreal to try to pry Wil Cordero from the Expos, Montreal's front office insisted on receiving Suppan in return.[17] The request was rejected.

Over the next two seasons, Suppan shuttled between Pawtucket and Boston. In 1996 he won 10 games for the PawSox to earn promotion to Boston. In his first start, Suppan pitched one-hit ball through six innings against the Minnesota Twins. "He should, and I think he does, feel good about the way he threw the ball," praised his manager, Kevin Kennedy.[18] In 1997 Suppan was 5-1 at Pawtucket, then made 22 starts for the Red Sox and compiled a 7-3 record.

During the winter of 1997-98, the major leagues added two expansion teams, the Tampa Bay Devil Rays and the Arizona Diamondbacks. Buck Showalter was hired to manage the Diamondbacks and embarked on an ambitious plan to construct the new club. "Arizona hired a lot of scouts the year before," recalled Los Angeles Dodgers advance scout John Van Ornum. "They had guys out scouting at every level of the minor leagues from A ball to Triple A."[19] The Diamondbacks placed a premium on young pitchers, and on the day of the expansion draft, the second player they chose was Jeff Suppan. "I was surprised," Suppan recalled. "I'd been told I was Boston's number-one prospect."

The change of organizations represented a new opportunity. Suppan's standing with his new club turned sour before the team had ever played its first game. "I got chicken pox. I got the flu twice. I had a bad spring. I got sent down," Suppan recounted. What impacted his performance most, however, was a bout of tendinitis in his right shoulder.

Four weeks into the 1998 season, Suppan's position in the big leagues became tenuous. He had lost all three of his decisions. His earned-run average was in the 7's. Pitching to avoid demotion, he impressed Showalter with six strong innings in a start against the Florida Marlins. It proved only a temporary stay. Over the next two months Suppan shuttled between Phoenix and the Diamondbacks' Triple-A team at Tucson. Finally, on September 3, the Diamondbacks sold Suppan's contract to the Kansas City Royals.

With Kansas City, Suppan found stability and success. He became a mainstay of the Royals' starting rotation. As Suppan's career blossomed, his life away from the game brought bliss as well. In 1996 he had met Dana Ozark. After dating long-distance for four years, the couple married in November 2000.

Suppan spent four seasons with Kansas City. He pitched an average of 213 innings per year. In three of those four years, Suppan led the Royals pitching staff in wins.

The winter of 2002-2003 put Suppan on the free-agent market for the first time. He accepted a one-year offer from the Pittsburgh Pirates for a reported $1 million.[20] Expectations were not high in the Steel City for either Suppan or the Pirates, but the newcomer won over fans by winning his first four starts. By the All-Star break, rumors were rampant that the Pirates were shopping several of their veteran players. Suppan, with eight wins, was mentioned prominently.[21] On July 28, Suppan pitched a shutout to beat the St. Louis Cardinals 3-0. Three days later, at the July 31 nonwaiver-trade deadline, Pittsburgh dealt Suppan to his original organization, the Boston Red Sox, in a five-player swap that brought Mike Gonzalez and Freddy Sanchez to the Pirates.

When Suppan rejoined the Red Sox, they were chasing the New York Yankees for the American League East championship. Boston trailed the Yankees by 3½ games and had fallen into what would become a four-game losing skid. Suppan's first start came against the California Angels, who managed to score seven times against him over five innings. In his next start, Suppan pitched into the seventh inning but surrendered five runs in a loss to Baltimore. On August 15, the Seattle Mariners scored four times in five innings against Suppan. "He can't pitch in the American League," a scout observed.[22] Suppan didn't agree but said, "I felt like the National League suited my style better. The American League is more of a stuff league. Those hitters are swinging for the fences. The National League is more situational. There's more bunting. There's more taking. You have a pitcher you pitch to. I enjoy that game." Suppan finished 2003 with

13 wins, 10 with Pittsburgh and three with Boston.

Again, Suppan found himself on the free-agent market during the offseason. This time, however, his 13-win season brought larger offers and from several teams. The Detroit Tigers and Pittsburgh Pirates tried to entice the pitcher.[23] The offer that Suppan elected to accept, however, distinctly changed his career – it was from the Cardinals.

It was in St. Louis that Suppan would flourish and his career would reach a zenith. The change of scenery did not change Suppan's habit of starting slowly. He lost his first two starts with the Cardinals but soon turned things around in a big way. Suppan won four of his next six decisions, then cemented himself as a new fan favorite with a brilliant performance against the Seattle Mariners on the Fourth of July 2004. That afternoon, Suppan pitched into the eighth inning. He scattered four hits, walked just two batters, struck out seven, and induced eight groundball outs in a 2-1 St. Louis victory.[24] "Having four or five Gold Glovers behind you was great for a contact pitcher," he said. In his next start, Suppan beat the Chicago Cubs, 5-2, for his eighth win in 13 decisions, which helped to push the Cardinals out to an eight-game lead in the National League Central Division.

"I really liked the way he worked," recalled advance scout Van Ornum. "He had the four pitches. None of them was really outstanding, but he got the most from what he had. He flat got you out." Mixing superior control with an ability to change speeds and locations, Suppan won 16 games, which led the Cardinals staff and tied Randy Johnson, Greg Maddux, and Carlos Zambrano for fifth best in the National League.

St. Louis won the Central Division title, and for the first time in his career, Suppan pitched under the bright lights of the postseason. His first playoff experience came against his hometown team, the Los Angeles Dodgers, in Dodger Stadium. The Cardinals had won the first two games of the best-of-five National League Division Series, in St. Louis. When the series moved to Los Angeles, the Dodgers won Game Three. Suppan drew the start for Game Four. Knowing that his parents, brothers, sister, and many friends would be in the stands, Suppan allowed himself a brief 10-minute pregame interlude to listen for encouraging shouts, wave to fans, and soak up the excitement of the moment, then he calmly shut it all out to focus his attention on the challenge before him.

The early innings of the game were back and forth. The second batter Suppan faced, Jayson Werth, hit a home run that gave Los Angeles a 1-0 lead. In the third inning, St. Louis scored a run to go on top, 2-1. Their lead was short-lived, however. In the bottom half of the inning, the Dodgers evened the score on a walk, a single by Steve Finley, and a sacrifice fly by Adrian Beltre. Whatever fervor was building about Dodger Stadium, however, soon evaporated. Finley was the last Dodger to reach base against Suppan. Albert Pujols crushed a three-run home run one inning later, and Suppan retired 13 Dodgers in a row before exiting the game for a pinch-hitter in the top of the eighth inning. St. Louis triumphed, 6-2, to win the series and advance to the National League Championship Series.

Following the final out the visitors' clubhouse erupted in revelry. At the center of the celebration was a jubilant Jeff Suppan. Donning goggles, the pitching hero was drenched with champagne and showered with praise. "This is probably the biggest and best outing of his career, something he'll remember forever," said fellow pitcher Matt Morris, who added, "I'm proud of him."[25]

The Cardinals faced Houston in the NLCS. Suppan made two starts in the series. He was defeated by Houston in Game Three, then with a trip to the World Series on the line, was given the ball to start the decisive seventh game against the Astros ace, Roger Clemens. The first batter of the game, Houston's Craig Biggio, tagged Suppan for a home run. Once the cheers of the Astros fans abated, their decibel level never rose again. For six innings Suppan changed speeds and mixed pitch locations to keep the Astros at bay. When he walked off the mound after the sixth inning, he had surrendered just three hits, walked only two, allowed one earned run, and struck out six. All around Busch Stadium, 52,140 Cardinals fans were chanting "Soup! Soup! Soup!" Nine outs later, the Cardinals had won, 5-2, and were on their way to the World Series. "You need to give credit to Suppan," said Cardinals first baseman Albert Pujols. "I mean, this guy made some pitches out there."[26]

The 2004 World series was a historic and emotional event. It was the 100th World Series. The American League champion Boston Red Sox had not won the World Series since 1918. Suppan drew the start against his former team in Game Three. After retiring the first two batters, he surrendered a home run to Manny Ramirez, and the Cardinals fell behind. David Ortiz then singled. Though Suppan shrugged it off and retired seven of the next eight batters, it was a miscue on the basepaths that he would be most remembered for in the Series. In the bottom of the third inning, Suppan beat out a roller toward third base for the Cardinals' second hit of the game. Edgar Renteria then doubled, sending Suppan to third base. The next hitter, Larry Walker, hit a smash to second base and was thrown out at first. On the play, protocol called for Suppan to dash for home on a ball hit to the second-base side of the diamond. However, the pitcher thought that instead of "Go!" he heard the Cardinals third-base coach yell "No!", so he stopped. After a momentary pause, he broke for home but again stopped then tried to retreat to third base. Seeing the mistake, Boston's first baseman, David Ortiz, fired the ball across the diamond and Suppan was tagged out as he dove toward the third-base bag. "It was a big break, and we took advantage of it," said Boston's pitcher, Pedro Martinez, who would retire 13 Cardinals in a row after the gaffe.[27] The Red Sox won, 4-1, and went on to sweep the Cardinals and claim baseball's crown.

In 2005 Suppan was again a mainstay of the Cardinals pitching staff and among the top hurlers in the National League. He replicated his 2004 feat of 16 wins. The Cardinals again won the National League Central Division. They swept San Diego in the Division Series, but in six games fell to Houston for the pennant. Suppan started Game Four and pitched five innings of three-hit ball with five strikeouts. He left with the game tied, 1-1. Houston added a run in the seventh inning to win, 2-1.

Suppan helped the Cardinals make a third consecutive trip to the postseason in 2006. He won 12 games during the regular season to help St. Louis win its third straight National League Central Division title. Against San Diego in the Division Series, Suppan was given the start in Game Three. His teammates had little success against San Diego's pitching that afternoon and lost, 3-1. The following night, however, St. Louis won to eliminate the Padres. The National League Championship Series elevated Suppan to a stage to which few players ascend. After his teammates had split the first two games of the NLCS with the New York Mets, Suppan's heroics almost single-handedly changed the momentum. In the top of the second inning of Game Three, Suppan sent a long fly ball over the outstretched glove of New York left fielder Endy Chavez. It bounced off the top of the wall and caromed over for a home run. "I swung, it ran into my bat. I don't know why that is," Suppan said after the game.[28]

On the mound Suppan was even better. For eight innings he did not allow the Mets to score. When he left the game for a pinch-hitter, he had scattered three hits and did not allow a walk until the eighth inning. St. Louis won the game, 5-0.

Five nights later Suppan went to the mound trying to send the Cardinals into the World Series for the second time in three years. A crowd of more than 56,000 packed New York's Shea Stadium for the deciding seventh game of the series. Suppan pitched seven innings. He allowed only two hits and one first-inning run. The Cardinals triumphed, 3-1. For his efforts, Suppan was named the Most Valuable Player of the NLCS.

In the World Series, Suppan started Game Four against the Detroit Tigers. He pitched six strong innings and the Cardinals won, 5-4. The next night St. Louis prevailed, 4-2, and claimed its first World Series championship in 24 years.

While the 2006 season brought awards and rewards, away from the ballpark it brought pain. When the Cardinals were in San Diego during the season for a series with the Padres, Larry and Kathleen Suppan traveled to visit their son. It was there that Kathleen Suppan broke the news to her son: She had been diagnosed with cancer. Her optimism was reassuring. And subsequent updates were positive.

After the World Series, Suppan's contract with the Cardinals expired, and he again became a free agent. Several teams extended offers, but one made by the Milwaukee Brewers proved too good to pass up. The pitcher agreed to a four-year contract worth $42 million.[29] "He gives us a big-game pitcher," Brewers general manager Doug Melvin told reporters.[30]

After losing his first two starts for the Brewers, he won his next five starts of the 2007 season. His third start as a Brewer came in St. Louis, where the Cardinals presented him with his World Series ring. Then Suppan went out and pitched strong baseball into the seventh inning to help Milwaukee win, 3-2. As hot as he was to start the season, Suppan soon went cold. He lost four consecutive starts. He rallied to win 12 games, which was tied for tops on the Milwaukee pitching staff.

During the winter of 2007-2008, the Suppans' world collapsed. Kathleen Suppan, whose condition had greatly improved since her 2006 cancer diagnosis, took a turn for the worse. On January 2, 2008, Jeff's 33rd birthday, his mother succumbed to pancreatic cancer. "It was devastating for our whole family," Suppan said. "She prayed for me before every game. We talked all the time. We had a great relationship. It was a big hit." Though he felt he was giving his all on the mound throughout the season, Suppan admitted that grief shadowed him: "I was sort of going through the motions. I was not really there." In late May elbow pains began to bother him. On July 7, he was placed on the 15-day disabled list. He finished the season with a 10-10 record and an earned-run average of 4.96.

In 2009 Suppan struggled. He gave up six runs in four innings and lost on Opening Day to the San Francisco Giants. The Chicago Cubs parlayed six walks into five runs and chased Suppan in the fourth inning of his next start. His skills were beginning to wane from age. (Suppan was 34 years old.) He was routinely booed. Suppan received regular criticism from the media. "Rich Donnelly once said, 'There are two types of players in this game. Those who have been humbled and those who are going to be humbled.' That was a humbling experience," Suppan said. The pitcher felt the weight of the big-money contract. He sought advice and perhaps internalized too much of it. The pitcher finished the season with a 7-12 record.

When Suppan's form did not improve after the first two months of the 2010 season, the Milwaukee Brewers bought out the remainder of his contract and released him. The Cardinals took a chance and signed Suppan for the remainder of the 2010 campaign. With St. Louis his form improved. He had left Milwaukee with a 7.84 earned-run average in 15 games pitched. With the Cardinals, he pitched 15 games and had an earned-run average of 3.84. On the final day of the season, Suppan showed flashes of his old self. He pitched six innings against the Colorado Rockies, did not allow a run, walked only one batter, and helped St. Louis to a 6-1 victory.

During the offseason, Suppan was left to wonder if his win over the Rockies was his final game in the major leagues. There were no calls with offers of a major-league contract. He accepted an offer of a minor-league deal with the San Francisco Giants. When the Giants informed him late in spring training that they wanted to send him to the minor leagues, Suppan asked for his release. Days later, Kansas City offered a similar deal, and Suppan spent 2011 with their Triple-A club in Omaha, where he went 11-8.

Before the 2012 season the San Diego Padres offered

Suppan a minor-league contract. He accepted but told his agent, "This season is it; I'm done." In spring training Suppan suffered an injury to his right triceps. While he was still nursing the injury in the minor leagues with Tucson, the Padres were beset with injuries to several pitchers. At the end of April, Suppan received a phone call from his agent. "Hey Soup," he blurted, "They want you for a start in the big leagues."

On May 2, needing all the guile he could muster to make an 87-mph fastball an effective weapon, Suppan beat the Milwaukee Brewers, 5-0. The performance drew a second opportunity, and on May 8, Suppan pitched the Padres to a 3-1 win over Colorado. He remained in the Padres' starting rotation through the month of May before a downturn in results brought a phone call from the Padres' general manager, Josh Byrnes, with Suppan's release.

Six months later Suppan asked his agent to submit his retirement papers to Major League Baseball. He asked that the end of his 17-year career be dated January 2 at 2:00 P.M. Pacific Time, the anniversary of his mother's passing in 2008.

During his minor-league season in the Kansas City organization, in 2011 the Royals gauged Suppan's interest about working for the club once he retired. In 2013 he attended scout school but felt he wasn't cut out for the role. In 2015 he accepted an offer from the Royals and became the pitching coach for their short-season Class-A farm club at Idaho Falls. In 2018 he entered his fourth season in the role.

In 2007, Jeff and Dana Suppan entered the restaurant business when they opened Soup's Sports Grill in Woodland Hills, California. The restaurant was popular with locals. In 2016 Suppan was approached by a real-estate investor who made an offer for the building that housed the restaurant, and the decision was made to sell and close.

Suppan has been actively involved in his alma mater, Crespi High School. He has served on the school's board of directors and for three seasons coached freshman baseball.

Jeff and Dana Suppan are parents of one son and one daughter. Jeff helps to coach his son's youth baseball team and his daughter's softball team.

As of 2018 the Suppans continued to call the San Fernando Valley home, residing in Calabasas, California.

## Sources

In addition to the sources cited in the Notes, the author also consulted Retrosheet.org and Baseball-Reference.com.

The author wishes to thank Jeff Suppan for his time and participation in this project.

## Notes

1 Unless otherwise noted, information for this story is from a telephone conversation with Jeff Suppan on February 14, 2018.

2 Eric Sondheimer, "Valley Newsbeat," *Los Angeles Times*, January 5, 1998.

3 Jeff Fletcher, "It All Falls Into Place for Suppan," *Los Angeles Times*, April 7, 1993.

4 Bob Bishop, telephone interview with author, February 21, 2018.

5 Jeff Fletcher, "Crespi's Suppan Has Turned on the Power," *Los Angeles Times*, May 5, 1993.

6 George Genovese with Dan Taylor, *A Scout's Report. My 70 Years in Baseball* (Jefferson, North Carolina: McFarland and Company, 2015), 210.

7 Ibid.

8 Ibid.

9 "Atmosphere Is Businesslike at Quartz Hill," *Los Angeles Times*, May 7, 1993.

10 Different editions of the *Los Angeles Times* reported his ERA as 0.85 and 0.92.

11 "Crespi's Suppan Named Division I Player of the Year," *Los Angeles Times*, June 27, 1993.

12 Jeff Fletcher, "Area Supplies Ample 2nd Helpings in Draft," *Los Angeles Times*, June 4, 1993.

13 Ibid.

14 Jeff Fletcher, "Crespi's Suppan Agrees to Sign with Red Sox," *Los Angeles Times*, June 29, 1993.

15 Mike Hiserman, "Suppan Wins Faster by Throwing Slower," *Los Angeles Times*, June 12, 1994.

16 "A Notes," *The Sporting News*, June 20, 1994.

17 Bob Nightengale, "Baseball Report," *The Sporting News*, January 15, 1996.

18 Joe Giuliotti, "Suppan's Start," *The Sporting News*, August 12, 1996.

19 John Van Ornum, telephone interview with author, February 15, 2018.

20  Dennis Tuttle, "Spring Training Preview," *The Sporting News*, February 17, 2003.

21  Ken Rosenthal, "Short on Starters," *The Sporting News*, July 21, 2003.

22  Ken Rosenthal, "Inside Dish," *The Sporting News*, August 25, 2003.

23  Ed Engle, "Team Reports," *The Sporting News*, December 1, 2003.

24  backtobaseball.com.

25  Bill Shaikin, "Suppan Gets the Job Done," *Los Angeles Times*, October 11, 2004.

26  Ben Bolch, "Cards Are All In," *Los Angeles Times*, October 22, 2004.

27  Mike DiGiovanna, "Riding a One-Away Train," *Los Angeles Times*, October 27, 2004.

28  Tim Brown, "Cardinals Pounce on Mets Early for 5-0 Win," *Los Angeles Times*, October 15, 2006.

29  "Suppan Goes from Series to Brewers," *Los Angeles Times*, December 25, 2006.

30  Ibid.

# HOW TAMPA BAY GOT ITS TEAM

## BY PETER M. GORDON

"If there's a greater day in the history of Tampa Bay, I don't know what it is," proclaimed Tampa Bay Devil Rays principal owner Vince Naimoli on March 20, 1995, the day the American League awarded a franchise to the group he headed.[1] After many years of city leaders striving to bring a team to the Tampa Bay area, Naimoli's group had finally achieved that goal.

Naimoli led the ownership group, but it was a community effort. After they received the official word, an editorial in the *St. Petersburg Times* said that St. Petersburg City Administrator Rick Dodge "should get a medal for fifteen years of thankless diligence quest to bring a major-league franchise to the area."[2] Major League Baseball rebuffed seven different attempts from various groups during those 15 years before finally awarding a franchise in 1995 to begin play in 1998.

Although the quest to bring a major-league franchise to the Tampa Bay area intensified in the early 1980s, it is not an exaggeration to say that it started at the turn of the twentieth century. Tampa Bay is a large harbor on the Florida Gulf Coast a little more than halfway down the length of the state. There is no city named Tampa Bay; the "Tampa Bay" in the names of sports franchises like the Rays, Buccaneers (football), and Lightning (hockey), mean they represent the geographic area and municipalities surrounding the Bay.

The two largest cities are Tampa, at the northeast extreme end of the bay, and St. Petersburg, on the southeast corner, bordered on the west by the Gulf of Mexico and on the south and east by Tampa Bay. Tampa is in Hillsborough County, and St. Petersburg is in Pinellas County. The municipalities in the area do cooperate on several projects, but in the case of the Devil Rays, the local effort to bring major-league baseball to the area started in St. Petersburg in the early twentieth century. During the late 1960s and early 1970s, St. Petersburg city officials, managers, and *St. Petersburg Times* publisher Jack Lang kept the dream of a major-league franchise alive. This leadership is one of the main reasons why Tampa Bay's major-league baseball franchise had its stadium in St. Petersburg.

St. Petersburg supported semipro baseball since its founding in the late nineteenth century. The semipro St. Petersburg Saints started regular play in 1902, and major-league teams

Opening Day program, March 31, 1998. The visiting Detroit Tigers beat the Devil Rays, 11-6. (Courtesy of the Tampa Bay Rays)

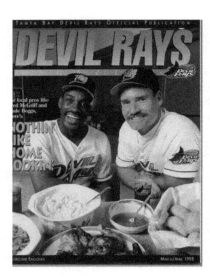

Fred McGriff and Wade Boggs on a 1998 Devil Rays' magazine. Both players grew up in the Tampa area (Courtesy of the Tampa Bay Rays)

began to play exhibition games in the area a few years later. In 1914 the St. Louis Browns, managed by Branch Rickey, became the first team to hold spring training in St. Petersburg. The Browns and Cubs played the first game between two major-league teams in the city. (The Cubs won, 3-2.) Either the financial arrangements or the competition wasn't to the Browns' liking, because they decided to train elsewhere in 1914.[3]

That might have been all for spring training in the area but for the efforts of one of the city's most prominent citizens, Al Lang. Lang had moved to St. Petersburg from Pittsburgh in 1910. His networking skills enabled him to rise through the city's political structure so quickly that by 1916 Lang was elected mayor. One of his endearing qualities for his fellow citizens was his effort to attract major-league teams to town. Once the Browns left, Lang persuaded the Phillies to train in St. Petersburg for the 1915 season. After the Phillies, led by Grover Cleveland Alexander and Gavvy Cravath, won the 1915 National League pennant, they trained in the city for the next three years.

For the next 70 years St. Petersburg was seldom without one, and sometimes two, baseball teams during spring training. During the 1940s one of the spring-training ballparks was named Al Lang Field in his honor. Games are still played there today.[4]

While Lang pushed to keep spring training in St. Petersburg, the dream of a major-league franchise seemed impossible. There had only been 16 major-league franchises since the turn of the twentieth century. When the leagues expanded in 1961 and 1962, they awarded franchises in the Northeast and Southwest and on the West Coast. Florida's growing population supported spring training,

but other cities got the prize.

In 1976 the NFL awarded the city of Tampa the expansion franchise that became the Buccaneers. The Bucs won the Super Bowl in January 2003, bringing the Tampa area its first major sports championship. The NHL Tampa Bay Lightning won the Stanley Cup in 2004. After the Bucs began playing, *St. Petersburg Times* publisher Jack Lake became a strong booster in editorials for a major-league-baseball franchise. Partly due to Lake's efforts, in 1983 a group of local businessmen formed the Tampa Bay Baseball Group (TBBG) to coordinate efforts to bring a major-league franchise to the area.[5]

One of the first teams the group approached was the Minnesota Twins. Calvin Griffith, whose family had owned the franchise since it was the Washington Senators, made his living from the team's profits. The Twins moved to the indoor Metrodome in 1982 but had an escape clause in their lease that they could trigger if the team failed to draw 800,000 fans in two of three seasons between 1982 and 1984. Twins attendance was over 900,000 in 1982 and over 800,000 in 1983. Nothing came of the discussions.

A pattern would soon emerge: A club that needed a new ballpark would dangle the fat wallets of the TBBG in front of city councils and state legislatures reluctant to approve new funding, in the hope that the competition would lead to more funding.

In 1985 TBBG approached the Oakland A's, only to find the team's interest wane as soon as the city provided upgrades to the Oakland Coliseum. Some cities would not commit to funding a ballpark until they had a team, but the St. Petersburg City Council thought it would help land a team if the city built the ballpark first. In 1985 the City Council appropriated $85 million to build a domed stadium. Its projected cost soon rose to $138 million. Commissioner Peter Ueberroth advised against building a ballpark on speculation, but the City Council decided to proceed.[6]

To demonstrate that local commitment went beyond the City Council, 20,000 fans pledged $50 each for seat licenses in the still-unbuilt ballpark. The city broke ground for the ballpark in 1986. As soon as it started to take shape, baseball owners and executives toured it.

In 1988 the Tampa Bay Baseball Group tried to buy the Chicago White Sox, who had failed to receive funding for a new ballpark. The threat of a move to Tampa Bay led

Illinois' governor, Big Jim Thompson, to literally stop the clocks in the Illinois State Assembly to keep the legislature in session until it approved a stadium funding bill.

The new Florida Suncoast Dome opened for business in 1990. The building soon got the nickname The Thunderdome, because its first major tenant was the NHL Tampa Bay Lightning. A baseball team remained elusive, but not for lack of trying. In 1990 the TBBG made a bid to buy the Kansas City Royals, but in the end the Royals received more support from Kansas City and decided to stay. The TBBG also made a strong bid to receive one of the new baseball expansion franchises awarded in 1991 to start play in 1993, but Major League Baseball awarded a franchise instead to a group from Miami led by Wayne Huizenga.

In 1992, local businessman and turnaround artist Vince Naimoli became the leader of the the Tampa Bay Baseball Group. Naimoli made his fortune buying money-losing companies, restructuring them, and turning them into profitable enterprises. If he couldn't make them profitable, he would sell the assets for as much as he could get. He was used to pushing hard to get what he wanted and persuading people to go along with his plans. After the city of San Francisco turned down the Giants' request for a new ballpark to replace cold, windy Candlestick Park, Naimoli agreed to buy the Giants for $115 million and move them to Tampa. It appeared that Tampa Bay's long quest for a franchise was finally over.

With the loss of the Giants staring them in the face, San Francisco city leaders pledged to fund a new ballpark to keep the team. National League President Bill White joined the last-minute effort to keep the Giants and found a San Francisco group led by Peter Magowan to buy the team for $100 million, or $15 million less than Naimoli offered. The Giants and the National League accepted the lower bid, the team stayed in San Francisco, and plays in the privately financed ballpark now known as AT&T Park.

Naimoli and other local leaders sued the major leagues for interfering in this transaction. In a move that was perhaps even more threatening to baseball's business, Florida Senator Connie Mack III, grandson of the legendary baseball manager and owner, and St. Petersburg Congressman C.W. Bill Young, started congressional investigations into whether it remained in the public interest for baseball to retain its antitrust exemption.

In March 1995, baseball owners approved two new franchises, one in Arizona and one, finally, in the Tampa Bay area to the group headed by Naimoli. Soon after the announcement was made, Mack and Young ended their investigations. Naimoli wanted to call the team the Sting Rays, but found there was a winter-league team in Hawaii that owned the name. Rather than purchase the name from that team, Naimoli decided to call the team the Devil Rays. That caused so much controversy that the team commissioned a poll to prove that the fans accepted the name change.[7] The team did not have a winning season until it dropped "Devil" to become the Rays in 2008.

In July 1995 Naimoli named Chuck LaMar the Devil Rays' first general manager. He worked for several successful organizations during the 1980s and 1990s, including the Reds, Pirates, and Braves in scouting and player development. LaMar had never worked as a general manager, and he was now starting one of the most difficult jobs a general manager could have.

LaMar planned to build the team through young players and the draft, with a plan to contend in five to seven years. Naimoli, who made his fortune quickly turning around companies, did not have the same patience. When it came to conflicts between the owner and his first-time general manager, the owner would usually get his way.

On September 26 LaMar signed the team's first player, Adam Sisk, a 6-foot-4 right-handed pitcher from Edison Community College in Fort Myers, Florida. Sisk would never pitch in the majors, but it was a start. In November the Devil Rays unveiled their new uniforms.

In 1996 Paul Wilder, an outfielder and first baseman, became the team's first draft pick during the amateur draft held on June 4. The Rays stocked their farm system with 97 players, which was the fifth-highest total in draft his-

Tampa Bay Devil Rays' 1998 autographed baseball (Courtesy of the Tampa Bay Rays)

tory to that time. The Gulf Coast Rays began to play that summer when right-hander Pablo Ortega threw the first pitch in club history – a ball.

On October 3, 1996, the Rays announced the sale of ballpark naming rights to Tropicana, a relationship that still existed in 2018. In January of 1997, the major-league owners voted to put the new franchise into the American League, adding it to what was arguably the most competitive division in baseball, the American League East. The Devil Rays would struggle for years to compete with the deep-pocketed New York, Boston, Toronto, and Baltimore franchises.

Throughout 1997 Naimoli and LaMar continued to add minor-league teams, players, and staff. The player evaluation team scouted major-league players likely to be available in the November 18 expansion draft. On November 7, the Devil Rays hired Larry Rothschild to be their first manager. Rothschild, the Florida Marlins' pitching coach, had never managed before, and returned to coaching after his turn at the Rays' helm.

The Devil Rays' inexperienced leadership continued to learn on the job throughout the expansion draft. On draft day, the National League expansion Diamondbacks picked first. LaMar's first draft pick was left-handed pitcher Tony Saunders from the Florida Marlins. The 24-year-old started regularly for the team during its freshman year, finished with a won-lost record of 6-15, and led the league in walks with 111. As of 2018, Saunders still held the team record for most walks allowed in a season.

They picked Quinton McCracken second. He had a decent year in 1998, earning 2.1 WAR, and played in the majors for another eight years. The Devil Rays' third pick was a gem: They plucked Bobby Abreu from the Houston system. Abreu earned 60 bWAR for his career and in 1998 hit .312/.409/.497 and slugged 17 home runs – for

Tampa Bay Devil Rays' 1998 seat cushion (Courtesy of the Tampa Bay Rays)

the Phillies.[8]

Chuck LaMar had arranged with the Phillies to trade Abreu for shortstop Kevin Stocker after the draft. Stocker was 28 in 1998 and had been solid if unspectacular for the Phillies for the previous five years. LaMar said the Rays needed a shortstop to help his pitchers, so he traded a player with a lifetime bWAR of 60 for one (Stocker) with a lifetime bWAR of 6, over half of which he had already earned. This trade was so lopsided that Rob Neyer wrote about it in his *Big Book of Baseball Blunders*.[9]

Vince Naimoli told his young general manager that it was imperative for the first-year team to lose fewer than 100 games. Consequently, after the Stocker trade, LaMar purchased the contract of slugger Fred McGriff from Atlanta, while trading shortstop Andy Sheets and pitcher Brian Boehringer to San Diego for backup catcher John Flaherty. LaMar also signed free-agent closer Roberto Hernandez, and gave up another solid pro when he traded the eighth pick, Dmitri Young, to the Reds to complete a deal for Mike Kelly.

LaMar told *USA Today Baseball Weekly* after the draft, "We think we have a great combination of young players and experienced players. We're going to try to be as competitive as we can, as quick as we can, and never lose sight of our long-term goals."[10]

Other free agents the Rays signed before the start of the season included starter Rolando Arrojo ($170,000 plus $45,000 performance bonus), 40-year-old Wade Boggs (for $1.1 million and a $650,000 performance bonus), starter Wilson Alvarez (5 years, $35 million), and Dave Martinez (3 years, $4.5 million). None of these players were signed because they were building blocks for the future. In a pattern that would repeat throughout the Naimoli era, they were signed to make a bad team a little less awful. At least Martinez would contribute to the Rays as a bench coach after his playing career ended. These players were long gone when the Rays won their first pennant in 2008. As of 2018, Roberto Hernandez still held the franchise record for career saves, with 101.

Fans were still excited to have major-league baseball, and Opening Day tickets sold out in just 17 minutes. More than 2.4 million tickets were sold during the season. Perhaps the team's veteran leadership helped the Devil Rays get off to a fast start. They opened their inaugural season on March 31, 1998, against the Detroit Tigers at Tropicana Field.

Four Hall of Famers with ties to the Tampa Bay area — Ted Williams, Stan Musial, Monte Irvin, and Al Lopez — each threw out a first ball on March 31. The Devil Rays Opening Day lineup was Quinton McCracken, CF, Miguel Cairo, 2B, Wade Boggs, 3B, Fred McGriff, 1B, Mike Kelly, LF, Paul Sorrento, DH, John Flaherty, C, Dave Martinez, RF, Kevin Stocker, SS. Wilson Alvarez was the starting pitcher. That lineup contained one future Hall of Famer (Boggs), one player whose career could be considered "Hall of Fame caliber" (McGriff), and several solid major leaguers.

In the first game the Tigers scored six runs and knocked out Alvarez in the second inning, going on to win, 11-6. Martinez got the first hit in Devil Rays history, a single in the third inning, and Wade Boggs hit the first home run, in the sixth inning. Boggs in 1999 became the first Ray to reach 3,000 hits. (Most of his hits came in a Boston Red Sox uniform.)

The next day, April 1, the Devil Rays recorded their first win, 11-8. Rolando Arrojo started, holding the Tigers to four runs through six innings to earn the win. He was aided by an 18-hit attack that included a home run by Rich Butler and a triple from Kevin Stocker. The expansion team took the series from the Tigers with a 7-1 win on April 2. Tony Saunders allowed a run in the first but held the Tigers scoreless for the next five innings. Esteban Yan replaced him at the start of the seventh inning, and got the win when the Devil Rays broke through with six runs in the bottom of the inning.

Tigers manager Buddy Bell said, "I don't think they're even close to being your typical expansion team. With the talent they have they are certainly better than expansion teams from the past." Baseball pundits wrote articles saying the Devil Rays might break the win record for expansion teams, which was held by the 1961 Los Angeles Angels with 70.[11]

The Devil Rays got the first shutout in team history on April 5. Wilson Alvarez earned his first win, blanking the White Sox for $6\frac{2}{3}$ innings, followed by Esteban Yan and Jim Mecir. Quinton McCracken and Miguel Cairo each got two hits. Cairo drove in two runs with a bases-loaded single. McGriff doubled in a run with two outs in the bottom of the fifth.

The Devil Rays continued their winning ways for the next couple of weeks. Roberto Hernandez earned the first of his 101 saves for the franchise on April 12. After beating the Angels on April 19, the team had a 10-6 record. No other expansion team in history reached four games over .500 at any time during its first year.[12] On April 23 the team sported an 11-8 record. It's a testament to the strength of the American League East in 1998 that this fine early performance put the Rays in fourth place in the division. The Yankees, at the top of the pack, were on their way to a 114-win season.

It looked as if the club's investment in free agents was paying off. If all the veterans could find one more good year from somewhere, maybe the team could go all the way. Unfortunately for the fans, April 23 was the high point of the season. After their win that day, they lost 10 of their next 12 games.

Twenty years after their inaugural season the Rays brought several players to back Tropicana Field for a celebration, and several of them said they remembered 1998 as a year they became a family that competed hard to win every game.

Closer Roberto Hernandez said, "It was exciting ... lots of emotions. Fans that came were outstanding. We tried to play hard, play to win, and leave everything out on the field. We gave it all."[13]

Backup catcher Mike DeFelice said, "The Rays were one of the tightest knit teams I ever played on. At the end of the year we didn't want to leave each other."[14]

The Devil Rays did have some impressive wins amid all those losses. On May 12, 1998, in a day game at Tropicana Field, they beat the defending American League champion Cleveland Indians, 6-5 in 14 innings. The Rays took advantage of some Indians fielding mistakes to get out to a four-run lead in the bottom of the first. The Indians scored four during the middle innings to tie it up, and it looked over when Kenny Lofton tripled in the top of the 14th and came home on a fly ball by Manny Ramirez.

In the bottom of the 14th, Aaron Ledesma singled to right, and after an out, Kevin Stocker justified the team's faith in him by hitting a walk-off, two-run homer.

The Devil Rays followed that win with two losses and then a four-game win streak that took them to third place, behind the Red Sox in second and the Yankees in first. That was as high as the team rose in 1998; the bottom was about to fall out.

The team lost steadily in June, July, and August. The Rays

suffered a 10-game losing streak from late June to early July. At least on July 5 they contributed to baseball history when Randy Winn became Roger Clemens' 3,000th strikeout victim in a 2-1 loss to the Toronto Blue Jays.

After they broke the streak with a 5-4 win against the Red Sox on July 14, the Devil Rays lost the next day, won on July 16, and dropped four more. They won only nine games in July, the fewest of any month that season. In August they won 10, against 20 losses. The team bounced back slightly in September with 10 wins against 16 losses.

The team's most common batting order in 1998 was Randy Winn, CF, Wade Boggs, 3B, Quinton McCracken, LF, Fred McGriff, 1B, Bubba Trammell, RF, Paul Sorrento, DH, Miguel Cairo, 2B, John Flaherty, C, Kevin Stocker, SS. McGriff had the best offensive season on the team, slashing .284/.371/.443 and leading the team in home runs (19) and RBIs (81). respectively. He earned 2.9 bWAR. Miguel Cairo earned 3.2 bWAR due to his fielding contributions and his .268/.307/.367 slash line, 19 stolen bases, 49 runs scored and 46 RBIs. Quinton McCracken became a fan favorite by leading the team in runs scored with 77 and leading the regulars in batting average with .292. He slashed .292/.355/.410 with 7 home runs and 59 RBIs.

Closer Roberto Hernandez had a good year, saving 26 games, or half the team's wins. He earned 0.8 bWAR. The two top starters in wins above replacement value were Rolando Arrojo with 4.1 and the team's first draft pick, Tony Saunders, with 3.1. Saunders was only 24 and might have become an even better pitcher as he gained experience. But he ruptured a tendon in his arm during a game in 1999, and never pitched again.

The Devil Rays did achieve Naimoli's goal of not losing 100 games. All of their free-agent signings and draft picks combined to produce a record of 63 wins and 99 losses. They finished last in the American League East, 51 games behind the first-place Yankees, and 16 games behind the fourth-place Orioles. As one would expect for a first-year expansion team, the Devil Rays had the worst won-lost record in the league.

In 1999 the Devil Rays' record would improve to 69-93, close to the worst record in the league. The 1999 draft yielded one of the best players in the team's history, Carl Crawford, in round two. Their first-round pick, Josh Hamilton, also went on to star in major-league baseball – for other teams.

By this time the road to landing a franchise had already cost millions of dollars and was about to cost even more. During the offseason Naimoli ended the honeymoon for the team in Tampa Bay when he told the St. Petersburg City Council that if they didn't pay for multimillion-dollar renovations to Tropicana Field, the club might move. Naimoli continued to micromanage the team, while feuding with advertisers, city and county officials, players, and, worst of all, fans. After the team set its all-time attendance record of 2,506,293 in 1998, attendance at Tropicana Field dropped every year until 2006, when Naimoli sold the Devil Rays to a group headed by investment banker Stuart Sternberg. That group celebrated the Devil Rays' 10th-anniversary season in 2008 by improving 31 games over their 2007 season, going from worst to first in the A.L. East, winning the American League pennant, and making the team's only World Series appearance to date. The Rays lost to the Philadelphia Phillies.

Chuck LaMar remained general manager from 1998 through 2007. The Devil Rays never achieved a winning record, and won as many as 70 games only once, in 2004, with Lou Piniella at the helm. LaMar summed up his time as general manager under Naimoli this way: "The only thing that kept this organization from being recognized as one of the finest in baseball is wins and losses at the major-league level."[15]

### Sources

In addition to the sources cited in the Notes, the author consulted Baseball-Reference.com, Retrosheet.org, and SABR.org, as well as Jonah Keri, *The Extra 2%: How Wall Street Strategies Took a Major League Baseball Team from Worst to First* (New York: Ballantine Books, 2011).

Thanks to the National Baseball Hall of Fame Library and the Orange County (Florida) Library

### Notes

1 Associated Press, *Oneonta Star*, March 10, 1995, from National Baseball Hall of Fame files.

2 Editorial page, *St. Petersburg Times*, March 10, 1995, from National Baseball Hall of Fame files.

3 Will Michaels, *The Making of St. Petersburg* (Charleston, South Carolina: History Press, 2012), 101-103.

4 Michaels, 104. *The Making of St. Petersburg* provides a detailed histo-

5  Kevin M. McCarthy, *Baseball in Florida* (Sarasota: Pineapple Press, 1996), 175-176.

6  McCarthy, 176-177.

7  Marc Topkin, "Twenty Things We've Hated Over the Years." *Tampa Bay Times*, March 25, 2018. Topkin, a longtime Rays beat reporter, produced a series of articles commemorating the team's 20th anniversary.

8  Mel Antonen, "Devil Rays Lean to Pitching Youth," *USA Today*, November 19, 1997.

9  Rob Neyer, *Rob Neyer's Big Book of Baseball Blunders* (New York: Simon & Schuster, 2006), 258-260.

10  Bill Koenig, "Deals Help Devil Rays Grow Up," *USA Today Baseball Weekly*, November 20, 1997: 22.

11  Pete Williams, "Rays Fans Juiced Over the Trop," *USA Baseball Weekly*, April 14, 1998: 14.

12  Adam Sanford, "20 Years of Rays Baseball: 1998," draysbay.com. draysbay.com/2017/10/16/16431104/tampa-bay-rays-20-years-remembering-inaugural-season (accessed July 4, 2018).

13  Interview with Roberto Hernandez on Rays telecast, March 31, 2018.

14  Interview with Mike DeFelice on Rays telecast, March 31, 2018.

15  Neyer, 260.

## TAMPA BAY DEVIL RAYS EXPANSION

PICK  PLAYER                    POSITION FORMER TEAM

### ROUND 1

| | | | |
|---|---|---|---|
| 1 | Tony Saunders | p | Florida Marlins |
| 2 | Quinton McCracken | of | Colorado Rockies |
| 3 | Bobby Abreu | of | Houston Astros |
| 4 | Miguel Cairo | 2b | Chicago Cubs |
| 5 | Rich Butler | of | Toronto Blue Jays |
| 6 | Bobby Smith | 3b | Atlanta Braves |
| 7 | Jason Johnson | p | Pittsburgh Pirates |
| 8 | Dmitri Young | 1b | Cincinnati Reds |
| 9 | Esteban Yan | p | Baltimore Orioles |
| 10 | Mike DiFelice | c | St. Louis Cardinals |
| 11 | Bubba Trammell | of | Detroit Tigers |
| 12 | Andy Sheets | ss | Seattle Mariners |
| 13 | Dennis Springer | p | Anaheim Angels |
| 14 | Dan Carlson | p | San Francisco Giants |

### ROUND 2

| | | | |
|---|---|---|---|
| 15 | Brian Boehringer | p | New York Yankees |
| 16 | Mike Duvall | p | Florida Marlins |
| 17 | John LeRoy | ss | Atlanta Braves |
| 18 | Jim Mecir | c | Boston Red Sox |
| 19 | Bryan Rekar | p | Colorado Rockies |
| 20 | Rick Gorecki | p | Los Angeles Dodgers |
| 21 | Ramon Tatis | p | Chicago Cubs |
| 22 | Kerry Robinson | of | St. Louis Cardinals |
| 23 | Steve Cox | 1b | Oakland A's |
| 24 | Albie Lopez | p | Cleveland Indians |
| 25 | Jose Paniagua | p | Montreal Expos |
| 26 | Carlos Mendoza | of | New York Mets |
| 27 | Ryan Karp | p | Philadelphia Phillies |
| 28 | Santos Hernandez | p | San Francisco Giants |

### ROUND 3

| | | | |
|---|---|---|---|
| 29 | Randy Winn | c | Florida Marlins |
| 30 | Terrell Wade | of | Atlanta Braves |
| 31 | Aaron Ledesma | of | Baltimore Orioles |
| 32 | Brooks Kieschnick | p | Chicago Cubs |
| 33 | Luke Wilcox | p | New York Yankees |
| 34 | Herbert Perry | 3b | Cleveland Indians |
| 35 | Vaughn Eshelman | of | Oakland A's |
| 34 | Scott Fredrickson | p | San Diego Padres |
| 35 | Braulio Castillo | of | Philadelphia Phillies |

# DENNIS SPRINGER

## By Rob Neyer

Over the course of roughly two decades, Dennis Springer's baseball travels took him practically everywhere in the U.S. and Canada, but he spent all his formative years in and around Fresno, California, and that's where he's made his second professional career in the years since his often-unreliable knuckleball finally became too unreliable.

Dennis LeRoy Springer was born in Fresno on February 12, 1965. His father was a teacher and football coach at suburban Washington Union High School, and so young Dennis first gravitated toward football. "I followed him around," Springer recalled. "It wasn't until I was nine [that] I started playing little league baseball."[1]

But he took to baseball quickly, and his favorite team was the Dodgers, because he would watch baseball games on television with his grandfather and the Dodgers were his favorite team. After going to the same high school where his dad coached, Springer pitched for two more local schools: two-year Reedley College, followed by a season

at Fresno State University. After a junior season in which he went 6-5 with a 3.92 ERA for the Bulldogs, Springer got a nice surprise: His Los Angeles Dodgers thought he had the makings of a pro.

"I didn't think I was going to be drafted at all," he later said, "so when I got the phone call from our family friend who was actually the Dodger scout, I was really excited."[2]

Perhaps Springer was drafted because of that family friend; on the other hand, he wasn't exactly a late-round flier, going to the Dodgers in the 21st round of a draft in which they drafted 30 players after him. Still, the 21st round isn't where you find the can't-miss prospects. Springer had fooled around with a knuckleball in college, and upon showing his stuff in the minors, he recalled, "the coaches told me that the knuckleball would be my ticket to the majors."[3]

What they probably didn't tell him what while his knuckleball ultimately was his ticket to the majors, it would take many years for that ticket to be punched.

Springer's first pro season was in the Rookie-level Pioneer League. He thrived there, and thrived again the next season in Class A, especially after being told, "We'll give you a shot to start, but you have to throw [the knuckleball] all the time." Along the way, he also received some tips from Charlie Hough, the longtime major leaguer who'd also gotten his start in the Dodgers' farm system, 20-some years earlier.[4]

In Springer's third pro season, he split his time between the Dodgers' Double-A and Triple-A clubs: heady stuff for a late-round draftee who hadn't expected to get so far. But for all of 1989 and the next five seasons, that's as far as Springer got, bouncing back and forth between those levels. In fact, after the 1993 season – in which he'd gone 3-8 with a 5.99 ERA for Triple-A Albuquerque – Springer drew his release from the Dodgers after seven seasons, and signed as a free agent with the Phillies … who exiled him to Double-A Reading for all of the '94 season.

And in '95, it was yet another long stint in the minors for Springer, who racked up a 10-11 record with Triple-A Scranton/Wilkes-Barre. Finally, though, his patience and hard work was rewarded with a September call-up. Springer debuted on the 13th with a start (and loss) in Montreal, and remained in the Phillies' rotation for the rest of the season. Alas, he went just 0-3, with his best outing (against the Marlins) resulting in a no-decision.

That winter the Phillies cut him loose, but Springer signed with the California Angels, and spent most of the next two seasons in the majors. In 1996, he joined the Angels' rotation after the All-Star break, and went 5-6 in 14 starts the rest of the way; the highlight came on August 25, when he shut out the Orioles in Baltimore, allowing just five hits. Springer spent nearly all of '97 in the Angels' rotation, despite a worrisome strikeout rate, and finished 9-9 for the season. Again, there was one highlight. Shortly after a rough July outing that goosed his ERA for the season to 6.31, Springer was advised by Hall of Fame knuckleballer Phil Niekro – in a Fenway Park tutorial also attended by Tim Wakefield – that he might be throwing his knuckleball too hard; Wakefield opined that changing speeds might help, especially against Springer's next opponent, the Indians. And sure enough, Springer tossed a nifty eight-hit shutout in Cleveland, one of four shutouts in his career.[5]

That November, the Angels left Springer unprotected in the expansion draft, and the Tampa Bay Devil Rays snagged him with the 26th pick. The idea was that Springer would, at the very least, relieve the pressure on the first-year franchise's shaky pitching staff, much as Charlie Hough had done for the Florida Marlins five years earlier. That didn't actually happen this time, though; in early July, Springer was demoted to the minors with a 2-11 record (5.67 ERA). He did return to the Devil Rays in August, but pitched largely in lost causes, his only decision (a victory) coming in a spot start against the Tigers.

After the season Springer was on the move once more, this time signing a free-agent deal with Florida. The good news: For the first and only time in his professional career, Springer spent the entire season in the majors, and set his career high with 196⅓ innings pitched. He also threw a couple of shutouts, first against the cross-state Devil Rays and later – sweetest of them all – a gem against the Braves to beat Greg Maddux, 2-0. Springer was also one-half of a historical oddity: For the first month of the season, Springer was joined on the Marlins' staff by fellow knuckleballer Kirt Ojala. In one game, Ojala relieved Springer; in another, Springer relieved Ojala. The bad news: Springer finished the season 6-16, with a 4.86 ERA (and Ojala was dispatched to the minors in early May, and never pitched in the majors again).[6]

That winter, Springer signed with the New York Mets. "We feel we've added to our pitching depth," said Mets general manager Steve Phillips. "He's versatile and proved he can throw a lot of innings."[7]

True enough, but the Mets didn't have much use for Springer's innings, nearly all of which he tossed in Triple-A; he did start twice for the big club in April, but the latter appearance included 13 hits, four walks, and eight runs, after which it was back to Norfolk for the rest of the season. With no call-up in September.

After which, another winter, another job hunt. But this one lasted far longer than the others, as Springer didn't actually sign a contract for the 2001 season until May … but at least it was with the Dodgers, whom he would later describe as "truly the best organization in baseball."

Springer began his delayed season back with Las Vegas, the Dodgers' Triple-A affiliate. But he finally, so many years later, made his Dodgers debut on July 19, going four innings in Dodger Stadium against the Brewers.

Five days later Springer started again, this time in Milwaukee, and sparkled: seven innings, five hits, and one run, good enough for his first victory in the majors since 1999. Two days later, though, Springer lost both his spot in the rotation and his spot on the 25-man roster, when the Dodgers traded for veteran starter James Baldwin. "This was a good situation and I had a good time," Springer told the Los Angeles Times. "Hopefully, I can get back here; if not before September, then in September."[8]

Springer did make it back that fall, but didn't actually pitch until October. On the 4th, he pitched a scoreless inning in San Diego. And on the 7th, the last day of the regular season, Springer started against the Giants in San Francisco … and threw the most famous pitch of his career.

In the bottom of the first inning, Springer walked leadoff man Marvin Benard, then retired Rich Aurilia on a fly to center field. Which brought up Barry Bonds, sitting on 72 home runs for the season. Two days earlier against the Dodgers, Bonds had broken Mark McGwire's single-season record with his 71st homer, then hit another in the game for good measure.

Unlike a lot of teams, and with nothing but their pride on the line, the Dodgers had decided to pitch to Bonds throughout the season-ending series, home runs be damned. So first came those two blasts in game one, then just a pinch-hit single in game two, which left Bonds with 72 homers when he stepped to the plate in the first inning against Springer.

The knuckleballer's fifth pitch was a ball, but Benard somehow decided to take off for second base and was thrown out stealing, catcher to shortstop. Springer's next pitch just hung there, and … well, here is Duane Kuiper's call: Here's the payoff, a floater to Bonds – and he hits it high, he hits it deep, and it is … outta here!

There are probably thousands of Giants fans who weren't there but say they were, and there are probably thousands who were there and say the baseball landed in McCovey Cove. It didn't. The ball landed toward the rear of the stands just above and beyond the high right-field wall (Bonds' home run was caught and then lost by a fan with a glove; ultimately that fan and the one who retrieved it shared in the proceeds of an auction that ended with collector Todd McFarlane bidding the highest: $450,000).

What's forgotten (of course) is that Springer actually pitched quite well in that start, getting stuck with the loss despite allowing only two runs in seven innings (the Giants' Kirk Rueter and four relievers held the Dodgers to just four hits and one run).

"The home run by Barry Bonds was my claim to fame," Springer said in 2013. "It doesn't bother me now and it didn't bother me then. It was just one homer that I gave up. It just happened to be the last one of his year."[9]

It was also the last homer Springer gave up in the major leagues, as he would make just one more appearance in the majors. After starting 2002 in the minors, he was recalled in May, made a single relief appearance and took the loss, and was sent right back to Triple-A Las Vegas, where he finished the season with a 5.85 ERA in 143 innings. And so ended Dennis Springer's professional baseball career, at 37.

Springer certainly didn't think, way back when he was drafted, that he'd spend 16-odd years playing pro baseball. "I thought I would play a couple of years," he said later, "and then come back to Fresno and be a teacher and a coach like my dad."[10]

As of 2013, Springer did coach baseball. But instead of teaching, he's been with the Hanford (California) Fire Department for nearly 15 years, roughly as long as he got paid to throw knuckleballs. "I have always wanted to be a firefighter," Springer said, "and that is what I went into, as soon as I retired from baseball."[11]

### Notes

1 Larry Ham, "Former Major League Pitcher Speaks at Reedley College," *Kings River Life*, January 17, 2013.

2 Ibid.

3 Ibid.

4 Elliott Teaford, "Hough Says Springer Can Help in Relief," *Los Angeles Times*, April 7, 1996.

5 "Springer Knuckles (Way) Down," *Los Angeles Times*, July 29, 1997.

6 David O'Brien, "Knuckleball Sandwich," *South Florida Sun Sentinel*, April 3, 1999.

7 Tyler Kepner, "Mets Sign a Workhorse to a Minor League Deal," *New York Times*, February 5, 2000.

8 Bill Shaikin, "Springer Gets Ticket for a Return to Vegas," *Los Angeles Times*, July 27, 2001.

9 Ham.

10 Ibid.

11 Ibid.

# BROOKS KIESCHNICK

## BY RICK SCHABOWSKI

Michael Brooks Kieschnick was a rare combination relief pitcher (74 major-league games) and outfielder (50 games), who also played a couple of games at first base, as a designated hitter, and pinch-hit. He batted from the left side and threw right-handed. He was 6-foot-4 and listed at 225 pounds.

Kieschnick was born in Robstown, Texas on June 6, 1972. Father Michael Lee Kieschnick sold drill bits oil fields. He worked in Houston and also abroad in Doha, Qatar for 8 years. His mother Karen Kelley LaBarbera "worked in insurance when I was growing up. She had her own company. Kennedy and Kieschnick Insurance. More recently for the last 15 years she has worked for the school district as an information and technology specialist." He added, "One other interesting point is that my Dad named me after Brooks Robinson."[1] Brooks attended Mary Carroll High School in Corpus Christi, Texas. Perhaps inspired by his father's interest in baseball, he received a baseball scholarship to the University of Texas at Austin.

There were no freshman jitters for Kieschnick at U.T. in 1991. Playing left field, he had a .358 batting average, along with 14 home runs and 66 RBIs. He maintained a high performance level when he took the mound, starting 12 games, posting a 7-1 record with a sparkling 2.58 ERA. *Baseball America* named Kieschnick their Freshman Player of the Year.

Kieschnick's sophomore year in 1992 was another great season. He batted .345 with 10 home runs and 68 RBIs. There was no letdown when Kieschnick toed the pitching rubber. He went 11-3, posting a 3.13 ERA, along with 81 strikeouts. His performance helped lead Texas to the College World Series. He also won the Dick Howser Award, awarded to the Collegiate Player of the Year.

In his junior year, 1993, after posting a 16-4 record, with a 3.25 ERA along with 126 strikeouts, batting .374 with 19 home runs, and 81 RBIs, Kieschnick repeated the honor he won the year before, winning the Howser Award again. (He is the only player ever to win the award in consecutive seasons.) He was also named *Baseball America's* 1993 Player of the Year. He helped lead Texas back to the College World Series, and in a 6-5 victory over Oklahoma State on June 5, he threw 172 pitches.

Texas associate head coach Tommy Harmon had high praise for Kieschnick: "I don't know too many people who have had 15 wins and 15 home runs in the same season. He wanted to be in the game and just because he was hurt didn't mean he wasn't going to be in there. He was the ultimate team guy. Whether it was the manager or the bullpen catcher, Brooks respected everyone. He didn't have any kind of star syndrome. He wasn't a prima donna or an elitist whatsoever. He was just one of the guys, a true leader." [2]

While playing for the University of Texas between 1991 and 1993, in addition to winning the Dick Howser Award twice, he was also a three-time All-American and earned Southwest Conference Player of the Year honors all three seasons. His career statistics in his three seasons at Texas were great. He had a 34-8 record with a 3.05 ERA and batted .360 with 43 home runs and 215 RBIs.

In later years, on March 28, 2009, in a ceremony before a game against Texas Tech, Texas retired his jersey. Kieschnick was pleased with the honor. "In all honesty, I don't think it's actually hit me yet. When I do think about it, that no one will ever wear my jersey again, it's very overwhelming. It's truly an unbelievable honor… But to know that number 23 will never be worn again is just… if you could describe it I would love to hear it because I can't." [3]

Kieschnick decided to forego his senior season at the university and was selected on June 3 with the 10th pick of the 1993 amateur free-agent draft by the Chicago Cubs. The Cubs did not plan to use Kieschnick as a pitcher, but he didn't mind. "Oh, I'd love to hit and to pitch, that would be awesome. But, I'm in the hands of the Cubs." [4]

Al Goldis, who was the Cubs head of scouting and player development, thought that Kieschnick was "the best hitter in the country, a potential .300 hitter and 25 home run hitter in the major leagues." [5]

Kieschnick was looking forward to playing for the Cubs. "I'm very signable, I just want what's fair. I'm not out to set the signing record. I'm sure I'll miss pitching, but I'll get over that, too. I want to concentrate on one thing. Right now, that's hitting." [6] On July 23, 1993, he signed his contract, which called for a $650,000 signing bonus. When asked where he wanted to play in the outfield, he answered, "I'm not going to choose, they can choose, put me there and say, 'Hey, let's go.'" [7]

After signing his contract with the Cubs, he reported to a rookie league team at St. Lucie. He had been a designated hitter and pitcher while playing at Texas, but the Cubs planned to use him as an outfielder. Cubs scouting

director Goldis said, "Brooks was worked out and drafted for the sole purpose of playing right field for the Cubs. He has power, hits for average and has a strong throwing arm." [8] He didn't stay very long at St. Lucie, and in 25 games at Double-A Orlando, he batted .341 with two home runs and 10 RBIs in 98 at-bats. After the season concluded at Orlando, he joined the Cubs in Houston. During a batting practice in Houston he hit a home run over the center-field wall. After the 1993 season ended, he played some third and first base in the Arizona Fall League in October and November.

In 1994, Kieschnick played outfield for the Orlando Cubs in the Southern League. Appearing in 126 games, he posted a .282 batting average in 509 at-bats, along with 14 home runs and 55 runs batted in. Moving up to the Triple-A Iowa Cubs for the 1995 season, Kieschnick, playing in 138 games, with 570 at-bats, batted .295 and led the league with 23 home runs.

After an impressive spring training, Kieschinck opened the 1996 season with the Cubs. He wasn't expected to stay long, probably being sent down when Cubs third baseman Dave Magadan returned to the active roster after arthroscopic hand surgery, but Kieschinck was excited. "It's an awesome feeling. My mom's going to flip out when I tell her." [9] Kieschnick made his major-league debut on April 3, 1996 at Wrigley Field. Pinch hitting for Turk Wendell in the sixth inning, he struck out against the Padres' Willie Blair. He got his first major-league hit at Dodger Stadium on April 7, when pinch-hitting for pitcher Frank Castillo in the fifth inning, he had an RBI single off of Ismael Valdez.

As expected, Kieschnick was sent down to Iowa and hit 18 home runs, batting .259 in 480 at-bats. He was called up after Iowa's season ended and hit his first major-league home run on September 24, off Cincinnati's Curt Lyons. His 1996 statistics for the Cubs were impressive, batting .345 in 29 at-bats.

After a great 1997 spring training in which Kieschnick batted .362 with three homers in 47 ABs, he was surprised to be sent down to Iowa on March 26. Brant Brown, a left-handed hitter who posted a near .400 batting average throughout the exhibition season, got the starting job in left field. Kieschnick was eager to contribute when called on. "I know I can play. Don't count me out. I've gone through this before. I got cut from the Olympic team (in 1992), and the next year I went out and had the best year of my life." [10] He was still a little upset about not staying with the Cubs to open the season. "If they don't feel I fit into their mix, maybe someone else will. Once I get between the lines, I'll play hard, whether at (Triple-A) Iowa or Chicago. But I wonder how many more numbers I have to put up to make them realize I belong."[11] Kieschnick was called up on April 11, and after Brant Brown was sent down to Iowa, Kieschnick started in left field. Kieschnick had a big game for the Cubs on April 29 in a 14-8 win over the Expos, going 3-for-4 with two home runs and six runs batted in, but he was sent down again on May 21 when Brown took over the left-field job. He played first, third, and left field at Iowa in 1997, posting a .258 batting average, with 21 home runs and 66 runs batted in.

Kieschnick had gone from being the Cubs' top-rated prospect, to being shopped around in a trade. After getting called up on September 1, 1997, Kieschnick commented, "Them calling me up shows me they're still interested in me, and that excites me. The Cubs are the team that drafted me, and this is the team I want to make it with."[12]

After the callup, Kieschnick snuck in some warm-up pitching. "Not many people know this, but I threw three or four bullpen sessions that year in September because they thought about making me a pitcher again. I had lost the left-field job to Brant Brown earlier in '97 and I remember Mark Grace coming down and watching me when they had me throw in the bullpen. Finally, I said to the Cubs, 'Hey, I'm not going to throw any more bullpens unless you're going to let me pitch in a game'."[13]

Major-league baseball held an expansion draft on November 18, 1997 and the Tampa Bay Devil Rays selected Kieschnick with the 64th pick of the draft. He spent the entire 1998 season in the minors playing for three different teams – the Gulf Coast League Devil Rays, the St. Petersburg Devil Rays in the Florida League (where he spent the majority of the season), and the Durham Bulls of the International League. His combined totals for the 1998 season were a .250 batting average with 28 runs batted in and eight home runs in 140 at-bats. The Devil Rays loaned the services of Kieschnick to the Anaheim Angels for the 1999 season and he spent a majority of the season with their Triple-A Pacific Coast League Edmonton Trappers. In 296 at-bats, Kieschnick batted .314 with 23 home runs and 73 runs batted in. The good season didn't help, as he was granted free agency on October 15, 1999.

On November 16, 1999, Kieschnick was signed by the Cincinnati Reds. For the 2000 season, they sent him to the Louisville Colonels, their Triple-A team in the Interna-

tional League. He had a decent season there, batting .277 with 25 home runs and 90 runs batted in 113 games with 440 at-bats. He didn't do well in his 12 at-bats with Cincinnati during the 1999 season, going hitless and striking out five times. On October 3, 2000, the Reds granted Kieschnick free agency, and on December 1, he was signed by the Colorado Rockies.

After the conclusion of spring training, Kieschnick was sent to the Rockies' Triple-A Pacific Coast League Colorado Springs team. He made his first appearance with the Rockies on May 2, 2001, and his best game was on May 29 when he went 2-for-2 (two home runs) and had three runs batted in in a 7-2 win versus the Dodgers. He had a .238 average in 42 at-bats, striking out 13 times with the Rockies. Despite batting .294, with 45 runs batted in 13 home runs in 252 at-bats for Colorado Springs for the 2001 season, he was granted free agency on October.

After being signed by the Cleveland Indians on February 1 and released a month and a half later, things changed again after the White Sox signed him on May 16. Starting the 2002 season, the emphasis was on staying up in the big leagues based on his pitching. Kieschnick discussed the change of strategy. "I had talked to a bunch of people who said, 'Hey, you ever think about pitching?' I was going up and down as a hitter. I didn't want to be sitting around when I was 40 years old wondering, 'What would have happened if I had pitched?"[14] He further elaborated, "I had to do something. I had to make myself more valuable. I pitched in college, and my arm was rested for 10 years, so that's what I wanted to do. I made the decision myself. If I couldn't do it, I couldn't do it."[15]

Kieschnick spent the entire 2002 season with the White Sox Triple-A affiliate Charlotte Knights. After pitching only three innings in his minor-league career, he pitched in 25 games, posting a 0-1 record with a 2.59 ERA, striking out 30 in 31 1/3 innings. He also did well at the plate. In 189 at-bats, he posted a .275 batting average with 13 home runs, 11 doubles, and 40 runs batted in.

The White Sox didn't have a roster spot available for Kieschnick, so he was released on October 15, 2002. White Sox general manager Ken Williams had high praise for Kieschnick: "His stuff was electric, and he competes like a lion. I can anticipate him not just being in somebody's bullpen, but in the back of the bullpen." [16]

On November 5, 2002, the Milwaukee Brewers signed Kieschnick. Brewers general manager Doug Melvin was excited about the scenario. "If a player like Brooks can be your 12th pitcher and a bat off the bench, he is performing two roles. He can hit for the pitcher in the fifth inning and stay out there. If he comes up and you don't want to make a change, he allows a manager to manage an American League game. We love the idea."[17]

Kieschnick obviously agreed with Melvin's assessment. "What Doug Melvin and Ned Yost (Brewers manager) saw was that it allowed them to keep an extra player because I was the 25th and 26th guy on the roster. That's a huge advantage."[18]

After starting the season with the Brewers' Triple-A Indianapolis Indians of the International League, Kieschnick was called up on April 30, 2003, and spent the remainder of the season with the Brewers. Versatility was the key word as Kieschnick was utilized as a pitcher, designated hitter, pinch-hitter, and left fielder.

Kieschnick struggled on the mound, posting a 1-1 record with a 5.26 ERA, appearing in 42 games. In his 53 innings of work, he struck out 39 while walking only 13 batters. Things went well at the plate as he batted .300, with 12 runs batted in, and seven home runs in 70 at-bats. He also became the first player in major-league history to hit home runs as a pitcher, designated hitter, and pinch-hitter all in the same season.

Brewers Director of Scouting Jack Zduriencik wasn't surprised about Kieschnick's performance. "He earned it. He excelled at both positions in college, so it wasn't a real stretch of the imagination to think that he might be able to do it in pro ball."[19]

Teammate Glendon Rusch thought that what Kieschnick accomplished was remarkable. "I don't think people realize how hard it is to be a major league player in the first place, and he did both (pitching and playing the outfield) and he did them well. It was awesome to be a part of."[20]

Brewers pitching coach Mike Maddux played a big role in Kieschnick's success, but he noticed that, "When he joined us last year, (2003) I guess you could say he was rushed up to the big leagues, and there's a learning curve for everyone, but he stood on the other side of the plate, and he knows what it takes to get a batter out. I think his strength is his aggressiveness."[21]

Brewers manager Ned Yost spoke highly of Kieschnick. "He's a great competitor. He just gives you what he's got every day. When you need an inning from him, he'll give you one, then be willing to give you one more."[22]

Yost had high hopes for Kieschnick in 2004. "What he did last year increased his value as a baseball player. Now, are we asking Brooks to be a better pitcher this year? Yeah, he's got to be. He's going to have to make it as a pitcher. I think he can do that. But, then again, in search for consistency out of the pen, we've got to take the guys who do the job."[23]

Kieschnick began the 2004 season with the Brewers and was used as a pitcher and pinch-hitter. One of his best performances of the season came on April 28 against the Reds as he worked three hitless innings, recording three strikeouts in a game in which the Brewers overcame a 9-0 deficit to win, 10-9. He was taken out of the pitching rotation on July 2 because of shoulder tightness. He continued his role as a pinch hitter. On August 2, he had an MRI on his shoulder. The Brewers placed him on the 15-day disabled list on August 12, retroactive to August 9. He was sent to Indianapolis for a rehab assignment.

After pitching a scoreless inning for Indianapolis on September 1, he was activated off the disabled list on September 3, 2004. He pitched in eight games for the remainder of the season. With the Brewers in 2004, he recorded a .270 batting average with one home run in 63 at-bats. He appeared in 32 games on the mound, working 43 innings, posting a 3.77 ERA, striking out 28 while walking 13 batters.

On March 29, 2005, near the end of spring training, the Brewers released Kieschnick. Brewers general manager Doug Melvin said, "We needed to evaluate him as a pitcher instead of both. Brooks knew that."[24] Kieschnick commented, "They didn't really say much about why they did it. I guess they want to go with younger, power arms."[25]

The Houston Astros signed him to a minor-league contract on April 9. He split the season between Triple-A Round Rock of the Pacific Coast League, and Double-A Corpus Christi of the Texas League. His combined pitching stats were a 2-4 record, with a 5.12 ERA, pitching 65 innings, and he batted .327 with three home runs. He was released by the Astros on October 15, 2005. On December 26, 2005 he signed with the Baltimore Orioles, but he decided to retire on February 15, 2006.

Reflecting on his career, Kieschnick was content with the effort he gave, and especially attempting to stay in the major leagues by pitching. "Now when I turn 40, I won't be lying awake wondering what I should have done. This has brought peace to the rest of my life."[26]

After retiring from baseball, Kieschnick worked for Biomet, a medical device manufacturer that specializes in spinal implants. The tireless work ethic he had during his baseball career carried over in his new job. Co-worker Bart Vanlandingham commented about Kieschnick, "His customers love him. He's persistent in what he does and works hard."[27]

In September 2014, along with friends Ray Fuchs, Jaime Gonzales, and country music singer Charlie Robison, Kieschnick opened an establishment in San Antonio called the Alamo Icehouse. Kieschnick's role at the bar is being a social person and helping to bring people there, but he believes the work ethic and drive he had during his baseball career is a must to make the bar/restaurant business a success.

## Sources

In addition to the sources cited in the Notes, the author drew on baseball data provided by www.retrosheet.org.

## Notes

1 Email Brooks Kieschnick to Bill Nowlin, July 24, 2018.

2 Jonathan Mann, *"Baseball Set to Retire Brooks Kieschnick's No. 23 on Saturday."* (http://www.texassports.com/sports/m-basebl/spec-rel/032709aab.html). TexasSports.com. March 27, 2009.

3 Ibid.

4 Bill Jauss, "Cubs get versatile No. 1 draft pick; Sox stick with pitching," *Chicago Tribune,* June 4, 1993: 4: 4.

5 Ibid.

6 Ibid.

7 "Cubs sign No. 1 pick Kieschnick," *Chicago Tribune,* July 23, 1993: 4-9.

8 Dave van Dyck, *The Sporting News,* August 2, 1993: 17.

9 "Kieschnick makes Cubs' roster," *Dubuque Telegraph-Herald,* March 27, 1996.

10 Barry Rozner, *The Sporting News,* April 7, 1997: 27.

11 Associated Press, "Cubs send Kieschnick back to Triple-A," *Dubuque Telegraph-Herald,* March 27, 1997: 3B.

12 Barry Rozner. *The Sporting News,* September 15, 1997: 45.

13 David Haugh, "Remember Brooks Kieschnick, the Cubs power hitter who could also pitch?" *Chicago Tribune.* December 8, 2017. (http://www.chicagotribune.com/sports/baseball/cubs/ct-spt-cubs-brooks-kieschnick-haugh-20171208-story-html.)

14 "Kieschnick takes a two-way road," *The Sporting News,* March 3, 2003: 55.

15 Doug Miller, "Before Ohtani, Kieschnick did it all for Brewers.,"December 16, 2017. https://www.mlb.com/news/brooks-kieschnick-played-both-ways-for-brewers/c-263664078.

16 "Kieschnick takes a two-way road."

17 Peter Gammons, "Kieschnick impresses Brewers," (www.espn.com/gammons/s/2003/0221/1512192.html) ESPN.com. February 21, 2003.

18 Haugh.

19 Miller.

20 Ibid.

21 Dave Caldwell. "For Two-Way Player, It's Perseverance," *New York Times.* May 9, 2004.

22 Ibid.

23 Tom Haudricourt, "Kieschnick likes traveling two-way street," JSOnline, March 8, 2004. A printout of this article is in Kieschnick's player file at the National Baseball Hall of Fame.

24 Tom Haudricourt, "Not quite up to speed," *Milwaukee Journal Sentinel,* March 30, 2005: C1.

25 Ibid.

26 Gammons.

27 Daniel Clay, "Where Are They Now? Baseball star Brooks Kieschnick," *The Daily Texan,* March 30, 2015. (http://www.daily-texanonline.com/2015/03/30/where-are-they-now-baseball-star-brooks-kieschnick)

# DMITRI YOUNG

## By Tom Cuggino

About one of every 200 high-school baseball players is drafted by a major-league team. Of those drafted, about 66 percent of first-round draft picks ever get to play in a major-league game, let alone make an Opening Day starting lineup.[1] Of the 18,911 players who have donned a big-league uniform, only four have hit three home runs on Opening Day, making it one of the rarest feats accomplished in the major leagues.[2] One of those fortunate men was Dmitri Young, then of the Detroit Tigers, who on a sun-soaked 68-degree afternoon in the Motor City cleared the fence thrice against the Kansas City Royals in an 11-2 Tigers victory to begin the 2005 campaign.

The first two came in Young's first two at-bats off Royals starter Jose Lima. The third time up, Young was hit by reliever Andy Sisco's (presumably innocent) pitch in the fifth inning. He singled off Shawn Camp in the seventh before cracking his third homer of the day, to deep right field in the bottom of the eighth, against Mike MacDougal. Young went 4-for-4 with 13 total bases and five runs batted in to kick off what was an otherwise forgettable 71-91 season for Detroit, the last for iconic franchise figure Alan Trammel as the team's manager.

Young could never have expected such a day, much less after a homerless spring training. "As far as Opening Day is concerned, it doesn't get any better than this," he said. "Four for four, we won, Bondo (winning pitcher Jeremy Bonderman) threw a great game for us." The home runs were also symbolic for Young as a father. "I hit three on the day, and I have three children," he said, referring to his sons, Owen and Damon, and his daughter, Layla. Young's teammates gave him high-fives, and pitching coach Bob Cluck gave him a big hug. "Dmitri's been the heart and soul of our club for three years," Cluck said. "We've got other stars in here now, but he's been the one constant since we've been here (referring to himself and Trammel). So I was pulling for him."[3] It was clear that day and often throughout his complex 13-year major-league career that Dmitri Young was born to hit a baseball very hard.

Dmitri Dell Young was born in Vicksburg, Mississippi, on October 11, 1973, the eldest child in an unusually gifted athletic family in which his brother Delmon also became a major-league player (and a number-one draft pick), and his sister DeAnn played softball at Oregon State University. Young's father, Larry, was a Delta Airlines pilot who had been one of the US Navy's first African-Americans to fly an FY-14 fighter jet. After a stint in Virginia Beach, Virginia, his family soon moved to Southern California, where Dmitri and his siblings grew up spraying line drives across Ventura County, a coastal area just north of Los Angeles. He never hit less than .400 during his days at Rio Mesa High School in Oxnard, and was an All-American his senior year. Young had originally committed to play ball at the University of Miami, but after being selected fourth in the first round of the 1991 draft by the St. Louis Cardinals, he decided to pursue the minor-league route to the major leagues. In stints with Johnson City, Springfield, Arkansas, St. Petersburg, and Louisville, Young was a four-time Baseball America Top 50 prospect from 1992-95, ranking as high as number 12 in 1993.

After being named the Cardinals' Minor League Player of the Year in 1996, when he hit .333 at Triple-A Louisville, Young got a late-season call-up to the majors, playing in 16 games. The Cardinals had finished fourth the season before but had brought in future Hall of Fame manager Tony La Russa to lead the team back to prominence. The challenge was that St. Louis already had solid players in the positions at which Young would logically fit. John Mabry, whom the Cardinals had drafted in the sixth round the same year they drafted Young in the first round, had hit .307 as a rookie in 1995 and was also a first baseman/outfielder. Veterans Ron Gant, Ray Lankford, and Brian Jordan all patrolled the outfield and were at or near the prime of their careers. Young also had earned some ill will while in the Texas League in 1995 when he had punched a heckler.

Young started 1997 back in Louisville, but a season-ending injury to Brian Jordan forced the Cardinals to make some early adjustments, one of which brought Young back up to the Cardinals. John Mabry was moved to Jordan's spot in right field, and Young was slotted at first base. The move was short-lived, though; the Cardinals made a blockbuster deal at the trade deadline to acquire slugging first baseman Mark McGwire from the Oakland A's, and Young was used mostly in the outfield for the remainder of '97, batting .258 in 110 games while the team slipped back below .500.

With Brian Jordan expected to return from his injury in 1998, the Cardinals had a long-term decision to make about its former top draft pick, and shortly after the 1997 season traded Young to the Cincinnati Reds for relief pitcher Jeff Brantley. In turn, the Reds made Young eligible for the coming expansion draft. (The major leagues were adding teams in Phoenix and Tampa.) Young was chosen by the Tampa Bay Devil Rays, but then was sent back to Cincinnati to complete a deal made between the two clubs the prior week, in which the Reds had sent outfielder Mike Kelly to Tampa. When the offseason was settled Young was back in the Queen City.

The Reds were also coming off a poor season in 1997, and had a blossoming first-base prospect of their own in Sean Casey. However, the Cincinnati outfield was a far murkier picture than the one Young left in St. Louis, which opened the door for him to win a platoon job in left field with Chris Stynes, who had hit a blistering .348 since being acquired in a mid-season trade with Kansas City. Young capitalized on Stynes's numbers returning to more natural levels in '98, got the lion's share of playing time, and led the team in hitting at .310 with 14 home runs, 83 RBIs, and an OPS of .864, second on the team only to future Hall of Famer Barry Larkin.

Young went on to hit .300 or better in each of his four seasons in Cincinnati as a corner outfielder, and became one of franchise's anchor players from 1998 to 2001 along with Casey and Aaron Boone. He was remarkably consistent, entirely unashamed emotionally, and a clubhouse leader. The team won 96 games in 1999 and 85 in 2000, but settled for second place both times as the Astros and Cardinals won division titles respectively. Skipper Jack McKeon won Manager of the Year in 1999 as the Reds stayed in the playoff hunt until the final day of the season despite operating with the 10th lowest payroll in the majors.

Despite his consistency, Young still didn't feel as though he had become a true fixture in the Reds organization, and always felt he was in the middle of trade discussions. General manager Jim Bowden had often seemed to pine for Deion Sanders since Sanders had converted his career to full-time pro football. During an interview prior to the 2000 season with rumors surrounding the addition of Sanders, Young told the Cincinnati Enquirer, "To this day, I don't know what that's about. When they first signed him, I thought, 'Here we go again.' I just thought to myself, 'I may never get 600 at-bats with this team. I may never get to show my stuff.' If Jim feels Deion serves more of a purpose on this team than I do, that's just the way he feels. Deion has so much to offer. He's a very positive force in the clubhouse. But you can't translate that as being the starting left fielder. I've dedicated pretty much my whole life to this."[4] After the 2000 season, Cincinnati fired McKeon and hired Bob Boone, a strange move in that Boone came in with just three sub-.500 seasons as manager of the Kansas City Royals on his résumé. He added another in 2001 as the Reds went 66-96 and went the way of a full-scale overhaul. It was in this reshuffling that Young's tenure with the team ended. He was dealt to the Tigers for Juan Encarnacion and Luis Pineda.

Landing in Detroit initially was akin to an exile for Young. The Tigers had also lost 96 games in 2001 but hadn't made any significant moves to improve the team under GM Randy Smith and manager Phil Garner. Both were shown the door early in the 2002 season, the latter replaced by Luis Pujols, who lasted just that season. Due to his below-average speed, Young was used mostly as a designated hitter, and was injured before the All-Star break that year to cap off a disappointing initial chapter in Motown.

The following year the Tigers lost an American League record 119 games under rookie manager Alan Trammel, a franchise icon who played his entire 20-year career as the team's shortstop. For Young, however, 2003 was his best season as a big leaguer. Splitting time between DH and left field, he achieved career highs in hits (167), triples (7), home runs (29), and OPS (.909), while batting .297 and being chosen for his first All-Star Game that summer. Although the team struggled mightily, Young relished becoming its veteran leader. At 29 years old, he had hit his prime in dramatic fashion.

The Tigers emerged slightly from their abyss in 2004 but still managed only 72 wins. Despite Young's stardom the year before, new GM Dave Dombrowski signed free agent Rondell White to be the team's new regular left fielder. White, originally a fleet-footed center fielder who suffered a knee injury a few years earlier, was older than Young but still a superior defender. Young was relegated to the DH role once

again, but adapted and hit a respectable .272 with 18 home runs and 60 RBIs and stayed consistent in 2005 with .271/21/72, including the aforementioned Opening Day heroics. The team also added star power during these two years by signing All-Star catcher Ivan Rodriguez away from the Florida Marlins, and right fielder Magglio Ordonez from the Chicago White Sox. It seemed Young would soon have a chance to play on a rebuilding contender.

Detroit launched high out of the gate in 2006, carrying baseball's best record a quarter of the way through the season at 27-13. Already with four separate winning streaks of five games of more, the Tigers were reminding their fans of their unthinkable start to 1984, in which they won 35 of their first 40 games on the way to a World Series championship. In unfortunate contrast, Young, who had by then become the very picture of consistency over eight seasons, was at his worst point since his rookie year and was starting to show signs of severe personal strife. On May 17 news broke of a misdemeanor domestic-abuse allegation against him by his ex-girlfriend, who claimed he had choked her while to two were at the Townsend Hotel in suburban Detroit. Young pleaded no contest after failing to appear at a pretrial hearing. "It's a bum deal," he told the Detroit Free Press. "Unfortunately it's public knowledge. I don't see this person anymore."[5] Within two weeks of these incidents, Dmitri's younger brother Delmon was suspended 50 games in the International League for throwing a bat that hit an umpire.[6] Dmitri also was enduring a divorce and had been treated for alcohol abuse and depression. After a month's absence, Young returned to the Tigers and apologized to the fans, and expressed his commitment to forever fighting his addiction.

Despite these recent troubles, Young had endeared himself to the fans in Detroit over the years as one of the few bright spots during an all-time low period for the franchise. So it came as a surprise when on September 6, in the middle of the team's first pennant race in almost two decades, the Tigers released him unconditionally. Detroit went on to win the American League pennant that year, and lose the World Series in five games to Young's former team, the Cardinals. Perhaps the only silver lining to the year for the Young family was that Delmon made his major-league debut with the Tampa Bay Devil Rays (on August 29, exactly 10 years to the day since Dmitri's debut).

After 36 years north of the border, the Montreal Expos had relocated in 2005 to Washington to become the Washington Nationals. By the end of 2006, the Nationals had posted two fifth-place finishes, and their blossoming young first baseman and leading hitter, Nick Johnson, had gone down with a broken leg and missed nearly a year of action. In order to fill the gap in the middle of their lineup, they took a chance on Young, offering him a minor-league contract heading into the 2007 season. "Dmitri Young has been through an awful lot personally over the last several years. He's been extremely apologetic for the mistakes he's made in his life. He has asked for a second chance in life," Nationals general manager Jim Bowden said. "He comes in knowing that the organization has zero tolerance on any incident whatsoever that may take place. If it does happen, he'll be released at that time. He understands that."[7]

After being invited to spring training by the Nationals, Young took full advantage of the opportunity, winning the first-base job and going on an offensive tear to start the season. In June the Tigers came to RFK Stadium to play the Nats in an interleague game, and honored Young by giving him a World Series ring from the prior year. Then, in a Fourth of July victory over the Chicago Cubs, Young hit his sixth career grand slam.

Finishing the first half hitting .339, Young was chosen for his second All-Star Game that summer as the team's only representative. (He had a hit in his only at-bat and scored on Alfonso Soriano's home run). He finished the season at .320, putting him in the top 10 in the National League and earning him the league's Comeback Player of the Year Award. The Nationals topped off Young's turnaround by signing him to a two-year, $10 million contract extension. The lovable bad boy known as "Da Meat Hook" had officially maximized his fresh start.

Despite this turnaround, Young's status as an everyday player was once again up for debate upon Nick Johnson's return in 2008. Johnson struggled mightily, though, and a third of the way into the year endured another season-ending injury, this time to his wrist. Young's health was also in question, however, as he had not reported to spring training in good shape and had also continued to battle the onset of Type 2 diabetes, which had begun to plague him during his infamous 2006 season and resulted in some time in the intensive-care unit of a hospital late that year.

Although Young was hitting a comfortable .280 in 2008, the rest of his production was waning, and he had been replaced at first base by his former Reds teammate Aaron Boone, by then an aging veteran himself who had signed with the club as a free agent during the previous winter.

After appearing in only 50 games, Young was placed on the 60-day disabled list because of his diabetes, and with that major setback, both his season and effectively his career came to a rather crushing end. He went on to battle his condition for over a year before finally announcing his retirement on March 18, 2010, at 36 years old.[8]

Young's 13-year career had spanned 1,364 games with four teams, and produced a career batting average of .292 with 1,389 hits, including 301 doubles and 171 home runs. Besides his Opening Day three-home-run highlight reel in 2005 with the Tigers, his career also boasted a 5-for-5 game in Baltimore on May 6, 2003, in which he collected two round-trippers, two triples, and a single. His second triple came in the ninth inning when he was just a double short of hitting for the cycle, but with the game tied, 6-6, he legged it out to third base instead, and in the process drove in Bobby Higginson with the winning run. "It crossed my mind, but since the game was close, my individual accomplishment took a back seat," he said. "The run is the important thing."[9] Despite a volatile career, this moment had perhaps best captured Young's spirit as both a truly professional hitter and a team player.

Given the challenges Young had been facing, his post-baseball life continued to be marked by some poor decisions accompanied by recurring redemption. After being named senior adviser of baseball operations for the Frontier League's Oakland County Cruisers on the same day he retired from the major leagues, Young's apparent comeback was squelched within 10 weeks when he was arrested at a Bloomington, Illinois, airport for possession of marijuana and related paraphernalia.[10] He offered his perspective on the situation on Sirius XM's MLB Network

Radio: "I am doing fine, and am not calling from jail. Without getting into the legalities that are still pending, I have the medical condition, of course being diabetic and having all these old aches and pains. Been to rehab before. And upon retirement been consulting with a doctor about having something to alleviate some of the pain that I've been going through in all my career." He was released on $100 bond and continued to pursue his role with the Cruisers.[11]

Over the next two years, however, Young underwent another turnaround in the form of an astounding physical-fitness overhaul. In addition to his other challenges, he had battled weight problems his entire career, his 6-foot-2 frame supporting 295 pounds by the end of his playing days. By the spring of 2012, though, Young had lost an Oprah Winfrey-esque 90 pounds and had become an inspiring shadow of his formerly hefty self. "I'm down to 205 pounds, and I did it the right way," he told Charlie Sloes on 106.7 The Fan in a 2014 interview. "I went to a doctor, a preventative doctor, and he told me, 'You want to get off the medicine, lose three inches.' I'm like, forget that, let's lose six. And then I started doing a lot of cardio, the weight started peeling off, and at that point I started working out. And I'm to this size right now, and very, very healthy. I still have to take a shot of NovoLog before each meal, but other than that I'm golden. I feel better, look better. I didn't look like this when I played."[12] After a brief and unsuccessful attempt to come back as a major-league player, Young continued his involvement in minor-league player development, as well as in various spring-training instruction roles.

Through all of his ups and downs, Young retained a boyish innocence and lightheartedness, as evidenced by his lifelong obsession with baseball cards. He started collecting them seriously in 2000 while with the Reds, when he and teammate Danny Graves were offered $2,000 to appear at a card show. In lieu of a cash payment for the appearance, Young instead asked for a Pete Rose rookie card that caught his eye, and the love affair had kicked into a new gear. After being introduced to memorabilia collector Dave Bailey some years later by Tigers teammate Robert Fick, Young went on to amass perhaps one of the most valuable card portfolios on record, including some 500 mint-condition rookie cards worth over $2 million. "I dove in headfirst into the deep end of the swimming pool with baseball," he told ESPN. "I was ingrained with Baseball Digest, the Baseball Encyclopedia, and what better way to learn the players than the baseball cards?" He said his two favorites were Hank Aaron and Willie Horton, Aaron having been his favorite player growing up, and Horton as a role model and grandfather figure to him during his time with the Tigers. "He was one of the few people who kept in contact with me and told me that it's not the mistakes a man makes, what makes a man is how he comes back from his mistakes."[13] Young eventually auctioned off many of the cards, several of which went for six figures, to help fund his Dmitri D. Young Foundation, which provides equipment, travel expenses, and instruction on baseball and life to underprivileged children in Ventura County, California, where as of 2018 he still resided.

## Sources

In addition to the sources cited in the Notes, the author also consulted Baseball-Reference.com.

## Notes

1 Emily Cornelius, "How Hard Is It to Make the Major Leagues," MLB.com, October 7, 2014.

huffingtonpost.com/emily-cornelius/how-hard-is-it-to-make-it_1_b_5947308.html.

2 Manny Randhawa and Matt Kelly, "3 HRs on Opening Day? Only 4 Have Done It," MLB.com, March 29, 2018. mlb.com/news/players-with-3-home-runs-on-opening-day/c-268442342.

3 George Sipple, "Opening Day Rewind: Dmitri Young's 3 HRs Live in Detroit Tigers Lore," *Detroit Free Press*, April 3, 2017. freep.com/story/sports/mlb/tigers/2017/04/03/opening-day-flashback-dmitri-youngs-3-hrs-live-detroit-tigers-lore/99707854/.

4 Tim Sullivan, "Young Fed Up With Trade Rumors," *Cincinnati Enquirer*, February 25, 2000. enquirer.com/editions/2000/02/25/spt_young_fed_up_with.html.

5 Associated Press, "Ex-Girlfriend Accuses Tigers' Young of Choking Her," ESPN, May 19, 2006. espn.com/mlb/news/story?id=2449289.

6 Associated Press, "Young Suspended 50 Games for Bat Toss," ESPN, May 9, 2006. espn.com/mlb/news/story?id=2438919.

7 Associated Press, "Nats Agree to Minor League Deal with Young," ESPN, February 14, 2007. espn.com/mlb/news/story?id=2765793.

8  Tom Dubberke, "Big D Retires," Bleacher Report, March 19, 2010. bleacherreport.com/articles/365988-big-d-retires.

9  Ibid.

10  James Schmehl, "Ex-Tiger Dmitri Young Arrested on Drug Charges," MLive.com, July 6, 2010. mlive.com/tigers/index.ssf/2010/07/ex-tiger_tiger_dmitri_young_ar.html.

11  Dan Steinberg, "Dmitri Young Says His Marijuana Was Medicinal," D.C. Sports Blog, July 7, 2010. voices.washingtonpost.com/dcsportsbog/2010/07/dmitri_young_says_his_marijuan.html.

12  Dan Steinberg, "Dmitri Young Explains His Amazing Weight Loss," D.C. Sports Blog, July 28, 2014. washingtonpost.com/news/dc-sports-bog/wp/2014/07/28/dmitri-young-explains-his-amazing-weight-loss/?utm_term=.e9fb326642af.

13  Jim Caple, "For Dmitri Young, It's All in the Cards," ESPN, May 2, 2012. espn.com/mlb/story/_/id/7881462/dmitri-young-selling-rookie-baseball-card-collection.

# CONTRIBUTORS

**Mark Armour** writes about baseball from his home in Corvallis, Oregon.

**John Bauer** resides with his wife and two children in Parkville, Missouri, just outside of Kansas City. By day, he is an attorney specializing in insurance regulatory law and corporate law. By night, he spends many spring and summer evenings cheering for the San Francisco Giants and many fall and winter evenings reading history. He is a past and ongoing contributor to other SABR projects.

**Richard Bogovich** is the author of *Kid Nichols: A Biography of the Hall of Fame Pitcher* and *The Who: A Who's Who,* both published by McFarland & Co. He has written chapters for various SABR books, including one in *Bittersweet Goodbye: The Black Barons, the Grays, and the 1948 Negro League World Series* and biographies of Freddie Sanchez and Dewon Brazelton for *Overcoming Adversity: Baseball's Tony Conigliaro Award.* He works for the Wendland Utz law firm in Rochester, Minnesota.

**Stephen D. Boren**, MD, MBA, FACEP is an emergency medicine physician, Assistant Professor of Emergency Medicine at the University of Illinois College of Medicine, and was stationed in the U.S. Army in Korea where M\*A\*S\*H took place (but 20 years afterwards). In addition to multiple publications in *Baseball Research Journal, The National Pastime,* and *Baseball Digest,* he has many medical publications include one of the most famous *New England Journal of Medicine* editorials. He has been a SABR member since 1979.

**Thomas J. Brown Jr**. is a lifelong Mets fan who became a Durham Bulls fan after moving to North Carolina in the early 1980s. He was a national board certified high school science teacher for 34 years before retiring in 2016. Tom still volunteers with the ELL students at his former high school, serving as a mentor to those students and the teachers who are now working with them. He also provides support and guidance for his former ELL students when they embark on different career paths after graduation. Tom has been a member of SABR since 1995 when he learned about the organization during a visit to Cooperstown on his honeymoon. He has become active in the organization since his retirement and has written numerous biographies and game stories, mostly about the NY Mets. Tom also enjoys traveling as much as possible with his wife and has visited major-league and minor-league baseball parks across the country on his many trips. He also loves to cook and makes all the meals for at his house while writing about those meals on his blog, Cooking and My Family.

**Alan Cohen** has been a SABR member since 2011, serves as Vice President-Treasurer of the Connecticut Smoky Joe Wood Chapter, and is the datacaster (stringer) for the Hartford Yard Goats, the Double-A affiliate of the Colorado Rockies. He has written more than 40 biographies for SABR's BioProject, and more than 30 games for SABR's Games Project. He has expanded his research into the Hearst Sandlot Classic (1946-1965), an annual youth All-Star game which launched the careers of 88 major-league players, including Hobie Landrith who played in the 1946 Esquire's Game and 1948 Hearst Game. He has four children and six grandchildren and resides in West Hartford, Connecticut with his wife Frances, cat (Morty) and dog (Sam).

**Warren Corbett**, a winner of the 2018 McFarland-SABR Baseball Research Award, is the author of *The Wizard of Waxahachie* and a contributor to SABR's BioProject.

**Rory Costello** is a lifelong fan of an expansion team, but in his case it's the Mets. He lives in Brooklyn with his wife Noriko and son Kai.

**Tom Cuggino** is a native of Bronxville, New York and currently lives in Wheaton, Illinois where he works as a financial controller for Cisco Systems and enjoys an active family life with his wife and three daughters. He is an avid consumer of New York and Chicago sports history, particularly that of the Yankees and Cubs, as well as rivalries, ballparks and their influence on cities, the Pacific Coast League, and Latin America's impact on baseball. In addition to authoring Dmitri Young's biography for the SABR BioProject, Tom also contributed an article on the 2014 Winter Meetings for SABR's recent publication of *Baseball's Business: The Winter Meetings, 1958-2016 (Volume Two)*, and on the great Met comeback known as "The Steve Henderson Game," as part of the SABR Baseball Games Project. He looks forward simply to more balls being put in play again someday, and to the unlikely understanding of the rationale by which a team chooses its home field dugout.

**John DiFonzo** grew up in Somerville, Massachusetts where he was the Sports Editor for his high school newspaper. He is a lifelong Red Sox fan and season-ticket holder since 2004 currently living in Beacon Hill with his wife Gabriella. John is a graduate of Tufts University and holds a Master of Science in Global Financial Analysis from Bentley University and is a CFA charterholder.

**Jeff Findley** is a native of Eastern Iowa where he did the logical thing growing up in the heart of the Cubs/Cardinals rivalry – he embraced the 1969 Baltimore Orioles and became a lifelong fan. An information security professional for a large financial services company in central Illinois, he also compiles a daily sports "Pages Past" column for his local newspaper.

**Adam Foldes** is an archivist at the Eastern Diocese of the Armenian Church of America. He is a member of the Casey Stengel Chapter of the Society of American Baseball Research. He is fortunate to be able to combine his love of baseball with his love of history and politics.

**Steve Friedman** has been a SABR member since 1990. He has resided in the Pacific Northwest since 1985 and has been a season ticket holder of the Seattle Mariners since 1995. His youth was spent in the San Francisco Bay Area where he followed his beloved Giants. Steve is currently retired after a career of over 35 years as an owner and operator of cable television systems.

**Danny Gallagher** played highly competitive baseball for 27 consecutive seasons from 1968-94 in adult leagues across Canada where he worked as a reporter. He has been covering major-league baseball since 1988 when he joined the staff of the *Montreal Daily News*. Over the years, Gallagher has written five books on the Expos, including his latest on the 1981 squad: *Blue Monday: The Expos, The Dodgers and the Home Run That Changed Everything. Blue Monday* was scheduled for release in the fall of 2018 by Dundurn Press. The softcover includes 74 interviews and will unveil secrets never told before. Danny co-authored *Remembering the Montreal Expos* and *Ecstasy to Agony* with fellow SABR member Bill Young. He lives in Uxbridge, Ontario with his wife Sherry.

**Paul Geisler** serves as pastor of Christ Lutheran Church in Lake Jackson, Texas, where he lives with his wife and their three children. For his entire life, Paul has enjoyed all aspects of baseball - playing, watching, coaching, researching, and writing.

**Brian Geller** is a lifetime Los Angeles Dodger fan and baseball fanatic. He lives in Long Beach, California with his wife and children who gladly support his fanaticism. When he is not out on the diamond playing in the Sunday hardball league, Brian is working his fantasy teams or playing baseball tabletop games. He also writes a daily blog called Dugout Chatter which can be found at www.dugoutchatter.net. Because no one can live on baseball alone, Brian is also lead singer of the world famous Atomic Punks---a tribute to classic Van Halen and hosts the podcast: Cover Your Ears.

**Peter M. Gordon** has over 35 years' experience creating and curating content for platforms ranging from live theater to digital video. He is a long-time member of SABR whose articles and player bios have appeared in more than 14 SABR publications and on SABR.org. Peter is also an award-winning poet whose most recent collection is

Let's Play Two: Poems about Baseball. He lives in Orlando, Florida, and teaches in Full Sail University's Film Production MFA program.

**Tom Hawthorn** is a freelance television, newspaper, and magazine writer from Victoria, B.C. He is the author of three books, most recently The Year Canadians Lost Their Minds and Found Their Country (Douglas and McIntyre, 2017). He has served on the selection committees for the British Columbia Sports Hall of Fame in Vancouver and the Canadian Baseball Hall of Fame at St. Marys, Ontario.

**Leslie Heaphy**, associate professor of history at Kent State University at Stark, is a lifelong Mets fan and author/editor of books on the Negro Leagues, women's baseball, and the New York Mets.

**Paul Hofmann**, a SABR member since 2002, is the Associate Vice President for International Programs at Sacramento State University. He is a native of Detroit, Michigan and lifelong Detroit Tigers fan. Paul currently resides in Folsom, California.

**Chuck Johnson** has been a SABR member since 1991 and is a co-founder of Arizona's Hemond-Delhi Chapter. Chuck has provided minor-league content for such media outlets as MLB.com, SB Nation and Bleacher Report and is a frequent contributor to SABR's Bio and Game Projects. A member of the Minor League Alumni Association through his work with the Eastern League, Chuck lives with his wife and daughter in Surprise, Arizona where he works as an official scorer for the Arizona Rookie League.

**Chris Jones** is an attorney at Phelps Dunbar where he practices in the area of commercial litigation, with a focus on property rights, eminent domain, real estate disputes and contract disputes. He is a lifelong baseball fan and a member of SABR since 2015. The highlight of his playing days was being drafted by the Toronto Blue Jays in the 2001 amateur draft. He resides in the Dallas/Fort Worth area with his wife and four children. For firm information please visit www.phelpsdunbar.com, or contact Chris directly at chris.jones@phelps.com.

**Maxwell Kates** is a CPA who lives and works in Toronto. He has worked in commercial radio and he writes a monthly column for the Houston-based *Pecan Park Eagle*. Maxwell's articles and essays have appeared in *The National Pastime* along with several SABR BioProjects. He served as Director of Marketing for the Hanlan's Point Chapter for 12 years and has spoken at SABR meetings and con-

ventions in Seattle, Montreal, and Houston. His baseball highlights include to have witnessed Magglio Ordonez' home run to win the 2006 American League Championship Series for the Detroit Tigers, along with the final out of the 2017 World Series. This is his first SABR project in an editorial capacity.

**Stephen Keeney** is a lifelong Reds fan and joined SABR in early 2015. He graduated from Miami University in 2010 with degrees in History and International Studies, and from Northern Kentucky University's Chase College of Law in 2013. After passing the bar exam he moved from his hometown of Cincinnati to Dayton, Ohio, where he works as a union staff representative and lives with his wife, Christine, and newborn son, Leo.

**Roger Kinney** is a Colorado native and he won three varsity letters playing baseball at the University of Colorado. He is a past President of the Colorado Sports Hall of Fame. Kinney was the Director of the Colorado Baseball Commission and he served on the Board of the Denver Metropolitan Stadium Authority. He was the first employee of the Colorado Rockies Baseball Club, where he served as the Director of Community Relations and the Executive Director of the Colorado Rockies Baseball Club Foundation. He retired from the Colorado Rockies in 2004 and now lives in Colorado where he enjoys coaching, writing, playing catch with his seven grandchildren, and rooting for the Rockies.

**Paul Ladewski** was the Chicago Baseball Museum communications director at the time he wrote the Ted Kluszewski biography for SABR. He was a former sportswriter who covered the Chicago scene for the better part of three decades. This Chicago native was a past winner of the prestigious Peter Lisagor Award, and in 2005, the Associated Press named him the top sports columnist in Illinois.

**Bob LeMoine** grew up in Maine, following the Red Sox on the radio or black and white TV. He joined SABR in 2013 and rarely finds a book project he doesn't like. His works include co-editing with Bill Nowlin, *Boston's First Nine: the 1871-75 Boston Red Stockings*. A future project will explore the Boston Beaneaters of the 1890s. Bob lives in Rochester, New Hampshire, where he is a high school librarian and adjunct professor.

**Len Levin**, a retired newspaper editor, has been the copyeditor for most SABR books in the last few years. He lives in Providence and has alternately exulted and suffered with the Red Sox.

**Max Mannis** is a diehard Yankees fan who has been a SABR member since 2013, when he, as an 11-year-old, began writing blogs as a special correspondent for Sports Illustrated for Kids covering the annual SABR conferences, conventions and other events. In 2016, he wrote a biography of Trevor Hoffman for SABR's BioProject. He currently covers SABR's many yearly events for SABR.org and also writes for unhingedyankees.com. He lives in New York City and attends the Abraham Joshua Heschel High School when he isn't attending games at Yankee Stadium. He is an avid baseball card and memorabilia collector. You can follow him on Twitter at @maxmannissabr or @MannisCards.

**Mel Marmer** has been a member of the Connie Mack chapter since 2003. He is an occasional contributor to the SABR BioProject and co-edited *The Year of the Blue Snow: The 1964 Phillies* (SABR, 2013).

**Michael Marsh** is a freelance writer based in Chicago, Illinois. A former staff writer for the *Chicago Reader*, he also covered high school sports for the *Chicago Sun-Times* and *Chicago Tribune*.

**Andy McCue** is a former president of SABR and winner of the 2007 Bob Davids Award. His *Mover and Shaker: Walter O'Malley, the Dodgers and Baseball's Westward Expansion* won the Seymour Medal for 2014. He's a retired newspaper reporter, editor, and columnist.

**Bill Mullins** is a 10-year SABR member. He received his Ph.D. in history from the University of Washington and is professor of history emeritus at Oklahoma Baptist University. This article is derived from his book *Becoming Big League: Seattle, the Pilots, and Stadium Politics* published by University of Washington Press in 2013.

**Rob Neyer** is a longtime national baseball writer, columnist, and blogger. His seventh book, *Power Ball: Anatomy of a Modern Baseball Game*, was published in 2018 by HarperCollins. Rob lives in Portland, Oregon, with his wife and daughter, and currently serves as Commissioner of the West Coast League, the premier collegiate summer baseball league west of the Mississippi River.

Heresy though it may be, **Bill Nowlin** confesses a certain irrational fondness for the original 16 teams of the National League and the American League (as a lifelong Red Sox fan, he does tend to favor the AL.) He was born in Boston and still lives in the area, which has a lot to do with the Red Sox fandom, was a co-founder of Rounder Records, and has helped edit a few dozen book for SABR.

**Carl Riechers** retired from United Parcel Service in 2012 after 35 years of service. With more free time, he became a SABR member that same year. Born and raised in the suburbs of St. Louis, he became a big fan of the Cardinals. He and his wife Janet have three children and is the proud grandpa of two.

**Joel Rippel**, a Minnesota native and graduate of the University of Minnesota, is the author or co-author of nine books on Minnesota sports history and has contributed to several SABR publications.

**John T. Saccoman** is Professor in the Department of Mathematics and Computer Science at Seton Hall University in New Jersey. His work has appeared in numerous SABR publications, including books *The Team that Time Won't Forget: The 1951 New York Giants*, *The Miracle has Landed: The Amazin' Story of How the 1969 Mets Shocked the World*, and *The Fenway Project*. He has contributed biographies of Gil Hodges and Willie Mays, among others, to the SABR Bio Project. A long-time member of SABR, John resides in northern New Jersey with Bosox-loving wife Mary. His son, and fellow Mets fan, Ryan, resides in the Hub City.

**Rick Schabowski** has been a SABR member since 1995. He is a retired machinist from Harley-Davidson Company, is currently an instructor at Wisconsin Regional Training Partnership in the Manufacturing Program, and is a certified Manufacturing Skills Standards Council instructor. He is President of the Ken Keltner Badger State Chapter of SABR, President of the Wisconsin Oldtime Ballplayers Association, Treasurer of the Milwaukee Braves Historical Association, a member of the Hoop Historians, and the Pro Football Research Association He lives in St. Francis, Wisconsin.

**Steven D. Schmitt** is the award-winning author of *A History of Badger Baseball – The Rise and Fall of America's Pastime at the University of Wisconsin* (UW Press, 2017). He has been a SABR member since 2010 and has written articles for SABR books and for the SABR BioProject. He is a graduate of the University of Wisconsin – Madison, with bachelor's and master's degrees in journalism and mass communication and a member of the Wisconsin Alumni Association.

**Andrew Sharp** grew up in the D.C. area as a fan of Washington Senators I and II, and spent 30-plus years in the wilderness as a New York Mets fan before happily regaining a Washington team to support. A retired newspaper editor, he began writing BioProject essays in 2017 and has written SABR's ownership histories of the Griffith era and the expansion Senators. He charts minor-league games on a free-lance basis for Baseball Info Solutions.

From an early age **David E. Skelton** developed a lifelong love of baseball when the lights from Philadelphia's Connie Mack Stadium shone through his bedroom window. Long removed from Philly, he resides with his family in central Texas where he is employed in the oil & gas industry. An avid collector, he joined SABR in 2012.

**Tal Smith** spent 54 working in major-league baseball front offices. In three separate stints with the Houston Colt .45s/Astros that spanned a total of 35 years, he held positions as the franchise's Farm System Director, Vice-President of Player Personnel, General Manager, and President of Baseball Operations. As an assistant to Judge Roy Hofheinz, the President of the Houston Astros, Tal helped to oversee the construction of the Astrodome and later was responsible for finding the stadium's synthetic playing surface that came to be known as AstroTurf. As general manager, he assembled the Astros' first playoff team, for which he was recognized as *The Sporting News'* Major League Executive of the Year in 1980. Tal and his wife, Jonnie, reside in Houston; they have two children, Valerie and Randy. Randy followed in his father's footsteps and, at age 29, became the youngest general manager in major-league history when he took the reins for the San Diego Padres in 1993.

**Glen Sparks** grew up in Santa Monica, California, and is a lifelong Dodgers fan. He recalls carrying a transistor radio and listening to Vin Scully describe the action from Chavez Ravine and points beyond. Glen has written for the SABR Biography Project and the Games Project. He and his wife, Pam, live deep in the heart of Cardinals country.

As a loyal fan of the New York Yankees for more than 40 years, **Mark S. Sternman** remembers exactly where he was during the two biggest moments in Joe Girardi's career. Game Six of the 1996 World Series took place during a party that Sternman attended in Somerville, Massachusetts. Sternman ignored the festivities and watched the entire game from a rocking chair. He apologizes to his fellow guests and his hosts, especially since Sternman wore grooves into the hosts' hardwood floor. Sternman spent the first part of Game Six of the

2009 World Series visiting his uncle, a fellow Yankee fan afflicted with ALS, at a long-term care facility in Waltham, Massachusetts. He returned to his apartment in Cambridge, Massachusetts for the final part of the game and, by standing near a window, managed to pick up John Sterling's call on New York radio of the final half inning of the 27th World Series title for the Yanks, a happy memory that Sternman later recounted to his uncle, who has since died from Lou Gehrig's disease.

**Jeb Stewart** is a lawyer in Birmingham, Alabama, who enjoys taking his sons (Nolan and Ryan) and his wife Stephanie to the Rickwood Classic each year. He has been a SABR member since 2012, and is a Board Member of the Friends of Rickwood Field. He is a regular contributor to the *Rickwood Time*s newspaper and has presented at the annual Southern Association Baseball Conference. He saw his first games at Yankee Stadium in 2006 and witnessed Derek Jeter get his 2,000th hit against the Kansas City Royals. On September 8, 2006 he saw Cory Lidle pitch at Baltimore's Camden Yards, although the Yankees lost, 9-4, as Lidle unraveled on the mound. He spent most of his youth pitching a tennis ball against his front porch steps, hoping a Yankees scout would happen by and discover him. Although he remains undiscovered, he still has a passion for baseball.

**John Struth** has been a SABR member since 2006. He lives in Ludlow, Massachusetts. A Mets fan, he grew up partial to fellow southpaw Jerry Koosman, though he never pitched a game growing up. He has only recently started to contribute to BioProject, this book containing his fourth effort.

**Dan Taylor** is a former award-winning television sportscaster. He is the author of three books which focus on baseball and baseball history. Mr. Taylor's first book, *The Rise of the Bulldogs: The Untold Story of one of the Greatest Upsets of All Time,* was released in June 2009 and chronicled the remarkable national championship achieved by the 2008 Fresno State baseball team. His second, *A Scout's Report: My 70 Years in Baseball* is the autobiography of the celebrated scout, George Genovese. In 2017, McFarland & Co. released his latest work, *Fates Take-Out Slide,* which tells the stories of 14 players who failed to achieve the stardom that was forecast. Mr. Taylor resides in Fresno, California.

**Eric Thompson** is a two-time presenter at SABR national conventions concerning baseball's first expansion between 1960 and 1962. A retired high school mathematics teacher and a life-long Cleveland Indians' fan, Thompson coached youth baseball and served as an assistant high school baseball coach for many years. Thompson played softball for nine years in The Babes of 1916 senior league for players 65 and over. Eric lives in Solon, Ohio, with Colleen, his wife for 50 years. He has three grown children and five grandchildren.

In Baseball's LOST Tradition, Thompson took on the challenge of researching and reporting the history of baseball's first organized expansion and then switched gears to a unique mathematical application to the statistical side of the game, all in the interest of his favorite topic, baseball.

**Joseph Thompson** joined the Houston Larry Dierker Chapter SABR in 2013. Married to his wife Susan and father of three wonderful children (Jordan, Josh, and Kayla), he is an Air Force veteran that served during Operation Desert Storm. A part-time lecturer at the University of Houston, he will complete his PhD in American History at the University of Houston this December. His doctoral dissertation focuses on drugs, vice, celebrity, and media in American culture and the national pastime. He is the 2018 Joseph Pratt Public History Prize winner for his book co-authored with Professor Richard Santillan called *Mexican-American Baseball in Houston and Southeast Texas*. Previously, he co-authored *Houston Baseball: The Early Years* with members from the Larry Dierker SABR chapter and several other chapter book selections on baseball history as well as various public history projects.

**Clayton Trutor** teaches U.S. History at Northeastern University. He is the chair of the Gardner-Waterman (Vermont) chapter of SABR and is a frequent contributor to the SABR Biography Project. You can follow him on Twitter: @ClaytonTrutor

**Dale Voiss** is a long-time Milwaukee Brewer fan who has been a SABR member since 2009. He has written several biographies for the SABR BioProject. Dale currently resides in Madison, Wisconsin.

**Mark Wernick.** George Wernick took his son Mark to his first Houston Colts .45s baseball game in 1962, and he still has all the programs from the 1962-2018 Colt .45s/Astros games he attended. To ensure continuity of the tradition, Mark took his son Aaron to the Astrodome to see his first Astros game at the age of 5. A member of SABR's Larry Dierker Chapter since 1997, Mark's biography of Bob Aspromonte is his first SABR publication. He

is kept busy by his day job, running a private practice in Clinical and Family Psychology in Houston, where he and his wife Luba also enjoy trying to figure out what garden plants can survive brutal heat, steaming humidity, subfreezing "blue northers," hurricane force winds, a panoply of insects, fungal diseases, birds, squirrels, possum, and raccoons. And that's where the Colt .45s played for three years in an uncovered stadium. Houston: where a domed stadium made sense.

A lifelong Pirates fans, **Gregory H. Wolf** was born in Pittsburgh, but now resides in the Chicagoland area with his wife, Margaret, and daughter, Gabriela. A professor of German studies and holder of the Dennis and Jean Bauman Endowed Chair in the Humanities at North Central College in Naperville, Illinois, he has edited eight books for SABR. He is currently working on projects about Wrigley Field and Comiskey Park in Chicago, and the 1982 Milwaukee Brewers. As of January 2017, he serves as co-director of SABR's BioProject, which you can follow on Facebook and Twitter.

CPSIA information can be obtained
at www.ICGtesting.com
Printed in the USA
LVHW061633110219
607149LV00027B/920/P